THE TRIAL OF JESUS

FROM A LAWYER'S STANDPOINT

BY
WALTER M. CHANDLER
OF THE NEW YORK BAR

Illustrated Edition

Illustrations
by
William M. McLane

THE HARRISON COMPANY, PUBLISHERS
3110 Crossing Park • Norcross. Georgia   30071

Illustrated Edition

Copyright 1976 By

THE HARRISON COMPANY

TO
MY MOTHER
WITH SENTIMENTS OF LOVE AND VENERATION
WHICH NO WORDS CAN EXPRESS

THE HEBREW TRIAL

VOLUME 1

CONTENTS OF VOLUME ONE

NOTES

TO

VOLUME ONE

Page 180

PREFACE TO VOLUME ONE

Many remarkable trials have characterized the judicial history of mankind.

The trial of Socrates before the dicastery of Athens, charged with corrupting Athenian youth, with blaspheming the Olympic gods, and with seeking to destroy the constitution of the Attic Republic, is still a sublime and thrilling chapter in the history of a wonderful people, among the ruins and wrecks of whose genius the modern world still wanders to contemplate, admire, and study the pride of every master and the perfection of every model.

The trial and execution of Charles the First of England sealed with royal blood a new covenant of British freedom, and erected upon the highway of national progress an enduring landmark to civil liberty. The entire civilized world stood aghast at the solemn and awful spectacle of the deliberate beheading of a king. And yet, today, the sober, serious judgment of mankind stamps the act with approval, and deems it a legitimate and righteous step in the heroic march of a brave and splendid people toward a complete realization of the inalienable rights of man. The philosopher of history declares these condemnatory and executory proceedings against a Stuart king worthy of all the epoch-making movements that have glorified the centuries of English constitutional growth, and have given to mankind the imperishable parchments of Magna Charta, the Bill of Rights, the Petition of Rights, and Habeas Corpus.

The trial of Warren Hastings in the hall of William Rufus has been immortalized by Lord Macaulay. This trial is a virtual reproduction in English history of the ancient Roman trial of Verres. England is substituted for Rome; Sicily becomes India; Hastings takes the place of Verres; and Burke is the orator instead of Cicero. The indictments are identical: Maladministration in the government of a province. In the impeachment of Hastings, England served notice upon her colonial governors and made proclamation to the world that English conquest was not intended to despoil and enslave, but was designed to carry to the inhabitants of distant lands her language, her literature, and her laws. This message to humanity was framed but not inspired by England. It was prompted by the success of the American Revolution, in which Washington and his Continentals had established the immortal principal, that the consent of the governed is the true source of all just powers of government.

The trial of Aaron Burr, omitting Arnold's treason, is the blackest chapter in the annals of our republic. Burr was the most extraordinary man of the first half century of American national history. His powerful and fascinating personality conquered men and enslaved women. He was the finest scholar of the Revolution excepting Thomas Jefferson. He was the greatest orator of the Revolution excepting Patrick Henry. His farewell address to the United States Senate caused his inveterate enemies to weep. His arraignment at the bar of public justice on the charge of high treason—that he had sought to destroy the Country of Washington, the Republic of Jefferson, which is today the Union of Lincoln—was the sad and melancholy close of a long and lofty life.

The trial of Alfred Dreyfus is still fresh in the minds and memories of men. Troubled political seas still surge and roll in France because of the hatred, prejudice, and passion that envelope the mysterious *bordereau*. The French Republic is still rent by two contending factions: Dreyfus and anti-Dreyfus. His friends still say that Dreyfus was a Prometheus who was chained to an ocean-girt rock while the vulture of exile preyed upon his heart. His enemies still assert that he was a Judas who betrayed not God or Christ, but France and the Fatherland. His banishment to the Island of the Devil; his wife's deathless devotion; the implacable hatred of his enemies; the undying loyalty of friends; and his own sufferings and woes are the warp and woof of the most splendid and pathetic epic of a century.

Other trials—of Mary Stuart, the beautiful and brilliant Scottish queen; of Robert Emmet, the grand and gifted Irish patriot martyr—thrilled the world in their day.

But these trials, one and all, were tame and commonplace compared with the trial and crucifixion of the Galilean peasant, Jesus of Nazareth. These were earthly trials, on earthly issues, before earthly courts. The trial of the Nazarene was before the high tribunals of both Heaven and earth; before the Great Sanhedrin, whose judges were the master-spirits of a divinely commissioned race; before the court of the Roman Empire that controlled the legal and political rights of men throughout the known world, from Scotland to Judea and from Dacia to Abyssinia.

The trial of Jesus was twofold: Hebrew and Roman; or Ecclesiastical and Civil. The Hebrew trial took place before the Great Sanhedrin, consisting of seventy-one members. The Roman trial was held before Pontius Pilate, Roman governor of Judea, and afterwards before Herod, Tetrarch of Galilee. These trials all made one, were links in a chain, and took place within a space of time variously estimated from ten to twenty hours.

The general order of events may be thus briefly described:

(1)   About eleven o'clock on the evening of April 6th, A.D. 30, Jesus and eleven of the Apostles left the scene of the Last Supper, which had been celebrated (probably in the home of Mark) on the outskirts of Jerusalem, to go to the Garden of Gethsemane.

(2)   Jesus was arrested about midnight in Gethsemane by a band of Temple officers and Roman soldiers guided by Judas.

(3)   Jesus was first taken to Annas, and was afterwards sent by Annas to Caiaphas. A private preliminary examination of Jesus was then had before one of these church dignitaries. St. John describes this examination, but does not tell us clearly whether it was Annas or Caiaphas who conducted it.

(4)   After His preliminary examination, Jesus was arraigned about two o'clock in the morning before the Sanhedrin, which had convened in the palace of Caiaphas, and was formally tried and condemned to death on the charge of blasphemy against Jehovah.

(5)   After a temporary adjournment of the first session, the Sanhedrin reassembled at the break of day to retry Jesus, and to determine how He should be brought before Pilate.

(6)   In the early morning of April 7th, Jesus was led before Pontius Pilate, who was then stopping in the palace of Herod on the hill of Zion, his customary residence when he came up from Caesarea to Jerusalem to attend the Jewish national festivals. A brief trial of Jesus by Pilate, on the charge of high treason against Caesar, was then had in front of and within the palace of Herod. The result was an acquittal of the prisoner by the Roman procurator, who expressed his verdict in these words: "I find in him no fault at all."

(7)   Instead of releasing Jesus after having found Him not guilty, Pilate, being intimidated by the rabble, sent the prisoner away to Herod, Tetrarch of Galilee, who was then in attendance upon the Passover Feast, and was at that moment residing in the ancient palace of the Asmoneans in the immediate neighborhood of the residence of Pilate. A brief, informal hearing was had before Herod, who, having mocked and brutalized the prisoner, sent Him back to the Roman governor.

(8)   After the return of Jesus from the Court of Herod, Pilate assembled the priests and elders, announced to them that Herod had found no fault with the prisoner in their midst, reminded them that he himself had acquitted Him, and offered to scourge and then release Him. This compromise and subterfuge were scornfully rejected by the Jews who had demanded the crucifixion of Jesus. Pilate, after much vacillation, finally yielded to the demands of the mob and ordered the prisoner to be crucified.

From this brief outline of the proceedings against Jesus, the reader will readily perceive that there were two distinct trials: a Hebrew and a Roman. He will notice further that each trial was marked by three distinct features or appearances. The Hebrew trial was characterized by:
(1)   The appearance before Annas.
(2)   The trial at the night session of the Sanhedrin.
(3)   The examination at the morning sitting of the same court.
The Roman trial was marked by:
(1)   The appearance of Jesus before Pilate.
(2)   His arraignment before Herod.
(3)   His reappearance before Pilate.
The first volume of this work has been devoted to the Hebrew trial of Jesus, and a distinctively Hebrew impress has been given to all its pages. The second volume has been devoted to the Roman trial, and a distinctively Roman impress has been given it. Each exhibits a distinct view of the subject. Taken together, they comprehend the most important and famous judicial transaction in history.

It is not the purpose of the author of these volumes to usurp the functions or the privileges of the ecclesiastic. To priests and preachers have been left the discussion and solution of theological problems: the divinity of Jesus, the immortality of the soul and kindred religious dogmas. "The Trial of Jesus from a *Lawyer's* Standpoint" is the expanded title of this work. A strict adherence to a secular discussion of the theme proclaimed has been studiously observed in the preparation of these pages. The legal rights of the *man* Jesus at the bar of *human* justice under Jewish and Roman law have marked the limitations of the argument. Any digression from this plan has been temporary and necessary.

A thorough understanding of any case, judicially considered, involves a complete analysis of the cardinal legal elements of the case: the element called Fact and the element called Law. Whether in ancient or modern times, in a Jewish or Gentile court, of civil or criminal jurisdiction, these elements have always entered into the legal conception of a case. Whether the advocate is preparing a pleading at his desk, is summing up before the jury, or addressing himself to the court, these elements are working forever in his brain. He is constantly asking himself these questions: What are the facts of this case? What is the law applicable to the facts? Do the facts and law meet and harmonize judicially? Do they blend in legal unison according to the latest decision of the court of last resort? If so, a case is made; otherwise, not.

Now many sermons might be differently preached; many books might be differently written. But an intelligent discussion of the trial and crucifixion of Jesus from a lawyer's point of view must be had upon the basis of an analytical review of the agreement or nonagreement of law and fact in the case sought to be made against the Christ.

The first question that naturally suggests itself to the inquiring mind, in investigating this theme, is this: Upon what facts was the complaint against Jesus based? A second question then logically follows: What were the rules and regulations of Hebrew and Roman law directly applicable to those facts in the trials of Jesus before the Sanhedrin and before Pilate? It is respectfully submitted that no clear and comprehensive treatment of the subject can be had without proper answers to these questions.

Having learned the facts of any case, and having determined what rules of law are applicable to them in regard to the controversy in hand, a third step in the proceedings, in all matters of review on appeal, is this: To analyze the record from the viewpoint of the juristic agreement or nonagreement of law and fact; and to determine by a process of judicial dissection and reformation the presence or absence of essential legal elements in the proceedings, with a view to affirmance in case of absence, or reversal of the verdict in the event of the discovery of the presence of error.

In obedience to this natural intellectual tendency and to the usual mode of legal procedure in reviewing and revising matters on appeal, the contents of Volume I have been divided into three parts, corresponding in a general way to the successive steps heretofore mentioned.

In Part I, the Record of Fact in the trial of Jesus has been authenticated; not, indeed, according to the strict provisions of modern statutes which regulate the authentication of legal documents, but in the popular sense of the word "authentication." Nevertheless, the authenticity of the Gospel narratives, which form the record of fact in the trial of Jesus, and the credibility of the Evangelists who wrote and published these narratives, have been subjected to the rigorous tests of rules of evidence laid down by Greenleaf and by Starkie. Such an authentication has been deemed necessary in a treatise of this kind.

Two main methods may be employed in investigating and proving the alleged occurrences of Sacred History: (1) The method which is based upon the evidence of spiritual consciousness and experience, derived from religious conversion and from communion with God; (2) the method that rests upon the application of historic facts and legal rules to the testimony of those who have asserted the existence of such occurrences.

It has been contended by many that the first of these methods is the supreme test, and the only proper one, in solving religious problems and in reaching full and final assurance of the existence of spiritual truths. It is confidently asserted by such persons that the true Christian who has accepted Jesus as his personal Redeemer and has thereby found peace with God, needs no assurance from Matthew that the Christ was the Heaven-begotten and Virgin-born. Such a Christian, it is said, has positive proof from within that Jesus was divine. It is further contended that all forms of religious truth are susceptible of the same kind of proof. It is argued that from despairing hope, born of the longing and the tears of a mother who, grief-stricken and broken-hearted, kneels in prayer beside the coffin of her firstborn, springs stronger evidence of a future life and of an everlasting reunion with loved ones, than comes from all the assurances of immortality handed down by saints and sages. The advocates of this theory contend that the fact of the Resurrection of Jesus should be proved mainly by the method of spiritual consciousness and experience, and only incidentally by the historical testimony of the sacred writers. They boldly maintain that the Resurrection was a spiritual fact born of a spiritual truth; and that within the soul of each true believer is the image of the risen Jesus, reflected from Heaven in as perfect form as that seen by Paul while journeying to Damascus.

It would be decidedly ungenerous and unjust to deny the force of the contention that spiritual consciousness and religious experience are convincing forms of proof. To do so would be to offer gratuitous insult to the intelligence and sincerity of millions of consecrated men and women who have repeatedly proclaimed and are still proclaiming that the Spirit of God and Christ within them attests the reality of religion.

But on the other hand the doctrine of religious consciousness, as a mode of proof, certainly has its limitations. Spiritual proofs are obviously the very best means of establishing purely spiritual truths. But not many truths of religion are purely spiritual. The most of them are encased within historic facts which may themselves be separately considered as historic truths. In a sense, all spiritual

truth is born of historic truth; that is, historic truths, in the order of our
acquisition of a knowledge of them, antedate and create spiritual truths. The
religious consciousness of the Resurrection of Jesus would never have been born
in our hearts if we had never read the historical records of the physical
Resurrection. Nor could we have ever had a religious experience of the divinity
of Jesus if we had never read the historical accounts of His miracles, of His Virgin
birth, His fulfillment of prophecy, and His Resurrection from the dead, unless
Jesus had personally communicated to us evidences of His divinity. These
separate and historic facts, of which spiritual truths are born, cannot be proved
by religious consciousness and experience.

The distinctions herein suggested are very aptly and beautifully expressed by
Professor Inge in his Bampton Lectures on Christian Mysticism, in which he
says: "The inner light can only testify to spiritual truths. It always speaks in the
present tense; it cannot guarantee any historical event, past or future. It cannot
guarantee either the Gospel history or a future judgment. It can tell us that
Christ is risen, and He is alive for evermore, but not that He rose again the third
day."

From the foregoing, then, it is clear that in dealing with the historical facts and
circumstances of the trial and crucifixion of Jesus, we cannot remotely employ
the method of proof which is based upon religious consciousness and experience,
since these events are matters of the past and not of the present. We have been
compelled, therefore, to resort to the legal and historical method of proof; since
we could not assume the correctness of the record, as such an assumption would
have been lacking in legal requirement and judicial fitness.

It has also been thought not to be within the scope of this treatise, or consistent
with the purpose of the author of these volumes, to enter into a discussion of the
question of inspiration in the matter of the origin of the New Testament Gospels,
as the record of fact in the trial of Jesus. As secular historians, rather than as
inspired writers, must the Evangelists be regarded in this connection; since the
title of this work suggests and demands a strictly legal treatment of the theme
proclaimed. The author would respectfully suggest, however, that the day is past
for complete reliance upon the theory of inspiration and a total rejection of all
analysis and investigation. That the Scriptures are sacred and inspired, and
neither need nor permit questions involving doubt and speculation as to origin
and authenticity will no longer meet the challenge or dissipate the fears of the
intellectual leaders of the human race. The Christianity of the future must be a
religion of reason as well as of faith, else it cannot and will not endure the shocks
of time, or survive the onward march of the soul. If the teachings of the Nazarene
are a faithful protrayal and a truthful expression of all the verities of Heaven and
earth, then Christianity has nothing to fear from the discoveries of Science, from
Roman catacombs, Arabian hieroglyphics, the sands of Egypt, or the ruins of
Nineveh and Babylon. Science is the High Priestess of Nature and Nature's
oracles, and no single revelation of Science can disprove or contradict the
simplest truth of Nature's God.

If, on the other hand, Christianity be fundamentally and essentially false, ignorance and bigotry will not preserve and perpetuate it; all the prayers of the faithful, all the martyrdom of the centuries, will not suffice to save it from death and annihilation.

But the Christian need have no fear of the results of scientific investigation or historic revelation. Assyriology, archaeology, and paleontology, interpreted and applied by the finest scholarship and the most superb intellects of earth, have spent all their stupendous and concentrated forces in the direction of the discovery of natural and historic facts that would confirm or destroy the Christian theory of things. And yet not one natural or historic fact has been discovered that seriously disturbs the testimony of the Evangelists or impairs the evidences of Christianity. A few unlettered fishermen, casting nets for a livelihood in the waters of Gennesaret, framed a message to humanity based upon the life and martyrdom of a Galilean peasant, their spiritual Lord and Master, and proclaimed it to the world; and all the succeeding centuries of scientific research and skeptical criticism have not shaken mankind's confidence in its truthfulness and its potency. If eighteen hundred years of scientific investigation have resulted only in proof and vindication of the historic asseverations of the Sacred Scriptures, and further investigation gives promise of still further proof and vindication, tending to remove all doubts and destroy all fears, nothing but rank stupidity and crass ignorance will place obstacles in the way of ultimate analysis and complete revelation.

In Part II of this volume, following the plan heretofore suggested, the element of Law has been considered. Hebrew criminal jurisprudence, based upon the Mosaic Code and upon the Talmud, has been outlined and discussed. A more exhaustive treatment has been given than the subject would seem to justify, but the writer is convinced that the Criminal Code of the Jews must be of surpassing interest to the general reader, regardless of whether certain peculiar rules therein contained have reference to the trial of Jesus or not. The bulk of this Code has been inserted in this work because it is felt that a comprehensive view of any system enables the student of a particular trial under that system to grasp more fully and to appreciate more keenly the merits of the proceedings.

In Part III the legal aspects of the trial of Jesus have been reviewed. The elements of Law and Fact have been combined in the form of a "Brief," in which "Points" have been made and errors have been discussed.

During the past decade, the author of this work has delivered occasionally, in the United States and in the Dominion of Canada, a lecture upon the subject, "The Trial of Jesus from a Lawyer's Standpoint." Numerous requests have been made, from time to time, for the lecture in printed form. To supply this demand is the purpose of the publication of these volumes. The voluminous treatment given has been in response to the demands of those who have asked for a topical treatment of the subject. Many auditors in his lecture audiences have asked for special treatment, from a lawyer's standpoint, of the New Testament Gospels. Many have requested an exhaustive handling of Hebrew criminal law. Others have asked for the insertion in this work of the Apocryphal Acts of Pilate. And still others have expressed a desire to have Graeco-Roman Paganism dealt with in its relationship to the trial of Jesus. In obedience to these various demands, certain chapters have been incorporated in the general work that may not seem to the average reader to have any direct bearing upon the subject treated. It is felt, however, that in every case at least a partial relevancy exists, and that in a large majority of cases the relevancy is perfect.

The writer wishes, at this time and place, to acknowledge his indebtedness and to express his thanks, for valuable assistance rendered, to all those authors mentioned under the title "Bibliography" at the end of Volume II.

Walter M. Chandler.

New York City, July 1, 1925.

THE GOSPEL NARRATIVES

THE GOSPEL NARRATIVES

MATTHEW

xxvi. 47—68; xxvii. 1—26.

AND while he yet spake, lo, Judas, one of the twelve, came, and with him a great multitude with swords and staves, from the chief priests and elders of the people. . . . Then came they, and laid hands on Jesus, and took him . . . . And they that had laid hold on Jesus led him away to Caiaphas the high priest, where the scribes and the elders were assembled . . . . Now the chief priests; and elders, and all the council, sought false witness against Jesus, to put him to death; But found none: yea, though many false witnesses came, yet found they none. At the last came two false witnesses, And said, This fellow said, I am able to destroy the temple of God, and to build it in three days. And the high priest arose, and said unto him, Answerest thou nothing? what is it which these witness against thee? But Jesus held his peace. And the high priest answered and said unto him, I adjure thee by the living God, that thou tell us whether thou be the Christ, the Son of God. Jesus saith unto him, Thou hast said: nevertheless I say unto you, Hereafter shall ye see the Son of man sitting on the right hand of power, and coming in the clouds of heaven. Then the high priest rent his clothes, saying, He hath spoken blasphemy; what further need have we of witnesses? behold, now ye have heard his blasphemy. What think ye? They answered and said, He is guilty of death. Then did they spit in his face, and buffeted him; and others smote him with the palms of their hands, Saying, Prophesy unto us, thou Christ, Who is he that smote thee?

When the morning was come, all the chief priests and elders of the people took counsel against Jesus to put him to death: And when they had bound him, they led him away, and delivered him to Pontius Pilate the governor . . . . And Jesus stood before the governor: and the governor asked him, saying, Art thou the King of the Jews? And Jesus said unto him, Thou sayest. And when he was accused of the chief priests and elders, he answered nothing. Then said Pilate unto him, Hearest thou not how many things they witness against thee? And he answered him to never a word; insomuch that the governor marvelled greatly. Now at that feast the governor was wont to release unto the people a prisoner, whom they would. And they had then a notable prisoner, called Barabbas. Therefore when they were gathered together, Pilate said unto them, Whom will ye that I release unto you? Barabbas, or Jesus which is called Christ? For he knew that for envy they had delivered him. When he was set down on the judgment seat, his wife sent unto him, saying, Have thou nothing to do with that just man: for I have suffered many things this day in a dream because of him. But the chief priests and elders persuaded the multitude that they should ask Barabbas, and destroy Jesus. The governor answered and said unto them, Whether of the twain will ye that I release unto you? They said, Barabbas. Pilate saith unto them, What shall I do then with Jesus which is called Christ? They all say unto him, Let him be crucified. And the governor said, Why, what evil hath he done? But they cried out the more, saying, Let him be crucified. When Pilate saw that he could prevail nothing, but that rather a tumult was made, he took water, and washed his hands before the multitude, saying, I am innocent of the blood of this just person: see ye to it. Then answered all the people, and said, His blood be on us, and on our children. Then released he Barabbas unto them: and when he had scourged Jesus, he delivered him to be crucified.

MARK

xiv. 43—65; xv. 1—15.

AND immediately, while he yet spake, cometh Judas, one of the twelve, and with him a great multitude with swords and staves, from the chief priests and the scribes and the elders. And he that betrayed him had given them a token, saying, Whomsoever I shall kiss, that same is he; take him, and lead him away safely. And as soon as he was come, he goeth straightway to him, and saith, Master, Master; and kissed him. And they laid their hands on him, and took him. And one of them that stood by drew a sword, and smote a servant of the high priest, and cut off his ear. And Jesus answered and said unto them, Are ye come out, as against a thief, with swords and with staves to take me? I was daily with you in the temple teaching, and ye took me not: but the scriptures must be fulfilled. And they all forsook him, and fled. And there followed him a certain young man, having a linen cloth cast about his naked body; and the young men laid hold on him: and he left the linen cloth, and fled from them naked. And they led Jesus away to the high priest: and with him were assembled all the chief priests and the elders and the scribes . . . . And the chief priests and all the council sought for witness against Jesus to put him to death; and found none. For many bare false witness against him, but their witness agreed not together. And there arose certain, and bare false witness against him, saying, We heard him say, I will destroy this temple that is made with hands, and within three days I will build another made without hands. But neither so did their witness agree together. And the high priest stood up in the midst, and asked Jesus, saying, Answerest thou nothing? what is it which these witness against thee? But he held his peace, and answered nothing. Again the high priest asked him, and said unto him, Art thou the Christ, the Son of the Blessed? And Jesus said, I am: and ye shall see the Son of man sitting on the right hand of power, and coming in the clouds of heaven. Then the high priest rent his clothes, and saith, What need we any further witnesses? Ye have heard the blasphemy: what think ye? And they all condemned him to be guilty of death. And some began to spit on him, and to cover his face, and to buffet him, and to say unto him, Prophesy: and the servants did strike him with the palms of their hands.

And straightway in the morning the chief priests held a consultation with the elders and scribes and the whole council, and bound Jesus, and carried him away, and delivered him to Pilate. And Pilate asked him, Art thou the King of the Jews? And he answering said unto him, Thou sayest it. And the chief priests accused him of many things: but he answered nothing. And Pilate asked him again, saying, Answerest thou nothing? behold how many things they witness against thee. But Jesus yet answered nothing; so that Pilate marvelled. Now at that feast he released unto them one prisoner, whomsoever they desired. And there was one named Barabbas, which lay bound with them that had made insurrection with him, who had committed murder in the insurrection. And the multitude crying aloud began to desire him to do as he had ever done unto them. But Pilate answered them, saying, Will ye that I release unto you the King of the Jews? For he knew that the chief priests had delivered him for envy. But the chief priests moved the people, that he should rather release Barabbas unto them. And Pilate answered and said again unto them, What will ye then that I shall do unto him whom ye call the King of the Jews? And they cried out again, Crucify him. Then Pilate said unto them, Why, what evil hath he done? And they cried out the more exceedingly, Crucify him. And so Pilate, willing to content the people, released Barabbas unto them, and delivered Jesus, when he had scourged him, to be crucified.

THE GOSPEL NARRATIVES

LUKE

xxii. 47—71; xxiii. 1—24.

AND while he yet spake, behold a multitude, and he that was called Judas, one of the twelve, went before them, and drew near unto Jesus to kiss him. But Jesus said unto him, Judas, betrayest thou the Son of man with a kiss? When they which were about him saw what would follow, they said unto him, Lord, shall we smite with the sword? And one of them smote the servant of the high priest, and cut off his right ear. And Jesus answered and said, Suffer ye thus far. And he touched his ear, and healed him. Then Jesus said unto the chief priests, and captains of the temple, and the elders, which were come to him, Be ye come out, as against a thief, with swords and staves? When I was daily with you in the temple, ye stretched forth no hands against me: but this is your hour, and the power of darkness. Then took they him, and led him, and brought him into the high priest's house. And Peter followed afar off . . . . And as soon as it was day, the elders of the people and the chief priests and the scribes came together, and led him into their council, saying, Art thou the Christ? tell us. And he said unto them, If I tell you, ye will not believe: And if I also ask you, ye will not answer me, nor let me go. Hereafter shall the Son of man sit on the right hand of the power of God. Then said they all, Art thou then the Son of God? And he said unto them, Ye say that I am. And they said, What need we any further witness? for we ourselves have heard of his own mouth.

And the whole multitude of them arose, and led him unto Pilate. And they began to accuse him, saying, We found this fellow perverting the nation, and forbidding to give tribute to Caesar, saying that he himself is Christ a King. And Pilate asked him, saying, Art thou the King of the Jews? And he answered him and said, Thou sayest it. Then said Pilate to the chief priests and to the people, I find no fault in this man. And they were the more fierce, saying, He stirreth up the people, teaching throughout all Jewry, beginning from Galilee to this place. When Pilate heard of Galilee, he asked whether the man were a Galilaean. And as soon as he knew that he belonged unto Herod's jurisdiction, he sent him to Herod, who himself also was at Jerusalem at that time. And when Herod saw Jesus, he was exceeding glad: for he was desirous to see him of a long season, because he had heard many things of him; and he hoped to have seen some miracle done by him. Then he questioned with him in many words; but he answered him nothing. And the chief priests and scribes stood and vehemently accused him. And Herod with his men of war set him at nought, and mocked him, and arrayed him in a gorgeous robe, and sent him again to Pilate. And the same day Pilate and Herod were made friends together: for before they were at enmity between themselves. And Pilate, when he had called together the chief priests and the rulers and the people, Said unto them, Ye have brought this man unto me, as one that perverteth the people: and, behold, I, having examined him before you, have found no fault in this man touching those things whereof ye accuse him: No, nor yet Herod: for I sent you to him, and, lo, nothing worthy of death is done unto him. I will therefore chastise him, and release him . . . . And they cried out all at once, saying, Away with this man, and release unto us Barabbas . . . . Pilate therefore, willing to release Jesus, spake again to them. But they cried, saying, Crucify him, crucify him. And he said unto them the third time, Why, what evil hath he done? I have found no cause of death in him: I will therefore chastise him, and let him go. And they were instant with loud voices, requiring that he might be crucified. And the voices of them and of the chief priests prevailed. And Pilate gave sentence that it should be as they required.

JOHN

xviii. 3—38; xix. 1—16.

JUDAS then, having received a band of men and officers from the chief priests and Pharisees, cometh thither with lanterns and torches and weapons . . . . Then the band and the captain and officers of the Jews took Jesus, and bound him, And led him away to Annas first; for he was father in law to Caiaphas, which was the high priest that same year . . . . The high priest then asked Jesus of his disciples, and of his doctrine. Jesus answered him, I spake openly to the world; I ever taught in the synagogue, and in the temple, whither the Jews always resort; and in secret have I said nothing. Why askest thou me? ask them which heard me, what I have said unto them: behold, they know what I said. And when he had thus spoken, one of the officers which stood by struck Jesus with the palm of his hand, saying, Answerest thou the high priest so? Jesus answered him, If I have spoken evil, bear witness of the evil: but if well, why smitest thou me? Now Annas had sent him bound unto Caiaphas the high priest. . . . Then led they Jesus from Caiaphas unto the hall of judgment: and it was early; and they themselves went not into the judgment hall, lest they should be defiled; but that they might eat the passover. Pilate then went out unto them, and said, What accusation bring ye against this man? They answered and said unto him, If he were not a malefactor, we would not have delivered him up unto thee. Then said Pilate unto them, Take ye him, and judge him according to your law. The Jews therefore said unto him, It is not lawful for us to put any man to death . . . . Then Pilate entered into the judgment hall again, and called Jesus, and said unto him, Art thou the King of the Jews? Jesus answered him, Sayest thou this thing of thyself, or did others tell it thee of me? Pilate answered, Am I a Jew? Thine own nation and the chief priests have delivered thee unto me: what hast thou done? Jesus answered, My kingdom is not of this world: if my kingdom were of this world, then would my servants fight, that I should not be delivered to the Jews: but now is my kingdom not from hence. Pilate therefore said unto him, Art thou a king then? Jesus answered, Thou sayest that I am a king. To this end was I born, and for this cause came I into the world, that I should bear witness unto the truth. Everyone that is of the truth heareth my voice. Pilate saith unto him, What is truth? And when he had said this, he went out again unto the Jews, and saith unto them, I find in him no fault at all.

Then Pilate therefore took Jesus, and scourged him. And the soldiers platted a crown of thorns, and put it on his head, and they put on him a purple robe, And said, Hail, King of the Jews! and they smote him with their hands. Pilate therefore went forth again, and saith unto them, Behold, I bring him forth to you, that ye may know that I find no fault in him . . . . The Jews answered him, We have a law, and by our law he ought to die, because he made himself the Son of God. When Pilate therefore heard that saying, he was the more afraid; And went again into the judgment hall, and saith unto Jesus, Whence art thou? But Jesus gave him no answer . . . . And from thenceforth Pilate sought to release him: but the Jews cried out, saying, If thou let this man go, thou art not Caesar's friend: whosoever maketh himself a king speaketh against Caesar. When Pilate therefore heard that saying, he brought Jesus forth, and sat down in the judgment seat in a place that is called the Pavement, but in the Hebrew, Gabbatha. And it was the preparation of the passover, and about the sixth hour: and he saith unto the Jews, Behold your King! But they cried out, Away with him, away with him, crucify him. Pilate saith unto them, Shall I crucify your King? The chief priests answered, We have no king but Caesar. Then delivered he him therefore unto them to be crucified. And they took Jesus, and led him away.

PART I
THE RECORD OF FACT

THE RECORD OF FACT

The Gospels of the New Testament form the record of fact in the trial of Jesus. There is not a line of authentic history in the literature of the world, sacred or profane, dealing originally and authoritatively with the facts and circumstances of the trial and crucifixion of the Christ, excepting these Gospels. A line from Philo—a dubious passage from Josephus—a mere mention by Tacitus—a few scattering fragments from the Talmud—all else is darkness, save the light that streams down through the centuries from Calvary and the Cross through the books of the Evangelists.

In dealing with the record of fact contained in the Gospels, in the trial of Jesus two questions naturally suggest themselves: (1) Are the Gospel narratives, such as we have them today, identical with those that were given to the world by the Evangelists in Apostolic times? That is, have these biographies of the Christ by the Evangelical writers been handed down to us through all the ages substantially uncorrupted and unimpaired?

(2) Are the Gospel writers—Matthew, Mark, Luke, and John—credible witnesses of the facts and circumstances recorded by them in the Gospel histories? That is, did they tell the truth when they wrote and published these narratives to the world? Satisfactory affirmative answers to these questions will establish and authenticate a perfect record of fact. The pages of Part I of this volume will be devoted to giving affirmative and satisfactory answers to these questions. And, in accomplishing this purpose, academic reasoning and metaphysical speculation will be rejected. Well-established rules of evidence, as employed in modern courts of law, will be rigorously applied. So-called "Higher Criticism" has no place in a treatise of this kind, since the critical niceties and dialectic quibbles of men like Strauss, Renan, and Baur would not be seriously considered in a modern judicial proceeding. Reasonable probability, and not mathematical certainty, is the legal test of adequacy in weighing human testimony with a view to a judicial determination.

The reader may ask: Why should not a Christian writer, in a Christian country, assume without argument that the testimony of Christian sacred writers is true? The answer is that such conduct would convert a purely legal treatise into a religious one, and substitute faith for logic. The writer of these volumes, as a Christian, believes that the Gospels relate the truth. As a lawyer, he is compelled to respect the opinions of a large proportion of mankind who differ with him, and to employ judicial methods in treating a legal theme.

The two questions above mentioned involve two distinct principles or features in the Law of Evidence: (1) Admissibility or relevancy of evidence; (2) Credibility of witnesses who have rendered testimony. All the pages of Part 1 will be devoted to a consideration of these features in their relationship to the testimony of the Evangelists.

The first question that naturally arises is this: Is there a well-established rule of the modern Law of Evidence under which the Gospels could be introduced as evidence in a modern judicial proceeding? Suppose that the question of the Resurrection of Jesus—that is, the fact of the truthfulness or falsity of the Resurrection—should become a material fact in issue in a suit in a modern court of law; could the testimony of the Evangelists relating to the Resurrection be introduced in evidence? It would probably be objected that their testimony was hearsay; that they had not been properly subjected to the cardinal tests of truth: an oath, a cross-examination, and personal demeanor while testifying. These objections might prevail if another rule of law could not be successfully invoked. Such a rule exists, and with it we have now to deal.

The author can conceive of no more satisfactory way of establishing the principle of the admissibility of the Gospels in evidence under modern law than by quoting at length from the celebrated treatise on the "Testimony of the Evangelists," by Mr. Simon Greenleaf, the greatest of all writers on the Law of Evidence. The opinion of Greenleaf on a subject of this kind is somewhat in the nature of a decision of a court of last resort, and his authority in matters of this import is unquestioned in every land where English law is practiced. The *London Law Magazine,* a few years ago, paid him the following splendid tribute: "It is no mean honor to America that her schools of jurisprudence have produced two of the first writers and best esteemed legal authorities of this century—the great and good man, Judge Story, and his worthy and eminent associate, Professor Greenleaf. Upon the existing Law of Evidence (by Greenleaf) more light has shone from the New World than from all the lawyers who adorn the courts of Europe."

Concerning the authenticity of the Sacred Scriptures and their admissibility in evidence, Greenleaf has thus written:

That the books of the Old Testament, as we now have them, are genuine; that they existed in the time of our Saviour, and were commonly received and referred to among the Jews as the sacred books of their religion; and that the text of the Four Evangelists has been handed down to us in the state in which it was originally written, that is, without having been materially corrupted or falsified, either by heretics or Christians, are facts which we are entitled to assume as true, until the contrary is shown.

The genuineness of these writings really admits of as little doubt, and is susceptible of as ready proof, as that of any ancient writings whatever. The rule of municipal law on this subject is familiar, and applies with equal force to all ancient writings, whether documentary or otherwise; and as it comes first in order, in the prosecution of these inquiries, it may, for the sake of mere convenience, be designated as our first rule.

Every document, apparently ancient, coming from the proper repository or custody, and bearing on its face no evident marks of forgery, the law presumes to be genuine, and devolves on the opposing party the burden of proving it to be otherwise.

An ancient document, offered in evidence in our courts, is said to come from the proper repository, when it is found in the place where, and under the care of persons with whom such writings might naturally and reasonably be expected to be found; for it is this custody which gives authenticity to documents found within it. If they come from such a place, and bear no evident marks of forgery, the law presumes that they are genuine, and they are permitted to be read in evidence, unless the opposing party is able successfully to impeach them. The burden of showing them to be false and unworthy of credit is devolved on the party who makes that objection. The presumption of law is the judgment of charity. It presumes that every man is innocent until he is proved guilty; that everything has been done fairly and legally until it is proved to have been otherwise; and that every document found in its proper repository, and not bearing marks of forgery, is genuine. Now this is precisely the case with the Sacred Writings. They have been used in the church from time immemorial, and are thus found in the place where alone they ought to be looked for. They come to us, and challenge our reception of them as genuine writings, precisely as Domesday Book, the Ancient Statutes of Wales, or any other of the ancient documents which have recently been published under the British Record Commission, are received. They are found in familiar use in all the churches of Christendom, as the sacred books to which all denominations of Christians refer, as the standard of their faith. There is no pretense that they were engraven on plates of gold and discovered in a cave, nor that they were brought from heaven by angels; but they are received as the plain narratives and writings of the men whose names they respectively bear, made public at the time they were written; and though there are some slight discrepancies among the copies subsequently made, there is no pretense that the originals were anywhere corrupted. If it be objected that the originals are lost, and that copies alone are now produced, the principles of the municipal law here also afford a satisfactory answer. For the multiplication of copies was a public fact, in the faithfulness of which all the Christian community had an interest; and it is a rule of law that

In matters of public and general interest, all persons must be presumed to be conversant, on the principle that individuals are presumed to be conversant with their own affairs.

Therefore it is that, in such matters, the prevailing current of assertion is resorted to as evidence, for it is to this that every member of the community is supposed to be privy. The persons, moreover, who multiplied these copies may be regarded, in some manner, as the agents of the Christian public, for whose use and benefit the copies were made; and on the ground of the credit due to such agents, and of the public nature of the facts themselves, the copies thus made are entitled to an extraordinary degree of confidence, and, as in the case of official registers and other public books, it is not necessary that they should be confirmed and sanctioned by the ordinary tests of truth. If any ancient document concerning our public rights were lost, copies which had been as universally received and acted upon as the Four Gospels have been, would have been received in evidence in any of our courts of justice, without the slightest hesitation. The entire text of the Corpus Juris Civilis is received as authority in all the courts of continental Europe, upon much weaker evidence of its genuineness; for the integrity of the Sacred Text has been preserved by the jealousy of opposing sects, beyond any moral possibility of corruption; while that of the Roman Civil Law has been preserved by tacit consent, without the interest of any opposing school, to watch over and preserve it from alteration.

These copies of the Holy Scriptures having thus been in familiar use in the churches from the time when the text was committed to writing; having been watched with vigilance by so many sects, opposed to each other in doctrine, yet all appealing to these Scriptures for the correctness of their faith; and having in all ages, down to this day, been respected as the authoritative source of all ecclesiastical power and government, and submitted to, and acted under in regard to so many claims of right, on the one hand, and so many obligations of duty, on the other; it is quite erroneous to suppose that the Christian is bound to offer any further proof of their genuineness or authenticity. It is for the objector to show them spurious; for on him, by the plainest rules of law, lies the burden of proof. If it were the case of a claim to a franchise, and a copy of an ancient deed or charter were produced in support of the title, under parallel circumstances on which to presume its genuineness, no lawyer, it is believed, would venture to deny either its admissibility in evidence or the satisfactory character of the proof. In a recent case in the House of Lords, precisely such a document, being an old manuscript copy, purporting to have been extracted from ancient Journals of the House, which were lost, and to have been made by an officer whose duty it was to prepare lists of the peers, was held admissible in a claim of peerage.[1]

Having secured the Gospel writings to be admitted in evidence under the rule laid down by Mr. Greenleaf, we are now ready to consider more at length the question of the credibility of the witnesses. The reader should bear in mind that there is a very important difference between the admission of testimony in evidence and belief in its truthfulness by the court or jury. Evidence is frequently deemed relevant and admissible, and goes to the jury for what it is worth. They may or may not believe it.

We are now ready to consider the credit that should be accorded the testimony of Matthew, Mark, Luke, and John concerning the trial and crucifixion of Jesus. And at the outset it should be borne in mind that there is a legal presumption that they told the truth. This presumption operates in their favor from the very moment that their testimony is admitted in evidence. Here, again, the opinion of Greenleaf—with all the weight and authority that such an opinion carries—is directly in point. In the "Testimony of the Evangelists" he says:

Proceeding further, to inquire whether the facts related by the Four Evangelists are proved by competent and satisfactory evidence, we are led, first, to consider on which side lies the burden of establishing the credibility of the witnesses. On this point the municipal law furnishes a rule which is of constant application in all trials by jury, and is indeed the dictate of that charity which thinketh no evil.

In the absence of circumstances which generate suspicion, every witness is to be presumed credible, until the contrary is shown, the burden of impeaching his credibility lying on the objector.

This rule serves to show the injustice with which the writers of the Gospels have ever been treated by infidels; an injustice silently acquiesced in even by Christians; in requiring the Christian affirmatively, and by positive evidence, *aliunde* to establish the credibility of his witnesses above all others, before their testimony is entitled to be considered, and in permitting the testimony of a single profane writer, alone and uncorroborated, to outweigh that of any single Christian. This is not the course in courts of chancery, where the testimony of a single witness is never permitted to outweigh the oath even of the defendant himself, interested as he is in the case; but, on the contrary, if the plaintiff, after having required the oath of his adversary, cannot overthrow it by something more than the oath of one witness, however credible, it must stand as evidence against him. But the Christian writer seems, by the usual course of the argument, to have been deprived of the common presumption of charity in his favor; and reversing the ordinary rule of administering justice in human tribunals, his testimony is unjustly presumed to be false, until it is proved to be true. This treatment, moreover, has been applied to them all in a body; and without due regard to the fact, that, being independent historians, writing at different periods, they are entitled to the support of each other; they have been treated, in the argument, almost as if the New Testament were the entire production, at once, of a body of men, conspiring by a joint fabrication, to impose a false religion upon the world. It is time that this injustice should cease; that the testimony of the evangelists should be admitted to be true, until it can be disproved by those who would impugn it; that the silence of one sacred writer on any point should no more detract from his own veracity or that of other historians, than the like circumstance is permitted to do among profane writers; and that the Four Evangelists should be admitted in corroboration of each other, as readily as Josephus and Tacitus, or Polybius and Livy.[2]

The reader will notice from the last extract that the eminent writer quoted has sought to establish the credibility of the Evangelists by a legal presumption in favor of their veracity. But it should be borne in mind that this presumption is a disputable one, and may be overturned by opposing evidence; that objections may be raised which will destroy the force of the presumption and shift the burden again to him who asserts the credibility of the witnesses. Now, let us suppose that such objections have been made, and that sufficient opposing evidence has been offered to accomplish this result; what has the Christian then to say in support of the credibility of the first historians of his faith? What proofs has he to offer, independent of legal presumption, that the first biographers of the Master were truthful men? Can he show that the application of legal tests to their credibility will save them in the eyes of a critical and unbelieving world? The writer believes that the Christian can do it, and will at once assume the task.

In "Starkie on Evidence" we find elaborated a rule of municipal law, at once concise and comprehensive, which furnishes a complete test of the credibility of witnesses. The various elements of this rule are constantly operating in the mind of the successful cross-examiner in the course of any extensive cross-examination.

The credit due to the testimony of witnesses depends upon, firstly, their honesty; secondly, their ability; thirdly, their number and the consistency of their testimony; fourthly, the conformity of their testimony with experience; and fifthly, the coincidence of their testimony with collateral circumstances. [3]

Let us apply these successive tests, in the order above enumerated, to the Evangelists.

(1) In the first place, let us consider the question of their *honesty.*

The meaning of the word "honesty," used in this connection, is peculiar. It relates rather to personal sincerity than to personal integrity, and suggests the idea of perjury rather than theft in criminal law. Were the witnesses honest? That is, were they sincere? Did they intend to tell the truth? That is, did they themselves believe what they testified? If so, they were honest witnesses, though their testimony was false, as a result of error in judgment or mistake of fact.

In the sense, then, of *sincerity* is the test of honesty to be applied to the Evangelists as witnesses of the facts which they relate in the New Testament narratives. And in making this test let us bear in mind the nature and scope of this work; that it is not a religious treatise, and that the question of inspiration must not be allowed to confuse a purely legal and historical discussion. As secular historians, and not as inspired writers, must the Evangelists be considered. And in testing their credibility, the customary standards employed in analyzing the motives and conduct of ordinary men in the usual experiences and everyday affairs of life must be applied. To regard them as strange or supernatural beings, subject to some awful influence, and acting under the guidance and protection of some god or hero, is decidedly foreign to the present purpose.

It is felt that only two considerations are needed in applying the test of sincerity to the Evangelists: (1) Character; (2) Motive. And this for the reason that honest character and righteous motive are the legitimate parentage of perfect sincerity. Then, as a primary consideration, in discussing their sincerity, it may be reasonably contended that the Gospel writers were either good men or bad. A middle ground is not possible in their case, since the issues joined and the results attained were too terrible and stupendous to have been produced by negative or indifferent forces. Were they good men, then they believed what they taught and wrote, and were sincere, else they deliberately palmed off an imposture on the world, which is inconsistent with the hypothesis that they were good. Were they bad men, then their lives and teachings furnish a contradiction in principle and an inversion in the nature and order of cause and effect which history has not elsewhere recorded, either before or since; for, in their discourses and their writings, they portrayed the divinest character and proclaimed the sublimest truths known to the children of men. Every serious, thoughtful mind at once inquires: Could bad men, conspirators and hypocrites, have painted such a character—one whose perfect purity and sinless beauty mock and shame the mental and spiritual attributes of every false prophet and of all heathen gods? The Olympian Zeus, the sovereign creation of the superb Greek intellect, was a fierce and vindictive deity—at times a faithless spouse and a drunken debauchee. Mahomet, whom two hundred millions of the human race worship as the Inspired of Allah, was cruel and treacherous in warfare, and base and sensual in private life. The Great Spirit of the Indian granted immortality to dogs, but denied it to women. Other hideous and monstrous attributes deformed the images and blurred the characters of pagan prophets and heathen divinities. But Jesus of Nazareth was a pure and perfect being who claimed to be sinless,[4] and whose claims have been admitted by all the world, believers and unbelievers alike. The great truths taught by the gentle Nazarene and transmitted by the Evangelists have brought balm and healing to the nations, have proclaimed and established universal brotherhood among men. Is it probable that such a character was painted and such truths proclaimed by dishonest and insincere men? Can Vice be the mother of Virtue? "Do men gather grapes of thorns or figs of thistles?" If Jesus was not really the pure and holy being portrayed by the Gospels, then the Evangelists have created a sublime character in a superb fiction which surpasses anything to be found in profane literature, and that evil-minded men could neither have conceived nor executed. It is impossible to derive from these reflections any other conclusion than the absolute honesty and perfect sincerity of the Evangelists. Besides, the mere perusal of their writings leaves a deep impression that they were pure and pious men.

Again, a second and more serious consideration than that of character, as affecting the sincerity of the Gospel writers, is the question of motive. If the Evangelists were insincere and did not believe their own story, what motive prompted them to tell it, to preach it, and to die for it? It is not believed that all men are now or have ever been wholly selfish, but it is contended that desire for compensation is the main inducement to human action, mental and manual. Reward is the great golden key that opens the door of the Temple of Labor, and some form of recompense, here or hereafter, explains all the bustling activity of men. The Apostles themselves acted in obedience to this law, for we find them quarreling among themselves as to place and precedence in the New Kingdom. They even demanded of the Master the exact nature of their reward for labors performed and sacrifices endured. To which reply was made that they should sit on twelve thrones and judge the Twelve Tribes of Israel.

Now let us apply this principle of expectation of reward to the conduct of the Evangelists in preaching and publishing the Gospel of the Nazarene, and let us note particularly the result as it affects the question of motive in human conduct. But first let us review, for a moment, the political and religious situation at the beginning of the Apostolic ministry. The Master and Savior of the first Christians had just perished as a malefactor on the cross. The religion which the Apostles began to preach was founded in the doctrine of repentance from sins, faith in the Crucified One, and belief in His resurrection from the dead. Christianity, of which these elements were the essentials, sought to destroy and supplant all other religions. No compromises were proposed, no treaties were concluded. The followers of the Nazarene raised a black flag against paganism and every heathen god. No quarter was asked and none was given. This strange faith not only defied all other religions, but mocked all earthly government not built upon it. The small but devoted band thus arrayed against themselves in the very beginning all the opposing religious and secular forces of the earth. Judaism branded the new creed as a disobedient and rebellious daughter. Paganism denounced it as a sham and a fraud, because its doctrines were unknown to the Portico and the Academy, and because its teachings were ridiculed by both Stoics and Epicureans. The Roman State cast a jealous and watchful eye upon the haughty pretensions of a religious system that taught the impotence of kings and sought to degrade earthly royalty.

In seeking, then, to establish the new faith and to inculcate its doctrines, what could and did the evangelists expect but the bitter opposition which they met? Did they seriously hope to see the proud and haughty Sadducee, who despised the common people, or the kingly aristocracy of Rome, that vaunted a superhuman excellence, complacently accept a religion that taught the absolute equality and the universal brotherhood of men? Did they not expect what they actually received—bitter persecution, horrible torture, and cruel death? Then we are led to ask: Was this the recompense which they sought? Again, we pose the question: What was the motive of these men in thus acting, if they were dishonest and insincere? If they knew that they were preaching a falsehood, what reward did they expect? Was it of an earthly or a heavenly kind? It is unreasonable to suppose that they looked forward to earthly recompense when their teachings arrayed against them every spiritual and temporal potentate who had honors to grant or favors to confer. Were they looking for heavenly reward? It is ridiculous to imagine that they hoped to gain this by preaching a falsehood in this world. Nothing could be, therefore, more absurd than the proposition that a number of men banded themselves together, repudiated the ancient faith of their fathers, changed completely their mode of life, became austere in professing and practicing principles of virtue, spent their entire lives proclaiming certain truths to mankind, and then suffered the deaths of martyrs—all for the sake of a religion which they knew to be false. If they did not believe it to be false, they were sincere, and one element of their credibility is established. It is not a question at this time as to the absolute correctness of their statements. These statements might have been false, though their authors believed them to be true—it is a question of sincerity at this point; and the test of sincerity, as an element of credibility, rests upon the simple basis that men are more disposed to believe the statement of a witness if it is thought that the witness himself believes it.

(2)   In the second place, let us consider the *ability* of the Evangelists as a test of their credibility as witnesses.

The text writers on the Law of Evidence are generally agreed that the ability of a witness to speak truthfully and accurately depends upon two considerations: (1) His natural powers of observation, which enable him to clearly perceive, and his strength of memory, which enables him to fully retain the matters of fact to which his testimony relates; (2) his opportunities for observing the things about which he testifies.

To what extent the Gospel writers possessed the first of these qualifications—that is, power of observation and strength of memory—we are not informed by either history or tradition. But we are certainly justified in assuming to be true what the law actually presumes: that they were at least men of sound mind and average intelligence. This presumption, it may be remarked, continues to exist in favor of the witness until an objector appears who proves the contrary by competent and satisfactory evidence. It is not believed that this proof has ever been or can ever be successfully established in the case of the Evangelists.

Aside from this legal presumption in their favor, there are certain considerations which lead us to believe that they were well qualified to speak truthfully and authoritatively about the matters relating to Gospel history. In the first place, the writings themselves indicate extraordinary mental vigor, as well as cultivated intelligence. The Gospels of Luke and John, moreover, reveal that elegance of style and lofty imagery which are the invariable characteristics of intellectual depth and culture. The "ignorant fishermen" idea is certainly not applicable to the Gospel writers. If they were ever very ignorant, at the time of the composition of the Evangelical writings they had outgrown the affliction. The fact that the Gospels were written in Greek by Hebrews indicates that they were not entirely illiterate.

Again, the occupations of two of them are very suggestive. Matthew was a collector at the seat of customs,[5] and Luke was a physician.[6] Both these callings required more than ordinary knowledge of men, as well as accurate powers of observation, discrimination, and analysis.

But it has been frequently urged that, regardless of their natural endowments, the Evangelists were biased in favor of Jesus and His teachings, and bitterly prejudiced against all opposing faiths. In other words, they were at the same moment both enthusiasts and fanatics. For this reason, it is contended, their testimony is unreliable. This is without doubt the weakest assault ever made upon the trustworthiness of the Gospel narratives. That the Gospel writers were neither fanatics nor enthusiasts is evident from the very tone and style of the Sacred Writings themselves. The language of fanaticism and enthusiasm is the language of rant and rage, of vituperation and of censure, on the one hand, and of eulogy and adulation on the other. The enthusiast knows no limit to the praise of those whose cause he advocates. The fanatic places no bounds to his denunciation of those whom he opposes. Now, the most remarkable characteristic of the New Testament histories is the spirit of quiet dignity and simple candor which everywhere pervades them. There is nowhere the slightest trace of bitterness or resentment. There is enthusiasm everywhere in the sense of religious fervor, but nowhere in the sense of unbecoming heat or impatient caviling. The three eventful years of the ministry of Jesus afforded many opportunities for the display of temper and for the use of invective in the Evangelical writings. The murder of the Baptist by Herod; his cunning designs against Jesus; the constant dogging of the footsteps of the Master by the spies of the Sanhedrin; and His crucifixion by the order of Pontius Pilate—what more could be desired to make the heart rage and the blood boil? But nowhere is there the slightest exhibition of violent feeling or extravagant emotion. A gentle forbearance, a mild equanimity, a becoming dignity, mark every thought and utterance. The character of Pilate, as portrayed in the New Testament, is a supreme illustration of the fairness and magnanimity of the Gospel writers. Philo and Josephus describe the Roman procurator as stubborn, cruel, and vindictive. The only kindly suggestion touching the character of Pilate that has come down from the ancient world, is that contained in the writings of men who, above all others, would have been justified in describing him as cowardly and craven. Instead of painting him as a monster, they have linked conscience to his character and stored mercy in his heart, by their accounts of his repeated attempts to release Jesus. Fanatics and enthusiasts would not have done this.

Again, the absence of both bias and prejudice in the minds and hearts of the Evangelists is shown by the fact that they did not hesitate to record their own ludicrous foibles and blunders, and to proclaim them to the world. A disposition to do this is one of the surest indications of a truthful mind. It is in the nature of "a declaration against interest," in the phraseology of the law; and such declarations are believed because it has been universally observed that "men are not likely to invent anecdotes to their own discredit." "When we find them in any author," says Professor Fisher in his "Grounds of Theistic and Christian Belief," "a strong presumption is raised in favor of his general truthfulness." Many passages of New Testament Scriptures place Jesus and the Apostles in a most unfavorable light before the world. The denial of the Master by Peter[7] and His betrayal by Judas;[8] the flight of the Eleven from the Garden at the time of the arrest;[9] the ridiculous attempt of Peter to walk upon the sea and his failure because of lack of faith;[10] the frequent childish contentions among the disciples for place and precedence in the affections of Jesus and in the New Kingdom;[11] the embassy from John the Baptist to Jesus asking if He, Jesus, was the Messiah, after the latter had already visited the former, and had been baptized by him;[12] the belief of the family of Jesus that He was mad;[13] and the fact that His neighbors at Nazareth threatened to kill Him by hurling Him from a cliff[14]—these various recitals have furnished a handle to skeptical criticism in every age. They might as well have been omitted from the Gospel histories; and they would have been omitted by designing and untruthful men.

Again, touching the question of bias and prejudice, it is worthy of observation that skeptics fail to apply the same rules of criticism to sacred that they employ in profane literature. It is contended by them that the Evangelists are unworthy of belief because their writings record the words and deeds of their own Lord and Master. It is asserted that this sacred and tender relationship warped and blinded their judgment, and disqualified them to write truthfully the facts and circumstances connected with the life and ministry of the founder of their faith. But these same critics do not apply the same tests of credibility to secular writers sustaining similar relationships. The Commentaries of Caesar and the Anabasis of Xenophon record the mighty deeds and brilliant achievements of their authors; but this fact does not destroy their reliability as historical records in the estimation of those who insist that the Gospel writers shall be rejected on grounds of bias and partiality. The Memorabilia of Xenophon, "Recollections of Socrates," is the tribute of an affectionate and admiring disciple; and yet, all the colleges and universities of the world employ this work as a textbook in teaching the life and style of conversation of the great Athenian philosopher. It is never argued that the intimate relationship between Xenophon and Socrates should affect the credibility of the author of the Memorabilia. The best biography in the English language is Boswell's "Life of Johnson." Boswell's admiration for Dr. Johnson was idolatrous. At times, his servile flattery of the great Englishman amounted to disgusting sycophancy. In spite of this, his work is a monumental contribution to historical literature. The "Encyclopedia Britannica" says that "Boswell has produced the best biography the world has yet seen"; but why not reject this book because of its author's spaniel-like devotion to the man whose life he has written? If Matthew, Mark, Luke, and John are to be repudiated on the ground of bias, why not repudiate Caesar, Xenophon, and Boswell? It is respectfully submitted that there is no real difference in logic between the tests of credibility applicable to sacred, and those required in the case of profane writers. A just and exact criticism will apply the same rules to both.

As to the second qualification above mentioned, under the second legal test of credibility laid down by Starkie, that is, the opportunity of observing facts and circumstances about which testimony is given, it may safely be said that the majority of the Evangelists possessed it in the highest degree. The most convincing testimony that can possibly be offered in a court of law is that of an eyewitness who has seen or heard what he testifies. Now, it is reasonably certain that all of the Gospel writers were eyewitnesses of most of the events recorded by them in the Gospel histories. Both Matthew and John were numbered among the Twelve who constantly attended the Master in all His wanderings, heard His discourses, witnessed the performance of His miracles, and proclaimed His faith after He was gone. It is very probable that Mark was another eyewitness of the events in the life and ministry of the Savior. It is now very generally agreed that the author of the Second Gospel was the young man who threw away his garment and fled at the time of the arrest in the Garden.[15] If Mark was actually present at midnight in Gethsemane peering through the shadows to see what would be done to the Nazarene by the mob, it is more than probable that he was also a witness of

many other events in the life and ministry of the great Teacher. But, whether this be true or not, it is very well settled that the Second Gospel was dictated to Mark by Peter, who was as familiar with all the acts and words of Jesus as was Matthew or John. The Christian writers of antiquity unanimously testify that Mark wrote the Gospel ascribed to him, at the dictation of Peter. If their testimony is true, Peter is the real author of the Second Gospel. That the Gospel of Mark was written by an eyewitness is the opinion of Renan, the skeptic, who says: "In Mark, the facts are related with a clearness for which we seek in vain amongst the other Evangelists. He likes to report certain words of Jesus in Syro-Chaldean. He is full of minute observations, coming doubtless from an eye-witness. There is nothing to prevent our agreeing with Papias in regarding this eye-witness, who evidently had followed Jesus, who had loved Him and observed Him very closely, and who had preserved a lively image of Him, as the Apostle Peter himself."[16] The same writer declares Matthew to have been an eyewitness of the events described by him. He says: "On the whole, I admit as authentic the four canonical Gospels. All, in my opinion, date from the first century, and the authors are, generally speaking, those to whom they are attributed; but their historic value is diverse. Matthew evidently merits an unlimited confidence as to the discourses; they are the Logia, the identical notes taken from a clear and lively remembrance of the teachings of Jesus."[16]

That Luke was an eyewitness of many of the things recorded by him, and that the others were related to him by eyewitnesses, is perfectly clear from the introductory verses of his Gospel. In addressing his royal patron. Theophilus, he assures him that those who communicated the information contained in the Gospel to him were eyewitnesses; and follows by saying that he himself had had "perfect understanding of all things from the very first."[17] The evident meaning of this is that, desiring full information for Theophilus, he had supplemented his own personal knowledge by additional facts secured from eyewitnesses to those things which, not being of the Twelve, he himself had not seen.

St. John was peculiarly well qualified to record the sayings and doings of the Christ. He was called "the disciple whom Jesus loved." He was admitted into the presence of the Savior, at all times, on terms of the utmost intimacy and friendship. At the Last Supper, his head reposed confidingly and lovingly upon the bosom of the Master. Together with Peter and James, he witnessed the resurrection of Jairus' daughter; was present at the Transfiguration on the Mount, and at the agony of the Savior in the Garden. From the cross, Jesus placed upon him the tender and pathetic burden of caring for His mother; and running ahead of Peter, he was the first among the Twelve to arrive at the open sepulcher. By means of a favorable acquaintance with the High Priest, he was enabled to gain access to the palace and to be present at the trial of Jesus, as well as to introduce Peter, his friend.

It is thus clearly evident that the Evangelists were amply able, from any point of view, to truthfully and accurately record the events narrated in the Gospel histories. As eyewitnesses, being on the ground and having the situation well in hand, they were certainly better qualified to write truthful history of the events then occurring than historians and critics who lived centuries afterwards.

But it is frequently contended that, if the Evangelists were eyewitnesses of the leading events which they recorded, they committed them to writing so long afterwards that they had forgotten them, or had confused them with various traditions that had in the meantime grown up. There may be some little truth in this contention, but not enough to destroy the credibility of the witnesses as to events such as the Crucifixion and Resurrection of Jesus. These are not matters to be easily forgotten or confused with other things. The date of the composition and publication of the different Gospels is not known. But Professor Holtzmann, of Heidleberg (a man who cannot be said to be favorable to Christianity, since he was for several years the leader of the freethinkers in the Grand Duchy of Baden), after many years of careful study of the subject, declared that the Synoptic Gospels, the first three, were committed to writing between the years 60 and 80 of our era.[18] This was only from thirty to fifty years after the death of Jesus. Could men of average memory and intelligence who had been almost daily preaching the life and deeds of Jesus during these thirty or fifty years have forgotten them? The testimony of Principal Drummond, of Oxford, is very pertinent at this point. He says: "If we suppose that the Synoptic Gospels were written from forty to sixty years after the time of Christ, still they were based on earlier material, and even after forty years the memory of characteristic sayings may be perfectly clear. . . . I have not a particularly good memory, but I can recall many sayings that were uttered forty, or even fifty, years ago, and in some cases can vividly recollect the scene."[19]

If the Evangelists were eyewitnesses, which the records seem clearly to indicate, they possessed one of the strongest tests of credibility.

(3)   In the third place, as to their *number* and the *consistency* of their testimony.

The credibility of a witness is greatly strengthened if his testimony is corroborated by other witnesses who testify to substantially the same thing. The greater the number of supporting witnesses, fraud and collusion being barred, the greater the credibility of the witness corroborated. But corroboration implies the presence in evidence of due and reasonable consistency between the testimony of the witness testifying and that of those corroborating. A radical discrepancy on a material point not only fails to strengthen, but tends to destroy the credibility of one or both the witnesses.

Now, the fierce fire of skeptical criticism during all the ages has been centered upon the so-called discrepancies of the Gospel narratives. It is asserted by many critics that these inconsistencies are so numerous and so palpable, that the Gospel records are worthless, even as secular histories. The authors of these writings, according to the skeptics, mutually destroy each other.

In considering this phase of the credibility of the Gospel writers, it must again be remembered that the question of inspiration has no place in this discussion; and that Matthew, Mark, Luke, and John must be regarded simply as secular historians. The reader is urged to consider the biographers of the Christ as he would consider ordinary witnesses in a court of law; to apply to them the same tests of credibility; to sift and weigh their testimony in the same manner; and to subject them to the same rules of cross-examination. If this is done, it is felt that the result will be entirely favorable to the veracity and integrity of the sacred writers.

In considering the subject of discrepancies it should be constantly kept in mind that contradictions in testimony do not necessarily mean that there has been falsehood or bad faith on the part of the witnesses. Every lawyer of experience and every adult citizen of average intelligence knows that this is true. Men of unquestioned veracity and incorruptible integrity are frequently arrayed against each other in both civil and criminal trials, and the record reveals irreconcilable contradictions in their testimony. Not only do prosecutions for perjury not follow, but, in many instances, the witnesses are not even suspected of bad faith or an intention to falsify. Defects in sight, hearing, or memory; superior advantage in the matter of observation; or a sudden change in the position of one or both the parties, causing distraction of attention, at the time of the occurrence of the events involved in litigation—all or any of these conditions, as well as many others, may create discrepancies and contradictions where there is a total absence of any intention to misrepresent. A thorough appreciation of this fact will greatly aid in a clear understanding of this phase of the discussion.

Again, an investigation of the charge of discrepancy against the Gospel writers shows that the critics and skeptics have classified mere *omissions* as contradictions. Nothing could be more absurd than to consider an omission a contradiction, unless the requirements of the case show that the facts and circumstances omitted were essential to be stated, or that the omission was evidently intended to mislead or deceive. Any other contention would turn historical literature topsy-turvy and load it down with contradictions. Dion Cassius, Tacitus, and Suetonius have all written elaborately of the reign of Tiberius. Many things are mentioned by each that are not recorded by the other two. Are we to reject all three as unreliable historians because of this fact? Abbott, Hazlitt, Bourrienne, and Walter Scott have written biographies of Napoleon Bonaparte. No one of them has recited all the facts recorded by the others. Are these omissions to destroy the merits of all these writers and cause them to be suspected and rejected? Grafton's Chronicles rank high in English historical literature. They comprise the reign of King John; and yet make no mention of the granting of Magna Charta. This is as if the life of Jefferson had been written without mention of the Declaration of Independence; or a biography of Lincoln without calling attention to the Emancipation Proclamation. Notwithstanding this strange omission, Englishmen still preserve Grafton's Chronicles as valuable records among their archives. And the same spirit of generous criticism is everywhere displayed in matters of profane literature. The opponents of Christianity are never embarrassed in excusing or explaining away omissions or contradictions, provided the writer is a layman and his subject secular. But let the theme be a sacred one, and the author an ecclesiastic—preacher, priest, or prophet—and immediately incredulity rises to high tide, engulfs the reason, and destroys all dispassionate criticism. Could it be forgotten for a moment that Matthew, Mark, Luke, and John were biographers of the Christ, a sacred person, no difficulties would arise in the matter of inconsistencies, no objections would be made to their credibility. The slight discrepancies that undoubtedly exist would pass unnoticed, or be forever buried under the weight of an overwhelming conviction that they are, in the main, accurate and truthful.

But the Evangelists were guided by inspiration, the skeptics say; and discrepancies are inconsistent with the theory of inspiration. God would not have inspired them to write contradictory stories. But the assumption is false that they claimed to be guided by inspiration; for, as Marcus Dods truthfully says, "none of our Gospels pretends to be infallible or even *inspired*. Only one of them tells us how its writer obtained his information, and that was by careful inquiry at the proper sources."[20]

But whether the Gospel writers were inspired or not is immaterial so far as the purpose of this chapter is concerned. The rules of evidence testing their credibility would be the same in either case.

A more pertinent observation upon the Gospel discrepancies has not been made than that by Paley in his "Evidences of Christianity," where he says:

I know not a more rash or more unphilosophical conduct of the understanding than to reject the substance of a story by reason of some diversity in the circumstances with which it is related. The usual character of human testimony is substantial truth under circumstantial variety. This is what the daily experience of courts of justice teaches. When accounts of a transaction come from the mouths of different witnesses it is seldom that it is not possible to pick out apparent or real inconsistencies between them. These inconsistencies are studiously displayed by an adverse pleader, but oftentimes with little impression upon the minds of the judges. On the contrary, a close and minute agreement induces the suspicion of confederacy and fraud. When written histories touch upon the same scenes of action, the comparison almost always affords ground for a like reflection. Numerous, and sometimes important, variations present themselves; not seldom, also, absolute and final contradictions; yet neither one nor the other are deemed sufficient to shake the credibility of the main fact. The embassy of the Jews to deprecate the execution of Claudian's order to place his statue in their temple, Philo places in the harvest, Josephus in seed-time; both contemporary writers. No reader is led by this inconsistency to doubt whether such an embassy was sent, or whether such an order was given. Our own history supplies examples of the same kind. In the account of the Marquis of Argyll's death, in the reign of Charles II, we have a very remarkable contradiction. Lord Clarendon relates that he was condemned to be hanged, which was performed the same day; on the contrary, Burnet, Woodrow, Heath, Echard, concur in stating that he was condemned upon the Saturday and executed upon a Monday. Was any reader of English history ever skeptic enough to raise from hence a question, whether the Marquis of Argyll was executed or not? Yet this ought to be left in uncertainty, according to the principles upon which the Christian history has sometimes been attacked.[21]

The reader should most carefully consider the useful as well as the damaging effect of Gospel inconsistencies in the matter of the credibility of the Evangelists. A certain class of persons have imagined the Gospel writers to be common conspirators who met together at the same time and place to devise ways and means of publishing a false report to the world. This is a silly supposition, since it is positively known that the authors of the Evangelical narratives wrote and published them at different times and places. Moreover, the style and contents of the books themselves negative the idea of a concerted purpose to deceive. And, besides, the very inconsistencies themselves show that there was no "confederacy and fraud"; since intelligent conspirators would have fabricated exactly the same story in substantially the same language.

Furthermore, a just and impartial criticism will consider not only the discrepant but also the corroborative elements in the New Testament histories. It should not be forgotten that the authors of the Gospels were independent historians who wrote at different times and places. Then, in all matters of fact in which there is a common agreement, they may be said to fully corroborate each other. And it may be contended without fear of successful contradiction that, when so considered, there will be found numerous cases of corroboration where there is one of discord or inconsistency.

The corroborative elements or features in the Evangelical narratives may be classified under three headings: (1) Instances in which certain historical events related by one of the Gospel writers are also told by one or more of the others. These are cases of ordinary corroboration. (2) Instances in which the recital of a certain fact by one of the Evangelists would be obscure or meaningless unless explained or supplemented by another. These may be regarded as examples of internal confirmation. (3) Instances in which the fact related by one Evangelist must be true from the nature of the case, regardless of what the others have said. This is the simple confirmation of logic or reason.

A few illustrations will serve to make clear this classification.

Under the first heading of "ordinary corroboration" may be mentioned the accounts of the miracle of feeding the five thousand. All the Evangelists tell us of this event, and each records the fact that the fragments taken up were *twelve baskets full.*[22]

Under the second heading of "internal confirmation" the following instances may be cited:

Matt. xxvi. 67, 68: "And others smote him with the palms of their hands, saying, Prophesy unto us, thou Christ, Who is he that smote thee?"

A caviling criticism would demand: Why ask of the Christ to *prophesy* to those in His presence? And the obscurity would be damaging, were it not for an additional sentence in Luke, who records the same circumstance. *"And when they had blindfolded him.* they struck him on the face, and asked him, saying Prophesy, Who is it that smote thee?"[23] The fact that Jesus was blindfolded, which is told by Luke, explains the use of the word "prophesy" by Matthew, which would otherwise be absurd.

Again, Matt. xiii. 2: "And great multitudes were gathered together with him, so that he went into the ship, and sat." Here, the definite article points to a particular ship which Matthew fails to mention. But Mark comes to his aid and clearly explains the statement: "And he spake to his disciples, that a small vessel should wait upon him because of the multitude, lest they should throng him."

These two passages taken together identify the ship.

Again, John vi. 5: "When Jesus lifted up his eyes, and saw a great company come to him, he saith unto Philip, Whence shall we buy bread that these may eat?" This is one of the only two places in the Gospel where Jesus addressed this Apostle. But why ask Philip instead of one of the others? Two other passages, one from John and one from Luke, furnish an explanation. In John i. 44 we read that "Philip was of Bethsaida." In Luke ix. 10 we learn that the scene of the event, the miracle of feeding the five thousand, was "a desert place belonging to the city called Bethsaida." The reason, then, for addressing Philip, instead of one of the other Apostles, is clear. Bethsaida was the home of Philip; and he would naturally, therefore, be more familiar with the location of the bread shops than the others. In John vi., where the question is asked, neither the place of the feeding nor the apostle questioned is even remotely connected with the city of Bethsaida; and in Luke the account of the miracle says nothing of Philip or the question put to him. But when the passages are connected the striking coincidence appears, and the explanation is complete.

Again, John xviii. 10: "Then Simon Peter, having a sword, drew it and smote the high priest's servant, and cut off his right ear. The servant's name was Malchus." It has been objected that there is nowhere an account of the arrest or punishment of Peter for this assault and resistance to armed authority; and that, therefore, there was no such occurrence. A passage from Luke explains the failure to arrest. "And Jesus answered and said, Suffer ye thus far, and he touched his ear and healed him."[1] The healing of the ear explains why no arrest followed; for, if charges had been made, there would have been no evidence of the gravity of the offense. Indeed, witnesses against Peter would have been completely confounded and humiliated by the result of the miracle; and might have been driven from court as malicious accusers. Then, the failure to arrest is a silent corroboration of the statement that the event occurred and that the miracle was performed.

Under the third heading, of the "confirmation of logic or reason," a single instance will suffice.

John xx. 4: "And the other disciple did outrun Peter and came first to the sepulchre." The "other disciple" was St. John, who is generally conceded to have been the youngest of the Apostles. And St. Peter, we may judge from John xxi. 18, was already past the meridian of life. What could be more natural than that the younger man should outrun the older and arrive first at the sepulcher? What better proof could be expected of the fact of the existence of that sweetness and modesty in youth which respects old age, and that endeared John to Jesus above all others, than we have here, where the younger man awaits the arrival of the older before beginning to explore the deserted tomb?

Examples similar to these might be multiplied at length, since the Gospel histories are filled with them; but those above mentioned are deemed sufficient to illustrate the theory of corroboration. The instances of internal confirmation in the New Testament narratives are especially convincing. They are arguments and proofs in the nature of undesigned coincidences which, from the very nature of the case, shut out all possibility of collusion or fraud. In most cases they are expressed in a single phrase and represent an isolated thought corroborative of some other elsewhere expressed. Though small, detached, and fragmentary, like particles of dynamite, they operate with resistless force when collected and combined.

Once more attention is called to the fact that these discrepancies negative completely the idea that the Gospel writers were conspirators, bent upon the common purpose of deceiving mankind by publishing a false history to the world. Nothing could be more absurd than to suppose that men conspiring to perpetrate a fraud, would neglect a fundamental principle underlying all successful conspiracy; that is, the creation and maintenance of a due and reasonable consistency between the words and deeds of the conspirators in formulating plans for carrying out the common purpose. Then, if there was no previous concert, the fact that four men, writing at different times and places, concurred in framing substantially the same history, is one of the strongest proofs of the credibility of the writers and the truthfulness of their narratives. And on this point the testimony of a very great writer may be quoted: that "in a number of concurrent testimonies, where there has been no previous concert, there is a probability distinct from that which may be termed the sum of the probabilities resulting from the testimonies of the witnesses; a probability which would remain, even though the witnesses were of such a character as to merit no faith at all. This probability arises from the concurrence itself. That such a concurrence should spring from chance is as one to infinite; that is, in other words, morally impossible. If, therefore, concert be excluded, there remains no cause but the reality of the fact."[25]

Apply the theory of probability, arising from concurrent testimonies, where there has been no previous concert, to the case of the Evangelists, and we are at once convinced that they were truthful and that their histories are true.

(4) Let us now consider the *conformity of the testimony of the Evangelists with human experience.* This is the fourth legal test of the credibility of witnesses prescribed by Starkie.

The conformity of testimony with experience is one of the most potent and universally applied tests of the credibility of witnesses. And it may be remarked that its application is not confined to judicial proceedings or to courts of law. It requires no professional attainments to make it effective. The blacksmith and carpenter, as well as the judge and jury, employ it in every mental operation where the statements of others are submitted to analysis and investigation. A new theory being proposed, the correctness of which is questioned, the test of experience is at once applied. If it is not in harmony with what we have seen and heard and felt, we usually reject it; or, at least, doubt it. If an explorer should return from the Arctic regions and tell us that he had seen oranges, such as we import from Florida, growing on trees near the North Pole, we would not believe him. Neither would we credit the statement of a traveler from South America that he had seen Polar bears browsing on the banks of the Amazon. These representations would be utterly inconsistent with what we know to be the essential conditions of orange culture, and with the well-known habits and climatic nature of the Polar bear. An ancient document, purporting to date from the time of Washington and the Revolution, and containing recitals about railways, telegraphs, telephones, and electric lights, would be recognized at once as spurious, because our own experience as well as facts of history would tell us that there were no such things in the days of Washington and the American Revolution. These are simple illustrations of the application of the test of experience in the mental processes of weighing and sifting the testimony of others.

Now, no serious objection to the credibility of the Gospel writers has been made under the test of the conformity of their statements with experience, except in the matter of miracles. It is generally admitted, even by skeptics, that the facts stated in the New Testament narratives might have happened in the due course of nature and in harmony with human experience, except where miracles are related.

A few skeptics have declared that a miracle is an impossibility and that the Evangelists were either deceivers or deceived when they wrote their accounts of the miraculous performances of the Christ; and that, whether deceivers or deceived, they are unworthy of belief. The great antagonist of the theory of miracles among those who assert their impossibility is Spinoza, who has thus written: "A miracle, whether contrary to or above nature, is a sheer absurdity. Nothing happens in nature which does not follow from its laws; these laws extend to all which enters the Divine mind; and, lastly, nature proceeds in a fixed and changeless course—whence it follows that the word 'miracle' can only be understood in relation to the opinions of mankind, and signifies nothing more than an event, a phenomenon, the cause of which cannot be explained by another familiar instance . . . I might say, indeed, that a miracle was *that,* the cause of which cannot be explained by our *natural understanding from the known principles of natural things."*

The radical antagonism of Spinoza to the doctrine of miracles, as taught in the New Testament scriptures, was the legitimate offspring of his peculiar philosophy. He was a pantheist and identified God with nature. He did not believe in a personal God, separate from and superior to nature. He repudiated the theory of a spiritual kingdom having a spiritual sovereign to whom earth and nature are subject and obedient. Therefore, every manifestation of power which he could not identify with a natural force he believed was unreal, if not actually deceptive and fraudulent; since he could not imagine anything superior to nature that could have created the phenomenon. His denial of miracles was, then, really nothing less than a denial of the existence of a personal God who spoke the earth into being in the very beginning; and has since, with a watchful paternal eye, followed its movements and controlled its destiny.

The question of miracles is really a matter of faith and not a problem of science.

It is impossible to either prove or disprove the nature of a miracle by physical demonstration. In other words, it is impossible to analyze a miracle from the standpoint of chemistry or physics. The performance of a miracle, nevertheless, may be proved by ordinary human testimony, as any other event may be proved. We may testify to the fact without being able to understand or to demonstrate the cause.

Those who believe that there are distinct spiritual as well as physical forces in the universe; that there is somewhere an omniscient and omnipotent Spiritual Being who has but to will the creation of a planet or the destruction of matter in order to accomplish the result desired, can easily believe in the exercise of miraculous power. Those who believe the Bible account of the creation, that God said in the beginning, "Let there be light: and there was light"—such persons find no difficulty in believing that Jesus converted water into wine or caused the lame to walk, if they believe that He was this same God "manifest in the flesh." A divinity who, in the morning of creation, spoke something out of nothing, would certainly not be impotent to restore life to Lazarus or sight to the blind Bartimeus.

The trouble with the philosophy of Spinoza is that his own high priestess—Nature—seems to be constantly working miracles under his own definitions; and miracles, too, that very closely resemble the wonders said to have been wrought by the Christ. Milk is taken into the stomach, subjected to various processes of digestion, is then thrown into the blood and finally becomes flesh and bone. The ultimate step in this process of transformation is unknown and, perhaps, unknowable to scientists. No deeper mystery is suggested by the New Testament scriptures. The conversion of water into wine is no stranger, no more incomprehensible than the transformation of milk into flesh and bone. It may be admitted that the chemical elements are the same throughout in one process and different in the other. Nevertheless, the results of both are perfectly described by Spinoza's definition, "that a miracle was *that,* the cause of which cannot be explained by our *natural understanding from the known principles of natural things.*"

It may be truthfully remarked that nature is everywhere and at all times working wonders in harmony with and parallel to the miracles wrought by the spiritual forces of the universe. God's sovereign miracle may be described as the changing of a man, with all his sins and imperfections, into a winged spirit, thus fitting him to leave the coarse and vulgar earth for life among the stars. Nature, in her feeble way, tries to imitate the wonder by transforming the caterpillar into a butterfly, thus fitting it to leave the dunghill for life among the flowers.

Spinoza insists that miracles are impossible because "nature proceeds in a fixed and changeless course." But is this really true? Are the laws of nature invariably uniform? Does not nature seem at times tired of uniformity and resolved to rise to liberty by the creation of what we call a miracle, or more vulgarly, a "freak"? Moving in what Spinzoa is pleased to call a "fixed and changeless course," nature ordinarily provides a chicken with two legs and a snake with one head. But what about chickens with three legs and snakes with two heads, such as are frequently seen? Was nature moving in a fixed and changeless course when these things were created? Could Spinoza have explained such phenomena by his "natural understanding from the known principles of natural things"? Would he have contented himself with calling them natural "accidents" or "freaks"? Nevertheless, they are miracles under his definition; and the entire subject must be discussed and debated with reference to some standard or definition of a miracle. If nature occasionally, in moments of sportiveness or digression, upsets her own laws and creates what we call "freaks," why is it unreasonable to suppose that the great God who created nature should not, at times, temporarily suspend the laws which He has made for the government of the universe, or even devote them to strange and novel purposes in the creation of those noble phenomena which we call miracles?

Other skeptics, like Renan, do not deny the possibility of miracles, but simply content themselves with asserting that there is no sufficient proof that such things ever happened. They thus repudiate the testimony of the Evangelists in this regard. "It is not," says Renan, "then, in the name of this or that philosophy, but in the name of universal experience, that we banish miracle from history. We do not say that miracles are impossible. We do say that up to this time a miracle has never been proved." Then the Breton biographer and philosopher gives us his idea of the tests that should be made in order to furnish adequate proof that a miracle has been performed. "If tomorrow," he says, "a thaumaturgus presents himself with credentials sufficiently important to be discussed and announces himself as able, say, to raise the dead, what would be done? A commission composed of physiologists, physicists, chemists, persons accustomed to historical criticism would be named. This commission would choose a corpse, would assure itself that the death was real, would select a room in which the experiment should be made, would arrange the whole system of precautions, so as to leave no chance of doubt. If, under such conditions, the resurrection were effected, a probability almost equal to certainty would be established. As, however, it ought to be possible always to repeat an experiment—to do over again that which has been done once; and as, in the order of miracle, there can be no question of ease or difficulty, the thaumaturgus would be invited to reproduce his marvelous act under other circumstances, upon other corpses, in another place. If the miracle should succeed each time, two things would be proved: first, that supernatural events happen in the world; second, that the power of producing them belongs or is delegated to certain persons. But who does not see that no miracle ever took place under these conditions? But that always hitherto the thaumaturgus has chosen the subject of the experiment, chosen the spot, chosen the public?"[1]

This is an extract from the celebrated "Life of Jesus" by Renan, and is intended to demolish the Gospel account of the miracles of the Christ. It is not too much to say that the great skeptic has failed to exhibit his usual fairness in argument. He has indirectly compared Jesus to a thaumaturgus, and has inferentially stated that in the performance of His miracles He "chose the subject of his experiment, chose the spot, chose the public." Every student of New Testament history knows that this is not true of the facts and circumstances surrounding the performance of miracles by Christ. It is true that vulgar curiosity and caviling incredulity were not gratified by the presence of specially summoned "physiologists, physicists, and chemists." But it is equally true that such persons were not prevented from being present; that there was no attempt at secrecy or concealment; and that no subject of experiment, particular spot, or special audience was ever chosen. The New Testament miracles were wrought, as a general thing, under the open sky, in the street, by the wayside, on the mountain slope, and in the presence of many people, both friends and enemies of Jesus. There was no searching or advertising for subjects for experiment. Far from choosing the subject, the spot, and the public, Jesus exercised His miraculous powers upon those who came voluntarily to Him suffering with some dreadful malady and asking to be cured. In some instances, the case of affliction was of long standing and well known to the community. The healing was done publicly and witnessed by many people.

Renan suggests that the thaumaturgus mentioned in his illustration would be required to repeat his performance in the matter of raising the dead before he would be fully believed. This reminds us that Jesus wrought many miracles. More than forty are recorded in the Gospel narratives; and in the closing verse of St. John, there is a strong intimation that He performed many that were never recorded. These, it is respectfully submitted, were amply sufficient to demonstrate His miraculous powers.

Whatever form infidelity may assume in its antagonism to the doctrine of miracles, it will be found that the central idea is that such things are not founded in experience; and that this test of credibility fails in the case of the Gospel writers, because they knowingly recorded impossible events. It would be idle to attempt to depreciate the value of this particular test; but it must be observed that nothing is more fallacious, unless properly defined and limited. It must be remembered that the experience of one man, nation, or generation is not necessarily that of another man, nation, or generation. The exact mechanical processes employed by the Egyptians in raising the pyramids are as much a mystery to modern scientists as a Marconigram would be to a savage of New Guinea. The Orient and the Occident present to each other almost miraculous forms of diversity in manners, habits, and customs, in modes of thought and life. "The Frenchman says, 'I am the best dyer in Europe: nobody can equal me, and nobody can surpass Lyons.' Yet in Cashmere, where the girls make shawls worth $30,000, they will show him three hundred distinct colors, which he not only cannot make, but cannot even distinguish." Sir Walter Scott, in his "Tales of the Crusaders," thrillingly describes a meeting between the Turkish Saladin and the English Richard Coeur-de-Lion. Saladin asked Richard to give him an exhibition of his marvelous strength. The Norman monarch picked up an iron bar from the floor of the tent and severed it. The Mahometan crusader was amazed. Richard then asked him what he could do. Saladin replied that he could not pull iron apart like that, but that he could do something equally as wonderful. Thereupon, he took an eider-down pillow from the sofa, and drew his keen, Damascus-tempered blade across it, which caused it to fall into two pieces. Richard cried in astonishment: "This is the black art; it is magic; it is the devil: you cannot cut that which has no resistance!" Here Occidental strength and Oriental magic met and wrought seeming miracles in the presence of each other. In his great lecture on "The Lost Arts," Wendell Phillips says that one George Thompson told him that he saw a man in Calcutta throw a handful of floss silk into the air, and that a Hindoo severed it into pieces with his saber. A Western swordsman could not do this.

Objectors to miracles frequently ask why they are not performed today, why we never see them. To which reply may be made that, under Spinoza's definition, miracles are being wrought every day not only by nature, but by man. Why call Edison "the magician" and "the wizard," unless the public believes this? But is it any argument against the miracles of Jesus that similar ones are not seen today? Have things not been done in the past that will never be repeated? We have referred to the pyramids of Egypt and to the lost art involved in their construction. A further illustration may be found in the origin of man. One of two theories is undoubtedly true: that the first man and woman came into the world without being born; or that man and woman are the products of evolution from lower orders of animals. No other theories have ever been advanced as to the origin of the human race. Now, it is certain that modern generations have never experienced either of these things, for all the human beings of today were undoubtedly born of other human beings, and it is certain that the process of evolution stopped long ago, since men and women were as perfect physically and mentally four thousand years ago as they are today. In other words, the processes which originated man are things of the past, since we have no Garden of Eden experiences today, nor is there any universal metamorphosis of monkeys going on. Therefore, to argue that the miracles of Jesus did not happen, because we do not see such things today, is to deny the undoubted occurrences of history and developments of human life, because such occurrences and developments are no longer familiar to us and our generation.

To denounce everything as false that we have not individually seen, heard, and felt, would be to limit most painfully the range of the mental vision. The intellectual horizon would not be greatly extended should we join with our own the experience of others that we have seen and known. Much information is reported by telegraphic despatch and many things are told us by travelers that we should accept as true; although such matters may have no relation to what we have ever seen or heard. Else, we should be as foolish as the king of Siam who rejected the story of the Dutch ambassador, that in Holland water was frequently frozen into a solid mass. In the warm climate of the East Indian tropics the king had never seen water so congealed and, therefore, he refused to believe that such a thing had ever happened anywhere.

Experience is a most logical and reasonable test if it is sufficiently extended to touch all the material phases of the subject under investigation. It is a most dangerous one if we insist upon judging the material and spiritual universe, with its infinite variety of forms and changes, by the limited experience of a simple and isolated life, or by the particular standards of any one age or race. A progressive civilization, under such an application of the test, would be impossible, since each generation of men would have to begin *de novo,* and be restricted to the results of its own experience. Furthermore, the enforcement of such a doctrine would prevent the acceptance of the truths of nature discovered by inventive genius or developed by physical or chemical research, until such truths had become matters of universal experience. Every man would then be in the position of the incredulous citizen who, having been told that a message had been sent by wire from Baltimore to Washington announcing the nomination of James K. Polk for the presidency, refused to believe in telegraphic messages until he could be at both ends of the line at once. The art of telegraphy was a reality, nevertheless, in spite of his incredulity and inexperience. The American savages who first beheld the ships of Columbus are said to have regarded them as huge birds from heaven and to have refused to believe that they were boats, because in their experience they had never seen such immense canoes with wings. Herodotus tells us of some daring sailors who crept along the coast of Africa beyond the limits usually visited at that time. They came back home with a wonderful account of their trip and told the story that they had actually reached a country where their shadows fell toward the south at midday. They were not believed, and their report was rejected with scorn and incredulity by the inhabitants of the Mediterranean coasts, because their only experience was that a man's shadow always pointed toward the north; and they did not believe it possible that shadows could be cast otherwise. But the report of the sailors was true, nevertheless.[27]

These simple illustrations teach us that beings other than ourselves have had experiences which are not only different from any that we have ever had, but are also either temporarily or permanently beyond our comprehension. And the moral of this truth, when applied to the statements of the Evangelists regarding miracles, is that the fortunate subjects and witnesses of the miraculous powers of Jesus might have had experiences which we have never had and that we cannot now clearly comprehend.

(5) In the fifth and last place, as to the *coincidence of their testimony with collateral circumstances.*

This is the chief test of credibility in all those cases where the witness, whose testimony has been reduced to writing, is dead, absent, or insane. Under such circumstances it is impossible to apply what may be termed personal tests on cross-examination; that is, to develop the impeaching or corroborating features of bias, prejudice, and personal demeanor to the same extent as when the witness is still living and testifies orally. When a written narrative is all that we have, its reliability can only be ascertained by a close inspection of its parts, comparing them with each other, and then with collateral and contemporaneous facts and circumstances. The value of this test cannot be overestimated, and Greenleaf has stated very fully and concisely the basis upon which it rests. "Every event," he says, "which actually transpires, has its appropriate relation and place in the vast complication of circumstances of which the affairs of men consist; it owes its origin to the events which have preceded it, is intimately connected with all others which occur at the same time and place, and often with those of remote regions, and in its turn gives birth to numberless others which succeed. In all this almost inconceivable contexture and seeming discord, there is perfect harmony; and while the fact which really happened tallies exactly with every other contemporaneous incident related to it in the remotest degree, it is not possible for the wit of man to invent a story, which, if closely compared with the actual occurrences of the same time and place, may not be shown to be false."[28]

This principle offers a wide field to the skill of the cross-examiner, and enables him frequently to elicit truth or establish falsehood when all other tests have failed. It is a principle also perfectly well known to the perjurer and to the suborner of witnesses. Multiplicity of details is studiously avoided by the false witness, who dreads particularity and feels that safety lies in confining his testimony as nearly as possible to a single fact, whose attendant facts and circumstances are few and simple. When the witness is too ignorant to understand the principle and appreciate the danger, his attorney, if he consents to dishonor his profession and pollute the waters of justice with corrupt testimony, may be depended upon to administer proper warning. The witness will be told to know as few things and to remember as little as possible concerning matters about which he has not been previously instructed. The result will be that his testimony, especially in matters in which he is compelled by the court to testify, will be hesitating, restrained, unequal, and unnatural. He will be served at every turn by a most convenient memory which will enable him to forget many important and to remember many unimportant facts and circumstances. He will betray a painful hesitancy in the matter of committing himself upon any particular point upon which he has not been already drilled. The truthful witness, on the other hand, is usually candid, ingenuous, and copious in his statements. He shows a willingness to answer all questions, even those involving the minutest details, and seems totally indifferent to the question of verification or contradiction. The texture of his testimony is, therefore, equal, natural, and unrestrained.

Now these latter characteristics mark every page of the New Testament histories. The Gospel writers wrote with the utmost freedom, and recorded in detail and with the utmost freedom, and recorded in detail and with the utmost particularity, the manners, customs, habits, and historic facts contemporaneous with their lives. The naturalness and ingenuousness of their writings are simply marvelous. There is nowhere any evidence of an attempt to conceal, patch up, or reconcile. No introductory exclamations or subsequent explanations which usually characterize false testimony appear anywhere in their writings. They were seemingly absolutely indifferent to whether they were believed or not. Their narratives seem to say: These are records of truth; and if the world rejects them it rejects the facts of history. Such candor and assurance are always overwhelmingly impressive; and in every forum of debate are regarded as unmistakable signs of truth.

The Evangelists, it must be assumed, were fully aware of the danger of too great particularity in the matter of false testimony, and would have hestiated to commit themselves on so many points if their statements had been untrue. We have already noted the opinion of Professor Holtzmann, of Heidelberg, that the Synoptic Gospels were committed to writing between the years 60 and 80 of our era. At that time it is certain that there were still living many persons who were familiar with the events in the life and teachings of the Savior, as well as with the numerous other facts and circumstances related by the sacred writers. St. Paul, in I Cor. xv. 6, speaks of five hundred brethren to whom the risen Jesus appeared at one time; and he adds, *"of whom the greater part remain unto this present, but some are fallen asleep."* And it must be remembered that this particular group of two hundred and fifty or more were certainly not the only persons then living who had a distinct remembrance of the Master, His teachings, and His miracles. Many who had been healed by Him, children who had sat upon His knee and been blessed by Him, and many members of the Pharisaic party and of the Sadducean aristocracy who had persecuted Him and had then slain Him, were doubtless still living and had a lively recollection of the events of the ministry of the Nazarene. Such persons were in a position to disprove from their personal knowledge false statements made by the Evangelists. A consciousness of this fact would have been, within itself, a strong inducement to tell the truth.

But not only are the Gospels not contradicted by contemporaneous writers; they are also not impeached or disproved by later scientific research and historical investigation. And at this point we come to make a direct application of the test of the coincidence of their testimony with collateral and contemporaneous history. For this purpose, as a matter of illustration, only facts in profane history corroborative of the circumstances attending the trial and crucifixion of the Master will be cited.

In the first place, the Evangelists tell us that Pontius Pilate sat in judgment on the Christ. Both Josephus and Tacitus tell us that Pilate was governor of Judea at that time.[29]

In John xviii. 31 we read: "Then said Pilate unto them, Take ye him, and judge him according to your law. The Jews therefore said unto him, *It is not lawful for us to put any man to death,*" From many profane historians, ancient and modern, we learn that the power of life and death had been taken from the Jews and vested in the Roman governor.[30]

In John xix. 16, 17 occurs this passage: "And they took Jesus, and led him away; and he, *bearing his cross,* went forth." This corroborative sentence is found in Plutarch: "Every kind of wickedness produces its own particular torment; just as every malefactor, when he is brought forth to execution, *carries his own cross."*[31]

In Matthew xxvii. 26 we read: "When he had scourged Jesus, he delivered him to be crucifixed." That scourging was a preliminary to crucifixion among the Romans is attested by many ancient writers, among whom may be mentioned Josephus and Livy. The following passages are taken from Josephus:

Whom, having *first scourged with whips,* he crucified.[32]

Being *beaten,* they were crucified opposite to the citadel.[33]

He was burned alive, *having been first beaten.*[34]

From Livy, a single sentence will suffice:

All were led out, *beaten with rods,* and beheaded.[35]

In John xix. 19, 20 we read: "And Pilate wrote a title and put it on the cross; and it was written in Hebrew, and Greek, and Latin." That it was a custom among the Romans to affix the accusation against the criminal to the instrument of his punishment appears from several ancient writers, among them Suetonius and Dion Cassius. In Suetonius occurs this sentence: "He exposed the father of the family to the dogs, with this *title,* 'A gladiator, impious in speech.' "[36] And in Dion Cassius occurs the following: "Having led him through the midst of the court or assembly, *with a writing signifying the cause of his death, and afterwards crucifying him.* "[37]

And finally, we read in John xix. 32: "Then came the soldiers and *brake the legs* of the first, and of the other which was crucified with him." By an edict of Constantine, the punishment of crucifixion was abolished. Speaking in commendation of this edict, a celebrated heathen writer mentions the circumstances of *breaking the legs.* "He was pious to such a degree," says this writer, "that he was the first to set aside that very ancient punishment, the cross, with the *breaking of legs.*[38]

If we leave the narrow circle of facts attendant upon the trial and crucifixion of Jesus with its corroborative features of contemporary history, and consider the Gospel narratives as a whole, we shall find that they are confirmed and corroborated by the facts and teachings of universal history and experience. An examination of these narratives will also reveal a divine element in them which furnishes conclusive proof of their truthfulness and reliability. A discussion of the divine or spiritual element in the Gospel histories would be foreign to the purpose of this treatise. The closing pages of Part I will be devoted to a consideration of the human element in the New Testament narratives. This will be nothing more than an elaboration of the fifth legal test of credibility mentioned by Starkie.

By the human or historical element of credibility in the Gospel histories is meant that likeness or resemblance in matters of representation of fact to other matters of representation of fact which we find recorded in secular histories of standard authority whose statements we are accustomed to accept as true. The relations of historic facts to each other, and the connections and coincidences of things known or believed to be true with still others sought to be proved, form a fundamental ground of belief, and are, therefore, reliable modes of proof. The most casual perusal of the New Testament narratives suggests certain striking resemblances between the events therein narrated and well-known historical occurrences related by secular historians whose statements are implicitly believed. Let us draw a few parallels and call attention to a few of these resemblances.

Describing the anguish of the Savior in the Garden, St. Luke says: "And being in an agony, He prayed more earnestly: And his sweat was as it were great drops of blood falling down to the ground."[39]

This strange phenomenon of the "bloody sweat" has been of such rare occurrence in the history of the world that its happening in Gethsemane has been frequently denied. The account of it has been ascribed to the overwrought imagination of the third Evangelist in recording the errors of tradition. And yet similar cases are well authenticated in the works of secular writers. Tissot reports a case of "a sailor who was so alarmed by a storm, that through fear he fell down, and his face sweated blood which, during the whole continuance of the storm, returned like ordinary sweat, as fast as it was wiped away."[40] Schenck cites the case of "a nun who fell into the hands of soldiers; and, on seeing herself encompassed with swords and daggers threatening instant death, was so terrified and agitated that she discharged blood from every part of her body, and died of hemorrhage in the sight of her assailants."[41] Writing of the death of Charles IX of France, Voltaire says: "The disease which carried him off is very uncommon; his blood flowed from all his pores. This malady, of which there are some examples, is the result either of excessive fear, furious passion, or of a violent and melancholic temperament."[42] The same event is thus graphically described by the old French historian, De Mezeray: "After the vigor of his youth and the energy of his courage had long struggled against his disease, he was at length reduced by it to his bed at the castle of Vincennes, about the 8th of May, 1574. During the last two weeks of his life his constitution made strange efforts. He was affected with spasms and convulsions of extreme violence. He tossed and agitated himself continually and his blood gushed from all the outlets of his body, even from the pores of his skin, so that on one occasion he was found bathed in a bloody sweat."[43]

If the sailor, the nun, and the king of France were afflicted with the "bloody sweat," why should it seem incredible that the man Jesus, the carpenter of Nazareth, should have been similarly afflicted? If Tissot, Schenck, and Voltaire are to be believed, why should we refuse to believe St. Luke? If St. Luke told the truth in this regard, why should we doubt his statements concerning other matters relating to the life, death, and resurrection of the Son of God? Does not Voltaire, the most brilliant and powerful skeptic who ever lived, corroborate in this particular the biographer of the Christ?

Let us pass to another instance of resemblance and corroboration. While describing the crucifixion, St. John wrote the following: "But one of the soldiers with a spear pierced his side, and forthwith came there out *blood and water.*"[44] Early skeptical criticism denied the account of the flowing of blood and water from the side of the Savior because, in the first place, the other Evangelists did not mention the circumstance; and, in the second place, it was an unscientific fact stated. But modern medical science has very cleverly demonstrated that Jesus, according to the Gospel accounts, died of rupture of the heart. About the middle of the last century, a celebrated English physician and surgeon, Dr. Stroud, wrote a treatise entitled, "Physical Cause of the Death of Christ." In this book, he proved very clearly that cardiac rupture was the immediate cause of the death of Jesus on the cross. Many arguments were adduced to establish this fact. Among others, it was urged that the shortness of time during which the sufferer remained upon the cross and His loud cry just before "He gave up the ghost," tended to prove that a broken heart was the cause of the death of the Man of Sorrows. But the strongest proof, according to the author of this work, was the fact that blood and water flowed from the dead man when a spear was thrust into His side. This, says Dr. Stroud, has happened frequently when the heart is suddenly and violently perforated after death from cardiac rupture. Within a few hours after death from this cause, he says, the blood frequently separates into its constituent parts or essential elements: *crassamentum,* a soft clotted substance of deep-red color, and *serum,* a pale, watery liquid—popularly called blood and water, which will flow out separately, if the pericardium and heart be violently torn or punctured. In this treatise numerous medical authorities are cited and the finished work is endorsed by several of the most famous physicians and surgeons of England.

It is very probable that St. John did not know the physical cause of the strange flow of blood and water from the side of Jesus. It seems that he was afraid that he would not be believed; for, in the following verse, he was careful to tell the world that he himself had personally seen it. "And he that *saw it* bare record, and his record is true: And he knoweth that he saith true that ye might believe."[45]

Here again modern medical science has corroborated, in the matter of the flowing of blood and water from the side of Jesus, the simple narrative of the gentle and loving Evangelist.

Still another illustration of resemblance, coincidence, and corroboration is furnished by the incident of the arrest of Jesus in the Garden. St. John says: "As soon, then, as he had said unto them, I am he, they went backward and fell to the ground."[46]

This is only one of several cases mentioned in history where ordinary men have been dazed and paralyzed in the presence of illustrious men against whom they were designing evil. When a Gallic trooper was sent by Sulla to Minturnae to put Marius to death, the old Roman lion, his great eyes flashing fire, arose and advanced toward the slave, who fled in utter terror from the place, exclaiming, "I cannot kill Caius Marius!"[47]

Again, we learn from St. Matthew that at the moment of the arrest in the Garden, "all the disciples forsook him and fled."

This is no isolated case of cowardice and desertion. It is merely an illustration of a universal truth: that the multitude will follow blindly and adore insanely the hero or prophet in his hour of triumph and coronation, but will desert and destroy him at the moment of his humiliation and crucifixion.

Note the burning of Savonarola. The patriot-priest of the Florentine Republic believed himself inspired of God; his heroic life and martyr death seemed to justify his claim. From the pulpit of St. Mark's he became the herald and evangel of the Reformation, and his devoted followers hung upon his words as if inspiration clothed them with messages from the skies. And yet when a wicked Inquisition had nailed him to the cross and fagots were flaming about him, this same multitude who adored him, now reviled him and jeered and mocked his martyrdom.

Note the career of Napoleon. When the sun of Austerlitz rose upon the world the whole French nation grew delirious with love and homage for their emperor, who was once a subaltern of Corsica. But when the Allies entered Paris after the battle of Leipsic, this same French nation repudiated their imperial idol, cast down his images, canceled his decrees, and united with all Europe in demanding his eternal banishment from France. The voyage to Elba followed. But the historic melodrama of popular fidelity and fickleness was not yet completely played. When this same Napoleon, a few months later, escaped from his islet prison in the Mediterranean and landed on the shores of France, this same French nation again grew delirious, welcomed the royal exile with open arms, showered him with his eagles, and almost smothered him with kisses. A hundred days passed. On the frightful field of Waterloo, "Chance and Fate combined to wreck the fortunes of their former king." Again the fickle French multitude heaped execrations upon their fallen monarch, declared the Napoleonic dynasty at an end and welcomed with acclamations of joy the return of the exiled Bourbon Louis XVIII.

And when the Evangelist wrote these words: "All the disciples forsook him and fled," he simply gave expression to a form of truth which all history reflects and corroborates.

Again, the parallels and resemblances of sacred and profane history do not seem to stop with mere narratives of facts. Secular history seems to have produced at times characters in the exact likeness of those in sacred history. The resemblance is often so striking as to create astonishment. For instance, who was St. Peter but Marshal Ney by anticipation? Peter was the leader of the Apostolic Twelve; Ney was the chief of the Twelve Marshals of Napoleon. Peter was impulsive and impetuous; so was Ney. Peter was the first to speak and act in all the emergencies of the Apostolic ministry; Ney, so Dumas tells us, was always impatient to open the battle and lead the first charge. Peter was probably the last to leave the garden in which the great tragedy of his Master had begun; Ney was the last to leave the horrors of a Russian winter in which the beginning of the end of the career of his monarch was plainly seen. Peter denied Jesus; Ney repudiated Napoleon, and even offered to bring him, at the time of his escape from Elba, in a cage to Louis XVIII. Peter was afterwards crucified for his devotion to Jesus whom he had denied; Ney was afterwards shot for loyalty to Napoleon whom he had once repudiated.

The examples heretofore given involve the idea of comparison and are based upon resemblance. These illustrations could be greatly extended, but it is believed that enough has been said in this connection. However, in closing this brief discussion of the human element in the sacred writings as evidenced by the coincidences and resemblances of their narratives to those of profane history, slight mention may be made of another test of truth which may be applied to the histories of the Evangelists. This test is not derived from a comparison which is focused upon any particular group of historic facts. It springs from an instantaneously recognized and inseparable connection between the statements made by the Gospel writers and the experience of the human race. A single illustration will suffice to elucidate this point. When Jesus was nailed upon the cross, the sad and pathetic spectacle was presented of the absence of the Apostolic band, with the exception of St. John, who was the only Apostle present at the crucifixion. The male members of the following of the Nazarene did not sustain and soothe their Master in the supreme moment of His anguish. But the women of His company were with Him to the end. Mary, his mother, Mary Magdalene, Mary, the wife of Cleophas, Salome, the mother of St. John the Evangelist, and others, doubtless among "the women that followed him from Galilee," ministered to His sufferings and consoled Him with their presence. They were the last to cling to His cross and the first to greet Him on the morning of the third day; for when the resurrection morn dawned upon the world, these same women were seen hastening toward the sepulcher bearing spices—fragrant offerings of deathless love. What a contrast between the loyalty and devotion of the women and the fickle, faltering adherence of the men who attended the footsteps of the Man of Sorrows in His last days! One of His Apostles denied Him, another betrayed Him, and all, excepting one, deserted Him in His death struggle. His countrymen crucified Him ignominiously. But "not one woman mentioned in the New Testament ever lifted her voice against the Son of God."

This revelation from the sacred pages of the devotion of woman is reflected in universal history and experience. It is needless to give examples. Suffice it to say that when Matthew, Mark, Luke, and John tell us of this devotion, we simply answer: yes, this has been ever true in all countries and in every age. We have learned it not only from history but from our own experience in all the affairs of life, extending from the cradle to the grave. The night of sorrow never grows so dark that a mother's love will not irradiate the gloom. The criminal guilt of a wayward son can never become so black that her arms will not be found about him. If we pass from loving loyalty to the individual, to patriotic devotion to the causes of the nations, woman's fidelity is still undying. The women of France are said to have paid the German war debt. The message of the Spartan mother to her soldier son is too well known to be repeated. When the legions of Scipio engirdled the walls of Carthage and desperation seized the inhabitants of the Punic city, Carthaginian women cut their long black hair to furnish bowstrings to the Carthaginian archers. Illustrations might be multiplied; but these will suffice to show that Mary and Martha and Salome, the women of the Gospels, are simply types of the consecrated women of the world.

When we come to summarize, we are led to declare that if the Gospel historians be not worthy of belief we are without foundation for rational faith in the secular annals of the human race. No other literature bears historic scrutiny so well as the New Testament biographies. Not by single chain, but by three great chains can we link our Bible of today with the Apostolic Bible. The great manuscripts: the Vatican, the Alexandrian, and the Sinaitic, dating from the middle of the fourth and fifth centuries, must have been copies of originals, or at least of first copies. The Bible is complete in these manuscripts today.

The Versions, translations of the original Scriptures from the language in which they were first written into other languages, form a perfect connection between the days of the Apostles and our own. The Vulgate, the celebrated Latin version of St. Jerome, was completed A.D. 385. In making this translation the great scholar has himself said that he used "ancient (Greek) copies." Manuscripts that were ancient, A.D. 385, must have been the original writings, or, at least, first copies. The Vulgate, then, is alone a perfect historic connection between the Bible that we read today and that studied by the first Christians.

Again, the Writings of the Church Fathers furnish a chain, without a single missing link, between the Bible of this generation and that of the first generation of the followers of the Christ. It has been truthfully said that if all the Bibles in the world were destroyed an almost perfect Bible could be reconstructed from quotations from these writings, so numerous and so exact are they. Beginning with Barnabas and Clement, companions of St. Paul, and coming down through the ages, there is not a single generation in which some prince or potentate of the Church has not left convincing evidence in writing that the Books of the Old and New Testament which we read today are identical with those read by the first propagators of our faith. The chain of proof forged from the Writings of the early Fathers is made up of a hundred links, each perfect within itself and yet relinked and welded with a hundred others that make each and all doubly strong. If these various testimonies, the Manuscripts, the Versions, and the Writings of the Church Fathers, be taken, not singly, but collectively, in support and corroboration of each other, we have then not merely a chain but rather a huge spiritual cable of many wires, stretching across the great sea of time and linking our Bible of today inseparable with that of the Apostolic Age.

If it be objected that these various writings might have been and probably were corrupted in coming down to us through the centuries, reply may be made that the facts of history repel such suggestions. As Mr. Greenleaf has suggested, the jealousy of opposing sects preserved them from forgery and mutilation. Besides these sects, it may be added, there were even in the earliest times, open and avowed infidels who assaulted the cardinal tenets of the Christian faith and made the Gospel histories the targets for their attacks. They, too, would have detected and denounced any attempt from any source to corrupt these writings.

Another and final, and probably the most cogent reason for the remarkable preservation of the books of the Bible, is the reverential care bestowed upon them by their custodians in every age. It is difficult for the modern world to fully appreciate the meaning and extent of this reverence and care. Before the age of printing, it must be remembered, the masses of the people could not and did not possess Bibles. In the Middle Ages it required a small fortune to own a single copy. The extreme scarcity enhanced not only the commercial value but added to the awful sanctity that attached to the precious volume; on the principle that the person of a king becomes more sacred and mysterious when least seen in public. Synagogues and monasteries were, for many centuries, the sole repositories of the Holy Books, and the deliberate mutilation of any portion of the Bible would have been regarded like the blaspheming of the Deity or the desecration of a shrine. These considerations alone are sufficient reason why the Holy Scriptures have come down to us uncorrupted and unimpaired.

These various considerations are the logical basis of that rule of law laid down by Mr. Greenleaf, under which the Gospel histories would be admitted into a modern court of law in a modern judicial proceeding.

Under legal tests laid down by Starkie, we have seen that the Evangelists should be believed, because: (1) They were honest and sincere, that is, they believed that they were telling the truth; (2) they were undoubtely men of good intelligence and were eyewitnesses of the facts narrated by them in the New Testament histories; (3) they were independent historians, who wrote at different times and places and in all essential details, fully corroborate each other; (4) excepting in the matter of miracles, which skepticism has never been able to fully disprove, their testimony is in full conformity with human experience; (5) their testimony coincides fully and accurately with all the collateral, social, historical, and religious circumstances of their time, as well as with the teachings and experience of universal history in every age.

Having received from antiquity an uncorrupted message, born of truth, we have, it is believed, a perfect record of fact with which to discuss the trial of Jesus.

PART II
HEBREW CRIMINAL LAW

CHAPTER I

HEBREW CRIMINAL LAW—MOSAIC AND TALMUDIC

The Pentateuch and the Talmud form the double basis of Hebrew jurisprudence. "The wisdom of the lawgiver," says Bacon, "consists not only in a platform of justice, but in the application thereof." The Mosaic Code, embodied in the Pentateuch, furnished to the children of Israel the necessary platform of justice; ancient tradition and Rabbinic interpretation contained in the Talmud, supplied needed rules of practical application. Employing classic terminology, it may be said that the ordinances of Moses were the substantive and the provisions of the Talmud were the adjective laws of the ancient Hebrews. These terms are not strictly accurate, however, since many absolute rights are declared and defined in the Talmud as well as in the Pentateuch. Another definition, following the classification of Roman legists, describes Mosaic injunction as the *lex scripta* and Talmudic provision as the *lex non scripta* of the Commonwealth of Israel. In other words, the Pentateuch was the foundation, the cornerstone; the Talmud was the superstructure, the gilded dome of the great temple of Hebrew justice.

Bible students throughout the world are familiar with the provisions of the Mosaic Code; but the contents of the Talmud are known to few, even among scholars and literary men. The most appalling ignorance has existed in every age among the Gentile uninitiated as to the nature and identity of this gigantic literary compilation. Henricus Segnensis, a pious monk of the Middle Ages, having heard and read many things about the despised heretical Talmud, conceived it to be a person and, in a transport of religious frenzy, declared that he would sooner or later have *him, the Talmud,* put to death by the hangmen![1]

For the benefit of the average reader, as well as to illuminate the general subject, a short description of the Talmud will be given.

Definition.— Many attempts have been made to define the Talmud, but all definition of this monumental literary production is necessarily inaccurate and incomplete because of the vastness and peculiarity of the matter treated. To describe it as an encyclopedia of the life and literature, law and religion, art and science of the Hebrew people during a thousand years would convey only an approximately correct idea of its true meaning, for it is even more than the foregoing descriptive terms would indicate. Emanuel Deutsch in his brilliant essay on the Talmud defines it as "a Corpus Juris, an encyclopedia of law, civil and penal, ecclesiastical and international, human and divine. It is a microcosm, embracing, even as does the Bible, heaven and earth. It is as if all the prose and poetry, the science, the faith and speculation of the Old World were, though only in faint reflections, bound up in it *in nuce.*"

Benny describes it as "the Talmud—that much maligned and even more misunderstood compilation of the rabbins; that digest of what Carlyle would term *allerlei-wissenschaften;* which is at once the compendium of their literature, the storehouse of their tradition, the exponent of their faith, the record of their acquirements, the handbook of their ceremonials and the summary of their legal code, civil and penal."

To speak of the Talmud as a book would be inaccurate. It is a small library, or collection of books. "Modern editions of the Talmud, including the most important commentaries, consist of about 3,000 folio sheets, or 12,000 folio pages of closely printed matter, generally divided into twelve or twenty volumes. One page of Talmudic Hebrew intelligibly translated into English would cover three pages; the translation of the whole Talmud with its commentaries would accordingly make a library of 400 volumes, each numbering 360 octavo pages."[2]

It would be well to bear in mind that the contents of the Talmud were not proclaimed to the world by any executive, legislative, or judicial body; that they were not the result of any resolution or mandate of any congregation, college, or Sanhedrin; that they were not, in any sense, formal or statutory. They were simply a great mass of traditionary matter and commentary transmitted orally through many centuries before being finally reduced to writing. Rabbinism claims for these traditions a remote antiquity, declaring them to be coeval with the proclamation of the Decalogue. Many learned doctors among the Jews ascribe this antiquity to the whole mass of traditional laws. Others maintain that only the principles upon which Rabbinic interpretation and discussion are based, can be traced back so far. But it is certain that distinct traditions are to be found at a very early period in the history of the children of Israel, and that on their return from Babylonian captivity these traditions were delivered to them by Ezra and his coadjutors of the Great Assembly.

This development of Hebrew jurisprudence along lines of written and oral law, Pentateuch and Talmud, Mosaic ordinance and time-honored tradition, seems to have followed in obedience to a general principle of juristic growth. *Lex scripta* and *lex non scripta* are classical Roman terms of universal application in systems of enlightened jurisprudence. A charter, a parchment, a marble column, a table of stone, a sacred book containing written maxims defining legal rights and wrongs are the beginnings of all civilized schemes of justice. Around these written, fundamental laws grow and cluster the race traditions of a people which attach themselves to and become inseparable from the prime organic structure. These oral traditions are the natural and necessary products of a nation's growth and progress. The laws of the Medes and Persians, at once unalterable and irrevocable, represent a strange and painful anomaly in the jurisprudence of mankind. No written constitution, incapable of amendment and subject to strict construction, can long survive the growth and expansion of a great and progressive people. The ever-changing, perpetually evolving forms of social, commercial, political, and religious life of a restless, marching, ambitious race, necessitate corresponding changes and evolutions in laws and constitutions. These necessary legal supplements are as varied in origin as are the nations that produce them. Magna Charta, wrung from John at Runnymede, became the written basis of English law and freedom, and around it grew up those customs and traditions that—born on the shores of the German Ocean, transplanted to the Isles of Britain, nurtured and developed through a thousand years of jucicial interpretation and application—became the great basic structure of the Common Law of England.

What the Mosaic Code was to the ancient Hebrews, what Magna Charta is to Englishmen, the Koran is to Mahometans: the written charter of their faith and law. Surrounding the Koran are many volumes of tradition, made up of the sayings of Mahomet, which are regarded as equally sacred and authoritative as the Koran itself. These volumes of Mahometan tradition are called the Sonna and correspond to the Talmud of the Hebrews. An analysis of any great system of jurisprudence will reveal the same natural arrangement of written and oral law as that represented by the Pentateuch and the Talmud of the Jews.

The word "Talmud" has various meanings, as it appears in Hebrew traditional literature. It is an old scholastic term, and "is a noun formed from the verb 'limmed' 'to teach.' It therefore means, primarily, 'teaching,' although it denotes also 'learning'; it is employed in this latter sense with special reference to the Torah, the terms 'Talmud' and 'Torah' being usually combined to indicate the study of the Law, both in its wider and its more restricted sense." [3]It is thus frequently used in the sense of the word "exegesis," meaning Biblical exposition or interpretation. But with the etymological and restricted, we are not so much interested as with the popular and general signification of the term "Talmud." Popularly used, it means simply a small collection of books represented by two distinct editions handed down to posterity by the Palestinian and Babylonian schools during the early centuries of the Christian era.

Divisions of the Talmud.— The Talmud is divided into two component parts: the Mishna, which may be described as the *text;* and the Gemara, which may be termed the *commentary.* [4]The Mishna, meaning tradition, is almost wholly law. It was, indeed, of old, translated as the Second or Oral Law—the δευτέρωσις — to distinguish it from the Written Law delivered by God to Moses. The relationship between the Mishna, meaning oral law, and the Gemara, meaning commentary, may be illustrated by a bill introduced into Congress and the debates which follow. In a general way, the bill corresponds to the Mishna, and the debates to the Gemara. The distinction, however, is that the law resulting from the passage of the bill is the effect and culmination of the debate; while the Mishna was already law when the Gemara or commentary was made.

As we have seen above, Hebrew jurisprudence in its principles and in the manner of their interpretation was chiefly transmitted by the living voice of tradition. These laws were easily and safely handed down from father to son through successive generations as long as Jewish nationality continued and the Temple at Jerusalem still stood. But, with the destruction of the Temple and the banishment of the Jews from Palestine (A.D. 70), the danger became imminent that in the loss of their nationality would also be buried the remembrance of their laws. Moved with pity and compassion for the sad condition of his people, Judah the Holy, called Rabbi for preeminence, resolved to collect and perpetuate for them in writing their time-honored traditions. His work received the name Mishna, the same which we have discussed above. But it must not be imagined that this work was the sudden or exclusive effort of Rabbi Judah. His achievement was merely the sum total and culmination of the labors of a long line of celebrated Hebrew sages. "The Oral Law had been recognized by Ezra; had become important in the days of the Maccabees; had been supported by Pharisaism; narrowed by the school of Shammai, codified by the school of Hillel, systematized by R. Akiba, placed on a logical basis by R. Ishmael, exegetically amplified by R. Eliezer, and constantly enriched by successive rabbis and their schools. Rabbi Judah put the coping-stone to the immense structure." [5]

Emanuel Deutsch gives the following subdivisions of the Mishna:

The Mishna is divided into six sections. These are subdivided again into 11, 12, 7, 9 (or 10), 11, and 12 chapters, respectively, which are further broken up into 524 paragraphs. We shall briefly describe their contents:

Section I.   Seeds: of Agrarian Laws, commencing with a chapter on Prayers. In this section, the various tithes and donations due to the Priests, the Levites, and the poor, from the products of the lands, and further the Sabbatical year and the prohibited mixtures in plants, animals, garments, are treated of.

Section II.   Feasts: of Sabbaths, Feast, and Fast days, the work prohibited, the ceremonies ordained, the sacrifices to be offered, on them. Special chapters are devoted to the Feast of the Exodus from Egypt, to the New Year's Day, to the Day of Atonement (one of the most impressive portions of the whole book), to the Feast of Tabernacles and to that of Haman.

Section III.   Women: of betrothal, marriage, divorce, etc., also of vows.

Section IV.   Damages: including a great part of the civil and criminal law. It treats of the law of trover, of buying and selling, and the ordinary monetary transactions. Further, of the greatest crime known to the law, viz., idolatry. Next of witnesses, of oaths, of legal punishments, and of the Sanhedrin itself. This section concludes with the so-called "Sentences of the Fathers, " containing some of the sublimest ethical dicta known in the history of religious philosophy.

Section V.   Sacred Things: of sacrifices, the first- born, etc.; also of the measurements of the Temple (Middoth).

Section VI.   Purifications: of the various levitical and other hygienic laws, of impure things and persons, their purification, etc. [6]

Recensions.— The Talmud exists in two recensions: the Jerusalem and the Babylonian. These two editions represent a double Gemara; the first (Jerusalem) being an expression of the schools in Palestine and redacted at Tiberias about 390 A.D.; the second (Babylonian) being an expression of the schools in Babylonia and redacted about 365-427 A. D.

The Mishna, having been formed into a code, became in its turn what the Pentateuch had been before it, a basis of discussion and development. The Gemara of the Jerusalem Talmud embodies the critical discussions and disquisitions on the Mishna by hundreds of learned doctors who lived in Palestine, chiefly in Galilee, from the end of the second till about the middle of the fifth century of the Christian era. The Gemara of the Babylonian Talmud embodies the criticisms and dissertations on the same Mishna of numerous learned doctors living in various places in Babylonia, but chiefly those of the two great schools of Sura and Pumbaditha.[7]The Babylonian Talmud is written in

"West Aramaean," is the product of six or seven generations of constant development, and is about four times as large as that of the Jerusalem Talmud, which is written in ▪ East Aramaean. ▪ [8] It should be kept clearly before the mind that the only difference between these two recensions is in the matter of commentary. The two sets of doctors whose different commentaries distinguish the two Talmuds dealt with the same Mishna as a basis of criticism. But decided differences are noticeable in the subject matter and style of the two Gemaras represented by the two recensions of the Talmud. The discussions and commentaries in the Jerusalem Talmud are simple, brief, and pointed; while those of the Babylonian Talmud are generally subtle, abstruse, and prolix. The dissertations in the Jerusalem Talmud are filled to overflowing with archaeology, geography, and history, while the Babylonian Talmud is more marked by legal and religious development.

But the reader should not form a wrong impression of the contents of the Talmud. They are a blending of the oral law of the Mishna and the notes and comments of the sages. The characteristics of both the editions are legal and religious, but a multitude of references are made in each to things that have no connection with either religion or law. "The Talmud does, indeed, offer us a perfect picture of the cosmopolitanism and luxury of those final days of Rome, such as but few classical or postclassical writings contain. We find mention made of Spanish fish, of Cretan apples, Bithynian cheese, Egyptian lentils and beans, Greek and Egyptian pumpkins, Italian wine, Median beer, Egyptian Zyphus; garments imported from Pelusium and India, shirts from Cilicia, and veils from Arabia. To the Arabic, Persian, and Indian materials contained, in addition to these, in the Gemara, a bare allusion may suffice. So much we venture to predict, that when once archaeological and linquistic science shall turn to this field, they will not leave it again soon."

Relation of Talmud to Mishna.— The relation of the Talmud, used in the popular sense, to the Mishna, raises the question of the relation of the whole to one of its parts. The varying meanings of Mishna, Gemara, and Talmud very easily confuse the ordinary reader. If these terms are considered separately in the order in which they appear in the preceding sentence, simple mathematical addition will greatly aid in elucidating matters. The Mishna is a vast mass of tradition or oral law which was finally reduced to writing about the close of the second century of the Christian era. The Gemara is the Rabbinical exposition of the meaning of the Mishna. The Talmud is the sum of the Mishna plus the Germara. In other words, the Talmud is the elaboration or amplification of the Mishna by manifold commentaries, designated as the Gemara. It frequently happens that the Talmud and the Mishna appear in the same sentence as terms designating entirely different things. This association in a different sense inevitably breeds confusion, unless we pause to consider that the Mishna has a separate existence from the Talmud and a distinct recension of its own. In this state it is simply a naked code of laws. But when the Gemara has been added to it the Talmud is the result, which, in its turn, becomes a distinct entity and may be referred to as such in the same sentence with the Mishna.

Relation of Talmud to Pentateuch.— As before suggested, the Pentateuch, or Mosaic Code, was the Written Law and the very foundation of ancient Hebrew jurisprudence. The Talmud, composed of the Mishna, i.e., Tradition, and the Gemara, i.e., Commentary, was the Oral Law, connected with, derived from, and built upon the Written Law. It must be remembered that the commonwealth of the Jews was a pure theocracy and that all law as well as all religion emanated directly or indirectly from Jehovah. This was as true of Talmudic tradition as of Mosaic ordinance. Hillel, who interpreted tradition, was as much inspired of God as was Moses when he received the Written Law on Sinai. Emanuel Deutsch is of the opinion that from the very beginning of the Mosaic law there must have existed a number of corollary laws which were used to interpret and explain the written rules; that, besides, there were certain enactments of the primitive Council of the Desert, and certain verdicts issued by the later "judges within the gates"—all of which entered into the general body of the Oral Law and were transmitted side by side with the Written Law through the ages.[9] The fourth book of Ezra, as well as other Apocryphal writings, together with Philo and certain of the Church Fathers, tells us of great numbers of books that were given to Moses at the same time that he received the Pentateuch. These writings are doubtless the source of the popular belief among the Jews that the traditional laws of the Mishna had existed from time immemorial and were of divine origin. "Jewish tradition traces the bulk of the oral injunctions, through a chain of distinctly named authorities, to 'Sinai itself.' It mentions in detail how Moses communicated those minutiae of his legislation, in which he had been instructed during the mysterious forty days and nights on the Mount, to the chosen guides of the people, in such a manner that they should forever remain engraven on the tablets of their hearts."[10] This direct descent of the Oral Law from the Sacred Mount itself would indicate an independent character and authority. Nevertheless, Talmudic interpretation of tradition professed to remain always subject to the Mosaic Code; to be built upon, and to derive its highest inspiration from it. But as a matter of fact, while claiming theoretically to be subordinate to it, the Talmud finally superseded and virtually displaced the Pentateuch as a legal and administrative code. This was the inevitable consequence and effect of the laws of growth and progress in national existence. Altered conditions of life, at home and in exile, necessitated new rules of action in the government of the Jewish commonwealth. The Mosaic Code was found inadequate to the ever-changing exigencies of Hebrew life. As a matter of fact, Moses laid down only general principles for the guidance of Hebrew judges. He furnished the body of the law, but a system of legal procedure was wholly wanting. The Talmud supplied the deficiency and completed a perfect whole. While yet in the Wilderness, Moses commanded the Israelites to establish courts and appoint judges for the administration of justice as soon as they were settled in Palestine.[11] This clearly indicates that the great lawgiver did not intend his ordinances and injunctions to be final and exclusive. Having furnished a foundation for the scheme, he anticipated that the piety, judgment, and learning of subsequent ages would do the rest. His expectations were fulfilled in the development of the traditions afterwards embodied in the Mishna, which is the principal component part of the Talmud.

As before suggested, with the growth in population and the ever-increasing complications in social, political, and religious life, and with the general advance in Hebrew civilization, Mosaic injunction began to prove entirely inadequate to the national wants. In the time intervening between the destruction of the first and second Temples, a number of Mosaic laws had become utter anachronisms; others were perfectly impracticable, and several were no longer even understood. The exigencies of an altered mode of life and the changed conditions and circumstances of the people rendered imperative the enactment of new laws unknown to the Pentateuch. But the divine origin of the Hebrew system of law was never for a moment forgotten, whatever the change and wherever made. The Rabbins never formally repealed or abolished any Mosaic enactment. They simply declared that it had fallen into desuetude. And, in devising new laws rendered necessary by changed conditions of life they invariably invoked some principle or interpretation of the Written Law.

In the declining years of Jewish nationality, many characteristic laws of the Pentateuch had become obsolete. The ordinance which determined the punishment of a stubborn and rebellious son; the enactment which commanded the destruction of a city given to idolatry; and, above all, the *lex talionis* had become purely matters of legend. On the other hand, many new laws appear in the Talmud of which no trace whatever can be discovered in the Pentateuch. "The Pharisees," says Josephus, "have imposed upon the people many laws taken from the tradition of the Fathers, which are not written in the law of Moses."[12] The most significant of these is the one providing for Antecedent Warning in criminal prosecutions, the meaning and purpose of which will be fully discussed in another chapter.

Vicissitudes of the Talmud.— An old Latin adage runs: "Habent sua fata libelli"[13] (Even books are victims of fate). This saying is peculiarly applicable to the Talmud, which has had, in a general way, the same fateful history as the race that created it. Proscription, exile, imprisonment, confiscation, and burning was its lot throughout the Middle Ages. During a thousand years, popes and kings vied with each other in pronouncing edicts and hurling anathemas against it. During the latter half of the sixteenth century it was burned not fewer than six different times by royal or papal decree. Whole wagonloads were consigned to the flames at a single burning. In 1286, in a letter to the Archbishop of Canterbury, Honorius IV described the Talmud as a "damnable book" (liber damnabilis), and vehemently urged that nobody in England be permitted to read it, since "all other evils flow out of it."[14] On New Year's day, 1553, numerous copies of the Talmud were burned at Rome in compliance with a decree of the Inquisition. And, as late as 1757, in Poland, Bishop Dembowski, at the instigation of the Frankists, convened a public assembly at Kamenetz-Podolsk, which decreed that all copies of the Talmud found in the bishopric should be confiscated and burned by the hangman.[15]

Of the two recensions, the Babylonian Talmud bore the brunt of persecution during all the ages. This resulted from the fact that the Jerusalem Talmud was little read after the closing of the Jewish academies in Palestine, while the Babylonian Talmud was the popular edition of eminent Jewish scholars throughout the world.

It is needless to say that the treatment accorded the venerable literary compilation was due to bitter prejudice and crass ignorance. This is well illustrated by the circumstance that when, in 1307, Clement V was asked to issue a bull against the Talmud, he declined to do so, until he had learned something about it. To his amazement and chagrin, he could find no one who could throw any light upon the subject. Those who wished it condemned and burned were totally ignorant of its meaning and contents. The surprise and disgust of Clement were so great that he resolved to found three chairs in Hebrew, Arabic, and Chaldee, the three tongues nearest the idiom of the Talmud. He designated the Universities of Paris, Salamanca, Bologna, and Oxford as places where these languages should be taught, and expressed the hope that, in time, one of these universities might be able to produce a translation of "this mysterious book."[16] It may be added that these plans of the Pope were never consummated.

The Message and Mission of the Talmud.— To appreciate the message and mission of the Talmud, its contents must be viewed and contemplated in the light of both literature and history. As a literary production it is a masterpiece—strange, weird, and unique—but a masterpiece, nevertheless. It is a sort of spiritual and intellectual cosmos in which the brain growth and soul burst of a great race found expression during a thousand years. As an encyclopedia of faith and scholarship it reveals the noblest thoughts and highest aspirations of a divinely commissioned race. Whatever the master spirits of Judaism in Palestine and Babylon esteemed worthy of thought and devotion was devoted to its pages. It thus became a great twin messenger, with the Bible, of Hebrew civilization to all the races of mankind and to all the centuries yet to come. To Hebrews it is still the great storehouse of information touching the legal, political, and religious traditions of their fathers in many lands and ages. To the Biblical critic of any faith it is an invaluable help to Bible exegesis. And to all the world who care for the sacred and the solemn it is a priceless literary treasure.

As an historical factor the Talmud has only remotely affected the great currents of Gentile history. But to Judaism it has been the cementing bond in every time of persecution and threatened dissolution. It was carried from Babylon to Egypt, northern Africa, Spain, Italy, France, Germany, and Poland. And when threatened with national and race destruction, the children of Abraham in every land bowed themselves above its sacred pages and caught therefrom inspiration to renewed life and higher effort. The Hebrews of every age have held the Talmud in extravagant reverence as the greatest sacred heirloom of their race. Their supreme affection for it has placed it above even the Bible. It is an adage with them that, "The Bible is salt, the Mischna pepper, the Gemara balmy spice," and Rabbi Solomon ben Joseoh sings:

"The Kabbala and Talmud hoar
Than all the Prophets prize I more;
For water is all Bible lore,
But Mischna is pure wine."

More than any other human agency has the Talmud been instrumental in creating that strangest of all political phenomena—a nation without a country, a race without a fatherland.

CHAPTER II

HEBREW CRIMINAL LAW—CRIMES AND PUNISHMENTS

Capital crimes, under Hebrew law, were classified by Maimonides according to their respective penalties His arrangement will be followed in this chapter.[1]

Hebrew jurisprudence provided four methods of capital punishment: (1) Beheading; (2) Strangling; (3) Burning; (4) Stoning.

Crucifixion was unknown to Hebrew law. This cruel and loathsome form of punishment will be fully discussed in the second volume of this work.

Thirty-six capital crimes are mentioned by the Pentateuch and the Talmud.

Beheading was the punishment for only two crimes:

(1)   Murder.

(2)   Communal apostasy from Judaism to idolatry.

Strangling was prescribed for six offenses:

(1)   Adultery.

(2)   Kidnaping.

(3)   False prophecy.

(4)   Bruising a parent.

(5)   Prophesying in the name of heathen deities.

(6)   Maladministration (the "Rebellious Elder").

Burning was the death penalty for ten forms of incest—criminal commerce:

(1)   With one's own daughter.

(2)   With one's own son's daughter.

(3)   With one's own daughter's daughter.

(4)   With one's own stepdaughter.

(5)   With one's own stepson's daughter.

(6)   With one's own stepdaughter's daughter.

(7)   With one's own mother-in-law.

(8)   With one's own mother-in-law's mother.

(9)   With one's own father-in-law's mother.

(10)   With a priest's daughter.[2]

Stoning was the penalty for eighteen capital offenses:

(1)   Magic.

(2)   Idolatry.

(3)   Blasphemy.

(4)   Pythonism.

(5)   Pederasty.

(6)   Necromancy.

(7)   Cursing a parent.

(8)   Violating the Sabbath.

(9)   Bestiality, practiced by a man.

(10)   Bestiality, practiced by a woman.

(11)   Sacrificing one's own children to Moloch.

(12)   Instigating individuals to embrace idolatry.

(13)   Instigating communities to embrace idolatry.

(14)   Criminal conversation with one's own mother.

(15)   Criminal conversation with a betrothed virgin.

(16)   Criminal conversation with one's own stepmother.

(17)   Criminal conversation with one's own daughter-in-law.

(18)   Violation of filial duty (making the "Prodigal Son").[3]

The crime of *false swearing* requires special notice. This offense could not be classified under any of the above subdivisions because of its peculiar nature. The Mosaic Code ordains in Deut. xix. 16—21: "If a false witness rise up against any man to testify against him that which is wrong . . . and, behold, if the witness be a false witness, and hath testified falsely against his brother; then shall ye do unto him, as he had thought to have done unto his brother . . . and thine eye shall not pity; but life shall go for life, eye for eye, tooth for tooth, hand for hand, foot for foot." Talmudic construction of this law awarded the same kind of death to him who had sworn falsely against his brother that would have been meted out to the alleged criminal, if the testimony of the false swearer had been true.

Imprisonment, as a method of punishment, was unknown to the Mosaic Code. Leviticus xxiv. 12 and Numbers xv. 34 seem to indicate the contrary; but the imprisonment therein mentioned undoubtedly refers to the mere detention of the prisoner until sentence could be pronounced against him. Imprisonment as a form of punishment was a creation of the Talmudists who legalized its application among the Hebrews. According to Mendelsohn, five different classes of offenders were punished by *imprisonment:*

(1)   Homicides; whose crime could not be legally punished with death, because some condition or other, necessary to produce a legal conviction, had not been complied with.

(2)   Instigators to or procurers of murder; such, for instance, as had the deed committed by the hands of a hireling.

(3)   Accessories to loss of life, as, for instance, when several persons had clubbed one to death, and the court could not determine the one who gave the death blow.

(4)   Persons who having been twice duly condemned to and punished with flagellation for as many transgressions of one and the same negative precept, committed it a third time.

(5)   Incorrigible offenders, who, on each of three occasions, had failed to acknowledge as many warnings antecedent to the commission of one and the same crime, the original penalty for which was excision.[4]

Flagellation is the only corporal punishment mentioned by the Pentateuch. The number of stripes administered were not to exceed forty and were to be imposed in the presence of the judges.[5] Wherever the Mosaic Code forbade an act, or, in the language of the sages, said "Thou shalt not," and prescribed no other punishment or alternative, a Court of Three might impose stripes as the penalty for wrongdoing. Mendelsohn gives the following classification:

Flagellation is the penalty of three classes of offenses:

(1)   The violation of a negative precept, deadly in the sight of heaven.

(2)   The violation of any negative precept, when accomplished by means of a positive act.

(3)   The violation of any one of the prohibitive ordinances punishable, according to the Mosaic law, with *excision,* to which, however, no capital punishment at the instance of a human tribunal is attached.[6]

The Mishna enumerates fifty offenses punishable by stripes, but this enumeration is evidently incomplete. Maimonides gives a full classification of all the offenses punishable by flagellation, the number of which he estimates to be two hundred and seven. The last three in his list are cases in which the king takes too many wives, accumulates too much silver or gold, or collects too many horses.[7]

Slavery was the penalty for *theft* under ancient Hebrew law. This is the only case where the Mosaic law imposed slavery upon the culprit as a punishment for his crime; and a loss of liberty followed only where the thief was unable to make the prescribed restitution. Exodus xxii. 1—3 says:

If a man shall steal an ox, or a sheep, and kill it, or sell it, he shall restore five oxen for an ox, and four sheep for a sheep . . . if he have nothing, then he shall be sold for his theft.

Penal servitude, or slavery, was imposed only on men, never on women. Slavery, as a penalty for theft, was limited to a period of six years in obedience to the Mosaic ordinance laid down in Exodus xxi. 2.

If thou buy a Hebrew servant, six years he shall serve: and in the seventh, he shall go free for nothing.

It should be remarked, in this connection, that slavery, as a punishment for crime, carried with it none of the odium and hardship usually borne by the slave. The humanity of Hebrew law provided that the culprit, thief though he was, should not be degraded or humiliated. He could be compelled to do work for his master, such as he had been accustomed to do while free, but was relieved by the law from all degrading employment, such as "attending the master to the bath, fastening or unfastening his sandals, washing his feet, or any other labor usually performed by the regular slave." Hebrew law required such kindly treatment of the convict thief by his master that this maxim was the result: "He who buys a Hebrew slave, buys himself a master."

Internment in a city of refuge was the punishment for accidental homicide. Mischance or misadventure, resulting in the slaying of a fellow-man, was not, properly speaking, a crime; nor was exile in a city of refuge considered by the Talmudists a form of punishment. But they are so classified by most writers on Hebrew criminal law. Among nearly all ancient nations there was a place of refuge for the unfortunate and downtrodden of the earth; debtors, slaves, criminals, and political offenders; some sacred spot—an altar, a grave, or a sanctuary dedicated and devoted to some divinity who threw about the hallowed place divine protection and inviolability. Such was at Athens the Temple of

Theseus, the sanctuary of slaves. It will be remembered that the orator Demosthenes took refuge in the Temple of Poseidon as a sanctuary, when pursued by emissaries of Antipater and the Macedonians.[8] Among the ancient Hebrews, there were six cities of refuge; three on either side of the Jordan. They were so located as to be nearly opposite each other. Bezer in Reuben was opposite Hebron in Judah; Schechem in Ephraim was opposite to Ramoth in Gad; and Golan in Manasseh was opposite to Kedesh in Naphtali.[9] Highways in excellent condition led from one to the other. Signposts were placed at regular intervals to indicate the way to the nearest city of refuge. These cities were designated by the law as asylums or sanctuaries for the protection of innocent slayers of their fellow-men from the "avenger of blood." Among nearly all primitive peoples of crude political development, such as the early Germans, the ancient Greeks and Slavs, certain North American savage tribes and the modern Arabs, Corsicans and Sicilians, the right of private vengeance was and is taught and tolerated. Upon the "next of kin," the "avenger of blood," devolved the duty of hunting down and slaying the guilty man. Cities of refuge were provided by Mosaic law for such an emergency among the Hebrews. This provision of the Mosaic Code doubtless sprang from a personal experience of its founder. Bible students will remember that Moses slew an Egyptian and was compelled to flee in consequence.[10] Remembering his dire distress on this occasion, the great lawgiver was naturally disposed to provide sanctuaries for others similarly distressed. But the popular notion of the rights of sanctuary under the Mosaic law is far from right. It is thought by many that a common murderer could, by precipitate flight, reach one of the designated places and be safe from his pursuers and the vengeance of the law. The observation of Benny on this point is apt and lucid:

Internment in one of the cities of refuge was not the scampering process depicted in the popular engraving: a man in the last stage of exhaustion at the gate of an Eastern town; his pursuers close upon him, arrows fixed and bows drawn; his arms stretched imploringly towards a fair Jewish damsel, with a pitcher gracefully poised upon her head. This may be extremely picturesque, but it is miserably unlike the custom in vogue among the later Hebrews. Internment in a city of refuge was a sober and judicial proceeding. He who claimed the privilege was tried before the Sanhedrin like any ordinary criminal. He was required to undergo examinations; to confront witnesses, to produce evidence, precisely as in the case of other offenders. He had to prove that the homicide was purely accidental; that he had borne no malice against his neighbor; that he had not lain in wait for him to slay him. Only when the judges were convinced that the crime was homicide by misadventure was the culprit adjudged to be interned in one of the sheltering cities. There was no scurrying in the matter; no abrupt flight; no hot pursuit, and no appeal for shelter. As soon as judgment was pronounced the criminal was conducted to one of the appointed places. He was accompanied the whole distance by two talmide-chachamin-disciples of the Rabbins. The avengers of the blood dared not interfere with the offender on the way. To slay him would have been murder, punishable with death.

Execution of Capital Sentences. (1) Beheading. — The Hebrews considered beheading the most awful and ignominious of all forms of punishment. It was the penalty for deliberate murder and for communal apostasy from Judaism to idolatry, the most heinous offenses against the Hebrew theocracy. Beheading was accomplished by fastening the culprit securely to a post and then severing his head from his body by a stroke with a sword.[11]

(2) Strangling.— The capital punishment of strangling was effected by burying the culprit to his waist in soft mud, and then tightening a cord *wrapped in a soft cloth* around his neck, until suffocation ensued.[12]

(3) Burning.— The execution of criminals by burning was not done by consuming the living person with fire, as was practiced in the case of heretics by prelates in the Middle Ages and in the case of white captives by savages in colonial days in America. Indeed, the term "burning" seems to be a misnomer in this connection, for the culprit was not really burned to death. He was simply suffocated by strangling. As in the case of strangling, the condemned man was placed in a pit dug in the ground. Soft dirt was then thrown in and battered down, until nothing but his head and chest protruded. A cord, wrapped in a soft cloth, was then passed once around his neck. Two strong men came forward, grasped each an end, and drew the cord so hard that suffocation immediately followed. As the lower jaw dropped from insensibility and relaxation, a lighted wick was quickly thrown into his mouth. This constituted the burning.[13] There is authority for the statement that instead of a lighted wick, molten lead was poured down the culprit's throat.[14]

(4) Stoning.— Death by stoning was accomplished in the following manner: The culprit was taken to some lofty hill or eminence, made to undress completely, if a man, and was then precipitated violently to the ground beneath. The fall usually broke the neck or dislocated the spinal cord. If death did not follow instantaneously the witnesses hurled upon his prostrate body heavy stones until he was dead. If the first stone, so heavy as to require two persons to carry it, did not produce death, then bystanders threw stones upon him until death ensued. Here, again, "stoning" to death is not strictly accurate. Death usually resulted from the fall of the man from the platform, scaffold, hill, or other elevation from which he was hurled. It was really a process of neck-breaking, instead of stoning, as burning was a process of suffocation, instead of consuming with fire.

These four methods of execution—beheading, strangling, burning, and stoning—were the only forms of capital punishment known to the ancient Hebrews. Crucifixion was never practiced by them; but a posthumous indignity, resembling crucifixion, was employed as an insult to the criminal, in the crimes of idolatry and blasphemy. In addition to being stoned to death, as a punishment for either of these crimes, the dead body of the culprit was then hanged in public view as a means of rendering the offense more hideous and the death more ignominious. This *hanging* to a tree was in obedience to a Mosaic ordinance contained in Deut. xxi. 22. The corpse was not permitted, however, to remain hanging during the night.

The burial of the dead body of the criminal immediately followed execution, but interment could not take place in the family burial ground. Near each town in ancient Palestine were two cemeteries; in one of them were buried those criminals who had been executed by beheading or strangling; in the other were interred those who had been put to death by stoning or burning. The bodies were required to remain, thus buried, until the flesh had completely decayed and fallen from the bone. The relatives were then permitted to dig up the skeletons and place them in the family sepulchers.

CHAPTER III

HEBREW CRIMINAL LAW—COURTS AND JUDGES

The Hebrew tribunals were three in kind: the Great Sanhedrin; the Minor Sanhedrin; and the Lower Tribunal, or the Court of Three.

The Great Sanhedrin, or Grand Council, was the high court of justice and the supreme tribunal of the Jews. It sat at Jerusalem, and numbered seventy-one members. Its powers were legislative, executive, and judicial. It exercised all the functions of education, of government, and of religion. It was the national parliament of the Hebrew Theocracy, the human administrator of the divine will. It was the most august tribunal that ever interpreted or administered religion to man.

The Name.— The word "Sanhedrin" is derived from the Greek (συνέδριον) and denotes a legislative assembly or an ecclesiastical council deliberating in a sitting posture. It suggests also the gravity and solemnity of an Oriental synod, transacting business of great importance. The etymology of the word indicates that it was first used in the later years of Jewish nationality. Several other names are also found in history to designate the Great Sanhedrin of the Jews. The Council of Ancients is a familiar designation of early Jewish writers. It is called Gerusia, or Senate, in the second book of Maccabees.[1] Concilium, or Grand Council, is the name found in the Vulgate.[2] The Talmud designates it sometimes as the Tribunal of the Maccabees, but usually terms it Sanhedrin, the name most frequently employed in the Greek text of the Gospels, in the writings of the Rabbins, and in the works of Josephus.[3]

Origin of the Great Sanhedrin.— The Historians are at loggerheads as to the origin of the Great Sanhedrin. Many contend that it was established in the Wilderness by Moses, who acted under divine commission recorded in Numbers xi. 16, 17: "Gather unto me seventy of the elders of Israel, whom thou knowest to be the elders of the people, and officers of them; and bring them unto the tabernacle of the congregation, that they may stand with thee; and I will take of the Spirit that is upon thee and will put it upon them; and they shall bear the burden of the people with thee, that thou bearest it not alone." Over the seventy elders, Moses is said to have presided, making seventy-one, the historic number of the Great Sanhedrin. Several Christian historians, among them Grotius and Selden, have entertained this view; others equally celebrated have maintained contrary opinions. These latter contend that the council of seventy ordained by Moses existed only a short time, having been established to assist the great lawgiver in the administration of justice; and that, upon the entrance of the children of Israel into the Promised Land, it disappeared altogether. The writers who hold this view contend that if the great assembly organized in the Wilderness was perpetuated side by side with the royal power, throughout the

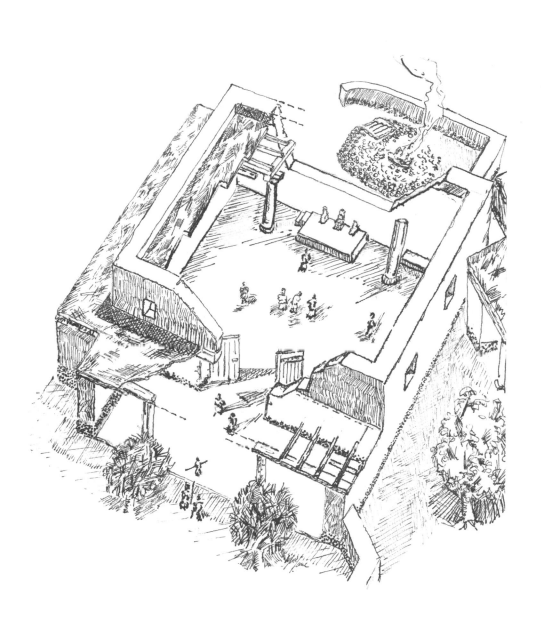

ages, as the Rabbis maintained, some mention of this fact would, in reason, have been made by the Bible, Josephus, or Philo.

The pages of Jewish history disclose the greatest diversity of opinion as to the origin of the Great Sanhedrin. The Maccabean era is thought by some to be the time of its first appearance. Others contend that the reign of John Hyrcanus, and still others that the days of Judas Maccabeus, marked its birth and beginning. Raphall, having studied with care its origin and progress, wrote: "We have thus traced the existence of a council of Zekenim or Elders founded by Moses, existing in the days of Ezekiel, restored under the name of Sabay Yehoudai, or Elders of the Jews, under Persian dominion; Gerusia, under the supremacy of the Greeks; and Sanhedrin under the Asmonean kings and under the Romans."[4]

Brushing aside mere theory and speculation, one historical fact is clear and uncontradicted, that the first Sanhedrin Council clothed with the general judicial and religious attributes of the Great Sanhedrin of the times of Jesus, was established at Jerusalem between 170 and 106 B.C.

Organization of the Great Sanhedrin. — The seventy-one members composing the Great Sanhedrin were divided into three chambers:

The chamber of priests;
The chamber of scribes;
The chamber of elders.

The first of these orders represented the religious or sacerdotal: the second, the literary or legal; the third, the patriarchal, the democratic or popular element of the Hebrew population. Thus the principal Estates of the Commonwealth of Israel were present, by representation, in the great court and parliament of the nation.

Matthew refers to these three orders and identifies the tribunal that passed judgment upon Christ: "From that time forth, began Jesus to shew unto his disciples, how that he must go unto Jerusalem, and suffer many things of the elders and chief priests and scribes, and be killed and raised again the third day."[5]

Theoretically, under the Hebrew constitution, the "seventy-one" of the three chambers were to be equally divided:

Twenty-three in the chamber of priests,
Twenty-three in the chamber of scribes,
Twenty-three in the chamber of elders.

A total of sixty-nine, together with the two presiding officers, would constitute the requisite number, seventy-one. But, practically, this arrangement was rarely ever observed. The theocratic structure of the government of Israel and the pious regard of the people for the guardians of the Temple, gave the priestly element a predominating influence from time to time. The scribes, too, were a most vigorous and aggressive sect and frequently encroached upon the rights and privileges of the other oders. Abarbanel, one of the greatest of the Hebrew writers, has offered this explanation: "The priests and scribes naturally predominated in the Sanhedrin because, not having like the other Israelites received lands to cultivate and improve, they had abundant time to consecrate to the study of law and justice, and thus became better qualified to act as judges."[6]

Qualifications of Members of the Great Sanhedrin.— The following qualifications were requisite to entitle an applicant to membership in the Great Sanhedrin:

(1)   He must have been a Hebrew and a lineal descendant of Hebrew parents. [7]

(2)   He must have been "learned in the law"; both written and unwritten.

His legal attainment must have included an intimate acquaintance with all the enactments of the Mosaic Code, with traditional practices, with the precepts and precedents of the colleges, with the adjudications of former courts and the opinions of former judges. He must have been familiar not only with the laws then actively in force, but also with those that had become obsolete.[8]

(3)   He must have had judicial experience; that is, he must have already filled three offices of gradually increasing dignity, beginning with one of the local courts, and passing successively through two magistracies at Jerusalem. [9]

(4)   He must have been thoroughly proficient in scientific knowledge.

The ancient Sanhedrists were required to be especially well grounded in astronomy and medicine. They were also expected to be familiar with the arts of the necromancer.[10] We are also led to believe from the revelations of the Talmud that the judges of Israel were well versed in the principles of physiology and chemistry, as far as these sciences were developed and understood in those days. History records that Rabbi Ismael and his disciples once engaged in experimental dissection in order to learn the anatomy of the human frame. On one occasion a deceitful witness tried to impose upon a Hebrew court by representing spermatic fluid to be the albumen of an egg. Baba bar Boutah was enabled, from his knowledge of the elements of chemistry, to demonstrate the fact of fraud in the testimony of the witness. Eighty disciples of the famous Academy of Hillel are said to have been acquainted with every branch of science known in those days.[11]

(5)   He must have been an accomplished linguist; that is, he must have been thoroughly familiar with the languages of the surrounding nations.

Interpreters were not allowed in Hebrew courts. A knowledge of several languages was, therefore, indispensable to the candidate who sought membership in the Great Sanhedrin. "In the case of a foreigner being called as a witness before a tribunal, it was absolutely necessary that two members should understand the language in which the stranger's evidence was given; that two others should speak to him; while another was required to be both able to understand and to converse with the witness. A majority of three judges could always be obtained on any doubtful point in the interpretation of the testimony submitted to the court. At Bither there were three Rabbins acquainted with every language then known; while at Jabneh there were said to be four similarly endowed with the gift of 'all the tongues.'"[12]

(6)   He must have been modest, popular, of good appearance, and free from haughtiness. [13]

The Hebrew mind conceived modesty to be the natural result of that learning, dignity, and piety which every judge was supposed to possess. The qualification of "popularity" did not convey the notion of electioneering hobnobbing and familiarity. It meant simply that the reputation of the applicant for judicial honors was so far above reproach that his countrymen could and would willingly commit all their interests of life, liberty, and property to his keeping. By "good appearance" was meant that freedom from physical blemishes and defects, and that possession of physical endowments that would inspire respect and reverence in the beholder. The haughty judge was supposed to be lacking in the elements of piety and humility which qualified him for communion with God. Haughtiness, therefore, disqualified for admission to the Great Sanhedrin.

(7)   He must have been pious, strong, and courageous. [14]

Piety was the preeminent qualification of a judge of Israel. Impiety was the negation of everything Israelitish. Strength and courage are attributes that all judges in all ages and among all races have been supposed to possess in order to be just and righteous in their judgments.

Disqualifications.— Disqualifications of applicants for membership in the Great Sanhedrin are not less interesting than qualifications. They are in the main mere negatives of affirmatives which have already been given, and would seem, therefore, to be superfluous. But they are strongly accentuated in Hebrew law, and are therefore repeated here.

(1)   A man was disqualified to act as judge who had not, or had never had, any regular trade, occupation, or profession by which he gained his livelihood.

The reason for this disqualification was based upon a stringent maxim of the Rabbins: "He who neglects to teach his son a trade is as though he taught him to steal!" A man who did not work and had never labored in the sweat of his brow for an honest livelihood, was not qualified, reasoned the Hebrew people, to give proper consideration or extend due sympathy to the cause of litigants whose differences arose out of the struggles of everyday life.

(2)   In trials where the death penalty might be inflicted, an aged man, a person who had never had any children of his own, and a bastard were disqualified to act as judge.

A person of advanced years was disqualified because according to the Rabbins old age is frequently marked by bad temper; and "because his years and infirmities were likely to render him harsh, perhaps obstinate and unyielding." On the other hand, youth was also a disqualification to sit in the Sanhedrin. According to the Rabbis, twenty-five years was the age which entitled a person to be called a Man;[15] but no one was eligible to a seat in the Sanhedrin until he had reached the age of forty years.[16] The ancient Hebrews regarded that period as the beginning of discretion and understanding.

A person without children was not supposed to possess those tender paternal feelings "which should warm him on behalf of the son of Israel who was in peril of his life."

The stain of birth and the degradation in character of a bastard were wholly inconsistent with the high ideals of the qualifications of a Hebrew judge.

(3)   Gamblers, dice players, bettors on pigeon matches, usurers, and slave dealers were disqualified to act as judges.

The Hebrews regarded gambling, dice playing, betting on pigeon matches, and other such practices as forms of thievery; and thieves were not eligible to sit as judges in their courts. No man who was in the habit of lending money in an usurious manner could be a judge. It was immaterial whether the money was lent to a countryman or a stranger. Slave dealers were disqualified to act as judges because they were regarded as inhuman and unsympathetic.

(4)   No man was qualified to be a judge who had dealt in the fruits of the seventh year.

Such a person was deemed lacking in conscience and unfitted to perform judicial functions.

(5)   No man who was concerned or interested in a matter to be adjudicated was qualified to sit in judgment thereon.

This is a universal disqualification of judges under all enlightened systems of justice. The weakness and selfishness of human nature are such that few men are qualified to judge impartially where their own interests are involved.

(6)   All relatives of the accused man, of whatever degree of consanguinity, were disqualified from sitting in judgment on his case.

This is only a variation of the disqualification of interest.

(7)   No person who would be benefited, as heir, or otherwise, by the death or condemnation of an accused man, was qualified to be his judge.

This, too, was a variation of the disqualification of interest.

(8)   The king could not be a member of the Sanhedrin.

Royalty disqualified from holding the place of judge because of the high station of the king and because his exercising judicial functions might hamper the administration of justice.

And, finally, in closing the enumeration of disqualifications, it may be added that an election to a seat obtained by fraud or any unfair means was null and void. No respect was shown for the piety or learning of such a judge; his judicial mantle was spat upon with scorn, and his fellow judges fled from him as from a plague or pest. Hebrew contempt for such a judge was expressed in the maxim: "The robe of the unfairly elected judge is to be respected not more than the blanket of an ass."

Officers of the Great Sanhedrin.— Two presiding officers directed the proceedings of the Great Sanhedrin. One of these, styled *prince* (nasi), was the chief and the president of the court. The other, known as the *father of the Tribunal* (ab-beth-din), was the vice-president.

There has been much discussion among the historians as to the particular chamber from which the president was chosen. Some have contended that the presidency of the Sanhedrin belonged by right to the high priest. But the facts of history do not sustain this contention. Aaron was high priest at the time when Moses was president of the first Sanhedrin in the Wilderness; and, besides, the list of presidents preserved by the Talmud reveals the names of many who did not belong to the priesthood. Maimonides has made the following very apt observation on the subject: "Whoever surpassed his colleagues in wisdom was made by them chief of the Sanhedrin."[17]

According to most Jewish writers, there were two scribes or secretaries of the Sanhedrin. But several others contend that there were three. Benny says: "Three scribes were present; one was seated on the right, one on the left, the third in the center of the hall. The first recorded the names of the judges who voted for the acquittal of the accused, and the arguments upon which the acquittal was grounded. The second noted the names of such as decided to condemn the prisoner and the reasons upon which the conviction was based. The third kept an account of both the preceding so as to be able at any time to supply omissions or check inaccuracies in the memoranda of his brother reporters."[18]

In addition to these officers, there were still others who executed sentences and attended to all the police work of legal procedure. They were called *shoterim.*[19]

There was no such officer as a public prosecutor or State's attorney known to the laws of the ancient Hebrews. The witnesses to the crime were the only prosecutors recognized by Hebrew criminal jurisprudence; and in capital cases they were the legal executioners as well.

There was also no such body as the modern Grand Jury known to ancient Hebrew criminal law. And no similar body or committee of the Sanhedrin performed the accusatory functions of the modern Grand Jury. The witnesses were the only accusers, and their testimony was both the indictment and the evidence. Until they testified, the man suspected was deemed not only innocent but unaccused.

The profession of the law, in the modern sense of the term, was no part of the judicial system of the ancient Hebrews. There were no advocates as we know them. There were, indeed, men learned in the law—Pharisees and Sadducees—who knew all the law. There were doctors of the law: men whom Jesus confounded when a youth in the Temple at the age of twelve.[20] But there were no lawyers in the modern sense: professional characters who accept fees and prosecute cases. The judges and disciples performed all the duties of the modern attorney and counselor-at-law. The prophets were the sole orators of Hebrew life, but they were never allowed to appear as defendants of accused persons. Indeed, they themselves were at times compelled to play the rôle of defendants. Jeremiah is an illustrious example.[21] Both Keim[22] and Geikie[23] speak of a Baal Rib, a counsel appointed to see that everything possible was done to secure the rights of an accused person at a Hebrew criminal trial. But these statements are not in accord with standard works on ancient Hebrew jurisprudence. Indeed, Friedlieb emphatically denies that there was any such person as a Baal Rib or Dominus Litis among the ancient Hebrews.[24] It seems that in the closing years of Jewish nationality, specially retained advocates were known, for St. Luke tells us that the Jews employed Tertullus, a certain orator, to prosecute St. Paul.[25] But this was certainly an exceptional case. It is historically

certain that in the early ages of the Jewish Commonwealth litigants pleaded their
own causes. This we learn from the case of the two women who appeared before
King Solomon, and laid before him their respective claims to a child.[26]

Compensation of Officers. — The judges of Israel were originally not paid
anything for their services. The honor of the office itself was considered sufficient
emolument for labors performed. Indeed, the office of teacher and judge in Israel
was so highly prized that the struggles and sacrifices of a lifetime were not
considered too great to pay for a place in the Great Sanhedrin. Such high station
was regarded as a sacred sphere into which the idea of material gain should not
enter. The regular court days were, therefore, spent by the judge on the bench,
without any expectation of reward for his services. The other days of the week he
spent in earning a livelihood. But in later years of the national life a change seems
to have taken place. The ancient rule was so far modified that when the services
of the judge were required on days when he was engaged in his private pursuits,
custom and the law gave him the right to claim a substitute during the time he
was occupied on the bench; or, in default of a substitute, to claim remuneration
for the time which he had lost. Another modification was that if his legal duties
required his entire time, the judge in Israel was entitled to support from the
communal treasury, and was even permitted to accept fees from litigants. This
practice was discouraged, however, by the Rabbis, who looked with disfavor
upon the appointment of judges who were not entirely able to support
themselves.

The secretaries and other officers of subordinate dignity were paid for their
services.[27]

Sessions of the Courts. — In the early days of the Hebrew Commonwealth the
laws provided for no regular court days. The Sanhedrin convened as occasion
required, to transact such business and dispose of such cases as came before it.
But this practice was oftentimes found to be expensive and annoying to litigants
who came into Jerusalem from the country and found no courts in session. To
accommodate the country folk, the farmers, and shepherds, Ezra and his
coadjutors of the Great Assembly designated Mondays and Thursdays as
regular court days. This enactment was not prohibitive, however. Court might be
held on any day of the week that necessity required. The reason assigned by the
Rabbins for the selection of Mondays and Thursdays as court days was that on
those days people from the country usually congregated in populous places, in
their houses of worship, to hear the law read and interpreted. While in
attendance upon these sacred services, it was thought that the time was both
convenient and propitious for the settlement of their legal difficulties.[28]

The authorities are divided as to the exact official hours of the day for holding
court. "The Sanhedrin sat from the close of the morning sacrifice to the time of
the evening sacrifice," is the language of the Jerusalem Talmud.[29] Mendelsohn
says: "The official hours for holding court were between the morning service and
noon; but a suit entered upon during the legal hours could be carried on until
evening, and civil cases could be continued even after nightfall."[30] But in no case

of a criminal nature could the court continue its session during the night.[31]

The Minor Sanhedrins in the provinces, as well as the local Courts of Three, usually held their sessions in the most public place, that is, at the city gate. The two Minor Sanhedrins of Jerusalem held their sessions at the entrance to the Temple-mound and to the woman's department respectively. The Great Sanhedrin convened in an apartment of the national temple at Jerusalem, known as the *Lishkath haggazith.* This apartment was the celebrated "Hall of Hewn Stones."[32]

Recruitments.— The young Hebrew disciple who possessed the necessary mental, spiritual, and personal qualifications for judicial honors was styled Haber, which means associate, fellow.[33] Such a disciple was first solemnly ordained and received the title of Zaken (elder) or Rabbi. This title rendered him eligible to membership in the different courts. But that he might acquire necessary experience for membership in the Great Sanhedrin and become a sage worthy of Israel, he was required to begin at the lowest rung of the judicial ladder and work gradually to the top. He was first appointed by the Great Sanhedrin to a place in one of the local courts, consisting of three members; he then served as a member of one of the provincial Sanhedrins; was then promoted to the first, and afterwards to the second Minor Sanhedrin at Jerusalem; and was elevated finally to the Great Sanhedrin itself.[34] After this manner, all the courts of the ancient Hebrews were recruited and replenished from time to time; the young aspirant to judicial favors beginning in the local Court of Three and rising by successive steps to the Great Sanhedrin at Jerusalem.

The exact method of filling vacancies and thus replenishing the membership of the Great Sanhedrin is not certainly known.[35] The following extract from the Talmud, however, is thought to be authoritative:

In front of them (the judges of the Great Sanhedrin) sat three rows of learned disciples; each of them had his own special place. Should it be necessary to promote one of them to the office of judge, one of those in the foremost row was selected. His place was then supplied by one in the second row, while one from the third was in turn advanced to the second. This being done, someone was then chosen from the congregation to supply the vacancy thus created in the third row. But the person so appointed did not step directly into the place occupied by the one last promoted from the third row, but into the place that beseemed one who was only newly admitted.[36]

Quorum of the Great Sanhedrin.— Twenty-three members constituted a quorum of the Great Sanhedrin. This was the full number of the membership of a Minor Sanhedrin.

Number of Votes Required to Convict.— "In criminal trials a majority of one vote is sufficient for an acquittal; but for a condemnation a majority of two is necessary," is the language of the Mishna.[37] The full membership of the Great Sanhedrin was seventy-one. A condemnation by thirty-five acquitted the accused; a condemnation by thirty-six also acquitted. At least thirty-seven votes were needed to convict. If a bare quorum was present, at least thirteen votes were necessary to condemn.

A very peculiar rule of Hebrew law provided that "a simultaneous and unanimous verdict of guilty rendered on the day of trial, had the effect of an acquittal."[38] Such a verdict was considered to be lacking in the element of mercy, and was thought to result more from conspiracy and mob violence than from mature judicial deliberation.

Jurisdiction of the Great Sanhedrin.— The jurisdiction of the Great Sanhedrin is briefly and concisely stated in the Mishna:

The judgment of the seventy-one is besought when the affair concerns a whole tribe or is regarding a false prophet or the high-priest; when it is a question whether war shall be declared or not; when it has for its object the enlargement of Jerusalem or its suburbs; whether tribunals of twenty-three shall be instituted in the provinces, or to declare that a town has become defiled, and to place it under ban of excommunication.[39]

Edward Gibbon has also defined the jurisdiction of the same court as follows:

With regard to civil objects, it was the supreme court of appeal; with regard to criminal matters, a tribunal constituted for the trial of all offences that were committed by men in any public station, or that affected the peace and majesty of the people. Its most frequent and serious occupation was the exercise of judicial power. As a council of state and as a court of justice, it possessed many prerogatives. Every power was derived from its authority, every law was ratified by its sanction.

The Great Sanhedrin possessed all the powers and attributes of a national parliament and a supreme court of judicature. It corresponded to the Areopagus of Athens and to the senate of Rome. It took cognizance of the misconduct of priests and kings. Josephus tells us that Herod the Great was arraigned as a criminal before its judges, and that King Hyrcanus himself obeyed its mandates and decrees.

Appeals.— Appeals were allowed from a Minor Sanhedrin to the Great Sanhedrin. But there was no appeal from a mandate, judgment, or decree of the Great Sanhedrin. "Its authority was supreme in all matters; civil and political, social, religious, and criminal."

It is believed that enough has been said touching the character, organization, and jurisdiction of the supreme tribunal of the ancient Hebrews to satisfy the average reader. Indeed, it may be that this limit has been exceeded. The remainder of this chapter will be devoted to a short review of the Minor Sanhedrins and the Courts of Three.

Minor Sanhedrins.— There was no fixed number of Minor Sanhedrins for the administration of justice in the Hebrew Commonwealth. Wherever and whenever, in any town or city inhabited by at least one hundred and twenty families, the people desired a Sanhedrin of three-and-twenty members, such a tribunal was established. For this purpose, an application was made to the Great Sanhedrin at Jerusalem, which dispatched a mandate to the town ordering the residents to assemble and to nominate from among themselves persons qualified to act as judges. The electors were expected to bear in mind the qualifications that would fit a judge for membership in the Great Sanhedrin, to which all local judges might eventually be elevated. Accordingly, only "good men and true" were chosen at the town mass meeting. Immediately upon receipt of the return to the mandate, an authorization was sent back from Jerusalem to the town or city which confirmed the election and constituted the judges selected a Sanhedrin of three-and-twenty members.[40]

Jurisdiction of the Minor Sanhedrins.— The jurisdiction of the Minor

Sanhedrins extended to nearly all criminal cases involving imprisonment or seclusion for life, internment in a city of refuge, and capital punishment. Adultery, seduction, blasphemy, incest, manslaughter, and murder belonged to these different classes. This court condemned an ox to be butchered that had gored a man to death. The condemnation proceedings were something in the nature of a trial of the beast; and the owner was severely fined where the evidence proved that he knew the vicious disposition and habits of the animal. The deliberations at the trial of the bull were most careful and solemn, since the value of a human life was involved in the proceedings and had to be estimated in the judgment.

Besides jurisdiction in criminal matters, the Sanhedrins of three-and-twenty members performed certain civil functions. They were the tax boards of the various provinces. They constituted the regular agencies of government for the distribution of public charity. The management and administration of public elementary schools were under their control. The legal standards of weights and measures were inspected by them and received their seals. Sanitary regulations, repairing the defenses of walled cities, and maintaining the public highways in good condition, were among the duties of the Minor Sanhedrins.

The qualifications of judges of these courts were the same as those required for membership in the Great Sanhedrin. This was true because the judges of the provincial courts might be promoted to the supreme tribunal at Jerusalem. The Minor Sanhedrins might be very aptly described as the *nisi prius* courts of the Commonwealth of Israel. It was in these courts of three-and-twenty members that the bulk of Hebrew litigation was disposed of. It seems that, though equal in number, they were not all regarded as equal in learning or authority. It is distinctly stated that appeals could be taken from one Minor Sanhedrin to another "deemed of superior authority."[41] The difference was probably due to the fact that in the larger towns were located colleges and schools, some of whose professors were doubtless either advisers or members of the local Sanhedrin. At any rate, when a difficult question, civil or criminal, could not be determined, for want of an authoritative and registered decision, by an ordinary Sanhedrin of three-and-twenty judges, the matter was referred to the nearest neighboring Sanhedrin thought to be of greater repute. If no authentic tradition offering a solution of the litigated question was in the possession of the Sanhedrin to which appeal had been taken, the matter was then referred to the first Minor Sanhedrin in Jerusalem which sat in the Har-habaith. If the judges of this court were themselves without precedent touching upon the litigated proposition, it was still further referred to the second Minor Sanhedrin of Jerusalem, located in the Azarah. If, again, this court was without the necessary tradition that would enable it to decide the question, the matter was finally brought before the Great Sanhedrin. If this august tribunal was without precedent and tradition that would enable its members to dispose of the question according to adjudicated cases, they then decided, nevertheless, in accordance with the sentiments and principles of natural justice.

It should be remembered that of the Minor Sanhedrins to which every town of one hundred and twenty families was entitled, two sat at Jerusalem. It was left optional with a litigant from the provinces to appeal to the local Sanhedrin or to one of the Minor Sanhedrins in Jerusalem. Local bias or prejudice was thus avoided.

Lower Tribunals.— The lowest order of Hebrew tribunal was the Court of Three, composed of judges selected by the litigants themselves. The plaintiff chose one member, the defendant selected another, and these two chose a third. A majority opinion decided all questions. In the later years of Jewish nationality, it was thought best to have at least one authorized jurist (mumcha) in the Court of Three. This particular judge was probably an appointee of the Great Sanhedrin from among the young disciples (Zaken or Rabbis). This appointment was doubtless intended to give repute to the local court and experience to the legal aspirant, as well as to furnish a possible recruit to the Great Sanhedrin.[42]

These courts corresponded very nearly to the modern courts of Justices of the Peace. Their jurisdiction extended to civil matters of small importance and to petty criminal offenses. They were not permanent, being more in the nature of referees or arbitrators, and sat only when occasion required. Their sessions were public and were held in the open air under trees, or at the city gate.

Thus much for the judicial system of courts and judges among the ancient Hebrews. It was simple in the extreme, democratic to the core, and seems to have been thoroughly reliable and effective. It was founded upon universal suffrage, subject only to the general supervision and occasional appointments of the Great Sanhedrin. The judges were ever in touch with the sympathies and the best interests of the people.

Peculiarities of the Hebrew System.— Certain very striking peculiarities marked the Hebrew system:

(1) There were no lawyers or advocates. These judicial disputants have been known to every other system of enlightened jurisprudence. But there were no Ciceros, Erskines, Choates among the ancient Hebrews. The judges were the defenders as well as the judges of the accused. It may be easily read between the lines that the framers and builders of the Hebrew judicial system regarded paid advocates as an abomination and a nuisance. King Ferdinand of Spain seems to have had the Hebrew notion when, more than a thousand years after Jerusalem fell, he sent out colonies to the West Indies, with special instructions "that no lawyers should be carried along, lest lawsuits should become ordinary occurrences in the New World."[43] Ferdinand evidently agreed with Plato that lawyers are the plague of the community.[44]

(2) There was no secret body, with the accusatory functions of the modern Grand Jury, connected with the ancient Hebrew judicial system. The witnesses were the accusers, and their testimony constituted both the indictment and the evidence.

(3) There were no public prosecutors or State's attorneys known to the Hebrew system. Here again, the witnesses were the informants, prosecutors, and,

in capital cases, executioners of the accused.

(4) No court among the ancient Hebrews could consist of a single judge. Three was the number of the lowest court; three-and-twenty, of the next highest; and seventy-one, of the Great Sanhedrin at Jerusalem. A single intelligence acting judicially would have been regarded as a usurpation of divine prerogative. The basis of this peculiar Hebrew notion is a single sentence from the Pirke Aboth, iv. 8: "Be not a sole judge, for there is no sole judge but One."[45]

CHAPTER IV

HEBREW CRIMINAL LAW—WITNESSES AND EVIDENCE

Competency.—The qualifications of a competent witness, under Hebrew law, were almost identical with those of a qualified judge, mentioned in a previous chapter. Self-evidently, all persons who were not incompetent, were competent.

Incompetency.—The following persons were incompetent to be witnesses: Gentiles, women,[1] minors, slaves,[2] idiots and lunatics, deaf mutes, blind men, gamblers, usurers, illiterate or immodest persons, persons who had been convicted of irreligion or immorality, relatives by affinity or consanguinity, and all persons directly interested in the case.

The witness must have been a Hebrew, though the Talmud mentions cases in which certain facts were allowed to stand proved upon statements "made innocently" by a Gentile; that is, not as a witness in court.

Women were not permitted to be witnesses ordinarily, because of the "levity and boldness of the sex."[3] In capital cases, they were not allowed to testify against the accused, because the law required the witnesses to become the executioners of the condemned man, and it was not deemed proper to impose this solemn and awful duty upon the weaker sex.

Puberty or adolescence marked the age which qualified a person to be a witness in criminal cases; that is, the thirteenth year must have been passed.

Immoral and irreligious persons were incompetent to testify. Such men were termed "wicked" in reference to the law as laid down in Exodus xxiii. 1: "Thou shalt not raise a false report: put not thine hand with the wicked to be an unrighteous witness." Under the stigma of the immoral and irreligious came dicers, usurers, pigeon fliers, and those who traded in the fruits of the Sabbatical year. Maimonides also mentions as incompetent "men who showed lack of self-respect by eating on the street, walking about naked at their work, or living openly on the charity of Gentiles."[4] Publicans—tax-gatherers—were usually classed with heathens and sinners as being among the immoral and irreligious. This class of persons were suspected by the Jews, not only because they were regarded as the official representatives of the Roman oppressors of Judea, but also because extortion and cruelty were frequently practiced by them. Theocritus being asked which was the most cruel of all beasts, replied: "Among the beasts of the wilderness, the bear and the lion are the most cruel, but among the beasts of the city, the Publican and the Parasite."[5]

The doctrine of interest as a disqualification to testify was carried to the limit of declaring a person incompetent to be a witness when he was the citizen of a town where claim of title to the public bath house or the square was made, until he had first divested himself of all share in the title to the litigated property.[6]

Number Required to Convict.—Under Hebrew law, both Mosaic and

Talmudic, at least two witnesses were required to convict an accused person. The prosecuting witness being included, three were necessary.

Concerning capital punishment, the Mosaic ordinance, referring to this rule, runs thus:

At the mouth of *two* witnesses, or *three* witnesses, shall he that is worthy of death be put to death; but at the mouth of *one* witness he shall not be put to death.[7]

Whoso killeth any person, the murderer shall be put to death by the mouth of witnesses; but *one* witness shall not testify against any person to cause him to die.[8]

From the Talmud we learn that this Mosaic provision was maintained with scrupulous fidelity in the administration of justice throughout all the years of Jewish nationality. It was a requirement of prudence and safety which commends itself to every logician and legist. It is not necessary to be a criminal lawyer of large experience to know that the blackest falsehood can almost always secure at least one champion. Pliny, the historian, knew this when he wrote: *"Nullum tam impudens mendacium est quod teste careat."*[9]

The requirement of two witnesses was not, however, peculiar to the jurisprudence of the Hebrews. Nearly every ancient code contained a similar enactment. It was especially prominent in Roman law.[10] But it can scarcely be found today in any modern legislation. In prosecutions for the crimes of treason and perjury under the Common Law of England, two witnesses were required; in almost all other cases, one positive witness was sufficient.[11]

The American Constitution requires two witnesses to the same overt act, to convict of treason.[12] And the penal laws of the majority of the American States have provisions requiring at least two witnesses, or one witness corroborated by circumstantial evidence, to establish guilt in the prosecution of certain crimes; notably, the sexual crimes of rape and seduction, the crime of perjury, as well as all crimes where it is sought to convict upon the testimony of an accomplice.

More than one hundred years ago, Montesquieu boasted of such a requirement in French law and declared that those laws which condemn a man to death on the testimony of a single witness are fatal to liberty.[13] The reason of the rule proclaimed by the great French writer is the same as that put forth by the ancient Rabbins. It was assumed that the defendant in a criminal case would plead not guilty and deny the facts of the crime. His plea and denial would simply counterbalance and destroy the testimony of a single witness swearing for the commonwealth. The testimony of a third witness was, therefore, indispensable to a decision. It may be objected that this rule was absurd, since a conviction was impossible unless the State could produce more witnesses than the accused. But we shall learn later that the doctrine of sifting testimony and weighing the credibility of witnesses did not obtain so strictly among the ancient Hebrew judges as it does in cases of modern trial by jury under English and American law.

Agreement of Witnesses.—The witnesses were required to agree in all essential details; else, their testimony was invalid and had to be rejected.

The Talmudic provision is: "If one witness contradicts another, the testimony is not accepted."[14]

The illustration of the rule given by Maimonides, in his commentary on this provision, is: "For instance, if one witness were to testify to having seen an Israelite in the act of worshiping the sun, and another to having seen the same man worshiping the moon, yet, although each of the two facts proves clearly that the man had committed the horrible crime of idolatry, the discrepancy in the statements of the witnesses invalidates their testimony and the accused is free."[15]

This rule of strict agreement, it is supposed, extended at first only to criminal cases, but it was undoubtedly afterwards applied to civil causes as well. An eminent contributor to the "Jewish Encyclopedia" says:

> In civil cases, however, it is not necessary that the two witnesses should agree very closely as to the time and place. Thus, if of two witnesses to a loan one should say, "A lent B a jar of oil," the other, "He lent him a jar of wine"; or, if one should say, "I was present when the money was paid at Jerusalem," the other, "I saw it paid at Hebron"; or, if one should say, "I saw it paid in the month of Nisan," the other, "I saw it paid in Iyyar," their testimony would be void. But if one says he saw it paid in the upper and the other in the lower story; or if he says on the first of the month and the other on the second of the month, such evidence is within the limit of fair mistake and the testimony stands. Even less does a disagreement as to circumstances other than time and place affect the testimony; for instance, if one say the money is black from usage, the other that it was new, this would be regarded as an immaterial circumstance, and the testimony would stand. Where the two witnesses vary only in the matter of quantity, the lesser quantity is sufficiently proved.[16]

One of the strangest provisions of Hebrew law was the requirement that the testimony of each witness to the transaction should cover the entire case. This was a Talmudic rule resulting from Rabbinic construction of the Mosaic ordinance, requiring at least two witnesses to establish a crime. The doctors of the law construed the rule to mean that the testimony of each witness was to be complete within itself and to extend to the whole case. Hebrew law did not permit the use of circumstantial evidence in criminal prosecutions. Only eyewitnesses of the crime were competent. Under English and American law a crime may be proven by any number of witnesses, each of whom testifies to a separate fact which constitutes a link in the chain of circumstantial evidence. But this method of proof was forbidden by both the Pentateuch and the Talmud. Under Hebrew law the capital crime of kidnaping was made up of the two elements of Abduction and Selling. The testimony of two witnesses—one to the fact of Abduction, the other to the fact of Selling—was insufficient to convict. Each had to testify to the facts of both Abduction and Selling. This Talmudic rule of criminal procedure was undoubtedly based upon a supreme regard for the sanctity of human life and upon the fact that the Hebrews rejected circumstantial evidence altogther in proving crime. The extreme of the rule is declared by Mendelsohn when he says: "And even where there appeared a legal number of duly qualified witnesses, the testimony was insufficient to convict, unless they agreed not only with regard to the prisoner's offense, but also with regard to the mode of committing it. Rabbinic law does not subject a person to capital, nor even to corporal punishment, unless all witnesses charge him with one and the same criminal act, their statements fully agreeing in the main circumstances, and declaring that they saw one another, while seeing him engaged in the crime."[17]

No Oath Required.—An oath, in the modern sense, was never administered to a Hebrew witness.

Testimony was given under the sanction of the Ninth Commandment: "Thou shalt not bear false witness against thy neighbor." This solemn prohibition of bearing false witness was regarded by both Moses and the Talmudists as a sufficient safeguard against perjury. It was a settled maxim of Talmudic law that: "Whosoever will not tell the truth without an oath, would not scruple to assert falsehood with an oath." The doctrine was carried still further by some of the Jewish philosophers who declared that swearing was injurious in itself; and that he who consents to swear should *ipso facto* be suspected of lacking credibility.[18]

In the place of an oath, the following solemn warning or adjuration was administered to each witness in the presence of the entire court:

Forget not, O witness, that it is one thing to give evidence in a trial as to money and another in a trial for life. In a money suit, if thy witness-bearing shall do wrong, money may repair that wrong. But in this trial for life, if thou sinnest, the blood of the accused and the blood of his seed to the end of time shall be imputed unto thee. . . . Therefore was Adam created one man and alone, to teach thee that if any witness shall destroy one soul out of Israel, he is held by the Scripture to be as if he had destroyed the world; and he who saves one such soul to be as if he had saved the world . . . . For a man from one signet ring may strike off many impressions, and all of them shall be exactly alike. But He, the King of the kings of kings, He the Holy and the Blessed, has struck off from His type of the first man the forms of all man that shall live, yet so that no one human being is wholly alike to any other. Wherefore let us think and believe that the whole world is created for a man such as he whose life hangs on thy words. But these ideas must not deter thee from testifying to what thou actually knowest. Scripture declares: "The witness who hath seen or known, and doth not tell, shall bear his iniquity." Nor must ye scruple about becoming the instrument of the alleged criminal's death. Remember the Scriptural maxim: "In the destruction of the wicked, there is joy."[19]

It will be observed that the two elements of this preliminary caution were, first, a solemn warning against injustice to the accused through false swearing and a reminder of the inevitable retribution of Heaven upon the perjured swearer and his remote descendants; second, a pointed admonition against timidity or fear in testifying.

Bound by this tremendous sanction, the Hebrew witness was prepared to testify. The method was unique, but seems to have been thoroughly effective. Students of law will not be struck by its peculiarity. They are well aware that any plan or mode is legal and effective that binds the conscience of the witness. Even under modern codes that impose an oath, no fixed form is imperatively demanded. In King v. Morgan, I Leach C. L. 54, a Mahometan was sworn upon the Koran; in Omychund v. Baker, I Atk. 21, a Gentoo was sworn by touching the foot of a Brahmin; in Reg v. Entrehman, I Car. & M. 248, a Chinese witness took an oath by kneeling down and breaking a saucer, the oath being administered through an interpreter in these words: "You shall tell the truth, the whole truth; the saucer is cracked, and if you do not tell the truth, your soul will be cracked like the saucer."

Examination of Witnesses.— As an act of caution against the admission of irrelevant testimony, and as a means of placing before the entire court, in the first instance, only such evidence as was deemed strictly legal, a preliminary examination of witnesses was conducted in private by a special committee of the Sanhedrin appointed for that purpose. All irrelevant testimony developed at this private examination was immediately declared inadmissible and was cast aside. The necessary result of this most sensible proceeding was the discovery, in advance, of discrepancies in the statements of witnesses and the eradication of all illegal testimony. The full court sitting in regular session were not, therefore, exposed to the danger of being prejudiced by the recital of facts that had no legal connection with the case. Modern jurists might easily learn something from the ancient Hebrews in this regard. Every sensible lawyer is perfectly well aware of the absurdity and injustice of the modern method of criminal procedure in allowing skilled and designing attorneys to propose certain kinds of irrelevant testimony in the presence of the jury, knowing very well that it will be overruled by the court. These attorneys frequently deliberately draw out such testimony from the witness with the expectation and understanding that it will be ordered stricken out. The rule of practice that allows incompetent testimony to be temporarily introduced upon a promise that a foundation will be laid or relevancy shown, is abortive instead of productive of justice. The mere clerical act of striking out incompetent testimony does not, as a matter of fact, remove the impression of prejudice from the brain of the judge or juror. The ancient Sanhedrists were men of brilliant education and superior natural endowments. They were trained in powers of logical analysis, and yet they were unwilling to trust themselves with the possession of prejudicial facts arising from incompetent testimony. It is respectfully submitted that the modern average juror, whose mind is usually undisciplined in logic and legal matters, is not able to sift and disentangle the relevant from the irrelevant in the record of a civil or criminal trial of two or more weeks' duration. Theoretically, he is; but practically, he is not. Every impression, good or bad, legal or illegal, received at the trial, affects his judgment and enters into the general summary of the case in reaching a verdict.

   Separation of Witnesses.—The witnesses were required to give their testimony separately and always in the presence of the accused.

   Daniel said to the people concerning the two old men who testified against Susanna: " *Separate* them, and I will examine them."[20]

   By this was meant that witnesses could not be examined until they had been separated in conformity with law. Under modern practice in most jurisdictions, witnesses may be separated and examined one at a time out of the presence of each other. The rule of separation is, however, generally optional with the litigant and discretionary with the court; the ruling of the court being usually reversed only in case of abuse of discretion. But among the Hebrews the requirement was mandatory and imperative. It had to be observed in every case.

   Mode of Examination of Witnesses.— The mode employed by the Hebrew judges in examining witnesses is without a precedent or parallel in the jurisprudence of the world. Two distinct sets of questions constituted the examination. The first set consisted of a series of interrogations relating to the *time* and *place* of the alleged crime. These questions were prescribed by law and could not be varied in the slightest. The technical name applied to the first set of questions was Hakiroth. The second set was termed Bedikoth[21] and included all interrogations touching the investigation of relevant circumstances and corroborative facts surrounding the case. The following seven questions, constituting the Hakiroth, the first set of questions, were propounded to each witness: "Was it during a year of jubilee? Was it in an ordinary year? In what month? On what day of the month? At what hour? In what place? Do you identify this person?"[22]

These seven questions were framed and applied in conformity with a fundamental principle of the Hebrew law of evidence that the testimony of any witness, if false, should admit of being impeached and overthrown by proof of an *alibi* against the witness. It seems, indeed, that proof of an *alibi* against the witness was the only method of impeachment known to Hebrew law. It may be readily seen that the only statements capable of being thus contradicted were confined to those relating to the details of *time* and *place*. To illustrate: Suppose that two witnesses had testified that the alleged crime was committed in a certain town at a certain hour; suppose that it subsequently appeared in evidence that, at the stated time, one or both these witnesses were in a neighboring town. In such a case, the witness or witnesses stood impeached, their testimony was overthrown and they, themselves, became subject to the pains and penalties of perjury.

The failure of any witness to answer satisfactorily any of the seven questions above mentioned entitled the accused to immediate acquittal. Any material disagreement between two or more witnesses required by the law in answer to any one of these questions, likewise entitled the prisoner to immediate discharge. These seven questions seem to have been framed not so much to develop truthful testimony and to promote the ends of justice from the standpoint of the State as to enable the defendant to attack and destroy the testimony of hostile witnesses. The rule and the reason thereof are thus clearly and succinctly stated by Mendelsohn:

The several particulars referring to time and place must be furnished with the greatest possible precision and certainty, and that by the whole party of witnesses. The slightest disagreement on the part of the witnesses in regard to any one of these particulars invalidates the entire testimony. Even where a number of witnesses greater than that required by law, as three, appear, and two agree on every point, but the third differs from them as to more than one day, or more than one hour in the day, the whole testimony is invalidated. For time and place are the only points which affect the person of the witness himself; he not being able to be at more than one spot at any one time; time and place are, accordingly, the only grounds on which the witness may be confuted and duly punished.

The second set of questions, termed the Bedikoth, embraced all matters not brought out by the Hakiroth, such as would form the basis of legitimate modern direct or cross examination. The following kinds of evidence, however, were not admissible under either set of questions: Evidence of character, good or bad; previous convictions of the accused; and evidence as to the prisoner's antecedents. Such matters were not relevant, under Hebrew law, and could not be urged against the prisoner.[23]

False Witnesses.—Hebrew law provided that false witnesses should suffer the penalty provided for the commission of the crime which they sought by their testimony to fix upon the accused.

The Scriptural authority for this rule is the following:

"And the judges shall make diligent inquisition; and, behold, if the witness be a false witness and hath testified falsely against his brother, then shall ye do unto him as he had thought to do unto his brother. . . . And thine eye shall not pity; but life shall go for life, eye for eye, tooth for tooth, hand for hand, foot for foot."[24]

"And they arose against the two elders, for Daniel had convicted them of false witness, by their own mouth; and according to the law of Moses, they did unto them in such a sort as they maliciously intended to do their neighbor; and they put them to death."[25]

The Accused as Witness.—The accused was never compelled, under Hebrew law, to testify against himself; but was permitted and encouraged to offer testimony in his own behalf. His confession of guilt was accepted in evidence and considered in connection with other facts of the case, but was never permitted, standing alone, to form the basis of a conviction.

The following is the commentary of Maimonides on this rule of law:

We have it as a fundamental principle of our jurisprudence that no one can bring an accusation against himself. Should a man make a confession of guilt before a legally constituted tribunal, such confession is not to be used against him, unless properly attested by two other witnesses. It is, however, well to remark that the death sentence issued against Achan was an exceptional case, brought about by the nature of the circumstances attending it, for our law never condemns on the single confession of an accused party.[26]

It is needless to suggest that the accused was never put under oath. His position in this regard was exactly the same as that of any other Hebrew witness. A special reason assigned for not swearing the accused is that offered in the celebrated maxim: "In most men religion is silent when interest speaks." Again, the inducement to perjury was so great that it was thought imprudent to allow the accused to confess under the solemnity of an oath.

The principle of law which rejects a bare confession of guilt as a basis of criminal conviction is one of the most merciful and benign known to jurisprudence. It is intended to protect the commonwealth against perjury and deception on the part of the accused. It is also intended to protect the prisoner against ignorance and rashness. It is a well-known fact that the masses of mankind are ignorant of law, both civil and criminal. Not one in a thousand in the most enlightened commonwealths can define successfully the elements of the crimes of the state of which he is a citizen. By refusing to allow an uncorroborated confession to be made the basis of a conviction, the State simply throws the mantle of charity and protection around the ignorance of the prisoner who confesses. It is also well known that men will frequently confess guilt when they are not guilty; sometimes, when they are even ignorant of the facts constituting the offense. This is one of the strangest things known to psychology and mental philosophy.[27] It is derived from the well-known and universally recognized weakness of the human will when confronted with a charge that threatens to blight and destroy life and character at a single blow. A celebrated modern writer, while discussing this rule of Hebrew law, wrote the following observations upon the origin and motive of confession of guilt under criminal charges:

The confession of the accused made no exception to the rule, showing how a confession could be made the result of weakness, or folly, or of interest-yes, even of interest. Some homicide on one occasion confessed himself to be guilty of robbery or arson in order to obtain proof of his innocence of some greater crime which he had committed at the same time; a husband persisted in declaring himself guilty of outrage upon a woman, really committed by some unknown person, on order that, by being sentenced on this account, he might prove his marital efficiency, which had been disputed by his wife, who was contemplating steps to annul her marriage. Some weak-minded people, unable to support the torture of a harassing examination, and eager to regain their liberty, make a full confession, accusing themselves in order not to be indicted, like those persons who, crossing a river on a plank bridge, throw themselves, through nervousness, into the rushing water, in order not to fall in. Fools, from want of responsibility, or through a boastful nature, accept, affirm, or confess everything of which they know nothing.[28]

The reasons above stated lie at the foundation of all modern provisions framed for the protection of the accused against precipitate self-condemnation. But, strange to say, these reasons were not urged by the framers or interpreters of Hebrew law. The explanation offered by the Talmud was simply this: "He is his own kin"; and, as we have seen, relatives were never permitted to be witnesses. A modern Jewish writer has assigned the following reason for the rule forbidding a confession to form the basis of a conviction: that, if the prisoner were innocent, he should not be permitted to incriminate himself by a false confession; if he were guilty, he was a wicked person, and, therefore, incompetent to testify under Hebrew law.[29] This rule was not enforced, however, against the defendant when testifying in his own behalf; an additional proof of the merciful regard of Hebrew law for the unfortunate position of a human being charged with crime. His testimony, though self-serving, was given due weight when urged in his own defense. Little attention was paid to it when he testified against himself.

Relevancy of Hebrew Evidence.—Hearsay evidence was irrelevant under Hebrew law. "Hearsay evidence was barred equally in civil as in criminal cases, no matter how strongly the witness might believe in what he heard and however worthy and numerous were his informants."[30]

Circumstantial evidence was irrelevant under Hebrew law. "The sages had very little more confidence in circumstantial evidence given for the purpose of 'taking money out of' the defendant's pocket, than in that given for the purpose of inflicting the penalty of death or stripes. Ket. ii. 10 has been cited, according to which a witness may testify that, when a boy, he saw a woman walk about in maidenly attire; the object being to prove that she married as a maiden, not as a widow, and is therefore entitled to a greater sum for her jointure. In discussing this clause, the Talmud remarks that this is only arguing from the majority of cases; for though in most cases those wearing maidens' attire are not widows, occasionally they are; and money ought not to be taken out of a man's pocket on reasoning from the greater number of cases. In fact, circumstantial evidence was generally rejected."[31]

There were occasional exceptions to the rule in the administration of Hebrew civil law, but none in criminal law. In criminal cases no Hebrew prisoner could be convicted upon circumstantial evidence. Every link in the chain of testimony had to be forged by the direct evidence of at least two competent witnesses; else the accused was acquitted and discharged.

Written, or documentary evidence, was not relevant, under Hebrew law, in criminal prosecution. The reason of this rule was derived from a literal interpretation of the Mosaic ordinance: "Whoso killeth any person, the murderer shall be put to death by the *mouth of witnesses.*"[32] The expression, "mouth of witnesses," was construed by the interpreters of the law to require oral testimony and to exclude writing in all criminal prosecutions.

Kinds of Oral Testimony.— Hebrew oral testimony is divided by the Mishna into three leading classes:[33]

(1)   Vain testimony.
(2)   Standing testimony.
(3)   Adequate testimony.

"Vain testimony" seems to have been wholly immaterial and irrelevant. It was not even conditionally admitted, but was instantly and permanently rejected. The New Testament seems to indicate that such testimony was rendered against Jesus by the "many false witnesses" who first came, and that this testimony was rejected.

"Standing testimony" seems to have been conditionally admitted and to have been allowed to remain in evidence until it was properly confirmed by and joined to other evidence which the law required. It was not valid, however, until so connected and confirmed. We must remember that at least two witnesses, agreeing in all essential details, were needed, under Hebrew law, to convict a prisoner. It is evident then that the testimony of the first witness against the accused was necessarily regarded as "standing testimony," until the second or confirming witness, which the law required, had testified. This testimony is also referred to in the New Testament when it is said that: "At the last, came two false witnesses, And said, This fellow said, I am able to destroy the temple of God and to build it in three days."[34] The testimony of the first of these witnesses was doubtless allowed to stand until it was shown that the second witness did not render testimony in agreement with it. Contradictory testimony was thrown out under Hebrew criminal procedure; and this was done regardless of the number of witnesses who testified against the accused. It seems that a rigid application of the principle of exclusion based upon contradictory statements would have shut out the testimony of any number of agreeing witnesses, if said testimony had been contradicted in a radical and material way by even a single witness. The sifting of evidence and the weighing of the credibility of witnesses, which is the peculiar prerogative of the modern jury, were no part of the duties of the ancient Sanhedrists. The testimony of all the witnesses against the accused had to agree in all material respects, else it was wholly rejected. Now it necessarily follows that all testimony against a prisoner was of the "standing" or provisional kind until the last witness had testified, and it was found that the evidence in its entirety was in legal agreement. Mark, using the almost exact technical expression of the law, tells us, concerning the false testimony against Jesus, that "their witness agreed not together."[35] This disagreement caused the "standing testimony" of the first witness to fall and the charge of threatening or attempting to destroy the Temple was abandoned, as we shall see in a later part of this work.

"Adequate testimony," under Hebrew criminal procedure, was evidence that was competent, material, and in legal agreement. When two or more witnesses, being the entire number, against the accused agreed in all essential details, their testimony was considered adequate, and if the judges believed it to be true they based a conviction upon it.

Antecedent Warning.— It is deemed appropriate in this chapter to call attention to and briefly discuss a very striking peculiarity of the law of evidence under Hebrew criminal procedure. In the chapter on Mosaic and Talmudic law, reference was made to the celebrated proviso, called "Antecedent Warning." This proviso was unknown to the Mosaic Code, being a creation of Talmudic law, and is without a parallel in the jurisprudence of the world. Briefly stated, Antecedent Warning, under Hebrew law, meant simply this: That no person charged with crime involving life and death, or even corporal punishment, could be convicted, unless it was shown by competent testimony that immediately before the commission of the crime the offender was warned that what he was about to do was a crime, and that a certain penalty was attached thereto. The warning was not effective if any time elapsed between the admonition and the commission of the offense. Furthermore, the warning was of no force unless it was shown that the alleged criminal had duly acknowledged it and had expressed a willingness to suffer corporal punishment or to die for the act. It must have been shown that, having received the warning, the would-be offender turned to his monitor and said, "I am very well aware of the nature of the act I am about to commit, of the rules of law applicable thereto, and of the inevitable consequences of my misdeed"—else the court could not consider the condition complied with.

This peculiar proviso seems to have been intended to serve three distinct purposes: (1) To protect the would-be offender against his own ignorance and rashness and to prevent the commission of crime by a timely warning; (2) to aid in establishing guilty intention, that is, criminal intent, at the trial of the prisoner, after the commission of the offense; (3) to enable the judges to determine the exact penalty to assess. The first two purposes are self-evident. The third merits a brief consideration. To complete the warning, it was essential that the offender be told the exact penalty attached to the crime which he was about to commit; whether the punishment was capital or corporal, and the exact kind, if capital; that is, whether beheading, burning, stoning, or strangling. Now, it often happened that two crimes were committed by the same person in one day; the penalty for one of which being flagellation and the other death. And it sometimes happened that two different crimes were the result of one criminal transaction. In such a case, the nature of the Antecedent Warning would guide the judges in decreeing punishment. To illustrate: The Mosaic Code forbids the killing of either a cow or a ewe "and her young both in one day";[36] and a violation of this prohibition, according to Rabbinic law, entails the punishment of flagellation. Another Mosaic ordinance imposes the penalty of death on the Jewish idolater.[37] Now, it might have happened that the last two offenses mentioned were committed by the same person at the same time, as when an Israelite slaughtered a ewe and her young and sacrificed them as an offering to an idol. The question would at once arise: Which penalty should be assessed, death for idolatry, or flagellation for killing the ewe and her young both on the same day? Here, the nature of the Warning would determine. If the prisoner had been told that flagellation would be the punishment, then stripes were administered. If he had been warned that death was the penalty, then capital punishment was meted out to him. If the caution had included both death and flagellation, then death would have been administered, because of the enormity of the crime of idolatry and for the reason that all lesser punishments are merged in death.

Another illustration of the third purpose above mentioned, that is, to enable the judges to determine the exact punishment to administer, is this: The ancient Nazarites made solemn vows of abstemiousness.[38] And when any Israelite took the Nazarite vow and violated it, he subjected himself to the penalty of flagellation if he drank a certain measure (1/4 log) of wine. If he drank several such measures in succession, the question would arise how he was to be punished. Again, the antecedent caution would decide. If the testimony showed that he had received due warning before each drink, then he was punished for each drink separately. If he had been admonished only once, he was punished only once for the whole debauch.[39]

The enforcement of this proviso established a rule of criminal procedure peculiar to the Hebrews, and recognized by no other nation. Such a requirement seems to be utterly subversive of the celebrated maxim that has found place in every other enlightened system of law: *Ignorantia juris, quod quisque tenetur scire, neminem excusat.* Among modern civilized nations, ignorance or mistake of fact in criminal law, as well as ignorance or mistake of the meaning and effect of civil or private law, has sometimes been permitted to operate as an excuse in favor of the victim of the ignorance or mistake; but ignorance of the criminal or public law has never been permitted to be pleaded as a defense to an indictment for crime. Such a plea would threaten the very existence of the state by rendering the proof of crime and the conviction of criminals impossible.

Other reasons besides those assigned above have been advanced to explain the invention of such a proviso by the Talmudists. None of them is entirely satisfactory. Rabbinowicz has urged with great force that the enactment was the offspring of a constantly increasing tendency on the part of the framers of the Talmud to mitigate the rigors of the Mosaic Code, and to abolish altogether the punishment of death by making the conviction of criminals practically impossible.[40] But this view has been ably and probably successfully combated by Benny and others. To say the least, it was a senseless provision when viewed from the standpoint of the state in maintaining order and preserving the commonwealth. The Rabbins framed several exceptions to its operation which were doubtless designed to stay the progress of certain forms of crime and to preserve the state. The false witness was excluded from the benefit of this proviso, as were also the instigator to idolatry and the burglar. The false witness was denied the benefit because of the impossibility of foreseeing that he would swear falsely and of forewarning him; the idolater was excepted because of the heinousness of the crime of idolatry under a theocratic commonwealth; and the burglar was denied the benefit of the caution for the very peculiar reason that the "breaking in," while committing the crime of burglary, was sufficient warning.[41]

Such a rule is utterly without foundation in logic or reason from the simple fact that crime in every age has been committed with every circumstance of caution and concealment that criminal ingenuity could devise; usually under the cover of night, often with a mask, frequently by the aid of accomplices to give notice of the appearance of the officers of the law, and nearly always with subsequent attempts to wipe out evidences of the commission of the offense. To require a preliminary caution, such as the Antecedent Warning of the Jews, was to handicap the state most seriously and to render almost impossible the apprehension and punishment of public malefactors.

CHAPTER V

HEBREW CRIMINAL LAW—MODE OF TRIAL AND EXECUTION IN CAPITAL CASES

The administration of Hebrew criminal law was marked by lofty conception of right and wrong, and was pervaded by a noble sentiment of justice and humanity. From the framing of the Decalogue to the latest years of Jewish nationality, each succeeding generation witnessed some humane and merciful modification of existing rules. Talmudic interpretation invented a series or collection of sayings that gave form and character to the whole body of later Hebrew law. These maxims were intended to mitigate the rigors of the Mosaic Code and to establish safeguards against negligence or injustice to the defendant in criminal trials. Indeed, every possible precaution was taken to render impossible the wrongful conviction of an accused person. The student of Hebrew law is at times astonished by the excessive caution inculcated in criminal procedure. Certain cautionary rules are no less than pedantic, and may be justly and aptly styled Judaical. The judges leaned always to the side of the defendant and gave him the advantage of every possible doubt. They went a step farther and sought pretext after pretext that would result in an acquittal. A sense of awful responsibility weighed upon the hearts and consciences of the judges. The services of the synagogue were not conducted with deeper fervor or greater religious solemnity than were the proceedings of a capital trial in the great Judgment Hall of the Sanhedrin. Certain sacred maxims flamed forever like beacon lights along the pathway of the members of the court during the solemn deliberations. "A judge," says the Talmud, "should always consider that a sword threatens him from above, and destruction yawns at his feet." The ancient adage, "the pen of the law fears the thunder of Heaven," though of Chinese origin, is Hebraic in spirit. "Thou shalt do no unrighteousness in judgment" was the leading aphorism of Hebrew jurisprudence. Among the earliest traditions of the Fathers, we read this maxim: "When a judge decides not according to truth, he makes the majesty of God to depart from Israel. But if he judges according to the truth, were it only for one hour, it is as if he established the whole world, for it is in judgment that the divine presence in Israel has its habitation." Hebrew horror of capital punishment and dread of taking human life are well expressed in the celebrated maxim of the Mishna: "The Sanhedrin, which so often as once in seven years, condemns a man to death, is a slaughter-house."[1] And more striking and startling still is the terrible sentence of Rabbi Meir: "What doth God say (if one may speak of God after the manner of men) when a malefactor suffers the anguish due to his crime? He says, *My head and my limbs are pained.* And if he so speaks of the suffering even of the guilty, what must he utter when the righteous is condemned?" The whole spirit of Talmudic caution is well illustrated by the principal rule of the Pirke Aboth, which says: "Be cautious and slow in judgment, send forth many disciples, and *make a fence round the law.*"²

In addition to the maxims above mentioned, which were more religious than legal, four cardinal rules of criminal procedure—"strictness in the accusation, publicity in the discussion, full freedom granted to the accused, and assurance against all dangers or errors of testimony"³—molded the judgment and guided the consciences of Hebrew judges. These sayings of the Fathers and maxims of the law were the touchstones of all their judicial inquiries and meditations at the trial of capital cases. With prayer in their hearts and these maxims upon their lips, they applied themselves to the solemn duties of their office.

A most interesting passage in the Mishna draws a striking contrast between capital trials and those involving questions of money only. The relevancy of the passage to this chapter is so great that it is deemed best to quote it entire:

Money trials and trials for life have the same rule of inquiry and investigation. But they differ in procedure in the following points: The former require only three, the latter three-and-twenty judges.

In the former it matters not on which side the judges speak who give the first opinions; in the latter, those who are in favor of acquittal must speak first.

In the former, a majority of one is always enough; in the latter, a majority of one is enough to acquit, but it requires a majority of two to condemn.

In the former, a decision may be quashed on review (for error), no matter which way it has gone; in the latter, a condemnation may be quashed, but not an acquittal.

In the former, disciples of the law present in the court may speak (as assessors) on either side; in the latter, they may speak in favor of the accused, but not against him.

In the former, a judge who has indicated his opinion, no matter on which side, may change his mind; in the latter, he who has given his voice for acquittal may not change.

The former (money trials) are commenced only in the daytime, but may be concluded after nightfall; the latter (capital trials) are commenced only in the daytime, and must also be concluded during the day.

The former may be concluded by acquittal or condemnation on the day on which they have begun; the latter may be concluded on that day if there is a sentence of acquittal, but must be postponed to a second day if there is to be a condemnation. And for this reason capital trials are not held on the day before a Sabbath or a feast day.⁴

The principal features of a Hebrew capital trial before the Great Sanhedrin were: (1) The Morning Sacrifice; (2) the Assembling of the Judges in the Lishkath haggazith, or the Hall of Hewn Stones; (3) the Examination of Witnesses; (4) the Debates and Balloting of the Judges on the guilt or the innocence of the accused. These successive steps will be briefly considered in this chapter.

The Morning Sacrifice.— It is not positively known what legal connection, if any, the morning sacrifice had with the trial of a capital case before the Great Sanhedrin at Jerusalem. Several writers contend that there was no essential legal connection; that the sacrifice was offered at the break of day whether a capital case was to be tried or not; and that the court was not dependent upon this religious observance for jurisdiction in the trial of criminal cases. Other writers hold opposite views, and contend that the morning sacrifice was essential to give jurisdiction to the court. MM. Lemann consider it an error in the trial of Jesus that the morning sacrifice was not offered before the commencement of proceedings.[5] Certain passages from the Mishna very strongly support this second view: that the court could not legally convene until the morning sacrifice had been offered. ▪The Sanhedrin sat from the close of the morning sacrifice to the time of the evening sacrifice."[6] . . . "Since the morning sacrifice was offered at the break of day, it was hardly possible for the Sanhedrin to assemble until an hour after that time."[7] These passages seem to indicate that the morning sacrifice was necessary before the court could legally convene. This question will be found more fully discussed under Point V of the Brief in this volume. The method of offering the morning sacrifice was as judicial in its precision as it was religious in its solemnity.

The Assembling of the Judges.— At the close of the morning sacrifice, the members of the court entered the judgment hall in solemn procession. They took their seats, "turbaned, on cushions or pillows, in oriental fashion, with crossed legs, and unshod feet, in a half-circle."[8] The high priest sat in the center with the other members of the court to the right and left of him. "His head was crowned with a turban of blue inwrought with gold. On his bosom hung the priestly breastplate, in which glittered twelve precious stones, emblems of the twelve tribes of Israel. A flowing robe of blue, gathered about his waist by a girdle of purple, scarlet, and gold embroidery, enveloped his person and set off the pure white linen of his capacious sleeves. The buttons of this costly robe were onyx stones. His slippered feet were half concealed beneath the long fringe of his pontifical vestments, which were curiously embroidered with pomegranates in gold and scarlet and crimson. No Roman Catholic pontiff ever wore robes more resplendent than those in which the high priest was attired on public and state occasions. Immediately before him sat the scribes or clerks of the court. The one on his left hand wrote down whatever testimony was adduced against the accused; what votes were cast for his condemnation. The one on the right transcribed what appeared in his favor."[9]

According to most writers, including Dr. Lyman Abbott, only two scribes were present having seats at each end of the semicircle. According to Benny, however, "three scribes were present; one was seated on the right, one on the left, the third in the center of the hall. The first recorded the names of the judges who voted for the acquittal of the accused and the arguments upon which the acquittal was grounded. The second noted the names of such as decided to condemn the prisoner and the reasons upon which the conviction was based. The third kept an account of both the preceding, so as to be able at any time to supply omissions or check inaccuracies in the memoranda of his brother reporters."

The prisoner was placed in front of the high priest, in a conspicuous position, where he could see all and could be seen by all.

Thus organized and arranged, the Sanhedrin began the work of the day.

Examination of Witnesses.— The examination of witnesses, who were also accusers, marked the beginning of proceedings. It is doubtful if the indictment against criminals was in writing. The first witness who was to testify was led into an adjoining room and solemnly warned. He was asked questions similar to the following: Is it not probable that your belief in the prisoner's guilt is derived from hearsay or circumstantial evidence? In forming your opinions concerning the guilt of the accused, have you or not been influenced by the remarks of persons whom you regard as reputable and trustworthy? Are you aware that you will be submitted to a most searching examination? Are you acquainted with the penalty attached to the crime of perjury?

After this preliminary warning, conveyed in these questions, had been given, the most learned and venerable of the judges administered to the witness the following impressive adjuration:

Forget not, O witness, that it is one thing to give evidence in a trial as to money, and another in a trial for life. In a money suit, if thy witness-bearing shall do wrong, money may repair that wrong. But in this trial for life, if thou sinnest, the blood of the accused, and the blood of his seed to the end of time, shall be imputed unto thee.... Therefore was Adam created one man and alone, to teach thee that if any witness shall destroy one soul out of Israel, he is held by the Scripture to be as if he had destroyed the world; and he who saves one such soul to be as if he had saved the world . . . . For a man from one signet-ring may strike off many impressions, and all of them shall be exactly alike. But He, the King of the kings of kings, He the Holy and the Blessed, has struck off from His type of the first man the forms of all men that shall live; yet so, that no one human being is wholly alike to any other. Wherefore let us think and believe that the whole world is created for a man such as he whose life hangs on thy words. But these ideas must not deter you from testifying from what you actually know. Scripture declares: "The witness who hath seen or known, and doth not tell, shall bear his iniquity." Nor must ye scruple about becoming the instrument of the alleged criminal's death. Remember the Scriptural maxim: "In the destruction of the wicked, there is joy."

At the close of this solemn exhortation, the examination of the witness commenced. The Hakiroth, seven questions prescribed by law, touching the identity of the prisoner and fixing the elements of time and place, were asked. They were as follows: Was it during a year of jubilee? Was it an ordinary year? In what month? On what day of the month? At what hour? In what place? Do you identify this person?

These questions being satisfactorily answered, the next step was a rigid examination into the facts and circumstances attending the commission of the crime and the connection of the accused therewith. This process of examination and cross-examination was termed the Bedikoth and embraced all questions not included in the Hakiroth which tended to establish the guilt or innocence of the prisoner at the bar.

When the witnesses for the Commonwealth of Israel had been examined, witnesses for the defendant were heard. The accused was also urged to say anything he wished in his own behalf. As we have before pointed out, the Hakiroth questions as to time and place could be rebutted only by establishing an alibi against the witnesses for the state. If such an alibi was proved, the defendant was acquitted and at once discharged. A contributor to the "Jewish Encyclopedia," discussing this point of procedure, says: "It has been shown under Alibi how a 'set' of witnesses may be convicted as 'plotters' by another set or sets proving an alibi on them. But the opposite party may prove an alibi on the convicting set or in some other way show that the facts testified to by the first set were impossible or untrue. Under such circumstances, a modern judge or jury would weigh the credibility of the witnesses and the probability of their stories and decide between them accordingly. The sages did not trust themselves or their successors with this discretion. If there were no indicia or fraud, they held that as some one was evidently lying they could not decide which of them it was, and that there was no evidence on the point."[10] The result was an acquittal.

If material contradictions in the testimony of the witnesses were shown by the Bedikoth, the trial was at once terminated and the accused was free. The failure of any witness to answer satisfactorily any of the seven questions above mentioned entitled the accused to immediate acquittal. Any material disagreement between the two or more witnesses required by the law in answer to any of these questions likewise entitled the prisoner to an immediate discharge. If the prosecuting witnesses relied upon documentary, circumstantial or hearsay evidence to convict, their testimony was at once rejected and the defendant was released.

But if the accused failed to establish an alibi against the prosecuting witnesses in the matter of the Hakiroth; and if the Bedikoth developed evidence fairly consistent and uncontradictory; and if the testimony of the witnesses was purely oral, that is, was not documentary, hearsay or circumstantial, then there was legally admissible evidence to lay before the Sanhedrin. The competent witnesses who could render relevant testimony were then led, one at a time, before the general body and required to testify.

The Debates and Balloting of the Judges.— All the evidence, pro and con, having been adduced, the tribunal began a full discussion of the case, preliminary to casting ballots. Arguments could be begun only on behalf of the accused. Nothing was permitted to be said against him until one of the judges had urged something in his behalf, and had said: "As I view the matter, and according to such and such evidence, it seems to me that the prisoner should be acquitted." The discussion became general for and against the accused. The entire record was then overhauled. Each item of evidence was carefully considered and subjected to the minutest criticism. Contradictions were noted and extenuating facts pleaded. If one of the disciples occupying one of the three rows of seats could offer any cogent or valid reason why the prisoner should not be convicted, he was invited to take his seat among the judges, and was regarded as a member of the court during the remainder of the day. If his argument resulted in the acquittal of the accused and saved a human life he was made a permanent member of the court. On the other hand, if one of the disciples had anything to say that would tend to injure the defendant he was not permitted to raise his voice.

When the entire case had been exhaustively discussed, the argument was closed and the balloting on the guilt or innocence of the accused commenced. The scribes were in readiness to record the votes and note the reasons assigned therefor. The youngest members of the tribunal were required to vote first, in order that they might not be unduly influenced by the example of their seniors in age and authority. The high priest, who was generally president of the Sanhedrin, addressed a gentle admonition to the youngest member, who was never less than forty years of age, to render a free and untrammeled verdict, and not to be awed or influenced by the patriarchs of the court. This admonition was repeated in the case of each youthful member of the tribunal. When the balloting commenced, each judge arose in his place and voted; at the same time making a short speech explanatory of his ballot. To secure a conviction it was not necessary that the members of the Sanhedrin should be unanimous. Indeed a peculiar rule of Hebrew law provided that if the verdict was instantaneous and unanimous it was invalid and could not stand. If the prisoner had not a single friend in court, the element of mercy was wanting in the verdict, said the ancient Hebrews, and the proceedings were regarded in the light of conspiracy and mob violence. A majority vote of at least two members was necessary to convict. A majority vote of one in his favor would acquit. Any majority amounting to two or more that did not reach unanimity was sufficient to condemn. If the accused was tried before a Minor Sanhedrin of three-and-twenty members or before the Great Sanhedrin with a bare quorum (twenty-three members, the same number as the full membership of a Minor Sanhedrin), a vote of thirteen members was necessary, in either case, to convict. If eleven judges were for conviction and twelve for acquittal, the prisoner was discharged at once; a majority of one vote being sufficient for that purpose. If twelve were in favor of conviction and eleven for acquittal, the condemnation of the accused was impossible; a majority of at least two being required to condemn. According to some writers, an acquittal was the result in such a case. According to others, in such a contingency the following novel expedient was employed to reach a verdict: From the first row of disciples two additional judges were selected and added to the original twenty-three members. Balloting then commenced anew. If the vote resulted in a majority of at least two against the prisoner, he stood convicted. If not, two more disciples were added from the first row in front and this process of increasing by twos the number of the Sanhedrin was continued until the requisite majority was secured. If it happened that the constant additions finally raised the number to seventy-one, the membership of the Great Sanhedrin, the process of increasing by twos was discontinued, and final balloting then began. If thirty-six voted for conviction and thirty-five for acquittal, the whole case was reargued for a reasonable time until one of the thirty-six yielded and declared in favor of acquittal. In case the thirty-six members persevered in their determination to convict, the prisoner was discharged.

At any stage of the trial, from the beginning with the three-and-twenty judges through all the successive additions of new members, a majority vote of one or more in favor of the accused would acquit; a majority of two or more, not amounting to unanimity, would convict.

In case of an acquittal the prisoner was immediately released and the trial was closed. In the event of conviction sentence could not be pronounced until the next afternoon and the session of the court was accordingly adjourned until the following day. Upon adjournment the members of the Sanhedrin with measured

step and solemn mien left the chamber in which the trial had been conducted.
Outside the judgment hall, in the open street, the judges formed themselves into
groups or knots of five or six to discuss the trial and to lament the awful
misfortune impending over Jerusalem; for such was the Hebrew conception of
the execution of a son of Israel. The nucleus of each group was formed of elders of
the Sanhedrin; the younger members came up from behind, leaned over between
the shoulders of the patriarchs, and listened attentively and devoutly to what
they were saying about the case. Gradually the groups broke up and the judges
linked arm in arm, by twos, walked slowly homeward, still discussing the facts
and arguments adduced at the trial. Finally they parted and retired to their
respective homes. No heavy food, like meat, and no intoxicating beverage, were
taken for the remainder of the day or during the night. Nothing was done that
would incapacitate them for correct thinking. At sunset they began to make calls
upon each other for the purpose of examining more carefully and debating more
fully the issues of the case. When these visits were concluded, in the early
evening, each judge retired to the privacy of his own home to sleep, meditate, and
pray. At the dawn of day, they arose and prepared to resume again the solemn
responsibilities of their office. The morning sacrifice was offered and the judges
again assembled at sunrise in the hall of justice. They reseated themselves in the
form of a semicircle; the prisoner was again led to the bar of the court; the
witnesses were again produced; and the scribes, bringing with them the minutes
of the former meeting, again took seats in their accustomed places.

The second part of the trial then began. It must be remembered that there were
two trials of every Hebrew capital case. The second day was not a trial *de novo;*
but was a proceeding in the nature of an appeal and was intended to accomplish a
review of the proceedings of the previous day. Additional testimony, however,
which had been discovered after the close of the first trial, might be introduced.
But the record of facts seems not to have been considered so important as the
question of the fixed opinions of the judges. Each member of the Sanhedrin was
required, on the second day, to vote again and to declare anew his notions
concerning the guilt or innocence of the accused. The statements of each judge
were carefully noted by the scribes and compared with his statements of the
previous day. If any judge voted for conviction at the second trial and founded
his judgment on reasons and arguments radically different from those of the first
day, his verdict was rejected. A member who had voted for acquittal on the first
day was not permitted to change his vote for conviction on the second day. But
one who had voted for condemnation at the first trial, might, by giving valid
reasons, vote on the second day for acquittal.[1]

A most striking peculiarity of Hebrew law is to be noted in their method of
counting votes and arriving at sums total in favor of or against the accused.
Certain peculiar rules were to be strictly applied in determining the ultimate
result. When upon examination of the record it was discovered that two or more
judges had advanced identical arguments, though each supported his contention
by different Biblical citations, their collective opinions were regarded as the

common expression of a single mind and all their votes were counted only as one. Father and son, teacher and pupil, being members of the same court, counted also as one, provided their votes and opinions were arrayed on the same side, but not when they were placed in antagonism.[1]

When the balloting was complete the number for and against the prisoner was again announced. If a majority of at least two votes were registered against him he stood convicted a second time. But the humane and indulgent spirit of Hebrew law continued to operate and deferred immediate sentence. The judges continued to deliberate. No one thought of quitting the judgment hall on the second day of the trial. No one ate anything, no one drank anything on this second day; for the day that was to condemn an Israelite to death was to be a fast day for those who condemned him. It was to be a day of prayerful meditation. Ancient maxims of the Fathers, framed for the protection of the accused, were reconsidered. All the merciful tendencies of Talmudic interpretation were invoked and pleaded by the judges, the defenders of the accused. It was hoped that a few hours' time would discover facts favorable to the doomed man. New arguments, it was thought, might be offered and new witnesses might be forthcoming in his behalf. As they continued to deliberate, the fatal hour approached. There was to be no thirty or sixty days, as in America, between sentence and execution, during which time the condemned man could make peace with God. The moment that saw the judgment finally pronounced witnessed the beginning of its execution. Sunset, Nature's symbol of the extinguishment of the light of life, was the time fixed for both.

The death march and the final circumstances attending the execution of a Hebrew prisoner are without parallel in the jurisprudence of the world. As the culprit was led away to his doom, a man, carrying in his hand a flag, was stationed at the entrance of the Sanhedrin Hall. A mounted officer of the court followed the procession at a convenient distance and kept his eyes constantly turned in the direction of the flag bearer on the hill. A herald, carrying aloft a staff from which fluttered a crimson banner, made proclamation to the gazing multitude along the way that a human being was about to be executed. He cried aloud: "AB is to be put to death on the testimony of CD and XY, on such and such a charge. If any man knows anything favorable to the accused, in the name of God let him come forth and speak, in order that the prisoner may be led back to the Sanhedrin Hall to be again confronted and tried by his judges."

If any witness, friend or stranger, came forth to furnish new evidence in favor of the condemned man, the procession was halted and the accused was led back to the Sanhedrin Chamber. If any member of the court still sitting in the hall of judgment bethought himself of any new argument in behalf of the accused that had not been offered at the trial, he arose quickly in his place and stated it to his fellow-judges. The flag at the gate was then waved and the mounted messenger, chosen for such an emergency, saw it waving and galloped forward to stop the execution.

The culprit himself could delay or prevent the accomplishment of the death sentence if he could give to the Rabbins who escorted him any valid reason why he should not be put to death. He was led back as often as he gave any good excuse, not exceeding five times, the number prescribed by law. If no new witnesses appeared and if the prisoner made no further plea for life, the procession proceeded to within a short distance of the place of execution. The convict was then exhorted to declare himself guilty of the crime of which he was charged and to make full confession of all his sins. He was told that a full confession would entitle him to a happy existence beyond this life, since the flood of death would wash away all stains of sin and cleanse the soul of all the iniquities of existence in this world. If the condemned man still refused to confess that he was guilty of the crime with which he was charged, he was then urged to say: "May my death prove an atonement for all my transgressions."

He was then led to the ground of execution. The death draught, consisting of a mixture of frankincense and myrrh, poured into a cup of vinegar or light wine, was then given him. Stupefaction followed, rendering the culprit unconscious of his impending doom and insensible to the agonies of death. In Jerusalem, this benumbing and stupefying mixture was furnished by the Hebrew women, whose tender and merciful regard for the wretched and unfortunate of earth has in all ages been a striking characteristic of the sex. As soon as the draught had been administered the execution took place. The prisoner was either stoned, strangled, burned, or beheaded, according to the nature of his crime. In case of blasphemy or idolatry the dead body was afterwards hung upon a gallows until dusk. But ordinarily the corpse was immediately interred after execution. On the outskirts of every town there were two graveyards for criminals; in one of these those who had been burned or stoned were buried; in the other were interred those who had been hanged or beheaded. As soon as decomposition had taken place—that is, when the flesh had decayed and fallen from the bones—the relatives were allowed to remove the skeleton and to deposit it in the family burial ground.

Soon after the execution the friends and relatives of the dead man made friendly calls upon the judges who had tried and sentenced him. These visits were intended to show that the visitors harbored no feelings of bitterness or revenge against those who, in condemning one of their loved ones to death, had only performed the high and righteous duties of just and honorable judges of Israel.

PART III
THE BRIEF

THE BRIEF

A number of difficult and confusing questions present themselves at the very beginning of any extensive and impartial investigation of the trial of Jesus.

Did the Great Sanhedrin exist at the time of Christ? If it existed, was it still a legally constituted court, having jurisdiction to try capital offenses? Did it have jurisdiction of the particular offense with which Jesus was charged? If the Great Sanhedrin was actually in existence, had criminal jurisdiction in capital cases, and was judicially empowered to try the offense with which Jesus was charged, did it actually try Him? Were the rules of criminal procedure, prescribed in the Mishna and cited in this Brief, in existence and actively in force in Judea at the time of the trial of Jesus? What was the nature of the charge brought against the Christ? Was He guilty as charged? Were forms of law duly observed in the trial of the accusation against Him? Answers to these questions, which will be considered in the Brief in the order above enumerated, will cover the legal aspects of the Hebrew trial of Jesus.

Did the Great Sanhedrin exist at the time of Christ? The answer to this question is of prime importance, since the existence of a court having jurisdiction of the person and subject matter of the suit is a fundamental consideration in all litigation. It is generally supposed that the Hebrew trial of Jesus took place before the Great Sanhedrin in Jerusalem. But many able writers, both Jewish and Gentile, deny that this court had any existence at the time of Christ. In the "Martyrdom of Jesus," Rabbi Wise says: "But this body did positively not exist at the time when Jesus was crucified, having been dissolved 30 A. C. In nowise, then, any passages of the Gospels must be understood to refer to the Great Sanhedrin." Many Jewish and several eminent Gentile authors agree with this contention, which is founded upon a passage in Josephus in which it is declared that King Herod had all the members of the Sanhedrin put to death.[1] It is contended by these writers that the supreme tribunal of the Jews was then abolished and was not restored until subsequent to the crucifixion. Opposed to this assertion, however, is the weight of both reason and authority. Schurer is of the opinion that Josephus did not mean literally "all" ($\pi\acute{a}\nu\tau\alpha\varsigma$) when he wrote that Herod had destroyed all the members of the Great Sanhedrin; since in the following book he relates that the same king caused to be put to death the forty-five most prominent members of the party of Antigonus, who must themselves have been members of this court; and forty-five are twenty-six fewer than seventy-one, the full membership of the Great Sanhedrin.[2] The same author asserts the existence and discusses the jurisdiction of this court in the following language: "As regards the area over which the jurisdiction of the Great Sanhedrin extended, it has already been remarked above that its civil authority was restricted, in the time of Christ, to the eleven toparchies of Judea proper. And, accordingly, for this reason it had no judicial authority over Jesus Christ so long as He remained in Galilee. It was only as soon as He entered Judea that He came directly under its jurisdiction."[3]

Again, Salvador, who may be justly styled the Jewish Blackstone, wrote concerning the condemnation of Jesus: "The *senate* declared that Jesus, son of Joseph, born at Bethlehem, had profaned the name of God in usurping it for himself, a simple citizen. The capital sentence was then pronounced." Now, the word "senate" is properly applied nowhere in literature to any other Hebrew court than the Great Sanhedrin. This High Court of the Jews has been frequently compared to the senate of Rome, to the Areopagus of the Greeks and to the parliament of England. It should be noted in this connection that the great Jewish writer not only styled the body that tried Jesus "senate" (Great Sanhedrin) but stated that it pronounced a capital sentence, thus declaring that the supreme tribunal of the Jews not only existed at the time of Jesus but had the right to decree capital punishment.

Edersheim, discussing the alleged abolition of the Sanhedrin by Herod, says: "The Sanhedrin did exist during his reign, though it must have been shorn of all real power, and its activity confined to ecclesiastical or semi-ecclesiastical causes. We can well believe that neither Herod nor the procurators would wish to *abolish* the Sanhedrin, but would leave to them the administration of justice, especially in all that might in any way be connected with purely religious questions. In short, the Sanhedrin would be accorded full jurisdiction in inferior and in religious matters; with the greatest show, but with the least amount of real rule or of supreme authority."[4] This is a powerful voice in favor of the existence of the supreme tribunal of the Jews at the time of Christ; for Edersheim's "Life and Times of Jesus the Messiah" is the best and most reliable biography of the Savior in any language.

Keim bases his advocacy of the existence of the Sanhedrin at the time of Christ on New Testament authority. "Not only," he says, "does the New Testament speak of Synedria in the time of Jesus and the Apostles, but Jesus Himself, in a well-established utterance, mentions the Synedrion (Sanhedrin) as the highest legally constituted tribunal and as having the right to pass the sentence of death."[5]

The strongest passage in the New Testament supporting the contention of the existence of the Great Sanhedrin at the time of the crucifixion is contained in Acts v. 21: "But the high priest came, and they that were with him, and called the *council* together, and all the *senate* of the children of Israel, and sent to the prison to have them brought." Here, the use of the words "high priest," "council," and "senate" in the same connection, strongly suggests, almost accurately describes, the president and members of the Great Sanhedrin; and besides, the words, "sent to the prison to have them brought," indicate that this body was exercising judicial functions.

Again, the utterance of Jesus above referred to by Keim is found in two passages of Matthew. The first is in Chap. xvi. 21 : "From that time forth began Jesus to shew unto His disciples, how that He must go unto Jerusalem, and suffer many things of the *elders* and *chief priests* and *scribes,* and be killed and be raised again the third day." The second is in Chap. xx. 18: "Behold, we go up to Jerusalem; and the Son of man shall be betrayed unto the chief priests and unto the scribes, and they shall condemn him to death." The "elders" and "chief priests" and "scribes" were the characteristic constituent elements of the Great Sanhedrin; and the prophecy, "they shall condemn him to death," ascribed to them the highest judicial prerogative, the right of passing the death sentence. In his brilliant essay on the Talmud, Emanuel Deutsch emphatically says: "Whenever the New Testament mentions the 'Priests, the Elders, and the Scribes' together, it means the Great Sanhedrin."[6]It is impossible to refrain from contrasting this statement of a most eminent and learned Jewish writer with that of Rabbi Wise, also very scholarly and pious, "In no wise, then, any passages of the Gospels must be considered to refer to the Great Sanhedrin." Suffice it to say that the weight of authority is with Emanuel Deutsch. And that which seems to conclusively disprove the whole theory of the nonexistence of the Great Sanhedrin at the date of the crucifixion, is the fact that Josephus—whose account of the alleged killing of all the members of the Sanhedrin by Herod is the very basis of the theory—in a subsequent chapter, relating to a subsequent event, describes the summoning of Hyrcanus, former king and high priest, before the Sanhedrin to be tried by them. As a result of the trial, Hyrcanus was put to death.[7]Such a personage could have been tried and condemned only by the Great Sanhedrin, which was in existence subsequent to the alleged destruction of all its members by Herod.

It is believed that enough has been said to show that the contention that the Great Sanhedrin did not exist at the time of Christ is not well founded. As a matter of reason, the mere destruction of the members of the court by Herod did not, of necessity, abolish the court itself. From what we know of the character and policy of Herod, he simply had the members of an old and unfriendly aristocracy put to death in order that he might make room in the court for an entirely new body friendly to him and devoted to his interests. Again, it is entirely improbable that the Roman masters, of whom Herod was but a subject prince and tool, would have permitted the destruction of the most important local institution of a conquered state. The policy of the Romans in this regard is well known. Whenever it was consistent with the dignity and safety of the Roman empire, local institutions were allowed to remain and undisturbed. We are not aware of any good historical reason why the Great Sanhedrin, the national parliament, and the supreme tribunal of the Jews, should have been abolished thirty years before Christ, as Rabbi Wise and other eminent scholars and theologians have contended. After all, it seems to be more a matter of dogma than of history. The majority of Jewish writers rest their case upon Josephus, with their peculiar construction of the passage; the majority of Christian writers quite naturally prefer the New Testament. But the line is not closely drawn. Dr. Geikie, the eminent Gentile author, supports the Jewish opinion, without reference, however, to the passage in Josephus. On the other hand, Salvador, Edersheim, and Deutsch, all writers of Jewish blood, support the Christian contention.

The assertion of Graetz that Jesus was arraigned before one of the Minor Sanhedrins,[8] of which there were two in Jerusalem, is not to be taken seriously, since these minor courts had no jurisdiction of the crime with which Jesus was charged.[9] It is very evident from the weight of authority that Jesus was tried before the Great Sanhedrin, and that this court had authority to pass sentence of death. Upon this theory, the author will proceed in framing the Brief.

Did the Great Sanhedrin have jurisdiction to try capital offenses at the time of the crucifixion? This question, involving great difficulty and much confusion in discussing the trial of Jesus, arises from the divergent opinions of Bible scholars as to the exact legal and political status of the Jews at the time of Christ. Many concede the existence of the Great Sanhedrin at this time, but insist that it had been shorn of its most important judicial attributes; that the right to try capital cases had been wholly taken from it; and that it retained the legal right to try only petty crimes and religious offenses not involving the death penalty. The Jews contend, and indeed the Talmud states that "forty years before the destruction of the Temple the judgment of capital causes was taken away from Israel." The great weight of authority, however, is registered against this view. The New Testament teachings on the subject have just been discussed in the beginning of the Brief. The opinion generally held by Bible scholars is that the Great Sanhedrin continued to exist after the Roman conquest of Judea and after the time of Herod; that its legislative, executive, and judicial powers remained substantially unimpaired in local matters pertaining to the internal affairs of the Jews; and that the Roman representatives intervened only when Roman interests required and the sovereignty of the Roman State demanded. The question of sovereignty presented itself, indeed, whenever the question of life and death arose; and Rome reserved to herself, in such cases, the prerogative of final judicial determination. Both Renan and Salvador hold the view that the Sanhedrin had the right of initiative, the *cognitio causae;* that is, the right to try the case. In the event of the acquittal of the accused the matter was finally ended without Roman interference, but in case of conviction the Roman legate or procurator certainly might review and probably was required to review the matter, and either affirm or reverse the sentence. This is the prevalent opinion among the best writers; and is plausible because it is at once consistent with the idea of the maintenance of Roman sovereignty and of the preservation of the local government of the Jews. However, many able writers, among them Rosadi and Dupin, assert that the Jews had lost the right, by virtue of Roman conquest, even to try capital cases. And it must be admitted that the logic of law is in their favor, though the facts of history and the weight of authority are against them.

Did the Great Sanhedrin have jurisdiction of the particular offense with which Jesus was charged? Admitting the existence of the Great Sanhedrin at the time of Christ, and its right to initiate and try proceedings in capital cases with reference to Roman authority, had it jurisdiction, under Hebrew law, of the special accusation against Christ? On this point there is little difference of opinion. Jesus was brought before the Sanhedrin on the charges of sedition and blasphemy, both of which crimes came within the cognizance of the supreme tribunal of the Jews.[10]

Was there a regular legal trial of Jesus before the Great Sanhedrin? Admitting that this court was in existence at the time of Christ, that it had competence, with reference to Roman authority, to try capital cases, and that it had jurisdiction under Hebrew law of the crime with which Jesus was charged, did it actually conduct a regular, formal trial of the Christ? Many able critics give a negative answer to this inquiry. Jost, one of the greatest and most impartial of Jewish historians, designates the crucifixion of Jesus "a private murder (Privat-Mord) committed by burning enemies, not the sentence of a regularly constituted Sanhedrin."[11] Edersheim supports this view as to the nature of the trial.[12]

A certain class of writers base their objection to a regular trial on the ground of the nonexistence of the Great Sanhedrin at the time of Christ. If this court did not exist, they say, there could not have been any regular judicial proceeding, since this body was the only Hebrew tribunal that had jurisdiction to try the offense with which Jesus was charged. Others, who hold similar views, maintain that the errors were so numerous and the proceedings so flagrant, according to the Gospel account, that there could have been no trial at all, and that it was simply the action of a mob. These writers contend that the members of the Sanhedrin acted more like a vigilance committee than a regularly organized tribunal. Of this opinion is Dr. Cunningham Geikie.

Still another class of critics insist that the Hebrew judges exercised only accusatory functions, and that the examination of Jesus at night was merely preparatory to charges to be presented to Pilate.

Others still apparently reverse the order, and insist that the Hebrew trial was the only one; that the duty of Pilate was merely to review, sanction, and countersign the verdict of the Sanhedrin. Of this class is Renan, who says: "The course which the priests had resolved to pursue in regard to Jesus was quite in conformity with the established law. The plan of the enemies of Jesus was to convict him, by the testimony of witnesses and by his own avowals, of blasphemy and of outrage against the Mosaic religion, to condemn him to death according to law, and then to get the condemnation sanctioned by Pilate."[13] Salvador and Stapfer agree with Renan that the Hebrew trial was regular and that the proceedings were legal. On the other hand, Rosadi, Dupin, Keim and many others denounce the proceedings in the trial of Jesus as outrageously illegal.

As to the number of trials, the authorities above cited seem to be exceptions to the rule. By far the greater number contend that there were two distinct trials: a Hebrew and a Roman, separate and yet dependent. The opinion of this class of writers is most clearly expressed by Innes, who says: "Whether it was legitimate or not for the Jews to condemn for a capital crime on this occasion, they did so. Whether it was legitimate or not for Pilate to try over again an accused whom they had condemned, on this occasion, he did so. There were certainly two trials."[14] This is the view of the writer of these pages; and he has, accordingly, divided the general subject into two trials, devoting a volume of the work to each. It may be answered, then, that there was a regular trial of Jesus before the Great Sanhedrin. The relation of this trial to the Roman proceeding will be more fully discussed in the second volume of this treatise.

Were the rules of criminal procedure prescribed in the Mishna and cited in this Brief, in existence and actively in force in Judea at the time of the trial of Jesus? This question has been answered in the negative by several writers of repute. Others have answered that the matter is in doubt. But it is very generally agreed that an affirmative answer is the proper one. Out of this question, two others arise: (1) Were the rules of criminal law, herein cited, obsolete at the time of the crucifixion? (2) Were they the legal developments of an age subsequent to that great event? In either case, their citation, in this connection, is without reason or justification.

It is a sufficient answer to the first of these questions that none of the standard works on Hebrew criminal law classes any of the rules herein stated as obsolete at the time of Christ. In support of a negative answer to this question, it may be urged that all of the aforesaid rules were the essential elements of an enlightened and humane criminal procedure in capital cases at the date of the crucifixion.

The answer to the second question above suggested is a more serious matter. It is historically true that the Mishna was not reduced to writing until two hundred years after the beginning of our era. The Jerusalem Talmud was not redacted until 390 A. D.; and the Babylonian Talmud, about 365-427 A. D. The question at once arises: Were the rules of criminal procedure, which we have herein invoked in the discussion of this case, the growth of the periods intervening between the crucifixion of Jesus and these dates? Two valid reasons give a negative answer to this question. In the first place, the criminal rules applied in the Brief are in nearly every case traceable to Mosaic provisions which were framed more than a thousand years before the trial of Jesus. In the second place, they could not have been the developments of a time subsequent to the crucifixion, because less than forty years, a single generation, intervened between that event and the fall of Jerusalem, which was followed by the destruction of Jewish nationality and the dispersion of the Jews. This short interval was a period of national decay and disintegration of the Jewish people and could not have been, under Roman domination, a formative period in legal matters. After the fall of Jerusalem, the additions and developments in Hebrew law were more a matter of commentary than of organic formation—more of Gemara than of Mosaic or Mishnic growth. The decided weight of authority, then, as well as the greater reason, is in favor of the proposition that the Hebrew criminal law had reached its full development and was still in active force at the time of which we write.

What was the nature of the charge brought against Christ at the trial before the Sanhedrin? Was He guilty as charged? The questions preceding these were secondary, though important. If the Great Sanhedrin did not exist at the time of Christ, we are forced to believe and admit that the men who arrested and examined Jesus at night were nothing more than an irresponsible rabble, acting without judicial authority or legal excuse. If it was without criminal jurisdiction, though in existence, we have erroneously spoken of a Hebrew trial. If the rules of criminal procedure which we have invoked were not in existence at the time of the crucifixion, we have proceeded upon a false hypothesis. Fortunately, the weight of authority, in every case, is so overwhelmingly in our favor, and our contention is, in each case, so well founded in reason, that we feel justified in now proceeding to a discussion of the real merits of the case, involved in answers to the questions: What was the nature of the charge or charges brought against Jesus at the Hebrew trial? Was He guilty as charged?

The accusations against Christ were numerous, both in and out of court; and it will help to simplify matters and to arrive at a clear understanding, if, in the very beginning, the distinction be made and held in mind between *judicial* and *extra-judicial* charges. By judicial charges are meant those made at the time of the examination of Jesus by the Sanhedrin, assembled at night in the palace of Caiaphas. By extra-judicial charges are meant those made out of court at divers times and places in Jerusalem, Galilee, and elsewhere by the accusers of the Christ, and especially by the spies who dogged His footsteps during the last days of His ministry on earth. Ordinarily, it would be proper, in a work of this kind, to consider only charges made after the trial of the accused had begun, and jeopardy had attached. All others are extra-judicial and are entitled to only passing notice. It would be proper to omit them altogether, if they did not serve to throw much light upon the specific charges at the trial. An excellent summary of the extra-judicial charges brought against Jesus at various times in His career, is given in Abbott's "Jesus of Nazareth," p. 118: "It was charged that He was a preacher of turbulence and faction; that he flattered the poor and inveighed against the rich; that He denounced whole cities, as Capernaum, Bethsaida, Chorazin; that He gathered about Him a rabble of publicans, harlots, and drunkards, under a mere pretense of reforming them; that He subverted the laws and institutions of the Mosaic commonwealth, and substituted an unauthorized legislation of His own; that He disregarded not only all distinctions of society, but even those of religion, and commended the idolatrous Samaritan as of greater worth than the holy priest and pious Levite; that, though He pretended to work miracles, He had invariably refused to perform them in the presence and at the request of the Rabbis of the Church; that He had condemned the solemn sanctions of their holy religion, had sat down to eat with publicans and sinners with unwashen hands, had disregarded the obligations of the Sabbath, had attended the Jewish feasts with great irregularity or not at all, had declared that God could be worshiped in any other place as well as in his Holy Temple, had openly and violently interfered with its sacred services by driving away the cattle gathered there for sacrifice."

These different charges were doubtless present in the minds and hearts of the members of the Sanhedrin at the time of the trial, and probably influenced their conduct and entered into their verdict. But only one or two of these accusations can be said to have any direct connection with the record in this case, and, consequently, can be only indirectly considered in discussing its merits.

We come now to examine the actual charges made at the night trial before the Sanhedrin. The subsequent charges before Pilate have no place in this volume. A review of the proceedings at the time of the examination in the palace of Caiaphas reveals two distinct charges: one preferred by witnesses who had been summoned by the Sanhedrin, the other preferred by Caiaphas himself.

First, according to Matthew, "At the last came two false witnesses, and said, This fellow said, I am able to destroy the temple of God, and to build it in three days."[15] The same testimony is thus reported by Mark: "And there arose certain, and bare false witness against him, saying, We heard him say, I will destroy this temple that is made with hands, and within three days, I will build another made without hands."[16] Luke and John do not discuss the night trial before the Sanhedrin, and therefore make no reference to the charges brought forward by the false witnesses. The second accusation made against Jesus is that by Caiaphas himself, who embodies his charge in the form of an oath or adjuration which he administered to the accused: "I adjure thee by the living God that thou tell us whether thou be the Christ, the Son of God." Then come the confession and condemnation. "Jesus saith unto him, Thou hast said: nevertheless I say unto you, Hereafter shall ye see the Son of man sitting on the right hand of power, and coming in the clouds of heaven. Then the high priest rent his clothes, saying, He hath spoken *blasphemy;* what further need have we of witnesses? behold, now ye have heard his blasphemy. What think ye? They answered and said, He is guilty of death."[17]

These few words of Scripture are the essential parts of the record of fact of the most awful trial in the history of the universe. An analysis of the evidence shows the existence of two distinct charges: that preferred by the false witnesses, accusing Jesus of sedition; and that of blasphemy made by Caiaphas himself.

Concerning the testimony adduced in support of the first charge, Mark says: "For many bare false witness against him, but their witness agreed not together."[18] Now, we have seen that the concurrent testimony of at least two witnesses, agreeing in all essential details, was necessary to sustain a conviction under Hebrew law. If one witness against the accused contradicted any other witness against the accused, all were rejected. Under this rule of law, when "their witness agreed not together," according to Mark, the charge of sedition was abandoned, and the accusation of blasphemy then followed, which resulted in a confession and condemnation. Later on, in another place, we shall dicuss the illegality of a double accusation, in the same breath and at the same trial. But at this point we have no further interest in the abandoned charge, except to say that the false witnesses, in their ignorance and blindness, failed to grasp the Master's allegorical language in reference to the destruction of the Temple. Their worldly-mindedness and purely physical conception of things centered their thoughts upon the Temple at Jerusalem, and gave a purely temporal and material interpretation to His words. "Forty and six years was this temple in building, and wilt thou rear it again in three days?"[19] This question asked by the original auditors, shows a total misconception of the true meaning of the language of Jesus. The spiritual allusion to the resurrection of His own body seems never to have penetrated their thoughts. Then, again, their general statement was, in effect, an absolute misrepresentation. By perverting His language, He was made to utter a deliberate threat against a national institution, around which clustered all the power, sanctity, and glory of the Hebrew people. He was made to threaten the destruction of the Temple at Jerusalem. But it is most reasonable to infer from the entire evidence as contained in the Sacred Writings that the words imputed to Jesus by the false witnesses were not those which He actually used. In reality, He did not say: *"I can destroy,"* or *"I will destroy";* but, simply, *"Destroy."* "Destroy this temple, and in three days I will raise it up."[20] This is evidently a purely hypothetical expression and is equivalent to *"Supposing you destroy this temple."* St. John, in whose presence, it seems, this language was used, correctly interprets the Savior's meaning when he says: ▪He spake of the temple of his body.▪[21]

The evidence of the false witnesses was so contradictory that even wicked judges were forced to reject it and to conduct the prosecution on another charge.

We come now to consider more closely the real accusation upon which Jesus was condemned to death. At first glance, there seems to be no difficulty in determining what this accusation was, since the Gospel record specifically mentions the crime of blasphemy. It was for this offense that Caiaphas pronounced judgment against Jesus with the unanimous approval of his fellow-judges. "Then the high priest rent his clothes and saith, What need we any further witnesses? ye have heard the *blasphemy:* what think ye? and they all condemned him to be guilty of death." But what had they heard that constituted blasphemy? Nothing more than His own confession that He was "the Christ, the Son of God." This seems simple enough upon its face; but a vast mass of acrimonious discussion has resulted from these few passages of Scripture. The main difficulty turns upon the meaning of the word "blasphemy," as used by the high priest in passing condemnation upon Jesus. The facts adduced at the trial, or rather the facts suggested by the oath or adjuration addressed to Jesus, as to whether or not he was "Christ, the Son of God," did not, in the opinion of many, constitute blasphemy under the definition of that term given in the Mosaic Code and interpreted by the Rabbinic writers whose opinions have been embodied in commentaries upon the Mishna. Eminent Jewish writers have ridiculed the idea of attempting to make a case of blasphemy out of a mere claim of being a "Son of God." Rabbi Wise, in "The Martyrdom of Jesus," has very tersely stated the Jewish position on the subject. "Had Jesus maintained," he says, "before a body of Jewish lawyers to be the Son of God, they could not have found him guilty of blasphemy, because every Israelite had a perfect right to call himself a son of God, the law (Deut. xiv. 1) stating in unmistakable words, 'Ye are sons of the Lord, your God.' When Rabbi Judah advanced the opinion, 'If ye conduct yourselves like the sons of God, ye are; if not, not,' there was Rabbi Mair on hand to contradict him: 'In this or in that case, ye are the sons of the Lord your God.' No law, no precedent, and no fictitious case in the Bible or the rabbinical literature can be cited to make of this expression a case of blasphemy. The blasphemy law is in Leviticus (xxiv. 15-20), which ordains, 'If any man shall curse his God (i.e., by whatever name he may call his God), he shall bear his sin,' but the law has nothing to do with it, dictates no punishment, takes no cognizance thereof. 'But he who shall curse the name of Jehovah, he shall surely be put to death,' be the curser native or alien. Another blasphemy law exists not in the Pentateuch. The ancient Hebrews expounded this law, that none is guilty of blasphemy in the first degree, unless he curses God himself by the name of Jehovah; or, as Maimonides maintains, by the name Adonai. The penalty of death is only threatened in the first degree. The Mishna states expressly as the general law, 'The blasphemer is not guilty, unless he (in cursing the Deity) has mentioned the name itself' (of Jehovah or Adonai), so that there can be no doubt whatever that such was the law in Israel. It is clear that the statements made by Mark, in the name of Jesus, had nothing in the world to do with the blasphemy laws of the Jews."[22]

Rabbi Wise was concededly an able and accomplished theologian; and in a general way the above extract states the truth. But it does not state the whole truth, and in one or two places is certainly erroneous. Leviticus xxiv. 15-20 is undoubtedly the blasphemy statute of the Mosaic Code. But Mr. Wise was assuredly wrong when he stated that "another blasphemy law exists not in the Pentateuch." For, if this were a correct statement, other eminent Jewish authorities, as well as many Gentile authors, would be all at sea. Besides, the New Testament use of the word "blasphemy," in many places, would only serve to illustrate the dense ignorance of the Jews of the time of Jesus as to the meaning of the term, if the author of "The Martyrdom of Jesus" were right.

In this connection, let us now consider another Jewish authority, as able and even more famous than the one just cited. In Salvador's celebrated treatise entitled "Histoire des Institutions de Moise," he devotes a chapter to the question of the judgment and condemnation of Jesus. Touching the nature of the charge against Christ and the real cause of His conviction, he says:"But Jesus, in presenting new theories and in giving new forms to those already promulgated, speaks of himself as God; his disciples repeat it; and the subsequent events prove in the most satisfactory manner that they thus understood him. This was *shocking blasphemy* in the eyes of the citizens: the law commands them to follow Jehovah alone, the only true God; not to believe in gods of flesh and bones, resembling men or women; neither to spare or listen to a prophet who, even doing miracles, should proclaim a new god, a god neither they nor their fathers had known. The question already raised among the people was this: Has Jesus become God? But the Senate having adjudged that Jesus, son of Joseph, born in Bethlehem, had profaned the name of God by usurping it to himself, a mere citizen, applied to him the law in the 13th Chapter of Deuteronomy and the 20th verse in Chapter 18, according to which every prophet, even he who works miracles, must be punished when he speaks of a god unknown to the Jews and their fathers: the capital sentence was pronounced."

Here we have the doctors divided; Wise saying that "another blasphemy law exists not in the Pentateuch," and Salvador contending that Jesus was legally convicted of blasphemy under the Mosaic Law as it was laid down, not in Leviticus xxiv. 15-20, but in Deuteronomy xiii.

The law in Deuteronomy is peculiarly impressive in its relationship to the charges against Jesus.

"If there arise among you a prophet, or a dreamer of dreams, and giveth thee a sign or a wonder, And the sign or the wonder come to pass, whereof he spake unto thee, saying, Let us go after other gods, which thou hast not known, and let us serve them; Thou shalt not hearken unto the words of that prophet, or that dreamer of dreams: for the Lord your God proveth you, to know whether ye love the Lord your God with all your heart and with all your soul. Ye shall walk after the Lord your God, and fear Him, and keep His commandments, and obey His voice, and ye shall serve Him, and cleave unto Him. And that prophet, or that dreamer of dreams, shall be put to death; because he hath spoken to turn you away from the Lord your God, which brought you out of the land of Egypt and redeemed you out of the house of bondage, to thrust thee out of the way which the Lord thy God commanded thee to walk in."[23]

The position of Rabbi Wise cannot be defended by trying to identify this passage with the one in Leviticus. The law in Deuteronomy has reference to that form of blasphemy which is nearly identical with idolatry, that is, seducing the people from their allegiance to Jehovah, and inducing them to go off after strange gods. The law in Leviticus applies peculiarly to profane epithets and to curses hurled at Jehovah Himself.

Again, Rabbi Wise ridicules the notion that Caiaphas and the Sanhedrists attempted to twist the use of the words "Son of God" into a crime. He is right when, quoting Deuteronomy xiv. 1, he says that "every Israelite had a perfect right to call himself a son of God." But here again the eminent theologian has stopped short of the entire truth. It is not at all probable that he would have contended that "every Israelite had a perfect right to call himself the son of God" in the sense of being equal with God Himself. Should reply be made that such would be an unwarranted construction of Christ's confession that he was "the Christ, the Son of God," then the opinion of Salvador would be again invoked. In a note to the "Jugement de Jesus," he says: "I repeat that the expression 'Son of God' includes here the idea of God Himself."

We are not in a position, nearly two thousand years after the event occurred, to tell exactly what was in the mind of Caiaphas at the time. But, in view of the condemnation which he passed, and of the language which he used in passing it, we are certainly justified in supposing that he deliberately and designedly connected the two titles—"the Christ" and "the Son of God"—to see if Jesus would assume responsibility for both, or if He would content himself with the simple appellation, "son of God," to which every pious Israelite was entitled.

The reply of Jesus, "Thou hast said," meaning "I am" the Christ, the Son of God, was an affirmation of His identity with the Father. The condemnation for blasphemy immediately followed. Such a sentence would have been inconsistent with any other theory than the assumption that Jesus had claimed equality with God, or had arrogated to Himself power and authority which belonged alone to Jehovah. This definition of blasphemy is certainly different from that laid down in Leviticus xxiv. 15-20.

As a matter of history, it is really true that both the Old and New Testaments reveal not only the existence of more than one blasphemy statute in the Mosaic Code, but also more than one conception and definition of blasphemy at different periods in the development of the Hebrew people.

In II Samuel xii. 14 the word "blaspheme" is used in the sense "to despise Judaism." In I Macc. ii. 6 blasphemy means "idolatry." In Job ii. 5; II Kings xix. 4-6; Hosea vii. 16, the term indicates "reproach," "derision."

Not only might God be blasphemed, but the king also, as his representative. The indictment against Naboth was: "Thou didst blaspheme God and the king."[24] The people of Jehovah and his Holy Land might also become victims of blasphemy.[25]

The New Testament writers frequently charge the Jews with blaspheming Jesus, when they use insulting language toward Him, or deny to Him the credit that is His due.[26]

In Revelation, St. John tells that he "saw a beast rise up out of the sea, having seven heads and ten horns, and upon his horns ten crowns, and upon his heads the name of blasphemy. And he opened his mouth in blasphemy against God, to blaspheme his name, and his tabernacles, and them that dwell in heaven."[27] This beast was the symbolical Antichrist, and his blasphemy was simply the treasonable opposition of the antichristian world to God and His kingdom.

A comprehensive meaning of "blasphemy," in the various senses above suggested, is conveyed by the definition of the term "treason" under the governments of Gentile commonwealths. A single statute, 25 Edw. iii. c. 2, defines seven different ways of committing treason against the king of England.[28] The *lex Julia majestatis,* promulgated by Augustus Caesar, was a single statute which comprehended all the ancient laws that had previously been enacted to punish transgressors against the Roman State.[29] There was no particular statute, as Rabbi Wise would have us believe, among the ancient Hebrews, that defined all forms of blasphemy against Jehovah. But a very clear notion of the various phases of blasphemy may be had if we will keep in mind the various definitions of treason under modern law.

It should not be forgotten that the ancient Hebrew Commonwealth was a pure theocracy; that Jehovah was king; that priests, prophets, and people were merely the subjects and servants of this king; that its government and its institutions were the products of his brain; and that the destinies of the people of Israel, the "chosen seed," were absolutely in his keeping and subject to his divine direction and control. It should also be remembered that the God of Israel was a most

jealous God; that the greatest irritant of His wrath was any encroachment upon His rights as ruler of men and creator of the universe; that for the protection of His sovereignty, He had proclaimed to His people through His servant Moses the most stringent statutes against any profanation of His name or disloyalty to His person. The Decalogue was the great charter of Jehovah for the government of His children. The first three commandments were special statutes intended to excite their gratitude and insure their attachment. He reminds them of the circumstances of their deliverance, and warns them, under severe penalty, against going off after strange gods.

But, not content with these, He had still other statutes proclaimed, furnishing safeguards against idolatry and insuring loyalty to His person.[30] At the time of the establishment of the Hebrew theocracy, idolatry was everywhere to be found. Not only were the neighboring peoples worshipers of idols, but the Israelites themselves were prone to idolatry and to running off after strange gods. The worship of the Golden Calf is a familiar illustration of this truth. Thus the Commonwealth of Jehovah was threatened not only with idolatrous invasion from without but with idolatrous insurrection from within. Hence the severity of the measures adopted for the protection of His kingdom, His person, and His name, not only against idolaters but against necromancers, witches, sorcerers, and all persons who pretended to supernatural powers that did not proceed directly from Jehovah Himself. The enforcement of and obedience to these various statutes required an acknowledgment of the power and authority of Jehovah in every case where prophecies were foretold, wonders worked, and supernatural powers of any kind exhibited. And throughout the Sacred Scriptures, in both the Old and New Testaments, we find traces of the operation of this law. Sometimes it is an instance of obedience, as when Pharaoh wanted to credit Joseph with the power of interpreting dreams. "And Joseph answered Pharaoh, saying, It is not in *me:* God shall give Pharaoh an answer of peace."[31] At other times, it is an act of disobedience. To satisfy the thirsty multitude Moses smote the rock and brought forth water at Meribah. But instead of giving the Lord credit for the act, Moses claimed it for Aaron and himself, saying, "Hear now, ye rebels: must *we* fetch you water out of this rock?" Whereupon Jehovah grew very angry and said to Moses and Aaron: "Because ye believe me not, to sanctify *me* in the eyes of the children of Israel, therefore ye shall not bring this congregation into the land which I have given them."[32] As punishment for this blasphemous conduct, neither Moses nor Aaron was permitted to enter the Promised Land.[33] And that this omission to give due acknowledgment to the Lord for the miraculous flow of water was treasonable or blasphemous under the wider interpretation of the term, cannot be doubted.

From the foregoing remarks it is clear that blasphemy among the ancient Hebrews was subject to a twofold classification: (1) A verbal renunciation and profane speaking of the name of Jehovah. To this kind of blasphemy the provision in Leviticus xxiv. 15-20 was applicable. This was blasphemy in its generally accepted but narrower and more restricted sense. This kind of blasphemy indicated a most depraved and malignant state of mind, and to secure a conviction it was necessary to show that the word "Jehovah" or "Adonai" had been pronounced. (2) "Every word or act, directly in derogation of the sovereignty of Jehovah, such as speaking in the name of another god, or omitting, on any occasion that required it, to give to Jehovah the honor due to His own name."[34] This form of blasphemy was nearly the same as treason under modern governments, and included all offenses that threatened the usurpation of the throne of Jehovah, the destruction of His institutions, and that withheld from Him due acknowledgment of His authority and authorship in all matters of miracle and prophecy.

Returning to the trial in the palace of Caiaphas, let us again consider the question: Was Jesus guilty of blasphemy under any of the definitions above given? Had He ever cursed the name of Jehovah and thereby brought Himself within the condemnation of the law, as laid down in Leviticus xxiv. 15-20? Certainly not. Every word uttered by Him at the trial, as well as every other expression elsewhere uttered at any time or place, was said with reverence and awe and love in praise and glorification of the name and person of Jehovah. Rabbi Wise ridicules the notion that Jesus was ever tried upon the charge of blasphemy, because it is not recorded anywhere that He ever used any but tender and affectionate language in speaking of the Heavenly Father.

Had Jesus blasphemed, in the sense of "despising Judaism," and thereby brought Himself within the purview of the rule as exemplified in II Sam. xii. 14? Certainly not. There is no record anywhere that He despised Judaism. Jesus revered both the Law and the Prophets. He claimed that He came to fulfill, not to destroy them.[35] He frequently denounced Pharisaic formalism and hypocrisy, but at the same time He was a most loyal Jew and a devoted son of Israel.

Had He blasphemed by working wonders in His own name, and omitting to give Jehovah credit for them; and did He thereby bring Himself within the condemnation of the rule exemplified by Moses and Aaron in the matter of striking water from the rock at Meribah? We are forced to answer this question in the affirmative. If we regard Jesus as a mere man, a plain citizen, like Moses, the New Testament discloses many infractions of the Law in His prophecies and miracles. It is true that in John v. 19 it is said, "Verily, verily, I say unto you, The Son can do nothing of himself, but what he seeth the Father do." Here He affirmed that the power was from God and not from Himself. Again, having raised Lazarus from the dead, Jesus said, "Father, I thank thee that thou hast heard me,"[36]thus acknowledging the intervention of Jehovah in the performance of the miracle. In several other places He gave the Father credit for the act of the Son. But these were exceptions, isolated cases. The Law required an express acknowledgment in every case of prophecy or miracle working. "Thus saith the Lord" was either the prologue or epilogue of every wonder-working performance. In all the miracles wrought by him in Egypt Moses had given due to Jehovah. But this was not enough. He was made an example for all time when he failed to make acknowledgement in the matter of striking the water from the rock. Now Jesus worked many miracles in no other name than His own, and in so doing brought Himself within the operation of the rule and of the precedent established in the case of Moses and Aaron. The curing of the bloody issue,[37] the stilling of the tempest,[38] the chasing of the devils into the sea,[39] the raising of Jairus' daughter,[40] and of the son of the widow of Nain[41] from the dead, were done without any mention of the power and guidance of Jehovah.

But these transgressions were extra-judicial offenses and have been discussed merely as an introduction throwing light upon the specific charge at the trial that Jesus had claimed to be "the Christ, the Son of God." The question of the high priest is meaningless, unless interpreted in the light of knowledge which we know the members of the Sanhedrin had regarding the wonder-working performances of the Christ. The failure of Jesus to acknowledge the power of Jehovah in working miracles might be interpreted as a tacit avowal that He Himself was Jehovah, and that therefore no acknowledgments were necessary. The silence itself was a proclamation of the divinity that was in Him, which placed Him above a law intended to govern the conduct of men like Moses and Aaron.

We are now prepared to consider the final question: Had Jesus blasphemed, when He confessed to the high priest that he was "the Christ, the Son of God"? Had He blasphemed in that wider sense which Salvador has interpreted as being the Jewish notion of blasphemy at the time of Christ; that is, by claiming at once the attributes of the Messiah and the Son of God? Had He asserted an equality with God which looked to a usurpation of His power and the destruction of His throne; that is, did the confession of Jesus that He was ∎Christ, the Son of God,∎ suggest a rivalry between Him and Jehovah which might result in the dethronement of the latter and the substitution of the former as the Lord and King and Ruler of Israel? Regarding Jesus as a mere man, a plain citizen, an affirmative answer to any one of these questions would convict Him of blasphemy, according to the Jewish interpretation of that term at the time of Christ; for the Hebrew Jehovah had repeatedly proclaimed that He was a jealous God, and that He would brook neither rivals nor associates in the government of His kingdom.

That Jesus had more than once identified Himself with Jehovah, and had claimed divine attributes and powers; and that the Jews regarded all these pretensions as blasphemous, is evident, and can be ascertained from more than one passage of New Testament Scripture. On one occasion the Savior said to one sick of palsy: ∎Son, be of good cheer; thy sins be forgiven thee. And, behold, certain of the Scribes said within themselves, This *man* blasphemeth."[42] According to Luke, they said; "Who is this man which speaketh blasphemies? Who can forgive sins but God alone?"[43] Here, according to the Scribes and Pharisees, Jesus had blasphemed by claiming the power which alone belonged to Jehovah, that of forgiving sins; or, at least, by exercising a supernatural power without acknowledging the authorship and guidance of the Almighty. It should be remembered that in this instance of alleged blasphemy Jesus had not remotely cursed or profaned the name of Jehovah; but, according to Jewish notions of the times, had exercised a prerogative, that of forgiving sins, which belonged solely to Jehovah, without giving credit.

Again, we read this passage in the New Testament: "Therefore the Jews sought the more to kill him, because he not only had broken the Sabbath, but said also that God was his Father, making himself equal with God."[44] Here we see that the Jews of the days of Jesus, as well as Salvador in our own day, construed the claims of Jesus to be "the Christ, the Son of God," as an assertion of equality with Jehovah.

Again, on another occasion, Jesus said emphatically: "I and my Father are one. Then the Jews took up stones again to stone him. Jesus answered them, Many good works have I shewed you from my Father; for which of those works do ye stone me? The Jews answered him, saying, For a good work, we stone thee not; but for blasphemy; and because that thou, being a man, makest thyself God."[45] Even before this bold declaration of His identity with Jehovah, He had intimated that He was of Heavenly origin and had enjoyed a divine preexistence. He had declared that He was the "Bread which came down from Heaven,"[46] and that "Before Abraham was, I am."[47] The Jews regarded His statement that He had lived before Abraham as blasphemy, and "took up stones to cast at him," this being the usual punishment for blasphemous conduct.

We have said enough to emphasize the point that there was another kind of blasphemy known to the Jews of the days of Jesus than that prescribed in Leviticus; and that the confession of being "Christ, the Son of God," as the Jews and Caiaphas interpreted the term, brought Jesus within the meaning of blasphemy, in its wider signification—that of assuming equality with God. The numerous illustrations above furnished were given to provide means of clear interpretation of the term blasphemy, as used in the condemnatory sentence of the high priest. For it is clearly evident that he and the other judges must have had many charges against Jesus in mind other than those that appear in the record of the trial. But we repeat, these extra-judicial charges must be considered only for purposes of correct interpretation and as a means of throwing light upon the actual proceedings in the night trial before the Sanhedrin. We further repeat that the New Testament furnishes abundant evidence that Jesus the man, the Jewish citizen, had, at divers times and places, committed blasphemy against Jehovah, under a strict interpretation of the law of God.

Mr. Simon Greenleaf, the great Christian writer on the Law of Evidence and the Harmony of the Gospels, has thus tersely and admirably summarized the matter from the lawyer's point of view: "If we regard Jesus simply as a Jewish citizen, and with no higher character, this conviction seems substantially right in point of law, though the trial were not legal in all its forms. For, whether the accusation were founded on the first or the second command in the Decalogue, or on the law laid down in the thirteenth chapter of Deuteronomy, or on that in the eighteenth chapter and the twentieth verse, he had violated them all by assuming to himself powers belonging alone to Jehovah. It is not easy to perceive on what ground his conduct could have been defended before any tribunal, unless upon that of his superhuman character. No lawyer, it is conceived, would think of placing his defense upon any other basis."[48]

But, at this point, the reader would do well to discriminate very carefully between certain matters touching the most vital features of the controversy. Certain well-defined distinctions must be observed, else an erroneous conclusion will inevitably follow.

In the first place, proper limitations must be applied to the person and character of Jesus before it can be truthfully said that His conviction by the Sanhedrin was "substantially right in point of law." It must be remembered that, in this connection, Jesus is regarded merely as a man, "a Jewish citizen," to use Greenleaf's phrase. His divine character, as the only-begotten Son of God, as the Second Person of the Trinity, as the Savior of the human race, is not considered. But the reader may object, and with reason, that this is begging the question; and is therefore an inexcusable evasion; since the real issue before the Sanhedrin was this: Is Jesus God? And to strike the Godhead of Jesus from the discussion is to destroy the real issue, and to place the judgment of the Sanhedrin upon an irrelevant and immaterial basis. There is much truth in this contention, since it is clearly evident that if Jesus was actually God, "manifest in the flesh," He was not guilty; if He was not God, He was guilty.

Fortunately for the purposes of this treatise, the legality or the illegality of the proceedings in the trial of Christ is not so much related to the question of substance as to that of form. Whether Jesus were God or not is a question involving His divinity, and is a problem peculiarly within the domain of the theologian. Whether legal rules were duly observed in the trial of Christ, were He man or God, is a question involving His civil rights, and belongs to the domain of the lawyer. Unless this distinction be recognized and held in mind, the treatment of this theme from a legal standpoint has no justification. This contention is all the more certainly true, since proof of the divinity of Jesus, a spiritual problem, would rest more upon the basis of religious consciousness and experience, than upon historical facts and logical inferences.

The author of these volumes believes that Jesus was divine, and that if He was not divine, Divinity has not touched this globe. The writer bases his conviction of this fact upon the perfect purity, beauty, and sinlessness of Jesus; upon the overwhelming historical evidence of His resurrection from the dead, which event "may unhesitatingly be pronounced that best established in history";[49] as well as upon the evident impress of a divine hand upon genuine Christian civilization in every age.

But the historic proofs of the divinity of Christ that have come down to us through twenty centuries were not before the Sanhedrin. A charitable Christian criticism will be slow in passing unmerciful judgment upon the members of that court for denying the claims of Jesus to identity with God, when His own disciples evidently failed to recognize them. The incidents of the Last Supper clearly prove that those who had been intimately associated with Him during three eventful years did not, at the close of His ministry, fully comprehend His character and appreciate His message and His mission.[50] Were comparative strangers to Him and His teachings expected to be more keenly discerning? After John had baptized Jesus in the Jordan and the Spirit of God, in the form of a dove, had descended upon Him, the Baptist seems to have had some doubts of the Messiahship of Christ and sent an embassy to Him to ask, "Art thou he that should come, or do we look for another?"[51] If the Forerunner of the Messiah did not know, are we justified in demanding perfect prescience and absolute infallibility of Caiaphas?

The most perfect proof of the divinity of Jesus is the fact of His resurrection from the dead, attested by Matthew, Mark, Luke, John, Peter, James, and Paul. And yet, although He had frequently foretold to them that He would rise again, Jesus had to personally appear before them and submit to physical tests before they would believe that His prophecies had been fulfilled.[52] And it must be remembered that the great proof of His divinity, His resurrection from the dead, was not before Caiaphas and his colleagues at the time of the trial.

The preceding suggestions and observations have not been made in order to excuse or palliate the conduct of the members of the Sanhedrin for their illegal conduct of the proceedings against Jesus. Under Point XI of the Brief we shall prove by Jewish testimony alone the utterly wicked and worthless character of these judges. Under Point XII we shall elaborate the proofs in favor of the Messiahship of Jesus and of His divine Sonship of the Father, as far as the scope of this work will permit. We have suggested above the perplexity of the members of the Sanhedrin and of the disciples of Jesus, concerning the divinity of the Nazarene, to illustrate to the reader how futile would be the task of attempting in a treatise of this kind to settle the question of the identity of Jesus with God, and thereby fix upon His judges in the palace of Caiaphas the odium of an unrighteous judgment. The question, after all, is one to be settled in the forum of conscience, illuminated by the light of history, and not at the bar of legal justice.

But whether Jesus were man or God, or man-God, we are justified in passing upon the question of the violation of forms of law which He was entitled to have observed in the trial of His claims. And at this point we return to a consideration of the phrase, "substantially right in point of law." This language is not intended to convey the notion that Jesus was legally convicted. It means simply that the claim of equality with God by a plain Jewish citizen was, under Hebrew law, blasphemy; the crime which Caiaphas and the Sanhedrin believed that Jesus had confessed, and for which they condemned Him.

Another distinction that must be made is that relating to the kind of law that is meant, when it is said that the conviction of Jesus was "substantially right in point of law." Ancient Hebrew law is meant, and as that law was interpreted from the standpoint of ancient Judaism. The policy and precepts of the New Dispensation inaugurated by Jesus can hardly be considered, in a legal sense, to have been binding upon Caiaphas and the Sanhedrin, since the very claims of Jesus to Messiahship and identity with God were to be tested by the provisions of the Mosaic Code and in the light of Hebrew prophecy. The Pentateuch, the

Prophets, and the Talmud were the legal guides, then, of the judges of Israel in judicial proceedings at this time, and furnished rules for determining the genuineness of His pretensions.

Mr. Greenleaf, the author of the phrase, "substantially right in point of law," asserts that the trial was not legal in all its forms, but he fails to enumerate the errors. The purpose of the Brief in this work is to name and discuss the errors and irregularities of the Hebrew trial, that is, the trial before the Sanhedrin.

But the question may be asked: Why be guilty of the inconsistency of discussing illegalities, when admission has already been made that the decision was "substantially right in point of law"? The answer is that a distinction must be made between that which is popularly and historically known or believed to be true, and that which has not been or cannot be proved in a court of law. Every lawyer is familiar with this distinction. The court may know that the accused is guilty, the jury may know it, the attorneys may be perfectly sure of it, but if the verdict of guilt returned by the jury into court is not based upon testimony that came from the witness stand from witnesses who were under oath, and that had submitted to cross-examination, such verdict would hardly be sustained on appeal. In other words, the lives and liberties of alleged criminals must not be endangered by extra-judicial and incompetent testimony. A legal verdict can be rendered only when a regular trial has been had before a competent court, having jurisdiction of the crime charged, and after all legal rules have been observed which the constitution and the laws have provided as safeguards for the protection of the rights of both the people and the prisoner. However heinous the offense committed, no man is, legally speaking, a criminal, until he has been legally tried and declared a criminal. The presumption of innocence, a substantial legal right, is thrown around him from the very beginning, and continues in his favor until it is overthrown by competent and satisfactory evidence. Unless such evidence is furnished, under legal forms, no man, however morally guilty, can be denominated a criminal, in a juristic sense, in the face of the perpetual continuance of this presumption of innocence.

If these rules and principles be applied to the trial of Jesus, either before the Sanhedrin or before Pilate, it can be easily demonstrated that while He might have been abstractly and historically guilty of the crime of blasphemy, in the wider acceptation of that term, He was not remotely a criminal. because He was never legally tried and convicted. In other words, his condemnation was not based upon a legal procedure that was in harmony with either the Mosaic Code or the Mishna. The pages of human history present no stronger case of judicial murder than the trial and crucifixion of Jesus of Nazareth, for the simple reason that all forms of law were outraged and trampled under foot in the proceedings instituted against Him. The errors were so numerous and the proceedings so flagrant that many have doubted the existence of a trial. Others have sought to attack the authenticity of the Gospel narratives and the veracity of the Gospel writers by pointing to the number of errors committed as evidence that no such proceedings ever took place. As Renan would say, this is a species of "naive impudence," to assert that a trial was not had, because numerous errors are alleged; as if a Hebrew court could not either intentionally or unintentionally commit blunders and many of them. Every lawyer of extensive practice anywhere knows from experience that judges of great ability and exalted character conduct lengthy trials, in both civil and criminal cases, with the most painstaking care, and are aided by eminent counsel and good and honest jurors; the whole purpose of the proceedings being to reach a just and righteous verdict; and yet, on appeal, it is frequently held that not one but many errors have been committed.

At this point, a few preliminary observations are necessary as a means of introduction to the discussion of errors. Certain elementary principles should be clearly understood at the outset. In the first place, an analysis of the word "case," used in a juristic sense, shows the existence of two cardinal judicial elements: the element called Fact, and the element called Law. And whether the advocate is preparing a pleading at his desk, is making a speech to the jury, or addressing himself to the court, these elements are ever present in his mind. He is continually asking these questions: What are the facts of this case? What is the law applicable to these facts? Do the facts and the law meet, harmonize, blend, according to the latest decision of the court of last resort? If so, a case is made; otherwise, not.

It is impossible to frame any legal argument upon any other basis than that of the agreement or nonagreement of law and fact, in a juristic sense; and upon this plan errors will be discussed and the Brief will be framed.

In the second place, it must not be forgotten that, in matters of review on appeal, errors will not be presumed; that is, errors will not be considered that do not appeal affirmatively upon the record. The law will rather presume and the court will assume that what should have been done, has been done. In conformity with this principle, only such errors will be discussed in these pages that affirmatively appear in the New Testament Gospels which form the record in this case. By "affirmatively appear" is meant that the error is clearly apparent or may be reasonably inferred.

In Part II of the preceding pages of this volume, Hebrew criminal law, which was actively in force at the time of Christ, was outlined and discussed. In Part I the Record of Fact was reviewed in the light of judicial rules. It is the present purpose, in Part III, to enumerate, in the form of a Brief, the errors committed by the Hebrew judges of Jesus, as the result of their failure to make the facts of their trial conform with the legal rules by which they were bound in all criminal proceedings where human life was at stake. The plan proposed is to announce successive errors in brief statements which will be designated "Points," in imitation of the New York method on appeal. Following the statement of error will be given a short synopsis of the law applicable to the point suggested. Then, finally, will follow the fact and argument necessary to elaboration and proof. Accordingly, in pursuance of this method, let us consider the points in order.

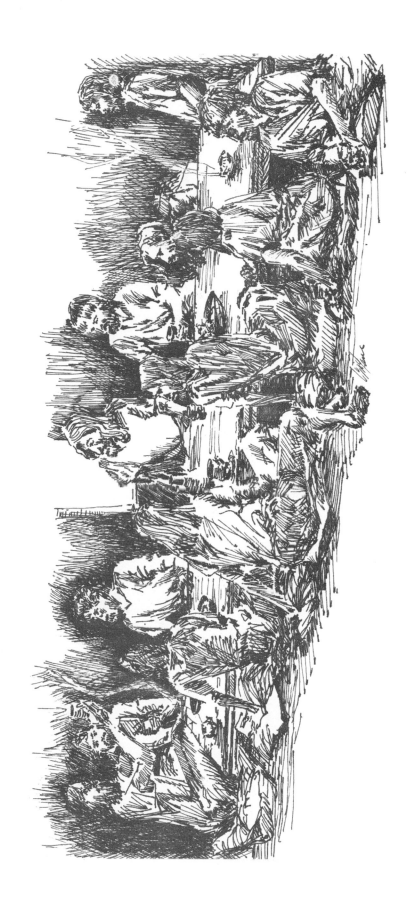

POINT I

THE ARREST OF JESUS WAS ILLEGAL

LAW

"Now the Jewish law prohibited *all proceedings by night.*"— DUPIN, "Jesus Devant Caiphe et Pilate."

"The testimony of an accomplice is not permissible by Rabbinic law both *propter affectum* and *propter delictum,* and no man's *life,* nor his *liberty,* nor his *reputation* can be endangered by the malice of one who has confessed himself a criminal."—MENDELSOHN, "Criminal Jurisprudence of the Ancient Hebrews," n. 274.

"Thou shalt not go up and down as a talebearer among thy people: neither shalt thou stand against the blood of they neighbor. Thou shalt not hate thy brother in thine heart: Thou shalt not avenge or bear any grudge against the children of thy people, but thou shalt love thy neighbor as thyself."—LEVITICUS xix. 17, 18.

FACT AND ARGUMENT

The Bible record discloses three distinct elements of illegality in the arrest of Jesus: (1) The arrest took place at night in violation of Hebrew law; (2) it was effected through the agency of a traitor and informer, in violation of a provision in the Mosaic Code and of a Rabbinic rule based thereon; (3) it was not the result of a legal mandate from a court whose intentions were to conduct a legal trial for the purpose of reaching a righteous judgment. These elements of illegality will be apparent when the facts of the arrest are briefly stated.

It was the 14th Nisan, according to the Jewish calendar; or April 6th, A. D. 30, according to our calendar. The Paschal Feast was at hand. The eyes of all Israel were centered upon the Metropolis of Judaism. From Judea, from Samaria, from Galilee and Perea, from all parts of the world where Jews were resident, pilgrims came streaming into the Holy City to be present at the great national festival. It was to be an occasion of prayer and thanksgiving, of sweet memories and happy reunions. Then and there offerings would be made and purifications obtained. In the great Temple, with its gorgeous ritual, Judaism was to offer its soul to Jehovah. The national and religious feelings of a divinely commissioned race were to be deeply stirred by memories that reminded them of the first, and by hopes that looked forward to the final great deliverance.

It was probably in the home of Mark, on the outskirts of Jerusalem, that Jesus gathered with the Twelve, on the evening of this day, to eat the Paschal lamb. In the Upper Room, the sacred feast was spread and the little band were gathered. Only the genius of a da Vinci could do justice to that scene. There was Peter, hot-headed, impetuous, bravado-like. There was John, as gentle, pure-minded, and loving as a woman. There was Judas, mercenary, lowbrowed, and craven-hearted. There were others who, with Peter and John, were to have temples dedicated in their names. In their midst was the Master of them all, "God manifest in the flesh," who "with His pierced hands was to lift empires off their hinges, and turn the stream of centuries from its channel." No moment of history was so fraught with tragic interest for the human race. There the seal of the New Covenant was affixed, the bond of the new human spiritual alliance was made. The great law of love was proclaimed which was to regenerate and sanctify the world. "These things I command you, that ye love one another. And I have declared unto them thy name, and will declare it; that the love wherewith thou hast loved me, may be in them, and I in them." Thus the great law of love was to be the binding tie, not only among the little brotherhood there assembled but was to be the cementing bond between the regenerate of earth, the Mediator, and the great Father of love, Himself. There, too, was given the great example of humility which was to characterize true Christian piety throughout the ages. The pages of history record no other spectacle so thrilling and sublime, and at the same time tender and pathetic, as that afforded by the Paschal Meal, when Jesus, the Savior of men, the Son of God, the Maker of all the shining worlds, sank upon His knees to wash the feet of ignorant, simple-minded Galilean fishermen, in order that future ages might have at once a lesson and an example of that genuine humility which is the very life and soul of true religion.

During the evening, a bitter anxiety, an awful melancholy, seized the devoted ban, whose number, thirteen, even today inspires superstitious dread. In the midst of the apprehension the heart of the Master was so deeply wrung with agony that He turned to those about him and said: "Verily, verily, I say unto you that one of you shall betray me." This prediction only intensified the sadness that had already begun to fall over the Sacred Meal and the loving disciples began to ask: "Lord, is it I?" Even the betrayer himself joined with the others, and, with inconceivable heartlessness and effrontery, asked: "Lord, is it I?" At the moment of greatest dread and consternation, Peter, bolder than the rest, leaned across the table and whispered to John, who was resting upon the bosom of Jesus, and suggested that he ask the Master who it was. Accordingly, John whispered and asked the Savior: "Lord, who is it?" "Jesus answered, He it is, to whom I shall give a sop, when I have dipped it. And when he had dipped the sop, he gave it to Judas Iscariot, the son of Simon. And after the sop Satan entered into him. Then said Jesus unto him, That thou doest, do quickly." Judas then arose from the feast and vanished from the room. When he was gone, the Master began to deliver to His "little children,"[1] to those who had loved and followed Him, those farewell words which St. John alone records, and that are so "rarely mixed of sadness and joys, and studded with mysteries as with emeralds."

There, too, doubts and fears began to burst from the hearts and lips of the members of the little company. The knowledge that the gentle Jesus, whose ministry had thrilled and glorified their simple peasant lives, and promised to them crowns of glory in the world to come, was about to leave them, and in a most tragic way, filled them with solicitude and dread. Their anxiety manifested itself by frequent questioning which excites our wonder that men who had been

with Him so long in the Apostolic ministry should have been so simple-minded and incredulous. "They said, therefore, What is this that he saith, A little while? We cannot tell what he saith." This verse is a simple illustration of the continued misapprehension, on this night, upon the part of the Apostles, of everything said by the Master. Peter was anxious to know why he could not follow the Lord. Thomas wanted to know the exact way, evidently failing to comprehend the figurative language of the Christ. Judas Lebbaeus also had his doubts. He became muddled by mixing the purely spiritual with the physical powers of sight. "Lord, how is it," he asked, "that thou wilt manifest thyself to us and not to the world?" Philip of Bethsaida desired to see the Father. "Lord, show us the Father," he said, "and it sufficeth us." Philip seems to have been so dense that he had no appreciation of the spiritual attributes and invisible existence of the Father.

It was thus that several hours were spent in celebrating the great Feast; in drinking wine; in eating the Paschal lamb, the unleavened bread, and the bitter herbs; in singing hymns, offering prayers, and performing the sacred rites; in delivering discourses which in every age have been the most precious treasures of Christians, and in expressing doubts and fears that have excited the astonishment and even the ridicule of the exacting and supercilious of all the centuries.

At the approach of midnight, Jesus and the Eleven left the Upper Chamber of the little house and stepped out into the moonlight of a solemn Passover night. They began to wend their way toward the Kedron that separated them from the olive orchard on the Mount. Less than an hour's journey brought them to the Garden of Gethsemane. The word "Gethsemane" means "oil press." And this place doubtless derived its name from the fact that in it was located an oil press which was used to crush olives that grew abundantly on the trees that crowned the slopes. Whether it was a public garden or belonged to some friend of Jesus, we do not know, but certain it is that it was a holy place, a sanctuary of prayer, where the Man of Sorrows frequently retired to pray and commune with His Heavenly Father. At the gateway Jesus left eight of the Apostles and took with Him the other three: Peter, James, and John. These men seem to have been the best beloved of the Master. They were with Him at the raising of Jairus' daughter, at the Transfiguration on the Mount, and were now selected to be nearest Him in the hour of His agony. Proceeding with them a short distance, He suddenly stopped and exclaimed: "My soul is exceedingly sorrowful, even unto death: tarry ye here, and watch with me." Then, withdrawing Himself from them a stone's cast, He sank upon His knees and prayed; and in the agony of prayer great drops of sweat resembling blood rolled from His face and fell upon the ground. Rising from prayer, He returned to His disciples to find them asleep. Sorrow had overcome them and they were mercifully spared the tortures of the place and hour. Three times did He go away to pray, and as many times, upon His return, they were found asleep. The last time He came He said to them: "Rise, let us be going: behold he is at hand that doth betray me." At this moment were heard the noise and tramp of an advancing multitude. "Judas then, having received a band of men and officers from the chief priests and Pharisees, cometh thither with lanterns and torches and weapons." This midnight mob, led by Judas, was made up of Roman soldiers, the Temple guard, and stragglers from along the way. It is probable that the traitor walked ahead of the mob by several paces. "And forthwith he came to Jesus, and said, Hail, master, and kissed him and Jesus said unto him, Friend, wherefore art thou come? Then came they and laid hands on Jesus and took him." But the arrest was not accomplished without incidents of pathos and of passion. "Whom seek ye?" asked the Master. "Jesus of Nazareth," they answered. "I am he," replied the Savior. Then, dazed and bewildered, they fell backward upon the ground. "Then asked he them again, whom seek ye? and they said, Jesus of Nazareth. Jesus answered, I have told you that I am he: if, therefore, ye seek me, let these go their way." John says that this intercession for the disciples was to the end that prophecy might be fulfilled.[2] Doubtless so; but this was not all. Nowhere in sacred literature do we find such pointed testimony to the courage and manliness of Jesus. His tender solicitude for the members of the little band, for those who had quit their homes and callings to link their destinies with His, was here superbly illustrated. He knew that He was going to immediate condemnation and then to death, but He ardently desired that they should be spared to live. And for them He threw Himself into the breach.

The furious and the passionate, as well as the tender and pathetic, mark the arrest in the garden. "Then Simon Peter having a sword drew it, and smote the high priest's servant, and cut off his right ear. The servant's name was Malchus." This was bloody proof of that fidelity which Peter loudly proclaimed at the banquet board, but which was soon to be swallowed up in craven flight and pusillanimous denial.

"Then the band and the captain and officers of the Jews took Jesus, and bound him."

At this point the arrest was complete, and we now return to the discussion of the illegalities connected with it.

It was a well-established and inflexible rule of Hebrew law that proceedings in capital trials could not be had at night. This provision did not apply simply to the proceedings of the trial after the prisoner had been arraigned and the examination had been begun. We have it upon the authority of Dupin that it applied to the entire proceedings, from the arrest to the execution. The great French advocate explicitly states that the arrest was illegal because it was made at night.[3] Deference to this rule seems to have been shown in the arrest of Peter and John on another occasion. "And they laid hands upon them and put them in hold unto the next day: for it was now *eventide.*"[4] That Jesus was arrested at night is clearly evident from the fact that those who captured Him bore " *lanterns* and *torches and weapons.* "

The employment of Judas by the Sanhedrin authorities constitutes the second element of illegality in the arrest. This wretched creature had been numbered among the Twelve, had been blessed and honored, not merely with discipleship

but with apostleship, had himself been sent on holy missions by the Master, had been given the power to cast out devils, had been appointed by his Lord the keeper of the moneys of the Apostolic company, and, if Edersheim is to be believed, had occupied the seat of honor by the Master at the Last Supper.[5] This craven and cowardly Apostate was employed by the Sanhedrin Council to betray the Christ. It is clearly evident from the Scriptures that the arrest of Jesus would not have taken place on the occasion of the Passover, and therefore probably not at all, if Judas had not deserted and betrayed Him. The Savior had appeared and preached daily in the Temple, and every opportunity was offered to effect a legal arrest on legal charges with a view to a legal determination. But the enemies of Jesus did not want this. They were waiting to effect His capture in some out-of-the-way place, at the dead of night, when His friends could not defend Him and their murderous proceedings would not reach the eye and ear of the public. This could not be accomplished as long as His intimates were faithful to Him. It was, then, a joyful surprise to the members of the Sanhedrin when they learned that Judas was willing to betray his Master. "And when they heard it, they were glad, and promised to give him money."

In modern jurisdictions, accomplice testimony has been and is allowed. The judicial authorities, however, have always regarded it with distrust, and we might say with deep-seated suspicion. At the common law in England a conviction for crime might rest upon the uncorroborated testimony of an accomplice, after the jury had been warned that such testimony was to be closely scrutinized. In the American States the testimony of an accomplice is admissible, but must be corroborated in order to sustain a conviction. This is the general rule. The weakness of such evidence is shown by the nature of the corroboration required by several states. In some of them the corroborating testimony must not only tend to prove the commission of the crime but must also tend to connect the defendant with such commission. Another evidence of the untrustworthiness of such testimony is that in several states an accomplice is not permitted to corroborate another accomplice, so as to satisfy the statutes.[6] The admission of such testimony seems to rest, in great measure, upon the supreme necessity of the preservation of the state, which is only possible when the punishment of crime is possible; and in very many instances it would be impossible to punish crime if guilty confederates were not allowed and even encouraged to give state's evidence.

But notwithstanding this supreme consideration of the necessity of the preservation of the state, the ancient Hebrews forbade the use of accomplice testimony, as we have seen from the extract from "The Criminal Jurisprudence of the Ancient Hebrews," by Mendelsohn, cited on page 219.

The arrest of Jesus was ordered upon the supposition that He was a criminal; this same supposition would have made Judas, who had aided, encouraged, and abetted Jesus in the propagation of His faith, an accomplice. If Judas was not an accomplice, Jesus was innocent, and His arrest was an outrage, and therefore illegal.

The Hebrew law against accomplice testimony must have been derived, in part at least, from the following rule laid down in Leviticus xix. 16-18: "Thou shalt not go up and down as a talebearer among thy people: neither shalt thou stand against the blood of thy neighbor. Thou shalt not hate thy brother in thine heart: Thou shalt not avenge, or bear any grudge against the children of thy people, but thou shalt love thy neighbor as thyself." It may be objected that this is only a moral injunction and not a legal rule; to which reply must be made that there was no difference between morality and law among the ancient Hebrews. Their religion was founded upon law, and their law upon religion. The two ideas of morality and law were inseparable. The ancient Hebrew religion was founded upon a contract of the strictest legal kind. The Abrahamic covenant, when properly interpreted, meant simply that Jehovah had agreed with the children of Israel that if they would obey the law as He gave it, they would be rewarded by Him. The force of this contention will be readily perceived when it is reflected that the Decalogue is nothing but ten moral injunctions, which are nevertheless said to be the law which God gave to Moses.

Every provision in the rule laid down in Leviticus is, moreover, directly applicable to the character and conduct of Judas, and seems to have been intended as a prophetic warning to him. Let us consider the different elements of this rule in order.

"Thou shalt not go up and down as a talebearer among thy people."

Was not Judas a talebearer among his people? Did he not go to the chief priests to betray his Master unto them? Was he not a "talebearer" if he did nothing more than communicate to the chief priests the whereabouts of the Savior, that Gethsemane was His accustomed place of prayer and that He might be found and arrested there at midnight? Are we not justified in supposing that Judas told the enemies of Jesus much more than this? Is it not reasonable to infer that the blood-money was paid to secure more evidence than that which would merely lead to the arrest of the Nazarene? Is it not probable that Judas detailed to the chief priests many events in the ministry of Jesus which, it is known, He communicated only to the Twelve? If he did these things, was he not a "talebearer" within the meaning of the rule?

"Neither shalt thou stand against the blood of thy neighbor."

Did not Judas stand against the blood of his nearest and dearest neighbor when he consented to be the chief instrument of an arrest which he knew would result in death?

"Thou shalt not hate thy brother in thy heart."

Is it possible to suppose that anything less than hatred could have induced Judas to betray the Christ? This question is important, for it involves a consideration of the real character of the betrayer and the main motive for the betrayal. Judas was from Kerioth in Judea and was the only Judean among the Twelve. Why Judas was selected as a member of the Apostolic company is too deep a mystery to be solved by the author of these pages. Besides, the consideration of the elements of predestination in his case is foreign to the purpose of this work. His character as a purely human agency is sufficient to answer the present design. Judas had undoubtedly demonstrated business capacity in some way before his appointment to the treasury portfolio of the little band. It cannot be doubted that greed was his besetting sin. This trait, coupled with political ambition, undoubtedly accounts for his downfall and destruction. He was one of those simple-minded, short-sighted individuals of his day who believed that a political upheaval was at hand which would result in the restoration of the independence of Israel as a separate kingdom. He believed that this result would be brought about through the agency of a temporal Messiah, an earthly deliverer of almost divine qualities. He thought at first that he saw in Jesus the person of the Messiah, and in the Apostolic band the nucleus of a revolution. He was gratified beyond measure at his appointment to the treasury position, for he felt sure that from it promotion was in sight. He was perfectly contented to carry for a while the "little bag," provided there was reasonable assurance that later on he would be permitted to carry a larger one.

As the months and years rolled by, heavy scales began to fall from his stupid eyes and he began to be deceived not by but in Jesus. We are justified in believing that Judas never even remotely appreciated the spiritual grandeur of the Christ. He probably had intellect and soul enough to be charmed and fascinated by the lofty bearing and eloquent discourse of Jesus, but after all he perceived only the necessary qualifications of a great republican leader and successful revolutionist. And after a while he doubtless began to tire of all this when he saw that the revolution was not progressing and that there was no possibility of actual and solid results. It is probable that disaffection and treachery were born and began to grow in his mind and heart at Capernaum, when Jesus was deserted by many of His followers and was forced to effect a realignment along spiritual lines. Judas was not equal to the spiritual test, and it was doubtless then that the disintegration of his moral nature began, which stopped only with betrayal, infamy, and death.

But by what process, we may ask, was the mercenary disposition of Judas converted into hatred against Jesus? The process was that of disappointment. When Judas became convinced that all the years of his connection with the Apostolic company had been lost, his will became embittered and his resentment was aroused. In the denseness of his ignorance and in the baseness of his soul he probably thought that Jesus had deceived His followers as to His true mission and he felt enraged because he had been duped. He had looked forward to worldly promotion and success. He had fondly hoped that the eloquence of Jesus would finally call around Him an invincible host of enthusiastic adherents who would raise the standard of revolt, drive the Romans from Judea, and establish the long-looked-for kingdom of the Jews. He had noted with deep disappointment and unutterable chagrin the failure of Jesus to proclaim Himself king when, at Bethphage, the multitude had greeted His entrance into Jerusalem with Hosannas and acclamations. And now, at the Last Supper, he became convinced from the conduct and discourses of the Master that his worst fears were true, that Jesus was sincere in His resolution to offer Himself as a sacrifice for the sake of a principle which he, Judas, did not approve because he could not understand. In other words, he witnessed in the resolve of Jesus to die at once the shipwreck of his hopes, and he made haste to vent his wrath upon the author of his disappointment.

The writer agrees with Renan that the thirty pieces of silver were not the real or leading inducement to this black and monumental betrayal. Having taken the fatal step, by leaving the Upper Room in the home of Mark, to deliver his Lord and Master into the hands of enemies, a bitter hatred was formed at once against the innocent victim of his foul designs, on the well-known principle of human nature that we hate those who have induced us to do that which causes us to despise and hate ourselves.

"Thou shalt not avenge or bear any grudge against the children of thy people."

Where, in the annals of the universe, do we find another such case of vengeance and grudge as this of Judas against Jesus?

"But thou shalt love thy neighbor as thyself."

This commandment of the Mosaic law was also the great commandment of the Master of Galilee, and in violating it by consenting to betray and sacrifice Jesus, Judas assaulted and destroyed in his own soul the cardinal principle of the two great religious dispensations of his race.

And yet this informer, conspirator, and malefactor was employed by the chief priests in effecting the arrest of Jesus. Was not a fundamental rule of Mosaic law violated? Will it be urged that the rule operated against Judas but not against the chief priests? If so, it must be remembered that no wicked instrument could be used in promoting Hebrew justice. Officers of the law were not permitted to require a citizen to do an act which was forbidden by law. If Jesus was innocent, then the arrest was illegal. If He was guilty, then Judas, his Apostle and fellow-worker, was an accomplice; and no accomplice could be utilized in furtherance of justice, under Hebrew law, either in the matter of arrest or in the establishment of guilt as a witness at the trial.

According to the Talmud, there was at least one seeming exception to this rule. Renan describes it with peculiar clearness and succinctness. "The procedure," he says, "against the 'corrupter' (mesith), who sought to attain the purity of religion, is explained in the Talmud, with details, the naive impudence of which provokes a smile. A judicial ambush is therein erected into an essential part of the examination of criminals. When a man was accused of being a 'corrupter,' two witnesses were suborned who were concealed behind a partition. It was arranged to bring the accused into a contiguous room, where he could be heard by these two witnesses without his perceiving them. Two candles were lighted near him, in order that it might be satisfactorily proved that the witnesses 'saw him.' (In criminal matters, eyewitnesses alone were admitted. Mishna, Sanhedrin VI. 5.) He was then made to repeat his blasphemy; next urged to retract it. If he persisted, the witnesses who had heard him conducted him to the Tribunal and he was stoned to death. The Talmud adds that this was the manner in which they treated Jesus; that he was condemned on the faith of two witnesses who had been suborned, and that the crime of 'corruption' is, moreover, the only one for which the witnesses are thus prepared."[7]

Most Gentile writers ridicule this statement of the Talmud, and maintain that it was a Rabbinic invention of post-Apostolic days, and was intended to offer an excuse for the outrageous proceedings against the Christ. Schurer dismisses the whole proposition with contempt. Many Jewish scholars also refuse it the sanction of their authority. But even if it was a Talmudic rule of law in force at the time of Christ, its constitutionality, so to speak, might be questioned, in the first place; since it was, in spirit at least, repugnant to and subversive of the Mosaic provision in Leviticus cited above. It must not be forgotten that the Mosaic Code was the constitution, the fundamental law of Judaism, by which every Rabbinic interpretation and every legal innovation was to be tested.

Again, such a law would have been no protection to the chief priests and to Judas against the operation of this Mosaic injunction. If such a rule of procedure could be justified upon any ground, it would require disinterested men acting from honorable motives, in promoting the maintenance of law and order. Officers of the law have sometimes, as pretended accomplices, acted in concert with criminals in order to secure and furnish evidence against them. But they were officers of the law, and the courts have held that their evidence was not accomplice testimony requiring corroboration. It is very clear that Judas was not such a disinterested witness, acting in the interest of public justice. He was a fugitive from the Last Supper of his Master, a talebearer within the meaning of the provision in Leviticus; and his employment by the Sanhedrin was a violation of a fundamental provision in the Mosaic Code.

The third illegality in the arrest of Jesus was that His capture was not the result of a legal mandate from a court whose intentions were to conduct a legal trial for the purpose of reaching a righteous judgment. "This arrest," says Rosadi, "effected in the night between Thursday and Friday, the last day of the life of Jesus, on Nisan 14, according to the Hebrew calendar, was the execution of an illegal and factious resolution of the Sanhedrin. There was no idea of apprehending a citizen in order to try him upon a charge which after sincere and regular judgment might be found just or unfounded; the intention was simply to seize a man and do away with him. The arrest was not a preventive measure such as might lawfully precede trial and condemnation; it was an executive act, accomplished in view of a sentence to be pronounced without legal justification."

POINT II

THE PRIVATE EXAMINATION OF JESUS BEFORE ANNAS (OR CAIAPHAS) WAS ILLEGAL

LAW

"Now the Jewish law prohibited *all proceedings by night.*" —DUPIN, "Jesus Devant Caiphe et Pilate."

"Be not a sole judge, for there is no sole judge but One."—MISHNA, Pirke Aboth IV. 8.

"A principle perpetually reproduced in the Hebrew scriptures relates to the two conditions of *publicity* and liberty. An accused man was never subjected to private or secret examination, lest, in his perplexity, he furnished damaging testimony against himself."—SALVADOR, "Institutions de Moise," pp. 365, 366.

FACT AND ARGUMENT

The private examination before Annas (or Caiaphas) was illegal for the following reasons: (1) The examination was conducted at night in violation of Hebrew law; (2) no judge or magistrate, sitting alone, could interrogate an accused judicially or sit in judgment upon his legal rights; (3) private preliminary examinations of accused persons were not allowed by Hebrew law.

The general order of events following the arrest in the garden was this: (1) Jesus was first taken to the house of Annas; (2) after a brief delay He was sent by Annas to Caiaphas, the high priest, in whose palace the Sanhedrin, or a part thereof, had already assembled; (3) He was then brought before this body, tried and condemned; (4) He remained, during the rest of the night, in the high priest's palace, exposed to the insults and outrages of His keepers; and was finally and formally sentenced to death by the Sanhedrin which reconvened at the break of day.

That Jesus was privately examined before His regular trial by the Sanhedrin is quite clear. But whether this preliminary examination took place before Annas or Caiaphas is not certainly known. John alone records the private interrogation of Jesus and he alone refers to Annas in a way to connect him with it. This Evangelist mentions that they "led him away to Annas first."[1] Matthew says that after the arrest of Jesus, they "led him away to Caiaphas the high priest,"[2] without mentioning the name of Annas. Mark tells us that "they led Jesus away to the high priest";[3] but he does not mention either Annas or Caiaphas. Luke records that they "took him, and led him, and brought him into the high priest's house,"[4] without telling us the name of the high priest.

"The high priest then asked Jesus of his disciples and of his doctrine."[5] This was the beginning of the examination. But who was the examiner—Annas or Caiaphas? At first view we are inclined to declare that Caiaphas is meant, because he was undoubtedly high priest in that year. But Annas is also designated as high priest by Luke in several places.[6] In Acts iv. 6 he mentions Caiaphas without an official title, but calls Annas high priest. It is therefore not known to whom John refers when he says that the "high priest asked Jesus of his disciples and of his doctrine." For a lengthy discussion of this point, the reader is referred to Andrew's "Life of Our Lord," pp. 505—510.

But it is absolutely immaterial, from a legal point of view, whether it was Annas or Caiaphas who examined Jesus, as the proceedings would be illegal in either case. For whether it was the one or the other, neither had the right to sit alone as judge; neither had the right to conduct any judicial proceeding at night; neither had the right to institute a secret preliminary examination by day or night.

Attention has been called to the matter as involving a question of historical rather than of legal consequence. A knowledge of the true facts of the case might, however, throw light upon the order and connection of the proceedings which followed the same night. For if the private examination recorded by John was had before Annas, it was doubtless separated by a certain interval of place and time from the later proceedings before Caiaphas. Then it is reasonable to suppose that the examination of witnesses, the confession and condemnation which took place at the regular trial before the Sanhedrin over which Caiaphas presided, happened later in the night, or even toward morning, and were of the nature of a regular public trial. If, on the other hand, Annas sent Jesus without delay to Caiaphas, who examined Him, it is reasonable to conclude that witnesses were at once produced, and that the adjuration and condemnation immediately followed. If such were the case, a considerable interval of time must have intervened between these proceedings and the meeting of the Sanhedrin which was had in the morning to confirm the judgment which had been pronounced at the night session. But these considerations are really foreign to the question of legal errors involved, which we come now to discuss.

In the first place, the private examination of Jesus, whether by Annas or Caiaphas, took place at night; and we have learned from Dupin that *all proceedings at night in capital cases* were forbidden.

In the second place, no judge or magistrate, sitting alone, could interrogate an accused person judicially or sit in judgment upon his legal rights. We have seen in Part II of this volume that the Hebrew system of courts and judges provided no single magistrates who, sitting alone, could adjudicate causes. The lowest Hebrew court consisted of three judges, sometimes called the Court of Three. The next highest tribunal was the Minor Sanhedrin of three-and-twenty members. The supreme tribunal of the Jews was the Great Sanhedrin of seventy-one members. There was no such thing among the ancient Hebrews as a court with a single judge. "Be not a sole judge, for there is no sole judge but One," is one of the most famous aphorisms of the Pirke Aboth. The reason of this rule is founded not only in a religious exaction born of the jealousy of Jehovah, but in the principle of publicity which provides for the accused, in the very number of judges, a public hearing. The same principle is suggested by the number of witnesses required by both the Mishna and Mosaic Code for the conviction of a prisoner. At least "two or three witnesses" were required to appear publicly and give testimony against the accused, else a conviction could not follow.

Again, preliminary examinations of accused persons were not allowed by Hebrew law. In the American states and in some other countries, a man suspected of crime and against whom an information or complaint has been lodged, is frequently taken before and examining magistrate to determine whether he should be discharged, admitted to bail, or sent to prison to await the action of a Grand Jury. At such hearing, the prisoner is usually notified that he is at liberty to make a statement regarding the charge against him; that he need not do so unless he desires; but that if he does, his testimony may be subsequently used against him at the regular trial of the case. But such proceedings, according to Salvador, were forbidden by ancient Hebrew law. The preliminary examination, therefore, by Annas or Caiaphas was illegal. The reason of the rule, as above stated, was to protect the prisoner against furnishing evidence that might be used against him at the regular trial of his case. The private examination of Jesus illustrates the justice of the rule and the necessity of its existence, for it was undoubtedly the purpose of Annas or Caiaphas to gather material in advance to lay before the regularly assembled Sanhedrin and thereby expedite the proceedings at the expense of justice.

If it be contended that the leading of Jesus to Annas first, which St. John alone relates, was merely intended to give the aged Sanhedrist an opportunity to see the prisoner who had been causing such commotion in the land for several years; and that there was no examination of Jesus before Annas—the interrogation by the high priest concerning the disciples and the doctrine of Jesus being construed to refer to an examination by Caiaphas, and being identical with the night trial referred to by Matthew and Mark—reply may be made that, under any construction of the case, there was at least an illegal appearance before Annas, as mere vulgar curiosity to see a celebrated prisoner was no excuse for the violation of the spirit if not the letter of the law. It is inconceivable, however, to suppose that Annas did not actually interrogate Jesus concerning His disciples, His doctrine, and His personal pretensions. To suppose that he demanded to see Jesus for no other reason than to get an impression of His looks, is to insult common sense. If Annas examined the prisoner, though only slightly, concerning matters affecting the charges against Him that might endanger His life or liberty, he had violated a very important rule of Hebrew criminal procedure. The question of the amount of examination of the accused is immaterial.

It is not known whether Annas at this time sat in the Great Sanhedrin as a judge. He had been deposed from the high priesthood nearly twenty years before by the procurator Valerius Gartus, for imposing and executing capital sentences. But he was, nevertheless, still all-powerful in the great Council of the Jews. Edersheim says that though "deprived of the Pontificate, he still continued to preside over the Sanhedrin."[7] Andrews is of the opinion that "he did in fact hold some high official position, and this probably in connection with the Sanhedrin, perhaps as occasional president."[8] Basing his criticism upon the words in Luke, "Annas and Caiaphas being the high priests,"[9] Dr. Plummer believes "that between them they discharged the duties, or that each of them in different senses was regarded high priest, Annas *de jure,* and Caiaphas *de facto.* "[10] This is a mere supposition, however, since there is no historical evidence that Annas was restored to the pontificate after his deposition by Valerius Gratus, A.D. 14.[11] The phrase, "Annas and Caiaphas being high priests," refers to the fifteenth year of the reign of Tiberius Caesar, which was A.D. 26.

After all, it is here again an historical more than a legal question, whether Annas was an official or not at the time of the appearance of Jesus before him. In either case his preliminary examination of the Christ was illegal. If he was a member of the Sanhedrin, the law forbade him to hold an informal preliminary examination at night. He certainly could not do this while sitting alone. If he was not a magistrate, as Dupin very properly contends, this fact only added to the seriousness of the illegality of subjecting a prisoner to the whimsical examination of a private citizen.

Whether a member of the Sanhedrin or not, Annas was at the time of Christ and had been for many years its dominating spirit. He himself had been high priest. Caiaphas was his son-in-law, and was succeeded in the high priesthood by four sons of Annas. The writer does not believe that Annas had any legal connection with the Sanhedrin, but, like many American political bosses, exercised more authority than the man that held the office. He was simply the political tool of the Roman masters of Judea, and the members of the Sanhedrin were simply figureheads under his control.

Again, the private examination of Jesus was marked by an act of brutality which Hebrew jurisprudence did not tolerate. This was not enumerated above as an error, because it was not probably a violation of any specific rule of law. But it was an outrage upon the Hebrew sense of justice and humanity which in its normal state was very pure and lofty.

"The high priest then asked Jesus of his disciples and of his doctrine. Jesus answered him, I spake openly to the world; I ever taught in the Synagogue, and in the Temple, whither the Jew always resort; and in secret have I said nothing. Why askest thou me? ask them which heard me, what I have said unto them: behold, they know what I said." In this reply Jesus planted Himself squarely upon His legal rights as a Jewish citizen. "It was in every word the voice of pure Hebrew justice, founded upon the broad principle of their judicial procedure and recalling an unjust judge to the first duty of his great office."

"And when he had thus spoken, one of the officers which stood by struck Jesus with the palm of his had, saying , Answerest thou the high priest so?" Again the Nazarene appealed for protection to the procedure designed to safeguard the rights of the Hebrew prisoner. "Jesus answered him, If I have spoken evil, bear witness of the evil: but if well, why smitest thou me?"[12]

We have seen that, under Hebrew law, the witnesses were the accusers, and their testimony was at once the indictment and the evidence. We have also seen that a Hebrew prisoner could not be compelled to testify against himself, and that his uncorroborated confession could not be made the basis of a conviction. *"Why askest thou me? ask them that heard me,* what I have said unto them." This was equivalent to asking: Do you demand that I incriminate myself when our law forbids such a thing? Why not call witnesses as the law requires? If I am an evil-doer, bear witness of the evil, that is, let witnesses testify to the wrongdoing, that I may be legally convicted. If I am not guilty of a crime, why am I thus maltreated?

Is it possible to imagine a more pointed and pathetic appeal for justice and for the protection of the law against illegality and brutal treatment? This appeal for the production of legal testimony was not without its effect. Witnesses were soon forthcoming—not truthful witnesses, indeed—but witnesses nevertheless. And with the coming of these witnesses began the formal trial of the Christ, and a formal trial, under Hebrew law, could be commenced only by witnesses.

POINT III

THE INDICTMENT AGAINST JESUS WAS, IN FORM, ILLEGAL

LAW

"The entire criminal procedure of the Mosaic Code rests upon four rules: *certainty in the indictment;* publicity in the discussion; full freedom granted to the accused; and assurance against all dangers or errors of testimony."—SALVADOR, "Institutions de Moise," p. 365.

"The Sanhedrin did not and could not originate charges; it only investigated those brought before it."—EDERSHEIM, "Life and Times of Jesus the Messiah," vol. i. p. 309.

"The evidence of the leading witnesses constituted the charge. There was no other charge: no more formal indictment. Until they spoke, and spoke in the public assembly, the prisoner was scarcely an accused man. When they spoke, and the evidence of the two agreed together, it formed the legal charge, libel, or indictment, as well as the evidence for its truth."—INNES, "The Trial of Jesus Christ," p. 41.

"The only *prosecutors* known to Talmudic criminal jurisprudence are the witnesses to the crime. Their duty is to bring the matter to the cognizance of the court, and to bear witness against the criminal. In capital cases, they are the legal executioners also. Of an official accuser or prosecutor there is nowhere any trace in the laws of the ancient Hebrews."—MENDELSOHN, "The Criminal Jurisprudence of the Ancient Hebrews," p. 110.

FACT AND ARGUMENT

The gospel records disclose two distinct elements of illegality in the indictment against Jesus: (1) The accusation, at the trial, was twofold, vague, and indefinite, which Mosaic law forbade; (2) it was made, in part, by Caiaphas, the high priest, who was one of the judges of Jesus; while Hebrew law forbade any but leading witnesses to present the charge.

A thorough understanding of Point III depends upon keeping clearly in mind certain well-defined elementary principles of law. In the first place, it should be remembered that in most modern jurisdictions an indictment is simply an accusation, carries with it no presumption of guilt, and has no evidentiary force. Its only function is to bring the charge against the prisoner before the court and jury, and to notify the accused of the nature of the accusation against him. But not so under the ancient Hebrew scheme of justice. Under that system there was no such body as the modern Grand Jury, and no committee of the Sanhedrin exercised similar accusatory functions. The leading witnesses, and they alone, presented charges. It follows then, of necessity, that the ancient Hebrew indictment, unlike the modern indictment, carried with it a certain presumption of guilt and had certain evidentiary force. This could not be otherwise, since the testimony of the leading witnesses was at once the indictment and the evidence offered to prove it.

Again, in the very nature of things an indictment should, and under any enlightened system of jurisprudence, does clearly advise the accused of the exact nature of the charge against him. Under no other conditions would it be possible for a prisoner to prepare his defense. Most modern codes have sought to promote clearness and certainty in indictments by requiring the charging of only one crime in one indictment, and in language so clear and simple that the nature of the offense charged may be easily understood.

Now Salvador says that "certainty in the indictment" was one of the cardinal rules upon which rested the entire criminal procedure of the Mosaic Code. Was this rule observed in framing the accusation against Jesus at the night trial before the Sanhedrin? If so, the Gospel records do not disclose the fact. It is very certain, indeed, that the learned of no age of the world since the crucifixion have been able to agree among themselves as to the exact nature of the indictment against the Christ. This subject was too exhaustively discussed in the beginning of the Brief to warrant lengthy treatment here. Suffice it to say that the record of the night trial before Caiaphas discloses two distinct charges: the charge of sedition—the threat to destroy a national institution and to seduce the people from their ancient allegiance, in the matter of the destruction of the Temple; and the charge of blasphemy preferred by Caiaphas himself in the adjuration which he administered to Jesus. When the false witnesses failed to agree, their contradictory testimony was rejected and the charge of sedition was abandoned. And before Jesus had time to answer the question concerning sedition, another distinct charge, that of blasphemy, was made in almost the same breath.[1] Did this procedure tend to promote "certainty in the indictment"? Did it not result in the complete destruction of all clearness and certainty? Are we not justified in supposing that the silence of Jesus in the presence of His accusers was at least partially attributable to His failure to comprehend the exact nature of the charges against Him?

Again, the accusation was, in part, by Caiaphas, the high priest, who was also one of the judges of Jesus;[2] while Hebrew law forbade any but leading witnesses to present the charge. Edersheim tells us that "the Sanhedrin did not and could not originate charges; it only investigated those brought before it." If the Sanhedrin as a whole could not originate charges, because its members were judges, neither could any individual Sanhedrist do so. When the witnesses "agreed not together" in the matter of the charge of sedition, this accusation was abandoned. Caiaphas then deliberately assumed the role of accuser, in violation of the law, and charged Jesus, in the form of an adjuration, with blasphemy, in claiming to be "the Christ, the Son of God." Confession and condemnation then followed. Only leading witnesses could prefer criminal charges under Hebrew law. Caiaphas, being a judge, could not possibly be a witness; and could not, therefore, be an accuser. Therefore, the indictment against Jesus was illegally presented.

The writer believes that the above is a correct interpretation of the nature and number of the charges brought against the Christ, and that the legal aspects of the case are as above stated. But candor and impartiality require consideration of another view. Several excellent writers have contended that there were, in fact, not two charges preferred against Jesus but only one under different forms. These writers contend that Caiaphas and his colleagues understood that Jesus claimed supernatural power and identity with God when He declared that He was *able* to destroy the Temple and to build it again in three days,[3] and that the question of the high priest, "I adjure thee by the living God, that thou tell us whether thou be the Christ, the Son of God," flowed naturally from and had direct reference to the charge of being able to destroy the Temple. The advocates of this view appeal to the language of the original auditors to sustain their contention. "Forty-and-six years was this temple in building, and wilt thou rear it again in three days?" It is insisted that these words convey the idea that those who heard Jesus understood Him to mean that He had supernatural power. There is certainly much force in the contention but it fails to meet other difficulties. In the first place, it is not clear that a threat to destroy the Temple implied a claim to supernatural power; in which case there would be no connection between the first charge and that in which it was suggested that Jesus had claimed to be the Christ, the Son of God. In the second place, the contention that the two charges are substantially the same ignores the language of Mark, "But neither so did their witness agree together,"[4] which was certainly not injected by the author of the second Gospel as a matter of mere caprice or pastime. This language, legally interpreted, means that the testimony of the false witnesses, being contradictory, was thrown aside, and that the charge concerning the destruction of the Temple was abandoned. This is the opinion of Signor Rosadi and is very weighty.

Those writers who maintain that there was only one charge, that of blasphemy, under different forms, rely upon the passage in Matthew, "I am *able* to destroy the temple of God and to build it again in three days," and interpret it as a claim to supernatural power in the light of the language used by those who heard it: "Forty-and-six years was this temple in building, and wilt thou rear it again in three days?" Those who hold the opposite view, that there were two distinct charges, rely upon the passage in Mark, "I *will* destroy this temple that is made with hands, and within three days I will build another made without hands," and interpret it in the light of a similar accusation against Stephen a few months afterwards: "For we have heard him say, that this Jesus of Nazareth *shall destroy this place,* and *shall change the customs* which Moses delivered us."[5] This second interpretation, which we believe to be the better, establishes the existence at the trial of Christ of two distinct charges: that of sedition, based upon a threat to assault existing institutions; and that of blasphemy, founded upon the claim of equality with God. And, in the light of this interpretation, the illegality in the form of the indictment against Jesus has been urged.

If the first construction be the true one, then the error alleged in Point III is not well founded, since the accusation was presented by witnesses, as the law required; unless it could be successfully urged that the witnesses, being *false* witnesses, were no more competent to accuse a prisoner than to convict him upon their false testimony. In such a case the substance as well as the form of the indictment would be worthless, and the whole case would fall, through failure not only of competent testimony to convict but also of a legal indictment under which to prosecute.

Neither the Mishna nor the Gemara mentions written indictments among the ancient Hebrews. "The Jewish Encyclopedia" says that accusations were probably in writing, but that it is not certain.[6] A passage in Salvador seems to indicate that they were in writing. "The papers in the case," he says, "were read, and the accusing witnesses were then called." "The papers" were probably none other than the indictment. But of this we are not sure, and cannot, therefore, predicate the allegation of an error upon it. From the whole context of the Scriptures, however, we are led to believe that only oral charges were preferred against Jesus.

POINT IV

THE PROCEEDINGS OF THE SANHEDRIN AGAINST JESUS WERE ILLEGAL BECAUSE THEY WERE CONDUCTED AT NIGHT

LAW

"Let a capital offence be tried during the day, but suspend it at night."—MISHNA, Sanhedrin IV. 1.

"Criminal cases can be acted upon by the various courts during day time only, by the Lesser Synhedrions from the close of the morning service till noon, and by the Great Synhedrion till evening."—MENDELSOHN, "Criminal Jurisprudence of the Ancient Hebrews," p. 112.

"The reason why the trial of a capital offense could not be held at night is because, as oral tradition says, the examination of such a charge is like the diagnosing of a wound—in either case a more thorough and searching examination can be made by daylight."—MAIMONIDES, Sanhedrin III.

FACT AND ARGUMENT

Hebrew jurisprudence positively forbade the trial of a capital case at night. The infraction of this rule involves the question of jurisdiction. A court without jurisdiction can pronounce no valid verdict or judgment. A court has no jurisdiction if it convenes and acts at a time forbidden by law.

One is naturally disposed to deride the reason assigned by Maimonides for the existence of the law against criminal proceedings at night. But it should not be forgotten that in the olden days surgery had no such aids as are at hand today. Modern surgical apparatus had not been invented and electric lights and the Roentgen Rays were unknown. In the light of this explanation of the great Jewish philosopher the curious inquirer after the real meaning of things naturally asks why the Areopagus of Athens always held its sessions in the night and in the dark.[1]

We have seen that Jesus was arrested in Gethsemane about midnight and that His first ecclesiastical trial took place between two and three o'clock in the morning.[2] St. Luke tells us that there was a daybreak meeting,[3] which was evidently intended to give a semblance of legality and regularity to that rule of Hebrew law that required two trials of the case.

The exact time of the beginning of the night session of the Sanhedrin is not known. It is generally supposed that the arrest took place in the garden between midnight and one o'clock. The journey to the house of Annas must have required some little time. Where this house was located nobody knows. According to one tradition Annas owned a house on the Mount of Olives close to the booths or bazaars under the "Two Cedars." Stapfer believes that Jesus was taken to that place. According to another tradition the house of Annas was located on the

"Hill of Evil Counsel." Barclay believes that this was the place to which Jesus was conducted. But the tradition which is most generally accepted is that which places the palace of Annas on Mount Zion near the palace of Caiaphas. It is believed by many that these two men, who were related, Annas being the father-in-law of Caiaphas, occupied different apartments in the same place. But these question are mere matters of conjecture and have no real bearing upon the present discussion, except to show, in a general way, the length of time probably required to conduct Jesus from Gethsemane to Annas; from Annas to Caiaphas, if the latter was the one who privately examined Jesus; and thence to the meeting of the Sanhedrin. It is reasonable to suppose that at least two hours were thus consumed, which would bring Jesus to the palace of Caiaphas between two and three o'clock, if the arrest in the garden took place between twelve and one o'clock. But here, again, a difference of one or two hours would not affect the merit of the proposition stated in Point IV. For it is beyond dispute that the first trial before the Sanhedrin was had at night, which was forbidden by law.

The question has been frequently asked: Why did the Sanhedrin meet at night in violation of law? The answer to this is referable to the treachery of Judas, to the fact that he "sought opportunity to betray him unto them in the absence of the multitude," and to the thought of the Master: "But this is your hour, and the power of God." Luke tells us that the members of the Sanhedrin "feared the people."[4] Mark informs us that they had resolved not to attempt the arrest and execution of Jesus at the time of the Passover, "lest there be an uproar of the people."[5]

Jesus had taught daily in the Temple, and had furnished ample opportunity for a legal arrest with a view to a legal trial. But His enemies did not desire this. "The chief priests and scribes sought how they might take him by craft, and put him to death."[6] The arrival of Judas from the scene of the Last Supper with a proposition of immediate betrayal of the Christ was a glad surprise to Caiaphas and his friends. Immediate and decisive action was necessary. Not only the arrest but the trial and execution of Jesus must be accomplished with secrecy and dispatch. The greatest festival of the Jews had just commenced. Pilgrims to the feast were arriving from all parts of the Jewish kingdom. The friends and followers of Jesus were among them. His enemies had witnessed the remakable demonstration in His honor which marked His entrance into Jerusalem only a few days before. It is not strange, then, that they "feared the people" in the matter of the summary and illegal proceedings which they had resolved to institute against Him. They knew that the daylight trial, under proper legal forms, with the friends of Jesus as witnesses, would upset their plans by resulting in His acquittal. They resolved, therefore, to act at once, even at the expense of all forms of justice. And it will be seen that this determination to arrest and try Jesus at night, in violation of law, became the parent of nearly every legal outrage that was committed against Him. The selection of the midnight hour for such a purpose resulted not merely in a technical infraction of law, but rendered it impossible to do justice either formally or substantially under rules of Hebrew criminal procedure.

POINT V

THE PROCEEDINGS OF THE SANHEDRIN AGAINST JESUS WERE ILLEGAL BECAUSE THE COURT CONVENED BEFORE THE OFFERING OF THE MORNING SACRIFICE

LAW

"The Sanhedrin sat from the close of the morning sacrifice to the time of the evening sacrifice."—TALMUD, Jerus., Sanhedrin I. fol. 19.

"No session of the court could take place before the offering of the morning sacrifice."—MM. LeMANN, "Jesus Before the Sanhedrin," p. 109.

"Since the morning sacrifice was offered at the dawn of day, it was hardly possible for the Sanhedrin to assemble until the hour after that time."—MISHNA, "Tamid, or of the Perpetual Sacrifice," C. III.

FACT AND ARGUMENT

The fact that the Sanhedrin convened before the offering of the morning sacrifice constitutes the fifth illegality. This error is alleged upon the authority of MM. Lemann, who, in their admirable little work entitled "Jesus Before the Sanhedrin," have called attention to it. It is very difficult, however, to determine whether this was a mere irregularity, or was what modern jurists would call a material error. From one point of view it seems to be merely a repetition of the rule forbidding the Sanhedrin to meet at night. The morning sacrifice was offered at the break of day and lasted about an hour. A session of the court before the morning sacrifice would, therefore, have been a meeting at night, which would have been an infringement of the law. But this was probably not the real reason of the rule. Its true meaning is doubtless to be found in the close connection that existed between the Hebrew law and the Hebrew religion. The constitution of the Hebrew Commonwealth was an emanation of the mind of Jehovah, the Temple in which the court met was His residence on earth, and the judges who formed the Great Sanhedrin were the administrators of His will. It is most reasonable, then, to suppose that an invocation, in sacrifice and prayer, of His guidance and authority would be the first step in any judicial proceedings conducted in His name.

It is historically true that a session of the Sanhedrin in the palmiest days of the Jewish Commonwealth was characterized by all the religious solemnity of a service in the synagogue or the Temple. It is entirely probable, therefore, that the morning sacrifice was made by law an indispensable prerequisite to the assembling of the supreme tribunal of the Jews for the transaction of any serious business. On any other supposition the rules of law cited above would have no meaning. We have reason to believe, then, that the offering of the morning sacrifice was a condition precedent to the attachment of jurisdiction, and without jurisdiction the court had no authority to act. That the morning sacrifice was offered each day, whether the court assembled or not, as a religious requirement, does not alter the principle of law above enunciated.

But it may be asked: How do we know that the morning sacrifice was not offered? The answer is that the whole context of the Scriptures relating to the trial shows that it could not have been offered. Furthermore, a simple and specific reason is that the time prescribed by law for conducting the morning service was between the dawn of day and sunrise. Then, if the court convened between two and three o'clock in the morning, it is very certain that the sacrifice had not been offered. It is true that there was a morning session of the Sanhedrin. But this was held simply to confirm the action of the night session at which Jesus had been condemned. In other words, the real trial was at night and was held before the performance of the religious ceremony, which was, in all probability, a prerequisite to the attachment of jurisdiction.

POINT VI

THE PROCEEDINGS AGAINST JESUS WERE ILLEGAL BECAUSE THEY WERE CONDUCTED ON THE DAY PRECEDING A JEWISH SABBATH; ALSO ON THE FIRST DAY OF THE FEAST OF UNLEAVENED BREAD AND THE EVE OF THE PASSOVER

LAW

"Court must not be held on the Sabbath, or any holy day."—"Betza, or of the Egg," Chap. V. No. 2.

"They shall not judge on the eve of the Sabbath, nor on that of any festival."—MISHNA, Sanhedrin IV. 1.

"No court of justice in Israel was permitted to hold sessions on the Sabbath or any of the seven Biblical holidays. In cases of capital crime, no trial could be commenced on Friday or the day previous to any holiday, because it was not lawful either to adjourn such cases longer than over night, or to continue them on the Sabbath or holiday."—RABBI WISE, "Martyrdom of Jesus," p. 67.

FACT AND ARGUMENT

No Hebrew court could lawfully meet on a Sabbath or a feast day, or on a day preceding a Sabbath or a feast day.

Concerning the Sabbath day provision Maimonides offers the following reason for the rule: "As it is required to execute the criminal immediately after the passing of the sentence, it would sometimes happen that the kindling of a fire would be necessary, as in the case of one condemned to be burned; and this act would be a violation of the law of the Sabbath, for it is written, 'Ye shall kindle no fire in your habitations on the Sabbath day.' "[1] (Exodus XXXV. 3.)

Under modern practice, sessions of court may be adjourned from day to day, or, if need be, from week to week. But under the Hebrew system of criminal procedure the court could not adjourn for a longer time than a single night. Its proceedings were, so to speak, continuous until final judgment. As the law forbade sessions of court on Sabbath and feast days, it became necessary to provide that courts should not convene on the day preceding a Sabbath or a feast day, in order to avoid either an illegal adjournment or an infringement of the rule relating to the Sabbath and feast days.

Now Jesus was tried by the Sanhedrin on both a feast day and a day preceding the Sabbath. And, at this point, a clear conception of the ancient Jewish mode of reckoning time should be had. The Jewish day of twenty-four hours began at one sunset and ended with the next. But this interval was not divided into twenty-four parts or hours of equal and invariable length. Their day proper was an integral part of time and was reckoned from sunrise to sunset. Their night proper was likewise a distinct division of time and was measured from sunset to sunrise. An hour of time, according to modern reckoning, is invariably sixty minutes. But the ancient Jewish hour was not a fixed measure of time. It varied in length as each successive day and night varied in theirs at different seasons of the year. Neither did the Jews begin their days and nights as we do. Our day of twenty-four hours always begins at midnight. Their day of twenty-four hours always began at one sunset and ended with the next.

Now Jesus was tried by the Sanhedrin on the 14th Nisan, according to the Jewish calendar; or between the evening of Thursday, April 6th, and the afternoon of Friday, April 7th, A.D. 30, according to our calendar. The 14th Nisan began on sunset on April 6th and lasted until sunset on April 7th. This was a single Jewish day, and within this time Jesus was tried and executed. According to our calendar, the trial and execution of Jesus took place on Friday, April 7th. This was the day preceding the Jewish Sabbath, which came on Saturday, according to our reckoning. And on a day preceding the Sabbath no Jewish court could lawfully convene. This is the first error suggested under Point VI.

Again, it is beyond dispute that the Feast of Unleavened Bread had begun and that the Passover was at hand when Jesus was tried by the Sanhedrin.[2] This was in violation of a specific provision of Hebrew law, and constitutes the second error alleged under Point VI.

There seems to be some conflict among the authorities as to whether Jesus was tried on the first day of the celebration of the feast of the Passover or on the day preceding. But the question is immaterial from a legal point of view, as the law forbade a trial either on a feast day or on the day preceding, for reasons above stated.

This violation of the law relating to the Sabbaths and feast days, like that relating to night sessions of the Sanhedrin, resulted in still other errors. It is necessary to mention only one of these at this point. The proceedings of the Sanhedrin were recorded by two scribes or clerks. Their records were to be used on the second day of the trial in reviewing the proceedings of the first. But Hebrew law forbade any writing on a Sabbath or a holy day. How was it possible, then, to keep a record of the proceedings, if Jesus was tried on a Sabbath and also on a feast day, without violating a rule of law? If no minutes of the meeting were kept, a most glaring irregularity is apparent.

POINT VII

THE TRIAL OF JESUS WAS ILLEGAL BECAUSE IT WAS CONCLUDED WITHIN ONE DAY

LAW

"A criminal case resulting in the acquittal of the accused may terminate the same day on which the trial began. But if a sentence of death is to be pronounced, it can not be concluded before the following day."—MISHNA, Sanhedrin IV. 1.

FACT AND ARGUMENT

Care and conservatism, precaution and delay, were the characteristic features of the criminal procedure of the ancient Hebrews. The principal aphorism of the Pirke Aboth is this: *"Be cautious and slow in judgment,* send forth many disciples, and *make a fence around the law."*[1] The length and seriousness of their deliberations in criminal proceedings of a capital nature were due to their supreme regard for human life. "Man's life belongs to God, and only according to the law of God may it be disposed of." "Whosoever preserves one worthy life is as meritorious as if he had preserved the world." These and similar maxims guided and controlled Hebrew judges in every capital trial. Their horror of death as the result of a judicial decree is shown by the celebrated saying: "The Sanhedrin which so often as once in seven years condemns a man to death, is a slaughter-house."[2]

To assure due deliberation and reflection in a case where a human life was at stake, Hebrew law required that the trial should last at least two days, in case of the conviction of the accused. In case of an acquittal the trial might terminate within a single day. Before condemnation could be finally decreed a night had to intervene, during which time the judges could sleep, fast, meditate, and pray. At the close of the first day's trial they left the judgment hall and walked homeward, arm in arm, discussing the merits of the case. At sunset they began to make calls upon each other, again reviewing among themselves the facts in evidence. They then retired to their homes for further mediation. During the intervening night they abstained from eating heavy food and from drinking wine. They carefully avoided doing anything that would incapacitate them for correct thinking. On the following day they returned to the judgment hall and retried the case. The second trial was in the nature of a review and was intended to detect errors, if there were any, in the first trial.[3] It was not until the afternoon of this day that a final decree could be made and that a capital sentence could follow.

Now the Gospel record very clearly discloses the fact that Jesus was arrested, tried, and executed within the limits of a single day. Neither the exact hour of His arrest, nor of His trial, nor of His execution is known. But is it positively certain that all took place between sunset, the beginning of Nisan 14, and sunset, the beginning of Nisan 15. This was the interval of a single Jewish day, Nisan 14.

And within such an interval of time it was illegal to finally condemn a man to death under Hebrew law. Even Stapfer, who contends that the trial was legal and that forms of law were generally observed, admits this error. He asserts that the precipitate conduct of the members of the Sanhedrin was not only opposed to the spirit of Hebrew conservatism in the matter of criminal procedure but was a breach of a specific provision of the criminal code.[4]

It is true that there were two distinct trials: one between 2 and 3 A.M., Friday, April 7th, which is recorded by Matthew[5] and Mark,[6] and a second about daybreak of the same day, recorded by Matthew,[7] Mark,[8] and Luke.[9] But both these trials were had within one day—indeed, within six hours of each other. The judges did not try the case and then retire to their homes for sleep, prayer, and meditation until the following day, as the law required. Even if they had done so, they would not have avoided an illegal procedure, inasmuch as the trial had been illegally begun on a feast day and the eve of the Sabbath, and it would have been impossible to avoid the error alleged in Point VII. For if they had deferred the sentencing and execution of Jesus until the following day it would still have been illegal, since the next day was both a Sabbath and a holy day (the Passover).

Several writers who contend that there was a regular trial of Jesus assert that the morning meeting of the Sanhedrin was intended to give a semblance of legality and regularity to that rule of Hebrew law which required at least two trials. But it will readily be seen that this was a subterfuge and evasion, since both trials were had on the same day, whereas the law required them to be held on different days.

POINT VIII

THE SENTENCE OF CONDEMNATION PRONOUNCED AGAINST JESUS BY THE SANHEDRIN WAS ILLEGAL BECAUSE IT WAS FOUNDED UPON HIS UNCORROBORATED CONFESSION

LAW

"We have it as a fundamental principle of our jurisprudence that no one can bring an accusation against himself. Should a man make confession of guilt before a legally constituted tribunal, such confession is not to be used against him unless properly attested by two other witnesses."—MAIMONIDES, Sanhedrin IV. 2.

"Not only is self-condemnation never extorted from the defendant by means of torture, but no attempt is ever made to lead him on to self-incrimination. Moreover, a voluntary confession on his part is not admitted in evidence, and therefore not competent to convict him, unless a legal number of witnesses minutely corroborate his self-accusation."—MENDELSOHN, "Criminal Jurisprudence of the Ancient Hebrews," p. 133.

FACT AND ARGUMENT

More than one system of jurisprudence has refused to permit a conviction for crime to rest upon an uncorroborated confession. But it remained for the ancient Hebrews to discover the peculiar reason for the rule, that the witness who confessed was "his own relative"; and relatives were not competent witnesses under Hebrew law. Modern Jewish writers, however, have assigned other reasons for the rule. Rabbi Wise says: "Self-accusation in cases of capital crime was worthless. For it not guilty he accuses himself of a falsehood; if guilty he is a wicked man, and no wicked man, according to Hebrew law, is permitted to testify, especially not in penal cases.∎ [1] Mendelsohn says that "the reason assigned for this enactment is the wish to avoid the possibility of permitting judicial homicide on self-accusing lunatics, or on persons who, in desperation, wish to cut short their earthly existence, and to effect this falsely accuse themselves of some capital crime."[2]

Modern jurists have assigned still other reasons for the rule as it has existed in modern law.[3] Men have been known to confess that they were guilty of one crime to avoid punishment for another. Morbid and vulgar sentimentality, such as love of newspaper notoriety, have induced persons of inferior intelligence, who were innocent, to assume responsibility for criminal acts.

But whatever the reason of the rule, Jesus was condemned to death upon His uncorroborated confession, in violation of Hebrew law.

"For many bare false witness against him, but their witness agreed not together. And there arose certain, and bare false witness against him, saying, We heard him say, I will destroy this temple that is made with hands, and within three days I will build another made without hands. But neither so did their witness agree together. And the high priest stood up in the midst, and asked Jesus, saying, Answerest thou nothing? what is it which these witness against thee? But he held his peace, and answered nothing. Again the high priest asked him, and said unto him, Art thou the Christ, the Son of the Blessed? An Jesus said, I am: and ye shall see the Son of Man sitting on the right hand of power, and coming in the clouds of Heaven. Then the high priest rent his clothes, and saith, What need we any further witnesses? ye have heard the blasphemy: what think ye? And they all condemned him to be guilty of death. And some began to spit on him, and to cover his face, and to buffet him, and to say unto him, Prophesy."[4]

It will be seen from a perusal of this report of the trial that it was sought to condemn Jesus first on the charge of sedition, that is, that He had threatened the destruction of the Temple and thereby endeavored to seduce the people from their national allegiance. "But their witness agreed not together"; and under Hebrew law they were required to reject contradictory testimony and discharge the prisoner, if the state was unable to prove its case. This is what should have been done at this point in the trial of Jesus. But, instead, the judges, in their total disregard of law, turned to the accused and said: "Answerest thou nothing? what is it which these witness against thee?" "But he held his peace, and answered nothing." By remaining silent, Jesus only exercised the ordinary privilege of a Jewish prisoner to refuse to incriminate himself. The modern rule that the accused cannot be made to testify against himself, unless he first voluntarily takes the witness stand in his own behalf, was substantially true among the ancient Hebrews. But here we find Caiaphas insisting that Jesus incriminate Himself. And he continues to insist in the matter of the second charge, that of blasphemy. "And the high priest asked him, and said unto him, Art thou the Christ, the Son of the Blessed?" That question was illegal, because it involved an irregular mode of criminal procedure, and because it asked for a confession of guilt to be made the basis of a conviction. The false witnesses had failed to agree and had evidently been rejected and dismissed. The judges were then without witnesses to formulate a charge and furnish proof of its truth. They were thus forced to the despicable and illegal method of asking the accused to condemn Himself, when they knew that no confession could be made the basis of a conviction. They were also guilty of the illegality of formulating a charge without witnesses. We have seen that only leading witnesses could present an indictment, but here the judges became the accusers, in violation of law.

In answer to the high priest's question, Jesus, feeling that He could not afford at such an hour and in such a place to conceal His Messiahship, answered boldly and emphatically: "I am."[5] "And they all condemned him to be guilty of death." It will thus be seen that upon his own confession and not upon the testimony of at least two competent witnesses agreeing in all essential details, as the law required, was the Nazarene condemned to death.

If it be argued, as it had been, that the two charges of threatening to destroy the

Temple and of pretending to be the "Christ, the Son of God," were in fact but different phases of the same charge of blasphemy, and that the two witnesses were the corroborators of the confession of Jesus, then reply must be made that the witnesses were not competent, being false witnesses, nor was their testimony legally corroborated, because it was false and contradictory.

Again, it was the rule of Hebrew law that both witnesses had to testify to all the essential elements of a complete crime. One could not furnish one link, and another another link, in order to construct a chain of evidence. Each had to testify to all the essential elements necessary to constitute the legal definition of a crime. But the false witnesses did not do this. Under any view of the case, then, the testimony of these witnesses was wholly worthless, and the confession of Jesus was the solitary and illegal basis of His conviction.

The failure of the Sanhedrin to secure sufficient and competent evidence to convict Jesus must not be regarded as accidental, or as attributable to the hour and to the surroundings. The popularity of the Nazarene, outside the narrow circle of the Temple authorities, was immense. The friendship of Nicodemus and Joseph of Arimathea is proof that He had standing even in the Sanhedrin itself. It was therefore difficult to find witnesses who were willing to testify against Him. Besides, the acts of His ministry, while in no sense cowardly or hypocritical, had been, in general, very cautious and diplomatic. He seems to have retired, at times, into the desert or the wilderness to avoid disagreeable and even dangerous complications with the civil and ecclesiastical authorities.[6] Jesus was in no sense a politician, but He was not lacking in mother wit and practical resources. He saw through the designs of Herod Antipas, who wished to get Him out of his dominions. It will be remembered that certain Pharisees, pretending friendship for Him, warned Him to flee from Galilee to avoid being killed by Herod. The courage and manliness of Jesus are shown by the fact that He remained in His native province, and even sent a contemptuous message to the Tetrarch, whom He styled "that fox."[7]

At other times, Christ was compelled to defend Himself against the swarm of spies that hovered over His pathway through Samaria, along the Jordan, and around the Sea of Galilee. In His discussions with His enemies who sought to entrap Him, He displayed consummate skill in debate. His pithy sayings and incomparable illustrations usually left His questioners defenseless and chagrined. Oftentimes in these encounters He proclaimed eternal and universal truths which other nations and later ages were to develop and enjoy. When, holding in His hand a penny with Caesar's image upon it, He said, "Render therefore unto Caesar the things which are Caesar's, and unto God the things that are God's" he foretold and stamped with approval the immortal principle that was to be embodied in the American constitution and to remain the cornerstone of the American Commonwealth; a truth repeated by Roger Williams when in the forests of Rhode Island he declared that the magistrate should rule in civil matters only and that man was answerable for his religious faith to God alone. This declaration of the Nazarene is the spiritual and intellectual basis of the sublime doctrine of civil liberty and religious freedom that finds its highest expression in that separation of the Church and State which enables men of different creeds and different parties to live side by side as patriots and religionists and as comrades, though antagonists.

The replies of Jesus to those who came to "entangle him in his talk" usually left them disconcerted and defeated, and little disposed to renew their attacks upon Him.[8] The efforts of the Pharisees to entrap Him seem to have resulted in failure everywhere and at all times. And at the trial the Sanhedrin found itself in possession of a prisoner but with no competent evidence to establish His guilt. It was least of all prepared to convict Him of the crime of blasphemy as founded upon the claim of Messiahship, for Jesus had been exceedingly cautious, during His ministry, in declaring Himself to be the Messiah. Except in the presence of the woman of Samaria, who came to draw water from the well, there is no recorded instance of an avowal of His Messiahsip outside the immediate circle of the disciples.[9] He forbade the devils whom He had cast out, and that recognized Him, to proclaim His Messiahship.[10] When the Jews said to Him, "How long dost thou make us doubt? if thou be the Christ, tell us plainly," Jesus simply referred them to His works, and made no further answer that could be used as testimony against Him.[11] He revealed Himself to His followers as the Messiah, and permitted them to confess Him as such, but forbade them to make the matter public. "Then charged he his disciples that they should tell no man that he was Jesus, the Christ."[12]

It will thus be seen that probably no two witnesses who were legally competent to testify could have been secured to condemn Jesus upon the charge preferred at the trial. In their desperation, then, the members of the Sanhedrin were compelled to employ false testimony and a confession which was equally illegal.

POINT IX

THE CONDEMNATION OF JESUS WAS ILLEGAL BECAUSE THE VERDICT OF THE SANHEDRIN WAS UNANIMOUS

LAW

"A simultaneous and unanimous verdict of guilt rendered on the day of the trial has the effect of an acquittal."—MENDELSOHN, "Criminal Jurisprudence of the Ancient Hebrews," p. 141.

"If none of the judges defend the culprit, i. e., all pronounce him guilty, having no defender in the court, the verdict of guilty was invalid and the sentence of death could not be executed."—RABBI WISE, "Martyrdom of Jesus," p. 74.

FACT AND ARGUMENT

Few stranger rules can be found in the jurisprudence of the world than that provision of Hebrew law which forbade a conviction to rest upon the unanimous vote of the judges. A comparison instantaneously and almost inevitably arises in the mind between the Saxon and Hebrew requirement in the matter of unanimity in the verdict. The finest form of mind of antiquity, with the possible exception of the Greek and Roman, was the Hebrew. One of the finest types of intellect of the modern world is that of the Anglo-Saxon. The Hebrew organized the Sanhedrin, and, under God, endowed it with judicial and spiritual attributes. The Anglo-Saxon, on the shores of the German Ocean, originated the modern jury and invested it with its distinctive legal traits. With the Anglo-Saxon jury a unanimous verdict is necessary to convict, but with the Hebrew Sanhedrin unanimity was fatal, and resulted in an acquittal. A great modern writer[1] has declared that law is the perfection of reason. But when we contemplate the differences in Hebrew and Saxon laws we are inclined to ask, in seeking the degree of perfection, whose law and whose reason?

But, after all, the Jewish rule is not so unreasonable as it first appears, when we come to consider the reason of its origin. In the first place, as we have seen in Part II, there were no lawyers or advocates, in the modern sense, among the ancient Hebrews. The judges were his defenders. Now if the verdict was unanimous in favor of condemnation it was evident that the prisoner had no friend or defender in court. To the Jewish mind this was almost equivalent to mob violence. It argued conspiracy, at least. The element of mercy, which was required to enter into every Hebrew verdict, was absent in such a case.

Again, this rule of unanimity was only another form or statement of the requirement that the court defer final action, in case of conviction, to the next day in order that time for deliberation and reflection might intervene. In other words, Hebrew law forbade precipitancy in capital proceedings. And what could be more precipitate than an instantaneous and unanimous verdict? "But where all suddenly agree on conviction, does it not seem," asks a modern Jewish writer, "that the convict is a victim of conspiracy and that the verdict is not the result of sober reason and calm deliberation?"

But how did they convict under Hebrew law? By a majority vote of at least two. A majority of one would acquit. A majority of two, or any majority less than unanimity, would convict.[2] If the accused had one friend in court, the verdict of condemnation would stand, since the element of mercy was present and the spirit of conspiracy or mob violence was absent. Seventy-one constituted the membership of the Great Sanhedrin. If all the members were present and voted, at least thirty-seven were required to convict. Thirty-six would acquit. If a bare quorum, twenty-three members, was present, at least thirteen were required to convict. Twelve would acquit.

This rule seem ridiculous and absurd, when viewed in the light of a brutal and undeniable crime. If the facts constituting such a crime had been proved against a Jewish prisoner beyond any possibility of doubt, if such facts were apparent to everybody, still it seems that the rule above stated required that the defendant have at least one advocate and one vote among the judges; else, the verdict was invalid and could not stand. Such a procedure could be justified on no other ground than that exceptional cases should not be permitted to destroy a rule of action that in its general operation had been found to be both generous and just.

Now the condemnation of Jesus was illegal because the verdict of the Sanhedrin was unanimous. We learn this from Mark, who says: "Then the high priest rent his clothes and saith, What need we any further witnesses? ye have heard the blasphemy: what think ye? And they *all* condemned him to be guilty of death."[3] If they *all* condemned Him, the verdict was unanimous and therefore illegal. The other Evangelists do not tell us that the verdict was unanimous; neither do they deny it. Mark's testimony stands alone and uncontradicted; therefore we must assume that it is true.

Rabbi Wise[4] and Signor Rosadi[5] call attention to the fact that the verdict was unanimous. The former seeks to ridicule Mark as an authority because a unanimous verdict was illegal under Hebrew law, and the distinguished Hebrew writer does not conceive that Hebrew judges could have made such a mistake. Such argument, reduced to ultimate analysis, means, according to Rabbi Wise, that there were certain rules of Hebrew law that could not be and were never violated.

In this connection, it has been frequently asked: Was the entire Sanhedrin present at the night trial of Jesus? Were Nicodemus and Joseph of Arimathea present? If they were present, did they vote against Jesus? These questions can be answered only in the light of the authorities. Only two of the Gospel writers, Matthew and Mark, tell us of the night trial. Both declare that "all the council" were present.[6] The "council" (concilium) is the Vulgate, the Latin New Testament designation of the Great Sanhedrin. Then, if all the "council" were present, the Great Sanhedrin were all present.

Concerning the number of judges at the second or daybreak meeting of the Sanhedrin, both Matthew and Mark again declare that the full membership was present. Matthew says: "When the morning was come *all* the chief priests and elders of the people took counsel against Jesus to put him to death."[7] Mark says: "And straightway in the morning the chief priests held a consultation with the elders and scribes and the *whole council,* and bound Jesus, and carried him away, and delivered him to Pilate."[8] It should be remembered that neither Luke nor John contradicts even remotely the statements of Matthew and Mark concerning the full attendance of the members of the Sanhedrin at either the night or morning trial. The first and second Gospel writers therefore corroborate each other, and the presumption of the law is that each told the truth.

And yet most commentators and writers seem to be of the opinion that all the members of the Sanhedrin were not present at the night trial of Jesus. They insist that both Matthew and Mark were employing a figure of speech, synecdoche, when they said that "all the council" were present. But these same writers seem to think that these same Evangelists were in earnest and speaking literally when they declared that *"all* the chief priests and elders" and the *"whole* council" were present at the morning trial. We shall not attempt to settle the question but will leave it to the reader to draw his own inferences. Suffice it to say that as far as the rule stated in connection with Point IX is concerned, it was immaterial whether the full council was present at either meeting. The rule against unanimity applied to a bare quorum or to any number less than the full Sanhedrin. It was the unanimity itself, of however few members, that carried with it the spirit and suggestion of mob violence and conspiracy against which Hebrew law protested.

The question of the number of members that were present at the different meetings of the Sanhedrin has been discussed in the light of history, and as bearing upon the conduct of Nicodemus and Joseph of Arimathea, who were friends of Jesus. Nicodemus was certainly a member of the Great Sanhedrin. This we learn from two passages of New Testament scripture.[9] It is also believed that Joseph of Arimathea was a member from a mere suggestion in another passage.[10] Did these friends of the Christ vote against Him? If they were members of the court; if Matthew and Mark wrote literally when they said that "all the council" were present; and if Mark wrote literally and truthfully when he said that "they *all* condemned him to be guilty of death"; then it naturally and inevitably follows that both Nicodemus and Joseph voted against Jesus.

A number of arguments have been offered against this contention. In the first place, it is said that at a previous meeting of the Sanhedrin Nicodemus defended Jesus by asking his fellow-judges this question: "Doth our law judge any man before it hear him and know what he doeth?"[11] It is asserted that there is no good reason to believe that Nicodemus defended Jesus at this meeting and turned against Him at a subsequent one, that there is a presumption of a continuance of fidelity. But is this good reasoning? Did not Peter cut off the ear of the high priest's servant, Malchus, in defense of Jesus at midnight, in the garden, and then within three hours afterwards deny that he knew Jesus? There is no good reason to believe that Nicodemus was braver or more constant than Peter, for the former seems to have been either ashamed or afraid to express his affection for the

Master during the daytime, but preferred to do it at night.[12]

Concerning the part taken by Nicodemus in the final proceedings, Rosadi says: "The verdict was unanimous. The members of the Sanhedrin who were secretly favorable to the Accused were either absent or else they voted against him. Nicodemus was amongst the absentees, or amongst those that voted against him. At all events, he did not raise his voice against the pronouncement expressed by acclamation."

If Joseph of Arimathea was a member of the Great Sanhedrin, it seems that he "had not consented to the counsel and the deed of them."[13] But it is impossible to tell certainly to which one of the three meetings of the Sanhedrin, held within the six months preceding the crucifixion, this language refers. The defense of Jesus offered by Nicodemus was certainly not at the final meeting which condemned Jesus. It may be that the reference to the protest of Joseph of Arimathea also referred to a prior meeting. Its connection in Luke seems to make it refer to the last trial, but this is not certain. Neither is it certain that Joseph was a member of the Great Sanhedrin, and his failure to consent if he were not a member, would not disturb the contention made in Point IX of the Brief. Even if he were a member, his failure to consent would not destroy the contention, since ancient Hebrew judges, like modern American jurors, could have first protested against their action and then have voted with them. The polling of the jury, under modern law, has reference, among other things, to this state of affairs.

But we may admit that both Nicodemus and Joseph of Arimathea, as well as many others, were absent, as Rosadi suggests, and still contend that the verdict against Jesus was illegal because it was unanimous, as Mark assures us, since the number of judges present was immaterial, provided there was a quorum of at least twenty-three and their verdict was unanimous against the accused. According to the second Gospel writer, there seems to be no doubt that this was the case in the judgment pronounced against Jesus.

POINT X

THE PROCEEDINGS AGAINST JESUS WERE ILLEGAL IN THAT: (1) THE SENTENCE OF CONDEMNATION WAS PRONOUNCED IN A PLACE FORBIDDEN BY LAW; (2) THE HIGH PRIEST RENT HIS CLOTHES; (3) THE BALLOTING WAS IRREGUALR

LAW

"After leaving the hall Gazith no sentence of death can be passed upon anyone soever."—TALMUD, Bab., Abodah Zarah, or of Idolatry, Chap. I. fol. 8.

"A sentence of death can be pronounced only so long as the Sanhedrin holds it sessions in the appointed place."—MAIMONIDES, Sanhedrin XIV.

"And he that is the high priest among his brethren, upon whose head the anointing oil was poured, and that is consecrated to put on the garments, shall not uncover his head, nor rend his clothes."—LEVITICUS xxi. 10.

"And Moses said unto Aaron, and unto Eleazar, and unto Ithamar, his sons, Uncover not your heads, neither rend your clothes; lest ye die, and lest wrath come upon all the people."—LEVITICUS x. 6.

"Let the judges each in his turn absolve or condemn."—MISHNA, Sanhedrin XV. 5.

"The members of the Sanhedrin were seated in the form of a semicircle at the extremity of which a secretary was placed, whose business it was to record the votes. One of these secretaries recorded the votes in favor of the accused, the other those against him."—MISHNA, Sanhedrin IV. 3.

"In ordinary cases the judges voted according to seniority, the oldest commencing; in a capital trial, the reverse order was followed. That the younger members of the Sanhedrin should not be influenced by the views or arguments of their more mature, more experienced colleagues, the junior judge was in these cases always the first to pronounce for or against a conviction."—BENNY, "Criminal Code of the Jews," pp. 73, 74.

FACT AND ARGUMENT

In the trial of capital cases, the Great Sanhedrin was required to meet in an apartment of the National Temple at Jerusalem, known as the Hall of Hewn Stones (Lishkhath haggazith). Outside of this hall no capital trial could be conducted and no capital sentence could be pronounced.[1] This place was selected in obedience to Mosaic injunction: "Thou shalt do according to the tenor of the sentence, which they may point out to thee *from the place which the Lord shall choose.*"[2] The Rabbis argued that the Great Council could not try a capital case or pronounce a death sentence, unless it met and remained in the place chosen by God, which, they contended, should be an apartment of the Great Temple. The Lishkhath haggazith was chosen, and continued for many years to be the meeting place of the supreme tribunal.

But Jesus was not tried or condemned to death in the Hall of Hewn stones, as Hebrew law required. It is clearly evident, from the Gospels, that He was tried and sentenced in the palace of Caiaphas, probably on Mount Zion. It is contended by the Jews, however, that soon after the Roman conquest of Judea the Great Sanhedrin removed from the sacred place to Bethany, and from there to other places, as occasion required. And there is a Jewish tradition that the court returned to accustomed place on the trial and condemnation of Jesus.[3]

In opposition to this, Edersheim says: "There is truly not a tittle of evidence for the assumption of commentators that Christ was led from the palace of Caiaphas into the Council Chamber (Lishkhath haggazith). The whole proceedings took place in the former, and from it Christ was brought to Pilate."[4] St. John emphatically declares: "Then led they Jesus from Caiaphas into the hall of judgment."[5] This Hall of Judgment was the Praetorium of Pilate.

The first irregularity, then, noted under Point X is that Jesus was tried and condemned in the palace of Caiaphas instead of the Hall of Hewn Stones, the regular legal meeting place of the Great Sanhedrin.

The second error noted under Point X is that which relates to the rending of garments by the high priest. "An ordinary Israelite could, as an emblem of bereavement, tear his garments, but to the high priest it was forbidden, because his vestments, being made after the express orders of God, were figurative of his office."[6]

When Jesus confessed that He was Christ the Son of God, Caiaphas seems to have lost his balance and to have committed errors with all the rapidity of speech. "Then the high priest rent his clothes, and saith, What need we any further witnesses? ye have heard the blasphemy: what think ye? And they all condemned him to be guilty of death."[7] In this language and conduct of the son-in-law of Annas there were several irregularities in procedure. The first was the rending of garments reported by Matthew and Mark, which act was forbidden by the provisions of the Mosaic Code, recorded in Leviticus and cited above.

But it is only fair to state the dissenting opinion on this point. In the times of Christ it seems to have been the custom among the Jews to rend the garments as a sign of horror and execration, whenever blasphemous language was heard. Edersheim states the rule: "They all heard it—and, as the law directed, when blasphemy was spoken, the high priest rent both his outer and inner garment, with a rent that might never be repaired.[8] The law here referred to, however, is the Rabbinic or Talmudic and not the Mosaic law. It should be remembered that the Mosaic Code was the constitution or fundamental law of the ancient Hebrews. The Talmudic law embodied in the Mishna was, in a sense, a mere commentary upon the Mosaic law. We have seen in Chapter I of Part II of this volume that the traditional law was based upon, derived from, and inspired by the written law contained in the Pentateuch. It is true that the Talmud, while professing subordination to the Pentateuch, finally virtually superseded it as an administrative code. But the doctors never repealed a Mosaic injunction, since it was an emanation of the mind of Jehovah and could not be abrogated by human intelligence. When an ancient ordinance ceased to be of practical value the Jewish legists simply declared that it had fallen into desuetude. And whenever a new law was proclaimed to meet an emergency in the life of the Hebrew people the Rabbins declared that it was derived from and inspired by some decree which God had handed down to Moses for the benefit of the nation. In other words, the Mosaic Code was Israel's divine constitution which was to serve as a standard for all future legislation. And as the Jewish lawmakers were not permitted to repeal a Mosaic ordinance, neither were they allowed to establish a rule in contravention of it. Now the Pentateuch forbade the rending of garments. Then did the Talmudists have a right to declare that the law might be changed or broken in the case of blasphemy? That they did is denied by many writers.

But admitting the validity of the Talmudic rule, it is nevertheless beyond dispute that the high priest was forbidden to rend his clothes on Sabbaths and holidays. And as Jesus was condemned on both a Sabbath and a festival day, the high priest's action in rending his clothes on that day was illegal.[9]

Again, the proceedings against Jesus were illegal because the balloting was irregular. This is the third error noted under Point X.

The Hebrew law required that each judge, when his time came to vote upon the guilt or innocence of the accused, should rise in his place, declare his vote, and state his reasons for so voting. In capital cases the youngest judge was required to vote first, in order that he might not be unduly influenced by the example of his seniors in age and authority. The balloting continued in this manner from the youngest member to the high priest, who was generally among the oldest. Two scribes—according to some writers, three—were present to record the votes and to note the reasons stated. These records were to be used on the second day of the trial in comparing the arguments of the judges on that day with those offered on the first day. Judges who had voted for acquittal on the first day could not change their votes on the second day. Those who had voted for conviction on the first day might change their votes on the second day, by assigning good reasons. Those who had voted for conviction on the first day could not vote for conviction on the second day, if the reasons assigned on the second day were radically different from those assigned on the first day.[10] It will thus be seen how very essential were the records of the scribes and how important it was that they should be correctly kept. Hence the necessity, according to Benny, of a third scribe whose notes might be used to correct any discrepancies in the reports of the other two.

Now are we justified in assuming that this was the method employed in counting votes at the trial of Jesus? The law will not permit us to presume errors. We must rather assume that this was the method employed, unless the Gospel record indicates, either by plain statement or by reasonable construction, that it was not the method used.

In this connection, let us review the language of the Scriptures. "Ye have heard the blasphemy: what think ye? And they all condemned him to be guilty of death." Is it not clearly evident, from this passage, that the balloting was not done singly, the youngest voting first, as Hebrew law required? Can it not be seen at a glance that the judges voted *en masse?* If they did, was it possible for the scribes to record the votes and make a note of the reasons assigned, as the law required? If these things were not done, were the proceedings regular?

According to Matthew, Caiaphas, before calling for the votes exclaimed: "He hath spoken blasphemy."[11] Instead of doing this, should he not, under the law, have carefully concealed his opinion until the younger members of the court had voted? Is it not a matter of history that the opinion of the high priest was regarded as almost infallible authority among the ancient Hebrews? Did not this premature declaration of guilt on the part of the high priest rob the subordinate judges of freedom of suffrage?

The conduct of the case at the close, when the balloting took place, seems to justify the view of those writers who assert that there was no regular trial of Jesus, but rather the action of a mob.

POINT XI

THE MEMBERS OF THE GREAT SANHEDRIN WERE LEGALLY DISQUALIFIED TO TRY JESUS

LAW

"The robe of the unfairly elected judge is to be respected not more than the blanket of the ass."—MENDELSOHN, "Hebrew Maxims and Rules," p. 182.

"As Moses sat in judgment without the expectation of material reward, so also must every judge act from a sense of duty only."—MENDELSOHN, "Hebrew Maxims and Rules," p. 177.

"Nor must there be on the judicial bench either a relation, or a particular friend, or an *enemy* of either the accused or of the accuser."—MENDELSOHN, "Criminal Jurisprudence of the Ancient Hebrews," p. 108.

"He (the Hebrew judge) was, in the first instance, to be modest, of good repute among his neighbors, and generally liked."—BENNY, "Criminal Code of the Jews," p. 38.

"Nor under any circumstances, was a man known to be *at enmity with the accused person* permitted to occupy a position among his judges."—BENNY, "Criminal Code of the Jews," p. 37.

FACT AND ARGUMENT

The Gospel records disclose the fact that the members of the Great Sanhedrin were legally disqualifed to try Jesus. This disqualification was of two kinds: (1) A general disqualification, under Hebrew law, to act as judges in any case; (2) a special disqualification to sit in judgment upon the life of Jesus.

Among all the great systems of jurisprudence of the world the ancient Hebrew system was the most exacting matter of judical fitness. In the palmiest days of the Hebrew Commonwealth the members of the Great Sanhedrin represented the most perfect mental, moral, and physical development of the Hebrew people. A man could not be a member of this court who had any serious mental, moral, or physical defect. He must have been "learned in the law," both written and unwritten. He must have had judicial experience; that is, he must have filled three offices of gradually increasing dignity, beginning with one of the local courts and passing successively through two magistracies at Jerusalem. He must have been an accomplished linguist; that is, he must have been thoroughly familiar with the languages of the surrounding nations. He must have been modest, popular, of good appearance, and free from haughtiness. He must have been pious, strong, and courageous. And above all, he must have been friendly in his attitude toward the accused.[1]

These were the qaulifications of Israel's judges before Roman politics had corrupted them. But at the time of Christ they had grown to be time-serving, degenerate, and corrupt. Judea was then passing through a period of religious and political revolution. At such a time in any state, as all history teaches us, the worst elements of society generally get the upper hand and control the political currents of the day. Many members of the Sanhedrin had themselves been guilty of criminal acts in both public and private life. Many of them held office by purchase—they had bought their seats. They were thus unfitted to be judges in any case; especially in one involving the great question of life and death.

In order to show the general disqualification, under the test of Hebrew law, of the members of the Great Sanhedrin, at the time of Christ, to exercise judicial functions, it is necessary to quote only Jewish authorities. In "The Martyrdom of Jesus," Rabbi Wise says: "The chief priests, under the iron rule of Pilate and his wicked master, Sejan, were the tools of the Roman soldiers who held Judea and Samaria in subjection. Like the high priest, they were appointed to and removed from office by the Roman governor of the country, either directly or indirectly. They purchased their commissions for high prices and, like almost all Roman appointees, used them for mercenary purposes. They were considered wicked men by the ancient writers and must have stood very low in the estimation of the people over whom they tyrannized. The patriots must have looked upon them as hirelings of the foreign despot whose rule was abhorred. Although there was, here and there, a good, pious and patriotic man among them, he was an exception. As a general thing, and under the rule of Pilate, especially, they were the corrupt tools of a military despotism which Rome imposed upon enslaved Palestine."

Again, the Talmud, in which we never look for slurs upon the Hebrew people, where slurs are not deserved, contains this bitter denunciation of the high-priestly families of the times of Christ: "What a plague is the family of Simon Boethus; cursed be their lances! What a plague is the family of Ananos; cursed be their hissing of vipers! What a plague is the family of Cantharus; cursed be their pens! What a plague is the family of Ismael ben Phabi; cursed be their fists! They are high priests themselves, their sons are treasurers, their sons-in-law are commanders, and their servants strike the people with staves."

In like manner the Talmud, in withering rebuke and sarcasm, again declares that "The porch of the sanctuary cried out four times. The first time, Depart from here, descendants of Eli; ye pollute the Temple of the Eternal! The second time, Let Issachar ben Keifar Barchi depart from here, who polluted himself and profaneth the victims consecrated to God! The third time, Widen yourselves, ye gates of the sanctuary and let Israel ben Phabi, the wilful, enter that he may discharge the functions of the priesthood! Yet another cry was heard, Widen yourselves, ye gates, and let Ananias ben Nebedeus, the gourmand, enter, that he may glut himself on the victims."[2]

It should be borne in mind that the high-priestly families so scathingly dealt with by the Talmud were the controlling spirits in the Great Sanhedrin at the time of Christ. Were they legally qualified, then, under the ancient and honorable tests of Hebrew law, to be members of the highest court in the land? If they bought their offices and used them for mercenary purposes, as Wise asserts, were they worthy of the great exemplar, Moses, who "sat in judgment without the expectation of material reward"? If they thus secured their places and prostituted them to selfish purposes, were their robes to be respected any more than the blanket of the ass?

The ancient Hebrew judges, in the days of Israel's purity and glory, submitted their claims to judicial preferment to the suffrage of a loving and confiding people.[3] They climbed the rungs of the judicial ladder by slow and painful degrees. Integrity and ability marked each advance toward the top. Was this the process of promotion in the case of Caiaphas and his fellow-judges? Did their bought and corrupted places not brand them with the anathema of the law?

We come now to consider the special disqualifications of members of the Sanhedrin to sit in judgment upon the life of Jesus. The reasons for these disqualifications were two: (1) The members of this court were, in the language of Jost, "burning enemies" of Jesus, and were therefore disqualified, under Hebrew law, to act as His judges; (2) they had determined upon His guilt, and had sentenced Him to death before the trial began; and had thus outraged not only a specific provision of Hebrew law but also a principle of universal justice.

The various causes of the hatred of the members of the Sanhedrin for Jesus are too numerous and profound to admit of exhaustive treatment here. A thorough analysis of these causes would necessitate a review of the life of Christ from the manger to the sepulcher. A few reasons will suffice.

But at this point a distinction should be made between that personal hatred which disqualifies and the hatred and loathing of the crime that do not disqualify. Every just and righteous judge should loathe and hate the crime itself; and a certain amount of loathing and dislike for the criminal is most natural and almost inevitable. But no judge is qualified to sit in judgment upon the rights of life, liberty, or property of another whom he hates as the result of a personal grudge, born of personal experience with the prisoner at the bar. The hatred that disqualified the members of the Sanhedrin, under Hebrew law, was that kind of hatred that had been generated by personal interest and experience. The most merciless invective, barbed with incomparable wit, ridicule, and satire, had been daily hurled at them by Jesus with withering effect. With a touch more potent than that of Ithuriel's spear He had unmasked their wicked hypocrisy and had blazoned it to the skies. Every day of His active ministry, which lasted about three years, had been spent in denouncing their shameless practices and their guilty lives. The Scribes and Pharisees were proud, haughty, and conceited beyond description. They believed implicitly in the infallibility of their authority and in the perfection of their souls. How galling, then, to such men must have been this declaration of an obscure and lowly Nazarene: "Verily, I say unto you, That the publican and the harlots go into the kingdom of God before you."[4] What impetuous invective this: "Woe unto you, scribes and Pharisees, hypocrites! for ye devour widows' houses, and for a pretense make long prayer: therefore ye shall receive the greater damnation. Woe unto you, scribes and

Pharisees, hypocrites! for ye compass sea and land to make one proselyte, and when he is made, ye make him twofold more the child of hell than yourselves."[5] We can well imagine how these fiery darts pierced and tore the vanity of a haughty and contemptuous priesthood.

Consider for a moment the difference in the spheres of Jesus and of His enemies. He, an obscure prophet from Nazareth in Galilee; they, the leaders of Israel and the guardians of the Temple at Jerusalem. He, the single advocate of the New Dispensation; they, the manifold upholders of the Old. He, without earthly authority in the propagation of His faith; they, clothed with the sanction of the law and the prestige of a mighty past. Imagine, then, if you can, the intensity of the hatred engendered by the language and the conduct of Jesus.

That we may fully appreciate the tension of the situation let us cast a single glance at the character of the Scribes. Edersheim has written these wonderfully graphic lines about them:

He pushes to the front, the crowd respectfully giving way, and eagerly hanging on his utterances, as those of a recognized authority. He has been solemnly ordained by the laying on of hands; and is the Rabbi, "my great one," Master, amplitudo. Indeed, his hyper-ingenuity in questioning has become a proverb. There is not measure of his dignity, nor yet limit to his importance. He is the "lawyer," the "well-plastered pit," filled with the water of knowledge, "out of which not a drop can escape," in opposition to the "weeds of untilled soil" of ignorance. He is the divine aristocrat, among the vulgar herd of rude and profane "country people," who "know not the law," and are "cursed." Each scribe outweighed all the common people, who must accordingly pay him every honor. . . . Such was to be the respect paid to their sayings that they were to be absolutely believed, even if they were to declare that to be at the right hand which was at the left, or vice-versa.[6]

What could, then, be more terrific than the hatred of such a character for an unlettered Galilean who descended from the mountains of His native province to rebuke and instruct the "divine aristocrats" in religious matters and heavenly affairs? Imagine his rage and chagrin when he heard these words: "Woe unto you, scribes and Pharisees, hypocrites] for ye are like unto whited sepulchers, which indeed appear beautiful outward, but are within full of dead men's bones, and all uncleanness. . . . Woe unto you, scribes and Pharisees, hypocrites! because ye build the tombs of the prophets, and garnish the sepulchers of the righteous, And say, If we had been in the days of our fathers, we would not have been partakers with them in the blood of the prophets. Wherefore ye be witnesses unto yourselves, that ye are the children of them which killed the prophets. Fill ye up then the measure of your fathers. Ye serpents, ye generation of vipers, how can ye escape the damnation of hell?"[7]

"His exquisite irony," says Renan, "His stinging remarks, always went to the heart. They were everlasting stings, and have remained festering in the wound. This Nessus-shirt of ridicule which the Jew, son of the Pharisees, has dragged in tatters after him during eighteen centuries, was woven by Jesus with a divine skill. Masterpieces of fine raillery, their features are written in lines of fire upon the flesh of the hypocrite and the false devotee. Incomparable traits worthy of a Son of God! A god alone knows how to kill in this way. Socrates and Moliere only grazed the skin. The former carried fire and rage to the very marrow."[8]

Are we not now justified in asserting, with Jost, that the members of the Sanhedrin, who were none other than the Scribes and Pharisees above described by Jesus, were the "burning enemies" of the prisoner at the bar? If they were, were they legally qualified to be His judges?

But it may be argued that their hatred was simply a form of righteous indignation provoked by His repeated assaults upon the national religion and the national institutions; that it was their duty as guardians of both to both hate and try Him; and that they would have been derelict in duty if they had not done so. But it is apparent from the record and is evident to any fair-minded reader that the enmity of the judges toward Jesus was more personal than political, more a private than a public affair. In support of this contention, in addition to the withering language addressed to them, the matter of the purification of the Temple may be mentioned. It will be remembered how Jesus, with a scorpion lash, scourged the money changers and traders from the Sanctuary. Now it is historically true that Annas and Caiaphas and their friends owned and controlled the stalls, booths, and bazaars connected with the Temple and from which flowed a most lucrative trade. The profits from the sale of lambs and doves, sold for sacrifice, alone were enormous. When Jesus threatened the destruction of this trade He assaulted the interests of Annas and his associates in the Sanhedrin in a vital place. This grievance was certainly not so religious as it was personal. The driving of the cattle from the stalls was probably more effective in compassing the destruction of the Christ than any miracle that He performed or any discourse that He delivered. But whatever the cause the fact is historic and indisputable that the Sanhedrists were enemies of Jesus, and therefore disqualified under Hebrew law to try Him.

A second reason for the special disqualification of the members of the Sanhedrin to sit as judges at the trial of Christ was the fact that they had determined upon His guilt and had sentenced Him to death before the trial began. This point needs no extensive argument or illustration. Under every enlightened system of justice the first great qualification of judges has been that they should be unbiased and unprejudiced. Judicial proceedings are murderous and no better than mob violence when judges and jurors enter upon the trial of the case with a determination to convict the accused, regardless of the testimony. The principles underlying this proposition are fundamental and self-evident.

Now the Gospel narratives disclose the fact that three different meetings of the Sanhedrin were held in the six months preceding the crucifixion, to discuss the miracles and discourses of Jesus, and to devise ways and means to entrap Him and put Him to death.

The first meeting was held in the latter part of the month of September, A.D. 29, about six months before the night trial in the palace of Caiaphas. This meeting is recorded by St. John in Chap. vii., verses 37—53. The occasion was the Feast of Tabernacles, when Jesus made many converts by His preaching, and at the same time caused much apprehension among the Pharisees, who assembled the Sanhedrin to adopt plans to check His career. It was on this occasion that Nicodemus defended Christ and asked the question that shows the nature of the proceedings at that time. "Doth our law judge any man before it hear him and know what he doeth?" This was the voice, not only of Hebrew but of universal justice demanding a hearing before a condemnation. Nothing definite seems to have been accomplished at this meeting.

The second session of the Sanhedrin took place in the month of February, A.D. 30, about six weeks before the crucifixion. The occasion of this meeting was the resurrection of Lazarus, an account of which is given in John xi. 41—53. The chief priests and Pharisees seem to have been seized with consternation by the reports of the progress of the propaganda of Jesus. They had often listened contemptuously and in sullen silence to the accounts of His miraculous performances. But when He began to raise the dead to life, they decided that it was about time to act. At this meeting Caiaphas appealed to his associates in the name of the common weal. "Ye know nothing at all," he said, "nor consider that it is expedient for us, that one man should die for the people, and that the whole nation perish not."[9] This seems to have been a form of condemnation in which the other judges joined. "Then from that day forth they took counsel together for to put him to death."[10] At this second session of the Sanhedrin the death of Jesus seems to have been decreed in an informal way and an opportunity was awaited for its accomplishment.

The third meeting of the Sanhedrin took place just a few days before the Paschal Feast.

"Now the feast of unleavened bread drew nigh, which is called the Passover. And the chief priests and scribes sought how they might kill him; for they feared the people."[11] "Then assembled together the chief priests, and the scribes, and the elders of the people, unto the palace of the high priest, who was called Caiaphas, and consulted that they might take Jesus by subtilty, and kill him. But they said, Not on the feast day, lest there be an uproar among the people."[12]

At this third session of the court it was agreed that the arrest and execution of Jesus should be accomplished at the earliest possible date.

It will be seen that at these different sessions of the Sanhedrin in the six months preceding the regular trial the judges had resolved that Jesus should be done away with at the first convenient opportunity. In short, and in fact, their hatred was formed and their determination fixed in the matter of the proceedings to be instituted against Him. Were they, then, legally qualified to act as His judges?

Again, besides prejudging Him to death had they not demonstrated their total unfitness for any righteous administration of justice by seeking false witnesses against Him? Hebrew law forbade them to seek for witnesses of any kind. They were the defenders of the accused and, under the Hebrew system, were required to search for pretexts to acquit and not for witnesses to condemn.[13] It was a maxim that "the Sanhedrin was to save, not to destroy life."[14] Much more were they forbidden to seek for false witnesses. Hebrew law denounced false witnesses and condemned them to the very punishment prescribed for those whom they sought to convict.

"And the judges shall make diligent inquisition; and, behold, if the witness be a false witness, and hath testified falsely against his brother; then shall ye do unto him, as he had thought to do unto his brother. . . . And thine eye shall not pity; but life shall go for life, eye for eye, tooth for tooth, hand for hand, foot for foot."[15]

But here we find the judges actually seeking testimony which the law pointedly prohibited. This matter alone establishes their utter unfitness to try Jesus, and is explicable only on the ground of the degradation into which they had fallen at the time of Christ and on the hypothesis that their burning hatred had overwhelmed their judgment and sense of justice.

If it be objected that the points of disqualification above alleged were not applicable to all the judges, a single sentence of Scripture meets the objection: "And the chief priests and *all the council* sought for witness against Jesus to put Him to death."[16] The fact that "all the council" were willing to outrage a provision of the fundamental law is sufficient proof that they were all disqualified to try Christ.

Another conclusive proof of the total unfitness of the members of the Sanhedrin to try Jesus is the fact that they so far forgot themselves that they abandoned all sense of self-respect and judicial dignity by brutally striking Him and spitting in His face. We would like to believe that this outrageous conduct was limited to the servents of the priests, but the Gospel of St. Mark, Chap. xiv., verse 65, clearly indicates that the judges themselves were also guilty.

POINT XII

THE CONDEMNATION OF JESUS WAS ILLEGAL BECAUSE THE MERITS OF THE DEFENSE WERE NOT CONSIDERED

LAW

"Then shalt thou inquire, and make search, and ask diligently."—DEUTERONOMY xiii. 14.

"The judges shall weigh the matter in the sincerity of their conscience."—MISHNA, Sanhedrin IV. 5.

"The primary object of the Hebrew judicial system was to render the conviction of an innocent person impossible. All the ingenuity of the Jewish legists was directed to the attainment of this end."—BENNY, "Criminal Code of the Jews," p. 56.

FACT AND ARGUMENT

The actual trial of any criminal case shows, upon the record, two essential parts: (1) The accusation; (2) the defense. The absence of the elements of defense makes the proceeding *ex parte;* and there is really no trial. And it is impossible to conceive a proper administration of justice where a defense is not allowed, since the right to combat the allegations of the indictment is the essential principle of liberty under the law. The destruction of this right is the annihilation of freedom by subjecting the individual citizen to the whims and caprices of the governing power. An ideal code of criminal procedure would embody rules of evidence and practice perfectly adapted to establish truth in the matter at issue between the commonwealth and the prisoner. Neither the people nor the accused would be favored or prejudiced by the admission or exclusion of any kind of evidence. An exact interpretation and administration of this code would result in a perfect intellectual balance between the rights of the state and the defendant. But such a code has never been framed, and if one were in existence, it would be impossible to enforce it, as long as certain judges insisted on aiding the prosecution and others on helping the accused, in violation of standard rules of evidence.

Now, the ancient Hebrew system of criminal procedure was no such ideal one as that above described. It should be remembered that there was no body, under that system, corresponding to our modern Grand Jury, to present indictments. There were no prosecuting officers and no counselors-at-law, in the modern sense. The leading witnesses preferred charges and the judges did the rest. They examined and cross-examined witnesses, did the summing up and were, above all, the defenders of the accused. The rights of the defendant seem to have alone been seriously considered. This startling maxim was a constant menace to the integrity of the government and to the rights of the commonwealth: "The Sanhedrin which so often as once in seven years condemns a man to death, is a slaughter-house."[1] Lightfoot is of the opinion that the Jews did not lose the power of capital punishment as the result of the Roman conquest, but that they voluntarily abandoned it because the rules of criminal procedure which they had from time to time adopted finally became wholly unfitted for convicting anyone. This view is unsupported by historic fact, but it is nevertheless true that the legal safeguards for the protection of the rights of the accused had, in the later years of Jewis nationality, become so numerous and stringent that a condemnation was practically impossible. The astonishing provision of Hebrew law to which we have referred in Part II known as Antecedent Warning had the effect of securing an acquittal in nearly every case. It is contended by many that this peculiar provision was intended to abolish capital punishment by rendering conviction impossible.

In the light of the principles above suggested let us review the action of the Sanhedrin in condemning Jesus to death upon His uncorroborated confession. The standard of thoroughness in investigating criminal matters is thus prescribed in the Mosaic Code: "Then shalt thou inquire, and make search, and ask diligently." The Mishna supplements the fundamental law by this direction: "The judges shall weigh the matter in the sincerity of their conscience." From what we know of the peculiar tendency of the Hebrew system to favor the accused we are justified in assuming that the two rules just cited were framed for the protection of the prisoner more than for the security of the commonwealth.

Now at this point we are led to ask: Were these rules applied in the trial of Jesus in any sense either for or against the accused? Did Caiaphas and the other members of the Sanhedrin "inquire, and make search and ask diligently" concerning the facts involved in the issue between Jesus and the Hebrew people? Did they weigh the whole matter "in the sincerity of their conscience"? Is it not clearly evident from the record that the false witnesses contradicted themselves, were rejected and dismissed, and that Jesus was then condemned upon His uncorroborated confession that He was the Christ, the Son of God? The usual and natural proceeding in a Jewish criminal trial was to call witnesses for the defendant, after the leading witnesses had testified for the people. Was this done in the case of Jesus? His own apostles deserted Him in the garden, although two of them seem to have returned to the scene of the trial. Is it probable, in the light of the record, that witnesses were called for the defendant? We have seen that they could not legally convict Him upon His own confession. And there is nowhere the faintest suggestion that witnesses other than the false ones were called to testify against Him. The record is clear and unequivocal that the conviction of Jesus was upon His uncorroborated confession. This was illegal. When Caiaphas said, "I adjure thee by the living God that thou tell us whether thou be the Christ, the Son of God," Jesus answered, "Thou hast said"; that is, "I am," according to Mark. Here was an issue squarely joined between the Commonwealth of Israel and Jesus of Nazareth. It was incumbent upon the state to establish His guilt by two competent witnesses who agreed in all essential details. If these witnesses were not present, or could not be secured, it was the duty of the court to discharge Christ at once. This the law provided and demanded. But this was not done.

If, as has been contended, the false witnesses were relied upon by the Sanhedrin to corroborate the confession of Jesus, then under Hebrew law the judges should at least have sought witnesses in His behalf, or should have allowed His friends time to find them and bring them in. In other words, His defense should have been considered. However overwhelming the conviction of the judges of the Sanhedrin that the claims of Jesus were false and blasphemous, they were not justified in refusing to consider the merits of His pretensions. If a midnight assassin should stealthily creep into the room of a sleeping man and shoot him to death, a judge would be legally justified in instructing the jury, at the close of the people's case, to bring in a verdict of guilty, on the ground that nothing that the defendant could prove would help his case. However weak and ridiculous his defense, the prisoner should at least be heard; and a failure to accord him a hearing would certainly result in reversal on appeal. A refusal to consider the defense of a prisoner under ancient Hebrew law was nothing less than an abrogation of the forms of government and a proclamation of mob violence in the particular case, for it must be remembered that Hebrew criminal law was framed especially for the protection of the accused.

It should also be kept in mind that it would not have been incumbent upon Caiaphas and his fellow-judges to acquit Jesus simply because a defense had been made. In other words, they were not bound to accept His explanations and arguments. If they had heard Him and His witnesses, they could have rejected His pretensions as false and blasphemous, although they were truthful and righteous, without incurring the censure of mankind and the curse of Heaven, for it would be preposterous to require infallible judgment of judicial officers. All that can be demanded of judges of the law is that they act conscientiously with the lights that are in from of them. The maledictions of the human race have been hurled at Caiaphas and his colleagues during nineteen centuries, not because they pronounced an illegal judgment, but because they outraged rules of law in their treatment of the Christ; not because they misinterpreted His defense, but because they denied Him all defense.

We should constantly keep in mind that Jesus was entitled to have the two requirements, "Then shalt thou inquire, and make search, and ask diligently," and "The judges shall weigh the matter in the sincerity of their conscience," applied not only for but against Him. That is, before the Hebrew Commonwealth rested its case against Him, He had a right to demand that a *prima facie* case be made, or in case of failure to do so, that He be at once discharged. This rule was as pointed and imperative under ancient as under modern law, and before the merits of the defense were required to be considered the state had to close its case against the defendant, with a presumption of guilt against Him, as a result of the introduction of competent and satisfactory evidence.

If rules of law had been properly observed in the trial of Jesus the question of the merits of His defense would never have been raised; for it was practically impossible to convict Him under the circumstances surrounding the night trial in the palace of Caiaphas. As has been before suggested, Jesus was very popular outside the circle of the Temple authorities. So great was His popularity that it is almost certain that two competent witnesses could not have been secured to convict Him of blasphemy in the sense that He had claimed to be the Messiah. We have seen, under Point VIII, that Jesus had confessed His Messiahship to no one excepting the Samaritan woman, outside the Apostolic company. Judas, then, was probably the only witness who had heard Him declare Himself to be the Messiah that could have been secured; and his testimony was incompetent, under Hebrew law, because, under the supposition that Jesus was a criminal, Judas, His apostle, was an accomplice. As to the charge of blasphemy in the broader sense of having claimed equality with God, upon which, according to Salvador, Jesus was convicted, it seems from the Gospel record that there would have been no difficulty in legally convicting Him , if the Sanhedrin had met regularly and had taken time to summon witnesses in legal manner. For on many occasions Jesus had said and done things in the presence of both friends and enemies that the Jews regarded as blasphemous; such as claiming that He and His Father were one; that He had existed before Abraham; and that He had power to forgive sins. But these charges were not made at the trial, and we have no right to consider them except as a means of interpreting the mind of Caiaphas in connection with the meaning of the claim of Jesus that He was the Christ, the Son of God. If Caiaphas was justified in construing these words to mean that Jesus claimed identity with Jehovah, then he was justified in inferring that Jesus had spoken blasphemy, for from the standpoint of ancient Judaism and considering Jesus simply as a Jewish citizen, blasphemy was the crime that resulted from such a claim. But even from this point of view Caiaphas was not justified in refusing Jesus ample opportunity to prove His equality with Jehovah, or at least that He was gifted with divine power. This was all the more true because the claim of Jesus was that of Messiahship, and according to one line of authorities in Hebrew Messianic theology the Messiah was to be clothed with divine authority and power as the messenger and vicegerent of Jehovah on earth.

But it is clearly certain that a *prima facie* case of guilt was not made by the Sanhedrin against Jesus; and, as a matter of law, He was not called upon to make any defense. He could have refused to say a word in answer to the accusation. He could have asserted His legal rights by objecting that a case against Him had not been made, by demanding that the charges against Him be dismissed and that He be set at liberty at once. But Jesus did not do this. He simply confessed His Messiahship and Sonship of the Father. This confession was not legal evidence upon which He could have been convicted, but it did help to create an issue, the truth or falsity of which should have been investigated by the court.

Now, let us suppose, for argument's sake, that a *prima facie* case of guilt against Jesus was made before the Sanhedrin. What was the next legal step under Hebrew law? What should the judges have done after hearing the witnesses against Him? It is beyond dispute that they should have begun at once to "inquire, and make search, and ask diligently" concerning all matters pertaining to the truthfulness and righteousness of His claims to Messiahship. They should have assisted Him in securing witnesses whose testimony would have helped to establish those claims. Having secured such testimony, they should have weighed it "in the sincerity of their conscience." But this they did not do.

It may be asked: What proofs could have been offered that Jesus was "the Christ, the Son of God," if complete rights of defense had been accorded? That question is difficult to answer, nearly two thousand years after the trial. But if a *prima facie* case of guilt had been made against Him, shifting the burden of proof, and requiring that His claims be proved, it may be reasonably contended that a complete defense would have necessitated proofs: (1) That Jesus was the Christ, that is, that He was the Messiah; (2) that he was also the Son of God, that is, that He was identical with God Himself. Let us consider these two phases of the subject and their attendant proofs in order.

And first, what evidence could have been offered that Jesus was the Christ, that is, the Messiah? What method of procedure should have been employed by the Sanhedrin in investigating His claims? Let us suppose that Caiaphas understood that Jesus claimed to be the long-looked-for Messiah who had come from Jehovah with divine authority to redeem mankind and to regenerate and rule the world. Let us not forget that the Jews were expecting a Messiah, and that the mere claim of Messiahship was not illegal. Such a claim merely raised an issue as to its truth or falsity which was to be investigated like any other proposition of theology or law. It was not one to be either accepted or rejected without demonstration. Then when Jesus acknowledged His Messiahship in answer to the high priest's question it was the duty of the court either to admit His claim and discharge Him at once, or to summon competent witnesses, by daylight, to prove that His pretensions were false and blasphemous. Having rested their case, it was their duty to aid the prisoner in securing witnesses to substantiate His claims, and according to the spirit of Hebrew law to view rather favorably then unfavorably such claims. It was also incumbent upon them to apply to Jesus all the Messianic tests of each and every school. It should be remembered that at the time of Christ there were radically different views of the attributes of the expected Messiah. No two schools agreed upon all the signs by which the future Deliverer would be recognized. Only one sign was agreed upon by all—that He would be a scion of the House of David. The followers of Judas of Galilee believed that the Messiah would be an earthly hero of giant stature—a William Tell, a Robert Bruce, an Abraham Lincoln—who would emancipate the Jews by driving out the Romans and permanently restoring the kingdom of David on the earth. The school of Shammai believed that he would be not only a great statesman and warrior, but a religious zealot as well; and that to splendid victories on the battlefield, he would add the glorious triumphs of religion. Radically different from both these views, were the teachings of the gentle Hillel and his disciples. According to these, the Messiah was to be a prince of peace whose sublime and holy spirit would impress itself upon all flesh, would banish all wars, and make of Jerusalem the grand center of international brotherhood and love. But even these conceptions were not exhaustive of the various

Messianic ideas that were prevalent in Palestine in the days of Jesus. Some of the Messianic notions were not only contradictory but diametrically opposite in meaning. A "prince of peace" and a "gigantic warrior" could not well be one and the same person. And for this reason it is apparent that, had an examination been made, the claims of Jesus to the Messiahship could not have been rejected by Caiaphas and the Sanhedrin, simply because this or that attribute did not meet the approval of this or that sect or school.

Instead of condemning Him to death for blasphemy, when Jesus answered that He was the Christ, the Son of God, Caiaphas should have asked a second question: "What sign shewest thou then, that we may see and believe thee?" It has been contended by Jewish writers that, far from denying Jesus the privilege of proving His Messiahship, He was frequently asked to give signs and perform wonders. The reply to this is that as far as the legal merits of the case are concerned Jesus was not invited at the trial in the palace of Caiaphas to show signs or give proofs of His Messiahship. And as to the chances afforded Him at other times and places, they were extra-judicial and were mere street affairs in which Jesus probably refused to gratify vulgar curiosity and by which He was not remotely bound legally or religiously. It is only when properly arraigned and accused that a citizen under modern law can be compelled to answer a charge of crime. The rule was more stringent under the ancient Hebrew dispensation. Private preliminary examinations, even by judicial officers, were not permitted by Hebrew law, as Salvador explicitly states. It was only when confronted by proper charges before a legally constituted tribunal in regular session, that a Hebrew prisoner was compelled to answer. And at the regular trial before the full Sanhedrin Jesus was not asked to give evidence that would serve to exculpate Him. What Caiaphas should have done was to notify Jesus, at the time of the arraignment in his own house, that His life was at stake and that now was the time to produce testimony in His own behalf. It was the duty, furthermore, of the high priest and his associates to consult the sacred books to see if the Messianic prophecies therein contained were fulfilled in the birth, life, and performances of Jesus, as these matters were developed at the trial by witnesses duly summoned in His behalf.

It was a matter personally within the knowledge of the judges that the time was ripe for the appearance of the Deliverer. Not only the people of Israel, but all the surrounding nations were expecting the coming of a great renovator of the world. Of such an arrival Virgil had already sung at Rome.[2]

A great national misfortune had already foreshadowed the day of the Messiah more potently than had any individual event in the life of Jesus. When Jacob lay dying upon his deathbed, he called around him his twelve sons and began to pronounce upon each in turn the paternal and prophetic blessing. When the turn of Judah came, the accents of the dying patriarch became more clear and animated, as he said: "Judah, thou art he whom thy brethren shall praise: thy hand shall be in the neck of thine enemies; thy father's children shall bow down before thee. Judah is a lion's whelp: from the prey, my son, thou art gone up: he

stooped down, he couched as a lion, and as an old lion; who shall rouse him up? The *sceptre* shall not depart from Judah, nor a lawgiver from between his feet, until Shiloh come; and unto him shall the gathering of the people be."[3] The Jewish Rabbinical commentators of antiquity were unanimously of the opinion that this prophecy of Jacob referred to the day of the Messiah. And for ages the people had been told to watch for two special signs which would herald the coming of the great Deliverer: (1) The departure of the scepter from Judah; (2) the loss of the judicial power.

The Talmudists, commenting on the above passage from Genesis, say: "The son of David shall not come unless the royal power has been taken from Judah"; and in another passage: "The son of David shall not come unless the judges have ceased in Israel."[4] Now both these signs had appeared at the time of the Roman conquest, shortly before the birth of Christ. At the deposition of Archelaus, A.D. 6, Judea became a Roman province with a Roman procurator as governor. Sovereignty then passed away forever from the Jews. And not only was sovereignty taken from them, but its chief attribute, the power of life and death in judicial matters, was destroyed. Thus the legal and historical situation was produced that had been prophesied by Jacob. The *scepter* had passed from Judah and the *lawgiver* from between his feet, when Jesus stood before the Sanhedrin claiming to be the Messiah.

A fair trial in full daylight, it is believed, would have called before His judges a host of witnesses friendly to Jesus, whose testimony would have established an exact fulfillment of ancient Messianic prophecy in His birth, life, arrest, and trial. A judicial record would have been made of which the following might be regarded as an approximately correct transcript:

(1)   That the Messiah was to be born in Bethlehem:

PROPHECY—But thou, Bethlehem Ephratah, though thou be little among the thousands of Judah, yet out of thee shall he come forth unto me that is to be ruler in Israel; whose goings forth have been from of old, from everlasting.—MICAH v. 2.

FULFILLMENT—Now when Jesus was *born in Bethlehem* of Judea in the days of Herod the king, behold, there came wise men from the east to Jerusalem.—MATT. ii, 1.

And Joseph also went up from Galilee, out of the city of Nazareth, into Judea, unto the city of David, which is called Bethlehem (because he was of the house and lineage of David), To be taxed with Mary his espoused wife, being great with child. And so it was, that, while they were there, the days were accomplished that she should be delivered. And she brought forth her first-born son, and wrapped him in swaddling clothes, and laid him in a manger; because there was no room for them in the inn.—LUKE ii. 4—7.

(2)   That the Messiah was to be born of a virgin:

PROPHECY—Therefore the Lord himself shall give you a sign; Behold, a virgin shall conceive, and bear a son, and shall call his name Immanuel.—ISA. vii. 14.

FULFILLMENT—And in the sixth month the angel Gabriel was sent from God unto a city of Galilee, named Nazareth, To a virgin espoused to a man whose name was Joseph, of the house of David; and the virgin's name was Mary. . . . And the angel said unto her, Fear not, Mary: for thou hast found favor with God. And, behold, thou shalt conceive in thy womb, and bring forth a son, and shalt call his name Jesus.—Luke i. 26—30. Then Joseph being raised from sleep did as the angel of the Lord had bidden him, and took unto him his wife: and knew her not till she had brought forth her firstborn son: and he called his name Jesus.—MATT. i. 24, 25.

(3) *That the Messiah was to spring from the house of David:*

PROPHECY—Behold, those days come, saith the Lord, that I will raise unto David a righteous Branch, and a King shall reign and prosper, and shall execute judgment and justice in the earth. In his days Judah shall be saved, and Israel shall dwell safely: and this is his name whereby he shall be called, THE LORD OUR RIGHTEOUSNESS.—Jer. xxiii. 5, 6.

FULFILLMENT—He shall be great, and shall be called the Son of the Highest; and the Lord God shall give unto him the throne of his father David.—LUKE i. 32. But while he thought on these things, behold, the angel of the Lord appeared unto him in a dream, saying, Joseph, thou son of David, fear not to take unto thee Mary thy wife: for that which is conceived in her is of the Holy Ghost.—MATT. i. 20.

(4) *That the Messiah should not come until the scepter had departed from Judah and the lawgiver from between his feet:*

PROPHECY—The sceptre shall not depart from Judah, nor a lawgiver from between his feet, until Shiloh come.—GEN. xlix. 10.

FULFILLMENT—And he saith unto them, Whose is this image and superscription? They say unto him, Caesar's. Then saith he unto them, Render therefore unto Caesar the things which are Caesar's; and unto God the things that are God's.—Matt. xxii 20, 21.

Then said Pilate unto them, Take ye him, and judge him according to your law. The Jews therefore said unto him, It is not lawful for us to put any man to death.—JOHN xviii. 31.

(5) *That a forerunner like unto Elijah should prepare the way of the Messiah:*

PROPHECY—Behold, I will send my messenger, and he shall prepare the way before me: and the Lord, whom ye seek, shall suddenly come into his temple, even the messenger of the covenant, whom ye delight in: behold, he shall come, saith the Lord of hosts.—Mal. iii. 1.

The voice of him that crieth in the wilderness, Prepare ye the way of the Lord, make straight in the desert a highway for our God.—ISA. xl. 3.

FULFILLMENT—In those days came John the Baptist, preaching in the wilderness of Judea, And saying, Repent ye: for the kingdom of heaven is at hand. For this is he that was spoken of by the prophet Esaias, saying, The voice of one crying in the wilderness, Prepare ye the way of the Lord, make his paths straight.—MATT. iii. 1-3.

This is he, of whom it is written, Behold, I send my messenger before thy face, which shall prepare thy way before thee. For I say unto you, Among those that are born of women there is not a greater prophet than John the Baptist.—LUKE vii. 27, 28.

(6) That the Messiah should begin to preach in Galilee:

PROPHECY—In Galilee of the nations, the people that walked in darkness have seen a great light.—ISA. ix. 1, 2.

FULFILLMENT—Now when Jesus had heard that John was cast into prison, He departed into Galilee. . . . The people which sat in darkness, saw great light; and to them which sat in the region and shadow of death light is sprung up. From that time, Jesus began to preach, and to say, Repent: for the kingdom of heaven is at hand.—Matt. iv. 12-17.

(7) That the Messiah should perform many miracles:

PROPHECY—Then the eyes of the blind shall be opened, and the ears of the deaf shall be unstopped. Then shall the lame man leap as a hart, and the tongue of the dumb sing: for in the wilderness shall waters break out, and streams in the desert.—ISA. xxxv, 5, 6.

FULFILLMENT—Then was brought unto him one possessed with a devil, blind, and dumb, and he healed him, insomuch that the blind and dumb both spake and saw.—MATT. xii. 22.

But that ye may know that the Son of man hath power upon earth to forgive sins (he said unto the sick of the palsy), I say unto thee, Arise, and take up thy couch, and go into thine house. And immediately he rose up before them, and took up that whereon he lay, and departed to his own house, glorifying God.—LUKE v. 24, 25.

Jesus answered and said unto them, Go and shew John again those things which ye do hear and see: The blind receive their sight, and the lame walk, the lepers are cleansed, and the deaf hear, the dead are raised up, and the poor have the gospel preached to them.—MATT. xi. 4, 5.

(8) That the Messiah should make his public entry into Jerusalem riding upon an ass:

PROPHECY—Rejoice greatly, O daughter of Zion; shout, O daughter of Jerusalem: behold, thy King cometh unto thee: he is just, and having salvation; lowly, and riding upon an ass, and upon a colt the foal of an ass.—ZECH. ix. 9.

FULFILLMENT—And the disciples went, and did as Jesus commanded them, And brought the ass, and the colt, and put on them their clothes, and they set him thereon. And a very great multitude spread their garments in the way; others cut down branches from the trees, and strewed them in the way. And the multitudes that went before, and that followed, cried, saying, Hosanna to the Son of David: Blessed is he that cometh in the name of the Lord; Hosanna in the highest.—MATT. xxi. 6-9.

(9) That the Messiah should be betrayed by one of his followers for thirty pieces of silver which would finally be thrown into the potter's field:

PROPHECY—Yea, mine owner familiar friend, in whom I trusted, which did eat of my bread, hath lifted up his heel against me.—Psa. xli. 9.

And I said unto them, If ye think good, give me my price; and if not, forbear. So they weighed for my price thirty pieces of silver. And the Lord said unto me, Cast it unto the potter: a goodly price that I was prized at of them. And I took the thirty pieces of silver, and cast them to the potter in the house of the Lord.—ZECH. xi. 12, 13.

FULFILLMENT—Then one of the twelve, called Judas Iscariot, went unto the chief priests, And said unto them, What will ye give me, and I will deliver him unto you? And they convenanted with him for thirty pieces of silver.—MATT. xxvi. 14, 15.

Then Judas, which had betrayed him, when he saw that he was condemned, repented himself, and brought again the thirty pieces of silver to the chief priests and elders, Saying, I have sinned in that I have betrayed the innocent blood. And they said, What is that to us? see thou to that. An he cast down the pieces of silver in the temple, and departed, and went and hanged himself. And the chief priests took the silver pieces, and said, It is not lawful for to put them into the treasury, because it is the price of blood. And they took counsel, and bought with them the potter's field, to bury strangers in.—MATT. xxvii. 3-8.

(10)   That the Messiah should be a man of poverty and of suffering; and should be despised and rejected of men:

PROPHECY—He is despised and rejected of men; a man of sorrows, and acquainted with grief: and we hid as it were our faces from him; he was despised, and we esteemed him not.—ISA. liii. 3.

FULFILLMENT—And Jesus said unto him, Foxes have holes, and birds of the air have nests; but the Son of man hath not where to lay his head.—LUKE ix. 58.

And they smote him on the head with a reed, and did spit upon him, and bowing their knees worshipped him. And when they had mocked him, they took off the purple from him, and put his own clothes on him, and led him out to crucify him.—MARK xv. 19, 20.

Through reasonable diligence, witnesses might have been secured to testify to a majority, at least, of the points above enumerated, touching Messianic prophecy and fulfillment. Besides these are many others too numerous to mention in a treatise of this kind.

The question then arises at once: Admitting that all the evidence above suggested, marked "Prophecy" and "Fulfillment," could have been introduced in evidence at the trial before the Sanhedrin; were the judges morally and legally bound to acquit and release Jesus, if they believed this testimony to be true? We answer unhesitatingly, yes; as far as the count in the accusation relating to Messiahship was concerned. But we must remember that the charge against Jesus was not limited to His claims to Messiahship. The indictment against Him was that He claimed to be "the Christ, the Son of God." "Christ" is the English form of the Greek translation of the word meaning "Messiah." The real nature of the charge against the prisoner, then, was that He claimed to be not only the

Messiah but also the Son of God. We have seen that "Son of God" conveyed to the Sanhedrin the notion of divine origin and of equality with Jehovah. Even today there is no dispute between Jews and Christians in regard to this construction. Jews charge that Jesus made such a claim and Christians agree with them. They are compelled to do so, indeed, or else abjure the fundamental dogma of their faith—the doctrine of the Trinity.

Now we approach the consideration of a phase of the subject where theology and law meet and blend. It has been sought to ridicule the contention that Jesus should have been heard on the charge of being the Son of God, in the sense that He was God Himself, because such a claim was not only ridiculous and frivolous as a plea, but because it was blasphemous upon its face; as being opposed, by bare assertion, to the most fundamental and sacred precept of the Mosaic Code and of the teachings of the Prophets: that God was purely and wholly spiritual; that He was not only incorporeal but invisible, indivisible, and incomprehensible. The advocates of this theory declare that Jesus asserted, in the face of this primary belief of the Hebrews, a plurality of gods of which He was a member, and that this assertion destroyed the very cornerstone of Judaism, founded in the teaching of the celebrated passage: "Hear, O Israel: The Lord our God is one Lord." They further declare that when Jesus presented Himself in the flesh, and declared that He was God, He insulted both the intelligence and religious consciousness of His judges by a complete anthropomorphism; and that when He did this, He was not entitled to be heard.

One of the most radical of this class is Rabbi Wise who, in "The Martyrdom of Jesus," says: "Had Jesus maintained before a Jewish court to be the Son of God, in the trinitarian sense of the terms, viz., that He was part, person, or incarnation of the Diety, He must have said it in terms to be understood to that effect, as ambiguous words amount to nothing. But if even clearly understood, the court could only have found Him insane, but not guilty of any crime." This is strong language, indeed, and deserves serious consideration. It means nothing less than that Jesus, upon His confession of equality and identity with God, should have been committed as a lunatic, and not tried as a criminal. And the real meaning of this too extreme view is that the claims of Jesus, being a man in the flesh, to membership in a plurality of gods was such an outrageous and unheard-of thing that it amounted to insanity; and that an insane person was not one to be listened to, but to be committed and protected. The purpose of the distinguished Hebrew theologian was to show by the absurdity of the thing that Jesus was never tried before a Hebrew court; that He never claimed to be the Son of God, and that the Evangelical narratives are simply false. The same writer thus continues in the same connection: "Mark reports furthermore, that Jesus did not simply affirm the high priest's question but added: 'And ye shall see the Son of Man sitting on the right hand of power, and coming in the clouds of heaven.' Jesus cannot have said these words. Our reasons are: they are not true; none of the judges and witnesses present ever did see him either sitting on the right hand of power or coming in the clouds of heaven. These words could have originated only after the death of Jesus, when the Jewish Christians expected his immediate return as the Messiah and restorer of the kingdom of heaven, so that those very men could see him coming in the clouds of heaven. Besides, Jesus, the Pharisean Jew, could not have entertained the anthropomorphism that God had a *right hand.* "[5] It is only necessary to add that Rabbi Wise may be right, if the Gospel writers were untruthful men. Suffice it to say that we have said enough in support of the veracity of the Evangelists in Part I of this volume. If we are right that they were truthful historians when they published these biographies to the world, Rabbi Wise is wrong; for according to these writers the Sanhedrin did not take the view that Jesus was a crazy man, but that He was a criminal. They accordingly tried Him to the extent of bringing an accusation against Him and of supporting it with a certain kind and amount of testimony, and by then leading Him away to be crucified by the Romans. Our contention is that the trial was not complete, in that His judges did not consider the merits of the defense of Jesus in the proceedings which they conducted against Him.

It would be entirely consistent with the plan of this treatise and of the special treatment of this theme to ignore completely the question of the divinity of Jesus; since we have announced a legal and not a theological consideration of the subject. But we repeat that the theological and the legal are inseparably interwoven in a proper handling of Point XII. If Rabbi Wise and others are right that the anthropomorphic pretensions of Jesus robbed Him of the protection of the law, in the sense that His claims to be God in the flesh were not worthy of consideration by a Hebrew court, then we are wrong in making the point that the merits of His defense should have been considered.

Our contention is that the claims of Jesus were not so strange and shocking as to place Him without the pale of the law and to deny Him its ordinary protection; that His pretensions were not those of an insane man; that if He was not the Son of God He was guilty of blasphemy; and that if He was the Son of God he was innocent. We further contend that all these things were subjects of legitimate judicial examination by Hebrew judges under Hebrew law, and that Jesus should have had His day in court.

A very brief examination of the question of anthropomorphism in its connection with the claims of Jesus will demonstrate the fallacy of the arguments of Rabbi Wise and of those who agree with him. Candor compels us to admit that the Jewish conception of Jehovah at the time of the crucifixion was very foreign to the notion of a God of flesh and bone. Hebrew monotheism taught the doctrine of one God who was purely spiritual, and therefore invisible, intangible, and unapproachable. Judaism delighted to lift its deity above the sensual, material, and corporeal things of earth, and to represent Him as a pure and sinless spirit in a state of awful and supreme transcendence. Our first impression, then, is that this dogma of divine unity and spirituality must have received a dreadful shock when Jesus, a carpenter of Nazareth, whose mother, father, brothers, and sisters were known, confronted the high priest and declared to him that He was God. But the shock was certainly not so great that Caiaphas and his colleagues, after a moment's composure and reflection, could not have concluded that the pretensions of Jesus were not wholly at variance with the revelations of Hebrew theology in the earlier years of the Commonwealth of Israel. They might have judged His claims to be unfounded, but they were certainly not justified in pronouncing Him insane, or in ignoring His rights under the law to be heard and to have His defense considered. Their arrest and trial of the prisoner was the consummation of a number of secret meetings in which the astounding personality and marvelous performances of Jesus were debated and discussed with fear and trembling. The raising of Lazarus from the dead had created a frightful panic among the Sadducean oligarchy. Far from regarding Him as an obscure person whose claims were ridiculous and whose mind was unbalanced, the priests feared lest all men might believe on Him, and boldly declared that such was the influence of His deeds that His single life might be balanced against the existence of a whole nation.[6]

What the judges of the Sanhedrin should have done in examining the merits of the defense of Jesus was: (1) To consider whether, in the light of Hebrew scripture and tradition, a god of flesh and bone, representing the second person of a Duality or a Trinity of gods, was possible; (2) to weigh thoroughly the claims of Jesus, in the light of testimony properly adduced at the trial, that He was this second person of a Duality or Trinity of gods.

In making this examination, let us bear in mind, the members of the court were not to look forward, but backward. They were to examine the past, not the future, in reference to the present. Furthermore, they were not to consider so much a Trinity as a Duality of gods; for it must be remembered that the Holy Ghost was not a feature of the trial. The Athanasian creed and the proceedings of the Nicene Council were not binding upon Caiaphas and his fellow-judges. Nor were the teachings of the New Testament scriptures published to the world more than a generation after the trial. They were to consider the divine pretensions of Jesus in the light of the teachings and revelations of the Law and the Prophets. They were to measure His claims by these standards in the light of the evidence adduced before them.

With a view to a thorough and systematic examination of the merits of the defense of Jesus, Caiaphas, as presiding officer of the Sanhedrin, should have propounded to his fellow-judges the following initial questions: (1) Do the Law and the Prophets reveal the doctrine of a plurality of gods among the Israelites? That is, has Jehovah ever begotten, or has He ever promised to beget, a Son of equal divinity with Himself? Was this Son to be, or is He to be born of a woman; and to have, therefore, the form of a man and the attributes of a human being? Was this Son to be, or is He to be at any time identical with the Father? Do the Law and the Prophets tell us unmistakably that Jehovah ever appeared upon the earth in human form and exhibited human attributes? Do they contain a promise from the Father that He would send His Son to the earth to be the Redeemer of men and the Regenerator of the world? (2) Do the credentials of Jesus, the prisoner at the bar, in the light of the evidence before us, entitle Him to be considered this Son and Ambassador of God, sent from the Father to redeem mankind?

It follows logically and necessarily that if affirmative answers were not given to the first set of questions an examination of the second would be useless. Let us conceive, then, that the judges of the Sanhedrin had employed this method. What answers, we may ask, would they have developed to these questions from the Sacred Books?

At the outset it is safe to say that negative answers would have been given, if the judges had considered the claims of Jesus with reference alone to the prevailing Pharisaic teachings of the days of Jesus. And in this connection let us note that the Hebrew conception of Jehovah had materially changed in the time intervening between the Mosaic dispensation and the coming of the Christ. The spiritual growth of the nation had been characterized at every step by marked aversion to anthropomorphism—the ascription to God of human form and attributes. In the Pentateuch there is a prevailing anthropomorphic idea of Jehovah. He is frequently talked about as if He were a man. Human passions and emotions are repeatedly ascribed to Him. This was inevitable among a primitive people whose crude religious consciousness sought to frame from the analogy of human nature a visible symbol of the Deity and a sensible emblem of religious faith. All early religions have manifested the same anthropomorphic tendencies. Both Judaism and Christianity have long since planted themselves upon the fundamental proposition that God is a spirit. But both these systems of religion have in all ages been compelled to run the gantlet of two opposing tendencies: one of which sought by a living, personal communion with God through Moses and through Christ, by means of human attributes and symbols, an intimate knowledge and immediate benefit of the divine nature; the other, from a horror of anthropomorphism, tending to make God purely passionless and impersonal, thus reducing Him to a bare conception without form or quality, thus making Him a blank negation.

The successive steps in the progress of weeding out anthropomorphisms from the Pentateuch may be clearly traced in later Hebrew literature. The Prophets themselves were at times repelled by the sensuous conceptions of God revealed by the writings of Moses. The great lawgiver had attributed to Jehovah the quality of repentance, a human attribute. "An it *repented* the Lord that he had made man on the earth, and it grieved him at his heart," says Genesis vi. 6. But a later writer, the prophet Samuel, denied that God had such a quality. "And also the Strength of Israel will not lie nor repent: for he is not a man, that he should repent."[7] And the prophet Hosea affirms this declaration when he places in the mouth of Jehovah the affirmation: "For I am God and not man."[8]

At a still later age, when the notion of the supreme transcendence of Jehovah had become prevalent, it was considered objectionable to make God say, "I will dwell in you midst"; as a substitute, "I shall cause you to dwell" was adopted. "To behold the face of God" was not a repulsive phrase in the ancient days of Hebrew plainness and simplicity, but later times sought to eradicate the anthropomorphism by saying instead, "to appear before God."

The Septuagint, the Greek version of the Bible in use at the time of Christ, reveals the same tendency toward paraphrasing or spiritualizing the anthropomorphic phrases of the older Bible. In this translation the "image of God" of the older Hebrew literature becomes "the glory of God," and "the mouth of God" is expressed by "the voice of the Lord."

The Septuagint was written more than a century before the birth of Jesus, and we may safely assert that at the beginning of our era the Jews not only affirmatively proclaimed the doctrine of divine unity and pure spirituality, in relation to the person and character of Jehovah, but that they boldly and indignantly denied and denounced any attempt to make of God a man or to attribute to Him human qualities. But when we say "the Jews," we mean the dominant religious sect of the nation, the Pharisees. We should not forget, in this connection, that the primary difference between the Sadducees and the Pharisees was in the varying intensity with which they loved the Law of Moses and adhered to its teachings. We have seen in Part II of this volume that the Mishna, the oral law, was really more highly esteemed by the Pharisaic Jews than was the Mosaic Code. But the Sadducees planted themselves squarely upon the Pentateuch and denied that the traditions of the Scribes were of binding force. "The Sadducees were a body of aristocrats opposed to the oral law and the later developments of Judaism."

Now what views, we may ask, did the Sadducees entertain of the possibility of God appearing to men in the flesh? In other words, what was their notion, at the time of Christ, of the anthropomorphisms of the Pentateuch, which was their ultimate guide and standard in all matters of legal and religious interpretation? These questions are important in this connection, since Caiaphas and the large majority of his colleagues in the Great Sanhedrin were Sadducees and held the fate of Jesus in their hands. Candor compels us to admit that we believe that the Sadducees agreed with the Pharisees that Jehovah was a pure and sinless spirit. But we feel equally sure that their knowledge of the Pentateuch, in which at times anthropomorphism is strongly accentuated, taught them that Jehovah had not only appeared in the flesh among men in olden times, but that it was not at all impossible or unreasonable that He should come again in the same form. But this much is certain: that in determining whether Jesus could be both man and God the Sadducees would be disposed to ignore the traditions of the Pharisees and "the later developments of Judaism," and appeal direct to the law of Moses. Jesus Himself, if Sanhedrin.— About three hours after the close of the He had been disposed to make a defense of His claims, and His judges had been disposed to hear Him, would have appealed to the same legal standard. Christ more than once manifested a disposition to appeal to the Mosaic Code, as a modern citizen would appeal from mere statutes and the decisions of the courts, to the constitution, as the fundamental law of the land. Mark tells us that in denouncing the Pharisees, He used this language: "And he said unto them, Full well ye reject the commandment of God, that ye may keep your own tradition. . . .

Making the word of God of none effect through your tradition, which ye have delivered: and many such like things do ye.'"[9] Hebrew sacred literature is filled with anecdotes, often characterized by raillery and jests, of how the Sadducees denounced the Pharisees for their attempts to nullify Mosaic injunction by their peculiar interpretation.

Now in view of what we have just said, are we not justified in assuming that if the judges had accorded Jesus full liberty of defense He would have appealed to the Pentateuch, with the approbation of His judges, to show that God had appeared among men in the flesh, and that a plurality in the Godhead was plainly taught? Would He not then have appealed to the Prophets to show that Jehovah had spoken of a begotten Son who was none other than Almighty God Himself? Would He not have shown from both the Law and the Prophets that the angel of Jehovah, who was none other than Himself, had frequently, in ages past, acted as the ambassador of God in numerous visits to the earth, on missions of love and mercy among men? Would He not have proved to them that this angel of Jehovah had been at certain times in the past none other than Jehovah Himself? Could He not have pointed out to them that their whole sacred literature was filled with prophecies foretelling the coming of this Son and Ambassador of God to the earth to redeem fallen man? Could He not then have summoned a hundred witnesses to prove His own connection with these prophecies, to show His virgin birth, and to give an account of the numerous miracles which He had wrought, and that were the best evidence of His divine character?

Let us imagine that Caiaphas, as judge, had demanded of Jesus, the prisoner, to produce Biblical evidence that God had ever begotten or had promised to beget a Son who was equal with Himself. The following passages might have been produced:

Psa. ii. 7: Thou art my son; this day have I begotten thee.

Isa. ix. 6: For unto us a child is born, unto us a son is given: and the government shall be upon his shoulder: and his name shall be called Wonderful, Counselor, The mighty God, The everlasting Father, The Prince of Peace.

What closer identity, we may ask, could be demanded between the Father and the Son than is revealed by this language of Isaiah, "and his (the son's) name shall be called The mighty God, The everlasting Father?" What more exact equality could be asked than the same words suggest? What stronger proof of plurality in the Godhead could be demanded?

Again, let us suppose that His judges had demanded of Jesus scriptural proof that the divine Son of God was to be born of a woman, and was to have, therefore, the form of a man and the attributes of a human being. The following passages might have been produced:

Isa. vii. 14: Therefore the Lord himself shall give you a sign; Behold, a virgin shall conceive, and bear a son, and shall call his name Immanuel.

Gen. iii. 15: And I will put enmity between thee and the woman, and between thy seed and her seed; it shall bruise thy head, and thou shalt bruise his heel.

Enoch lxii. 5: And one Portion of them will look on the other, and they will be terrified, and their countenance will fall, and pain will seize them when they see *that Son of Woman* sitting on the throne of his glory.

The first of these passages needs no comment. It is perfectly clear and speaks for itself. Regarding the second, it may be observed that after the fall of Adam and Eve in the Garden of Eden it was announced that the seed of the woman should bruise the serpent's head. This announcement contained, when viewed in the light of subsequent revelations, both a promise and a prophecy; a promise of a Redeemer of fallen man, and a prophecy that He would finally triumph over all the powers of sin and darkness whose father was Satan, who had entered into the serpent. The "seed of the woman" foretold that the Redeemer would have a human nature; His triumph over Satan suggested His divine origin and power.

Again, continuing the examination, let us suppose that Caiaphas had informed Jesus that His pretensions to be God in the flesh were not only not sanctioned by but were offensive to the current teachings of Judaism in relation to the person and character of Jehovah. Let us suppose, further, that the high priest had informed the prisoner that he and his fellow-judges, who were Sadducees in faith and a majority in number of the Sanhedrin, did not feel themselves bound by Pharisaic tradition and "the later developments of Judaism"; that they preferred the Mosaic Code as a standard of legal and religious judgment; that the anthropomorphisms of the Pentateuch were not particularly offensive to them, for the reason that they had not been to Moses; and that if He, the prisoner at the bar, could cite instances related by Moses where Jehovah had appeared among men, having the form of a human being, His case would be greatly strengthened; on the ground that if God had ever appeared in the flesh on one occasion it was not unreasonable, or at least impossible, that He should so appear again.

In proof that God had appeared in the flesh, or at least in Human form, among men, the following passages might have been adduced:

Gen. xviii. 1—8: And the Lord appeared unto him in the plains of Mamre: and he sat in the tent door in the heat of the day; And he lifted up his eyes and looked, and, lo, three men stood by him: and when he saw them, he ran to meet them from the tent door, and bowed himself toward the ground, And said, My Lord, if now I have found favor in thy sight, pass not away, I pray thee, from thy servant: . . . And Abraham ran unto the herd, and fetched a calf tender and good, and gave it unto a young man; and he hasted to dress it. And he took butter, and milk, and the calf which he had dressed, and set it before them; and he stood by them under the tree, and they did eat.

Gen. xvi 10—13: And the angel of the Lord said unto her, I will multiply thy seed exceedingly, that it shall not be numbered for multitude. And the angel of the Lord said unto her, Behold, thou art with child, and shalt bear a son, and shalt call his name Ishmael; because the Lord hath heard thy affliction. . . . And she called the name of the Lord that spake unto her, Thou God seest me: for she said, Have I also here looked after him that seeth me?

Gen. xxii. 11, 12: And the angel of the Lord called unto him out of heaven, and said, Abraham, Abraham: and he said, Here am I. And he said, Lay not thine hand upon the lad, neither do thou any thing unto him: for now I know that thou fearest God, seeing thou hast not withheld thy son, thine only son, from me.

Ex. iii. 2—6: And the Angel of the Lord appeared unto him in a flame of fire out of the midst of a bush: and he looked, and, behold, the bush burned with fire, and the bush was not consumed. And Moses said, I will not turn aside, and see this great sight, why the bush is not burnt. And when the Lord saw that he turned aside to see, God called unto him out of the midst of the bush, and said, Moses, Moses. And he said, Here am I. And he said, Draw not nigh hither: put off thy shoes from off thy feet; for the place whereon thou standest is holy ground. Moreover he said, I am the God of thy father, the God of Abraham, the God of Isaac, and the God of Jacob. And Moses hid his face; for he was afraid to look upon God.

From the first passage above cited it is clear that Jehovah, in the form of a man, appeared to Abraham in the plains of Mamre. A contributor to "The Jewish Encyclopedia" declares that these three men were angels in the shape of human beings of extraordinary beauty but that they were not at once recognized as angels.[10] The Christian commentators are generally agreed that it was Jehovah who was present in human form.[11] The other members of the company are declared by some of them to be the second and third persons of the Trinity. Plausibility is given to this contention by the fact that Abraham first saw one person, the Lord; then he looked up and saw three; he then advanced to meet the three, and, addressing them, used a singular epithet, "My Lord." The form of the address, together with the movements of Abraham, seem to suggest three in one and one in three. But with this theory we are not seriously concerned, as our present purpose is to show that Jehovah occasionally appeared in human form upon the earth in the olden days. A plurality of gods is suggested, however, by the passage, if Christian interpretation be applied; for if one of these men was Jehovah, as Abraham's language seems to indicate, and as modern Christian interpretation generally maintains, why could not the other two men have also been gods in the form of the Son and the Holy Spirit? If the Jewish commentator's opinion, to which we have referred heretofore, be plausible—that the three men were angels in human form—why is it not equally as plausible to suppose that a god or gods should also appear in human form? But at all events these three men were not ordinary human beings. He who maintains that they were assaults the intelligence of either the translators of the Bible or of Abraham, or both; for the Hebrew patriarch believed that Jehovah was present as a guest in his house, and he spread a hospitable meal for him. The language of Genesis very clearly indicates as much. And the question may be asked: If Abraham could not recognize Jehovah, who could or can?

In the second of the above extracts from Genesis the angel of the Lord appeared unto Hagar and said to her: "I will multiply thy seed exceedingly, that it shall not be numbered for multitude." And Hagar made reply: "And she called the name of the Lord that spake unto her, Thou God seest me." This passage plainly teaches that the angel of the Lord and Jehovah were sometimes identical.

The third passage heretofore cited from Genesis also teaches the identity of the angel of the Lord and of God Himself, in the matter of the attempted sacrifice of Isaac by Abraham. It was the same voice, that of the angel of the Lord, that said: "For now I know that thou fearest God, seeing thou hast not withheld thy son, thine only son from me."

Again, the identity of the angel of the Lord and of Jehovah is unmistakably shown from the account of the voice that cried from the burning bush: "I am the God of thy father, the God of Abraham, the God of Isaac, and the God of Jacob. And Moses hid his face, for he was afraid to look upon God."

Concerning the manifestation of Jehovah to men in angelic and human form a modern writer says; "Much has been written concerning a certain Mal'akh

Yaweh (messenger of Jehovah) who appears in the Old Testament. I say 'a certain' Mal'akh Yaweh, because it is not every Mal'akh Yaweh that appears to which I refer. In most passages the Mal'akh Yaweh is simply an angel sent by the Almighty to communicate his will or purposes to men. These angels are distinctly apprehended as created intelligences, wholly separate and diverse from God. But there is a class of passages in which the Mal'akh Yaweh appears as a self-manifestation of God. He appears indeed in human form and speaks of God in the third person. But those to whom he appears are oppressed by the consciousness that they have seen God and must die. They see in him an impersonation of Deity such as is found in no other angel. He is to their minds not merely a messenger from God but the revelation of the being of God. The Christian fathers for the most part identify him with the Logos of the New Testament. But there is as much reason to adopt the opinion of many modern writers who hold that he is Jehovah himself appearing in human form, for he is explicitly addressed as Jehovah (Judges vi. 11—24.)"[12]

The identity of the angel of Jehovah and of Jehovah Himself could not be more conclusively proved than in the appearance to Gideon, related in the passage above cited, Judges vi. 11—24. The absolute identity is revealed in verses 22, 23: "And when Gideon perceived that he was an angel of the Lord, Gideon said, Alas, O Lord God! for because I have seen an angel of the Lord face to face. And the Lord said unto him, Peace be unto thee; fear not: thou shalt not die."

Now let us suppose that Caiaphas and the Sanhedrin had received these passages favorably; that they had become convinced that Jehovah had appeared in the olden days in the form of angels and of men; that at one time He was identical with a man, and at another with an angel whom He had sent. Let us suppose further that the judges of Jesus had demanded of Him a passage of ancient Scriptures connecting Him even remotely with this messenger of God. The following passage might have been produced:

Ex. xxiii. 20, 21: Behold, I send an Angel before thee, to keep thee in the way, and to bring thee into the place which I have prepared. Beware of him, and obey his voice, provoke him not; for he will not pardon your transgressions: for my name is in him.

The concluding paragraph of the last cited passage, "My name is in him," is equivalent to "I am in him." The mere name of God is often used to denote God Himself as manifested. For instance, in I Kings viii. 29 is contained the statement, "My name shall be there"; that is, "There will I dwell." And when it is said that the name of Jehovah would be in the angel of Jehovah it is equivalent to saying that Jehovah Himself would be present in His messenger which He had sent before Him. The passage further teaches that the messenger of Jehovah to the earth bore a commission to pardon sin, or not to, according to his pleasure. The Sanhedrin were undoubtedly aware that Jesus claimed the same power by virtue of authority vested in Him by His Father.

But it may be imagined that Caiaphas was perfectly willing to concede that Jehovah had appeared in human form upon the earth, but was not inclined to believe that He had ever manifested human passions and emotions, as Jesus had done when He denounced on several occasions the hypocrisy of the Pharisees;

and, above all, when He overthrew the tables in the Temple, and, applying a lash to their backs, drove out the money-changers.[13] Let us imagine that the high priest demanded of the prisoner proof from the ancient Scriptures that Jehovah was possessed of ordinary human attributes; and particularly that He was at times disposed to fight. Jesus might have produced the following passages to show that Jehovah, His Father, had manifested in times past the ordinary human passions and emotions of repentance, grief, jealousy, anger, graciousness, love, and hate:

Ex. xv. 3, 6: The Lord is a man of war. . . . Thy right hand, O Lord, is become glorious in power: thy right hand, O Lord, hath dashed in pieces the enemy.

Gen. vi. 6: And it *repented* the Lord that he had made man on the earth, and it grieved him at his heart.

Deut. vi. 15: For the Lord thy God is a *jealous* God among you, lest the anger of the Lord thy God be kindled against thee, and destroy thee from off the face of the earth.

Psa. cxi. 4: He hath made his wonderful works to be remembered: the Lord is *gracious* and full of *compassion.*

I Kings x. 9: Because the Lord *loved* Israel forever, therefore made he thee king, to do judgment and justice.

Prov. vi. 16: These six things doth the Lord *hate:* yea, seven are an abomination unto him.

And as a final step in the examination let us imagine that Caiaphas and his colleagues had stated to Jesus that they were satisfied, from the authorities cited, that Jehovah had, in ancient days, appeared upon the earth in human form and had exhibited human attributes; that Jehovah had begotten a Son who was equal in power and majesty with Himself: that this Son had been begotten of a woman and possessed, therefore, human form and attributes; that this Jehovah had sent an angel messenger to the earth with a commission to pardon sins. Let us imagine further that the judges had demanded of the prisoner that He present and prove His credentials as the divine ambassador of God from heaven to men on earth; that He conform His personal claims to heavenly Messiahship to ancient prophecy by producing evidence before them in court. What facts, we may ask, could Jesus have shown to establish His claims to Messiahship and to Sonship of the Father?

To attempt to originate a defense for Jesus would be unnecessary, if not actually impertinent and sacrilegious. We are fully justified, however, in assuming that if called upon to prove His claims to Messiahship He would have made the same reply to the Sanhedrin that He had already made to the Jews out of court who asked Him: "What sign shewest thou, then, that we may see, and believe thee? what dost thou work?"[14] "How long dost thou make us to doubt? If thou be the Christ, tell us plainly. Jesus answered them, I told you, and ye believed not: *the works that I do in my Father's name, they bear witness of me.*"[15] Again, He would have doubtless made the same reply to Caiaphas that He did to the embassy from John the Baptist who came to inquire if He was really the Messiah. "Jesus answered and said unto them, Go and shew John again those things which ye do hear and see: The blind receive their sight, and the lame walk, the lepers are cleansed, and the deaf hear, the dead are raised up, and the poor have the gospel preached to them."[16]

Under a fair trial, in daylight, with full freedom of defense to the accused, abundant evidence could have been secured of the miraculous powers of Jesus and of the truthfulness of His pretensions to a divine origin. Testimony could have been introduced that would have been not only competent but entirely satisfactory. The New Testament narratives tell us of about forty miracles that Jesus performed during His life. The closing verse of St. John intimates that He performed many that were never reported. The circumstances surrounding the working of these wonders were such as to make them peculiarly competent as evidence and to carry conviction of their genuineness, when they were once introduced.

In the first place, miracles were entirely capable of being proved by testimony. If those persons who had known Lazarus intimately during his lifetime saw him dead on one day, and on the fourth day afterwards saw him alive and walking the streets, the senses would be perfectly competent to decide and the fact that a miracle had been performed would be conclusively proved. And it may be added that a dozen witnesses who were entirely competent to testify could have been summoned to the defense of Jesus in the matter of raising Lazarus from the dead.

Again, we must remember that the miracles of Jesus were performed in the most public manner, in the street, on the highway, in far-away Galilee, and at the very gates of Jerusalem. Both His friends and enemies, men and women, were witnesses of their performance. The number and publicity of these wonder-working performances rendered it possible for the Sanhedrin to call before them hundreds and thousands of competent witnesses who had seen and felt the manifestation of the divine power of the prisoner in their presence.

Again, the miracles of Jesus were such as to render them subject to the test of the senses, when submitted to examination. If Caiaphas and his fellow-judges had decided that there was fraud in the matter of the alleged raising of Lazarus from the dead, because the brother of Martha and Mary was not really dead, but simply swooned or slept; if they had decided that the man sick of the palsy was not cured by miracle, but by faith; nevertheless, they could not have charged fraud and faith cure in the matter of the stilling of the tempest or the feeding of the five thousand or the walking on the sea. They would have been forced to conclude that the witnesses had lied or that miracles had been wrought. In the case of the feeding of the five thousand, the witnesses would have been too numerous to brand with falsehood.

But, we may ask, was the performance of miracles by Jesus, if believed by the Sanhedrin, sufficient evidence of the divine origin of Jesus? This question we are not prepared to answer positively, either yes or no. We can only venture the personal opinion that the act of raising a person indisputably dead, to life again, would be an astounding miracle, an achievement that could be wrought by the hand of a God alone. The trouble with the question is that men like Elijah raised the dead.[17] It is true that there is no pretension that Elijah was divine or that he wrought the miracle by virtue of any peculiar power within himself. The Scriptures plainly state that he asked God to raise the dead to life through him.

The same is true of the raising of Lazarus by Jesus.[18] But Christ seems to have raised the daughter of Jairus[19] and the son of the widow of Nain[20] from the dead by virtue of the strength of His own divinity; for there is no suggestion that the power of God was either previously invoked or subsequently acknowledged.

As to the weight which the testimony of the miracles of Jesus should have had with Caiaphas and the other members of the court, we have a valuable indication in the opinion expressed by Nicodemus, who was himself a member of the Sanhedrin, when he said to Jesus: "We know that thou art a teacher come from God: for no man can do these miracles that thou doest, except God be with him."[21] If Nicodemus, "a ruler of the Jews" and one of the leading members of their highest tribunal, believed that Jesus was divine because of the wonders that He had wrought, why should not a knowledge of these miracles by the other members of the Sanhedrin have produced the same impression? Nicodemus, it is true, was a friend of Jesus, but he was not a disciple. And the very timidity with which he expressed his friendship, having come at night to pay him compliments to the Master, demonstrates the deep impression that the miraculous powers of the Christ had made upon him.

But the judges of Jesus were not limited to the evidence of miracles as a proof of the divinity of the prisoner in their midst. They should have weighed "in the sincerity of their conscience" the fact that Jesus was born in Bethlehem in fulfillment of the prophecy contained in Micah v. 2; that He was sprung from the House of David in conformity with the teachings in Jeremiah xxiii. 5, 6; that John the Baptist was His forerunner like unto Elijah, who had come to prepare the way according to the prophecy in Malachi iii. 1; that He had begun to preach in Galilee, as foretold in Isaiah ix. 1, 2; that the scepter had departed from Judah and the lawgiver from between his feet, as prophesied in Genesis xlix. 10, which fact it was believed would herald the approach of the Messiah; that He had made His public entry into Jerusalem riding upon an ass, as foretold in Zechariah ix. 9; and that He had been betrayed into their hands by one of His own friends, in fulfillment of prophecies contained in Psalms xli. 9 and Zechariah xi. 12, 13.

This cumulative evidence, this collective proof, must have carried overwhelming conviction to the minds and the hearts of fair and impartial judges. More than one Nicodemus would have arisen to plead the case of Jesus if this testimony had been adduced before a free-minded, open-hearted, disinterested tribunal. More than one Joseph of Arimathea would have refused assent to a hostile verdict against a prisoner in whose favor the record of fact was so pronounced.

In determining the weight that this evidence should have had in affecting the decision of the judges we must not forget that a Jewish prisoner was not required to prove his innocence. It was incumbent upon the Commonwealth of Israel to establish guilt beyond all doubt. We should also remember that the peculiar tendency of the Hebrew system of criminal procedure was in the direction of complete protection to the accused. Not reasonable doubt merely, but all doubt was resolved in his favor. It was a maxim of the Hebrew law that "the Sanhedrin

was to save, not to destroy life." Pretext after pretext was sought to acquit. "The primary object of the Hebrew judicial system," says Benny, "was to render the conviction of an innocent person impossible. All the ingenuity of the Jewish legists was directed to the attainment of this end." If this generous and merciful tendency of Hebrew law had been duly observed, would not the production of the evidence above noted have resulted in the acquittal of Jesus?

But, at this point, let us return to the consideration of the real meaning of the objection urged in Point XII. The irregularity therein alleged is that the Sanhedrin paid no attention whatever to the defense of Jesus. And herein was the real error. The members of that court might have rejected as false the claims of the Nazarene to Messiahship. They might have denounced as fraudulent his pretensions to miraculous powers. They could not for this reason have been charged with judicial unfairness, if they had first heard his defense and had then "weighed it in the sincerity of their conscience." Infallibility of judgment cannot be demanded of judicial officers.

In closing the discussion of errors committed at the night trial in the palace of Caiaphas, the reader should be reminded that the twelve Points above mentioned are not exhaustive of the irregularities. Others might be mentioned. It seems that Jesus, being the accused, should not have been put under oath.[22] On the days on which capital verdicts were pronounced Hebrew judges were required to mourn and fast.[23] But there was evidently no mourning and fasting by Caiaphas and his colleagues at the time of the condemnation of Jesus. Again, there is no evidence that Antecedent Warning was properly administered. Still other errors might be noted, if a legal presumption in favor of the correctness of the record did not prevent. The irregularities which we have heretofore discussed, it is believed, exhaust all the material errors committed at the first session of the Sanhedrin. At least, no others are revealed by the Gospel records.

The Morning Session of the Sandedrin. — About three hours after the close of the night session in the palace of Caiaphas, that is about six o'clock in the morning, the Sanhedrin reconvened in a second session. In the interval between these sittings Jesus was brutalized by His keepers. Exactly what the priests were doing we do not know. There were probably busily engaged in perfecting plans for the destruction of the prisoner in their charge.

The daylight meeting is thus reported in Matthew xxvii. 1: "When the morning was come, all the chief priests and elders of the people took counsel against Jesus to put him to death." In Mark xv. 1 the same session is thus recorded: "And straightway in the morning the chief priests held a consultation with the elders and scribes and the whole council, and bound Jesus, and carried him away, and delivered him to Pilate."

The exact nature of this morning sitting, whether a regular trial or an informal gathering, is not certainly known. Meyer, Ellicott, and Lichtenstein maintain that this second session was nothing more than a prolongation of the night trial, perhaps with a brief recess, and that its special object was to convene for consultation concerning the carrying out of the sentence which had already been pronounced against Jesus.[24] But this view is entirely exceptional. It is maintained by the greater number of reputable authorities that the second sitting was in the nature of a second trial. The solution of the difficulty seems to turn upon the account given by St. Luke, for St. John records the details of neither the night nor the morning session. St. Luke describes a regular trial, but it is not positively known whether his account refers to the night or to the morning meeting. If his report refers to the same trial as that described in Matthew xxvi. 57—68 and in Mark xiv. 53—65, then we have only the brief notices in Matthew xxvii. 1 and in Mark xv. 1 concerning the morning session, which indicate only a very brief and informal meeting of the Sanhedrin at daybreak. On the other hand, if the report of St. Luke refers to the daylight meeting of the Sanhedrin referred to by St. Matthew and St. Mark then we have received from the third Evangelist a description of a regular trial at the second session of the Sanhedrin. Andrews has thus expressed himself very cogently concerning this matter:

Our decision as to a second and distinct session of the Sanhedrin will mainly depend upon the place we give to the account in Luke xxii. 66—71. Is this examination of Jesus identical with that first session of Matthew xxvi. 57—68, and of Mark xiv. 53—65? Against this identity are some strong objections: First, The mention of time by Luke: "As soon as it was day." This corresponds well to the time of the morning session of Matthew and Mark, but not to the time when Jesus was first led before the Sanhedrin, which must have been two or three hours before day. Second, The place of the meeting: "They led Him into their council," ἀνήγαγον αὐτὸν εἰς τὸ συνέδριον ἑαυτῶν. This is rendered by some: "They led Him up into their council chamber," or the place where they usually held their sessions. Whether this council chamber was the room Gazith at the east corner of the court of the temple is not certain. Lightfoot (on Matthew xxvi. 3) conjectures that the Sanhedrin was driven from this its accustomed seat half a year or thereabout before the death of Christ. But if this were so, still the "Tabernae," where it established its sessions, were shops near the gate Shushan, and so connected with the temple. They went up to that room where they usually met. Third, The dissimilarity of the proceedings, as stated by Luke, which shows that this was no formal trial. There is here no mention of witnesses—no charges brought to be proved against Him. He is simply asked to tell them if He is the Christ ("If thou art the Christ, tell us," R. V.); and this seems plainly to point to the result of the former session. Then, having confessed Himself to be the Christ, the Son of God, He was condemned to death for blasphemy. It was only necessary now that He repeat His confession, and hence this question is put directly to Him: "Art thou the Christ? tell us." His reply, "If I tell you, ye will not believe; and if I also ask you, ye will not answer me, nor let me go," points backward to his former confession. To His reply they only answer by asking, "Art thou then the Son of God?" The renewed avowal that He is the Son of God, heard by them all from His own lips, opens the way for His immediate delivery into Pilate's hands. Fourth, The position which Luke gives (xxii. 63—65) to the insults and abuse heaped upon Jesus. There can be no doubt that they are the same mentioned by Matthew and Mark as occurring immediately after the sentence had been first pronounced.

From all this it is probable, though not a certain conclusion, that Luke (xxii. 66—71) refers to the same meeting of the Sanhedrin mentioned by Matthew (xxvii. 1) and Mark (xv. 1), and relates, in part, what then took place. (Alford thinks that Luke has confused things and relates as happening at the second session what really happened at the first.) This meeting was, then, a morning session convened to ratify formally what had been done before with haste and informality. The circumstances under which its members had been earlier convened, at the palace of Caiaphas, sufficiently show that the legal forms, which they were so scrupulous in observing, had not been complied with.[25]

If then the second session of the Sanhedrin was in the nature of a regular trial, what were the facts of the proceedings? St. Luke says: "And as soon as it was day, the elders of the people and the chief priests and the scribes came together, and led him into their council, saying, Art thou the Christ? tell us. And he said unto them, If I tell you, ye will not believe: And if I also ask you, ye will not answer me, nor let me go. Hereafter shall the Son of man sit on the right hand of the power of God. Then said they all, Art thou then the Son of God? And he said unto them, Ye say that I am. And they said, What need we any further witness? for we ourselves have heard of his own mouth."[26]

The reader will readily perceive the source of the difficulty which we have just discussed. This report of St. Luke points both ways, toward both the night and morning sessions. *"And as soon as it was day"* clearly indicates a daybreak meeting, but the remainder of the account bears a most striking resemblance to the reports of the night trial given by St. Matthew and St. Mark. This seeming discrepancy is very easily reconciled, however, when we reflect that the second trial required by Hebrew law to be held in every case where a verdict of guilt had been pronounced, was virtually a repetition of the first trial. Benny tells us that the second trial was a critical examination of the trial of the first day, in which the questions and answers originally asked and made were carefully reviewed and reexamined.[27] Is it very strange, then, that at the morning trial described by St. Luke substantially the same questions are asked and answers given as are found in the reports of the night trial by St. Matthew and St. Mark?

We may now ask: What was the purpose of this second trial? Why did not the first trial suffice? According to the most reliable authorities, the answer to this question is to be found in that provision of the Hebrew law which required two trials instead of one, in every case where the prisoner had been found guilty at the first trial. Not only were there to be two trials, but they were to be held on different days. The morning session of the Sanhedrin was intended, therefore, to give a semblance of legality and regularity to this requirement of Hebrew law. But we shall see how completely the Sanhedrin failed in this design. "What legitimacy," says Keim, "might be lacking in the proceedings of the nocturnal sitting of the Sanhedrin, was to be completely made up by the morning sitting, without prejudice to the authority and the—in the main point—decisive action of the former. . . . There nevertheless was no lack of illegality. The most striking instance of this was the fact that though they wished to bring about an extension of the procedure over two days they had in fact only two sittings, and not two separate days. But contempt of the legal ordinances was much more seriously shown by the absence of any investigation into the circumstances of the case at the second sitting, although *both law and tradition demanded such an investigation.* "[28]

If "both law and tradition demanded such an investigation," that is, if the second trial of the case on the second day of the proceedings was required to be formal and in the nature of an action *de novo;* if the second trial was required by law to be characterized by all the formality, solemnity, and legality of the first trial; what errors, we may ask, are disclosed by the reports of St. Luke, St. Matthew, and St. Mark in the proceedings against Jesus conducted by the

Sanhedrin at the morning session? To be brief, reply may be made that the irregularites were virtually the same as those that occurred at the night trial. The same precipitancy that was forbidden by Hebrew law is apparent. This haste prevented, of course, that careful deliberation and painstaking investigation of the case which the Mosaic Code as well as the rules of the Mishna imperatively demanded. It is true that the second trial was not conducted at night. But the Passover Feast was still in progress, and no court could legally sit at such a time. The Sanhedrin at the second session seems to have been still sitting in the palace of Caiaphas instead of the Hall of Hewn Stones, the legal meeting place of the court. This we learn from a passage in St. John.[29] Again, no witnesses seem to have been summoned and the accused was convicted upon his uncorroborated confession.

And finally, the verdict at the second trial, as was the case in that of the first, seems to have been unanimous, and therefore illegal. This unanimity is indicated by the combined reports of St. Matthew, St. Mark, and St. Luke. St. Matthew says:"When the morning was come, *all* the chief priests and elders of the people took counsel against Jesus to put Him to death." St. Mark says: "And straightway in the morning, the chief priests held a consultation with the elders and scribes and the *whole council,* and bound Jesus and carried him away, and delivered him to Pilate." These accounts of the first two Evangelists very clearly state that the full Sanhedrin was present at the morning trial. Then St. Luke very explicitly explains the nature and manner of the verdict: "Then said they *all,* Art thou then the Son of God? And he said unto them, Ye say that I am. And they said, What need we any further witness? for we ourselves have heard of his own mouth."

It may be objected that no formal verdict was pronounced at the second trial. Such a verdict would have been expressed in these words: "Thou, Jesus, art guilty."[30] While such words are not expressly reported by the Evangelists, the account of St. Luke taken in connection with the report of St. Mark of the night trial, which the morning session was intended to confirm, clearly indicates that such a verdict must have been pronounced. A reasonable inference from the whole context of the synoptic writers in describing both trials certainly justifies such a conclusion.

The question again arises: If the full Sanhedrin was present at the morning session and if all the members condemned Jesus, either with or without a formal verdict, is it not true that both Nicodemus and Joseph of Arimathea, who were doubtless members of the court, were arrayed against the Christ? If they were hostile in their attitude toward Him, either openly or by acquiescence at the morning session, does this fact not help to support the contention made under Point IX that they voted against Him at the night trial? We are well aware that there is much opposition to this view, but we are, nevertheless, compelled to agree rather reluctantly with Keim that "it is a pure supposition that members of the council who were secret friends of Jesus—whose existence, moreover, cannot be established—either raised an opposition in one of the sessions, or abstained from voting, or were not present."[31] The plain language of the Scriptures indicates: (1) That both Nicodemus[32] and Joseph of Arimathea[33] were members of the Great Sanhedrin; (2) that they were both present at both trials;[34] and (3) that they both either voted against Him or tacitly acquiesced in the judgments pronounced against Him.[35] We have already discussed under Point IX the passage in Luke xxiii. 51 referring to the fact that Joseph of Arimathea "had not consented to the counsel and deed of them," which seems to furnish refutation of the contention which we have made, as far as such contention relates to Joseph of Arimathea. Suffice it to note the opinion of Keim that "the passage in itself can be held to refer to absence or to dissent in voting."[36]

"And the whole multitude of them arose, and led him unto Pilate."

The reader may ask: Why did the Jews lead Jesus away to Pilate? When they had condemned Him to death on the charge of blasphemy, why did they themselves not put Him to death? Why did they invoke Roman interference in the matter? Why did they not stone Jesus to death, as Hebrew law required in the case of culprits convicted of blasphemy? Stephen was stoned to death for blasphemy.[37] What was the difference between his case and that of Jesus? Why was Jesus crucified instead of being put to death by stoning?

The stoning of Stephen as a blasphemer by the Jews has been explained as an irregular outbreak of fanatical priests, a sort of mob violence. It has also been contended that the case of Stephen was one of the rare instances in which Roman procurators permitted the Jews to execute the death sentence. In any event it was an exceptional proceeding. At the time of the crucifixion of Jesus and of the martyrdom of Stephen the Jews had lost the right of enforcing the death penalty. Judea was a subject province of the Roman empire. The Jews were permitted by the Romans to try capital cases. If an acquittal was the result, the Romans did not interfere. If a verdict of guilty was found, the Jews were compelled to lead the prisoner away to the Roman governor, who reviewed or retried the case as he saw fit. Accordingly, having condemned Him to death themselves, the Jews were compelled to lead Jesus away to the palace of Herod on the hill of Zion in which Pilate was stopping on the occasion of the Paschal Feast, to see what he had to say about the matter, whether he would reverse or affirm the sentence which they had pronounced.

The Roman trial of Jesus will be treated in the second volume of this work.

END OF VOL. I

NOTES
TO
VOLUME I

PART I
THE RECORD OF FACT

1 "Testimony of the Evangelists," pp. 7-11.
2 "Testimony of the Evangelists," pp. 25, 26.
3 "Starkie on Evidence," pp. 480-545.
4 John x. 30: "I and my Father are one."
5 Matt. ix. 9.
6 Col. iv. 14: "Luke, the beloved physician."
7 Matt. xxvi. 70-72.
8 Matt. xxvi. 46-50.
9 Matt. xxvi. 56.
10 Matt. xiv. 28-31.
11 Mark x. 35-42; Matt. xx. 20-25.
12 Matt. xi. 2, 3.
13 Mark iii. 21.
14 Luke iv. 28, 29.
15 Mark xiv. 51, 52.
16 "Intro. Vie de Jesus."
17 Luke i. 2, 3.
18 "Die synoptischen Evangelien," pp. 412-14.
19 Marcus Dods, "The Bible, Its Origin and Nature," p. 184.
20 An opposite doctrine seems to be taught in Luke xii. 11, 12; xxiv. 48, 49.
21 "Evidences of Christianity," p. 319.
22 Matt. xiv. 12-20; Mark vi. 34-43; Luke ix. 12-17; John vi. 5-13.
23 Luke xxii. 64.
24 Luke xxii. 51.
25 Campbell's "Philosophy of Rhetoric," c. v. b. 1, Part III, p. 125.
26 "Intro. Vie de Jesus," p. 62.
27 D. L. Moody, "Sermon on the Resurrection of Jesus."
28 See also 1 "Starkie on Evidence," pp. 496-99.
29 "Ant.," XVIII. 3, 1.
30 See authorities cited in "The Brief."
31 "De iis qui sero puniuntur," p. 554.
32 P. 1080, edit. 45.
33 P. 1247, edit. 24, Huds.
34 P. 1327, edit. 43.
35 "Productique omnes, virgisque caesi, ac securi percussi," Lib. XI. c. 5.
36 Domit. Cap. X. "Patremfamilias—canibus objecit, cum hoc *titulo,* Impie locutas, parmularius."
37 Book LIV.
38 "Aur. Vict. Ces.," Cap. XLI. "Eo pius, ut etiam vetus veterrimumque supplicium, patibulum, et cruribus suffringendis, primus removerit." Also see Paley's "Evidences of Christianity," pp. 266-68.
39 Luke xxii. 44.
40 Tissot, "Traite des Nerfs," pp. 279, 280.
41 Joannes Schenck a Grafenberg, "Observ. Medic.," Lib. III. p. 458.

42 Voltaire, "Oeuvres completes," vol. xvii. op. 531, 532.

43 De Mezeray, "Histoire de France," vol. iii. p. 306.

44 John xix. 34.

45 John xix. 35.

46 John xviii. 6.

47 "Encyc. Brit.," vol. xv. p. 550.

PART II

CHAPTER I HEBREW CRIMINAL LAW—MOSAIC AND TALMUDIC

1 Mendelsohn, "Criminal Jurisprudence of the Ancient Hebrews," p. 191.

2 Mendelsohn, p. 189, n. 1.

3 "Jewish Encyc.," vol. xii. p. 1.

4 Emanuel Deutsch, "The Talmud," p. 26.

5 Farrar, "Hist. of Interpretation."

6 Emanuel Deutsch, "The Talmud," p. 47.

7 "Encyc. Brit.," vol. xxiii. p. 35.

8 Emanuel Deutsch, "The Talmud," p. 58.

9 Emanuel Deutsch, "The Talmud," p. 27.

10 Emanuel Deutsch, "The Talmud," p. 27.

11 Deut. xvi. 18.

12 "Ant.," XIII. 10, 6.

13 Horace.

14 Emanuel Deutsch, "The Talmud," p. 12.

15 "Jewish Encyc.," vol. xii. p. 22.

16 Emanuel Deutsch, "Talmud," p. 12.

CHAPTER II HEBREW CRIMINAL LAW—CRIMES AND PUNISHMENTS

1 Maimon., "H. Sanh." xv. 10-13.

2 Mendelsohn, "Criminal Jurisprudence of the Ancient Hebrews," pp. 45-50.

3 Mendelsohn, "Criminal Jurisprudence of the Ancient Hebrews," pp. 45-50.

4 Mendelsohn, p. 43.

5 Mendelsohn, pp. 39, 40.

6 Mendelsohn, pp. 39, 40.

7 Maimonides ("Yad"), "Sanhedrin" xix.

8 Dr. Smith's "Hist. of Greece," p. 557.

9 "Jewish Encyc.," vol. ii. p. 257.

10 Ex. ii. 12-16.

11 "Sanh." 52b; Maim., "H. Sanh." xv. 4.

12 "H. Sanh." xv. 5.

13 Benny, "Crim. Code of the Jews," p. 90.

14 Mendelsohn, p. 159.

CHAPTER III HEBREW CRIMINAL LAW—COURTS AND JUDGES

1 Chap. I. 10; X. i, 2.

2 Matt. xxvi. 59.

3 "Ant.," XIV. Chap. V. 4; "Wars of the Jews," I. VIII. 5; "Talmud," "Sanhedrin."

4 "Post Bibl. Hist.," vol. i. p. 106.

5 Matt. xvi. 21.

6 "Commentary on the Law," vol. ccclxvi. recto.

7 "Sanhedrin" 32.

8 Benny.

9 Jose b. Halafta, I. c.

10 R. Johanan, "Sanhedrin" 19a.

11 Benny.

12 Benny.

13 "Sanhedrin" 17a; "Menahoth" 65a.

14 Sifre, Num. 92 (ed. Friedmann, p. 25b).

15 Yalkut, "Exodus," Sec. 167.

16 Sotah 22b.

17 "Const. of the Sanhedrin," Chap. I.

18 Benny, "The Criminal Code of the Jews," p. 71.

19 Saalschutz, "Das Mosaische Recht," p. 58; Deut. xx. 5, 6.

20 Luke ii. 46-51.

21 Jer. xxxvii., xxxviii.

22 "Jesus of Nazara," vol. vi. p. 45.

23 "The Life and Words of Christ," vol. ii. p. 517.

24 "Archaeol." 87.

25 Acts xxiv. 1, 2.

26 I Kings iii. 16-28.

27 Mendelsohn, "Criminal Jurisprudence of the Ancient Hebrews," pp. 102, 103.

28 Mendelsohn, pp. 96-98.

29 "Sanhedrin," Chap. I. fol. 19.

30 Mendelsohn, p. 97.

31 Mishna, "Sanhedrin," Chap. IV. 1.

32 Mendelsohn, p. 98.

33 "Sanhedrin" 8b, 41a, *et al.*

34 Mendelsohn, p. 101.

35 Schurer, "The Jewish People in the Time of Jesus Christ," 2d Div., 1.

36 "Sanhedrin" IV. 4.

37 "Sanhedrin" IV. 1.

38 "Sanhedrin" 17a, p. 176.

39 "Sanhedrin," Chap. I. 5.

40 Benny.

41 Benny.

42 Benny.

43 Mendelsohn, p. 140, n. 327.

44 Montaigne, "Essays," III. C. XIII.

45 "Un homme ne jugera jamais seul; cela n'appartient qu'a Dieu." "Ne sis judex unus; non est enim unicus judex, nisi unus."—Salvador, "Institutions de Moise," L. IV. Chap. II. p. 357.

CHAPTER IV HEBREW CRIMINAL LAW—WITNESSES AND EVIDENCE

1 "But let not the testimony of women be admitted, on account of the levity and boldness of their sex."—Josephus, "Ant.," IV. 8, 15.

2 "Nor let servants be admitted to give testimony, on account of the ignobility of their souls."—"Ant.," IV. 8, 15.

3 "Ant.," IV. 8, 15.

4 Maimonides, I. C. XI. 6, based on "Sanh." 26b.

5 Mendelsohn, p. 118.

6 "Talmud," B. B. 43a.

7 Deut. xvii. 6.

8 Num. xxxv. 30.

9 "Hist. Nat.," Lib. VIII. Cap. XXII.

10 L. 20, Dig. De quaestionibus, xlviii. 18.

11 Blackstone, iv. 357.

12 Con. U. S., Art. III, Sec. 3.

13 "Les lois qui font perir un homme sur la deposition d'un seul temoin, sont fatales a la liberte. La raison en exige deux; parce qu'un temoin qui affirme, et un accuse qui nie, font un partage; et il faut un tiers pour le vider. Les Grecs and les Romains exigeaient une voix de plus pour condamner. Nos lois francaises en demandent deux. Les Grecs pretendaient que leur usage avait ete etabli par les dieux; mais c'est le notre."—"De L'Esprit Des Lois," L. XII. C. III.

14 Mishna, "Sanhedrin," C. V. 2.

15 Maimonides, "Sanhedrin," Chap. XX.

16 "Jewish Encyc.," vol. v. p. 277.

17 "Criminal Jurisprudence of the Ancient Hebrews," p. 29.

18 Philo Judaeus, "De Decalogo," III.

19 Prov. xi. 10; Mishna, "Sanhedrin" IV. 5.

20 Apocrypha.

21 Benny.

22 Mishna, "Sanhedrin," Chap. V. 1.

23 Benny.

24 Deut. xix. 18-21.

25 Apocrypha.

26 Maimonides, Mishna, "Sanhedrin," Chap. IV. 2.

27 Munsterberg, "On the Witness Stand," "Untrue Confessions," pp. 137-171.

28 Rosadi.

29 Rabbi Wise, "Martyrdom of Jesus."

30 "Yad," Edut, xvii. 1.

31 "Jewish Encyc.," vol. v. p. 279.

32 Num. xxxv. 30.

33 Mishna, "Sanhedrin" V. 3, 4.

34 Matt. xxvi. 60.

35 Mark xiv. 56.

36 Lev. xxii. 28.

37 Deut. xvii. 5; "Sanhedrin" VII. 4.

38 Num. vi. 2-4.

39 "Jewish Encyc.," vol. vi. p. 260.

40 "Einleitung in der Gesetzgebung," p. 4.

41 "Jewish Encyc.," vol. vi. p. 260; Benny, "Criminal Code of the Jews," p. 97; Saalschutz, "Das Mosaische Recht," n. 560.

CHAPTER V HEBREW CRIMINAL LAW—MODE OF TRIAL AND EXECUTION IN CAPITAL CASES

1 Mishna, treatise Makhoth.

2 Mishna, "Capita Patrum," I. 1.

3 Salvador, "Institutions de Moise."

4 Mishna, "Sanhedrin" IV. 1.

5 "Jesus Before the Sanhedrin," p. 109.

6 "Talmud," Jerus., Sanh., C. I. fol. 19.

7 Mishna, "Tamid," C. III.

8 Geikie, vol. ii. p. 517.

9 Lyman Abbott, "Jesus of Nazareth," pp. 446, 447.

10 "Jewish Encyc.," vol. v. pp. 279, 280.

11 Benny.

12 Mendelsohn, p. 144.

PART III THE BRIEF

1 Josephus, "Ant.," XIV. 9, 4.

2 Schurer, 2d div., vol. i. p. 175.

3 Schurer, 2d div., vol. i. p. 184.

4 "Life and Times of Jesus the Messiah," vol. ii. p. 556.

5 "Jesus of Nazara," vol. vi. p. 37.

6 "The Talmud," p. 32.

7 "Ant." xv. 6, 2.

8 "History of the Jews," vol. ii. p. 163.

9 "Tribus, pseudo-propheta, sacerdos magnus, non nisi a septuaginta et unius judicum consessu judicantur."—"Mishna, De Synedriis," i. 5.

10 "Among the offenses of which it took cognizance were false claims to prophetic inspiration and blasphemy."—Andrews, "The Life of Our Lord," p. 510.

11 "Gesch. d. Judenth." vol. i. pp. 402-409.

12 "Life and Times of Jesus the Messiah," vol. ii. p. 553.

13 "Vie de Jesus." pp. 303, 304.

14 "Trial of Jesus Christ," p. 81.

15 Matt. xxvi. 60, 61.

16 Mark xiv. 57, 58.

17 Matt. xxvi. 64-66.

18 Mark xiv. 56.

19 John ii. 20.

20 John ii. 19.

21 John ii. 21.

22 "The Martyrdom of Jesus," pp. 75-77.

23 Deut. xiii. 1-5.

24 I Kings xxi. 10.

25 Isa. lii. 5; Ezek. xxxv. 12.

26 Luke xxii. 65; Acts xiii. 45; xviii. 6.

27 Revelation xiii. 1-6.

28 "Blackstone," vol. ii. pp. 75-84.

29 Greenidge, "Legal Procedure of Cicero's Time," pp. 427, 507, 518.

30 Deut. iv. 15, 16; Deut. xiii.

31 Gen. xli. 16.

32 Num. xx. 10-12.

33 Num xx. 20-24.

34 Greenleaf, "Testimony of the Evangelists," p. 555.

35 Matt. v. 17.

36 John xi. 41.

37 Matt. ix. 20-22; Mark v. 25-34; Luke viii. 43-48.

38 Matt. viii. 24-26; Mark iv. 37-39; Luke viii. 23-25.

39 Matt. viii. 28-32; Mark v. 1-13; Luke viii. 26-33.

40 Matt. ix. 18-26; Mark v. 22-42; Luke viii. 41-55.

41 Luke vii. 12-15.

42 Matt. ix. 2, 3.

43 Luke v. 21.

44 John v. 18.

45 John x. 30-33.

46 John vi. 41.

47 John viii. 58.

48 "Testimony of the Evangelists," p. 562.

49 Edersheim, "Life and Times of Jesus the Messiah," vol. ii. p. 629.

50 John xiii.-xvii.
51 Matt. xi. 3.
52 Luke xxiv. 39-43; John xx. 24-28.

Point I The Arrest of Jesus Was Illegal

1 John xiii. 33.
2 John xviii. 9.
3 "Jesus Devant Caiphe et Pilate."
4 Acts iv. 3.
5 "Life and Times of Jesus the Messiah," vol. ii. p. 494.
6 See Cooley's "Blackstone," vol. ii. p. 330, n. 6; also Greenleaf, "On Evidence," vol. i. pp. 531-35 (10th edition).
7 "Vie de Jesus," p. 303.

Point II The Private Examination of Jesus Before Annas (or Caiaphas) Was Illegal

1 John xviii. 13.
2 Matt. xxvi. 57.
3 Mark xiv. 53.
4 Luke xxii. 54.
5 John xviii. 19.
6 Luke iii. 2; Acts iv. 6.
7 "Life and Times of Jesus the Messiah," vol. i. p. 264.
8 "The Life of Our Lord," p. 142.
9 Luke iii. 2.
10 Plummer, St. Luke, in "International Critical Commentary," pp. 84, 515.
11 Josephus, "Ant.," XVIII. chap. ii. 2.
12 John xviii. 19-23.

Point III The Indictment Against Jesus Was, in Form, Illegal

1 Mark xiv. 58-61.
2 Matt. xxvi. 60-63.
3 Matt. xxvi. 63.
4 Mark xiv. 59.
5 Acts vi. 14.
6 "Jewish Encyc.," vol. i. p. 163.

Point IV The Proceedings of the Sanhedrin Against Jesus Were Illegal Because They Were Conducted at Night

1 Fiske, "Manual of Classical Literature," iii. Sec. 108; Smith, "Dictionary of Greek and Roman Antiquities," 89a.
2 See discussion of Point I.
3 Luke xxii. 66.
4 Luke xxii. 2.
5 Mark xiv. 2.
6 Mark xiv. i; Matt. xxvi, 4 (Consilium fecerunt ut Jesum dolo tenerent et occiderent).

Point VI The Proceedings Against Jesus Were Illegal Because They Were Conducted on the Day Preceding a Jewish Sabbath; also on the First Day of the Feast of Unleavened Bread and the Eve of the Passover

1 Maimonides, "Sanhedrin" II.
2 John xviii. 28; Luke xxii. 1; Mark xiv. 1; Matt. xxvi. 2.

Point VII The Trial of Jesus Was Illegal Because It Was Concluded Within One Day

1 Mishna, "Capita Patrum," I, 1.
2 Mishna, "Treatise Makhoth."
3 See Part II, Chap. V.
4 Edmund Stapfer, "Life of Jesus."
5 Matt. xxvi. 57-66.
6 Mark xiv. 55-64.
7 Matt. xxvii. 1.
8 Mark xv. 1.
9 Luke xxii. 66-71.

Point VIII The Sentence of Condemnation Pronounced Against Jesus By the Sanhedrin Was Illegal Because It Was Founded Upon His Uncorroborated Confession

1 "Martyrdom of Jesus," p. 74.
2 "Criminal Jurisprudence of the Ancient Hebrews," p. 133, n. 311.
3 See Part II, Chap. IV.
4 Mark xiv. 56-65.
5 Mark xiv. 62.
6 Matt. xii. 14-16; Mark iii. 7; ix. 29, 30.
7 Luke xiii. 31, 32.
8 Matt. xxii. 15.
9 John iv. 26.
10 Mark i. 34.
11 John x. 24.
12 Matt. xvi. 20.

Point IX The Condemnation of Jesus Was Illegal Because the Verdict of the Sanhedrin Was Unanimous

1 Blackstone.
2 Mendelsohn, p. 143.
3 Mark xiv. 63, 64.
4 "Martyrdom of Jesus," p. 74.
5 "The Trial of Jesus," p. 200.
6 Matt. xxvi. 59; Mark xiv. 55.
7 Matt. xxvii. 1.
8 Mark xv. 1.
9 John iii. 1; vii. 50.
10 Luke xxiii. 51.
11 John vii. 51.
12 John vii. 50; xix. 39.
13 Luke xxiii. 51.

Point X The Proceedings Against Jesus Were Illegal in That: (1) The Sentence of Condemnation Was Pronounced in a Place Forbidden by Law; (2) The High Priest Rent His Clothes; (3) The Balloting Was Irregular

1 Mendelsohn, p. 98.
2 Deut. xvii. 7, 8.
3 "It is important to notice that every time the necessities of the case required the Sanhedrin returned to the Hall Gazith, or of Hewn Stones, as in the case of Jesus and others."—"Thosephthoth, or Additions to the Talmud," Bab., "Sanhedrin," C. IV. fol. 37, recto.
4 Edersheim, "Life and Times of Jesus the Messiah," vol. ii. p. 556, n. 1.

5 John xviii. 28.

6 MM. Lemann, "Jesus Before the Sanhedrin," p. 140.

7 Mark xiv. 63, 64.

8 Edersheim, "Life and Times of Jesus the Messiah," vol. ii. p. 561.

9 Rabbi Wise, "Martyrdom of Jesus," p. 74.

10 Benny, "Criminal Code of the Jews," p. 81.

11 Matt. xxvi. 65.

Point XI The Members of the Great Sanhedrin Were Legally Disqualified to Try Jesus

1 See Part II, Qualifications of Judges.

2 "Talmud, Pesachim, or the Passover," fol. 57, verso; see also "Jesus Before the Sanhedrin," pp. 54, 55.

3 Benny, "Criminal Code of the Jews," pp. 28-41.

4 Matt. xxi. 31.

5 Matt. xxiii. 14, 15.

6 "Life and Times of Jesus the Messiah," vol. i. pp. 93, 94.

7 Matt. xxiii. 27, 29-33.

8 "Vie de Jesus," p. 267.

9 John xi. 49, 50.

10 John xi. 53.

11 Luke xxii. 1-3.

12 Matt. xxvi. 3-5.

13 Benny, "Criminal Code of the Jews," p. 56.

14 Geikie, "The Life and Words of Christ," vol. ii. p. 517.

15 Deut. xix. 18-21.

16 Mark xiv. 55.

Point XII The Condemnation of Jesus Was Illegal Because the Merits of the Defenses Were Not Considered

1 Mishna, Treatise "Makhoth."

2 "Afresh the mighty line of years unroll'd, The Virgin now, now Saturn's sway returns; Now the blest globe a heaven-sprung Child adorns, Whose genial power shall whelm earth's iron race, And plant once more the golden in its place."—Virgil, Eclogue IV.

3 Gen. xlix, 8-10.

4 "Sanhedrin," fol. 97, verso.

5 "Martyrdom of Jesus" p. 76.

6 John xi. 48-50.

7 I Sam. xv. 29.

8 Hosea xi. 9.

9 Mark vii. 9-13.

10 "Jewish Encyc.," vol. i. p. 583.

11 Hodge, "Systematic Theology," vol. i. p. 485.

12 Steenstra, "The Being of God as Unity and Trinity," pp. 192, 193.

13 John ii. 15.

14 John vi. 30.

15 John x. 24, 25.

16 Matt. xi. 4, 5.

17 I Kings xvii. 17-22.

18 John xi. 41.

19 Matt. ix. 18-26; Mark v. 22-42; Luke viii. 41-55.

20 Luke vii. 12-15.

21 John iii. 2.

22 See Friedlieb, Archaeol., 87; Dupin, 75; Keim, vol. iii. 327.

23 Bab. Sanh. f. 63, 1: "Cum synedrium quemquam moti adjudicavit, ne quidquam degustent illi isto die."

24 Andrews, "The Life of Our Lord," p. 522.

25 "The Life of Our Lord," pp. 523, 524.

26 Luke xxii. 66-71.

27 See Part II, Chap. V.; also Benny, "Crim. Code of the Jews," pp. 81-83.

28 Keim, "Jesus of Nazara," vol. vi. pp. 63, 64.

29 John xviii. 28.

30 "Thou, Reuben, art guilty! Thou, Simon, art acquitted, art not guilty!" were stereotyped forms of verdicts under Hebrew criminal procedure. Sanh. in Friedl., p. 89.

31 Keim, "Jesus of Nazara," vol. vi. p. 74.

32 John iii. 1; vii. 50.

33 Luke xxiii. 50, 51.

34 Matt. xxvi. 59; Mark xiv. 55; Matt. xxvii. 1; Mark xv. 1.

35 Mark xiv. 63, 64; Luke xxii. 70, 71.

36 Keim, "Jesus of Nazara," vol. vi. p. 74, n. 2.

37 Acts vi. 11; vii. 59.

THE ROMAN TRIAL

VOLUME II

CONTENTS OF VOLUME TWO

Preface to Volume Two

NOTES
TO
APPENDICES
Page 188

PREFACE TO VOLUME TWO

Sufficient was said concerning the entire work in the preface to volume one to warrant a very brief preface to volume two.

The reader will notice that the plan of treatment of the Roman trial of Jesus is radically different from that employed in the Hebrew trial. There is no Record of Fact in the second volume, for the reason that the Record of Fact dealt with in the first volume is common to the two trials. Again, there is no Brief of the Roman trial and no systematic and exhaustive treatment of Roman criminal law in the second volume, corresponding with such a treatment of the Hebrew trial, under Hebrew criminal law, in the first volume. This is explained by the fact that the Sanhedrin found Jesus guilty, while both Pilate and Herod found Him not guilty. A proper consideration then of the Hebrew trial became a matter of review on appeal, requiring a Brief, containing a complete statement of facts, an ample exposition of law, and sufficient argument to show the existence of error in the judgment. The nature of the verdicts pronounced by Pilate and by Herod rendered these things unnecessary in dealing with the Roman trial.

In Part II of this volume, Graeco-Roman Paganism at the time of Christ has been treated. It is evident that this part of the treatise has no legal connection with the trial of Jesus. It was added simply to give coloring and atmosphere to the painting of the great tragedy. It will serve the further purpose, it is believed, of furnishing a key to the motives of the leading actors in the drama, by describing their social, religious, and political environments. The strictly legal features of a great criminal trial are rarely ever altogether sufficient for a proper understanding of even the judicial aspects of the case. The religious faith of Pilate, the judge, is quite as important a factor in determining the merits of the Roman trial, as is the religious belief of Jesus, the prisoner. This contention will be fully appreciated after a careful perusal of Chapter VI of this volume.

Short biographical sketches of about forty members of the Great Sanhedrin who tried Jesus have been given under Appendix I at the end of this work. They were originally written by MM. Lemann, two of the greatest Hebrew scholars of France, and are doubtless authoritative and correct. These sketches will familiarize the reader with the names and characters of a majority of the Hebrew judges of Jesus. And it may be added that they are a very valuable addition to the general work, since the character of the tribunal is an important consideration in the trial of any case, civil or criminal.

The apocryphal Acts of Pilate have been given under Appendix II. But the author does not thereby vouch for their authenticity. They have been added because of their very intimate connection with the trial of Jesus; and for the further reason that, whether authentic or not, quotations from them are to be found everywhere in literature, sacred and secular, dealing with this subject. The mystery of their origin, the question of their genuineness, and the final disposition that will be made of them, render the Acts of Pilate a subject of surpassing interest to the student of ancient documents.

Walter M. Chandler.

New York City, July 1, 1925.

PART I
THE ROMAN TRIAL

Christus, Tiberio imperitante, per procuratorem
Pontium Pilatum supplicio affectus est. — Tacitus.

CHAPTER I

A TWOFOLD JURISDICTION

The Hebrew trial of Jesus having ended, the Roman trial began. The twofold character of the proceedings against the Christ invested them with a solemn majesty, an awful grandeur. The two mightiest jurisdictions of the earth assumed cognizance of charges against the Man of Galilee, the central figure of all history. "His tomb," says Lamartine, "was the grave of the Old World and the cradle of the New," and now upon His life before He descended into the tomb, Rome, the mother of laws, and Jerusalem, the destroyer of prophets, sat in judgment.

The Sanhedrin, or Grand Council, which conducted the Hebrew trial of Jesus was the high court of justice and the supreme tribunal of the Jews. It numbered seventy-one members. Its powers were legislative, executive, and judicial. It exercised all the functions of education, of government, and of religion. It was the national parliament of the Hebrew Theocracy, the human administrator of the divine will. It was the most august tribunal that ever interpreted or administered religion to man. Its judges applied the laws of the most peculiar and venerable system of jurisprudence known to civilized mankind, and condemned upon the charge of blasphemy against Jehovah, the most precious and illustrious of the human race. Standing alone, the Hebrew trial of Christ would have been the most thrilling and impressive judicial proceeding in all history. The Mosaic Code, whose provisions form the basis of this trial, is the foundation of the Bible, the most potent juridical as well as spiritual agency in the universe. In all the courts of Christendom it binds the consciences, if it does not mold the convictions, of judge and jury in passing judgment upon the rights of life, liberty, and property. The Bible is everywhere to be found. It is read in the jungles of Africa, while crossing burning deserts, and amidst Arctic snows. No ship ever puts to sea without this sacred treasure. It is found in the cave of the hermit, in the hut of the peasant, in the palace of the king, and in the Vatican of the pope. It adorns the altar where bride and bridegroom meet to pledge eternal love. It sheds its hallowing influence upon the baptismal font where infancy is christened into religious life. Its divine precepts furnish elements of morals and manliness in formative life to jubilant youth; cast a radiant charm about the strength of lusty manhood; and when life's pilgrimage is ended, offer to the dying patriarch, who clasps it to his bosom, a sublime solace as he crosses the great divide and passes into the twilight's purple gloom. This noble book has furnished not only the most enduring laws and the sublimest religious truths, but inspiration as well to the grandest intellectual triumphs. It is literally woven into the literature of the world, and few books of modern times are worth reading that do not reflect the sentiments of its sacred pages. And it was the Mosaic Code, the basis of this book, that furnished the legal guide to the Sanhedrin in the trial of the Christ. Truly it may be said that no other trial mentioned in history would have been comparable to this, if the proceedings had ended here. But to the Hebrew was added Roman cognizance, and the result was a judicial transaction at once unique and sublime. If the sacred spirit of the Hebrew law has illuminated the conscience of the world in every age, it must not be forgotten that "the written reason of the Roman law has been silently and studiously transfused" into all our modern legal and political life. The Roman judicial system is incomparable in the history of jurisprudence. Judea gave religion, Greece gave letters, and Roman gave laws to mankind. Thus runs the judgment of the world. A fine sense of justice was native to the Roman mind. A spirit of domination was the mental accompaniment of this trait. The mighty abstraction called Rome may be easily resolved into two cardinal concrete elements: the Legion and the Law. The legion was the unit of the military system through which Rome conquered the world. The law was the cementing bond between the conquered states and the sovereign city on the hills. The legion was the guardian and protector of the physical boundaries of the Empire, and Roman citizens felt contented and secure, as long as the legionaries were loyal to the standards and the eagles. The presence of barbarians at the gate created not so much consternation and despair among the citizens of Rome, as did the news of the mutiny of the soldiers of Germanicus on the Rhine. What the legion was to the body, the law was to the soul of Rome—the highest expression of its sanctity and majesty. And when her physical body that once extended from Scotland to Judea, and from Dacia to Abyssinia was dead, in the year 476 A.D., her soul rose triumphant in her laws and established a second Roman Empire over the minds and consciences of men. The Corpus Juris Civilis of Justinian is a text-book in the greatest universities of the world, and Roman law is today the basis of the jurisprudence of nearly every state of continental Europe. The Germans never submitted to Caesar and his legions. They were the first to resist successfully, then to attack vigorously, and to overthrow finally the Roman Empire. And yet, until a few years ago, Germans obeyed implicity the edicts and decrees of Roman praetors and tribunes. Is it any wonder, then, that the lawyers of all modern centuries have looked back with filial love and veneration to the mighty jurisconsults of the imperial republic? Is it any wonder that the tragedy of the Praetorium and Golgotha, aside from its sacred aspects, is the most notable event in history? Jesus was arraigned in one day, in one city, before the sovereign courts of the universe; before the Sanhedrin, the supreme tribunal of a divinely commissioned race; before the court of the Roman Empire that determined the legal and political rights of men throughout the known world. The Nazarene stood charged with blasphemy and with treason against the enthroned monarchs represented by these courts; blasphemy against Jehovah who, from the lightning-lit summit of Sinai, proclaimed His laws to mankind; treason against Caesar, enthroned and uttering his will to the world amidst the pomp and splendor of Rome. History records no other instance of a trial conducted before the courts of both Heaven and earth; the court of God and the court of man; under the law of Israel and the law of Rome; before Caiaphas and Pilate, as the representatives of these courts and administrators of these laws.

Approaching more closely the consideration of the nature and character of the Roman trial, we are confronted at once by several pertinent and interesting questions.

In the first place, were there two distinct trials of Jesus? If so, why were there two trials instead of one? Were the two trials separate and independent? If not, was the second trial a mere review of the first, or was the first a mere preliminary to the second?

Again, what charges were brought against Jesus at the hearing before Pilate? Were these charges the same as those preferred against Him at the trial before the Sanhedrin? Upon what charge was He finally condemned and crucified?

Again, what Roman law was applicable to the charges made against Jesus to Pilate? Did Pilate apply these laws either in letter or in spirit?

Was there an attempt by Pilate to attain substantial justice, either with or without the due observance of forms of law?

Did Pilate apply Hebrew or Roman law to the charges presented to him against the Christ?

What forms of criminal procedure, if any, were employed by Pilate in conducting the Roman trial of Jesus? If not legally, was Pilate politically justified in delivering Jesus to be crucified?

A satisfactory answer to several of these questions, in the introductory chapters of this volume, is deemed absolutely essential to a thorough understanding of the discussion of the trial proper which will follow. The plan proposed is to describe first the powers and duties of Pilate as presiding judge at the trial of Christ. And for this purpose, general principles of Roman provincial administration will be outlined and discussed; the legal and political status of the subject Jew in his relationship to the conquering Roman will be considered; and the exact requirements of criminal procedure in Roman capital trials, at the time of Christ, will, if possible, be determined. It is believed that in the present case it will be more logical and effective to state first what should have been done by Pilate in the trial of Jesus, and then follow with an account of what was actually done, than to reverse this order of procedure.

CHAPTER II

NUMBER OF REGULAR TRIALS

Were there two regular trials of Jesus? In the first volume of this work this question was reviewed at length in the introduction to the Brief. The authorities were there cited and discussed. It was there seen that one class of writers deny the existence of the Great Sanhedrin at the time of Christ. These same writers declare that there could have been no Hebrew trial of Jesus, since there was no competent Hebrew court in existence to try Him. This class of critics assert that the so-called Sanhedrin that met in the palace of Caiaphas was an ecclesiastical body, acting without judicial authority: and that their proceedings were merely preparatory to charges to be presented to Pilate, who was alone competent to try capital cases. Those who make this contention seek to uphold it by saying that the errors were so numerous and the proceedings so flagrant, according to the Gospel account, that there could have been no trial at all before the Sanhedrin: that the party of priests who arrested and examined Jesus did not constitute a court, but rather a vigilance committee.

On the other hand, other writers contend that the only regular trial was that before the Sanhedrin; and that the appearance before Pilate was merely for the purpose of securing his confirmation of a regular judicial sentence which had already been pronounced. Renan, the ablest exponent of this class, says: "The course which the priest had resolved to pursue in regard to Jesus was quite in conformity with the established law. The plan of the enemies of Jesus was to convict Him, by the testimony of witnesses and by His own avowals, of blasphemy and of outrage against the Mosaic religion, to condemn Him to death according to law, and then to get the condemnation sanctioned by Pilate."

Still another class of writers contend that there were two distinct trials. Innes thus tersely and forcibly states the proposition: "Whether it was legitimate or not for the Jews to condemn for a capital crime, on this occasion they did so. Whether it was legitimate or not for Pilate to try over again an accused whom they had condemned, on this occasion he did so. There were certainly two trials. And the dialogue already narrated expresses with a most admirable terseness the struggle which we should have expected between the effort of the Jews to get a mere countersign of their sentence, and the determination of Pilate to assume the full judicial responsibility, whether of first instance or of revision." This contention, it is believed, is right, and has been acted upon in dividing the general treatise into two volumes, and in devoting each to a separate trial of the case.

Why were there two trials of Jesus? When the Sanhedrists had condemned Christ to death upon the charge of blasphemy, why did they not lead Him away to execution, and stone Him to death, as their law required? Why did they seek the aid of Pilate and invoke the sanction of Roman authority? The answer to these questions is to be found in the historic relationship that existed, at the time of the crucifixion, between the sovereign Roman Empire and the dependent province of Judea. The student of history will remember that the legions of Pompey overran Palestine in the year 63 B.C., and that the land of the Jews then became a subject state. After the deposition of Archelaus, A.D.6, Judea became a Roman province, and was governed by procurators who were sent out from Rome. The historian Rawlinson has described the political situation of Judea, at the time of Christ, as "complicated and anomalous, undergoing frequent changes, but retaining through them all certain peculiarities which made that country unique among the dependencies of Rome. Having passed under Roman rule with the consent and by the assistance of a large party of its inhabitants, it was allowed to maintain for a while a sort of semi-independence. A mixture of Roman with native power resulted from this cause and a complication in a political status difficult to be thoroughly understood by one not native and contemporary."

The difficulty in determining the exact political status of the Jews at the time of Christ has given birth to the radically different views concerning the number and nature of the trials of Jesus. The most learned critics are in direct antagonism on the point. More than forty years ago Salvador and Dupin debated the question in France. The former contended that the Sanhedrin retained complete authority after the Roman conquest to try even capital crimes, and that sentence of death pronounced by the supreme tribunal of the Jews required only the countersign or approval of the Roman procurator. On the other hand, it was argued by Dupin that the Sanhedrin had no right whatever to try cases of a capital nature; that their whole procedure was a usurpation; and that the only competent and legitimate trial of Christ was the one conducted by Pilate. How difficult the problem is of solution will be apparent when we reflect that both these disputants were able, learned, conscientious men who, with the facts of history in front of them, arrived at entirely different conclusions. Amidst the general confusion and uncertainty, the reader must rely upon himself, and appeal to the facts and philosophy of history for light and guidance.

In seeking to ascertain the political relationship between Rome and Judea at the time of Christ, two important considerations should be kept in mind: (1) That there was no treaty or concordat, defining mutual rights and obligations, existing between the two powers; Romans were the conquerors and Jews were the conquered; the subject Jews enjoyed just so much religious and political freedom as the conquering Romans saw fit to grant them; (2) that it was the policy of the Roman government to grant to subject states the greatest amount of freedom in local self-government that was consistent with the interests and sovereignty of the Roman people. These two considerations are fundamental and indispensable in forming a correct notion of the general relations between the two powers.

The peculiar character of Judea as a fragment of the mighty Roman Empire should also be kept clearly in mind. Roman conquest, from first to last, resulted in three distinct types of political communities more or less strongly bound by ties of interest to Rome. These classes were: (1) Free states; (2) allied states; and

(3) subject states. The communities of Italy were in the main, free and allied, and were members of a great military confederacy. The provinces beyond Italy were, in the main, subject states and dependent upon the good will and mercy of Rome. The free states received from Rome a charter of privileges *(lex data)* which, however, the Roman senate might at any time revoke. The allied cities were bound by a sworn treaty *(foedus)*, a breach of which was a cause of war. In either case, whether of charter or treaty, the grant of privileges raised the state or people on whom it was conferred to the level of the Italian communes and secured to its inhabitants absolute control of their own finances, free and full possession of their land, which exempted them from the payment of tribute, and, above all, allowed them entire freedom in the administration of their local laws. The subject states were ruled by Roman governors who adminstered the so-called law of the province *(lex provinciae)*. This law was peculiar to each province and was framed to meet all the exigencies of provincial life. It was sometimes the work of a conquering general, assisted by a commission of ten men appointed by the senate. At other times, its character was determined by the decrees of the emperor and the senate, as well as the edicts of the praetor and procurator. In any case, the law of the province *(lex provinciae)* was the sum total of the local provincial law which Rome saw fit to allow the people of the conquered state to retain, with Roman decrees and regulations superadded. These added decrees and regulations were always determined by local provincial conditions. The Romans were no sticklers for consistency and uniformity in provincial administration. Adaptability and expediency were the main traits of the lawgiving and government-imposing genius of Rome. The payment of taxes and the furnishing of auxiliary troops were the chief exactions imposed upon conquered states. An enlightened public policy prompted the Romans to grant to subject communities the greatest amount of freedom consistent with Roman sovereignty. Two main reasons formed the basis of this policy. One was the economy of time and labor, for the Roman official staff was not large enough to successfully perform those official duties which were usually incumbent upon the local courts. Racial and religious differences alone would have impeded and prevented a successful administration of local government by Roman diplomats and officers. Another reason for Roman noninterference in local provincial affairs was that loyalty was created and peace promoted among the provincials by the enjoyment of their own laws and religions. To such an extent was this policy carried by the Romans that it is asserted by the best historians that there was little real difference in practice between the rights exercised by free and those enjoyed by subject states. On this point, Mommsen says: "In regard to the extent of application, the jurisdiction of the native courts and judicatories among subject communities can scarcely have been much more restricted than among the federated communities; while in administration and in civil jurisdiction we find the same principles operative as in legal procedure and criminal laws."[1] The difference between the rights enjoyed by subject and those exercised by free states was that the former were subject to the whims and caprices of Rome, while

the latter were protected by a written charter. A second difference was that Roman citizens residing within the boundaries of subject states had their own law and their own judicatories. The general result was that the citizens of subject states were left free to govern themselves subject to the two great obligations of taxation and military service. The Roman authorities, however, could and did interfere in legislation and in administration whenever Roman interests required.

Now, in the light of the facts and principles just stated, what was the exact political status of the Jews at the time of Christ? Judea was a subject state. Did the general laws of Roman provincial administration apply to this province? Or were peculiar rights and privileges granted to the strange people who inhabited it? A great German writer answers in the affirmative. Geib says: "Only one province . . . namely Judea, at least in the earlier days of the empire, formed an exception to all the arrangements hitherto described. Whereas in the other provinces the whole criminal jurisdiction was in the hands of the governor, and only in the most important cases had the supreme imperial courts to decide—just as in the least important matters the municipal courts did—the principle that applied in Judea was that at least in regard to questions of religious offenses the high priest with the Sanhedrin could pronounce even death sentences, for the carrying out of which, however, the confirmation of the procurator was required."

That Roman conquest did not blot out Jewish local self-government; and that the Great Sanhedrin still retained judicial and administrative power, subject to Roman authority in all matters pertaining to the local affairs of the Jews, is thus clearly and pointedly stated by Schurer: "As regards the area over which the jurisdiction of the supreme Sanhedrin extended, it has been already remarked above that its *civil* authority was restricted, in the time of Christ, to the eleven toparchies of Judea proper. And accordingly, for this reason, it had no judicial authority over Jesus Christ so long as He remained in Galilee. It was only as soon as He entered Judea that He came directely under its jurisdiction. In a certain sense, no doubt, the Sanhedrin exercised such jurisdiction over *every* Jewish community in the world, and in that sense over Galilee as well. Its orders were regarded as binding throughout the entire empire domain of orthodox Judaism. It had power, for example, to issue warrants to the congregations (synagogues) in Damascus for the apprehension of the Christians in that quarter (Acts ix. 2; xxii. 5; xxvi. 12). At the same time, however, the extent to which the Jewish communities were willing to yield obedience to the orders of the Sanhedrin always depended on how far they were favorably disposed toward it. It was only within the limits of Judea proper that it exercised any direct authority. There could not possibly be a more erroneous way of defining the extent of its jurisdiction as regards the kind of causes with which it was competent to deal than to say that it was the *spiritual or theological* tribunal in contradistinction to the civil judicatories of the Romans. On the contrary, it would be more correct to say that it formed, in contrast to the foreign authority of Rome, that *supreme native* court which here, as almost everywhere else, the Romans had allowed to continue as before, only imposing certain restrictions with regard to competency. To this tribunal then belonged all those judicial matters and all those measures of an administrative character which either could not be competently dealt with by the inferior or local courts or which the Roman procurator had not specially reserved for himself."[2]

The closing words of the last quotation suggest an important fact which furnishes the answer to the question asked at the beginning of this chapter, Why were there two trials of Jesus? Schurer declares that the Sanhedrin retained judicial and administrative power in all local matters which the "procurator had not specially reserved for himself." Now, it should be borne in mind that there is not now existence and that there probably never existed any law, treaty or decree declaring what judicial acts the Sanhedrin was competent to perform and what acts were reserved to the authority of the Roman governor. It is probable that in all ordinary crimes the Jews were allowed a free hand and final decision by the Romans. No interference took place unless Roman interests were involved or Roman sovereignty threatened. But one fact is well established by the great weight of authority: that the question of sovereignty was raised whenever the question of life and death arose; and that Rome reserved to herself, in such a case, the prerogative of final judicial determination. Even this contention, however, has been opposed by both ancient and modern writers of repute; and, for this reason, it has been thought necessary to cite authorities and offer arguments in favor of the proposition that the right of life or death, *jus vitae aut necis,* had passed from Jewish into Roman hands at the time of Christ. Both sacred and profane history support the affirmative of this proposition. Regarding this matter, Schurer says: "There is a special interest attaching to the question as to how far the jurisdiction of the Sanhedrin was limited by the authority of the Roman procurator. We accordingly proceed to observe that, inasmuch as the Roman system of provincial government was not strictly carried out in the case of Judea, as the simple fact of its being administered by means of a procurator plainly shows, the Sanhedrin was still left in the enjoyment of a comparatively high degree of independence. Not only did it exercise civil jurisdiction, and that according to Jewish law (which was only a matter of course, as otherwise a Jewish court of justice would have been simply inconceivable), but it also enjoyed a considerable amount of criminal jurisdiction as well. It had an independent authority in regard to political affairs, and consequently possessed the right of ordering arrests to be made by its own officers (Matt. xxvi. 47; Mark xiv. 43; Acts iv. 3; v. 17, 18). It had also the power of finally disposing, on its own authority, of such cases as did not involve sentence of death (Acts iv. 5-23; v. 21-40). It was only in cases in which such sentence of death was pronounced that the judgment required to be ratified by the authority of the procurator."[3]

The Jews contend, and, indeed, the Talmud states that "forty years before the destruction of the temple the judgment of capital cases was taken away from Israel."

Again, we learn from Josephus that the Jews had lost the power to inflict capital punishment from the day of the deposition of Archelaus, A.D. 6, when Judea became a Roman province and was placed under the control of Roman procurators. The great Jewish historian says: "And now Archelaus's part of Judea was reduced into a province, and Coponius, one of the equestrian order among the Romans, was sent as procurator, having the power of life and death put into his hands by Caesar."[4]

Again, we are informed that Annas was deposed from the high priesthood by the procurator Valerius Gratus, A.D. 14, for imposing and executing capital sentences. One of his sons, we learn from Josephus, was also deposed by King Agrippa for condemning James, the brother of Jesus, and several others, to death by stoning. At the same time, Agrippa reminded the high priest that the Sanhedrin could not lawfully assemble without the consent of the procurator.[5]

That the Jews had lost and that the Roman procurators possessed the power over life and death is also clearly indicated by the New Testament account of the trial of Jesus. One passage explicitly states that Pilate claimed the right to impose and carry out capital sentences. Addressing Jesus, Pilate said: "Knowest thou not that I have power to crucify thee and have power to release thee?"[6]

In another passage, the Jews admitted that the power of life and death had passed away from them. Answering a question of Pilate at the time of the trial, they answered: "It is not lawful for us to put any man to death."[7]

If we keep in mind the fact stated by Geib that "the principle that applied in Judea was that at least in regard to questions of religious offense the high priest with the Sanhedrin could pronounce even death sentences, for the carrying out of which, however, the confirmation of the procurator was required," we are then in a position to answer finally and definitely the question, Why were there two trial of Jesus?

In the light of all the authorities cited and discussed in this chapter, we feel justified in asserting that the Sanhedrin was competent to take the initiative in the arrest and trial of Jesus on the charge of blasphemy, this being a religious offense of the most awful gravity; that this court was competent not only to try but to pass sentence of death upon the Christ: but that its proceedings had to be retired or at least reviewed before the sentence could be executed. Thus two trials were necessary. The Hebrew trial was necessary, because a religious offense was involved with which Rome refused to meddle, and of which she refused to take cognizance in the first instance. The Roman trial was necessary, because, instead of an acquittal which would have rendered Roman interference unnecessary, a conviction involving the death sentence had to be reviewed in the name of Roman sovereignty.

Having decided that there were two trials, we are now ready to consider the questions: Were the two trials separate and independent? If not, was the second trial a mere review of the first, or was the first a mere preliminary to the second? No more difficult questions are suggested by the trial of Jesus. It is, in fact, impossible to answer them with certainty and satisfaction.

A possible solution is to be found in the nature of the charge preferred against Jesus. It is reasonable to suppose that in the conflict of jurisdiction between Jewish and Roman authority the character of the crime would be a determining factor. In the case of ordinary offenses it is probable that neither Jews nor Romans were particular about the question of jurisdiction. It is more than probable that the Roman governor would assert his right to try the case *de novo,* where the offense charged either directly or remotely involved the safety and sovereignty of the Roman state. It is entirely reasonable to suppose that the Jews would insist on a final determination by themselves of the merits of all offenses of a religious nature; and that they would insist that the Roman governor should limit his action to a mere countersign of their decree. It is believed that ordinarily these principles would apply. But the trial of Jesus presents a peculiar feature which makes the case entirely exceptional. And this peculiarity, it is felt, contains a correct answer to the questions asked above. Jesus was tried before the Sanhedrin on the charge of blasphemy. This was a religious offense of the most serious nature. But when the Christ was led before Pilate, this charge was abandoned and that of high treason against Rome was substituted. Now, it is certain that a Roman governor would not have allowed a Jewish tribunal to try an offense involving high treason against Caesar. This was a matter exclusively under his control. It is thus certain that Pilate did not merely review a sentence which had been passed by the Sanhedrin after a regular trial, but that he tried *ab initio* a charge that had not been presented before the Jewish tribunal at the night session in the palace of Caiaphas.

It will thus be seen that there were two trials of Jesus; that these trials were separate and independent as far as the charges, judges, and jurisdictions were concerned; and that the only common elements were the persons of the accusers and the accused.

CHAPTER III

POWERS AND DUTIES OF PILATE

What were the powers and duties of Pilate as procurator of Judea? What forms of criminal procedure, if any, were employed by him in conducting the Roman trial of Jesus? This chapter will be devoted to answering these questions.

The New Testament Gospels denominate Pilate the "governor" of Judea. A more exact designation is contained in the Latin phrase, *procurator Caesaris;* procurator of Ceasar. By this is meant that Pilate was the deputy, attorney, or personal representative of Tiberius Caesar in the province of Judea. The powers and duties of his office were by no means limited to the financial functions of a Roman quaestor, a *procurator fiscalis.* "He was a procurator *cum potestate;* a governor with civil, criminal, and military jurisdiction; subordinated no doubt in rank to the adjacent governor of Syria, but directly responsible to his great master at Rome."

A clear conception of the official character of Pilate is impossible unless we first thoroughly understand the official character of the man whose political substitute he was. A thorough understanding of the official character of Tiberius Caesar is impossible unless we first fully comprehend the political changes wrought by the civil wars of Rome in which Julius Caesar defeated Cneius Pompey at the battle of Pharsalia and made himself dictator and undisputed master of the Roman world. With the ascendency of Caesar the ancient republic became extinct. But liberty was still cherished in the hearts of Romans, and the title of king was detestable. The hardy virtues and democratic simplicity of the early republic were still remembered; and patriots like Cicero had dreamed of the restoration of the ancient order of things. But Roman conquest was complete, Roman manners were corrupt, and Roman patriotism was paralyzed. The hand of a dictator guided by a single intelligence was the natural result of the progressive degradation of the Roman state. The logical and inevitable outcome of the death of Caesar and the dissolution of the Triumvirate was the regime of Augustus, a monarchy veiled under republican forms. Recognizing Roman horror of absolutism, Roman love of liberty, and Roman detestation of kingly power, Augustus, while in fact an emperor, claimed to be only a plain Roman citizen intrusted with general powers of government. He affected to despise public honors, disclaimed every idea of personal superiority, and exhibited extreme simplicity of manners in public and private life. This was the strategy of a successful politician who sought to conceal offensive reality under the cloak of a pleasant deception. Great Caesar fallen at the foot of Pompey's statue was a solemn reminder to Augustus that the dagger of the assassin was still ready to defend the memory of freedom, after liberty was, in reality, dead. And the refusal by the greatest of the Romans, at the feast of the Lupercal, to accept a kingly crown when it was thrice offered him by Antony, was a model of discreet behavior and political caution for the first and most illustrious of the emperors. In short, Augustus dared not destroy the laws or assault the constitution of the state. But he accomplished his object, nevertheless. "He gathered into his own hands the whole honors and privileges, which the state had for centuries distributed among its great magistrates and representatives. He became perpetual Princeps Senatus, or leader of the legislative house. He became perpetual Pontifex Maximus, or chief of the national religion. He became perpetual Tribune, or guardian of the people, with his person thereby made sacred and inviolable. He became perpetual Consul, or supreme magistrate over the whole Roman world, with the control of its revenues, the disposal of its armies, and the execution of its laws. And lastly he became perpetual Imperator, or military chief, to whom every legionary throughout the world took the *sacramentum,* and whose sword swept the globe from Gibraltar to the Indus and the Baltic. And yet in all he was a simple citizen—a mere magistrate of the Republic. Only in this one man was now visibly accumulated and concentrated all that for centuries had broadened and expanded under the magnificent abstraction of Rome." The boundless authority of Rome was thus centered in the hands of a single person. Consuls, tribunes, praetors, proconsuls, and procurators were merely the agents and representatives of this person.

Tiberius Caesar, the political master of Pontius Pilate, was the successor of Augustus and the first inheritor of his constitution. Under this constitution, Augustus had divided the provinces into two classes. The centrally located and peacefully disposed were governed by proconsuls appointed by the senate. The more distant and turbulent were subjected by Augustus to his personal control, and were governed by procurators who acted as his deputies or personal representatives. Judea came in his second class, and the real governor of his province was the emperor himself. Tiberius Caesar was thus the real procurator of Judea at the time of the crucifixion and Pilate was his political substitute Who did his bidding and obeyed his will. Whatever Tiberius might have done, Pilate might have done. We are thus enabled to judge the extent of Pilate's powers; powers clothed with *imperium* and revocable only by the great procurator at Rome.

In the government of the purely subject states of a province, the procurator exercised the unlimited jurisdiction of the military *imperium.* No law abridged the single and sovereign exercise of his will. Custom, however, having in fact the force of law, prescribed that he should summon to his aid a council of advisers. This advisory body was composed of two elements: (1) Roman citizens resident in this particular locality where the governor was holding court; and (2) members of his personal staff known as the Praetorian Cohort. The governor, in his conduct of judicial proceedings, might solicit the opinions of the members of his council. He might require them to vote upon the question at issue; and might, if he pleased, abide by the decision of the majority. But no rule of law required him to do it; it was merely a concession and a courtesy; it was not a legal duty.

Again, when it is said that the procurator exercised the "unlimited jurisdiction

of the military *imperium,"* we must interpret this, paradoxical though it may seem, in a restricted sense: that is, we must recognize the existence of exceptions to the rule. It is unreasonable to suppose that Rome, the mother of laws, ever comtemplated the rule of despotism and caprice in the administration of justice in any part of the empire. It is true that the effect of the *imperium,* "as applied to provincial governship, was to make each *imperator* a king in his own domain"; but kings themselves have nearly always been subject to restrictions: and the authorities are agreed that the *imperium* of the Roman procurator of the time of Christ was hemmed in by many limitations. A few of these may be named.

In the first place, the rights guaranteed to subject states within the provincial area by the law of the province *(lex provinciae)* were the first limitations upon his power.

Again, it is a well-known fact that Roman citizens could appeal from the decision of the governor, in certain cases, to the emperor at Rome. Paul exercised this right, because he was a Roman citizen.[1] Jesus could not appeal from the judgment of Pilate, because He was not a Roman citizen.

Again, fear of an aroused and indignant public sentiment which might result in his removal by the emperor, exercised a salutary restraint upon the conduct, if it did not abridge the powers of the governor.

These various considerations bring us now to the second question asked in the beginning of this chapter: What forms of criminal procedure, if any, were employed by Pilate in conducting the Roman trial of Jesus?

It is historically true that Pilate exercised, as procurator of Judea, the unlimited jurisdiction of the military *imperium;* and that this *imperium* made him virtually an *"imperator,* a king in his own domain." It is also historically true that the inhabitants of the purely subject states of the province, who were not themselves Roman citizens, when accused of crime, stood before a Roman governor with no protection except the plea of justice against the summary exercise of absolute power. In other words, in the employment of the unlimited jurisdiction of the military *imperium,* a Roman governor, in the exercise of his discretion, might, in the case of non-Roman citizens of a subject state, throw all rules and forms of law to the wind, and decide the matter arbitrarily and despotically. It may be that Pilate did this in this case. But the best writers are agreed that this was not the policy of the Roman governors in the administration of justice in the provinces at the time of Christ. The lawgiving genius of Rome had then reached maturity and approximate perfection in the organization of its criminal tribunals. It is not probable, as before suggested, that despotism and caprice would be systematically tolerated anywhere in the Roman world. If the emperors at Rome were forced, out of regard for public sentiment, to respect the constitution and the laws, it is reasonable to infer that their personal representatives in the provinces were under the same restraint. We feel justified then in asserting that Pilate, in the trial of Jesus, should have applied certain laws and been governed by certain definite rules of criminal procedure. What were these rules? A few preliminary considerations will greatly aid the reader in arriving at an answer to this question. It should be understood:

(I)   That Pilate was empowered to apply either Roman law or the local law in the trial of any case where the crime was an offense against both the province and the empire, as in the crime of murder; but that in the case of treason with which Jesus was charged he would apply the law of Rome under forms of Roman procedure. It has been denied that Pilate had a right to apply Jewish law in the government of his province; but this denial is contrary to authority. Innes says: "The Roman governor sanctioned, or even himself administered, the old law of the region."[2] Schurer says: "It may be assumed that the administration of the civil law was wholly in the hands of the Sanhedrin and native or local magistrates: Jewish courts decided according to Jewish law. But even in the criminal law this was almost invariably the case, only with this exception, that death sentences required to be confirmed by the Roman procurator. In such cases, the procurator decided, if he pleased, according to Jewish law."[3] Greenidge says: "Even the first clause of the Sicilian *lex,* if it contained no reference to jurisdiction by the local magistrate, left the interpretation of the *native law* wholly to Roman *propraetors.*"[4] It is thus clearly evident that Roman procurators might apply either Roman or local laws in ordinary cases.

(2)   That Roman governors were empowered to apply the adjective law of Rome to the substantive law of the province. In support of this contention, Greenidge says: "The edict of the *propraetor* or pro-consul, . . . clearly could not express the native law of each particular state under its jurisdiction; but its generality and its expansiveness admitted, as we shall see, of an application of Roman forms to the substantive law of any particular city."[5]

(3)   That the criminal procedure employed by Pilate in the trial of Jesus should have been the criminal procedure of a capital case tried at Rome, during the reign of Tiberius Caesar. This fact is very evident from the authorities. The trial of capital cases at Rome furnished models for similar trials in the provinces. In the exercise of the unlimited jurisdiction of the military *imperium,* Roman governors might disregard these models. But, ordinarily, custom compelled them to follow the criminal precedents of the Capital of the empire. The following authorities support this contention.

Rosadi says: "It is also certain that in the provinces the same order was observed in criminal cases as was observed in cases tried at Rome."[6] This eminent Italian writer cites, in proof of this statement, Pothier, Pandect. XLVIII. 2, n. 28.

Greenidge says: "Yet, in spite of this absence of legal checks, the criminal procedure of the provinces was, in the protection of the citizen as in other respects, closely modelled on that of Rome."[7]

To the same effect, but more clearly and pointedly expressed, is Geib, who says: "It is nevertheless true that the knowledge which we have, imperfect though it may be, leaves no doubt that the courts of the Italian municipalities and provinces had, in all essential elements, the permanent tribunals *(quaestiones perpetuae)* as models; so that, in fact, a description of the proceedings in the permanent tribunals is, at the same time, to be regarded as a description of the proceedings in the provincial courts."[8]

These permanent tribunals *(quaestiones perpetuae)* were courts of criminal jurisdiction established at Rome, and were in existence at the time of the crucifixion. Proceedings in these courts in capital cases, were models of criminal procedure in the provinces at the time of Christ. It logically follows then that if we can ascertain the successive steps in the trial of a capital case at Rome before one of the permanent tribunals, we have accurate information of the exact form of criminal procedure, not that Pilate did employ, but which he should have employed in the trial of Jesus.

Fortunately for the purposes of this treatise, every step which Roman law required in the trial of capital cases at Rome is as well known as the provisions of any modern criminal code. From the celebrated Roman trials in which Cicero appeared as as advocate, may be gleaned with unerring accuracy the fullest information touching all the details of capital trials at Rome at the time of Cicero.

It should be observed, at this point, that the period of Roman jurisprudence just referred to was in the closing years of the republic; and that certain changes in the organization of the tribunals as well as in the forms of procedure were effected by the legislation of Augustus. But we have it upon the authority of Rosadi that these changes were not radical in the case of the criminal courts and that the rules and regulations that governed procedure in them during the republic remained substantially unchanged under the empire. The same writer tells us that the permanent tribunals for the trial of capital cases did not go out of existence until the third century of the Christian era.[9]

The following chapter will be devoted, in the main, to a description of the mode of trial of capital cases at Rome before the permanent tribunals at the time of Christ.

CHAPTER IV

MODE OF TRIAL IN ROMAN CAPITAL CASES

The reader should keep clearly and constantly in mind the purpose of this chapter: to describe the mode of trial in capital cases at Rome during the reign of Tiberius Caesar; and thus to furnish a model of criminal procedure which Pilate should have imitated in the trial of Jesus at Jerusalem. In the last chapter, we saw that the proceedings of the permanent tribunals *(quaestiones perpetuae) at Rome furnished models for the trial of criminal cases in the provinces. It is now only necessary to determine what the procedure of the permanent tribunals at the time of Christ was, in order to understand what Pilate should have done in the trial of Jesus. But the character of the quaestiones perpetuae,* as well as the rules and regulations that governed their proceedings, cannot well be understood without reference to the criminal tribunals and modes of trial in criminal cases that preceded them. Roman history discloses two distinct periods of criminal procedure before the organization of the permanent tribunals about the beginning of the last century of the Republic: (1) The period of the kings and (2) the period of the early republic. Each of these will be here briefly considered.

The Regal Period. —The earliest glimpses of Roman political life reveal the existence of a sacred and military monarchy in which the king is generalissimo of the army, chief pontiff of the national religion, and supreme judge in civil and criminal matters over the lives and property of the citizens. These various powers and attributes are wrapped up in the *imperium.* By virtue of the *imperium,* the king issued commands to the army and also exercised the highest judicial functions over the lives and fortunes of his fellow citizens. The kings were thus military commanders and judges in one person, as the consuls were after them. The monarch might sit alone and judge cases and impose sentences; but the trial was usually a personal investigation undertaken by him with the advise and aid of a chosen body of judges from the senate or the pontifical college. According to Dionysius, Romulus ordered that all crimes of a serious nature should be tried by the king, but that all lighter offenses should be judged by the senate.[1] Little confidence can be reposed in this statement, since the age and deeds of Romulus are exceedingly legendary and mythical. But it is historically true that in the regal period of Rome the kings were the supreme judges in all civil and criminal matters.

The Early Republican Period. —The abolition of the monarchy and the establishment of the republic witnessed the distribution of the powers of government formerly exercised by the king among a number of magistrates and public officers. Consuls, tribunes, praetors, aediles, both curule and plebeian, exercised, under the republic, judicial functions in criminal matters.

The consuls were supreme criminal judges at the beginning of the republic, and were clothed with unlimited power in matters of life and death. This is shown by the condemnation and execution of the sons of Brutus and their fellow-conspirators.[2] Associated with the consuls were, at first, two annually appointed quaestors whom they nominated. The functions of the quaestors were as unlimited as those of their superiors, the consuls; but their jurisdiction was confined chiefly to criminal matters and finance.

The tribunes, sacred and inviolable in their persons as representatives of the *plebs* and as their protectors against patrician oppression, exercised at first merely a negative control over the regular magistracies of the community. But, finally, they became the chief public prosecutors of political criminals.

The praetors, whose chief jurisdiction was in civil matters, Were potentially as fully criminal judges as the consuls, and there may have been a time when a portion of criminal jurisdiction was actually in their hands. In the later republic, they presided over the *quaestiones perpetuae,* permanent criminal tribunals.

The aediles are found in Roman history exercising functions of criminal jurisdiction, although their general powers were confined to the special duties of caring for the games, the market, and the archives.

But the criminal jurisdiction of the magistrates who replaced the king at the downfall of the monarchy was abridged and almost destroyed by the famous *lex Valeria (de provocatione).* This law was proposed 509 B.C. by Publius Valerius, one of the first consuls of Rome, and provided that no magistrate should have power to execute a sentence of death against a Roman citizen who had appealed to the judgment of the people in their public assembly. This *lex* was the *magna charta* of the Romans and was justly regarded by them as the great palladium of their civil liberty. And it was this law that inaugurated the popular jurisdiction of the *comitia.* The result was that for more than three hundred years the final determination of the question of life or death was in the hands of the people themselves. From the passage of the Valerian law the function of the magistrates was limited to the duty of convincing the people of the guilt of an alleged criminal against whom they themselves had already pronounced a preliminary sentence. The magistrates were, therefore, not so much judges as prosecutors; the people were the final judges in the case.

Mode of Trial in the Comitia, or Public Assembly. —On a certain day, the prosecuting magistrate, who had himself pronounced the preliminary sentence against an accused person who had appealed to the people in their public assembly, mounted the *rostra,* and called the people together by the voice of a herald. He then made a proclamation that on a certain day he would bring an accusation against a certain person upon a given charge. At the same time, he called upon this person to come forward and hear the charges against him. The defendant then presented himself, listened to the accusation, and immediately furnished bond for his appearance, or in default of bail, was thrown into prison. Upon the day announced at the opening of the trial, the prosecuting magistrate again mounted the *rostra,* and summoned the accused by a herald, if he was at large, or had him brought forth if he was in prison. The prosecutor then produced evidence, oral and documentary, against the prisoner. The indictment had to be in writing, and was published on three market days in the Forum. The prosecution came to an end on the third day, and the accused then began his defense by mounting the *rostra* with his patron and presenting evidence in his own behalf. The prosecutor then announced that on a certain day he would ask the people to render judgment by their votes. In the early years of the republic, the people voted by shouting their approval or disapproval of the charges made; but later a tablet bearing one of the two letters V. *(uti rogas)* or A. *(absolvo)* was used as a ballot.

The effect of popular jurisdiction in criminal processes at Rome was in the nature of a two-edged sword that cut both ways. It was beneficial in the limitations it imposed upon the conduct of single magistrates who were too often capricious and despotic. But this benefit was purchased at the price of a kind of popular despotism not less dangerous in its way. It has always been characteristic of popular assemblies that their decisions have been more the outcome of passion and prejudice than the result of calm wisdom and absolute justice. The trouble at Rome was that the people were both legislators and judges in their public assemblies; and it nearly always happened that the lawmakers rose above and trampled upon the very laws which they themselves had made. The natural offspring of this state of things is either anarchy or despotism; and it was only the marvelous vitality of the Roman Commonwealth that enabled it to survive.

The reports of the great criminal trials before the *comitia* reveal the inherent weakness of a system of popular jurisdiction in criminal matters. Personal and political considerations foreign to the merits of the case were allowed to take the place of competent evidence; and issues of right and expediency were too frequently mixed up. The accused, at times, trusted not so much in the righteousness of his cause as in the feelings of compassion and prejudice that moved the people as popular judges, and to excite these feelings the most ludicrous and undignified steps were sometimes taken. The defendant nearly always appeared at the trial in mourning garb, frequently let his hair and beard grow long, and often exhibited the scars and wounds received in battle whilst fighting for his country. He sometimes offered prayers to the immortal gods and wept bitterly; at other times he caused his children and other relatives to appear at the trial, wailing, and tearing their clothes. Not content with presenting all the pathetic features of his own life, he left nothing undone to expose his opponents to hatred and contempt. It thus happened that many of the great criminal causes of Rome were mere farcical proceedings. A few instances may be cited.

Horatius, though tried in the time of the third Roman king, was pardoned by the people for the murder of his sister because of his heroic deed in single combat with the three Curiatii, and because his father had lost three children in the service of the state.

In the year 98, Manlius Aquillius, the pacificator of Sicily, was tried for embezzlement. Marcus Antonius, his advocate, ended his argument for the defense by tearing the tunic of Aquillius to show the breast of the veteran warrior covered with scars. The people were moved to tears and Aquillius was aquitted, although the evidence was very clear against him.

In the trial of M. Manlius, 384 B.C., new tactics were employed. The accused refused to appear in mourning. There was no weeping in his behalf. On the other hand, Manlius relied upon his services to the state for acquittal. He brought forward four hundred citizens who by his generosity he had saved from bondage for debt; he exhibited the spoils taken from thirty slain enemies; also military decorations received for bravery in battle—among them two mural and eight civic crowns: he then produced many citizens rescued by him from the hands of the enemy; he then bared his breast and exhibited the scars received by him in wars; and, lastly, turning toward the Capitol, he implored Jupiter to protect him, and to infuse, at this moment, into the Roman people, his judges, the same spirit of courage and patriotism that had given him strength to save the city of Rome and his whole country from the hands of the Gauls. He begged the people to keep their eyes fixed on the Capitol while they were pronouncing sentence against him to whom they owed life and liberty. It is said that his prosecutors despaired of convicting him amidst such surroundings, and adjourned the trial to another place, where the Capitol could not be seen; and that thereupon the conviction of Manlius was secured and his condemnation pronounced.

In the year 185 B.C., the tribune M. Naevius, at the instigation of Cato, accused Scipio Africanus before the tribes of having been bribed to secure a dishonorable peace. It was clearly evident that a charge of this kind could not well be sustained by evidence; but it was believed that a conviction could be secured by an appeal to the passion and prejudice of the multitude. But this advantage operated as greatly in favor of Scipio as it did in favor of his accusers. And he did not fail to use the advantage to the fullest extent. In seeming imitation of M. Manlius, two hundred years before, he appealed for acquittal to the people on account of his public services. He refused to appear in mourning, offered no evidence in his own behalf, nor did he exhibit the usual humility of an accused Roman before his countrymen. With proud disdain, he spurned the unworthy imputation of bribery, and pointed the people to the magnificent achievements of his brilliant public career. He reminded them that the day of the trial was itself the anniversary of his victory over the greatest enemy that Rome ever had, at Zama. It was degrading, he exclaimed, both to him and to the Roman nation, to bring such a charge on this day against the man to whom it was due that the Commonwealth of Rome still existed. He refused to lower himself, he said, by listening to the insolent charges of a vulgar brawler who had never done anything for the state. He declared that instead he would repair at once to the temple of Jupiter and render thanks for his victory over Hannibal to the protecting gods of his country. With these words, he left the Forum and went to the Capitol and from there to his house, accompanied by the great majority of the people, while the accusing tribune and his official staff were left alone in the market place.

The inevitable result of these cases of miscarriage of justice, in which patriotic bravado and rhetorical claptrap took the place of legal rules, was a desire and demand for the reform of criminal procedure. Besides, it had ever been found troublesome and inconvenient to summon the whole body of the Roman people to try ordinary offenses. It was only in cases of great gravity that the ponderous machinery of the *comitia centuriata* could be set in motion. This difficulty was increased with the growth of the republic, in which crimes also grew in number and magnitude. The necessity for the reform of the criminal law resulted in the institution of permanent tribunals *(quaestiones perpetuae)*. A series of legal enactments accomplished this result. The earliest law that created a permanent *quaestio* was the *lex Calpurnia* of 149 B.C. And it was the proceedings in these courts, which we shall now describe, that should have guided Pilate in the trial of Jesus.

Mode of Trial in the Permanent Tribunals. —We shall attempt to trace in the remaining pages of this chapter the successive steps in the trial of criminal cases before the permanent tribunals at Rome.

First Stage (postulatio). —A Roman criminal trial before a *quaestio perpetua* commenced with an application to the presiding magistrate, the praetor or the *index quaestionis,* for permission to bring a criminal charge against a certain person. The technical Latin expression for this request to prosecute is *postulatio.* It should be here noted that State's attorneys or public prosecutors, in a modern sense, were not known to the Romans at this time. Private citizens took upon themselves public prosecutions in behalf of the state. They were encouraged to do this from motives of personal profit as well as patriotic interest in the welfare of the community. As young men in modern times, just admitted to the bar, often accept criminal cases by assignment from the court in order to make a beginning in their professional careers, so young Roman nobles in ancient times sought to make reputations for themselves by accusing and prosecuting public delinquents. And not only professional reputation, but financial compensation as well could be gained in this way. The Roman laws of the time of Cicero provided that a successful prosecutor should receive one-fourth part of the property confiscated or the fine imposed. A Macedonian inscription offered a reward of 200 denarii to the prosecutor who should bring to justice the desecrators of a tomb.[3]

Second Stage (divinatio). —It often happened that more than one accuser desired to prosecute a single offense; but more than one prosecutor was not permitted by Roman law unless there was more than one crime charged. Then, in case of a concurrence of would-be accusers, a preliminary trial was had to determine which one of these was best fitted to bring the accusation. This initial hearing was known in Roman law as the *divinatio.* It was indeed more than a mere hearing; it was a regular trial in which the question of the fitness of the different candidates for the position of *delator* was argued before the president and the jury. This jury was in many cases distinct from the one that finally tried the case on the merits. The purpose of the whole proceeding known as the *divinatio* was to secure a prosecutor who was at once both able and sincere; and both these qualities were generaliy very strenuously urged by all those who desired to assume the role of accuser. Indeed all personal qualifications involving the mental and moral attributes of the would-be prosecutors were pointedly urged. At the hearing, the different candidates frequently became animated and even bitter opponents of each other. Crimination and recrimination then followed as a natural consequence. An applicant might show that he was thoroughly familiar with the affairs of a province, as a special fitness in the prosecution of a public official for extortion in that province. An opponent, on the other hand, might show that said applicant had been, and was now, said official in the government of the province and had been, and was now, on the friendliest terms with him. After the meritorious qualifications of all the claimants had been presented, the president and jury rendered their decision. The details of the evidence affecting the merits of the charge were not considered at this preliminary trial. Only such facts were considered as affected the personal qualifications of the different candidates for the place of accuser. When these qualifications were about equally balanced in point of merit between two applicants, the abler speaker was generally chosen.

Third Stage (nominis delatio). —It frequently happened that the *postulatio,* the request to prosecute, was not followed by the *divinatio,* the preliminary hearing on the merits of different applicants, because there was only one would-be accuser; and his qualifications were beyond dispute. In such a case, when a request to bring a criminal charge against a certain person had been presented by a citizen to the praetor, there followed, after a certain interval of time, a private hearing before the president of the court for the purpose of gaining fuller and more definite information concerning the charge. This private proceeding was styled the *nominis* or *criminis delatio,* and took place before the president alone. Its main object was to secure a specification of the personality of the accused as well as of the charges brought against him. At this stage of the trial the presence of the accused person was necessary, unless he was absent under valid excuse. The *lex Memmia,* passed in the year 114 B.C., permitted a delinquent to plead that he was absent from Rome on public business, as an excuse for not appearing at the *nominis delatio.* In the year 58 B.C., the tribune L. Antistius impeached Julius Caesar. But the colleagues of Antistius excused Caesar from personal attendance because he was absent in the service of the state in Gaul. But, if the accused appeared at the *nominis delatio,* the prosecutor interrogated him at length concerning the facts of the crime. The purpose of this interrogation *(interrogatio)* was to satisfy the president that there was a prima facie case to carry before the regular tribunal on open trial. The proceedings of the *nominis delatio* were thus in the nature of a modern Grand Jury investigation, instituted to determine if a serious prosecution should be had.

Fourth Stage (inscriptio). —If the interrogation convinced the president that the prosecutor had a prima facie case to take before the permanent tribunal, he framed a form of indictment called the *inscriptio.* This indictment was signed by the chief prosecutor and also by a number of witnesses against the accused called *subscriptores.* The charge was now definitely fixed; and, from this moment, it was the only offense that could be prosecuted at the trial. The drawing up of this charge by the president was similar to the framing of an indictment by a modern Grand Jury.

Fifth Stage (nominis receptio). —After the indictment or inscription had been framed, it was formally received by the president. This act was styled the *nominis receptio* and corresponds, in a general way, with the presentment of an indictment by a modern Grand Jury. When the *nominis receptio* was complete, the case was said to be *in judicio,* and the accused was said to be *in reatu.* The president then fixed a day certain for the appearance of the accused and the beginning of the trial. The time fixed was usually ten days from the *nominis receptio.* However, a longer time was allowed if evidence had to be secured from beyond the sea. Thirty days were allowed the accusers in the prosecution of Scaurus. Cicero was given one hundred and ten days to secure evidence against Verres; but he actually employed only sixty. The time granted the prosecutor was also required by the law to be utilized by the defendant in preparing his case.

The preliminary steps in the prosecution were now complete, and the accused awaited the day of trial. In the meantime, he was allowed to go at large, even when charged with a grave offense like murder. Imprisonment to prevent escape had almost ceased at the time of which we write. If the evidence against the accused was weak, it was felt that he would certainly appear at the trial. If the evidence against him was very strong, it was thought that he would seek to escape a sentence of death in voluntary exile, a step which Romans always encouraged, as they were averse, at all time, to putting a Roman citizen to death.

Sixth Stage (citatio). —At the expiration of the time designated by the president for the beginning of the trial, the proceedings before the judges began. All the necessary parties, including the judges or jurors, were summoned by a herald to appear. This procedure was termed the *citatio.* Strange to say, if the accused failed to appear the case could proceed without him. The reason for the requirement of his presence at the *nominis delatio,* but not at the trial is not clear; especially when viewed in the light of a modern trial in which the defendant must be present at every important step in the proceedings. Under Roman procedure, the presence of the defendant was not necessary, whether he was in voluntary exile, or was obstinately absent. In 52 B.C., Milo was condemned in his absence; and we read in Plutarch that the assassins of Caesar were tried in their absence, 43 B.C.

Excusable absence necessitated an adjournment of the case. The chief grounds for an adjournment were: (1) Absence from the city in the public service; (2) that the accused was compelled to appear in another court on the same day; (3) illness.

The absence of the accused did not prevent the prosecution of the case, but the nonappearance of the prosecutor on the day fixed for the beginning of the trial usually terminated the proceedings at once. The fact that the case had to be dismissed if the accuser failed to appear only serves to illustrate how dependent the state was on the sincerity of the citizen who undertook the prosecution. The obligations of the prosecutor honestly and vigorously to follow up a suit which he had set in motion were felt to be so serious a matter by the Romans that special laws were passed to hold him in the line of duty. The *lex Remmia* provided that if any citizen knowingly accused another citizen falsely of a crime, the accuser should be prosecuted for calumny *(calumnia)*. It further provided that, in case of conviction, the letter K should be branded on the forehead of the condemned. Such laws were found necessary to protect the good name of Roman citizens against bad men who desired to use the legal machinery of the state to gratify private malevolence against their enemies. It may thus be seen that the system which permitted public prosecutions on the motion of private citizens was attended by both good and bad results. Cicero regarded such a system as a positive benefit to the state.[4] Its undoubted effect was to place a check upon corruption in public office by subjecting the acts of public officials to the scrutiny and, if need be, to the censure of every man in the nation. On the other hand, accusers in public prosecutions came finally to be identified, in the public mind, with coarse and vulgar informers whose only motive in making public accusations was to create private gain. So thoroughly were they despised that one of the parasites of Plautus scornfully exclaims that he would not exchange his vocation, though low and groveling, with that of the man who makes a legal proceeding "his net wherein to catch another man's goods."[5]

Seventh Stage (impaneling the judges). —But if the prosecutor appeared in due time, the trial formally began by the impaneling of the judges. This was usually done by the praetor or *iudex quaestionis* who, at the beginning of the trial, placed the names of the complete panel of jurors, inscribed on white tablets, into an urn, and then drew out a certain number. Both prosecutor and accused had the right to challenge a limited number, as the names were being drawn. The number of challenges allowed varied from time to time.

Eighth Stage (beginning of the trial). —When the judges had been impaneled, the regular proceedings began. The place of trial was the Forum. The curule chair of the praetor and the benches of the judges, constituting the tribunal, were here placed. On the ground in front of the raised platform upon which the praetor and judges sat, were arranged the benches of the parties, their advocates and witnesses. Like the ancient Hebrew law, Roman law required that criminal cases should be tried only by daylight, that is, between daybreak and one hour before sunset. At the opening of the trial, the prosecutor, backed by the *subscriptores,* and the accused, supported by his patrons and advocates, appeared before the tribunal.

In a modern criminal trial the case is opened by the introduction of testimony which is followed by regular speeches of counsel for the people and the defendant. In those jurisdictions where opening addresses are required before the examination of the witnesses, the purpose is to inform the jury of the facts which it is proposed to prove. Argument and characterization are not permitted in thes opening speeches. The real speeches in which argument and illustration are permitted come after the evidence has been introduced. The purpose of these closing speeches is to assist the jury in determining matters of fact from conflicting testimony.

Under the Roman system of trial in criminal cases, the order was reserved. The regular speeches containing argument, characterization, and illustration, as well as a statement of the facts proposed to be proved, were made in the very beginning. Evidence was then introduced to show that the orators had told the truth in their speeches.

It is not practicable in this place to discuss the kinds and relevancy of evidence under Roman criminal procedure. Suffice it to say that slaves were always examined under torture.

The close of the evidence was followed by the judgment of the tribunal.

Ninth Stage (voting of the judges). —The judges voted by ballot, and a majority of votes decided the verdict. The balloting was done with tablets containing the letters A. *(absolvo),* C. *(condemno)* and N.L. *(non liquet).* When the votes had been cast, the tablets were then counted by the president of the tribunal. If the result indicated a condemnation, he pronounced the word *fecisse;* if an acquittal, the phrase, *non fecisse videtur;* if a doubtful verdict *(non liquet),* the words *amplius esse cognoscendum.* The result of a doubtful *(non liquet)* verdict was a retrial of the case at some future time.

Such were the main features of the trial of a capital case at Rome at the date of the crucifixion. Such was the model which, according to the best authorities, Pilate was bound to follow in the trial of Jesus. Did he imitate this model? Did he observe these rules and regulations? We shall see.

CHAPTER V

ROMAN FORMS OF PUNISHMENT

According to Gibbon, the laws of the Twelve Tables, like the statutes of Draco, were written in blood. These famous decrees sanctioned the frightful principle of the *lex talionis;* and prescribed for numerous crimes many horrible forms of punishment. The hurling from the Tarpeian Rock was mild in comparison with other modes of execution. The traitor to his country had his hands tied behind his back, his head shrouded in a veil, was then scourged by a lictor, and was afterwards crucified, in the midst of the Forum by being nailed to the *arbor infelix.* A malicious incendiary, on a principle of retaliation, was delivered to the flames. He was burned to death by being wrapped in a garment covered with pitch which was then set on fire.[1] A parricide was cast into the Tiber or the sea, inclosed in a sack, to which a cock, a viper, a dog, and a monkey had been successively added as fit companions in death.[2]

But the development of Roman jurisprudence and the growth of Roman civilization witnessed a gradual diminution in the severity of penal sanctions, in the case of free citizens, until voluntary exile was the worst punishment to which a wearer of the toga was compelled to submit. The Porcian and Valerian laws prohibited the magistrates from putting any Roman citizen to death. The principle underlying these laws was the offspring of a proud and patriotic sentiment which exempted the masters of the world from the extreme penalties reserved for barbarians and slaves. Greenidge, interpreting Cicero, very elegantly expresses this sentiment: "It is a *facinus* to put a Roman citizen in bonds, a *scelus* to scourge him, *prope parricidium* to put him to death."

The subject of this volume limits the discussion in this chapter to a single Roman punishment: Crucifixion. Around this word gather the most frightful memories and, at the same time, the sweetest and sublimest hopes of the human race. A thorough appreciation of the trial of Jesus, it is felt, renders necessary a comparatively exhaustive treatment of the punishment in which all the horrors and illegalities of the proceedings against Him culminated.

History. —Tradition attributes the origin of crucifixion, the most frightful and inhuman form of punishment ever known, to a woman, Semiramis, Queen of Assyria. We are reminded by this that quartering, drawing at a horse's tail, breaking on the wheel, burning and torture with pincers, were provisions in a codex bearing the name of a woman: Maria Theresa.[3]

Crucifixion was practiced by the ancient Egyptians, Carthaginians, Persians, Germans, Assyrians, Greeks, and Romans. The Romans employed this form of punishment on a colossal scale. The Roman general Varus crucified 2,000 Jews in one day at the gates of Jerusalem. The close of the war with Spartacus, the gladiator, witnessed the crucifixion of 10,000 slaves between Capua and Rome.

Crucifixion as a form of punishment was unknown to the ancient Hebrews.

The penalty of death was enforced among them by burning, strangling, decapitation, and stoning. The "hanging" of criminals "on a tree," mentioned in Deut. xxi. 22, was a posthumous indignity offered the body of the criminal after death by stoning, and struck horror to the soul of every pious Israelite who beheld it. Among the Romans also degradation was a part of the infliction, since crucifixion was peculiarly a *supplicium servile.* Only the vilest criminals, among free men, such as were guilty of robbery, piracy, assassination, perjury, sedition, treason, and desertion from the army, met death in this way. The *jus civitatis* protected Roman citizens against this punishment.

Mode of Crucifixion. —A sentence of death having been pronounced by a Roman magistrate or tribunal, scourging became a preliminary to execution. This was done with the terrible *Flagellum* into which the soldiers frequently stuck nails, pieces of bone, and other hard substances to heighten the pain which was often so intense as to produce death. The victim was generally bound to a column to be scourged. It was claimed by Jerome, Prudentius, Gregory of Tours, and others that they had seen the one to which Jesus was bound before His scourging began. After the flagellation, the prisoner was conducted to the place of execution. This was outside the city, often in some public road, or other conspicuous place like the Campus Martius at Rome. The criminal was compelled to carry his own cross; and when he had arrived at the place of crucifixion, he was compelled to watch the preparations for his torture. Before his eyes and in his presence, the cross was driven into the ground; and, after having been stripped naked, he was lifted upon and nailed to it. It sometimes happened that he was stretched upon it first and then lifted with it from the ground. The former method was the more common, however, as it was desired to strike terror into the victim by the sight of the erection of the cross. The body was fastened to the cross by nails driven into the hands and sometimes into the feet; more frequently, however, the feet were merely bound by cords.

The pictures of crosses in works of art are misrepresentations, in that they are too large and too high. The real cross of antiquity was very little longer than the victim, whose head was near the top, and whose feet often hung only twelve or fifteen inches from the ground. Pictorial art is also false because it fails to show the projecting beam from near the center of the cross upon which the criminal sat. That there was such a beam is attested by the almost unanimous voice of antiquity.

Crucifixion was conducted, under Roman auspices, by a *carnifex,* or hangman, assisted by a band of soldiers. At Rome, execution was done under the supervision of the *Triumviri Capitales.* The duty of the soldiers was not only to erect the cross and nail the victim to it, but also to watch him until he was dead. This was a necessary precaution to prevent friends and relatives from taking the criminal down and from carrying him away, since he sometimes continued to live upon the cross during several days. If taken down in time, the suffering man might easily be resuscitated and restored to health. Josephus tells us that three victims were ordered to be taken down by Titus at his request, and that one of them recovered. "In the later persecutions of the Christians, the guards remained four or six days by the dead, in order to secure them to the wild beasts and to cut off all possibility of burial and resurrection; and in Lyons the Christians were not once able by offers of much gold to obtain the privilege of showing compassion upon the victims of the pagan popular fury. Sometimes, however, particularly on festival days, e.g., the birthdays of the emperors, the corpse was given up to the friends of the deceased, either for money or without money, although even Augustus could be cruel enough to turn a deaf ear to the entreaties of the condemned for sepulture."[4]

Roman records tell us that the soldiers frequently hastened death by breaking the legs of the criminal; at other times, fires were built about the cross beneath him; and, again, wild beasts were turned loose upon him.

It was the general custom to allow the body to remain and rot upon the cross, or to be devoured by wild beasts and birds of prey. "Distracted relatives and friends saw the birds of prey attack the very faces of those whom they loved; and piety often took pains to scare away the birds by day and the beasts by night, or to outwit the guards that watched the dead."[5]

Sepulture was generally forbidden by law, though there were exceptions to the rule. At the request of Joseph of Arimathea, Pilate consented that Jesus should be taken down and buried.[6] A national exception seems also to have been made in the case of the Jews on account of the requirements of Deut. xxi. 22, 23.

Pathology. —The following pathological phases of death by crucifixion are from a treatise by the celebrated physician, Richter (in John's "Bibl. Arch."), which have been reproduced in Strong and McClintock's "Cyclopedia":

"(1)   The unnatural position and violent tension of the body, which cause a painful sensation from the least motion.

"(2)   The nails, being driven through parts of the hands and feet which are full of nerves and tendons (and yet at a distance from the heart) create the most exquisite anguish.

"(3)   The exposure of so many wounds and lacerations brings on inflammation, which tends to become gangrene, and every movement increases the poignancy of suffering.

"(4)   In the distended parts of the body, more blood flows through the arteries than can be carried back into the veins: hence too much blood finds its way from the aorta into the head and stomach, and the blood vessels of the head become pressed and swollen. The general obstruction of circulation which ensues causes an intense excitement, exertion, and anxiety more intolerable than death itself.

"(5)   The inexpressible misery of *gradually increasing* and lingering anguish.

"(6)   Burning and raging thirst.

"Death by crucifixion (physically considered) is, therefore, to be attributed to the sympathetic fever which is excited by the wounds, and aggravated by exposure to the weather, privation of water, and the painfully constrained position of the body. Traumatic fever corresponds, in intensity and in character, to the local inflammation of the wound, is characterized by heat, swelling, and great pain, the fever is highly inflammatory, and the sufferer complains of heat, throbbing headache, intense thirst, restlessness, and anxiety. As soon as suppuration sets in, the fever somewhat abates, and partially ceases as suppuration diminishes and the stage of cicatrization approaches. But if the wound be prevented from healing and suppuration continues, the fever assumes a hectic character, and will sooner or later exhaust the powers of life. When, however, the inflammation of the wound is so intense as to produce mortification, nervous depression is the immediate consequence; and, if the cause of this excessive inflammation of the wound still continues, as is the case in crucifixion, the sufferer rapidly sinks. He is no longer sensible of pain, but his anxiety and sense of prostration are excessive; hiccough supervenes, his skin is moistened with a cold clammy sweat, and death ensues. It is in this manner that death on the cross must have taken place in an ordinarily healthy constitution."

The intense sufferings and prolonged agony of crucifixion can be best illustrated by an account of several cases of this form of punishment taken from history.

From the "Chrestomathia Arabica" of Kosegarten, published in 1828, is taken the following story of the execution of a Mameluke. The author of this work gleaned the story from an Arabic manuscript entitled

"The Meadow of Flowers and the Fragrant Odour":

" It is said that he had killed his master for some cause or other, and he was crucified on the banks of the river Barada under the castle of Damascus, with his face turned toward the East. His hands, arms, and feet were nailed, and he remained so from midday on Friday to the same hour on Sunday, when he died. He was remarkable for his strength and prowess; he had been engaged with his master in sacred war at Askelon, where he slew great numbers of the Franks; and when very young he had killed a lion. Several extraordinary things occurred at his being nailed, as that he gave himself up without resistance to the cross, and without complaint stretched out his hands, which were nailed and after them his feet: he in the meantime looked on, and did not utter a groan, or change his countenance or move his limbs. I have heard this from one who witnessed it, and he thus remained till he died, patient and silent, without wailing, but looking around him to the right and the left upon the people. But he begged for water, and none was given him, and he gazed upon it and longed for one drop of it, and he complained of thirst all the first day, after which he was silent, for God gave him strength."

Describing the punishments used in Madagascar, Rev. Mr. Ellis says: "In a few cases of great enormity, a sort of crucifixion has been resorted to; and, in addition to this, burning or roasting at a slow fire, kept at some distance from the sufferer, has completed the horrors of this miserable death. . . . In the year 1825, a man was condemned to crucifixion, who had murdered a female for the sake of stealing her child. He carried the child for sale to the public market, where the infant was recognized, and the murderer detected. He bore his punishment in the most hardened manner, avenging himself by all the violence he was capable of exercising upon those who dragged him to the place of execution. Not a single groan escaped him during the period he was nailed to the wood, nor while the cross was fixed upright in the earth."[7]

More horrible still than punishment by crucifixion was that of impalement and suspension on a hook. The following description of the execution, in 1830, at Salonica, of Chaban, a captain of banditti, is given by Slade: "He was described by those who saw him as a very fine-looking man, about thirty-five. As a preparatory exercise, he was suspended by his arms for twelve hours. The following day a hook was thrust into his side, by which he was suspended to a tree, and there hung enduring the agony of thirst till the third evening, when death closed the scene; but before that about an hour the birds, already considering him their own, had alighted upon his brow to pick his eyes. During this frightful period he uttered no unmanly complaints, only repeated several times, 'Had I known that I was to suffer this infernal death, I would never have done what I have. From the moment I led the klephte's life I had death before my eyes, and was prepared to meet it, but I expected to die as my predecessors, by decapitation.' "[8]

The Cross. —The instrument of crucifixion, called the Cross, was variously formed. Lipsius and Gretser have employed a twofold classification: the *crux simplex,* and the *crux composita* or *compacta.* A single upright stake was distinguished as a *crux simplex.* The *crux composita,* the compound or actual cross, was subject to the following modifications of form: *Crux immissa,* formed as in the figure **†**; *crux commissa* thus formed **T**; and the *crux decussata,* the cruciform figure set diagonally after the manner of the Roman letter X. It is generally thought that Jesus was crucified upon the *crux immissa,* the "Latin cross."

According to the well-known legend of the "Invention of the Cross," the actual cross on which Jesus was crucified was discovered in the year 326 A.D. by the Empress Helena, the mother of Constantine the Great. As the story goes, while visiting Jerusalem and the scenes of the passion, she was guided to the summit of Calvary by an aged Jew. Here an excavation was made, and, at a considerable depth, three crosses were found; and, with them, but lying aside by itself, was the inscription, in Hebrew, Latin, and Greek, placed above the head of Christ at the time of the crucifixion. To determine which of the three crosses was the one upon which Jesus suffered, it was decided, at the suggestion of Macarius, bishop of Jerusalem, to employ a miracle. The sick were brought and required to touch the three. According to the legend, the one upon which the Savior died immediately imparted miraculous healing. A church was at once built above the excavation and in it was deposited the greater part of the supposed real cross, and the remainder was sent to Byzantium, and from there to Rome, where it was placed in the church of Santa Croce in Gerusalemme, built especially to receive the precious relic. The genuineness of this relic was afterwards attested by a Bull of Pope Alexander III.

In connection with the legend of the discovery of the actual cross upon which Christ was crucified, goes a secondary story that the nails used at the crucifixion were also found at the same time and place. Later tradition declared that one of these was thrown by Helena into the Adriatic when swept by a terrific storm, and that this was followed by an instantaneous calm.

The popular impression among Christians that the cross is exclusively a Christian religious symbol, seems to be without historical foundation. It is quite certain, indeed, that it was a religious emblem among several ancient races before the beginning of the Christian era.

The ancient Egyptians adored the cross with the most holy veneration; and this sacred emblem was carved upon many of their monuments. Several of these monuments may be seen today in the British Museum.[9] A cross upon a Calvary may also be seen upon the breast of one of the Egyptian mummies in the Museum of the London University.[10] The ancient Egyptians were accustomed to putting a cross on their sacred cakes, just as the Christians of today do, on Good Friday.[11]

The cross was also adored by the ancient Greeks and Romans, long before the crucifixion of Christ. Greek crosses of equal arms adorn the tomb of Midas, the ancient Phrygian king.[12] One of the early Christian Fathers, Minucius Felix, in a heated controversy with the pagan Romans, charged them with adoration of the cross. "As for adoration of the cross," said he to the Romans, "which you object against us, I must tell you that we neither adore crosses nor desire them. You it is, ye Pagans, who worship wooden gods, who are the most likely people to adore wooden crosses, as being part of the same substance with your deities. For what else are your ensigns, flags, and standards, but crosses, gilt and beautiful? Your victorious trophies *not only represent a cross, but a cross with a man upon it.*"[13]

It also seems that, at a time antedating the early Romans, Etruscans and Sabines, a primitive race inhabited the plains of Northern Italy, "to whom the cross was a religious symbol, the sign beneath which they laid their dead to rest; a people of whom history tells nothing, knowing not their name; but of whom antiquarian research has learned this, that they lived in ignorance of the arts of civilization, that they dwelt in villages built on platforms over lakes, and that they trusted to the cross to guard, and maybe to revive, their loved ones whom they committed to the dust."

The cross was also a sacred symbol among the ancient Scandinavians. "It occurs," says Mr. R. P. Knight, "on many Runic monuments found in Sweden and Denmark, which are of an age long anterior to the approach of Christianity to those countries, and, probably, to its appearance in the world."[14]

When the Spanish missionaries first set foot on the soil of Mexico, they were amazed to find that the Aztecs worshiped the cross as an object of supreme veneration. They found it suspended as a sacred symbol and an august emblem from the walls of all the Aztec temples.[15] When they penetrated farther south and entered Peru, they found that the Incas adored a cross made out of a single piece of jasper.[16] "It appears," says "Chambers's Encyclopedia," "that the sign of the cross was in use as an emblem having certain religious and mystic meanings attached to it, long before the Christian era; and the Spanish conquerors were astonished to find it an object of religious veneration among the nations of Central and South America."[17]

That the ancient Mexicans should have worshiped the cross and also a crucified Savior, called Quetzalcoatle,[18] is one of the strangest phenomena of sacred history. It is a puzzle which the most eminent theologians have found it impossible to solve. They have generally contented themselves with declaring the whole thing a myth built upon primitive superstition and ignorance. This worship of the cross and Quetzalcoatle was going on before Columbus discovered America, and it seems impossible to establish any historical or geographical connection between it and the Christian worship of the cross and the crucified Jesus.

Several writers of eminence have contended that the widespread adoration of the cross, as a sacred symbol among so many races of mankind, ancient and modern, proves a universal spiritual impulse, culminating in the crucifixion of Jesus as the common Savior of the world. "It is more than a coincidence," says the Rev. S. Baring-Gould, "that Osiris by the cross should give life eternal to the spirits of the just; that with the cross Thor should smite the head of the great Serpent, and bring to life those who were slain; that beneath the cross the Muysca mothers should lay their babes, trusting to that sign to secure them from the power of evil spirits; that with that symbol to protect them, the ancient people of Northern Italy should lay them down in the dust."[19]

But it is not with the mythical crucifixions of mythical gods that we have to deal. The real, historical death of Jesus upon the cross with its accompanying incidents of outrageous illegality is the purpose of this treatise; and to the accomplishment of that design we now return.

CHAPTER VI

ROMAN LAW APPLICABLE TO THE TRIAL OF JESUS

What was the law of Rome in relation to the trial of Jesus? The answer to this question is referable to the main charge brought against the Master before Pilate. A single verse in St. Luke contains the indictment: "And they began to accuse him, saying, We found this fellow perverting the nation, and forbidding to give tribute to Caesar, saying that he himself is Christ a King." Three distinct elements are wrapped up in this general accusation; but they are all interwoven with and culminate in the great charge that Jesus claimed to be "Christ a King." Of this accusation alone, Pilate took cognizance. And there is no mistake as to its nature and meaning. It was High Treason against Caesar—the most awful crime known to Roman law. This was the charge brought by the priests of the Sanhedrin against the Nazarene. What then was the law of Rome in relation to the crime of high treason? The older Roman law, *crimen per duellionis,* applied chiefly to offenses committed in the military service. Deserters from the army were regarded as traitors and punished as public enemies either by death or interdiction of fire and water. Later Roman law broadened the definition of treason until it comprehended any offense against the Roman Commonwealth that affected the dignity and security of the Roman people. Ulpian, defining treason, says: *"Majestatis crimen illud est quod adversus populum Romanum vel adversus securitatem ejus committitur."*[1] Cicero very admirably describes the same crime as: *"Majestatem minuere est de dignitate aut amplitudine aut potestate populi aut eorum quibus populus potestatem dedit aliquid derogare."*[2] The substance of both these definitions is this: Treason is an insult to the dignity or an attack upon the sovereignty and security of the Roman State. From time to time, various laws were passed to define this crime and to provide penalties for its commission. Chief among these were the *lex Julia Majestatis,* 48 B.C. Other laws of an earlier date were the *lex Cornelia,* 81 B.C.; *lex Varia,* 92 B.C.; and the *lex Appuleia,* 100 B.C. The *lex Julia* was in existence at the time of Christ, and was the basis of the Roman law of treason until the closing years of the empire. One of its provisions was that every accusation of treason against a Roman citizen should be made by a written libel. But it is not probable that provincials were entitled to the benefit of this provision; and it was not therefore an infraction of the law that the priests and Pilate failed to present a written charge against Jesus.

In studying the trial of Jesus and the charge brought against Him, the reader should constantly remind himself that the crucifixion took place during the reign of Tiberius Caesar, a morbid and capricious tyrant, whose fretful and suspicious temper would kindle into fire at the slightest suggestion of treason in any quarter. Tacitus records fifty-two cases of prosecution for treason during his reign. The enormous development of the law of *majestas* at this time gave rise to a class of professional informers, *delatores,* whose infamous activity against private citizens helped to blacken the name of Tiberius. The most harmless acts were at times construed into an affront to the majesty or into an assault upon the safety of this miserable despot. Cotta Messalinus was prosecuted for treason because it was alleged "that he had given Caligula the nickname of Caia, as contaminated by incest"; and again on another charge that he had styled a banquet among the priests on the birthday of Augusta, a "funeral supper"; and again on another charge that, while complaining of the influence of Manius Lepidus and Lucius Arruntius, with whom he had had trouble in court, he had said that "they indeed will be supported by the senate, but I by my little Tiberius."[3]

Manercus Scaurus was prosecuted for treason because he wrote a tragedy in which were certain lines that might be made to apply in an uncomplimentary manner to Tiberius. We are told by Dio that this tragedy was founded on the story of Atreus; and that Tiberius, believing himself referred to, said, "Since he makes me another Atreus, I will make him an Ajax," meaning that he would compel him to destroy himself.[4]

"Nor," says Tacitus, "were even women exempt from danger. With designs to usurp the government they could not be charged; their tears are therefore made treason; and Vitia, mother to Fusius Geminus, once consul, was executed in her old age for bewailing the death of her son."[5]

An anecdote taken from Seneca but related in Tacitus, illustrates the pernicious activity of the political informers of this age. At a banquet in Rome, one of the guests wore the image of Tiberius on his ring. His slave, seeing his master intoxicated, took the ring off his finger. An informer noticed the act, and, later in the evening, insisted that the owner, to show his contempt of Tiberius, was sitting upon the figure of the emperor. Whereupon he began to draw up an accusation for high treason and was getting ready to have it attested by subscribing witnesses, when the slave took the ring from his own pocket, and thus demonstrated to the whole company that he had had it in his possession all the time. These instances fully serve to illustrate the political tone and temper of the age that witnessed the trial and crucifixion of Jesus. They also suggest the exceedingly delicate and painful position of Pilate when sitting in judgment upon the life of a subject of Tiberius who claimed to be a king.

It is deemed entirely appropriate, in this place, to discuss a peculiar phase of the law of treason in its relationship to the trial of Jesus. It is easily demonstrable that the teachings of Christ were treasonable under Roman public law. An essential and dominating principle of that law was that the imperial State had the right to regulate and control the private consciences of men in religious matters. It was held to be an attribute of the sovereignty of Rome that she had the right to create or destroy religions. And the theory of the Roman constitution was that the exercise of this right was not a religious but a governmental function. The modern doctrine of the separation of Church and State had no place in Roman politics at the time of Christ. Tiberius Caesar, at the beginning of his reign, definitely adopted the principle of a state religion, and as Pontifex Maximus, was bound to protect the ancient Roman worship as a matter of official duty.

Roman treatment of foreign religions, from first to last, is a most interesting and fascinating study. Polytheistic above all other nations, the general policy of the Roman empire was one of toleration. Indeed she not only tolerated but adopted and absorbed foreign worships into her own. The Roman religion was a composite of nearly all the religions of the earth. It was thus natural that the imperial State should be indulgent in religious matters, since warfare upon foreign faiths would have been an assault upon integral parts of her own sacred system. It is historically true that attempts were made from time to time by patriotic Romans to preserve the old Latin faith in its original purity from foreign invasion. The introduction of Greek gods was at first vigorously opposed, but the exquisite beauty of Greek sculpture, the irresistible influence of Greek literature, and the overwhelming fascination of Greek myths, finally destroyed this opposition, and placed Apollo and Aesculapius in the Roman pantheon beside Jupiter and Minerva.

At another time the senate declared war on the Egyptian worship which was gradually making its way into Rome. It had the images of Isis and Serapis thrown down; but the people set them up again. It decreed that the temples to these deities should be destroyed, but not a single workman would lay hands upon them. Aemilius Paulus, the consul, was himself forced to seize an ax and break in the doors of the temple. In spite of this, the worship of Isis and Serapis was soon again practiced unrestrained at Rome.[6]

It is further true that Rome showed not only intolerance but mortal antagonism to Druidism, which was completely annihilated during the reign of the Emperor Claudius.

A decree of the Roman senate, during the reign of Tiberius, ordered four thousand freemen charged with Egyptian and Jewish superstitions out to Sardinia to fight against and be destroyed by the banditti there, unless they saw fit to renounce these superstitions within a given time.[7]

But it must be remembered that these are exceptional cases of intolerance revealed by Roman history. The general policy of the empire, on the other hand, was of extreme tolerance and liberality. The keynote of this policy was that all religions would be tolerated that consented to live side by side and in peace with all other religions. There was but one restriction upon and limitation of this principle, that foreign religions would be tolerated only in their local seats, or, at most, among the races in which such religions were native. The fact that the worship of Serapis was left undisturbed on the banks of the Nile, did not mean that the same worship would be tolerated on the banks of the Tiber. An express authorization by Rome was necessary for this purpose. Said authorization made said worship a *religio licita*. And the peregrini, or foreigners in Rome, were thus permitted to erect their own altars, and to assemble for the purpose of worshiping their own gods which they had brought with them. The reverse side of this general principle of religious tolerance shows that Roman citizens were not only permitted but required to carry the Roman faith with them throughout the world. Upon them, the Roman state religion was absolutely binding; and for all the balance of the world it was the dominant cult. "The provinces," says Renan, "were entirely free to adhere to their own rights, on the sole condition of not interfering with those of others." "Such toleration or indifference, however," says Dollinger, "found its own limits at once whenever the doctrine taught had a practical bearing on society, interfered with the worship of the state gods, or confronted their worship with one of its own; as well as when a strange god and *cultus* assumed a hostile attitude toward Roman gods, could be brought into no affinity or corporate relation with them, and would not bend to the supremacy of Jupiter Capitolinus."

Now, the principles declared by Renan and Dollinger are fundamental and pointed in the matter of the relationship between the teachings of Jesus and the theory of treason under Roman law. These principles were essential elements of Roman public law, and an attempt to destroy them was an act of treason under the definitions of both Ulpian and Cicero. The Roman constitution required that a foreign religion, as a condition of its very existence, should live in peace with its neighbors; that it should not make war upon or seek to destroy other religions; and that it should acknowledge the dominance and superior character of the imperial religion. All these things Jesus refused to do, as did his followers after Him. The Jews, it is true, had done the same thing, but their nationality and lack of aggressiveness saved them until the destruction of Jerusalem. But Christianity was essentially aggressive and proselytizing. It sought to supplant and destroy all other religions. No compromises were proposed, no treaties concluded. The followers of the Nazarene raised a black flag against paganism and every heathen god. Their strange faith not only defied all other religions, but mocked all earthly government not built upon it. Their propaganda was nothing less than a challenge to the Roman empire in the affairs of both law and religion. Here was a faith which claimed to be the only true religion; that proclaimed a monotheistic message which was death to polytheism; and that refused to be confined within local limits. Here was a religion that scorned an authorization from Rome to worship its god and prophet; a religion that demanded acceptance and obedience from all the world—from Roman and Greek, as well as Jew and Egyptian. This scorn and this demand were an affront to the dignity and a challenge to the laws of the Roman Commonwealth. Such conduct was treason against the constitution of the empire.

"The substance of what the Romans did," says Sir James Fitz-James Stephen, "was to treat Christianity by fits and starts as a crime."[8] But why a crime? Because the Roman religion, built upon polytheism, was an integral and inseparable part of the Roman State, and whatever menaced the life of the one, threatened the existence of the other. The Romans regarded their religion as "an engine of state which could not be shaken without the utmost danger to their civil government." Cicero further says: "The institutions of the fathers must be defended; it is the part of wisdom to hold fast the sacred rites and ceremonies."[9] Roman statesmen were fully aware of the truthfulness of the statement of a modern writer that, "wherever the religion of any state falls into disregard and comtempt it is impossible for that state to subsist long." Now, Christianity was monotheistic, and threatened destruction to polytheism everywhere. And the Romans treated it as a crime because it was regarded as a form of seditious atheism whose teachings and principles were destructive of the established order of things. The Roman conception of the nature of the crime committed by an attack upon the national religion is well illustrated by the following sentence from Dollinger: "If an opinion unfavorable to the apotheosis of any member of the imperial dynasty happened to be dropped, it was dangerous in itself as falling within the purview of the law of high treason; and so it fell out in the case of Thrasea Paetus, who refused to believe in the deification of Poppaea." If it was high treason to refuse to believe in the deification of an emperor or an empress, what other crime could be imputed to him whose design was to destroy an entire religious system, and to pile all the gods and goddesses—Juno and Poppaea, Jupiter and Augustus—in common ruin?

From the foregoing, it may be readily seen that it is impossible to appreciate the legal aspects of the trial of Jesus before Pilate, unless it is constantly kept in mind that the Roman constitution, which was binding upon the whole empire, reserved to the state the right to permit or forbid the existence of new religious faiths and the exercise of rights of conscience in religious matters. Rome was perfectly willing to tolerate all religions as long as they were peaceful and passive in their relations with other religions. But when a new and aggressive faith appeared upon the scene, proclaiming the strange dogma that there was but one name under heaven whereby men might be saved, and demanding that every knee bow at the mention of that name, and threatening damnation upon all who refused, the majesty of Roman law felt itself insulted and outraged; and persecution, torture, and death were the inevitable result. The best and wisest of the Roman emperors, Trajan and the Antonines, devoted to the ax or condemned to crucifixion the early Christians, not because Christianity was spiritually false, but because it was aggressive and intolerant, and they believed its destruction necessary to the maintenance of the supremacy and sovereignty of the Roman State.

An interesting correspondence between Pliny and Trajan, while the former was governor of Bithynia, reveals the Roman conception of and attitude toward Christianity. Pliny wrote to Trajan: "In the meanwhile, the method I have observed toward those who have been brought before me as Christians is this: I asked them whether they were Christians; if they admitted it, I repeated the question twice, and threatened them with punishment; if they persisted, I ordered them to be at once punished, for I was persuaded, whatever the nature of their opinions might be, a contumacious and inflexible obstinacy certainly deserved correction. There were others also brought before me possessed with the same infatuation, but being Roman citizens, I directed them to be sent to Rome."

To this, Trajan replied: "You have adopted the right course, my dearest

Secundus, in investigating the charges against the Christians who were brought before you. It is not possible to lay down any general rule for all such cases. Do not go out of your way to look for them. If, indeed, they should be brought before you, and the crime is proved, they must be punished; with the restriction, however, that where the party denies he is a Christian, and shall make it evident he is not, by invoking our gods, let him (notwithstanding any former suspicion) be pardoned upon his repentance."[10] Here the magnanimous Trajan called Christianity a crime, and this was the popular Roman conception of it during the first two centuries of its existence.

Now, it is true that Christianity was not on trial before Pilate; but the Author of Christianity was. And the same legal principles were extant and applicable that afterwards brought the Roman State and the followers of the Nazarene into mortal conflict. For the prisoner who now stood before the procurator to answer the charge of high treason asserted substantially the same claims and proclaimed the same doctrines that afterwards caused Rome to devote His adherents to flames and to wild beasts in the amphitheater. The record does not disclose that Pilate became fully acquainted at the trial of Jesus with His claims and doctrines. On the other hand, it is clear that he became convinced that the claim of Jesus to be "Christ a King" was not a pretension to earthly sovereignty. But, nevertheless, whatever might have been the information or the notions of the deputy of Tiberius, the teachings of Jesus were inconsistent and incompatible with the public law of the Roman State. Pilate was not necessarily called upon to enforce this law, since it was frequently the duty of Roman governors, as intimated by Trajan in his letter to Pliny, to exercise leniency in dealing with religious delinquents.

To summarize, then: it may be said that the Roman law applicable to the trial of Jesus was the *lex Julia Majestatis,* interpreted either in the light of claims to actual kingship made by Jesus, or to kingship of a religious realm whose character and existence were a menace to the religion and laws of Rome. In the light of the evidence adduced at the hearing before Pilate, these legal principles become mere abstract propositions, since there seems to have been neither necessity nor attempt to enforce them; but they were in existence, nevertheless, and were directly applicable to the trial of Jesus.

CHAPTER VII

PONTIUS PILATE

His Name. — The praenomen or first name of Pilate is not known. Rosadi calls him Lucius, but upon what authority is not stated. His nomen or family name indicates that he was connected either by descent or by adoption with the gens of the Pontii, a tribe first made famous in Roman history in the person and achievements of C. Pontius Telesinus, the great Samnite general. A German legend, however, offers another explanation. According to this story, Pilate was the natural son of Tyrus, King of Mayence. His father sent him to Rome as a hostage, and there he was guilty of murder. Afterwards he was sent to Pontus, where he distinquished himself by subduing certain barbarian tribes. In recognition of his services, it is said, he received the name Pontius. But this account is a pure fabrication. It is possible that it was invented by the 22d legion, which was assigned to Palestine at the time of the destruction of Jerusalem, and was afterwards stationed at Mayence. The soldiers of this legion might have been "either the bearers of this tradition or the inventors of the fable."

It is historically almost certain that Pilate was a native of Seville, one of the cities of Baetic Spain that enjoyed rights of Roman citizenship. In the war of annihilation waged by Agrippa against the Cantabrians, the father of Pilate, Marcus Pontius, acquired fame as a general on the side of Rome. He seems to have been a renegade to the cause of the Spaniards, his countrymen. And when Spain had been conquered by Rome, as a reward for service, and as a mark of distinction, he received the pilum (javelin), and from this fact his family took the name of Pilati. This is the common explanation of the origin of the cognomen Pilatus.

Others have sought to derive the word Pilate from *pileatus,* which, among the Romans, was the cap worn as a badge of servitude by manumitted slaves. This derivation would make Pontius Pilate a *libertus,* or the descendant of one.

Of his youth, very little is known. But it is believed that, after leaving Spain, he entered the suite of Germanicus on the Rhine and served through the German campaigns; and that, when peace was concluded, he went to Rome in search of fortune and in pursuit of pleasure.

His Marriage. — Soon after his arrival in Rome, Pilate was married to Claudia, the youngest daughter of Julia, the daughter of Augustus. Julia was a woman of the most dissolute and reckless habits. According to Suetonius, nothing so embittered the life of the Roman emperor as the shameful conduct of the mother of the wife of the procurator of Judea. He had reared her with the utmost care, had accustomed her to domestic employments such as knitting and spinning, and had sought to inculcate principles of purity and nobility of soul by requiring her to speak and act openly before the family, that everything which was said and done might be put down in a diary. His guardianship of the attentions paid her by young men was so strict that he once wrote a letter to Lucius Vinicius, a handsome young man of good family, in which he said: "You have not behaved very modestly, in making a visit to my daughter at Baiae." Notwithstanding this good training, Julia became one of the lewdest and coarsest women in Rome. Augustus married her first to Marcellus; then, after the death of Marcellus, to Marcus Agrippa; and, finally, to Tiberius. But in spite of the noble matches that had been made for her, her lewdness and debaucheries became so notorious that Augustus was compelled to banish her from Rome. It is said that he was so much ashamed of her infamous conduct that for a long time he avoided all company, and even had thoughts of putting her to death. His sorrow and humiliation are shown from the circumstance that when one Phoebe, a freedwoman and confidante of hers, hanged herself about the time the decree of banishment was passed by the senate, he said: "I had rather be the father of Phoebe than of Julia." And whenever the name of Julia was mentioned to him, during her exile, Augustus was wont to exclaim: "Would I were wifeless, or had childless died."[1]

Such was the character of Julia, mother-in-law of Pilate. In exile, she bore Claudia to a Roman knight. In her fifteenth year, the young girl met the Spaniard in Rome and was courted by him. Nothing better illustrates the character of Pilate than his union with this woman with whose origin and bringing up he was well acquainted. It was a servile and lustful rather than a noble and affectionate eye which he cast upon her. Having won the favor of Tiberius and the consent of Claudia, the marriage was consummated. After the nuptial rites, tradition has it that Pilate desired to follow the bride in the imperial litter; but Tiberius, who had acted as one of the twelve witnesses required by the law, forced him back, and drawing a paper from his bosom, handed it to him and passed on. This paper contained his commission as procurator of Judea; and the real object of the suit paid to Claudia was attained.

Pilate proceeded at once to Caesarea, the headquarters of the government of his province. His wife, who had been left behind, joined him afterwards. Caesar's permission to do this was a most gracious concession, as it was not generally allowed that governors of provinces should take their wives with them. At first it was positively forbidden. But afterwards a *senatus consult,* which is embodied in the Justinian text, declared it better that the wives of proconsuls and procurators should not go with them, but ordaining that said officials might take their wives with them provided they made themselves personally responsible for any transgressions on their part. Notwithstanding the numerous restrictions of Roman law and customs, it is very evident that the wives of Roman officers frequently accompanied them to the provinces. From Tacitus we hearn that at the time of the death of Augustus, Germanicus had his wife Agrippina with him in Germany; and afterwards, in the beginning of the reign of Tiberius, she was also with him in the East. Piso, the praefect of Syria, took his wife with him at the same time. These facts are historical corroborations of the Gospel accounts of the presence of Claudia in Jerusalem at the time of the crucifixion and of her warning dream to Pilate concerning the date of the Master.

His Procuratorship.— Pontius Pilate was the sixth procurator of Judea. Sabinus, Coponius, Ambivus, Rufus, and Gratus had preceded him in the government of the province. Pilate's connection with the trial and crucifixion of Jesus will be dealt with in succeeding chapters of this volume. Only the chief acts of his public administration, in a purely political capacity, will be noticed here. One of the first of these acts serves well to illustrate the reckless and tactless character of the man. His predecessors in office had exercised great care in the matter of the religious prejudices of the Jews. They had studiously avoided exhibiting flags and other emblems bearing images of the emperor that might offend the sacred sentiments of the native population. Even Vitellius, the legate of Syria, when he was marching against the Arabian king Aretas, ordered his troops not to carry their standards into Jewish territory, but to march around it. Pilate, on the other hand, in defiance of precedent and policy, caused the garrison soldiers of Jerusalem to enter the city by night carrying aloft their standards, blazoned with the images of Tiberius. The news of this outrage threw the Jews into wild excitement. The people in great numbers flocked down to Caesarea, where Pilate was still stopping, and begged him to remove the standards. Pilate refused; and for five days the discussion went on. At last he became enraged, summoned the people into the race course, had them surrounded by a detachment of soldiers, and served notice upon them that he would have them put to death if they did not become quiet and disperse. But, not in the least dismayed, they threw themselves upon the ground, laid bare their necks, and, in their turn, served notice upon Pilate that they, the children of Abraham, would rather die, and that they would die, before they would willingly see the Holy City defiled. The result was that Pilate finally yielded, and had the standards and images withdrawn from Jerusalem. Such was the Roman procurator and such the people with whom he had to deal. Thus the very first act of this procuratorship was a blunder which embarrassed his whole subsequent career.

A new storm burst forth when, on another occasion, Pilate appropriated funds from the Corban or sacred treasury to complete an aqueduct for bringing water to Jerusalem from the "Pools of Solomon." This was certainly a most useful enterprise; and, ordinarily, would speak well for the statesmanship and administrative ability of the procurator. But, in this instance, it was only another exhibition of tactless behavior in dealing with a stubborn and peculiar people. The Jews had a very great reverence for whatever was set apart for the Corban, and they considered it a form of awful impiety to devote its funds to secular purposes. Pilate, we must assume, was well acquainted with their religious scruples in this regard, and his open defiance of their prejudices was an illustration not of courage, but of weakness in administrative matters. Moreover, his final conduct in the matter of the aqueduct revealed a malignant quality in the temper of the man. On one occasion when he was getting ready to go to Jerusalem to supervise the building of this work, he learned that the people would again importune him, as in the case of the standards and the images. He then deliberately caused some of his soldiers to be disguised as Jewish citizens, had them armed with clubs and daggers, which they carried concealed beneath their upper garments; and when the multitude approached him to make complaints and to present their petitions, he gave a preconcerted signal, at which the assassins beat down and cut to pieces great numbers of the helpless crowds. Pilate was victorious in this matter; for the opposition to the building of the aqueduct was thus crushed in a most bloody manner. But hatred against Pilate was stirred up afresh and intensified in the hearts of the Jews.

A third act of defiance of the religious prejudices of the inhabitants of Jerusalem illustrates not only the obstinacy but the stupidity as well of the deputy of Caesar in Judea. In the face of his previous experiences, he insisted on hanging up in Herod's palace certain gilt shields dedicated to Tiberius. The Jews remonstrated with him in vain for this new outrage upon their national feelings. They were all the more indignant because they believed that he had done it, "less for the honor of Tiberius than for the annoyance of the Jewish people." Upon the refusal of Pilate to remove the shields, a petition signed by the leading men of the nation, among whom were the four sons of Herod, was addressed to the emperor, asking for the removal of the offensive decorations. Tiberius granted the request and the shields were taken from Jerusalem and deposited in the temple of Augustus at Caesarea—"And thus were preserved both the honor of the emperor and the ancient customs of the city."[2]

The instances above cited are recounted in the works of Josephus [3] and Philo. But the New Testament also contains intimations that Pilate was a cruel and reckless governor in his dealings with the Jews. According to St. Luke xiii. 1 : "There were present at that season some that told him of the Galileans, whose blood Pilate had mingled with their sacrifices." Nothing definite is known of this incident mentioned by the Evangelist. But it probably refers to the fact that Pilate had put to the sword a number of Galileans while they were offering their sacrifices at Jerusalem.

His Character. — The estimates of the character of Pilate are as varied as the races and creeds of men. Both Josephus and Philo have handed down to posterity a very ugly picture of the sixth Roman procurator of Judea. Philo charges him with "corruptibility, violence, robberies, ill-treatment of the people, grievances, continuous executions without even the form of a trial, endless and intolerable cruelties." If we were to stop with this, we should have a very poor impression of the deputy of Tiberius; and, indeed at best, we can never either admire or love him. But there is a tender and even pathetic side to the character of Pilate, which is revealed to us by the Evangelists of the New Testament. The pure-hearted, gentle-minded authors of the Gospels, in whose writings there is not even a tinge of bitterness or resentment, have restored "for us the man within the governor, with a delicacy, and even tenderness, which make the accusing portrait of Philo and Josephus look like a hard, revengeful daub." Instead of painting him as a monster, they have linked conscience to his character and placed mercy in his heart, by their accounts of his repeated attempts to release Jesus. The extreme of pity and of pathos, derived from these exquisitely merciful side touches of the gentle biographers of the Christ, is manifested in the opinion of Tertullian that Pilate was virtually a Christian at heart.[4]

A further manifestation is the fact that the Abyssinian Church of Christians has canonized him and placed his name in the calendar on June 25th.

A still further revelation of this spirit of regarding Pilate merely as a sacred instrument in the hands of God is shown by the Apocryphal Gospel of Nicodemus which speaks of him as "uncircumcised in flesh but circumcised in heart."

Renan has called him a good administrator, and has sought to condone his brutal treatment of the Jews by pointing to the necessity of vigorous action in dealing with a turbulent and fanatical race. But the combined efforts of both sacred and secular apologists are still not sufficient to save the name of Pilate from the scorn and reprobation of mankind. That he was not a bad man in the worst sense of the term is manifest from the teachings of the Gospel narratives. To believe that he was wholly without conscience is to repudiate the revelations of these sacred writings. Of wanton cruelty and gratuitous wickedness, he was perhaps incapable. But the circumstances of his birth and breeding; his descent from a renegade father; his adventurous life in the army of Germanicus; his contact with and absorption of the skepticism and debauchery of Rome; his marriage to a woman of questionable virtue whose mother was notoriously coarse and lewd—all these things had given coloring to the character of Pilate and had stricken with inward paralysis the moral fiber of his manhood. And now, in the supreme moment of his life and of history, from his nerveless grasp fell the reins of fate and fortune that destiny had placed within his hands. Called upon to play a leading role in the mighty drama of the universe, his craven cowardice made him a pitiable and contemptible figure. A splendid example this, the conduct of Pilate, for the youth of the world, not to imitate but to shun! Let the young men of America and of all the earth remember that a crisis is allotted to every life. It may be a great one or a small one, but it will come either invited or unbidden. The sublime courage of the soul does not avoid, but seeks this crisis. The bravest and most holy aspirations leap at times like angels from the temple of the brain to the highest heaven. Never a physician who does not long for the skill that dicovers a remedy for disease and that will make him a Pasteur or a Koch; never a poet who does not beseech the muse to inspire him to write a Hamlet or a Faust; never a general of armies who would not fight an Austerlitz battle. Every ambitious soul fervently prays for strength, when the great crisis comes, to swing the hammer of the Cyclop with the arm of the Titan. Let the young aspirant for the glories of the earth and the rewards of heaven remember that youth is the time for the formation of that courage and the gathering of that strength of which victory is born. Let him remember that if he degrades his physical and spiritual manhood in early life, the coming of the great day of his existence will make him another Pilate— cringing, crouching, and contemptible.

The true character of the Roman judge of Jesus is thus very tersely given by Dr. Ellicott: "A thorough and complete type of the later Roman man of the world: stern, but not relentless; shrewd and world-worn, prompt and practical, haughtily just, and yet, as the early writers correctly perceived, self-seeking and cowardly; able to perceive what was right, but without moral strength to follow it out."[5]

His End. — Pilate's utter recklessness was the final cause of his undoing. It was an old belief among the Samaritans that Moses buried the sacred vessels of the temple on Mt. Gerizim. An impostor, a sort of pseudo-prophet, promised the people that if they would assemble on the top of the mountain, he would unearth the holy utensils in their presence. The simple-minded Samaritans assembled in great numbers at the foot of the Mount, and were preparing to ascend, when Pilate on the pretense that they were revolutionists, intercepted them with a strong force of horse and foot. Those who did not immediately submit were either slain or put to flight. The most notable among the captives were put to death. The Samaritans at once complained to Vitellius, the legate in Syria at that time. Vitellius at once turned over the administration of Judea to Marcellus and ordered Pilate to leave for Rome in order to give an account to the emperor of the charges brought against him by the Jews.[6] Before he arrived in Italy, Tiberius had died; but Pilate never returned to the province over which he had ruled during ten bloody and eventful years.

"Paradosis Pilati." — The death of Pilate is clouded in mystery and legend. Where and when he died is not known. Two apocryphal accounts are interesting, though false and ridiculous. According to one legend, the "Paradosis Pilati," the emperor Tiberius, startled and terrified at the universal darkness that had fallen on the Roman world at the hour of the crucifixion, summoned Pilate to Rome to answer for having caused it. He was found guilty and condemned to death; but before he was executed, he prayed to Jesus that he might not be destroyed in eternity with the wicked Jews, and pleaded ignorance as an excuse for having delivered the Christ to be crucified. A voice from heaven answered his prayer, and assured him that all generations would call him blessed, and that he should be a witness for Christ at his second coming to judge the Twelve Tribes of Israel. He was then executed; an angel, according to the legend, received his head; and his wife died from joy and was buried with him.

"Mors Pilati" — According to another legend, the "Mors Pilati," Tiberius had heard of the miracles of healing wrought by Jesus in Judea. He ordered Pilate to conduct to Rome the man possessed of such divine power. But Pilate was forced to confess that he had crucified the miracle worker. The messenger sent by Tiberius met Veronica who gave him the cloth that had received the impress of the divine features. This was taken to Rome and given to the emperor, who was restored to health by it. Pilate was summoned immediately to stand trial for the execution of the Christ. He presented himself wearing the holy tunic. This acted as a charm upon the emperor, who temporarily relented. After a time, however, Pilate was thrown into prison, where he committed suicide. His body was thrown into the Tiber. Storms and tempests immediately followed, and the Romans Were compelled to take out the corpse and send it to Vienne, where it was cast

into the Rhone. But as the storms and tempests came again, the body was again removed and sent to Lucerne, where it was sunk in a deep pool, surrounded by mountains on all sides. Even then, it is said, the water of the pool began to boil and bubble strangely.

This tradition must have had its origin in an early attempt to connect the name of Pilate with Mt. Pilatus that overlooks Lake Lucerne. Another legend connected with this mountain is that Pilate sought to find an asylum from his sorrows in its shadows and recesses; that, after spending years in remorse and despair, wandering up and down its sides, he plunged into the dismal lake which occupies its summit. In times past, popular superstition was wont to relate how "a form is often seen to emerge from the gloomy waters, and go through the action of washing his hands; and when he does so, dark clouds of mist gather first round the bosom of the Infernal Lake (such as it has been styled of old) and then wrapping the whole upper part of the mountain in darkness, presage a tempest or hurricane which is sure to follow in a short space."[7]

The superstitious Swiss believed for many centuries that if a stone were thrown into the lake a violent storm would follow. For many years no one was permitted to visit it without special authority from the officers of Lucerne. The neighboring shepherds bound themselves by a solemn oath, which they renewed annually, never to guide a stranger to it.[8] The strange spell was broken, however, and the legend exploded in 1584, when Johannes Muller, cure of Lucerne, was bold enough to throw stones into the lake, and to stand by complacently to await the consequences.[9]

CHAPTER VIII

JESUS BEFORE PILATE

At the close of their trial, according to Matthew[1] and Mark,[2] the high priest and the entire Sanhedrin led Jesus away to the tribunal of the Roman governor. It was early morning, probably between six and seven o'clock, when the accusing multitude moved from the judgment seat of Caiaphas to the Praetorium of Pilate. Oriental labor anticipates the day because of the excessive heat of noon; and, at daybreak, Eastern life is all astir. To accommodate the people and to enjoy the repose of midday, Roman governors, Suetonius tells us, mounted the *bema* at sunrise. The location of the judgment hall of Pilate in Jerusalem is not certainly known. It may have been in the Castle of Antonia, a frowning fortress that overlooked the Temple and its courts. Much more probably, however, it was the magnificent palace of Herod, situated in the northwest quarter of the city. This probability is heightened by the fact that it was a custom born of both pride and pleasure, for Roman procurators and proconsuls to occupy the splendid edifices of the local kings. The Roman propraetor of Sicily dwelt in the Castle of King Hiero; and it is reasonable to suppose that Pilate would have passed his time while at Jerusalem in the palace of Herod. This building was frequently called the "King's Castle," sometimes was styled the "Praetorium," and was often given the mixed name of "Herod's Praetorium." But, by whatever name known, it was of gorgeous architecture and magnificent proportions. Keim describes it as "a tyrant's stronghold and in part a fairy pleasure-house." A wall thirty cubits high completely encircled the buildings of the palace. Beautiful white towers crowned this wall at regular intervals. Three of these were named in honor of Mariamne, the wife; Hippicus, the friend; and Phasaelus, the brother of the king. Within the inclosure of the wall, a small army could have been garrisoned. The floors and ceilings of the palace were decorated and adorned with the finest woods and precious stones. Projecting from the main building were two colossal marble wings, named for two Roman imperial friends, the Caesareum and the Aegrippeum. To a person standing in one of the towers, a magnificent prospect opened to the view. Surrounding the castle walls were beautiful green parks, intercepted with broad walks and deep canals. Here and there splashing fountains gushed from brazen mouths. A hundred dovecots, scattered about the basins and filled with cooing and fluttering inmates, lent charm and animation to the scene. And to crown the whole, was the splendid panorama of Jerusalem stretching away among the hills and valleys. Such was the residence of the Roman knight who at this time ruled Judea. And yet, with all its regal splendor and magnificence, he inhabited it only a few weeks in each year. The Jewish metropolis had no fascination whatever for the tastes and accomplishments of Pilate. "The saddest region in the world," says Renan, who had been imbued, from long residence there, with its melancholy character, "is perhaps that which surrounds Jerusalem." "To the Spaniard," says Rosadi, "who had come to Jerusalem, by way of Rome, and who was also of courtly origin, there could have been nothing pleasing in the parched, arid and colorless nature of Palestine, much less in the humble, mystic, out-at-elbows existence of its people. Their superstition, which would have nothing of Roman idolatry, which was their sole belief, their all, appeared to him a reasonable explanation, and a legitimate one, of their disdain and opposition. He therefore detested the Jews, and his detestation was fully reciprocated." It is not surprising, then, that he preferred to reside at Caesarea by the sea where were present Roman modes of thought and forms of life. He visited Jerusalem as a matter of official duty, "during the festivals, and particularly at Easter with its dreaded inspirations of the Jewish longing for freedom, which the festival, the air of spring and the great rendezvous of the nation, charmed into activity." In keeping with this custom, Pilate was now in the Jewish Capital on the occasion of the feast of the Passover.

Having condemned Him to death themselves, the Sanhedrin judges were compelled to lead Jesus away to the Praetorium of the Roman governor to see what he had to say about the case; whether he would reverse or affirm the condemnation which they had pronounced. Between dawn and sunrise, they were at the palace gates. Here they were compelled to halt. The Passover had commenced, and to enter the procurator's palace at such a time was to incur Levitic contamination. A dozen judicial blunders had marked the proceedings of their own trial in the palace of Caiaphas. And yet they hesitated to violate a purely ritual regulation in the matter of ceremonial defilement. This regulation was a prohibition to eat fermented food during the Passover Feast, and was sacred to the memory of the great deliverance from Egyptian bondage when the children of Israel, in their flight, had no time to ferment their dough and were compelled to consume it before it had been leavened. Their purposes and scruples were announced to Pilate; and, in a spirit of gracious and politic condescension, he removed the difficulty by coming out to meet them. But this action was really neither an inconvenience nor a condescension; for it was usual to conduct Roman trials in the open air. Publicity was characteristic of all Roman criminal proceedings. And, in obedience to this principle, we find that the proconsul of Achaia at Corinth, the city magistrates in Macedonia, and the procurators at Caesarea and Jerusalem, erected their tribunals in the most conspicuous public places, such as the market, the race course, and even upon the open highway.[3] An example directly in point is, moreover, that of the procurator Florus who caused his judgment seat to be raised in front of the palace of Herod, A.D. 66, and, enthroned thereon, received the great men of Jerusalem who came to see him and gathered around his tribunal. To the same place, according to Josephus, the Jewish queen Bernice came barefoot and suppliant to ask favors of Florus.[4] The act of Pilate in emerging from the palace to meet the Jews was, therefore, in exact compliance with Roman custom. His judgment seat was doubtless raised immediately in front of the entrance and between the great marble wings of the palace. Pilate's tribune or *bema* was located in this space on the elevated spot called Gabaatha, an Aramaic Word signifying an eminence, a "hump." The same place in Greek was called Lithostroton, and signified "The Pavement," because it was laid with Roman marble mosaic. The location on an eminence was in accordance with a maxim of Roman law that all criminal trials should be directed from a raised tribunal where everybody could see and understand what was being said and done. The ivory curule chair of the procurator, or perhaps the ancient golden royal chair of Archelaus was placed upon the tessellated pavement and was designed for the use of the governor. As a general thing, there was sitting room on the tribunal for the assessors, the accusers and the accused. But such courtesies and conveniences were not extended to the despised subjects of Judea; and Jesus, as well as the members of the Sanhedrin, was compelled to stand. The Latin language was the official tongue of the Roman empire, and was generally used in the administration of justice. But at the trial of Jesus it is believed that the Greek language was the medium of communication. Jesus had doubtless become acquainted with Greek in Galilee and probably replied to Pilate in that tongue. This is the opinion, at least, of both Keim[5] and Geikie.[6] The former asserts that there was no interpreter called at the trial of Christ. It is also reasonably certain that no special orator like Tertullus, who informed the governor against Paul, was present to accuse Jesus.[7] Doubtless Caiaphas the high priest played this important role.

When Pilate had mounted the *bema,* and order had been restored, he asked: "What accusation bring ye against this man?"

This question is keenly suggestive of the presence of a judge and of the beginning of a solemn judicial proceeding. Every word rings with Roman authority and administrative capacity. The suggestion is also prominent that accusation was a more important element in Roman criminal trials than inquisition. This suggestion is reenforced by actual *dictum* from the lips of Pilate's successor in the same place: "It is not the manner of the Romans to deliver any man to die, before that he which is accused have the accusers face to face, and have license to answer for himself concerning the crime laid against him."[8]

The chief priests and scribes sought to evade this question by answering:

"If he were not a malefactor, we would not have delivered him up unto thee."[9]

They meant by this that they desired the procurator to waive his right to retry the case; accept their trial as conclusive; and content himself with the mere execution of the sentence. In this reply of the priests to the initial question of the Roman judge, is also revealed the further question of that conflict of jurisdiction between Jews and Romans that we have already so fully discussed. "If he were not a malefactor, we would not have delivered him up unto thee." These words from the mouths of the priests were intended to convey to the mind of Pilate the Jewish notion that a judgment by the Sanhedrin was all-sufficient; and that they merely needed this countersign to justify execution. But Pilate did not take the hint or view the question in that light. In a tone of contemptuous scorn he simply replied:

"Take ye him, and judge him according to your law."

This answer indicates that Pilate did not, at first, understand the exact nature of the proceedings against Jesus. He evidently did not know that the prisoner had been charged with a capital offense; else he would not have suggested that the Jews take jurisdiction of the matter. This is clearly shown from the further reply of the priestly accusers:

"It is not lawful for us to put any man to death."[10]

The advice of Pilate and the retort of the Jews have been construed in two ways. A certain class of critics have contended that the procurator granted to the Jews in this instance the right to carry out capital punishment, as others have maintained was the case in the execution of Stephen. This construction argues that Pilate knew at once the nature of the accusation.

Another class of writers contend that the governor, by this language, merely proposed to them one of the minor penalties which they were already empowered to execute. The objection to the first interpretation is that the Jews would have been delighted to have such power conferred upon them, and would have exercised it; unless it is true, as has been held, that they were desirous of throwing the odium of Christ's death upon the Romans. The second construction is entirely admissible, because it is consonant with the theory that jurisdiction in capital cases had been withdrawn from the Sanhedrin, but that the trial and punishment of petty offenses still remained with it. A third and more reasonable interpretation still is that when Pilate said, "Take ye him and judge him according to your law," he intended to give expression to the hatred and bitterness of his cynical and sarcastic soul. He despised the Jews most heartily, and he knew that they hated him. He had repeatedly outraged their religious feelings by introducing images and shields into the Holy City. He had devoted the Corban funds to unhallowed purposes, and had mingled the blood of the Galileans with their sacrifices. In short, he had left nothing undone to humiliate and degrade them. Now here was another opportunity. By telling them to judge Jesus according to their own laws, he knew that they must make a reply which would be wounding and galling to their race and national pride. He knew that they would have to confess that sovereignty and nationality were gone from them. Such a confession from them would be music to his ear. The substance of his advice to the Jews was to exercise their rights to a certain point, to the moment of condemnation; but to stop at the place where their sweetest desires would be gratified with the exercise of the rights of sovereignty and nationality.

Modern poetry supports this interpretation of ancient history. "The Merchant of Venice" reveals the same method of heaping ridicule upon a Jew by making him impotent to execute the law. Shylock, the Jew, in contracting a usurious loan, inserted a stipulation that if the debt should not be paid when due, the debtor must allow a pound of flesh to be cut from his body. The debt was not discharged at the maturity of the bond, and Shylock made application to the Doge to have the pound of human flesh delivered to him in accordance with the

compact. But Portia, a friend of the debtor, though a woman, assumed the garb and affected the speech of a lawyer in his defense; and, in pleading the case, called tauntingly and exultingly to the Jew:

> This bond doth give thee here no jot of blood;
> The words expressly are, a pound of flesh:
> Take then thy bond, take thou thy pound of flesh;
> But, in the cutting it, if thou dost shed
> One drop of Christian blood, thy lands and goods
> Are by the laws of Venice confiscate
> Unto the State of Venice.[11]

But whatever special interpretation may be placed upon the opening words passed between the priestly accusers and the Roman judge, it is clearly evident that the latter did not intend to surrender to the former the right to impose and execute a sentence of death. The substance of Pilate's address to the Jews, when they sought to evade his question concerning the accusation which they had to bring against Jesus, was this: I have asked for a specific charge against the man whom you have brought bound to me. You have given not a direct, but an equivocal answer. I infer that the crime with which you charge him is one against your own laws. With such offenses I do not with to meddle. Therefore, I say unto you: "Take ye him and judge him according to your law." If I am not to know the specific charge against him, I will not assume cognizance of the case. If the accusation and the facts relied upon to support it are not placed before me, I will not sentence the man to death; and, under the law, you cannot.

The Jews were thus thwarted in their designs. They had hoped to secure a countersign of their own judgment without a retrial by the governor. They now found him in no yielding and accommodating mood. They were thus forced against their will and expectation to formulate specific charges against the prisoner in their midst. The indictment as they presented it, is given in a single verse of St. Luke:

"And they began to accuse him, saying, We found this fellow perverting the nation, and forbidding to give tribute to Caesar, saying that he himself is Christ, a King."[12]

It is noteworthy that in this general accusation is a radical departure from the charges of the night before. In the passage from the Sanhedrin to the Praetorium, the indictment had completely changed. Jesus had not been condemned on any of the charges recorded in this sentence of St. Luke. He has been convicted on the charge of blasphemy. But before Pilate he is now charged with high treason. To meet the emergency of a change of jurisdiction, the priestly accusers converted the accusation from a religious into a political offense. It may be asked why the Sanhedrists did not maintain the same charges before Pilate that they themselves had considered before their own tribunal. Why did they not lead Jesus into the presence of the Roman magistrate and say: O Governor, we have here a Galilean blasphemer of Jehovah. We want him tried on the charge of blasphemy, convicted and sentenced to death. Why did they not do this? They were evidently too shrewd. Why? Because, in legal parlance, they would have had no standing in court. Why? Because blasphemy was not an offense against Roman law, and Roman judges would generally assume cognizance of no such charges.

The Jews understood perfectly well at the trial before Pilate the principle of Roman procedure so admirably expressed a few years later by Gallio, proconsul of Achaia, and brother of Seneca: "If it were a matter of wrong or wicked lewdness, O ye Jews, reason would that I should bear with you: but if it be a question of words and names, and of your law, look ye to it; for I will be no judge of such matters."[13] This attitude of Roman governors toward offenses of a religious nature perfectly explains the Jewish change of front in the matter of the accusation against Jesus. They merely wanted to get themselves into a Roman court on charges that a Roman judge would consent to try. In the threefold accusation recorded by the third Evangelist, they fully accomplished this result.

The first count in the indictment, that He was perverting the nation, was vague and indefinite, but was undoubtedly against Roman law, because it was in the nature of sedition, which was one of the forms of treason under Roman jurisprudence. This charge of perverting the nation was in the nature of the revival of the accusation of sedition which they had first brought forward by means of the false witnesses before their own tribunal, and that had been abandoned because of the contradictory testimony of these witnesses.

The second count in the indictment, that He had forbidden to give tribute to Caesar, was of a more serious nature than the first. A refusal, in modern times, to pay taxes or an attempt to obstruct their collection, is a mild offense compared with a similar act under ancient Roman law. To forbid to pay tribute to Caesar in Judea was a form of treason, not only because it was an open defiance of the laws of the Roman state, but also because it was a direct denial of Roman sovereignty in Palestine. Such conduct was treason under the definitions of both Ulpian and Cicero. The Jews knew the gravity of the offense when they sought to entrap Jesus in the matter of paying tribute to Caesar. They believed that any answer to the question that they had asked would be fatal to Him. If He advised to pay the imperial tribute, He could be charged with being an enemy to His countrymen, the Jews. If He advised not to pay the tribute, He would be charged with being a rebellious subject of Caesar. His reply disconcerted and bewildered them when He said: "Render therefore unto Caesar the things which are Caesar's; and unto God the things that are God's."[14] In this sublime declaration, the Nazarene announced the immortal principle of the separation of church and state, and of religious freedom in all the ages. And when, in the face of His answer, they still charged Him with forbidding to pay tribute to Caesar, they seem to have been guilty of deliberate falsehood. Keim calls the charge "a very flagrant lie." Both at Capernaum,[15] where Roman taxes were gathered, and at Jerusalem,[16] where religious dues were offered, Jesus seems to have been both a good citizen and a pious Jew. "Jesus bon citoyen" (Jesus a good citizen) is the title of a chapter in the famous work of Bossuet entitled "Politique tiree de l'Ecriture sainte." In it the great French ecclesiastic describes very beautifully the law-abiding qualities of the citizen-prophet of Galilee. In pressing the false charge that he had advised not to pay taxes to Rome, the enemies of Jesus revealed a peculiar and wanton malignity.

The third count in the indictment, that the prisoner had claimed to be "Christ a King," was the last and greatest of the charges. By this He was deliberately accused of high treason against Caesar, the gravest offense known to Roman law. Such an accusation could not be ignored by Pilate as a loyal deputy of Tiberius. The Roman monarch saw high treason in every word and act that was uncomplimentary to his person or dangerous to his power. Fifty-two prosecutions for treason, says Tacitus, took place during his reign.

The charges of high treason and sedition against Jesus were all the more serious because the Romans believed Palestine to be the hotbed of insurrection and sedition, and the birthplace of pretenders to kingly powers. They had recently had trouble with claimants to thrones, some of them from the lowest and most ignoble ranks. Judas, the son of Hezekiah, whom Herod had caused to be put to death, proclaimed royal intentions, gathered quite a multitude of adherents about him in the neighborhood of Sepphoris in Galilee, raised an insurrection, assaulted and captured the palace of the king at Sepphoris, seized all the weapons that were stored away in it, and armed his followers with them. Josephus does not tell us what became of this royal pretender; but he does say that "he became terrible to all men, by tearing and rending those that came near him."[17]

In the province of Perea, a certain Simon, who was formerly a slave of Herod, collected a band of followers, and had himself proclaimed king by them. He burned down the royal palace at Jericho, after having plundered it. A detachment under the command of the Roman general Gratus made short work of the pretensions of Simon by capturing his adherents and putting him to death.[18]

Again, a certain peasant named Athronges, formerly a shepherd, claimed to be a king, and for a long time, in concert with his four brothers, annoyed the authorities of the country, until the insurrection was finally broken up by Gratus and Ptolemy.[19]

In short, during the life of Jesus, Judea was passing through a period of great religious and political excitement. The Messiah was expected and a king was hoped for; and numerous pretenders appeared from time to time. The Roman governors were constantly on the outlook for acts of sedition and treason. And when the Jews led Jesus into the presence of Pilate and charged Him with claiming to be a king, the recent cases of Judas, Simon, and Athronges must have arisen in his mind, quickened his interest in the pretensions of the prisoner of the Jews, and must have awakened his sense of loyalty as Caesar's representative. The lowliness of Jesus, being a carpenter, did not greatly allay his fears; for he must have remembered that Simon was once a slave and that Athronges was nothing more than a simple shepherd.

When Pilate had heard the accusations of the Jews, he deliberately arose from his judgment seat, gathered his toga about him, motioned the mob to stand back, and beckoned Jesus to follow him into the palace. St. John alone tells us of this occurrence.[20]

At another time, in the Galilean simplicity and freedom of His nature, the Prophet of Nazareth had spoken with a tinge of censure and sarcasm of the rulers of the Gentiles that lorded it over their subjects,[21] and had declared that "they that wear soft clothing are in kings' houses."[22] Now the lowly Jewish peasant was entering for the first time a palace of one of the rulers of the Gentiles in which were soft raiment and royal purple. The imagination is helpless to picture the historical reflections born of the memories of that hour. A meek and lowly carpenter enters a king's palace on his way to an ignominious death upon the cross; and yet the greatest kings of all the centuries that followed were humble worshipers in their palaces before the cross that had been the instrument of his torture and degradation. Such is the irony of history; such is the mystery of God's providence; such is the mystic ebb and flow of the tides and currents of destiny and fate.

Of the examination of Jesus inside the palace, little is known. Pilate, it seems brushed the first two charges aside as unworthy of serious consideration; and proceeded at once to examine the prisoner on the charge that he pretended to be a king. "If," Pilate must have said, "the fellow pretends to be a king, as Simon and Athronges did before him; if he says that Judea has a right to have a king other then Caesar, he is guilty of treason, and it is my solemn duty as deputy of Tiberius to ascertain the fact and have him put to death."

The beginning of the interrogation of Jesus within the palace is reported by all the Evangelists in the same words. Addressing the prisoner, Pilate asked: "Art thou the King of the Jews?" "Jesus answered him, Sayest thou this thing of thyself, or did others tell it thee of me?"[23]

This was a most natural and fitting response of the Nazarene to the Roman. It was necessary first to understand the exact nature of the question before an appropriate answer could be made. Jesus simply wished to know whether the question was asked from a Roman or a Jewish, from a temporal or a spiritual standpoint. If the interrogation was directed from a Roman, a temporal point of view, His answer would be an emphatic negative. If the inquiry had been prompted by the Jews, it was then pregnant with religious meaning, and called for a different reply; one that would at once repudiate pretensions to earthly royalty, and, at the same time, assert His claims to the Messiahship and heavenly sovereignty.

"Pilate answered, Am I a Jew? Thine own nation and the chief priests have delivered thee unto me: What hast thou done?"

To this Jesus replied: "My kingdom is not of this world: if my kingdom were of this world, then would my servants fight, that I should not be delivered to the Jews: but now is my kingdom not from hence."[24]

This reply of the Master is couched in that involved, aphoristic, strangely beautiful style that characterized His speech at critical moments in His career. Its import is clear, though expressed in a double sense: first from the Roman political, and then from the Jewish religious side.

First He answered negatively: "My kingdom is not of this world."

By this He meant that there was no possible rivalry between Him and Caesar. But, in making this denial, He had used two words of grave import: My Kingdom. He had used one word that struck the ear of Pilate with electric force: the word Kingdom. In the use of that word, according to Pilate's reasoning, Jesus stood self-convicted. For how, thought Pilate, can He pretend to have a Kingdom, unless He pretends to be a king? And then, as if to cow and intimidate the prisoner, as if to avoid an unpleasant issue of the affair, he probably advanced threateningly upon the Christ, and asked the question which the Bible puts in his mouth: "Art thou a king then?"

Rising from the simple dignity of a man to the beauty and glory and grandeur of a God, Jesus used the most wonderful, beautiful, meaningful words in the literature of the earth: "Thou sayest that I am a king. To this end was I born, and for this cause came I into the world, that I should bear witness unto the truth. Everyone that is of the truth heareth my voice."[25]

This language contains a perfectly clear description of the kingdom of Christ and of His title to spiritual sovereignty. His was not an empire of matter, but a realm of truth. His kingdom differed widely from that of Caesar. Caesar's empire was over the bodies of men; Christ's over their souls. The strength of Caesar's kingdom was in citadels, armies, navies, the towering Alps, the all-engirdling seas. The strength of the kingdom of the Christ was and is and will ever be in sentiments, principles, ideas, and the saving power of a divine word. But, as clever and brilliant as he must have been, Pilate could not grasp the true meaning of the words of the Prophet. The spiritual and intellectual grandeur of the Galilean peasant was beyond the reach of the Roman lord and governor. In a cynical and sarcastic mood, Pilate turned to Jesus and asked: "What is truth?"[26]

This pointed question was the legitimate offspring of the soul of Pilate and a natural product of the Roman civilization of his age. It was not asked with any real desire to know the truth; for he turned to leave the palace before an answer could be given. It was simply a blank response born of mental wretchedness and doubt. If prompted by any silent yearning for a knowledge of the truth, his conduct indicated clearly that he did not hope to have that longing satisfied by the words of the humble prisoner in his charge. "What is truth?" An instinctive utterance this, prompted by previous sad reflections upon the wrecks of philosophy in search of truth.

We have reason to believe that Pilate was a man of brilliant parts and studious habits. His marriage into the Roman royal family argued not only splendid physical endowments, but rare intellectual gifts as well. Only on this hypothesis can we explain his rise from obscurity in Spain to a place in the royal family as husband of the grandaughter of Augustus and foster daughter of Tiberius. Then he was familiar, if he was thus endowed and accomplished, with the despairing efforts of his age and country to solve the mysteries of life and to ascertain the end of man. He had doubtless, as a student, "mused and mourned over Greece, and its search of truth intellectual—its keen and fruitless search, never-ending, ever beginning, across wastes of doubt and seas of speculation lighted by uncertain stars." He knew full well that Roman philosophy had been wrecked and stranded amidst the floating debris of Grecian thought and speculation. He had thought that the *ultima ratio* of Academicians and Peripatetics, of Stoics and Epicureans had been reached. But here was a new proposition—a kingdom of truth whose sovereign had as subjects mere vagaries, simple mental conceptions called truths—a kingdom whose boundaries were not mountains, seas, and rivers, but clouds, hopes, and dreams.

What did Pilate think of Jesus? He evidently regarded Him as an amiable enthusiast, a harmless religious fanatic from whom Caesar had nothing to fear. While alone with Jesus in the palace, he must have reasoned thus with himself, silently and contemptuously: The mob outside tells me that this man is Rome's enemy. Foolish thought! We know who Caesar's enemies are. We have seen and heard and felt the enemies of Rome—barbarians from beyond the Danube and the Rhine—great strong men, who can drive a javelin not only through a man, but a horse, as well. These are Caesar's enemies. This strange and melancholy man, whose subjects are mere abstract truths, and whose kingdom is beyond the skies, can be no enemy of Caesar.

Believing this, he went out to the rabble and pronounced a verdict of acquittal: "I find in him no fault at all."

Pilate had tried and acquitted Jesus. Why did he not release Him, and, if need be, protect Him with his cohort from the assaults of the Jews? Mankind has asked for nearly two thousand years why a Roman, with the blood of a Roman in him, with the glorious prestige and stern authority of the Roman empire at his back, with a Roman legion at his command, did not have the courage to do the high Roman act. Pilate was a moral and intellectual coward of arrant type. This is his proper characterization and a fitting answer to the world's eternal question.

The Jews heard his sentence of acquittal in sullen silence. Desperately resolved to prevent His release, they began at once to frame new accusations.

"And they were the more fierce, saying, He stirreth up the people, teaching throughout all Jewry, beginning from Galilee to this place."[27]

This charge was intended by the Jews to serve a double purpose: to strengthen the general accusation of high treason recorded by St. Luke; and to embitter and poison the mind of the judge against the prisoner by telling Pilate that Jesus was from Galilee. In ancient times Galilee was noted as the hotbed of riot and sedition. The Galileans were brave and hardy mountaineers who feared neither Rome nor Judea. As champions of Jewish nationality, they were the fiercest opponents of Roman rule; and in the final catastrophe of Jewish history they were the last to be driven from the battlements of Jerusalem. As advocates and preservers of the purity of the primitive Jewish faith, they were relentless foes of Pharisaic and Sadducean hypocrisy as it was manifested by the Judean keepers of the Temple. The Galileans were hated, therefore, by both Romans and Judeans; and the Sanhedrists believed that Pilate would make short work of Jesus if he learned that the prisoner was from Galilee. But a different train of thought was excited in the mind of the Roman governor. He was thinking about one thing, and they about another. Pilate showed himself throughout the trial a craven coward and contemptible timeserver. From beginning to end, his conduct was a record of cowardice and subterfuge. He was constantly looking for loopholes of escape. His heart's desire was to satisfy at once both his conscience and the mob. The mention of Galilee was a ray of light that fell across the troubled path of the cowardly and vacillating judge. He believed that he saw an avenue of escape. He asked the Jews if Jesus was a Galilean. An affirmative reply was given. Pilate then determined to rid himself of responsibility by sending Jesus to be tried by the govenor of the province to which He belonged. He felt that fortune favored his design; for Herod, Tetrarch of Galilee, was at that very moment in Jerusalem in attendance upon the Passover feast. He acted at once upon the happy idea; and, under the escort of a detachment of the Praetorian Cohort, Jesus was led away to the palace of the Maccabees where Herod was accustomed to stop when he came to the Holy City.

CHAPTER IX

JESUS BEFORE HEROD

It was still early morning when Jesus, guarded by Roman soldiers and surrounded by a jeering, scoffing, raging multitude of Jews, was conducted to the palace of the Maccabees on the slope of Zion, the official residence of Herod when he came to Jerusalem to attend the sacred festivals. This place was to the northeast of the palace of Herod and only a few streets distant from it. The journey must have lasted therefore only a few minutes.

But who was this Herod before whom Jesus now appeared in chains? History mentions many Herods, the greatest and meanest of whom was Herod I, surnamed the Great, who ordered the massacre of the Innocents at Bethlehem. At his death, he bequeathed his kingdom to his sons. But being a client-prince, a *rex socius,* he could not finally dispose of his realm without the consent of Rome. Herod had made several wills, and, at his death, contests arose between his sons for the vacant throne of the father. Several embassies were sent to Rome to argue the rights of the different claimants. Augustus granted the petitioners many audiences; and, after long delay, finally confirmed practically the last will of Herod. This decision gave Judea, Samaria, and Idumea, with a tribute of six hundred talents, to Archelaus. Philip received the regions of Gaulanitis, Auranitis, Trachonitis, Batanea, and Iturea, with an income of one hundred talents. Herod Antipas was given the provinces of Galilee and Perea, with an annual tribute of two hundred talents and the title of Tetrarch. The title of Ethnarch was conferred upon Archelaus.

Herod Antipas, Tetrarch of Galilee, was the man before whom Jesus, his subject, was now led to be judged. The pages of sacred history mention the name of no more shallow and contemptible character than this petty princeling, this dissolute Idumaean Sadducee. Compared with him, Judas is eminently respectable. Judas had a conscience which, when smitten with remorse, drove him to suicide. It is doubtful whether Herod had a spark of that celestial fire which we call conscience. He was a typical Oriental prince whose chief aim in life was the gratification of his passions. The worthlessness of his character was so pronounced that it excited a nauseating disgust in the mind of Jesus, and disturbed for a moment that serene and lofty magnanimity which characterized His whole life and conduct. To Herod is addressed the only purely contemptuous epithet that the Master is ever recorded to have used. "And he said unto them, Go ye, and tell *that fox,* Behold, I cast out devils, and I do cures to-day and to-morrow, and the third day I shall be perfected."[1]

The son of a father who was ten times married and had murdered many of his wives; the murderer himself of John the Baptist; the slave of a lewd and wicked woman—what better could be expected than a cruel, crafty, worthless character, whose attributes were those of the fox?

But why was Jesus sent to Herod? Doubtless because Pilate wished to shift the responsibility from his own shoulders, as a Roman judge, to those of the Galilean Tetrarch. A subsidiary purpose may have been to conciliate Herod, with whom, history says, he had had a quarrel. The cause of the trouble between them is not known. Many believe that the murder of the Galileans while sacrificing in the Temple was the origin of the unpleasantness. Others contend that this occurrence was the result and not the cause of the quarrel between Pilate and Herod. Still others believe that the question of the occupancy of the magnificent palace of Herod engendered ill feeling between the rival potentates. Herod had all the love of gorgeous architecture and luxurious living that characterized the whole Herodian family. And, besides, he doubtless felt that he should be permitted to occupy the palace of his ancestors on the occasion of his visits to Jerusalem. But Pilate would naturally object to this, as he was the representative of almighty Rome in a conquered province and could not afford to give way, in a matter of palatial residence, to a petty local prince. But, whatever the cause, the unfriendliness between them undoubtedly had much to do with the transfer of Jesus from the Praetorium to the palace of the Maccabees.

"And when Herod saw Jesus, he was exceeding glad: for he was desirous to see him for a long season, because he had heard many things of him; and he hoped to have seen some miracle done by him."[2]

This passage of Scripture throws much light upon Herod's opinion and estimate of Jesus. Fearing that he was the successor and imitator of Judas the Gaulonite, Herod at first sought to drive Him from his province by sending spies to warn Him to flee. The courageous and contemptuous reply of Jesus, in which he styled Herod "that fox," put an end to further attempts at intimidation.

The notions of the Galilean Tetrarch concerning the Galilean Prophet seem to have changed from time to time. Herod had once regarded Jesus with feelings of superstitious dread and awe, as the risen Baptist. But these apprehensions had now partially passed away, and he had come to look upon the Christ as a clever impostor whose claims to kingship and Messiahship were mere vulgar dreams. For three years, Galilee had been ringing with the fame of the Miracleworker; but Herod had never seen his famous subject. Now was his chance. And he anticipated a rare occasion of magic and merriment. He doubtless regarded Jesus as a clever magician whose performance would make a rich and racy programme for an hour's amusement of his court. This was no doubt his dominant feeling regarding the Nazarene. But it is nevertheless very probable that his Idumaean cowardice and superstition still conjured images of a drunken debauch, the dance of death, and the bloody head; and connected them with the strange man now before him.

No doubt he felt highly pleased and gratified to have Jesus sent to him. The petty and obsequious vassal king was caught in Pilate's snare of flattery. The sending of a noted prisoner to his judgment seat by a Roman procurator was no ordinary compliment. But Herod was at once too serious and too frivolous to assume jurisdiction of any charges against this prisoner, who had offended both the religious and secular powers of Palestine. To condemn Jesus would be to incur the ill will and resentment of his many followers in his own province of Galilee. Besides, he had already suffered keenly from dread and apprehension, caused by the association of the names of John and Jesus, and he had learned that from the blood of one murdered prophet would spring the message and mission of another still more powerful and majestic. He was, therefore, unwilling to embroil himself and his dominions with the heavenly powers by condemning their earthly representatives.

Again, though weak, crafty and vacillating, he still had enough of the cunning of the fox not to wish to excite the enmity of Caesar by a false judgment upon a noted character whose devoted followers might, at any moment, send an embassy to Rome to make serious and successful charges to the Emperor. He afterwards lost his place as Tetrarch through the suspicions of Caligula, who received news from Galilee that Herod was conspiring against him.[3] The premonitions of that unhappy day probably now filled the mind of the Idumaean.

On the other hand, Herod was too frivolous to conduct from beginning to end a solemn judicial proceeding. He evidently intended to ignore the pretensions of Jesus, and to convert the occasion of His coming into a festive hour in which languor and drowsiness would be banished from his court. He had heard much of the miracles of the prisoner in his presence. Rumor had wafted to his ears strange accounts of marvelous feats. One messenger had brought news that the Prophet of Nazareth had raised from the dead a man named Lazarus from Bethany, and also the son of the widow of Nain. Another had declared that the laws of nature suspended themselves on occasion at His behest; that when He walked out on the sea, He did not sink; and that He stilled the tempests with a mere motion of His hand. Still another reported that the mighty magician could take mud from the pool and restore sight; that a woman, ill for many months, need only touch the hem of His garment to be made whole again; and that if He but touched the flesh of a leper, it would become as tender and beautiful as that of a new-born babe. These reports had doubtless been received by Herod with sneers and mocking. But he gathered from them that Jesus was a clever juggler whose powers of entertainment were very fine; and this was sufficient for him and his court.

"Then he questioned with him in many words; but he answered him nothing."[4]

Herod thus opened the examination of Jesus by interrogating Him at length. The Master treated his insolent questions with contemptuous scorn and withering silence. No doubt this conduct of the lowly Nazarene greatly surprised and nettled the supercilious Idumaean. He had imagined that Jesus would be delighted to give an exhibition of His skill amidst royal surroundings. He could not conceive that a peasant would observe the contempt of silence in the presence of a prince. He found it difficult, therefore, to explain this silence. He probably mistook it for stupidity, and construed it to mean that the pretensions of Jesus were fraudulent. He doubtless believed that his captive would not work a miracle because He could not; and that in His failure to do so were exploded His claims to kingship and Messiahship. At all events, he was evidently deeply perplexed; and this perplexity of the Tetrarch, in its turn, only served to anger the accusing priests who stood by.

"And the chief priests and scribes stood and vehemently accused him."[5]

This verse from St. Luke clearly reveals the difference in the temper and purposes of the Sanhedrists on the one hand, and of Herod on the other. The latter merely intended to make of the case of Jesus a farcical proceeding in which the jugglery of the prisoner would break the monotony of a day and banish all care during an idle hour. The priests, on the other hand, were desperately bent upon a serious outcome of the affair, as the words "vehemently accused" suggest. In the face of their repeated accusations, Jesus continued to maintain a noble and majestic silence.

Modern criticism has sought to analyze and to explain the behavior of Christ at the court of Herod. "How comes it," asks Strauss, "that Jesus, not only the Jesus without sin of the orthodox school, but also the Jesus who bowed to the constituted authorities who says 'Give unto Caesar that which is Caesar's'—how comes it that he refuses the answer due to Herod?" The trouble with this question is that it falsely assumes that there was an "answer due to Herod." In the first place, it must be considered that Herod was not Caesar. In the next place, we must remember that St. Luke, the sole Evangelist who records the event, does not explain the character of the questions asked by Herod. Strauss himself says that they "displayed simple curiosity." Admitting that Jesus acknowledged the jurisdiction of Herod, was He compelled to answer irrelevant and impertinent questions? We do not know what these questions were. But we have reason to believe that, coming from Herod, they were not such as Jesus was called upon to answer. It is very probable that the prisoner knew His legal rights; and that He did not believe that Herod, sitting at Jerusalem, a place without his province, was judicially empowered to examine Him. If he was not legally compelled to answer, we are not surprised that Jesus refused to do so as a matter of graciousness and accommodation; for we must not forget that the Man-God felt that He was being questioned by a vulgar animal of the most cunning type.

But what is certain from the Scriptural context is that Herod felt chagrined and mortified at his failure to evoke from Jesus any response. He was enraged that his plans had been foiled by one of his own subjects, a simple Galilean peasant. To show his resentment, he then resorted to mockery and abuse.

"And Herod with his men of war set him at nought, and mocked him, and arrayed him in a gorgeous robe, and sent him again to Pilate."[6]

We are not informed by St. Luke what special charge the priests brought against Jesus at the judgment seat of Herod. He simply says that they "stood and vehemently accused him." But we are justified in inferring that they repeated substantially the same accusations which had been made before Pilate, that He had claimed to be Christ a King. This conclusion best explains the mockery which they sought to heap upon Him; for in ancient times, when men became candidates for office, they put on white gowns to notify the people of their candidacy. Again, Tacitus assures us that white garments were the peculiar dress of illustrious persons; and that the tribunes and consuls wore them when marching before the eagles of the legions into battle.[7]

The meaning of the mockery of Herod was simply this: Behold O Pilate, the illustrious candidate for the kingship of the Jews! Behold the imperial gown of the royal peasant pretender!

The appearance before Herod resulted only in the humiliation of Jesus and the reconciliation of Pilate and Herod.

"And the same day Pilate and Herod were made friends together: for before they were at enmity between themselves."[8]

CHAPTER X

JESUS AGAIN BEFORE PILATE

The sending of Jesus to Herod had not ended the case; and Pilate was undoubtedly very bitterly disappointed. He had hoped that the Galilean Tetrarch would assume complete jurisdiction and dispose finally of the matter. On the contrary, Herod simply mocked and brutalized the prisoner and had him sent back to Pilate. The Roman construed the action of the Idumaean to mean an acquittal, and he so stated to the Jews.

"And Pilate, when he had called together the chief priests and the rulers and the people, Said unto them, Ye have brought this man unto me, as one that perverteth the people: and, behold, I, having examined him before you, have found no fault in this man touching those things whereof ye accuse him: No, nor yet Herod: for I sent you to him; and, lo, nothing worthy of death is done unto him. I will therefore chastise him, and release him."[1]

The proposal to scourge the prisoner was the second of those criminal and cowardly subterfuges through which Pilate sought at once to satisfy his conscience and the demands of the mob. The chastisement was to be a sop to the rage of the rabble, a sort of salve to the wounded pride of the priests who were disappointed that no sentence of death had been imposed. The release was intended as a tribute to justice, as a soothing balm and an atoning sacrifice to his own outraged sense of justice. The injustice of this monstrous proposal was not merely contemptible, it was execrable. If Jesus was guilty, He should have been punished; if innocent, He should have been set free and protected from the assaults of the Jews.

The offer of scourging first and then the release of the prisoner was indignantly rejected by the rabble. In his desperation, Pilate thought of another loophole of escape.

The Evangelists tell us that it was a custom upon Passover day to release to the people any single prisoner that they desired. St. Luke asserts that the governor was under an obligation to do so.[2] Whether this custom was of Roman or Hebrew origin is not certainly known. Many New Testament interpreters have seen in the custom a symbol of the liberty and deliverance realized by Israel in its passage from Egypt at the time of the first great Passover. Others have traced this custom to the Roman practice of releasing a slave at the Lectisternia, or banquets to the gods.[3] Aside from its origin, it is interesting as an illustration of a universal principle in enlightened jurisprudence of lodging somewhere, usually with the chief executive of a race or nation, a power of pardon which serves as an extinction of the penal sanction. This merciful principle is a pathetic acknowledgment of the weakness and imperfection of all human schemes of justice.

Pilate resolved to escape from his confusion and embarrassment by delivering

Jesus to the people, who happened to appear in great numbers at the very moment when Christ returned from Herod. The multitude had come to demand the usual Passover deliverance of a prisoner. The arrival of the crowd of disinterested strangers was inopportune for the priests and elders who were clamoring for the life of the prisoner in their midst. They marked with keen discernment the resolution of the governor to release Jesus. They were equal to the emergency, and began to whisper among the crowd that Barabbas should be asked.

"And they had then a notable prisoner, called Barabbas. Therefore when they were gathered together, Pilate said unto them, Whom will ye that I release unto you? Barabbas, or Jesus which is called Christ? For he knew that for envy they had delivered him."[4]

Pilate believed that the newly arrived multitude would be free from the envy of the priests, and that they would be satisfied with Jesus whom they had, a few days before, welcomed into Jerusalem with shouts of joy. When they demanded Barabbas, he still believed that if he offered them the alternative choice of a robber and a prophet, they would choose the latter.

"But the chief priests and elders persuaded the multitude that they should ask Barabbas, and destroy Jesus. The governor answered and said unto them, Whether of the twain will ye that I release unto you? They said, Barabbas. Pilate saith unto them, What shall I do then with Jesus which is called the Christ? They all say unto him, Let him be crucified."[5]

"Barabbas, or Jesus which is called the Christ?" Such was the alternative offered by a Roman governor to a Jewish mob. Barabbas was a murderer and a robber. Jesus was the sinless Son of God. An erring race wandering in the darkness of sin and perpetually tasting the bitterness of life beneath the sun, preferred a criminal to a prophet. And to the ghastliness of the choice was added a touch of the irony of fate. The names of both the prisoners were in signification the same. Barabbas was also called Jesus. And Jesus Barabbas meant Jesus the Son of the Father. This frightful coincidence was so repugnant to the Gospel writers that they are generally silent upon it. In this connection, Strauss remarks: "According to one reading, the man's complete name was $\iota\eta\sigma o\hat{v}s$ $\beta\alpha\rho\alpha\beta\beta\alpha s$, which fact is noted only because Olshausen considers it noteworthy. Barabbas signifies 'son of the father,' and consequently Olshausen exclaims: 'All that was essential to the Redeemer appears ridiculous in the assassin!' and he deems applicable the verse: *'Ludit in humanis divina potentia rebus.'* We can see nothing in Olshausen's remark but a *ludus humanae impotentiae.*"[6]

Amidst the tumult provoked by the angry passions of the mob, a messenger arrived from his wife bearing news that filled the soul of Pilate with superstitious dread. Claudia had had a dream of strange and ill-boding character.

"When he was set down on the judgment seat, his wife sent unto him, saying, Have thou nothing to do with that just man: For I have suffered many things this day in a dream because of him."[7]

This dream of Pilate's wife is nothing strange. Profane history mentions many similar ones. Calpurnia, Caesar's wife, forewarned him in a dream not to go to the senate house; and the greatest of the Romans fell beneath the daggers of Casca and Brutus, because he failed to heed the admonition of his wife.

In the apocryphal report of Pilate to the emperor Tiberius of the facts of the crucifixion, the words of warning sent by Claudia are given: "Beware said she to me, beware and touch not that man, for he is holy. Last night I saw him in a vision. He was walking on the waters. He was flying on the wings of the winds. He spoke to the tempest and to the fishes of the lake; all were obedient to him. Behold! the torrent in Mount Kedron flows with blood, the statues of Caesar are filled with the filth of Gemoniae, the columns of the Interium have given away and the sun is veiled in mourning like a vestal in the tomb. O, Pilate, evil awaits thee if thou wilt not listen to the prayer of thy wife. Dread the curse of the Roman Senate, dread the powers of Caesar."

This noble and lofty language, this tender and pathetic speech, may appear strange to those who remember the hereditary stigma of the woman. If this dream was sent from heaven, the recollection is forced upon us that the medium of its communication was the illegitimate child of a lewd woman. But then her character was probably not worse than that of Mary Magdalene, who was very dear to the Master and has been canonized not only by the church, but by the reverence of the world.

It is certain, however, that the dream of Claudia had no determining effect upon the conduct of Pilate. Resolution and irresolution alternately controlled him. Fear and superstition were uppermost in both mind and heart. The Jews beheld with anxious and discerning glance the manifestation of the deep anguish of his soul. They feared that the governor was about to pronounce a final judgment of acquittal. Exhibiting fierce faces and frenzied feelings, they moved closer to him and exclaimed: "We have a law, and by our law he ought to die, because he made himself the Son of God."[8]

Despairing of convicting Jesus on a political charge, they deliberately revived a religious one, and presented to Pilate substantially the same accusation upon which they had tried the prisoner before their own tribunal.

"He made himself the Son of God!" These words filled Pilate's mind with a strange and awful meaning. In the mythology and ancient annals of his race, there were many legends of the sons of the gods who walked the earth in human form and guise. They were thus indistinguishable from mortal men. It was dangerous to meet them; for to offend them was to provoke the wrath of the gods, their sires. These reflections, born of superstition, now swept through Pilate's mind with terrific force; and the cries of the mob, "He made himself the Son of God," called from out the deep recesses of his memory the half-forgotten, half-remembered stories of his childhood. Could not Jesus, reasoned Pilate, be the son of the Hebrew Jehovah as Hercules was the son of Jupiter? Filled with superstitious dread and trembling with emotion, Pilate called Jesus inside the Temple a second time; and, looking with renewed awe and wonder, asked:

"Whence art thou?"[9] But Jesus answered him nothing.

Pilate came forth from the judgment hall a second time determined to release the prisoner; but the Jews, marking his decision, began to cry out: "Away with him, away with him, crucify him!"[10] Maddened by the relentless importunity of the mob, Pilate replied scornfully and mockingly:

"Shall I crucify your king?"

The cringing, hypocritical priests shouted back their answer:

"We have no king but Caesar."[11]

And on the kingly idea of loyalty to Roman sovereignty they framed their last menace and accusation. From the quiver of their wrath they drew the last arrow of spite and hate, and fired it straight at the heart of Jesus through the hands of Pilate:

"If thou let this man go, thou art not Caesar's friend: whosoever maketh himself a king speaketh against Caesar."[12]

This last maneuver of the mob sealed the doom of the Christ. It teaches also most clearly that Pilate was no match for the Jews when their religious prejudices were aroused and they were bent on accomplishing their desires. They knew Pilate and he knew them. They had been together full six years. He had been compelled to yield to them in the matter of the standards and the eagles. The sacred Corban funds had been appropriated only after blood had been shed in the streets of Jerusalem. The gilt shields of Tiberius that he had placed in Herod's palace were taken down at the demands of the Jews and carried to the temple of Augustus at Caesarea. And now the same fanatical rabble was before him demanding the blood of the Nazarene, and threatening to accuse him to Caesar if he released the prisoner. The position of Pilate was painfully critical. He afterwards lost his procuratorship at the instance of accusing Jews. The shadow of that distant day now fell like a curse across his pathway. Nothing was so terrifying to a Roman governor as to have the people send a complaining embassy to Rome. It was especially dangerous at this time. The imperial throne was filled by a morbid and suspicious tyrant who needed but a pretext to depose the governor of any province who silently acquiesced in traitorous pretensions to kingship. Pilate trembled at these reflections. His feelings of self-preservation suggested immediate surrender to the Jews. But his innate sense of justice, which was woven in the very fiber of his Roman nature, recoiled at the thought of Roman sanction of judicial murder. He resolved, therefore, to propitiate and temporize. The frenzied rabble continued to cry: "Crucify him! Crucify him!" Three times, in reply, Conscience sent to Pilate's trembling lips the searching question: "Why, what evil hath he done?" "Crucify him! Crucify him!" came back from the infuriated mob.

Pilate finally resolved to do their bidding and obey their will. But he seems to have secretly cherished the hope that scourging, which was the usual preliminary to crucifixion, might be made to satisfy the mob. But this hope was soon dispelled; and he found himself compelled to yield completely to their wishes by delivering the prisoner to be crucified. Before this final step, however, which was an insult to the true courage of the soul and an outrage upon all the charities of the heart, he resolved to apply a soothing salve to wounded conscience. He resolved to perform a ceremonial cleansing act. Calling for a basin of water, he washed his hands before the multitude, saying : "I am innocent of the blood of this just person: see ye to it."[13]

This was a simple, impressive, theatrical act; but little, mean, contemptible, cowardly. He washed his hands when he should have used them. He should have used them as Brutus or Gracchus or Pompeius Magnus would have done, in pointing his legion to the field of duty and of glory. He should have used them as Bonaparte did when he put down the mob in the streets of Paris. But he was too craven and cowardly; and herein is to be found the true meaning of the character and conduct of Pilate. He believed that Jesus was innocent; and that the accusations against Him were inspired by the envy of His countrymen. He had declared to the Jews in an emphatic verdict of acquittal that he found in Him no fault at all. And yet this very sentence, "I find in him no fault at all," was the beginning of that course of cowardly and criminal vacillation which finally sent Jesus to the cross. "Yet was this utterance," says Innes, "as it turned out, only the first step in that downward course of weakness the world knows so well: a course which, beginning with indecision and complaisance, passed through all the phases of alternate bluster and subserviency; persuasion, evasion, protest, and compromise; superstitious dread, conscientious reluctance, cautious duplicity, and sheer moral cowardice at last; until this Roman remains photographed forever as the perfect feature of the unjust judge, deciding 'against his better knowledge, not deceived.' "

"Then released he Barabbas unto them: and when he had scourged Jesus, he delivered him to be crucified. Then the soldiers of the governor took Jesus into the common hall, and gathered unto him the whole band of soldiers. And they stripped him, and put on him a scarlet robe. And when they had platted a crown of thorns, they put it upon his head, and a reed in his right hand: And they bowed the knee before him, and mocked him, saying, Hail, King of the Jews! And they spit upon him, and took the reed, and smote him on the head. And after that they had mocked him, they took the robe off from him, and put his own raiment on him, and led him away to crucify him."[14]

Thus ended the most memorable act of injustice recorded in history. At every stage of the trial, whether before Caiaphas or Pilate, the prisoner conducted Himself with that commanding dignity and majesty so well worthy of His origin, mission, and destiny. His sublime deportment at times caused His judges to marvel greatly. And through it all, He stood alone. His friends and followers had deserted Him in His hour of greatest need. Single-handed and unaided, the Galilean peasant had bared His breast and brow to the combined authority, to the insults and outrages, of both Jerusalem and Rome. "Not a single discordant voice was raised amidst the tumultuous clamour: not a word of protest disturbed the mighty concord of anger and reviling; not the faintest echo of the late hosannas, which had wrung with wonder, fervour, and devotion, and which had surrounded and exalted to the highest pitch of triumph the bearer of good tidings on his entry into the Holy City. Where were the throngs of the hopeful and believing, who had followed His beckoning as a finger pointing toward the breaking dawn of truth and regeneration? Where were they, what thinking and why silent? The bands of the humble and poor, of the afflicted and outcast who had entrusted to His controlling grace the salvation of soul and body—where were they, what thinking and why silent? The troops of women and youths, who had drawn fresh strength from the spell of a glance or a word from the Father of all that liveth—where were they, what thinking and why silent? And the multitudes of disciples and enthusiasts who had scattered sweet-scented boughs and joyous utterances along the road to Sion, blessing Him that came in the name of the Lord—where were they, what thinking and why silent? Not a remembrance, not a sign, not a word of the great glory so lately His. Jesus was alone."

CHAPTER XI

LEGAL ANALYSIS AND SUMMARY OF THE ROMAN TRIAL OF JESUS

In the preceding pages of this volume we have considered the elements of both Law and Fact as related to the Roman trial of Jesus. Involved in this consideration were the powers and duties of Pilate as procurator of Judea and as presiding judge at the trial; general principles of Roman provincial administration at the time of Christ; the legal and political status of the subject Jew in his relationship to the conquering Roman; the exact requirements of criminal procedure in Roman capital trials at Rome and in the provinces at the date of the crucifixion; the Roman law applicable to the trial of Jesus; and the facts of said trial before Pilate and Herod.

We are now in a position to analyze the case from the view point of the juristic agreement or nonagreement of Law and Fact; and to determine by a process of judicial dissection and re-formation, the presence or absence of essential legal elements in the proceedings. We have learned what should have been done by Pilate acting as a Roman judge in a criminal matter involving the life of a prisoner. We have also ascertained what he actually did. We are thus enabled to compare the requirements with the actualities of the case; and to ascertain the resemblances in the proceedings against Jesus to a legally conducted trial under Roman law.

But, in making this summary and analysis, a most important consideration must be constantly held in mind: that, in matters of review on appeal, errors will not be presumed; that is, errors will not be considered that do not appear affirmatively upon the record. The law will rather presume and the court will assume that what should have been done, was done. In conformity with this principle, the presumption must be indulged that Pilate acted in strict obedience to the requirements of Roman law in trying Jesus, unless the Gospels of the New Testament, which constitute the record in the case, either affirmatively or by reasonable inference, disclose the absence of such obedience. A failure to note this presumption and to keep this principle in mind, has caused many writers upon this subject to make erroneous statements concerning the merits and legal aspects of the trial of Christ.

Laymen frequently assert the essential principle of this presumption without seeming to be aware of it. Both Keim and Geikie declare that assessors or assistants were associated with Pilate in the trial of Jesus. The Gospel records nowhere even intimate such a thing; and no other original records are in existence to furnish such information. And yet one of the most celebrated of the biblical critics, Dr. Theodor Keim, writing on the trial of Christ by Pilate, says: "Beside him, upon benches, were the council or the assessors of the court, sub-officials, friends, Roman citizens, whose presence could not be dispensed with, and who were not wanting to the procurators of Judea, although our reports do not mention them."[1] To the same effect, Dr. Cunningham Geikie thus writes: "The assessors of the court—Roman citizens—who acted as nominal members of the judicial bench, sit beside Pilate—for Roman law required their presence."[2]

These statements of the renowned writers just quoted are justified not only on the ground of logical historical inference, but also on the principle of actual legal presumption. The closest scrutiny of the New Testament narratives nowhere discovers even an intimation that a bench of judges helped Pilate to conduct the trial of Jesus. And yet, as Geikie says, "Roman law required their presence," and the legal presumption is that they were in and about the Praetorium ready to lend assistance, and that they actually took part in the proceedings. This inference is strengthened by the fact that Pilate, after he had learned the nature of the accusation against Jesus, called Him into the palace to examine Him. Why did Pilate do this? Why did he not examine the prisoner in the presence of His accusers in the open air? Geikie tells us that there was a judgment hall in the palace in which trials were usually conducted.[3] Is it not possible, nay probable, that the assessors and Pilate were assembled at an early hour in this hall to hear the usual criminal charges of the day, or, perhaps, to try the accusation against Jesus, of whose appearance before them they had been previously notified; and that, when the governor heard that the religious scruples of the Jews would not permit them to enter the judgment hall during the Passover feast, he went out alone to hear the accusation against the prisoner; and that he then returned with the accused into the hall where the bench of judges were awaiting him, to lay before them the charges and to further examine the case? It is admitted that this theory and the statement of Geikie that there was a hall in the palace where trials were generally held, are seemingly refuted by the fact that Roman trials were almost always conducted in the open air. But this was not invariably true; and the case of Pilate and his court might have been an exception.

It has been sought to lay particular stress upon the doctrine of legal presumption that what should have been done, was done, unless the record affirmatively negatives the fact, because it is impossible to appreciate fully the legal aspects of the trial of Jesus, unless this doctrine is understood and kept constantly in view.

A casual perusal of the New Testament narratives leaves the impression upon the mind of the reader that the proceedings against Jesus before Pilate were exceedingly irregular and lacking in all the essential elements of a regular trial. As a matter of fact, this impression may be grounded in absolute truth. It may be that the action of Pilate was arbitrary and devoid of all legal forms. This possibility is strengthened by the consideration that Jesus was not a Roman citizen and could not, therefore, demand the strict observance of forms of law in His trial. A Jewish provincial, when accused of crime, stood before a Roman governor with no other rights than the plea of justice as a defense against the summary exercise of absolute power. In other words, in the case of Jesus, Pilate was not bound to observe strictly rules of criminal procedure prescribed by Roman law. He could, if he saw fit, dispense with forms of law and dispose of the case either equitably or as his whims suggested. Nor was there a right of appeal in such a case, from the judgment of the procurator to the emperor at Rome. The decision of the governor against a provincial was final. The case of Paul before Felix and before Festus was entirely different. Paul was a Roman citizen and, as such, was entitled to all the rights involved in Roman citizenship, which included the privilege of an appeal to Caesar against the judgment of a provincial officer; and he actually exercised this right.[4] It was incumbent, therefore, upon Roman officials to observe due forms of law in proceeding against him. And St. Luke, in Acts xxiv., indicates the almost exact precision and formality of a Roman trial, in the case of Paul.

But the fact that Jesus was not a Roman citizen does not prove that due forms of law were not observed in His trial. It is hardly probable, as before observed, that despotism and caprice were tolerated at any time, in any part of the Roman world. And, besides, Roman history and jurisprudence are replete with illustrations of complete legal protection extended by Roman officials to the non-Roman citizens of subject states. It is, moreover, a legitimate and almost inevitable inference, drawn from the very nature of the Roman constitution and from the peculiar character of Roman judicial administration, that no human life belonging to a citizen or subject of Rome would be permitted to be taken without due process of law, either imperial or local.

In forming an opinion as to the existence or nonexistence of a regular trial of Jesus before Pilate, the meager details of the New Testament histories must not alone be relied upon. Nor must it be forgotten that the Gospel writers were not lawyers or court officers reporting a case to be reviewed on appeal. They were laymen writing a general account of a judicial transaction. And the omissions in their narratives are not to be considered as either discrepancies or falsehoods. They simply did not intend to tell everything about the trial of Jesus; and the fact that they do not record the successive steps of a regular trial does not mean that these steps were not observed.

It is respectfully submitted that if a modern layman should write a newspaper or book account of one of the great criminal trials of this century, with no intention of making it a strictly judicial report, this account would not reveal the presence of more essential legal elements than are disclosed by the reports of the Evangelists of the proceedings against Jesus.

The majority of writers on the subject express the opinion that the appearance of the Christ before the Roman governor was nothing more than a short hearing in which a few questions were asked and answers made; that the proceedings were exceedingly brief and informal; and that the emergencies of the case rather than forms of law guided the judgment and controlled the conduct of Pilate. As a layman, the author of these volumes would take the same view. But as a lawyer, treating the subject in a judicial manner, and bound by legal rules, regulations, and presumptions, in reviewing the merits of the case, he feels constrained to dissent from the prevalent opinion and to declare that the New Testament records, though meager in details, exhibit all the essential elements of an ordinary criminal trial, whether conducted in ancient or modern times. He further asserts that if the affirmative statements of the Evangelists that certain things were done, be supplemented by the legal presumption that still other things were done because they should have been done, and because the record does not affirmatively declare that they were not done, an almost perfect judicial proceeding can be developed from the Gospel reports of the trial of Jesus before Pilate. These reports disclose the following essential elements of all ancient and modern criminal trials:

1.   The Indictment, or *Nominis Delatio.*

"What accusation bring ye against this man?"

"And they began to accuse him, saying, We found this fellow perverting the nation, and forbidding to give tribute to Caesar, saying that he himself is Christ a King."

2.   The Examination, or *Interrogatio.*

"Art thou the King of the Jews?"

"Art thou a King then?"

3.   The Defense, or *Excusatio.*

"My kingdom is not of this world: if my kingdom were of this world, then would my servants fight, that I should not be delivered to the Jews: but now is my kingdom not from hence...To this end was I born and for this cause came I into the world, that I should bear witness unto the truth. Everyone that is of the truth heareth my voice."

4.   The Acquittal, or *Absolutio.*

"I find in him no fault at all."

Here we have clearly presented the essential features of a criminal trial: the Indictment, the Examination of the charge, the Defense, and the Judgment of the tribunal, which, in this case, was an Acquittal.

To demonstrate that Pilate intended to conduct the proceedings against Jesus seriously and judicially, at the beginning of the trial, let us briefly review the circumstances attendant upon the successive steps just enumerated. And to this end, let us proceed in order:

1.   The Indictment, or *Nominis Delatio.*

When Pilate had seated himself in the ivory curule chair of the procurator of Judea, at an early hour on Friday morning, the day of the crucifixion of Jesus, a Jerusalem mob led by the Sanhedrin confronted him with the prisoner. His first recorded words are: "What accusation bring ye against this man?" As before suggested, this question is very keenly indicative of the presence of the judge and of the beginning of a solemn judicial proceeding. Every word rings with Roman authority and strongly suggests administrative action.

The accusing priests sought to evade this question by answering: "If he were not a malefactor, we would not have delivered him up unto thee."

If Pilate had adopted the Jewish view of the merits of the matter, that his countersign was the only thing necessary to justify the final condemnation and punishment of the prisoner; or, if he had been indifferent to the legal aspects of the case, he would simply have granted their request at once, and would have ordered the prisoner to execution. But this was not the case; for we are assured that he insisted on knowing the nature of the accusation before he would assume jurisdiction of the affair. The mere information that He was a "malefactor" did not suffice. The conduct of the Roman judge clearly indicated that accusation was a more important element of Roman criminal procedure than was inquisition. To meet the emergency, the Jews were compelled, then, to make the formal charge, that:

"We found this fellow perverting the nation, and forbidding to give tribute to Caesar, saying that he himself is Christ a King."

Here we have presented the indictment, the first step in a criminal proceeding; and it was presented not voluntarily, but because a Roman judge, acting judicially, demanded and forced its presentment.

2.   The Examination, or *Interrogatio. Not content with knowing the nature of the charges against the prisoner, Pilate insisted on finding out whether they were true or not. He accordingly took Jesus inside the palace and interrogated Him. With true judicial tact, he brushed aside the first two accusations as unimportant, and came with pointed directness to the material question:*

"Art thou the King of the Jews?"

This interrogation bears the impress of a judicial inquiry, touching a matter involving the question of high treason, the charge against the prisoner. It clearly indicates a legal proceeding in progress. And when Jesus made reply that seemed to indicate guilt, the practiced ear of the Roman judge caught the suggestion of a criminal confession, and he asked impatiently:

"Art thou a King then?"

This question indicates seriousness and a resolution to get at the bottom of the matter with a view to a serious judicial determination of the affair.

3.   The Defense, or *Excusatio.*

In reply to the question of the judge, the prisoner answered:

"My kingdom is not of this world."

This language indicates that Jesus was conscious of the solemnity of the proceedings; and that he recognized the right of Pilate to interrogate Him judicially. His answer seemed to say: "I recognize your authority in matters of this life and this world. If my claims to kingship were temporal, I fully appreciate that they would be treasonable; and that, as the representative of Caesar, you would be justified in delivering me to death. But my pretensions to royalty are spiritual, and this places the matter beyond your reach."

The defense of Jesus was in the nature of what we call in modern pleading a Confession and Avoidance: "A plea which admits, in words or in effect, the truth of the matter contained in the Declaration; and alleges some new matter to avoid the effect of it, and shows that the plaintiff is, notwithstanding, not entitled to his action."

It may be analyzed thus:

Confession: Inside the palace, Pilate asked Jesus the question: "Art thou the King of the Jews?" According to St. Matthew, Jesus answered: "Thou sayest";[5] according to St. Mark: "Thou sayest it";[6] according to St. Luke: "Thou sayest it";[7] according to St. John: "Thou sayest that I am a king."[8]

All these replies are identical in signification, and mean: Thou sayest it, because I am really a king. In other words, He simply confessed that He was a king. Then came His real defense.

Avoidance: "My kingdom is not of this world: if my kingdom were of this world, then would my servants fight, that I should not be delivered to the Jews: but now is my kingdom not from hence.... To this end was I born and for this cause came I into the world, that I should bear witness of the truth. Everyone that is of the truth heareth my voice."

After having confessed claims to kingship, and having thereby made Himself momentarily liable on the charge of high treason, He at once avoids the effect of the declaration by alleging new matter which exempted Him from the operation of the *crimen Laesae Majestatis.* He boldly declares His kingship, but places His kingdom beyond the skies in the realm of truth and spirit. He asserts a bold antithesis between the Empire of Caesar and the Kingdom of God. He cheerfully acknowledges the procuratorship of Pilate in the first, but fearlessly proclaims His own Messiahship in the second.

4.   The Acquittal, or *Absolutio.*

It is more than probable that Pilate's heathen soul mocked the heavenly claims of the lowly prisoner in his presence, but his keenly discerning Roman intellect marked at once the distinction between an earthly and a heavenly kingdom. He saw clearly that their boundaries nowhere conflicted, and that treasonable contact was impossible. He judged that Jesus was simply a gentle enthusiast whose pretensions were harmless. Accordingly, he went out to the mob and pronounced a verdict of "not guilty." Solemnly raising his hand, he proclaimed the sentence of acquittal:

"I find in him no fault at all."

This language is not the classical legal phraseology of a Roman verdict of acquittal. The Latin word for a single ballot was *absolvo;* the words of a collective judgment of a bench of judges was *non fecisse videtur.* The language of St. John, though that of a layman, is equally as effectual, if not so formal and judicial.

More than any other feature of the case, the verdict of acquittal, "I find in him no fault at all," indicates the regularity and solemnity of a judicial proceeding. Standing alone, it would indicate the close of a regular trial in which a court having jurisdiction had sat in judgment upon the life or liberty of an alleged criminal.

If to these essential elements of a trial which the Gospel records affirmatively disclose be added other necessary elements of a regular Roman trial which legal presumption supplies, because these records do not deny their existence, we have then in the proceedings against Jesus all the important features of Roman criminal procedure involving the question of life or death. That several essential elements are absent is evident from a reasonable construction of the statements of the Evangelists. That which most forcibly negatives the existence of a regular trial was the precipitancy with which the proceedings were conducted before Pilate. We have seen that ten days were allowed at Rome after the *nominis receptio* to secure testimony and prepare the case before the beginning of the trial. This rule was certainly not observed at the trial of Jesus. But several irregularities which are apparent from a perusal of the Gospel histories may be explained from the fact that Jesus was not a Roman citizen and was not, therefore, entitled to a strict observance of Roman law in the proceedings against him.

The foregoing analysis and summary apply only to the proceedings of the first appearance of Jesus before Pilate. It was at this time that the real Roman trial took place. All subsequent proceedings were irregular, tumultuous and absolutely illegal. The examination of Jesus by Herod cannot, strictly speaking, be called a trial. The usual explanation of the sending of the prisoner to Herod is that Pilate learned that He was a native and citizen of Galilee; and that, desiring to rid himself of an embarrassing subject, he determined to transfer the accused from the *forum apprehensionis* to the *forum originis vel domicilii*. It has frequently been asserted that it was usual in Roman procedure to transfer a prisoner from the place of arrest to the place of his origin or residence. There seems to be no authority for this contention. It may or may not have been true as a general proposition. But it was certainly not true in the case of the transfer of Jesus to Herod. In the first place, when Pilate declared, "I find no fault in him at all," a verdict of acquittal was pronounced, and the case was ended. The proceedings had taken form of *res adjudicata*, and former jeopardy could have been pleaded in bar of further prosecution. It might be differently contended if Pilate had discovered that Jesus was from Galilee before the proceedings before him were closed. But it is clear from St. Luke, who alone records the occurrence of the sending of the prisoner to Herod, that the case was closed and the verdict of acquittal had been rendered before Pilate discovered the identity of the accused.[9] It was then too late to subject a prisoner to a second trial for the same offense.

Rosadi denies emphatically that Herod had jurisdiction of the offense charged against Jesus. In this connection, he says: "His prosecutors insisted tenaciously upon His answering to a charge of *continuous* sedition, as lawyers call it. This offence had been begun in Galilee and ended in Jerusalem—that is to say, in Judaea. Now it was a rule of Roman law, which the procurator of Rome could neither fail to recognize nor afford to neglect, that the competence of a court territorially constituted was determined either by the place in which the arrest was made, or by the place in which the offence was committed. Jesus had been arrested at the gates of Jerusalem; His alleged offence had been committed for the most part, and as far as all the final acts were concerned, in the city itself and in other localities of Judaea. In continuous offences competence was determined by the place in which the last acts going to constitute the offence had been committed. Thus no justification whatever existed for determining the court with regard to the prisoner's origin. But this investigation upon a point of Roman law is to all intents superfluous, because either Pilate, when he thought of Herod, intended to strip himself of his inalienable judicial power, and in this case he ought to have respected the jurisdiction and competence of the Grand Sanhedrin and not to have busied himself with a conflict as to cognizance which should only have been discussed and resolved by the Jewish judicial authorities; or else he had no intention of abdicating his power, and in this case he ought never to have raised the question of competence between himself, Governor of Judaea, and Herod, Regent of Galilee, but between himself and the Roman Vice-Governor of Galilee, his colleague, if there had been such an one. It is only between judges of the same judicial hierarchy that a dispute as to territorial competence can arise. Between magistrates of different States there can only exist a contrast of power and jurisdiction. The act of Pilate cannot then be interpreted as a scruple of a constitutional character. It is but a miserable escape for his irresolution, a mere endeavour to temporize."

The second and final appearance of Jesus before Pilate bears little resemblance to a regular trial. The characteristic elements of an ordinary Roman criminal proceeding are almost wholly wanting. The pusillanimous cowardice of the procurator and the blind fury of the mob are the chief component parts. A sort of wild phantasmagoria sweeps through the multitude and circles round the tribunal of the governor. Pilate struggles with his conscience, and seeks safety in subterfuge. He begins by declaring to the assembled priests and elders that neither he nor Herod has found any fault in the man; and then, as a means of compromise and conciliation, makes the monstrous proposal that he will first scourge and then release the prisoner. This infamous proposal is rejected by the mob. The cowardly procurator then adopts another mean expedient as a way of escape. He offers to deliver Jesus to them as a Passover gift. Him they refuse and Barabbas, the robber, is demanded. Pilate's terror is intensified by superstitious dread, when the mob begins to cry: "He made himself the Son of God!" From out the anguish of his soul, the voice of Justice sends to his quivering lips the thrice-repeated question: "Why, what evil hath he done?" The mob continues to cry: "Crucify him! Crucify him!"

And as a final assault upon his conscience and his courage, the hypocritical priests warn him that he must not release a pretender to kingship, for such a man is an enemy to Caesar. The doom of the Nazarene is sealed by this last maneuver of the rabble. Then, as a propitiation to the great God of truth and justice, and as balm to his hurt and wounded conscience, he washes his hands in front of them and exclaims: "I am innocent of the blood of this just person: see ye to it."

The crucifixion followed Pilate's final determination; and thus ended the most famous trial in the history of the world. It began with the arrest of Jesus in Gethsemane at midnight, and ended with His crucifixion on Golgotha on the afternoon of the same day. As we have seen, it was a double trial, conducted within the jurisdictions of the two most famous systems of jurisprudence known to mankind. In both trials, substantially the right issue was raised. Before the

Sanhedrin, the prisoner was charged with blasphemy and convicted. Regarding Jesus as a mere man, a plain Jewish citizen, this judgment was "substantially right in point of law"; but was unjust and outrageous because forms of criminal procedure which every Jewish prisoner was entitled to have observed, were completely ignored.

The proceedings before Pilate, we have reason to believe, were conducted, in a general way, with due regard to forms of law. But the result was judicial murder, because the judge, after having acquitted Jesus, delivered Him to be crucified. "I find in him no fault at all" was the verdict of Pilate. But this just and righteous sentence was destroyed and obliterated by the following: "And they were instant with loud voices, requiring that he might be crucified. And the voices of them and of the chief priests prevailed. And Pilate gave sentence that it should be as they required."[10]

A horrible travesty on justice, this! *"Absolvo"* and *"Ibis ad crucem,"* in the same breath, were the final utterances of a Roman judge administering Roman law in the most memorable judicial transaction known to men.

The treatment of this great theme would be incomplete and unsatisfactory unless reference were made to the peculiar views of some who believe that political rather than legal considerations should govern in determining the justice or the injustice of the proceedings against Jesus before Pilate. A certain class of critics insist on regarding the Roman governor in the light of an administrator rather than a judge, and contend that the justice of his conduct and the righteousness of his motives should be tested by principles of public policy rather than by strict legal rules. It is insisted by such persons that various considerations support this contention. It is pointed out that Pilate exercised the unlimited jurisdiction of the military *imperium,* and was not, therefore, strictly bound by legal rules; that Jesus was not a Roman citizen, and, for this reason, was not entitled to the strict observance of forms of law; and that the stubborn, rebellious and turbulent temper of the Jewish people required the strong hand of a military governor, enforcing political obedience by drastic measures, rather than the action of a judge punctiliously applying rules of law. These peculiar views subject the conduct of Pilate to the pressure of public necessity rather than to the test of private right, and insist that sympathy rather than censure should hold the scales in which his deeds are weighed.

This view of the case was presented in the last generation by Sir James Fitz-James Stephen in a book of extraordinary strength and brilliancy entitled "Liberty, Equality, Fraternity." It was written in answer to John Stuart Mill, and is, without doubt, the most powerful assault in the English language on what men have been pleased to call in modern times "liberty of conscience." In his letters and essays, Mr. Mill, according to the interpretation of Mr. Stephen, "condemns absolutely all interference with the expression of opinion." When tried by this standard, the Athenian dicasts, who condemned Socrates; Marcus Aurelius, who persecuted the Christians; Pontius Pilate, who crucified Jesus; and Philip II, who sanctioned the tortures of the Spanish Inquisition, were simply violators of rights of personal opinion and of freedom of conscience. If you deny the right of liberty of conscience, Mr. Mill contends, you must not censure Marcus Aurelius and other persecutors of Christianity. On the contrary, you must approve such persecution; and you must go further, and find "a principle which would justify Pontius Pilate." This challenge was boldly accepted by Mr. Stephen, who says:

"Was Pilate right in crucifying Christ? I reply, Pilate's paramount duty was to preserve the peace in Palestine, to form the best judgment he could as to the means required for that purpose, and to act upon it when it was formed. Therefore, if and in so far as he believed in good faith and on reasonable grounds that what he did was necessary for the preservation of the peace of Palestine, he was right. It was his duty to run the risk of being mistaken, notwithstanding Mr. Mill's principle as to liberty. He was in the position of a judge whose duty it is to try persons duly brought before him for trial at the risk of error."[11]

This contention is founded upon the inexorable doctrine that what is, is right; that revolution, though righteous, must be nipped in the bud and destroyed; and that rights of private conscience must not be tolerated if they tend to disturb the peace of the community at large. The inevitable logic of the theory of Mr. Stephen is that the established order of things in Palestine under Roman rule was right, and that it was the duty of the Roman governor to regard all attempts at innovation or revolution in religion or government as a breach of the peace which was to be promptly suppressed by vigorous measures. There is undoubtedly a certain amount of truth in this contention, in so far as it implies that under a just and orderly plan of government, the rights of the commonwealth to peace and security are greater than the claims of the individual to liberty of conscience which conflict with and tend to destroy those rights. It is a truth, at once sovereign and fundamental, in both law and government, that the rights of the collective body are greater than those of any individual member; and that when the rights of the whole and those of a part of the body politic conflict, the rights of the part must yield and, if necessity requires it, be destroyed. Upon no other basis can the doctrine of majorities in politics and the right of Eminent Domain in law, rest. But the application of the principles involved in this theory must always be made with proper limitations, and with a due regard to the rights of minorities and individuals; else government becomes an engine of despotism instead of an expression of political freedom. A claim of privilege which every member of the community has a right to make, must be respected by the collective body; otherwise, a common right has been violated and destroyed. The complete recognition of this principle is imperative and fundamental, and is the corner stone of political freedom in free institutions among men.

But the trouble with the contention of Mr. Stephen is that it proceeds upon a wrong hypothesis. He intimates that Pilate might have "believed in good faith that what he did was necessary for the preservation of the peace of Palestine." This is a purely gratuitous and unhistorical suggestion. The Gospel records nowhere justify such an assumption. The very opposite is taught by these sacred writings. It is true that Caiaphas contended that it was expedient that one man should die rather than that the whole nation should perish. But this was a Jewish, not a Roman opinion. The Evangelical narratives are unanimous in declaring that Pilate believed Jesus to be innocent and that "for envy" He had been accused by His countrymen.

It is cheerfully conceded that occasions may present themselves, in the tumult and frenzy of revolution, when the responsible authorities of government may put to death a person whose intentions are innocent, but whose acts are incentives to riot and bloodshed. This may be done upon the principle of self-preservation, which is the first law of government as well as of nature. But no such necessity arose in the case of Jesus; and no such motives are ascribed by the Evangelists to Pilate. They very clearly inform us that the action of the Roman governor in delivering the prisoner to be crucified was prompted by private and not public considerations. He had no fears that Jesus would precipitate a revolution dangerous to the Roman state. He simply wished to quiet the mob and retain his position as procurator of Judea. The facts of history, then, do not support the contention of Mr. Stephen.

Continuing, in another place, the same eminent writer says: "The point to which I wish to direct attention is that Pilate's duty was to maintain peace and order in Judea and to maintain the Roman power. It is surely impossible to contend seriously that it was his duty, or that it could be the duty of any one in his position, to recognize in the person brought to his judgment seat, I do not say God Incarnate, but the teacher and preacher of a higher form of morals and a more enduring form of social order than that of which he himself was the representative. To a man in Pilate's position the morals and the social order which he represents are for all practical purposes final and absolute standards. If, in order to evade the obvious inference from this, it is said that Pilate ought to have respected the principle of religious liberty as propounded by Mr. Mill, the answer is that if he had done so he would have run the risk of setting the whole province in a blaze. It is only in very modern times, and under the influence of modern sophisms, that belief and action have come to be so much separated in these parts of the world that the distinction between the temporal and spiritual department of affairs even appears to be tenable; but this is a point for future discussion.

"If this should appear harsh, I would appeal again to Indian experience. Suppose that some great religious reformer—say, for instance, some one claiming to be the Guru of the Sikhs, or the Imam in whose advent many Mahommedans devoutly believe—were to make his appearance in the Punjab or the North-West Provinces. Suppose that there was good reason to believe—and nothing is more probable—that whatever might be the preacher's own personal intentions, his preaching was calculated to disturb the public peace and produce mutiny and rebellion: and suppose further (though the supposition is one which it is hardly possible to make even in imagination), that a British officer, instead of doing whatever might be necessary, or executing whatever orders he might receive, for the maintenance of British authority, were to consider whether he ought not to become a disciple of the Guru or Imam. What course would be taken towards him? He would be instantly dismissed with ignominy from the service which he would disgrace, and if he acted up to his convictions, and preferred his religion to his Queen and country, he would be hanged as a rebel and a traitor."[12]

These theories and illustrations are not only plausible but entirely reasonable when viewed in the light of the facts which they assume to be true. But here again, we must insist that they do not harmonize with the actual facts of the case to which they are intended to apply. In the extract above quoted, three suppositions are suggested. The first one is immaterial. Let us analyze the other two in the light of the Gospel histories. The second supposition is this: "Suppose that there was good reason to believe—and nothing is more probable—that whatever might be the preacher's own personal intentions, his preaching was calculated to disturb the public peace and produce mutiny and rebellion." What passage of Scripture, it may be asked, justifies this parallel with the case of Jesus before Pilate? There is, in fact, absolutely none. The nearest approach to one is Matthew xxvii. 24: "When Pilate saw that he could prevail nothing, but that rather a tumult was made, he took water, and washed his hands before the multitude, saying, I am innocent of the blood of this just person: see ye to it." The "tumult" here referred to means nothing more than the manifestation of agitated feelings on the part of the mob, who were enraged at the prospect of an acquittal by the governor. It does not remotely refer to the danger of a popular rebellion which might endanger the security and safety of Rome. To admit this supposition would be to elevate the motives of Pilate in consenting to the crucifixion of Jesus to the level of solicitude for the welfare of his country. This would not be justified by the record, which clearly reveals that Pilate was moved by personal selfishness rather than by a sense of official duty.

The third and last supposition above mentioned is this: "And suppose, further (though the supposition is one which it is hardly possible to make even in imagination), that a British officer, instead of doing whatever might be necessary, or executing whatever orders he might receive for the maintenance of British authority, were to consider whether he ought not to become a disciple of the Guru or Imam." Here again, we may ask, what passage of Scripture supports this parallel of a Mohammedan Guru before a British officer with Jesus Christ before Pontius Pilate? Where is it anywhere stated, or by reasonable inference implied, that Pilate considered whether he ought not to become a disciple of Jesus? The celebrated English author has simply argued his case from a radically defective record of fact.

On the other hand, let us draw what we conceive to be a true parallel. Let us take an illustration nearer home. Suppose that the Governor General of the Phillippine Islands was clothed with authority of life and death as a judge in criminal matters pertaining to the affairs of those islands. Suppose that a Mohammedan preacher should appear somewhere in the archipelago where Mohammedans are numerous, and begin to proclaim a new religious faith which was opposed not only to the ordinary tenets of Islamism, but also to the Christian religion which is the dominant faith of the rulers of the Philippines. Suppose that the coreligionists of this Mohammedan prophet should seize him, bring him before the Governor General, and lodge against him a threefold charge: That he was stirring up sedition in the islands; that he had advised the Filipinos not to pay taxes due to the United States government; and that he had said and done things that were treasonable against the United States. Suppose that the Governor General, after personal examination, became satisfied that the Mohammedan preacher was an innocent enthusiast, that the charges against him were false, and were due to the envy and hatred of his fellow-Mohammedans; that to quiet the passions, and satisfy the demands of the mob, he proposed to scourge him first and then release him; that, in the face of the vehement accusations of the rabble, he hesitated and vacillated for several hours; and that finally, when the Mohammedans threatened to send a complaint to President Roosevelt which might endanger his position, he ordered his innocent prisoner to death. Suppose this should happen beneath the American flag, what would be the judgment of the American people as to the merits of the proceedings? Would the Governor General retain his office by such a course of conduct?

But let us view it in another light. Let us assume that the Governor General believed that the Mohammedan preacher was innocent and that his "personal intentions" were not remotely hostile or treasonable, but felt that his preaching might stir up rebellion dangerous to the power of the American government in the Philippines; and that it was his duty as the guardian of American honor and security, to put the native preacher to death; and this not to punish past criminal conduct, but to prevent future trouble by a timely execution. Suppose that the Governor General should do this while sitting as a judge, would it not be judicial murder? Suppose that he should do it while acting as an administrator, would it be less an assassination? Would it not stamp with indelible shame the administration that should sanction or tolerate it? Would the press of America not denounce the act as murder, declare that despotism reigned in our Eastern possessions, and demand the removal and punishment of the man who had disgraced his office and brought odium upon the administrative justice of his country?

In closing the Roman trial of Jesus, let us repeat what we have already said: that the conduct of Pilate, when the prisoner was first brought before him, seems to have been marked by judicial regularity and solemnity; that the Roman procurator seems to have deported himself in a manner worthy of his office; that, in the beginning, he appears to have resolved to observe due forms of law in the proceedings, to the end that justice might be attained; and that, after a comparatively regular trial, he pronounced an absolute verdict of acquittal. Thus far the course of Pilate is manly and courageous. But with the return of the prisoner from Herod, unmanliness and cowardice begin.

This last act of the great drama presents a pitiable spectacle of Roman degeneracy. A Roman governor of courtly origin, clothed with *imperium,* with a

Praetorian Cohort at his command, and the military authority and resources of an empire at his back, cringes and crouches before a Jerusalem mob. The early Christian writers characterized Pilate with a single term ($\dot{\alpha}\nu\alpha\nu\delta\rho\dot{\iota}\alpha$), "unmanliness." They were right. This word is a summary, accurate and complete, of the character of the man.

There is inherent in the highest and noblest of the human species a quality of courage which knows no fear; that prefers death and annihilation to dishonor and disgrace; that believes, with Caesar, that it is better to die at once than to live always in fear of death; and, with Mahomet, that Paradise will be found in the shadow of the crossing of swords. This quality of courage is peculiar to no race of men and to no form of civilization. It has existed everywhere and at all times. It causes the spirit of man to tread the earth like a lion and to mount the air like an eagle. The ancient barbarians of Gaul believed that lightning was a menace from the skies; and amidst the very fury of the storm, from their great bows they sent arrows heavenward as a defiance to the gods. This quality of courage, which is natural to man, Pilate lacked. And when we think of his cowardly, cringing, crouching, vacillating conduct before a few fanatical priests in Jerusalem, another scene at another time comes up before us. The Tenth Legion rises in mutiny and defies Julius Caesar. The mighty Roman summons his rebellious soldiers to the Field of Mars, reads to them the Roman riot act, and threatens to dismiss them not only from his favor but from Roman military service. The veterans of a hundred Gallic battlefields are subdued and conquered by the tone and glance of a single man; and with tearful eyes, beg forgiveness, and ask to be permitted to follow once again him and his eagles to the feast of victory and of death. Imagine, if you can, Caesar in the place of Pilate. It is not difficult to conceive the fate of a vulgar rabble who persisted in annoying such a Roman by demanding the blood of an innocent man.

But the cowardice and pusillanimity of the Roman governor are not properly illustrated by comparison with the courage and magnanimity of a Roman general. At the trial of Jesus, Pilate was acting in a judicial capacity, and was essentially a judge. His character, then, may be best understood by contrasting it with another judge in another age and country. His craven qualities will then be manifest.

The greatest of the English jurists and judges was Sir Edward Coke. His legal genius was superb and his judicial labors prodigious. During the greater part of his professional career he slept only six hours each night, "and from three in the morning till nine at night he read or took notes of the cases tried in Westminster Hall with as little interruption as possible." He was great not only as a judge, but as an advocate as well. The consummate skill with which he argued the intricate cases of Lord Cromwell and Edward Shelley, brought him a practice never before equaled in England, and made him renowned as the greatest lawyer of the times. If his erudition was profound, his powers of advocacy brilliant, his personal and judicial courage was magnificent. He not only repeatedly defied and ridiculed his colleagues on the bench, but more than once excited the wrath and braved the anger of the king. He fearlessly planted himself upon the ancient and inalienable rights of Englishmen; and, time and time again, interposed his robe of office between the privileges of the Commons and the aggressions of the Crown. He boldly declared that a royal proclamation could not make that an offense which was not an offense before. His unswerving independence was well illustrated in a case brought before him in 1616. The question at issue was the validity of a grant made by the king to the Bishop of Lichfield of a benefice to be held *in commendam*. King James, through his attorney-general, Bacon, commanded the chief justice to delay judgment till he himself had discussed the question with the judges. Bacon, at Coke's request, sent a letter containing the same command to each of the judges. Coke then obtained their signatures to a paper declaring that the instructions of the attorney-general were illegal, and that they were bound to proceed with the case. The king became very angry, summoned the judges before him in the council chamber, declared to them his kingly prerogative, and forbade them to discuss his royal privileges in ordinary arguments before their tribunal. Coke's colleagues fell upon their knees, cowed and terrified before the royal bigot and despot, and begged his pardon for having expressed an opinion that had excited his displeasure. But Coke refused to yield, and, when asked if, in the future, he would delay a case at the king's order, he bravely replied that on all occasions and under any emergency, he would do nothing unworthy of himself or his office as an English citizen and judge. And rather than prostitute the high prerogatives of his court, he indignantly and contemptuously hurled his judicial mantle into the face of the Stuart king. How much grander and nobler was the conduct of Coke, the Englishman, than that of Pilate, the cowardly, pusillanimous Roman! Both were judges, both stood in the shadow of the majesty and menace of a throne, both were threatened with royal wrath, both held high judicial places under the governments of the most vast and glorious empires that this world has known. Coke preferred the dictates of his conscience to the decrees of his king; and his name remains forever enshrined in the minds and memories of men as the noblest type of a brave and righteous judge. For a miserable mess of Roman political potage, Pilate forfeited his birthright to the most splendid and illustrious example of judicial integrity and courage in the history of the earth; and his name remains forever a hissing and reproach, as the worst specimen of the corrupt and cowardly judge that mankind has known.

If it be objected that the position of Pilate was more painful and precarious than that of Coke, because the Roman was confronted by a wild and furious mob, reply must then be made that both the spirit and letter of Roman laws forbade surrender by Roman governors and administrators of the principles of justice to the blind passions of the multitude. This spirit was, in a later age, set forth in the laws of Justinian, when reproduction was made of the proclamations of the emperors Diocletian and Maximian, on the occasion of a public riot, that "the vain clamors of the people are not to be heeded, seeing that it is in no wise necessary to pay any attention to the cries of those desiring the acquittal of the guilty, or the condemnation of the innocent."[13]

Pilate yielded to the demands of the mob when his country's laws forbade it. His intellect willed the execution of an innocent man when his conscience condemned it. "Such was the man whose cowardice, made manifest in the most supreme and memorable act of injustice the world has ever known, was destined to earn him eternal infamy. To him and to no others pointed the poet as

'colui
Che fece per viltate il gran rifiuto;'

to him, the prototype of that long train of those who were never quite alive, who vainly sought glory in this world, vainly dreaded infamy; who, ever wavering betwixt good and evil, washed their hands; who, like the neutral angels of the threshold, were neither faithful nor rebellious; who are equally despised by pity and justice; who render themselves

'A Dio spiacenti ed ai nemici sui.'

And what man other than Pilate was ever placed so typically, in such accordance with the eyes of the poet, between the Son of God and His enemies, between justice and mercy, between right and wrong, between the Emperor and the Jews, and has refused either issue of the dilemma?

"Was it Celestine, Diocletian, or Esau? But they of two things chose the one; and who knows but that they chose the better? A hermitage and a mess of potage may under many aspects be better worth than the papacy renounced by Celestine, than the empire abdicated by Diocletian, or than the birthright bartered by Esau. But Pilate refused to choose, and his refusal was great—great enough to justify the antonomasia of Dante—and it was cowardly. He refused not only the great gift of free will, in a case when a free choice was his absolute duty. When admitted, like the fallen angels, to the great choice between good and evil, he did not cleave for ever to the good, as did S. Michael, or to the evil, as did Lucifer, but he refused a power which for him was the fount of duty and which cost the life of a man and the right of an innocent."

But was Pilate alone guilty of the crime of the crucifixion? Were the Jews wholly blameless? This raises the question: Who were the real crucifiers of the Christ, the Jews or the Romans? That the Jews were the instigators and the Romans the consummators of the crucifixion is evident from the Gospel narratives. The Jews made the complaint, and the Romans ordered and effected the arrest of the prisoner in Gethsemane. Having tried Him before their own tribunal, the Jews then led Jesus away to the Roman governor, and in the Praetorium accused Him and furnished evidence against Him. But the final act of crucifying was a Roman act. It is true that Jewish elements were present in the crucifixion of Jesus. The death draught offered Him on the cross suggests a humane provision of Hebrew law. This drink was usually administered among the Hebrews "so that the delinquent might lose clear consciousness through the ensuing intoxication." Again, the body of Jesus was removed from the cross and buried before it was night. This was in deference to an ancient custom of the Jews

to bury before sunset criminals who had first been executed by stoning for the crime of blasphemy and had then been subjected to the indignity of being hung upon a tree, in conformity with a Mosaic ordinance contained in Deut. xxi. 22. But these two incidents exhaust the Jewish features of the crucifixion; and, besides, these elements were merely physical. The spiritual or moral features, involving turpitude and crime, are entirely different considerations from those that are simply historical. The question still arises: Who were the morally guilty parties? Who were the directly responsible agents of the crucifixion, the Jews or the Romans? Upon whom should the greater blame rest, if both were guilty? A passage from St. John seems to indicate that the Jews were the bearers of the greater sin. Replying to a question of Pilate concerning the procurator's power to crucify Him, "Jesus answered, Thou couldest have no power at all against me, except it were given thee from above; therefore he that delivered me unto thee hath the greater sin."[14] According to many commentators, Jesus referred to Caiaphas; according to others, He spoke of Judas as the person who had the greater sin. But in any case it is certain that He did not intend to involve the whole Jewish nation in the crime of His arrest and execution. The language of the scriptural context indicates a single person. Pilate, on the one hand, is made the silent instrument in the hands of God for the accomplishment of the designs of Heaven. Caiaphas, on the other hand, is probably referred to as the one having the greater sin, because, being the high priest of the Sanhedrin, he better understood the questions involved in the religious charge of blasphemy, and was, therefore, the greater sinner against the laws of God, in the matter of the injustice then being perpetrated.

Aside from the religious questions involved, and speaking in the light of history and law, our own judgment is that the real crucifiers of the Christ were the Romans, and that Pilate and his countrymen should bear the greater blame. It is true that the Jews were the instigators, the accusers. But Pilate was the judge whose authority was absolute. The Jews were powerless to inflict the death penalty. Pilate had the final disposition of all matters of life and death. In short, he could have prevented the crucifixion of Jesus. He did not do so; and upon him and his countrymen should rest the censure of Heaven and the execration of mankind.

But, admitting that the priests of the Sanhedrin were equally guilty with Pilate and the Romans, does it follow that all Jews of the days of Jesus who were not participants in the crime against him, should suffer for the folly and criminal conduct of a mere fragment of a Sadducean sect? Is it not true that the Jewish people, as a race, were not parties to the condemnation and execution of the Christ? Is it not reasonable to suppose that the masses in Palestine were friendly to the democratic Reformer who was the friend of the poor, the lame, and the blind? Did not the reception of his miracles and his triumphal entry into Jerusalem indicate His popularity with the plain people? Is it not historically true that the great body of the Jewish population in Judea, in Galilee, in Samaria, and in Perea, was unfriendly to the members of the Sanhedrin, and regarded them as political renegades and religious delinquents? Is it not reasonably certain that a large majority of the countrymen of Jesus were his ardent well-wishers and sincerely regretted his untimely end? Is it possible to conceive that these friends and well-wishers were the inheritors of the curse of Heaven because of the crime of Golgotha? If not, is it rational to suppose that their innocent descendants have been the victims of this curse?

The cruel and senseless notion of the implacable wrath of Deity has prevailed in all the ages as an explanation of the destruction of Jerusalem and the dispersion and persecution of the Jews. It is worse than nonsense to see in this event anything but the operation of vulgar physical forces of the most ordinary kind. The fall of Jerusalem was a most natural and consequential thing. It was not even an extraordinary historical occurrence, even in Jewish history. Titus did not so completely destroy Jerusalem as did Nebuchadnezzar before him. Razing cities to the ground was a customary Roman act, a form of pastime, a characteristic Roman proceeding in the case of stubborn and rebellious towns. Scipio razed Carthage and drove Carthaginians into the most remote corners of the earth. Was any Roman or Punic god interested in this event? Caesar destroyed many Gallic cities and scattered Gauls throughout the world. Was any deity concerned about these things?

Roman admiration was at times enkindled, but Roman clemency was never gained by deeds of valor directed against the arms of Rome. Neither Hannibal nor Mithradates, Vercingetorix nor Jugurtha, the grandest of her enemies, received any mercy at her hands. To oppose her will, was to invite destruction; and the sequel was a mere question of "the survival of the fittest." The most turbulent, rebellious and determined of all the imperial dependencies was the province of Judea. The Jews regarded the Romans as idolaters; and, instead of obeying them as masters, despised and defied them as barbarians. When this spirit became manifest and promised to be perpetual, the dignity of the Roman name as well as the safety of the Roman State, demanded the destruction of Jerusalem and the dispersion of the Jews. And destruction and dispersion followed as naturally as any profane effect follows any vulgar cause.

The Irish, another splendid race, are being dispersed throughout the earth by the English domination of Ireland. Is anybody so keenly discerning as to see in Irish dispersion a divine or superhuman agency? Is it not, after all, the simple operation of the same brutal, physical forces that destroyed Carthage and Jerusalem, and, in a latter century, dismembered Poland?

But the advocates of the divine wrath theory quote Scriptures and point to prophecy in support of their contention. Then Scriptures must be pitted against Scriptures. The last prayer of the Master on the cross must be made to repeal every earlier Scriptural prophecy or decree. "Father, forgive them, for they know not what they do," is the sublimest utterance in the literature of the world. It is the epitome of every Christian virtue and of all religious truth. This proclamation from the cross repealed the Mosaic law of hereditary sin; placed upon a personal basis responsibility for offenses against God and man; and served notice upon future generations that those who "know not what they do" are entitled to be spared and forgiven. To believe that God ignored the prayer of Christ on the cross; and that the centuries of persecution of the Jews which followed, were but the fulfillment of prophecy and fate, is to assail the Messiahship of Jesus and to question the goodness and mercy of Jehovah. Jesus knew the full meaning of His prayer and was serious unto death. To believe that the Father rejected the petition of the Son is to destroy the equality of the persons of the Trinity by investing one with the authority and power to review, revise, and reject the judgments and petitions of the others. If the Christian doctrine be true that Christ was God "manifest in the flesh"; if the doctrine of the Trinity be true that God the Father, God the Son, and God the Holy Ghost, are one and the same, eternal and inseparable, then the prayer of Jesus on the cross was not a petition, but a declaration that the malefactors of the crucifixion, who, in the blindness of ignorance, had helped to kill the Son of Man, would receive at the Last Day the benefits of the amnesty of the Father of mercy and forgiveness.

If the perpetrators of the great injustice of the Sanhedrin and of the Praetorium are to be forgiven because they knew not what they did, is there any justice, human or divine, in persecuting their innocent descendants of all lands and ages? "When Sir Moses Montefiore was taunted by a political opponent with the memory of Calvary and described by him as one who sprang from the murderers who crucified the world's Redeemer, the next morning the Jewish philanthropist, whom Christendom has learned to honor, called upon his assailant and showed him the record of his ancestors which had been kept for two thousand years, and which showed that their home had been in Spain for two hundred years before Jesus of Nazareth was born." This half-humorous anecdote illustrates the utter absurdity and supreme injustice of connecting the modern Jew with ancient tragic history. The elemental forces of reason, logic, courage and sympathy, wrapped up and interwoven in every impulse and fiber of the human mind and heart, will be forever in rebellion against the monstrous doctrine of centuries of shame, exile and persecution visited upon an entire race, because of the sins and crimes of a handful of their progenitors who lived more than a thousand years before.

But, if the visitation of the sins of the fathers upon the sons is to be maintained, and perpetuated as a form of divine, if not of human justice, then, why not, at least, be consistent in the application of the principle? Many philosophers and critics have detected a striking kinship between the teachings of Socrates and those of Jesus. A celebrated historian closes a chapter of the history of Greece with this sentence: "Thus perished the greatest and most original of the Grecian philosophers (Socrates), whose uninspired wisdom made the nearest approach to the divine morality of the Gospel."[15] The indictments against the philosopher of Athens and the Prophet of Nazareth were strikingly similar. Socrates was charged with corrupting Athenian youth; Jesus, with perverting the nation. Socrates was charged with treason against Athens; Jesus, with treason against Rome. Both were charged with blasphemy; the Athenian, with blasphemy of the

Olympic gods; the Nazarene, with blaspheming Jehovah. Both sealed with their blood the faith that was in them. If the descendants of the crucifiers of the Christ are to be persecuted, brutalized, and exiled for the sins of the fathers, why not apply the same pitiless law of hereditary punishment to the descendants of the Athenian dicasts who administered hemlock to the greatest sage of antiquity? Why not persecute all the Greeks of the earth, wherever found, because of the injustice of the Areopagus?

Coming back from antiquity and the Greeks to modern times in America, let us express the hope that all forms of race prejudice and persecution will soon cease forever. It is a truth well known of all intelligent men that racial prejudice against the Jew has not completely vanished from the minds and hearts of Gentiles; that political freedom in an enlightened age has not brought with it full religious tolerance and social recognition; that the Jew enjoys the freedom of the letter, but is still under the ban of the spirit. It is not necessary to go to Russia to prove this contention. In 1896, Adolf von Sonnenthal, the greatest of modern actors, who has covered the Austrian stage with glory, celebrated the fortieth anniversary of his entrance into theatrical life. The City Council of Vienna refused to extend him the freedom of the city, because he was a Jew. In 1906, Madame Bernhardt, the most marvelous living woman, while acting in Canada, was insulted by having spoiled eggs thrown upon the stage amidst shouts of "Down with the Jewess]" This outrage called forth a letter of apology, which appeared in public print, from Sir Wilfred Laurier, Prime Minister of the Dominion. In the summer of 1907, the sister of Senator Isidor Rayner, of Maryland, was refused admission to an Atlantic City hotel because she was a Jewess. Be it remembered that these several acts of prejudice and persecution did not happen in the Middle Ages, or under the government of the Romanoffs. Two of them occurred at the beginning of the twentieth century, beneath the flags of two of the freest and most civilized nations of the globe. What have Americans to say of the exclusion of a virtuous, refined, intelligent sister of a great American senator from an American hotel for no other reason than that she was a Jewess; that is, that she was of the same race with the Savior of mankind?

There is certainly no place for religious intolerance and race prejudice beneath our flag. False and hypocritical our religion, if while professing faith in Jesus we continue to persecute those for whom He prayed! In vain did Washington, marching in Liberty's vanguard, "lead Freedom's eaglets to their feast"; in vain the proclamation of the Declaration of Independence and the adoption of the Constitution at Philadelphia, a hundred years ago; in vain the bonfires and orations of the nation's natal day, if our boasted liberties are to exist in theory, but not in practice, in fancy, but not in fact!

Let no persecutor of the Jew lay the unction to his soul that he is justified by the tragedy of Golgotha; for he who persecutes in the name of religion is a spiritual barbarian, an intellectual savage. Let this same persecutor not make the mistake of supposing that the Jews are wholly responsible for the persecution that has been heaped upon them. Before he falls into the foolish blunder of such a supposition, let him ponder the testimony of several Gentile experts upon the subject. Let him read "The Scattered Nation," a brilliant lecture on the Jew by the late Zebulon Vance, of North Carolina, in which occurs this sentence: "If the Jew is a bad job, in all honesty we should contemplate him as the handiwork of our own civilization." Let him find Shakespearean confirmation of this statement in "The Merchant of Venice," Act III, Scene i. If the Jew-baiter objects that this is the imagination of a poet, let us then point him to the testimony of a great historian and statesman to prove to him that the Gentile is in great measure responsible for the causes that have produced Jewish persecution.

In the British House of Commons, on April 17, 1833, a bill for the removal of the disabilities of the Jews was the subject of parliamentary discussion. Lord Macaulay took part in the debate and spoke as follows:

The honorable member for Oldham tells us that the Jews are naturally a mean race, a money-getting race; that they are averse to all honorable callings; that they neither sow nor reap; that they have neither flocks nor herds; that usury is the only pursuit for which they are fit; that they are destitute of all elevated and amiable sentiments.

Such, sir, has in every age been the reasoning of bigots. They never fail to plead in justification of persecution the vices which persecution has engendered. England has been legally a home to the Jews less than half a century, and we revile them because they do not feel for England more than a half patriotism.

We treat them as slaves, and wonder that they do not regard us as brethern. We drive them to mean occupations, and then reproach them for not embracing honorable professions. We long forbade them to possess land, and we complain that they chiefly occupy themselves in trade. We shut them out from all the paths of ambition, and then we despise them for taking refuge in avarice.

During many ages we have, in our dealings with them, abused our immense superiority of force, and then we are disgusted because they have recourse to that cunning which is the natural and universal defence of the weak against the violence of the strong. But were they always a mere money-changing, money-getting, money-hoarding race? Nobody knows better than my honorable friend, the member for the University of Oxford, that there is nothing in their national character which unfits them for the highest duties of citizens.

He knows that, in the infancy of civilization, when our island was as savage as New Guinea, when letters and art were still unknown to Athens, when scarcely a thatched hut stood on what was afterwards the site of Rome, this contemned people had their fenced cities and cedar palaces, their splendid Temple, their fleets of merchant ships, their schools of sacred learning, their great statesmen and soldiers, their natural philosophers, their historians and their poets.

What nation ever contended more manfully against overwhelming odds for its independence and religion? What nation ever, in its last agonies, gave such signal proofs of what may be accomplished by a brave despair? And if, in the course of many centuries, the depressed descendants of warriors and sages have degenerated from the qualities of their fathers; if, while excluded from the blessings of law and bowed down under the yoke of slavery, they have contracted some of the vices of outlaws and slaves, shall we consider this is a matter of reproach to them? Shall we not rather consider it as a matter of shame and remorse to ourselves? Let us do justice to them. Let us open to them the door of the House of Commons. Let us open to them every career in which ability and energy can be displayed. Till we have done this, let us not presume to say that there is no genius among the countrymen of Isaiah, no heroism among the descendants of the Maccabees.

If the persecutor of the Jew is not moved by the eloquence of Macaulay or by the satire and sarcasm of Shakespeare, then let him call the roll of Hebrew great names and watch the mighty procession as it moves. Abraham among patriarchs; Moses among lawgivers; Isaiah and Jeremiah among prophets; Philo,

Maimonides, Spinoza, and Mendelsohn among philosophers; Herschel, Sylvester, Jacobi, and Kroecker among mathematicians and astronomers; Josephus, Neander, Graetz, Palgrave, and Geiger among historians; Mendelssohn, Meyerbeer, Offenbach, Goldmark, Joachim, Rubinstein, and Strauss among musicians; Sonnenthal, Possart, Rachel, and Bernhardt among actors and actresses; Disraeli, Gambetta, Castelar, Lasker, Cremieux, and Benjamin among statesmen; Halevi and Heine among poets; Karl Marx and Samuel Gompers among labor leaders and political economists; the Rothschilds, Bleichroeders, Schiffs, and Seligmans among financiers; Auerbach and Nordau among novelists; Sir Moses Montefiore and Baron Hirsch among philanthropists!

But there are no Caesars, no Napoleons, no Shakespeares, no Aristotles among them, you say? Maybe so; but what of that? Admitting that this is true, is anything proved by the fact? These characters represented mountain peaks of intellect, and were the isolated products of different races and different centuries. It may be justly observed that, of their kind, no others were comparable to them. But if the "mountain-peak" theory is to govern as to the intellectuality of races, will it be seriously contended that any one of the last-mentioned characters was equal in either spiritual or intellectual grandeur to the Galilean peasant, Jesus of Nazareth? If colossal forms of intellect and soul be invoked, does not the Jew still lead the universe?

Jesus was the most perfect product of Jewish spiritual creation, the most precious gem of human life. The most brilliant and civilized nations of the earth worship Him as God, "manifest in the flesh, justified by the Spirit, seen of angels, preached unto the Gentiles, believed on in the world, received up into glory."[16]

Both skeptics and believers of all ages have alike pronounced His name with reverence and respect. Even the flippant, sarcastic soul of Voltaire was awed, softened and subdued by the sweetness of His life and the majesty of His character.[17]

"If the life and death of Socrates are those of a sage," said Rousseau, "the life and death of Jesus are those of a God."[18]

"Jesus of Nazareth," says Carlyle, "our divinest symbol! Higher has the human thought not yet reached. A symbol of quite perennial, infinite character, whose significance will ever demand to be anew inquired into, and anew made manifest."[19]

"Jesus Christ," says Herder, "is in the noblest and most perfect sense, the realized ideal of humanity."[20]

"He is," says Strauss, "the highest object we can possibly imagine with respect to religion, the Being without whose presence in the mind perfect piety is impossible."[21]

"The Christ of the Gospels," says Renan, "is the most beautiful incarnation of God in the most beautiful of forms. His beauty is eternal; His reign will never end."[22]

Max Nordau betrays secret Jewish pride in Jesus when he says: "Jesus is soul of our soul, even as he is flesh of our flesh. Who, then, could think of excluding him from the people of Israel? St. Peter will remain the only Jew who has said of the Son of David, 'I know not the man.' Putting aside the Messianic mission, this man is ours. He honors our race, and we claim him as we claim the Gospels—flowers of Jewish literature and only Jewish."

"Is it a truth," asks Keim, "or is it nothing but words, when this virtuous God-allied human life is called the noblest blossom of a noble tree, the crown of the cedar of Israel? A full vigorous life in a barren time, a new building among ruins, an erect strong nature among broken ones, a Son of God among the godless and the God-forsaken, one who was joyous, hopeful, generous among those who were mourning and in despair, a freeman among slaves, a saint among sinners—by this contradiction to the facts of the time, by this gigantic exaltation above the depressed uniformity of the century, by this compensation for stagnation, retrogression, and the sickness of death in progress, health, force and color of eternal youth—finally, by the lofty uniqueness of what he achieved, of his purity, of his God-nearness—he produces, even with regard to endless new centuries that have *through him* been saved from stagnation and retrogression, the impression of mysterious solitariness, superhuman miracle, divine creation."[23]

"Between Him and whoever else in the world," said Napoleon at St. Helena, "there is no possible term of comparison."[24]

Throughout Napoleonic literature two names constantly recur as exhibiting the Corsican's ideals of spiritual and intellectual perfection. These names are those of Jesus Christ and Julius Caesar. Napoleon's stupendous genius and incomprehensible destiny formed the basis of a secret conviction within his soul that with Jesus and Caesar displaced, he himself would be the grandest ornament of history. But in the mind of the emperor there was no element of equality or comparison between Jesus and Caesar. The latter he regarded as the crown and consummation of Roman manhood, the most superb character of the ancient world. The former he believed to be divine.

It was the custom of Napoleon while in exile at St. Helena to converse almost daily about the illustrious men of antiquity and to compare them with himself. On one occasion while talking upon his favorite theme with an officer, one of the companions of his exile, he suddenly stopped and asked: "But can you tell me who Jesus Christ was?" In reply, the officer candidly confessed that he had never thought much about the Nazarene. "Well, then," said Napoleon, "I will tell you." The illustrious captive then compared Jesus with the heroes of antiquity and finally with himself. The comparison demonstrated how paltry and contemptible was everything human when viewed in the light of the divine character and sublime achievements of the Man of Nazareth. "I think I understand somewhat of human nature," said Napoleon, "and I tell you all these were men, and I am a man, but not one is like Him; Jesus Christ was more than man. Alexander, Caesar, Charlemagne, and myself founded great empires; but upon what did the creations of our genius depend? Upon force. Jesus alone founded His empire upon love, and to this very day millions would die for Him."[25]

We have every reason to believe that the homage paid the character of Jesus by Napoleon was not merely the product of his brain, but was also the humble tribute of his heart. When the disasters of the Russian campaign broke upon his fortunes, when "the infantry of the snow and the cavalry of the wild blast scattered his legions like winter's withered leaves," the iron-hearted, granite-featured man who had "conquered the Alps and had mingled the eagles of France with the eagles of the crags," only laughed and joked. But, while contemplating the life and death of Jesus, he became serious, meditative and humble. And when he came to write his last will and testament, he made this sentence the opening paragraph: "I die in the Roman Catholic Apostolical religion, in the bosom of which I was born more than fifty years ago."[26] The Christianity of Napoleon has been questioned. It is respectfully submitted that only an ungenerous criticism will attribute hypocrisy to this final testimony of his religious faith. The imperial courage, the grandeur of character, and the loftiness of life of the greatest of the emperors negative completely the thought of insincerity in a declaration made at a time when every earthly inducement to misrepresentation had passed forever.

But Jesus was not the Christ, the Savior of warrior-kings alone, in the hour of death. On the battlefield of Inkerman a humble soldier fell mortally wounded. He managed to crawl to his tent before he died. When found he was lying face downward with the open Bible beside him. His right hand was glued with his lifeblood to Chapter XI., Verse 25 of St. John. When the hand was lifted, these words, containing the ever-living promise of the Master, could be clearly traced: "I am the resurrection and the life: he that believeth in me, though he were dead, yet shall he live."

PART II
GRAECO-ROMAN PAGANISM

GRAECO-ROMAN PAGANISM

Extent of the Roman Empire at the Time of Christ.— The policy of ancient Rome was to extend and hold her possessions by force of arms. She made demands; and if they were not complied with, she spurned the medium of diplomacy and appealed for arbitrament to the god of battles. Her achievements were the achievements of war.

Her glories were the glories of combat. Her trophies were the treasures of conquered provinces and chained captives bowed in grief and shame. Her theory was that "might makes right"; and in vindication and support of this theory she imbued her youth with a martial spirit, trained them in the use of arms from childhood to manhood, and stationed her legions wherever she extended her empire. Thus, military discipline and the fortune of successful warefare formed the basis of the prosperity of Rome.

At the period of which we write, her invincible legions had accomplished the conquest of the civilized earth. Britain, Gaul, Spain, Italy, Illyria, Greece, Asia Minor, Africa, Egypt, and the islands of the Mediterranean—six hundred thousand square leagues of the most fertile territory in the world—had been subdued to the Roman will and had become obedient to Roman decrees. "The empire of the Romans," says Gibbon, "filled the world, and when that empire fell into the hands of a single person, the world became a safe and dreary prison for his enemies. The slave of imperial despotism, whether he was compelled to drag his gilded chain in Rome and the Senate, or to wear out a life of exile on the barren rock of Seriphus, or on the frozen banks of the Danube, expected his fate in silent despair. To resist was fatal, and it was impossible to fly. On every side he was encompassed by a vast extent of sea and land, which he could never hope to traverse without being discovered, seized, and restored to his irritated master. Beyond the frontiers, his anxious view could discover nothing, except the ocean, inhospitable deserts, hostile tribes of barbarians, of fierce manners and unknown language, or dependent kings who would gladly purchase the emperor's protection by the sacrifice of an obnoxious fugitive. 'Wherever you are,' said Cicero to the exiled Marcellus, 'remember that you are equally within the power of the conqueror.' "

In obedience to a universal law of development and growth, when the Roman empire had reached the limits of physical expansion, when Roman conquest was complete, when Roman laws and letters had reached approximate perfection, and when Roman civilization had attained its crown and consummation, Roman decline began. The birth of the empire marked the beginning of the end. It was then that the shades of night commenced to gather slowly upon the Roman world; and that the Roman ship of state began to move slowly but inevitably, upon a current of indescribable depravity and degeneracy, toward the abyss. The Roman giant bore upon his shoulders the treasures of a conquered world; and Bacchus-like, reeled, crowned and drunken, to his doom.

No period of human history is so marked by lust and licentiousness as the history of Rome at the beginning of the Christian era. The Roman religion had fallen into contempt. The family instinct was dead, and the marital relation was a mockery and a shame. The humane spirit had vanished from Roman hearts, and slavery was the curse of every province of the empire. The destruction of infants and the gladiatorial games were mere epitomes of Roman brutality and degeneracy. Barbarity, corruption and dissoluteness pervaded every form of Roman life.

A perfect picture of the depravity of the times about which we write may be had from a perusal of the Roman satirists, Tacitus and Juvenal. The ordinary Roman debauchee was not the sole victim of their wrath. They chiseled the hideous features of the Caesars with a finer stroke than that employed by Phidias and Praxiteles in carving statues of the Olympic gods.

The purpose of Part II of this volume is to give coloring and atmosphere to the picture of the trial and crucifixion of Jesus by describing: (1) The Graeco-Roman religion; and (2) the Graeco-Roman social life, during the century preceding and the century following the birth of the Savior.

I.—THE GRAECO-ROMAN RELIGION

Origin and Multiplicity of the Roman Gods. —The Romans acquired their gods by inheritance, by importation, and by manufacture. The Roman race sprang from a union of Etruscans, Latins, and Sabines; and the gods of these different tribes, naturalized and adopted, were the first deities of Rome. Chief among them were Janus, Jupiter, Juno, and Minerva. Other early Roman deities were Sol, the Sun, and Luna the Moon, both of Sabine origin; Mater Matuta, Mother of Day; Divus Pater Tiberinus, or Father Tiber; Fontus, the god of fountains; Vesta, the goddess of the hearth; and the Lares and Penates, household gods.

These primitive Italian divinities were at first mere abstractions, simple nature-powers; but later they were Hellenized and received plastic form. The Greeks and Romans had a common ancestry and the amalgamation of their religions was an easy matter. The successive steps in the process of blending the two forms of worship are historical. From Cumae, one of the oldest Greek settlements in Italy, the famous Sibylline books found their way to Rome; and through these books the Greek gods and their worship established themselves in Italy. The date of the arrival of several of the Hellenic deities is well ascertained. The first temple to Apollo was vowed in the year 351 A.U.C. To check a lingering epidemic of pestilence and disease, the worship of Aesculapius was introduced from Epidaurus into Rome in the year 463. In 549, Cybele, the Idaean mother, was imported from Phrygia, in the shape of a black stone, and was worshiped at Rome by order of the Sibylline books.

In various ways, the Hellenization of the Roman religion was accomplished. The Decemviri, to whom the consulting of the Sibylline books was intrusted, frequently interpreted them to mean that certain foreign gods should be invited at once to take up their residence in Rome.

The introduction of Greek literature also resulted in the importation of Greek gods. The tragedies of Livius Andronicus and the comedies of Naevius, founded upon Greek legends of gods and heroes, were presented in Rome in the later years of the third century B.C. Fragments of Greek literature also began to make their way into the Capital about this time. Philosophers, rhetoricians, and grammarians flocked from Greece to Italy and brought with them the works of Homer, Hesiod and the Greek philosophers, whose writings were permeated with Greek mythology.

Grecian sculpture was as potent as Grecian literature in transforming and Hellenizing the religion of Rome. The subjugation of the Greek colonies in the south of Italy and the conquests of Greek cities like Syracuse and Corinth in the East, brought together in Rome the masterpieces of the Greek sculptors.

A determined effort was made from time to time by the patriotic Romans to destroy Hellenic influence and to preserve in their original purity early Roman forms of worship. But all attempts were futile. The average Roman citizen, though practical and unimaginative, was still enamored of the beautiful myths and exquisite statues of the Greek gods. And it was only by Hellenizing their own deities that they could bring themselves into touch and communion with the Hellenic spirit. The aesthetical and fascinating influence of the Greek language, literature and sculpture, was overwhelming. "At bottom, the Roman religion was based only on two ideas—the might of the gods who were friendly to Rome, and the power of the ceremonies over the gods. How could a religion, so poverty-stricken of thought, with its troops of phantom gods, beingless shadows and deified abstractions, remain unscathed and unaltered when it came in contact with the profusion of the Greek religion, with its circle of gods, so full of life, so thoroughly anthropomorphised, so deeply interwoven into everything human?"[1]

Not only from Greece but from every conquered country, strange gods were brought into Italy and placed in the Roman pantheon. When a foreign city was besieged and captured, the Romans, after a preliminary ceremony, invited the native gods to leave their temples and go to Rome where, they were assured, they would have much grander alters and would receive a more enthusiastic worship. It was a religious belief of the ancient masters of the world that gods could be enticed from their allegiance and induced to emigrate. In their foreign wars, the Romans frequently kept the names of their own gods secret to prevent the enemy from bribing them.

The gods at Rome increased in number just in proportion that the empire expanded. The admission of foreign territory brought with it the introduction of strange gods into the Roman worship.

When the Romans needed a new god and could not find a foreign one that pleased them, they deliberately manufactured a special deity for the occasion. In the breaking up and multiplication of the god-idea, they excelled all the nations of antiquity. It was the duty of the pontiffs to manufacture a divinity whenever an emergency arose and one was needed. The god-casting business was a regular employment of the Decemviri and the Quindecemviri; and a perusal of the pages of Roman history reveals these god-makers actively engaged in their workshops making some new deity to meet some new development in Roman life.

The extent of the polytheistic notions of the ancient Romans is almost inconceivable to the modern mind. Not only were the great forces of nature deified, but the simplest elements of time, of thought, and action. Ordinary mental abstractions were clothed with the attributes of gods. Mens (Mind), Pudicitia (Chastity), Pietas (Piety), Fides (Fidelity), Concordia (Concord), Virtus (Courage), Spes (Hope), and Voluptas (Pleasure), were all deities of the human soul, and were enthusiastically worshiped by the Romans. A single human action was frequently broken into parts each of which had a little god of its own. The beginning of a marriage had one deity and its conclusion, another. Cunina was the cradle-goddess of a child. Statilinus, Edusa, Potnia, Paventia, Fabelinus and Catius were other goddesses who presided over other phases of its infancy. Juventas was the goddess of its youth; and, in case of loss of parents, Orbona was the goddess that protected its orphanage.

Any political development in the Roman state necessitated a new divinity to mark the change. In the early periods of their history, the Romans used cattle as a medium of exchange in buying and bartering. Pecunia was then the goodness of such exchange. But when, in later times, copper money came into use, a god called Aesculanus was created to preside over the finances; and when, still later, silver money began to be used, the god Argentarius was called into being to protect the coinage. This Argentarius was naturally the son of Aesculanus.

Not only the beneficent but the malign forces of nature were deified. Pests, plagues, and tempests had their special divinities who were to be placated. "There were particular gods for every portion of a dwelling—the door, the threshold of the door, and even the hinges of the door. There was a special god for each different class—even the most menial and the most immoral; and a special divinity for those who were afflicted in a peculiar manner, such as the childless, the maimed or the blind. There was the god of the stable, and the goddess of the horses; there were gods for merchants, artists, poets and tillers of the soil. The gods must be invoked before the harvest could be reaped; and not even a tree could be felled in the forest without supplicating the unknown god who might inhabit it."[2]

The extreme of the Roman divinity-making process was the deification of mere negative ideas. Tranquillitas Vacuna was the goddess of "doing nothing."

Not only were special actions and peculiar ideas broken up and subdivided with an appropriate divinity for each part or subdivision, but the individual gods themselves were subdivided and multiplied. It is said that there were three hundred Jupiters in Rome. This means that Jupiter was worshiped under three hundred different forms. Jupiter Pluvius, Jupiter Fulgurator, Jupiter Tonans, Jupiter Fulminator, Jupiter Imbricitor, Jupiter Serenator, were only a few designations of the supreme deity of the Romans.

It will thus be seen that polytheism was insatible in its thirst for new and strange gods. When the god-casting business was once begun, there was no end to it. And when the Roman empire had reached its greatest expansion, and Roman public and private life had attained to complete development, the deities of the Roman religion were innumerable. No pantheon could hold them, and no Roman could remember the names of all. Temples of the gods were everywhere to be found throughout the empire; and where there were no altars or temples, certain trees, stones and rocks were decorated with garlands and worshiped as sacred places which the gods were supposed to frequent. Thus the Roman world became crowded with holy places, and the gods and goddesses became an innumerable host. Petronius makes a countrywoman from a district adjoining Rome declare that it was much easier to find a god in her neighborhood than a man. We shall see that the multiplicity of the gods was finally the cause of the decay and ruin of the Roman religion.

The Roman Priesthood.— The Roman priesthood was composed of several orders of pontiffs, augurs, keepers of the Sibylline books, Vestal virgins, epulos, salians, lupercals, etc.

Fifteen pontiffs exercised supreme control in matters of religion. They were consecrated to the service of the gods; and all questions of doubtful religious interpretation were submitted to the judgment of their tribunal.

Fifteen learned and experienced augurs observed the phenomena of nature and studied the flight of birds as a means of directing the actions of the state.

Fifteen keepers of the Sibylline books read the pages of their treasures and from them divined coming events.

Six Vestals, immaculate in their virginity, guarded the Roman sacred fire, and presided at the national hearthstone of the Roman race.

Seven epulos conducted the solemn processions and regulated the religious ceremonies at the annual festivals of the gods.

Fifteen flamens were consecrated to the service of separate deities. Those of Jupiter, Mars, and Quirinus were held in the highest esteem. The Flamen Dialis, or priest of Jupiter, was loaded down with religious obligations and restrictions. He was not permitted to take an oath, to ride, to have anything tied with knots on his person, to look at a prisoner, see armed men, or to touch a dog, a goat, or raw flesh, or yeast. He was not allowed to bathe in the open air; nor could he spend the night outside the city. He could resign his office only on the death of his wife. The Salians were priests of Mars, who, at festivals celebrated in honor of the war-god, danced in heavy armor, and sang martial hymns.

Roman Forms of Worship. —Roman worship was very elaborate and ceremonial. It consisted of sacrifices, vows, prayers, and festivals. With the exception of the ancient Hebrews, the Romans were the greatest formalists and ritualists of antiquity. Every act of Roman public and private life was supposed to be framed in accordance with the will of the gods. There was a formula of prayer adapted to every vicissitude of life. Caesar never mounted his chariot, it is said, that he did not repeat a formula three times to avert dangers.

A painful exactness in the use of words was required in the offering of a Roman prayer. A syllable left out or a word mispronounced, or the intervention of any disturbing cause of evil import, would destroy the merit of the formula. The Romans believed that the voice of prayer should not be interrupted by noises or bad omens. And that the sound of evil augury might not be heard at the moment of supplication, they were in the habit of covering their ears. Musical notes of favorable import were not objectionable, and frequently flutes were played while the prayer was being offered to chase away disturbing sounds. At other times, the priests had special assistants whose duty it was to maintain silence during the recital of the formula. But, if the ceremony was successful, if the language had been correctly pronounced, without the omission or addition of a word; if all disturbing causes and things of evil omen had been alienated from the services, then the granting of the prayer was assured, regardless of the motive or intention of the person praying. It should be remembered that piety and faith were not necessary to the efficacy of Roman prayer. Ceremonial precision, rather than purity of heart, was pleasing to the Roman gods. A peculiar element entered into the religions of both the ancient Romans and the ancient Hebrews. It was the principle of contract in an almost purely juristic sense. Both the Romans and the Hebrews believed that if the divine law was obeyed to the letter, their deities were under the strictest obligation to grant their petitions.

Under the Roman form of worship, a peculiar act of supplication was performed by the suppliant who kissed his right hand, turned round in a circle by the right, and then seated himself upon the ground. This was done in obedience to one of the laws of Numa. The circular movement of the earth, it was thought, was symbolized by the turning round in a circle; and the sitting down indicated that the suppliant was confidant that his prayer would be granted.

The Romans believed that prayers were more efficacious if said in the immediate presence and, if possible, in actual contact with the image of the god. The doorkeepers of the temple were frequently besieged by suppliants who begged to be admitted into the inclosures of the sacred places where they might pray to the deity on the spot.

On account of the vast numbers of the gods, the Romans were sometimes at a loss to know which one to address in prayer. Unlike the Greeks, they had no preferences among their deities. Each was supplicated in his turn according to the business in hand. But they were frequently in doubt as to the name of the god who had control of the subject-matter of their petitions. In such cases, the practical genius of the Roman people served them well. They had recourse to several expedients which they believed would insure success. When in doubt as to the particular divinity which they should address in supplication, they would, at times, invoke, in the first place, Janus, the god of all good beginnings, the doorkeeper, so to speak, of the pantheon, who, it was believed, would deliver the prayer to the proper deity. At other times, in such perplexity, they would address their petitions to a group of gods in which they knew the right one was bound to be. It sometimes happened that they did not know whether the deity to be supplicated was a god or goddess. In such an emergency, they expressed

themselves very cautiously, using the alternative proviso: "Be thou god or goddess." At other times, in cases of extreme doubt, they prayed to all the deities at once; and often, in fits of desperation, they dismissed the entire pantheon and addressed their prayers to the Unknown God.

Another mode of propitiating the gods was by sacrifice. Animals, the fruits of the fields, and even human beings were devoted to this purpose. In the matter of sacrifice, the practical genius of the Roman people was again forcibly manifested. They were tactful enough to adapt the sacrifice to the whims and tastes of the gods. A provision of the Twelve Tables was that "such beasts should be used for victims as were becoming and agreeable to each deity." The framers of these laws evidently believed that the gods had keenly whetted appetites and discriminating tastes in the matter of animal sacrifice. Jupiter Capitolinus was pleased with an offering of white cattle with gilded horns, but would not accept rams or bulls. Mars, Neptune and Apollo were, on the other hand, highly delighted with the sacrifice of bulls. It was also agreeable to Mars to have horses, cocks, and asses sacrificed in his honor. An intact heifer was always pleasing to the goddess Minerva. A white cow with moon-shaped horns delighted Juno Calendaris. A sow in young was sacrificed to the great Mother; and doves and sparrows to Venus. Unweaned puppies were offered as victims of expiation to the Lares and Penates. Black bulls were usually slaughtered to appease the infernal gods.

The most careful attention was given to the selection of the victims of sacrifice from the flocks and herds. Any serious physical defect in the animal disqualified. A calf was not fit for slaughter if its tail did not reach to the joint of the leg. Sheep with cloven tongues and black ears were rejected. Black spots on a white ox had to be rubbed white with chalk before the beast was available for sacrifice.

Not only animals were sacrificed, but human beings as well, to appease the wrath of the gods in time of awful calamity. In early Roman history, gray-headed men of sixty years were hurled from the Pons Sublicius into the Tiber as an offering to Saturn. In the year 227 B.C., the pontiffs discovered from the Sibylline books that the Gauls and Greeks were to attack and capture the city. To fulfill the prophecy and, at the same time to avert the danger, the senate decreed that a man and woman of each of these two nations should be buried alive in the forum as a form of constructive possession. This was nothing but a human sacrifice to the gods.

Again, two of Caesar's soldiers, who had participated in a riot in Rome, were taken to the Campus Martius and sacrificed to Mars by the pontiffs and the Flamen Martialis. Their heads were fixed upon the Regia, as was the case in the sacrifice of the October-horse. As an oblation to Neptune, Sextus Pompeius had live men and horses thrown into the sea at the time when a great storm was destroying the fleet of the enemy.

A near approach to human sacrifice was the custom of sprinkling the statue of Jupiter Latiaris with the blood of gladiators. A priest caught the blood as it gushed from the wound of the dying gladiator, and dashed it while still warm at the face of the image of the god.

Suetonius tells us that after the capture of Perugia, Augustus Caesar slaughtered three hundred prisoners as an expiatory sacrifice to Julius Caesar.

Thus at the beginning of the Christian era, human beings were still being sacrificed on the altars of superstition.

Ascertaining the Will of the Gods. —Various methods were employed by the Romans in ascertaining the will of the gods. Chief among these were the art of divination from the flight of birds and from the inspection of the entrails of animals; also from the observation of lightning and the interpretation of dreams. The Romans had no oracles like those of the Greeks, but they frequently sent messengers to consult the Delphic oracle.

Nothing is stranger or more disgusting in all the range of religious history than the practice of the Roman haruspices. That the ancient masters of the world should have felt themselves obliged to search in the belly of a beast for the will of Jupiter is one of the abominable enigmas of Pagan superstition. The inspection of the entrails of victims was a Tuscan science, early imported from Etruria, and naturalized at Rome. Tuscan haruspices accompanied the Roman armies everywhere, and determined by their skill whether a battle should be fought or a retreat ordered. When it was doubtful what to do, an animal was slaughtered, and the heart, lungs, liver, tongue, spleen, kidneys and caul were closely inspected with the aid of a small needle or knife. Various conditions and appearances of these parts were considered as signs of the pleasure or disfavor of the gods. Largely developed veins on the adverse side were considered tokens of extreme displeasure and an indication of pending misfortune. It was also considered gravely ominous when the head or protuberance in the right lobe of the liver was wanting. The Romans were too practical and indomitable, however, to allow a single bad omen to frustrate a great enterprise. If the inspection of the entrails of the first animal was not favorable, they slaughtered still others until a propitious sign was observed. At times, a score of beasts were slain before the gods gave assent to the enterprise in hand.

Divination from the flight and notes of birds was another method employed by the Romans in finding out the will of the gods. And it may be remarked that this was certainly a more rational and elevated form of divination than that which we have just discussed. An eagle swooping down from the skies would certainly be a more natural and pleasing suggestion of the thoughts and attributes of Jove than the filthy interior of the entrails of a bull.

The elements of divination from the flight of birds were derived either from the significant notes and sounds of their voices, or from the manner in which their wings were flapped or their flight conducted. If the bird flew from the left to the right of the augur, it was considered a happy omen; if the flight was in the opposite direction, the enterprise in hand had to be abandoned or at least delayed. Augury by flight was usually applied to eagles and vultures, while woodpeckers, ravens, crows, and screech owls announced the will of the gods by note. The direction from which the note came, usually determined the nature of the augury. But, in the case of the screech owl, the sounds were always of evil omen, from whatever side they came. And those who have been so unfortunate as to hear its mournful, desolate and Godforsaken tones will not be disposed to censure either the Romans or their gods for the low esteem in which they held this bird.

Again, it was a principle of Roman augury that auspices could be neutralized or overcome. If a crow furnished an omen, and an eagle gave another which was opposed to it, the first sign was wiped out, because the eagle was a larger and nobler bird than the crow. And, as in the case of prayer, so also in the matter of the auspices, a disturbing sound would destroy the effect of the augury. The squeak or cry of a mouse would destroy a message from Jupiter conveyed in the scream of an eagle.

But the most potent manifestation of the divine mind, among the ancient Romans, was that derived from thunder and lightning. Lightning to them was the sovereign expression of the will of the gods; and a single flash blotted out every other sign and token. It was an irrevocable presage and could not be remotely modified or evaded. It came directly from the hand of the deity and was an emphatic revelation of the divine mind. All places struck by lightning were considered sacred and were consecrated to the god who had sent the bolt. Upon the spot where it fell, an altar was raised and an inclosure formed. The service of consecration consisted in burying the lightning, that is, in restoring the earth thrown up by it, and in the sacrifice of a two-year-old sheep. All such places were considered hallowed spots and it was impious and sacrilegious to touch them or even look at them. The gods deprived of reason those who destroyed the altars and sacred inclosures of these places.

These various methods of ascertaining the will of the deities were employed in every important transaction of Roman public and private life. At times, all of them cooperated on occasions of vast import and when the lives and destinies of great men were involved.

The following single paragraph from Suetonius contains allusions to all the modes of divination which we have just discussed:

After the death of Caesar, upon his return from Apollonia as he was entering the city, on a sudden, in a clear and bright sky a circle resembling the rainbow surrounded the body of the sun; and immediately afterwards, the tomb of Julia, Caesar's daughter, was struck by lightning. In his first consulship whilst he was observing the auguries, twelve vultures presented themselves as they had done to Romulus. And when he offered sacrifice, the livers of all the victims were folded inward in the lower part; a circumstance which was regarded by those present, who had skill in things of that nature, as an indubitable prognostic of great and wonderful fortune.[3]

The interpretation of dreams also formed an important part in the determination of the will of the gods, not only among the Romans, but among all ancient nations. The literature of antiquity, both sacred and profane, is filled with dreams. Whether the biographer is Matthew or Plutarch, dreams appear on the pages of both. Chrysippus made a collection of prophetical dreams in order to explain their meaning. Both Galen and Hippocrates believed that dreams were sent by the gods to men. Artemidorus wrote a treatise on the subject, and in it he assures us that it was compiled at the express bidding and under the direction of Apollo himself.

It was in a dream that Joseph was warned not to put away Mary his wife.[4] It was also in a dream that an angel voice warned him to flee into Egypt with the infant Savior to escape the murderous designs of Herod.[5] Nearly every great event, both in Greek and Roman history, seems to have been heralded or attended by dreams. The following account is given by Suetonius of the dreams of Quintus Catulus and Marcus Cicero presaging the reign of Augustus:

Quintus Catulus had a dream, for two nights successively after his dedication of the Capitol. The first night he dreamt that Jupiter out of several boys of the order of the nobility who were playing about his altar, selected one, into whose bosom he put the public seal of the commonwealth, which he held in his hand; but in his vision the next night, he saw in the bosom of Jupiter Capitolinus, the same boy; whom he ordered to be removed, but it was forbidden by the God, who declared that it must be brought up to become the guardian of the state. The next day, meeting Augustus, with whom till that hour he had not the least acquaintance, and looking at him with admiration, he said he was extremely like the boy he had seen in his dream. Some gave a different account of Catulus's first dream, namely that Jupiter, upon several noble lads requesting of him that they might have a guardian, had pointed to one amongst them, to whom they were to prefer their requests; and putting his fingers to the boy's mouth to kiss, he afterwards applied them to his own.

Marcus Cicero, as he was attending Caius Caesar to the Capitol, happened to be telling some of his friends a dream which he had the preceding night, in which he saw a comely youth let down from heaven by a golden chain, who stood at the door of the Capitol, and had a whip put into his hands by Jupiter. And immediately upon sight of Augustus, who had been sent for by his uncle Caesar to the sacrifice, and was as yet perfectly unknown to most of the company, he affirmed that it was the very boy he had seen in his dream. When he assumed the manly toga, his senatorian tunic becoming loose in the seam on each side, fell at his feet. Some would have this to forebode, that the order of which that was the badge of distinction, would some time or other be subject to him.[6]

Omens also played an important role in molding the destiny of the Roman state. In his "Life of Caesar Augustus," Suetonius says:

Some signs and omens he regarded as infallible. If in the morning, his shoe was put on wrong, the left instead of the right, that boded some disaster. If when he commenced a long journey, by land or sea, there happened to fall a mizzling rain, he held it to be a good sign of a speedy and happy return. He was much affected likewise with anything out of the common course of nature. A palm-tree which chanced to grow up between some stones in the court of his house, he transplanted into a court where the images of the Household Gods were placed, and took all possible care to make it thrive. In the island of Capri, some decayed branches of an old ilex, which hung drooping to the ground, recovered themselves upon his arrival; at which he was so delighted, that he made an exchange with the Republic of Naples, of the island of Ischia, for that of Capri. He likewise observed certain days; as never to go from home the day after the Numdinae, nor to begin any serious business upon the nones; avoiding nothing else in it, as he writes to Tiberius, than its unlucky name.[7]

Any unusual happening and all the striking phenomena of nature were regarded by the Romans as prodigies or omens indicative of the will of the gods. The nature of the occurrence indicated the pleasure or the wrath of the deity. An eclipse of the sun and the moon, a shooting star, a rainbow of peculiar color, showers of stones and ashes, were regarded as awful prodigies, and generally threw the Roman Senate into a panic. On such occasions, the pontifical college called a hurried meeting. The augurs and haruspices were summoned to immediate duty; and everything was done to ascertain the will of the gods and to do their bidding. A two-headed snake or a three-legged chicken, such as we frequently see today, would have shaken the whole Roman religious system to the center.

Such was the credulity of the Roman people, that the most improbable and impossible stories, mere rummors born of lying imposture, were heard and believed. "Idols shed tears or sweated blood, oxen spoke, men were changed into women, cocks into hens, lakes or brooks ran with blood or milk, mice nibbled at the golden vessels of the temples, a swarm of bees lighted on a temple or in a public place." All such alleged occurrences required sacrifices and expiatory rites to conquer the fury and regain the favor of the gods.

Fall of the Early Roman Religion.— At the beginning of the Christian era, the old Roman religion, founded upon the institutions of Numa, had almost come to an end. The invasion of Italy by the Greek gods was the first serious assault upon the early Roman faith. The elegant refinement and fascinating influence of Greek literature, philosophy and sculpture, had incrusted with a gorgeous coating the rude forms of the primitive Roman worship. But, as time advanced, the old gods grew stale and new deities were sought. The human soul could not forever feed upon myths, however brilliant and bewitching. The mysterious and melancholy rites of Isis came to establish themselves by the side of those of Janus and Aesculapius. The somber qualities of the Egyptian worship seemed to commend it. Even so good and grand a man as Marcus Aurelius avowed himself an adorer of Serapis; and, during a sojourn in Egypt, he is reported to have conducted himself like an Egyptian citizen and philosopher while strolling through the temples and sacred groves of the banks of the Nile.[8]

The effect of the repeated changes from one form of religious faith to another was to gradually destroy the moral fiber of Roman worship and to shatter Roman faith in the existence and stability of the gods. The first manifestation of that disintegration which finally completely undermined and destroyed the temple of Roman worship was the familiarity with which the Romans treated their gods. Familiarity with gods, as with men, breeds contempt. A striking peculiarity of both the Roman and Greek mythologies was the intimate relationship that existed between gods and human beings. Sometimes it took the form of personal intercourse from which heroes sprang, as was the case with Jupiter and Alcmene, of whom Hercules was born. At other times, deities and human beings traveled together on long voyages, as was the case with Minerva and Telemachus on their trip to the island of Calypso. These were instances of what the Greeks regarded as that natural and sympathetic relationship that not only could but should exist between them and their divinities. But in time the Romans entered upon a career of frivolous fellowship and familiarity with their gods which destroyed their mutual respect, and hastened the dissolution of the bonds that had hitherto held them together. They began to treat their divinities as men, deserving of honor indeed, but nevertheless human beings with all the frailties and attributes of mortals. "Arnobius speaks of morning serenades sung with an accompaniment of fifes, as a kind of reveille to the sleeping gods, and of an evening salutation in which leave was taken of the deity with the wishing him a good night's rest."

The Lectisternia or banquets of the gods were ordinary religious functions to which the deities themselves were invited. These feasts were characterized at times by extreme exclusiveness. It was not right, thought the Romans, to degrade and humiliate the greater gods by seating them at the banquet board with smaller ones. So, a right royal fete was annually arranged in the Capitol in honor of Jupiter, Juno, and Minerva. The statue of the great god was placed reclining on a pillow; and the images of the two goddesses were seated upon chairs near him. At other times, the functions were more democratic, and great numbers of the gods were admitted, as well as a few select and distinquished mortals. On such occasions, the images of the gods were placed in pairs on cushions near the table. The Romans believed that the spirit of the god actually inhabited or occupied the statute. This we learned from Lucian. The happy mortals who were fortunate enough to be present at the banquet, actually believed that they were seated among the gods. Livy tells us that once the gods turned on their cushions and reversed themselves at the table, and that mice then came and devoured the meats.[9]

The Roman historians very seriously inform us that special invitations were extended the gods to attend these banquets. They fail to tell us, however, whether R.S.V.P. or any other directions were inserted in the cards of invitation. We are left completely in the dark as to the formality employed by the deities to indicate their acceptance or rejection of the proffered honor.

The purpose of the Lectisternia was at first undoubtedly to promote hospitality and fellowship, and to conciliate the good will of the gods. But finally such intimacy ripened into contempt and all kinds of indecencies began to be practiced against the deities. Speaking of the actions of certain Romans, Seneca says: "One sets a rival deity by the side of another god; another shows Jupiter the time of day; this one acts the beadle, the other the anointer, pretending by gesture to rub in the ointment. A number of coiffeurs attend upon Juno and Minerva, and make pretence of curling with their fingers, not only at a distance from their images, but in the actual temple. Some hold the looking-glass to them; some solicit the gods to stand security for them; while others display briefs before them, and instruct them in their law cases." This rude conduct was practiced by men. But Seneca, continuing, says: "Women, too, take their seats at the Capitol pretending that Jupiter is enamored of them, and not allowing themselves to be intimidated by Juno's presence."[10]

Roman Skepticism. — Of contempt of the gods, which was due to many causes, skepticism was born. The deities of every race had been brought to Rome and placed in the pantheon; and there, gazing into each other's faces, had destroyed each other. The multiplicity of the gods was the chief agency in the destruction of the Roman faith and ritual. The yoke and burden of endless ceremonials had been borne for centuries and were now producing intolerable irritation and nauseating disgust. The natural freedom of the soul was in open rebellion and revolt against the hollow forms and rigid exactions of the Roman ritual. The eagle of the human intellect was already preparing to soar above the clouds of superstition. Cicero gave expression to the prevalent sentiments of educated Romans of his day when he wrote:

I thought I should be doing an immense benefit both to myself and to my countrymen if I could entirely eradicate all superstitious errors. Nor is there any fear that true religion can be endangered by the demolition of this superstition; for as this religion which is united with the knowledge of nature is to be propagated, so, also, are all the roots of superstition to be destroyed; for that presses upon and pursues and persecutes you wherever you turn yourself, whether you consult a diviner or have heard an omen or have immolated a victim, or beheld a flight of birds; whether you have seen a Chaldaean or a soothsayer; if it lightens or thunders, or if anything is struck by lightning; if any kind of prodigy occurs; some of which things must be frequently coming to pass, so that you can never rise with a tranquil mind.

The completion of Roman conquest in the reign of Augustus was another potent influence in the destruction of the old Roman religion. The chief employment of the Roman gods had ever been as servants of the Roman state in the extension of the Roman empire. Their services were now no longer needed in this regard, and their ancient worshipers were ready to repudiate and dismiss them. The Hebrew characteristic of humility and resignation in the presence of divine displeasure was not a Roman trait. The ancient masters of the world reserved the right to object and even to rebel when the gods failed to do their duty after appropriate prayers had been said and proper ceremonies had been performed. Sacrilege, as the result of disappointment, was a frequent occurrence in Roman religious life. Bitter defiance of the heavenly powers sometimes followed a defeat in battle or a failure in diplomacy. Augustus, as supreme pontiff, chastised Neptune, the god of the sea, because he lost his fleet in a storm, by forbidding the image of the god to be carried in the procession of the next Circensian games. The emperor Julian was regarded as a most pious potentate, but he did not hesitate to defy the gods when he became displeased. At the time of the Parthian war, he was preparing to sacrifice ten select and beautiful bulls to Mars the Avenger, when nine of them suddenly lay down while being led to the altar, and the tenth broke his band. The fury of the monarch was aroused, and he swore by Jupiter that he would not again offer a sacrifice to Mars.[11] Claudius, the commander of the Roman fleet at Drepanum, ordered the sacred pullets to be thrown into the sea because they would not eat. When Germanicus was sick in Asia, his devoted admirers offered frequent prayers to the gods for his recovery. When the report of his death reached Rome, the temples of the unaccommodating deities were stoned, and their altars were overturned.[12]

The same feeling of angry resentment and defiance may be discerned in inscriptions on the graves of relatives prematurely snatched away by death. An epitaph on the monument of a child of five years was this: "To the unrighteous gods who robbed me of my life." Another on the tombstone of a maiden of twenty, named Procope, read as follows: "I lift my hand against the god who has deprived me of my innocent existence."[13]

The soil of familiarity, contempt and sacrilege which we have just described, was most fertile ground for the growth of that rank and killing skepticism which was destroying the vitals of the Roman faith at the time of Christ. This unbelief, it is true, was not universal. At the time of the birth of the Savior, the Roman masses still believed in the gods and goddesses of the Greek and Roman mythologies. Superstition was especially prevalent in the country districts of both Greece and Italy. Pausanias, who lived about the middle of the second century of the Christian era, tells us that in his time the olden legends of god and hero were still firmly believed by the common people. As he traveled through Greece, the cypresses of Alcmaeon, the stones of Amphion, and the ashes of the funeral piles of Niobe's children were pointed out to him. In Phocis, he found the belief still existing that larks laid no eggs there because of the sin of Tereus.[14] Plutarch, who lived about the middle of the first century of our era, tells us that the people were still modeling the gods in wax and clay, as well as carving them in marble and were worshiping them in contempt and defiance of philosophers and statesmen.[15] But this credulity was limited to the ignorant and unthinking masses. The intellectual leaders of both the Greek and Roman races had long been in revolt against the absurdity and vulgarity of the myths which formed the foundation of their popular faiths. The purity and majesty of the soul felt keenly the insult and outrage of enforced obedience to the obscene divinities that Homer and Hesiod had handed down to them. Five hundred years before Christ, Pindar, the greatest lyric poet of Greece, had denounced the vulgar tales told of the deities, and had branded as blasphemous the story of the cannibal feast spread for the gods by the father of Pelops. Xenophanes, also, in the sixth century before Christ, had ridiculed the mythical tales of the Homeric poems, and had called attention to the purely human character of popular religions. He had pointed out that the Ethiopians painted the images of their deities black, and gave them flat noses, in the likeness of themselves; that the Thracians, on the other hand, created their gods blue-eyed and red; and that, in general, every race had reflected its own physical peculiarities in the creation of its gods. He declared it to be his opinion that if the beasts of the field should attempt to produce a likeness of the gods, the horses would produce a resemblance of themselves, and that oxen and lions would ascribe to their own divinities their own images and peculiarities.

The whole structure of the Roman religion, built upon myths and adorned with fables, was ill fitted to stand the tests of analysis and criticism. It was destined to weaken and crumble the moment it was subjected to serious rational inquiry. Such inquiry was inevitable in the progress of that soul-growth which the centuries were sure to bring. Natural philosophy and historical study began to dissolve the sacred legends and to demand demonstration and proof where faith had before sufficed. Skeptical criticism began to dissect the formulae of prayer and to analyze the elements of augury and sacrifice. Reason began to revolt against the proposition that Jupiter was justified in rejecting a petition because a syllable had been omitted or a word mispronounced. Men began to ask: "What explanation could be given of the strange changes of mind in the gods, often threatening evil on the first inspection of the victim, and at the second promising good? How did it happen that a sacrifice to Apollo gave favorable, and one to Diana unfavorable signs? Why did the Etruscan, the Elan, the Egyptian, and the Punic inspectors of sacrifice interpret the entrails in an entirely different manner? Again, what connection in nature was there between a fissure in the liver of a lamb, and a trifling advantage to a man, an inheritance to be expected, or the like? And on a man's intending to sacrifice, did a change, corresponding to his circumstances, take place in the entrails of the beast; so that, supposing another person had selected the same victim, he would have found the liver in a quite different condition?"

The gods themselves became subject of inspection and analysis. Their origin and nature were studied historically, and were also reviewed in the light of natural and ethical products. Three hundred years before Christ, Evhemere of Messina boldly declared that the gods were simply ancient kings deified by fear and superstition after death. Anaxagoras sought to identify the several deities with the forces and phenomena of nature, thus converting the pantheon into an observatory, or into a physical and chemical laboratory. Metrodorus contended that the gods were deifications of mere abstract ethical precepts.

Instances are recorded in history, from time to time, where the philosophers attempted to explain to the people the natural meaning of those things which they believed were pregnant with supernatural import. On a certain occasion, a ram with one horn was found on the farm of Pericles; and, from this circumstance, an Athenian diviner, names Lampon, predicted that the party of the orator would triumph over the opposite faction and gain control of the government. Whereupon Anaxagoras dissected the skull, and demonstrated to the people the natural cause of the phenomenon in the peculiar shape of the animal's brain. But this former finally suffered the fate of other innovators, was prosecuted for impiety, and was only saved by the influence of Pericles.

At the beginning of the Christian era, the religion of Rome was privately ridiculed and repudiated by nearly all statesmen and philosophers of the empire, although they publicly professed it on grounds of public policy. Seneca, a contemporary of Jesus, advised observance of rites appointed by law, on patriotic grounds. "All which things," he says, "a wise man will observe as being commanded by the laws, but not as being pleasing to the gods." Again he says: "All that ignoble rabble of gods which the superstition of ages has heaped up, we shall adore in such a way as to remember that their worship belongs rather to custom than to reality." Ridiculing the popular notions of the matrimonial relations of the deities, the same eminent philosopher says: "And what of this, that we unite the gods in marriage, and that not even naturally, for we join brothers and sisters? We marry Bellona to Mars, Venus to Vulcan, Salacia to Neptune. Some of them we leave unmarried, as though there were no match for them, which is surely needless, especially when there are certain unmarried goddesses, as Populonia, or Fulgora, or the goddess Rumina, for whom I am not astonished that suitors have been wanting."

The prevailing skepticism of the times is well illustrated in a dialogue which

Cicero introduces into his first Tusculan Disputation between M, which may be interpreted Marcus, and A, which may be translated Auditor:

> Marcus: Tell me, are you not afraid of the three-headed Cerberus in the infernal regions, and the roaring of Cocytus, and the passage over Acheron, and Tantalus, dying with thirst, while water laves his chin, and Sisyphus,
>
>   "Who sweats with arduous toil in vain
>   The steepy summit of the mount to gain?"
>
> Perhaps you are also afraid of the inexorable judges, Minos and Rhadamanthus, because before them neither L. Crassus nor M. Antonius can defend you, and because appearing before Grecian judges, you will not be permitted to employ Demosthenes, but must plead for yourself before a very great crowd. All these things, perhaps, you fear, and therefore regard death as an eternal evil.
> Auditor: Do you think I'm such a fool as to give credence to such things?
> Marcus: What! You don't believe in them?
> Auditor: Truly, not in the least.
> Marcus: I am deeply pained to hear that.
> Auditor: Why?
> Marcus: Because, if occasion had offered, I could very eloquently have denounced them, myself.[16]

The contemptuous scorn of the cultivated Romans of his time is frequently revealed in the writings of Cicero. He refers more than once to the famous remark of Cato, who said that he could not explain why the haruspices did not laugh in each other's faces when they began to sacrifice.

At this point, it is worthy of observation that the prevalent unbelief was not limited to a simple denial of the existence of mythical divinities and of the efficacy of the worship rendered them. Roman skepticism sought to destroy the very foundation of all religious belief by denying not only the existence of the gods, but also the immortality of the soul. Cicero is said to have been the only great Roman of his time who believed that death was not the end. Students of Sallust are familiar with his account of the conspiracy of Cataline in which it is related that Julius Caesar, in a speech before the Roman senate, opposed putting the traitor to death because that form of punishment was too mild, since beyond the grave there was neither joy nor sorrow.[17]

Antagonism to the doctrine of the immortality of the soul reached a melancholy refinement in the strange contention that life after death was a cruel thought. Pliny expresses this sentiment admirably when he says:

What folly it is to renew life after death. Where shall created beings find rest if you suppose that shades in hell and souls in heaven continue to have any feeling? You rob us of man's greatest good—death. Let us rather find in the tranquillity which preceded our existence the pledge of the repose which is to follow it.

When skepticism had destroyed their faith in the gods, and had robbed them of the consolations of religion, educated Romans sought refuge and solace in Greek philosophy. Stoicism and Epicureanism were the dominant spiritual and intellectual forces of the Roman empire at the time of Christ. Epicureanism was founded by Epicurus, who was born of an Athenian family in the Island of Samos about 342 B. C. Stoicism originated with Zeno, a native of Cittium in Cyprus, born about the year 340 B. C.

The original design of the system of Epicurus was to found a commonwealth of happiness and goodness in opposition to the purely intellectual aristocracy of Plato and Aristotle. Men were beginning to tire of speculation and dialectics, and to long for a philosophy built upon human feeling and sensibility. As a touchstone of truth, it was proposed to substitute sensation for intellect. Whatever was pleasing to the natural and healthful senses was to be taken to be true. The pursuit of happiness was to be the chief aim of the devotees of this system. The avoidance of mental pain and physical suffering, as well as the cultivation of all pleasurable emotions, were to be the leading features of every Epicurean programme. In the beginning, Epicureanism inculcated principles of virtue as a means of happiness. The mode of life of the first followers of Epicurus was simple and abstemious. Barley-bread and water are said to have been their ordinary food and drink. But in time this form of philosophy became identified with the coarsest sensuality and the most wicked lust. This was especially true after it was transplanted from Greece to Italy. The doctrines of this school met with a ready response from the pleasure-seeking, luxury-loving Roman people who were now enriched by the spoils and treasures of a conquered world. "This philosophy therefore became at Rome a mere school of self-indulgence, and lost the refinement which, in Greece, had led it to recognize in virtue that which gave zest to pleasure and in temperance that which prolonged it. It called simply for a continuous round of physical delights; it taught the grossest sensuality; it proclaimed the inanity of goodness and the lawfulness of lust. It was the road—sure, steep and swift, to awful demoralization."

Stoicism, on the other hand, furnished spiritual and intellectual food to that nobler class of Romans who were at once the support and ornament of a magnificent but decadent civilization. This form of philosophy was peculiarly consonant with early Roman instincts and habits. In its teachings were perfectly reflected that vigor, austerity, and manly self-reliance which had made the Roman race undisputed masters of the world. Many of its precepts were not only moral and ennobling, but deeply religious and sustaining. A striking kinship between them and certain Christian precepts has been frequently pointed out. Justice, fortitude, prudence, and temperance were the four cardinal virtues of Stoicism. Freedom from all passions and complete simplicity of life, resulting in perfect purity of manners, was its chief aim. But the fundamental principles of both Epicureanism and Stoicism were destructive of those spiritual elements which furnish complete and permanent nourishment to the soul. Stoicism was pantheism, and Epicureanism was materialism. The Stoic believed that the human soul was corporeal, but that it was animated and illuminated by the universal soul. The Epicurean taught that the soul was composed of material atoms, which would perish when its component parts separated or dissolved. Epicureanism was materialistic in its tendency, and its inevitable result, in perverted form, was sensualism. Stoicism was pervaded throughout by a melancholy and desolating fatalism. It was peculiarly the philosophy of suicide; or, as a great French writer once described it, "an apprenticeship for death."[18] To take one's life was not only allowable but commendable in certain cases.

Zeno, the founder of the sect, taught that incurable disease was a sufficient excuse for suicide. Marcus Aurelius considered it an obligation of nature and of reason to make an end of life when it became an intolerable burden. "Kill thyself and die erect in the consciousness of thy own strength," would have been a suitable inscription over the doorway of every Stoic temple. Seneca furnished to his countrymen this Stoic panacea for all the ills of life:

> Seest thou yon steep height, that is the descent to freedom. Seest thou yon sea, yon river, yon well; freedom sits there in the depths. Seest thou yon low withered tree; there freedom hangs. Seest thou thy neck, thy throat, thy heart; they are the ways of escape from bondage.

And the Roman philosopher was not only conscientious but consistent in his teachings. He was heroic enough to take the medicine himself which he had prescribed for others. Indeed, he took a double dose; for he not only swallowed poison, but also opened his veins, and thus committed suicide, as other Stoics—such as Zeno, Cleanthes and Cato—had done before him.

It was not a problem of the Stoic philosophy,
> Whether 'tis nobler in the mind to suffer
> The slings and arrows of outrageous fortune,
> Or to take arms against a sea of troubles,
> And by opposing end them?[19]

A familiar illustration of the advocates of suicide among the Roman writers was that a human body afflicted with incurable disease, or a human mind weighed down with intolerable grief, was like a house filled with smoke. As it was the duty of the occupant of the house to escape from the smoke by flight, so it was the duty of the soul to leave the body by suicide.

But neither Epicureanism nor Stoicism could satisfy the natural longing of the soul for that which is above the earth and beyond the grave. It was impossible that philosophy should completely displace religion. The spiritual nature of the Roman people was still intact and vigorous after belief in myths was dead. As a substitute for their ancient faith and as a supplement to philosophy, they began to deify their illustrious men and women. The apotheosis of the emperors was the natural result of the progressive degradation of the Roman religion. The deification of Julius Caesar was the beginning of this servile form of worship; and the apotheosis of Diocletian was the fifty-third of these solemn canonizations. Of this number, fifteen were those of princesses belonging to the imperial family.

Divine honors began to be paid to Caesar before he was dead. The anniversary of his birth became a national holiday; his bust was placed in the temple, and a month of the year was named for him. After his assassination, he was worshiped as a god under the name of Divus Julius; and sacrifices were offered upon his altar. After Julius Caesar, followed the deification of Augustus Caesar. Even before his death, Octavian had consented to be worshiped in the provinces, especially in Nicomedia and Pergamus. After his death, his worship was introduced into Rome and Italy.

The act of canonizing a dead emperor was accomplished by a vote of the senate, followed by a solemn ceremony, in which an eagle was released at the funeral pile, and soaring upward, became a symbol of the ascent of the deceased to the skies. A Roman senator, Numerius Atticus, swore that he had seen Augustus ascending to heaven at the time of his consecration; and received from Livia a valuable gift of money as a token of her appreciation of his kindness.

Not only were grand and gifted men like Julius and Augustus Caesar, but despicable and contemptible tyrants like Nero and Commodus, raised to the rank of immortals. And, not content with making gods of emperors, the Romans made goddesses of their royal women. Caligula had lived in incestuous intercourse with his sister Drusilla; nevertheless, he had her immortalized and worshiped as a divine being. This same Caligula who was a monster of depravity, insisted on being worshiped as a god in the flesh throughout the Roman empire, although the custom had been not to deify emperors until after they were dead. The cowardly and obsequious Roman senate decreed him a temple in Rome. The royal rascal erected another to himself, and appointed his own private priests and priestesses, among whom were his uncle Claudius, and the Caesonia who afterwards became his wife. This temple and its ministry were maintained at an enormous expense. Only the rarest and most costly birds like peacocks and pheasants, were allowed to be sacrificed to him. Such was the impious conceit of Caligula that he requested the Asiatics of Miletus to convert a temple of Apollo into a shrine sacred to himself. Some of the noblest statuary of antiquity was mutilated in displacing the heads of gods to make places for the head of this wicked monster. A mighty descent this, indeed, from the Olympian Zeus of Phidias to a bust of Caligula!

Domitian, after his deification, had himself styled "Lord and God," in all documents, and required all his subjects to so address him. Pliny tells us that the roads leading into Rome were constantly filled with flocks and herds being drive to the Capital to be sacrificed upon his altar.[20]

The natural and inevitable result of the decay of the Roman religion was the corruption and demoralization of Roman social life. All experience teaches that an assault upon a people's religious system is an assault upon the entire social and moral organization. Every student of history knows that a nation will be prosperous and happy to the extent that it is religiously intelligent, and in proportion to its loyalty to the laws of social virtue, to the laws of good government, and the laws of God; and that an abandonment of its gods means the wreck and dissolution of its entire social structure. The annals of Rome furnish a striking confirmation of this fact.

The closing pages of this chapter will be devoted to a short topical review of Roman society at the time of Christ. Only a few phases of the subject can be presented in a work of this character.

II.—GRAECO-ROMAN SOCIAL LIFE

Marriage and Divorce. — The family is the unit of the social system; and at the hearthstone all civilization begins. The loosening of the domestic ties is the beginning of the dissolution of the state; and whatever weakens the nuptial bonds, tends to destroy the moral fiber of society. The degradation of women and the destruction of domestic purity were the first signs of decay in Roman life. In the early ages of the republic, marriage was regarded not only as a contract, but as a sacrament as well. Connubial fidelity was sacredly maintained. Matrons of the type of Cornelia, the mother of the Gracchi, were objects of national pride and affection. The spirit of desperation which caused the father of Virginia to plunge a butcher's knife into the chaste and innocent heart of his child to save her from the lust of Appius Claudius, was a tragic illustration of the almost universal Roman respect for virtue in the age of the Tarquins. To such an extent were the marital relations venerated by the early Romans that we are assured by Dionysius that five hundred and twenty years had passed before a single divorce was granted. Carvilius Ruga, the name of the first Roman to procure a divorce, has been handed down to us.[21]

If we are to believe Dollinger, the abandonment of the policy of lifelong devotion to the marriage relation and the inauguration of the system of divorce were due not to the faults of the men but to the dangerous and licentious qualities of the Roman women. In connection with the divorce of Carvilius Ruga, he discusses a widespread conspiracy of Roman wives to poison their husbands. Several of these husbands fell victims to this plot; and, as punishment for the crime, twenty married women were forced to take the poison which they had themselves prepared, and were thus put to death. And, about a half century after this divorce, several wives of distinguished Romans were discovered to be participants in the bacchanalian orgies. From all these things, Dollinger infers that the Roman men began to tire of their wives and to seek legal separation from them.[22]

But, whatever the cause, the marriage tie was so easily severed during the latter years of the republic, that divorce was granted on the slightest pretext. Q. Antistius Vetus divorced his wife because she was talking familiarly and confidentially to one of his freedmen. The wife of C. Sulpicius imprudently entered the street without a veil, and her husband secured a divorce on that ground. P. Sempronius Sophus put away his wife for going to the theater without his knowledge.

Cicero divorced his first wife that he might marry a younger and wealthier woman; and because this second one did not exhibit sufficient sorrow at the death of his daughter, Tullia, he repudiated her.

Cato, the stern Stoic moralist, was several times divorced. To accommodate his friend Hortensius he gave him his second wife Marcia, with her father's consent; and, after the death of the orator, he remarried her.

After being several times previously divorced, Pompey put away Mucia in order that he might wed Julia, Caesar's daughter, who was young enough to be the child of Pompey.

Caesar himself was five times married. He divorced his wife, Pompeia, because of her relationship to Clodius, a dashing and dissolute young Roman, who entered Caesar's house on the occasion of the celebration of the feast of the Bona Dea in a woman's dress, in order that he might pay clandestine suit to the object of his lust. Caesar professed to believe that the charges against Pompeia were not

true, but he divorced her nevertheless, with the remark that "Caesar's wife must be above suspicion." We are reminded by this that, in ancient as in modern times, society placed greater restrictions upon women than upon men; for Caesar, who uttered this virtuous and heroic sentiment, was a most notorious rake and profligate. Suetonius tells us that he debauched many Roman ladies of the first rank; among them "Lollia, the wife of Aulus Gabinius; Tertulla, the wife of Marcus Crassus; and Mucia, the wife of Cneius Pompey." It was frequently made a reproach to Pompey, "that to gratify him ambition, he married the daughter of a man upon whose account he had divorced his wife, after having had three children by her; and whom he used, with a deep sigh, to call Aegisthus." But the favorite mistress of Caesar was Servilia, the mother of Marcus Brutus. To consummate an intrigue with her, he gave Servilia a pearl which cost him six millions of sesterces. And at the time of the civil war he had deeded to her for a trifling consideration, several valuable farms. When people expressed surprise at the lowness of the price, Cicero humorously remarked: "To let you know the real value of the purchase, between ourselves, Tertia was deducted." It was generally suspected at Rome that Servilia had prostituted her daughter Tertia to Caesar; and the witticism of the orator was a *double entendre,* Tertia signifying the third (of the value of the farm), as well as being the name of the girl, whose virtue had paid the price of the deduction. Caesar's lewdness was so flagrant and notorious that his soldiers marching behind his chariot, on the occasion of his Gallic triumph, shouted in ribald jest, to the multitude along the way:

> Watch well your wives, ye cits, we bring a blade,
> A bald-pate master of the wenching trade.[23]

If this was the private life of the greatest Roman of the world, who, at the time of his death, was Pontifex Maximus, the supreme head of the Roman religion, what must have been the social life of the average citizen who delighted to style Caesar the demigod while living and to worship him as divine, when dead?

A thorough knowledge of the details of the most corrupt and abandoned state of society recorded in history may be had by a perusal of the Annals of Tacitus and the Satires of Juvenal. The Sixth Satire is a withering arraignment of Roman profligacy and wickedness. "To see the world at its worst estate," says Professor Jowett, "we turn to the age of the satirists and of Tacitus, when all the different streams of evil, coming from east, west, north, south, the vices of barbarism and the vices of civilization, remnants of ancient cults, and the latest refinements of luxury and impurity, met and mingled on the banks of the Tiber." Rome was the heart of the empire that pumped its filthy blood from the center to the extremities, and received from the provinces a return current of immorality and corruption. Juvenal complains that

> Long since the stream that wanton Syria laves,
> Has disembogued its filth in Tiber's waves.

Grecian literature and manners were the main cause of Roman dissoluteness.

The grandfather of Cicero is said to have made this declaration: "A Roman's wickedness increases in proportion to his acquaintance with Greek authors." It is undeniably true that the domestic immorality of the Greeks exercised a most baneful influence upon the social life of the Romans. Both at Athens and in Sparta marriage was regarded as the means to an end, the procreation of children as worshipers of the gods and citizens of the state. In this fundamental purpose were involved, the Greeks believed, the mission and the destiny of woman. Marriage was not so much a sacred institution, as it was a convenient arrangement whereby property rights were regulated and soldiers were provided for the army and the navy. This view was entertained by both the Athenians and the Spartans. The code of Lycurgus regulated the family relations to the end that healthy, vigorous children might be born to a military commonwealth. The Spartan maidens were required to exercise in the palestra, almost naked, in the presence of men and strangers. And so loose and extravagant were the ideas of conjugal fidelity among the Spartans that it was not regarded as an improper thing to borrow another man's wife for the purpose of procreating children, if there had already been born to the legitimate husband all the children that he desired. This we learn from Xenophon[24] and from Polybius,[25] who assure us that it often happened that as many as four Spartans had one woman, in common, for a wife. "Already in the time of Socrates, the wives of Sparta had reached the height of disrepute for their wantonness throughout the whole of Greece; Aristotle says that they lived in unbridled licentiousness; and, indeed, it is a distinctive feature in the female character there, that publicly and shamelessly they would speed a well-known seducer of a woman of rank by wishing him success, and charging him to think only of endowing Sparta with brave boys."[26]

At Athens the principle was the same, even if the gratification of lust was surrounded with a halo of poetry and sentiment which the Spartan imagination was incapable of creating. The Athenians were guilty of a strange perversion of the social instincts by placing a higher appreciation upon the charms of a certain class of lewd women that they did upon the virtuous merits of their own wives and mothers. These latter were kept in retirement and denied the highest educational advantages; while the former, the Hetairai, beautiful and brilliant courtesans, destined for the pleasure and entertainment of illustrious men, were accorded the utmost freedom, as well as all the advantages of culture in the arts and sciences. Demosthenes has classified the women of ancient Athens in this sentence: "We have Hetairai for our pleasure, concubines for the ordinary requirements of the body, and wives for the procreation of lawful issue and as confidential domestic guardians." The most renowned of the Hetairai was Aspasia, the mistress of Pericles. She was exceedingly beautiful and brilliantly accomplished. At her house in Athens, poets, philosophers, statesmen, and sculptors frequently gathered to do her honor. Pericles is said to have wept only three times in life; and one of these was when he defended Aspasia before the dicastery of Athens against the charge of impiety.

Another of the Hetairai scarcely less famous than Aspasia was the celebrated Athenian courtesan, Phryne. Praxiteles, the sculptor, was one of her adorers.

She, too, was tried for impiety before the dicastery. Hiperides, the Attic orator, defended her. To create a favorable impression upon the court, he bade her reveal her bosom to the judges. She did so, and was acquitted. So great was the veneration in which Phryne was held that it was considered no profanation to place her image in the sacred temple at Delphi. And so overwhelming was her beauty, that her statues were identified with the Aphrodite of Apelles and the Cnidian goddess of Praxiteles. At Eleusis, on the occasion of a national festival, she impersonated Venus by entering naked into the waves, in the presence of spectators from all the cities of Greece. She is said to have amassed such a fortune that she felt justified in offering to build the walls of Thebes.

Such was the esteem in which these elegant harlots were held, that we find recorded among their patrons on the pages of Greek history the names of Pericles, Demades, Lysias, Demosthenes, Isocrates, Aristotle, Aristippus, and Epicurus. So little odium attached to the occupation of this class of women that we read that Socrates frequently paid visits to one of them named Theodota and advised her as to the best method of gaining "friends" and keeping them.[27]

As the sculptors did not hesitate to carve the images of the Hetairai in marble and give them the names of the goddesses of Olympus, so the poets, orators, and historians did not fail to immortalize them in their poems, orations, and annals. Greek statuary and literature were then transported to Italy to corrupt Roman manners. It was not long before adultery and seduction had completely poisoned and polluted every fountain of Roman private life. "Liaisons in the first houses," says Mommsen, "had become so frequent, that only a scandal altogether exceptional could make them the subject of special talk; a judicial interference seems now almost ridiculous."

Roman women of patrician rank, not content with noblemen as lovers, sought out "lewd fellows of the baser sort" among slaves and gladiators, as companions of corrupt intrigues. Juvenal, in his Sixth Satire, paints a horrible picture of social depravity when he describes the lewdness of Messalina, the wife of Claudius I. This woman, the wife of an emperor, and the mother of the princely Britannicus, descends from the imperial bed, in the company of a single female slave, at the dead of night, to a common Roman brothel, assumes the name Lycisca, and submits to the embraces of the coarsest Roman debauchees.

The degradation of women was not peculiar to the Capital of the empire, but extended to every province. Social impurity was rankest in the East, but it was present everywhere. Virtue seemed to have left the earth, and Vice had taken her place as the supreme mistress of the world.

Luxury and Extravagance.— At the birth of Christ, the frontiers of the Roman empire comprised all the territory of the then civilized world. In extending her conquests, Rome laid heavy tribute upon conquered nations. All the wealth of the earth flowed into her coffers. The result was unexampled luxury and extravagance. A single illustration will serve to show the mode of life of the wealthy Roman citizen of the time of which we write. Lucullus, the lieutenant of Sulla, and the friend of Cicero and Pompey, had amassed enormous wealth in the

Mithradatic wars. This fortune he employed to inaugurate and maintain a style of social life whose splendor and extravagance were the astonishment and scandal of his age and race. The meals served upon his table, even when no guests were present, were marked by all the taste, elegance, and completeness of a banquet. On one occasion, when he happened to dine alone, the table was not arranged with the ordinary fullness and splendor; whereupon he made complaint to the servants, who replied that they did not think it necessary to prepare so completely when he was alone. "What! did you not know that Lucullus would dine with Lucullus?" was his answer. At another time, Cicero and Pompey met him in the Forum and requested that he take them with him to dine, as they desired to learn how his table was spread when no visitors were expected. Lucullus was embarrassed for a moment; but soon regained his composure, and replied that he would be delighted to have such distinguished Romans dine with him, but that he would like to have a day for preparation. They refused this request, however; nor would they consent that he send directions to his servants, as they desired to see how meals were served in his home when no guests were there. Lucullus then requested Cicero and Pompey to permit him to tell his servants, in their presence, in what room the repast should be served. They consented to this; and Lucullus then directed that the Hall of Apollo should be arranged for the dinner. Now the dining rooms in the home of Lucullus were graded in price; and it was only necessary to designate the room in order to notify the servants of the style and costliness of the entertainment desired. The Hall of Apollo called for an expenditure, at each meal, of fifty thousand drachmas, the equivalent of $10,000 in our money. And when Cicero and Pompey sat down at the table of Lucullus a few hours later, the decorations of the room and the feast spread before them, offered a spectacle of indescribable beauty and luxury. The epicure had outwitted the orator and the general.

Other anecdotes related by Plutarch also illustrate the luxurious life of Lucullus. Once when Pompey was sick, his physician prescribed a thrush for his meal; whereupon Pompey's servants notified him that a thrush could not be secured in Italy during the summer time, except in the fattening coops of Lucullus.

Cato despised the luxurious habits of Lucullus; and, on one occasion, when a young man was extolling the beauties of frugality and temperance in a speech before the senate, the Stoic interrupted him by asking: "How long do you mean to go on making money like Crassus, living like Lucullus and talking like Cato?"[28]

Lucullus was not the only Roman of his day who spent fabulous sums of money in luxurious living and in building palatial residences. M. Lepidus, who was elected Consul in 87 B.C., erected the most magnificent private edifice ever seen in Rome.

But the culmination of magnificence in Roman architecture was the Golden House of Nero. Its walls were covered with gold and studded with precious stones. The banquet rooms were decorated with gorgeous ceilings, and were so constructed that from them flowers and perfumes could be showered from above on the guests below.

Concerning the luxurious life of the later days of the republic, Mommsen says: "Extravagant prices, as much as one hundred thousand sesterces (M1,000) were paid for an exquisite cook. Houses were constructed with special reference to this subject. . . . A dinner was already described as poor at which the fowls were served up to the guests entire, and not merely the choice portions. . . . At banquets, above all, the Romans displayed their hosts of slaves ministering to luxury, the bands of musicians, their dancing-girls, their elegant furniture, their carpets glittering with gold, or pictorially embroidered, their rich silver plate."[29]

But the luxury and extravagance of the Romans were nowhere so manifest as in their public bathing establishments. "The magnificence of many of the thermae and their luxurious arrangements were such that some writers, as Seneca, are quite lost in their descriptions of them. The piscinae were often of immense size—that of Diocletian being 200 feet long—and were adorned with beautiful marbles. The halls were crowded with magnificent columns, and were ornamented with the finest pieces of statuary. The walls, it has been said, were covered with exquisite mosaics that imitated the art of the painter in their elegance of design and variety of color. The Egyptian syenite was encrusted with the precious green marbles of Numidia. The rooms contained the works of Phidias and Praxiteles. A perpetual stream of water was poured into capacious basins through the wide mouths of lions of bright and polished silver. 'To such a pitch of luxury have we reached,' says Seneca, 'that we are dissatisfied if we do not tread on gems in our baths.' "[30]

The circuses were scarcely inferior to the baths in magnificence. Caligula is said to have strewn them with gold dust.

The result of Roman luxury in the matter of food and drink was a coarse and loathsome gluttony which finds no parallel in modern life. Epicureanism had degenerated from barley-bread and water to the costliest diet ever known. Wealthy Romans of the age of Augustus did not hesitate to pay two hundred and fifty dollars for a single fish—the mullet. And that they might indulge their appetite to the fullest extent, and prolong the pleasures of eating beyond the requirements and even the capacity of nature, they were in the habit of taking an emetic at meal times. We learn from the letters of Cicero that Julius Caesar did this on one occasion when he went to visit the orator at his country villa. And the degeneracy of Roman life is nowhere more clearly indicated than in the Fourth Satire of Juvenal where he describes the gathering of the great men of the state, at the call of Domitian, to determine how a turbot should be cooked.

But the reader must not infer that all Romans were rich and that luxury was indulged in every home. In the Roman capital the extremes of wealth and poverty met. The city was filled with idlers, vagabonds and paupers from all quarters of the globe. In the early days of the Republic, sturdy farmers had tilled the soil of Italy and had filled the legions with brave and hardy warriors. The beginning of the empire witnessed a radical change. Hundreds of thousands of these farmers had been driven from their lands to furnish homes to the disbanded soldiers of conquerors like Sulla, Marius, and Caesar. Homeless and poverty-stricken, they wandered away to Rome to swell the ranks of mendicants and adventurers that crowded the streets of the imperial city. The soldiers themselves, finding agriculture distasteful and unprofitable, sold their lands to Roman speculators, and returned to the scene of the triumphs of their military masters. The inevitable consequence of this influx of strangers and foreigners, without wealth and without employment, was the degradation and demoralization of Roman social and industrial life. Augustus was compelled to make annual donations of money and provisions to 200,000 persons who wandered helpless about the streets. This state of things—fabulous wealth in the hands of a few, and abject poverty as the lot of millions—was the harbinger sure and swift to the destruction of the state.

Slavery.— At the beginning of the Christian era, slavery existed in every province of the Roman empire. Nearly everywhere the number of slaves was much greater than that of the free citizens. In Attica, according to the census of Demetrius Phalereus, about the beginning of the fourth century B.C., there were 400,000 slaves, 10,000 foreign settlers, and 20,000 free citizens. Zumpt estimates that there were two slaves to every freeman in Rome in the year 5 B.C. It frequently happened that a wealthy Roman possessed as many as 20,000 slaves. Slaves who gained their freedom might themselves become masters and own slaves. During the reign of Augustus, a freedman died, leaving 4,116 slaves. Crassus possessed so many that his company of architects and carpenters alone exceeded 500 in number.

The principal slave markets of Greece were those at Athens, Ephesus, Cyprus, and Samos. In the market place of each of these cities, slaves were exposed for sale upon wooden scaffolds. From the neck of each was hung a tablet or placard containing a description of his or her meritorious qualities, such as parentage, educational advantages, health and freedom from physical defects. They were required to strip themselves at the request of purchasers. In this way, the qualifications of slaves for certain purposes could be accurately judged. The vigorous, large-limbed Cappadocians, for instance, like our modern draft horses, were selected for their strength and their ability to lift heavy loads and endure long-continued work.

The property of the master in the slave was absolute. The owner might kill or torture his slave at will. Neither the government nor any individual could bring him to account for it. Roman law compelled female slaves to surrender themselves, against their will, to their master's lust. All the coarseness and brutality of the haughty, arrogant, and merciless Roman disposition were manifested in the treatment of their slaves. Nowhere do we find any mercy or humanity shown them. On the farms they worked with chains about their limbs during the day; and at night they were lodged in the *ergastula* —subterranean apartments, badly lighted and poorly ventilated. The most cruel punishment awaited the slave who attempted to escape. The *fugitavarii*— professional slave chasers—ran him down, branded him on the forehead, and brought him back to

his master. If the master was very rich, or cared little for the life of the slave, he usually commanded him to be thrown, as a punishment for his attempt to flee, to the wild beasts in the amphitheater. This cruel treatment was not exceptional, but was ordinary. Cato, the paragon among the Stoics, was so merciless in his dealings with his slaves that one of them committed suicide rather than await the hour of punishment for some transgression of which he was guilty.[31] It frequently happened that the slaves had knowledge of crimes committed by their masters. In such cases they were fortunate if they escaped death, as the probability of their becoming witnesses against their masters offered every inducement to put them out of the way. In his defense of Cluentius, Cicero speaks of a slave who had his tongue cut out to prevent his betraying his mistress.[32] If a slave murdered his master, all his fellow-slaves under the same roof were held responsible for the deed. Thus four hundred slaves were put to death for the act of one who assassinated Pedanius Secundus, during the reign of Nero.[33] Augustus had his steward, Eros, crucified on the mast of his ship because the slave had roasted and eaten a quail that had been trained for the royal quail-pit. Once a slave was flung to the fishes because he had broken a crystal goblet.[34] On another occasion, a slave was compelled to march around a banquet table, in the presence of the guests, with his hands, which had been cut off, hanging from his neck, because he had stolen some trifling article of silverware. Cicero, in his prosecution of Verres, recites an instance of mean and cowardly cruelty toward a slave. "At the time," he says, "in which L. Domitius was praetor in Sicily, a slave killed a wild boar of extraordinary size. The praetor, struck by the dexterity and courage of the man, desired to see him. The poor wretch, highly gratified with the distinction, came to present himself before the praetor, in hopes, no doubt, of praise and reward; but Domitius, on learning that he had only a javelin to attack and kill the boar, ordered him to be instantly crucified, under the barbarous pretext that the law prohibited the use of this weapon, as of all others, to slaves."

The natural consequence of this cruel treatment was unbounded hatred of the master by the slave. "We have as many enemies," says Seneca, "as we have slaves." And what rendered the situation perilous was the numerical superiority of the slave over the free population. "They multiply at an immense rate," says Tacitus, "whilst freemen diminish in equal proportion." Pliny the Younger gave expression to the universal apprehension when he wrote: "By what dangers we are beset! No one is safe; not even the most indulgent, gentlest master." Precautionary measures were adopted from time to time both by individuals and by the government to prevent concerted action among the slaves and to conceal from them all evidences of their own strength. To keep down mutiny among his slaves, Cato is said to have constantly excited dissension and enmity among them. "It was once proposed," says Gibbon, "to discriminate the slaves by a peculiar habit; but it was justly apprehended that there might be some danger in acquainting them with their own numbers."[35]

If the Roman masters maltreated and destroyed the bodies of their slaves, the slaves retaliated by corrupting and destroying the morals of their masters. The institution of slavery was one of the most potent agencies in the demoralization of ancient Roman manners. The education of children was generally confided to the slaves, who did not fail to poison their minds and hearts in many ways. In debauching their female slaves, the Roman masters polluted their own morals and corrupted their own manhood. The result teaches us that the law of physics is the law of morals: that action and reaction are equal, but in opposite directions.

Destruction of New-Born Infants.— The destruction of new-born children was the deepest stain upon the civilization of the ancient Greeks and Romans. In obedience to a provision of the code of Lycurgus, every Spartan child was exhibited immediately after birth to public view; and, if it was found to be deformed and weakly, so that it was unfit to grow into a strong and healthy citizen of the Spartan military commonwealth, it was exposed to perish on Mount Taygetus. The practice of exposing infants was even more arbitrary and cruel in Rome than in Greece. The Roman father was bound by no limitations; but could cast his offspring away to die, through pure caprice. Paulus, the celebrated jurist of the imperial period, admitted that this was a paternal privilege. Suetonius tells us that the day of the death of Germanicus, which took place A.D. 19, was signalized by the exposition of children who were born on that day.[36] This was done as a manifestation of general sorrow. The emperor Augustus banished his granddaughter Julia on account of her lewdness and licentiousness, as he had done in the case of his daughter, Julia. In exile, she gave birth to a child which Augustus caused to be exposed. It often happened that new-born babes that had been cast away to die of cold and hunger or to be devoured by dogs or wild beasts were rescued by miscreants who brought them up to devote them to evil purposes. The male children were destined to become gladiators, and the females were sold to houses of prostitution. Often such children were picked up by those who disfigured and deformed them for the purpose of associating them with themselves as beggars.

The custom of exposing infants was born of the spirit of fierceness and barbarity that characterized many ancient races. Its direct tendency was to make savages of men by destroying those tender and humane feelings for the weak and helpless which have been the most marked attributes of modern civilizations. Occasionally in our day one hears or reads of a proposition by some pseudo-philanthropist that the good of the race demands the destruction of certain persons—deformed infants, imbecile adults and the like. But the humanity of the age invariably frowns upon such proposals. The benign and merciful features of our Christian creed would be outraged by such a practice.

Gladiatorial Games.— The combats of gladiators were the culmination of Roman barbarity and brutality. All the devotees of vice and crime met and mingled at the arena, and derived strength and inspiration from its bloody scenes. The gatherings in the amphitheater were miniatures of Roman life. There, political matters were discussed and questions of state determined, as was once the case in the public assemblies of the people. Now that the gates of Janus were closed for the third time in Roman history, the combats of the arena took the place, on a diminutive scale, of those battles by which Romans had conquered the world. The processions of the gladiators reminded the enthusiastic populace of the triumphal entries of their conquerors into the Roman capital. Nothing so glutted the appetite and quenched the thirst of a cruel and licentious race as the gorgeous ceremonials and bloody butchery of the gladiatorial shows.

These contests, strange to say, first took place at funerals, and were intended to honor the dead. In 264 B.C., at the burial of D. Junius Brutus, we are told, three pairs of gladiators fought in the cattle market. Again, in 216 B.C., at the obsequies of M. Aemilius Lepidus, twenty-two pairs engaged in combat in the Forum. And, in 174 B.C., on the death of his father, Titus Flaminius caused seventy-four pairs to fight for three days.[37] It will thus be seen that the death of one Roman generally called for that of several others.

In time, the fondness of these contests had grown so great that generals and statesmen arranged them on a gigantic scale as a means of winning the favor and support of the multitude. The Roman proletariat demanded not only bread to satisfy their hunger, but games to amuse them in their hours of idleness. Augustus not only gave money and rations to 200,000 idlers, but inaugurated gladiatorial shows in which 10,000 combatants fought. Not only men but wild beasts were brought into the arena. Pompey arranged a fight of 500 lions, 18 elephants and 410 other ferocious animals, brought from Africa. In a chase arranged by Augustus, A.D. 5, 36 crocodiles were killed in the Flaminian circus, which was flooded for the purpose. Caligula brought 400 bears into the arena to fight with an equal number of African wild animals. But all previous shows were surpassed in the magnificent games instituted by Trajan, A.D. 106, to celebrate his victories on the Danube. These games lasted four months; and, in them, 10,000 gladiators fought, and 11,000 beasts were slain.

Such was the thirst for blood, and to such a pitch had the fury of the passions reached at the beginning of the empire that Romans were no longer satisfied with small fights by single pairs. They began to demand regular battles and a larger flow of blood. And to please the populace, Julius Caesar celebrated his triumph by a real battle in the circus. On each side were arrayed 500 foot soldiers, 300 cavalrymen, and 20 elephants bearing soldiers in towers upon their backs. This was no mimic fray, but an actual battle in which blood was shed and men were killed. To vary the entertainment, Caesar also arranged a sea fight. He caused a lake to be dug out on Mars Field, and placed battleships upon it which represented Tyrian and Egyptian fleets. These he caused to be manned by a thousand soldiers and 2,000 oarsmen. A bloody fight then ensued between men who had no other motive in killing each other than to furnish a Roman holiday. Augustus also arranged a sea fight upon an artificial lake where 3,000 men were engaged. But both these battles were eclipsed by the great sea fight which the emperor Claudius caused to be fought on Lake Fucinus, in the presence of a great multitude that lined the shore. Nineteen thousand men engaged in the bloody struggle. On an eminence overlooking the lake, the Empress Agrippina, in gorgeous costume, sat by the side of the emperor and watched the battle.

Announcement of gladiatorial fights in the amphitheater was made by posters on the walls of the city. In these advertisements, the number and names of the fighters were announced. On the day of the performance a solemn procession of gladiators, walking in couples, passed through the streets to the arena. The arrangements of the building and the manner of the fights were so ordered as to arouse to the highest pitch of excitement the passions and expectations of the spectators. The citizens were required to wear the white toga. The lower rows of seats were occupied by senators, in whose midst were the boxes occupied by the imperial family. The equestrian order occupied places immediately above the senators. The citizens were seated next after the equestrians; and in the topmost rows, on benches, were gathered the Roman rabble. An immense party-colored awning, stretched above the multitude, reflected into the arena its variegated hues. Strains of music filled the air while preparations for the combat were being made. The atmosphere of the amphitheater was kept cool and fragrant by frequent sprays of perfume. The regular combat was preceded by a mock fight with blunt weapons. Then followed arrangements for the life-and-death struggle. The manager of the games finally gave the command, and the fight was on. When one of the gladiators was wounded, the words "hoc habet" were shouted. The wounded man fell to the earth, dropped his weapon, and, holding up his forefinger, begged his life from the people. If mercy was refused him, he was compelled to renew the combat or to submit to the death stroke of his antagonist. Attendants were at hand with hot irons to apply to the victim to see that death was not simulated. If life was not extinct, the fallen gladiator was dragged out to the dead room, and there dispatched. Servants then ran into the arena and scattered sand over the blood-drenched ground. Other fighters standing in readiness, immediately rushed in to renew the contest. Thus the fight went on until the Roman populace was glutted with butchery and blood.

Gladiators were chosen from the strongest and most athletic among slaves and condemned criminals. Thracians, Gauls, and Germans were captured and enslaved for the purpose of being sacrificed in the arena. They were trained with the greatest care in gladiatorial schools. The most famous of these institutions was at Capua in Italy. It was here that Spartacus, a young Thracian, of noble ancestry, excited an insurrection that soon spread throughout all Italy and threatened the destruction of Rome. Addressing himself to seventy of his fellow-gladiators, Spartacus is said to have made a bitter and impassioned speech in which he proposed that, if they must die, they should die fighting their enemies and not themselves; that, if they were to engage in bloody battles, these battles should be fought under the open sky in behalf of life and liberty, and not in the amphitheater to furnish pastime and entertainment to their masters and oppressors. The speech had its effect. The band of fighters broke out of Capua, and took refuge in the crater of Mount Vesuvius (73 B.C.). Spartacus became the leader, with Crixus and Oenomaus, two Celtic gladiators, as lieutenants. Their ranks soon swelled to the proportions of an army, through accessions of slaves and desperadoes from the neighborhood of the volcano. During two years, they terrorized all Italy, defeated two consuls, and burned many cities. Crixus was defeated and killed at Mount Gargarus in Apulia by the praetor Arrius. Spartacus compelled three hundred Roman prisoners, whom he had captured, to fight as gladiators, following Roman custom, at the grave of his fallen comrade and lieutenant. Finally, he himself was slain, sword in hand, having killed two centurions before he fell. With the death of their leaders, the insurgents either surrendered or fled. Those who were captured were crucified. It is said that the entire way from Capua to Rome was marked by crosses on which their bodies were suspended, to the number of ten thousand.[38]

Throughout Italy were amphitheaters for gladiatorial games. But the largest and most celebrated of all was the Coliseum at Rome. Its ruins are still standing. It was originally called the Flavian Amphitheater. This vast building was begun A.D. 72, upon the site of the reservoir of Nero, by the emperor Vespasian, who built as far as the third row of arches, the last two rows being finished by Titus after his return from the conquest of Jerusalem. It is said that twelve thousand captive Jews were employed in this work, as the Hebrews were employed in building the Pyramids of Egypt, and that the external walls alone cost nearly four millions of dollars. It consists of four stories: the first, Doric; the second, Ionic; the third and fourth, Corinthian. Its circumference is nearly two thousand feet; its length, six hundred and twenty feet; and its width, five hundred and thirteen. The entrance for the emperor was between two arches facing the Esquiline, where there was no cornice. The arena was surrounded by a wall sufficiently high to protect the spectators from the wild beasts, which were introduced by subterranean passages, closed by huge gates from the side. The Amphitheater is said to have been capable of seating eighty-seven thousand people, and was inaugurated by gladiatorial games that lasted one hundred days, and in which five thousand beasts were slain. The emperor Commodus himself fought in the Coliseum, and killed both gladiators and wild beasts. He insisted on calling himself Hercules, was dressed in a lion's skin, and had his hair sprinkled with gold dust.

An oriental monk, Talemachus, was so horrified at the sight of the gladiatorial games, that he rushed into the midst of the arena, and besought the spectators to have them stopped. Instead of listening to him, they put him to death.

The first martyrdom in the Coliseum was that of St. Ignatius, said to have been the child especially blessed by our Savior, the disciple of John, and the companion of Polycarp, who was sent to Rome from Antioch when he was bishop. When brought into the arena, St. Ignatius knelt down and exclaimed: "Romans who are here present, know that I have not been brought into this place for any crime, but in order that by this means I may merit the fruition of the glory of God, for love of whom I have been made a prisoner. I am as the grain of the field and must be ground by the teeth of the lions that I may become bread fit for His table." The lions were then let loose, and devoured him, except the larger bones which the Christians collected during the night.

The spot where the Christian martyrs suffered was for a long time marked by a tall cross devoutly kissed by the faithful. The Pulpit of the Coliseum was used for the stormy sermons of Gavazzi, who called the people to arms from thence in the Revolution of March, 1848.

Graeco-Roman Social Depravity, Born of Religion and Traceable to the Gods.— The modern mind identifies true religion with perfect purity of heart and with boundless love. "Do unto others as you would have others do unto you" is the leading aphorism of both the Hebrew and Christian faiths. The Sermon on the Mount is the chart of the soul on the sea of life; and its beatitudes are the glorifications of the virtues of meekness, mercy, and peace. To the mind imbued with the divine precepts of the Savior, it seems incredible that religion should have ever been the direct source of crime and sin. It is, nevertheless, a well-established fact that the Roman and Greek mythologies were the potent causes of political corruption and social impurity in both Italy and Greece. Nothing better illustrates this truth than the abominable practice that found its inspiration and excuse in the myth of the rape of Ganymede. The guilty passion of Zeus for the beautiful boy whom he, himself, in the form of an eagle, had snatched up from earth and carried away to Olympus to devote to shameful and unnatural uses, was the foundation, in Greece, of the most loathsome habit that ever disgraced the conduct of men. Passionate fondness for beautiful boys, called paiderastia in Greek, termed sodomy in modern criminal law, was the curse and infamy of both Roman and Grecian life. This unnatural vice was not confined to the vulgar and degenerate. Men of letters, poets, statesmen and philosophers, debased themselves with this form of pollution. It was even legalized by the laws of Crete and Sparta. Polybius tells us that many Romans paid as much as a talent ($1,000) for a beautifully formed youth. This strange perversion of the sexual instincts was marked by all the tenderness and sweetness of a modern courtship or a honeymoon. The victim of this degrading and disgusting passion treated the beautiful boy with all the delicacy and feeling generally paid a newly wedded wife. Kisses and caresses were at times showered upon him. At other times, he became an object of insane jealousy.

An obscene couplet in Suetonius attributes this filthy habit to Julius Caesar in the matter of an abominable relationship with the King of Bithynia.[39] "So strong was the influence of the prevalent epidemic on Plato, that he had lost all sense of the love of women, and in his descriptions of Eros, divine as well as human, his thoughts were centered only in his boy passion. The result in Greece confessedly was that the inclination for a woman was looked upon as low and dishonorable, while that for a youth was the only one worthy of a man of education."[40]

A moment's reflection will convince the most skeptical of the progress of morality and the advance of civilization. That which philosophers and emperors not only approved but practiced in the palmiest days of the commonwealths of Greece and Rome, is today penalized; and the person guilty of the offense is socially ostracized and branded with infamy and contempt.

The above is only one of many illustrations of the demoralizing influence of the myths. The Greeks looked to the gods as models of behavior, and could see nothing wrong in paiderastia, since both Zeus and Apollo had practiced it. Nearly every crime committed by the Greeks and Romans was sought to be excused on the ground that the gods had done the same thing. Euthyphro justified mistreatment of his own father on the ground that Zeus had chased Cronos, his father, from the skies.

Homer was not only the Bible, but the schoolbook of Grecian boys and girls throughout the world; and their minds were saturated at an early age with the escapades of the gods and goddesses as told by the immortal bard. Plato, in the "Republic," deprecates the influence of Homeric myths upon the youth of Greece, when he says: "They are likely to have a bad effect on those who hear them; for everybody will begin to excuse his own vices when he is convinced that similar wickednesses are always being perpetrated by the kindred of the gods." And Seneca thus condemns the moral effect of the myth of Zeus and Alcmene: "What else is this appeal to the precedent of the gods for, but to inflame our lusts, and to furnish a free license and excuse for the corrupt act under shelter of its divine prototype?" "This," says the same author in another treatise, "has led to no other result than to deprive sin of its shame in man's eyes, when he saw that the gods were no better than himself."

We have seen that, in the matter of the multiplicity of the gods, there were deities of the baser as well as of the better passions, and of criminal as well as virtuous propensities. Pausanias tells us that, in his day, on the road to Pellene, there were statues of Hermes Dolios (the cheat), and that the worshipers of this god believed that he was always ready to help them in their intrigues and adventures. The same writer also tells us that young maidens of Troezene dedicated their girdles to Athene Apaturia, the deceiver, for having cunningly betrayed Aethra into the hands of Neptune. The festivals of Bacchus were far-famed in ancient times for the drunken debauches and degrading ceremonies that accompanied them. The Attic feasts of Pan were celebrated with every circumstance of low buffoonery. The solemnities of the Aphrodisia were akin to the bacchanalian orgies in all the features of inebriety and lust. The name of the goddess of love and beauty was blazoned across the portal of more than one Greek and Roman brothel. The Aphrodite-Lamia at Athens and the Aphrodite-Stratonikis at Smyrna were the favorite resorts of the most famous courtesans of antiquity. Venus was the recognized goddess of the harlots. A thousand of them guarded her temple at Corinth; and, when an altar was erected to her at the Colline gate in Rome, in the year 183 A.U.C., they celebrated a great feast in her honor, and dedicated chaplets of myrtle and roses, as a means of obtaining her favor as the guardian divinity of their calling.

What more could be expected, then, of the morality of the Greeks and Romans, when we consider the nature of their religion and the character of their gods? Jupiter and Apollo were notorious rakes and libertines; Venus and Flora were brazen-faced courtesans; Harmonia was a Phrygian dancer, who had been seduced by Cadmus; Hercules was a gladiator; Pan was a buffoon; Bacchus was a drunkard, and Mercury was a highway robber. And not only in the poems of Homer and Hesiod did the Greek and Roman youth learn these things, but from the plays of the theaters and from plastic art as well. If we except the gladiatorial fights in the amphitheaters, nothing was more cruel and unchaste than Greek and Roman tragedy and comedy. At the time of Christ, the tastes and appetites of the multitude had grown so fierce and depraved that ordinary spectacles were regarded as commonplace and insipid. Lifelike realities were demanded from the actors on the stage; and accordingly, the hero who played the role of the robber chief, Laureolus, was actually crucified before the spectators, and was then torn to pieces by a hungry bear. The burning of Hercules on Mount Oeta and the emasculation of Atys were sought to be realized on the stage by the actual burning and emasculation of condemned criminals. Lustful as well as cruel appetites were inflamed and fed by theatrical representations of the intrigues and adventures of the gods and goddesses. Pantomimes and mimic dances, with flute accompaniment, were employed to reproduce the amours and passionate devotions of the inhabitants of Olympus. The guilty loves of Aphrodite with Mars and Adonis, the adventures of Jupiter and Apollo with the wives and daughters of mortals, were the plays most frequently presented and most wildly applauded. And the ignorant rabble were not the only witnesses of these spectacles. "The sacerdotal colleges and authorities," says Arnobius, "flamens, and augurs, and chaste vestals, all have seats at these public amusements. There are seated the collective people and senate, consuls and consulars, while Venus, the mother of the Roman race, is danced to the life, and in shameless mimicry is represented as reveling through all the phases of meretricious lust. The great mother, too, is danced; the Dindymene of Pessinus, in spite of her age, surrendering herself to disgusting passion in the embraces of a cowherd. The supreme ruler of the world is himself brought in, without respect to his name or majesty, to play the part of an adulterer, masking himself in order to deceive chaste wives, and take the place of their husbands in the nuptial bed."[41]

Not only gladiatorial games and theatrical shows, but painting and sculpture as well, served to corrupt and demoralize Roman and Greek manners. Nor is there any prudery in this statement. The masterpieces of the Greek artists have been the astonishment and despair of all succeeding ages; and the triumphs of modern art have been but poor imitations of the models of the first masters. But it is, nevertheless, true that the embodiment in marble of certain obscene myths was destructive of ancient morals. The paintings in the temples and houses of the cities of Greece and Italy were a constant menace to the mental purity of those who gazed upon them. The statue of Ganymede at the side of Zeus was a perpetual reminder to the youth of Athens of the originator of the loathsome custom of paiderastia. The paintings of Leda and the swan, of the courtship of Dionysus and Ariadne, of the naked Aphrodite ensnared and caught in the net with Ares that adorned the walls and ceilings of Greek and Roman homes, were not too well calculated to inspire pure and virtuous thoughts in the minds and hearts of tender youths and modest maidens who looked upon and contemplated them. At Athens, especially, was the corrupting influence of painting and plastic art most deeply felt. "At every step," says Dollinger, "which a Greek or Roman took, he was surrounded by images of his gods and memorials of their mythic history. Not the temples only, but streets and public squares, house walls, domestic implements and drinking vessels, were all covered and incrusted with ornaments of the kind. His eye could rest nowhere, not a piece of money could he take into his hand without confronting a god. And in this way, through the magical omnipresence of plastic art, the memory of his gods had sunk into his soul indelibly, grown up with every operation of his intellect, and inseparably blended with every picture of his imagination."[42]

It can thus be easily imagined how close the connection between the social depravity and the religion of the Greeks and Romans. What was right in the conduct of the gods, men could not deem sinful in their own behavior. Indeed, lewd and lascivious acts were frequently proclaimed not only right, but sacred, because they had been both sanctioned and committed by the gods themselves. "As impurity," says Dollinger, "formed a part of religion, people had no scruples in using the temple and its adjoining buildings for the satisfaction of their lust. The construction of many of the temples and the prevalent gloom favored this. 'It is a matter of general notoriety,' Tertullian says, 'that the temples are the very places where adulteries were arranged, and procuresses pursue their victims between the altars.' In the chambers of the priests and ministers of the temple, impurity was committed amid clouds of incense; and this, Minucius adds, more frequently than in the privileged haunts of this sin. The sanctuaries and priests of Isis at Rome were especially notorious in this respect. 'As this Isis was the concubine of Jove herself, she also makes prostitutes of others,' Ovid said. Still more shameful sin was practiced in the temples of the Pessinuntine mother of the gods, where men prostituted themselves and made a boast of their shame afterwards."[43]

The Bacchanalian Orgies. — The most interesting passage of ancient literature dealing with social life in its relation to religious observances, is an extract from Livy, the most elegant of Roman historians. This passage describes the bacchanalian orgies, and gives exquisite touches to certain phases of ancient Roman social life. Its insertion here entire is excused on the ground of its direct bearing upon the subject matter of this chapter:

A Greek of mean condition came, first, into Etruria; not with one of the many trades which his nation, of all other the most skilful in the cultivation of the mind and body, has introduced among us, but a low operator in sacrifices, and a soothsayer; nor was he one who, by open religious rites, and by publicly professing his calling and teaching, imbued the minds of his followers with terror, but a priest of secret and nocturnal rites. These mysterious rites were, at first, imparted to a few, but afterwards communicated to great numbers, both men and women. To their religious performances were added the pleasures of wine and feasting, to allure a greater number of proselytes. When wine, lascivious discourse, night, and the intercourse of the sexes had extinguished every sentiment of modesty, then debaucheries of every kind began to be practiced, as every person found at hand that sort of enjoyment to which he was disposed by the passion predominant in his nature. Nor were they confined to one species of vice—the promiscuous intercourse of free-born men and women; but from this store-house of villainy proceeded false witnesses, counterfeit seals, false evidences, and pretended discoveries. From the same place, too, proceeded poison and secret murders, so that in some cases, even the bodies could not be found for burial. Many of their audacious deeds were brought about by treachery, but most of them by force; it served to conceal the violence, that on account of the loud shouting, and the noise of drums and cymbals, none of the cries uttered by the persons suffering violation or murder could be heard abroad.

The infection of this mischief, like that from the contagion of disease, spread from Etruria to Rome; where, the size of the city affording greater room for such evils, and more means of concealment, cloaked it at first; but information of it was at length brought to the consul, Postumius, principally in the following manner. Publius Aebutius, whose father had held equestrian rank in the army, was left an orphan, and his guardians dying, he was educated under the eye of his mother Duronia, and his stepfather Titus Sempronius Rutilus. Duronia was entirely devoted to her husband; and Sempronius, having managed the guardianship in such a manner that he could not give an account of the property, wished that his ward should be either made away with, or bound to compliance with his will by some strong tie. The Bacchanalian rites were the only way to effect the ruin of the youth. His mother told him, that, "During his sickness, she had made a vow for him, that if he should recover, she would initiate him among the Bacchanalians; that being, through the kindness of the gods, bound by this vow, she wished now to fulfil it; that it was necessary he should preserve chastity for ten days, and on the tenth, after he should have supped and washed himself, she would conduct him into the place of worship." There was a freedwoman called Hispala Fecenia, a noted courtesan, but deserving of a better lot than the mode of life to which she had been accustomed when very young, and a slave, and by which she had maintained herself since her manumission. As they lived in the same neighborhood, an intimacy subsisted between her and Aebutius, which was far from being injurious either to the young man's character or property; for he had been loved and wooed by her unsolicited; and as his friends supplied his wants illiberally, he was supported by the generosity of this woman; nay, to such a length did she go under the influence of her affection, that, on the death of her patron, because she was under the protection of no one, having petitioned the tribunes and praetors for a guardian, when she was making her will, she constituted Aebutius her sole heir.

As such pledges of mutual love subsisted, and as neither kept anything secret from the other, the young man jokingly bid her not be surprised if he separated himself from her for a few nights; as, "on account of a religious duty, to discharge a vow made for his health, he intended to be initiated among the Bacchanalians." On hearing this, the woman, greatly alarmed, cried out, "May the gods will more favorably!" affirming that "It would be better, both for him and her, to lose their lives than that he should do such a thing:" she then imprecated curses, vengeance, and destruction on the head of those who advised him to such a step. The young man, surprised both at her expressions and at the violence of her alarm, bid her refrain from curses, for "it was his mother who ordered him to do so, with the approbation of his stepfather." "Then," said she, "your stepfather (for perhaps it is not allowable to censure your mother), is in haste to destroy, by that act, your chastity, your character, your hopes and your life." To him, now surprised by such language, and inquiring what was the matter, she said, (after imploring the favor and pardon of the gods and goddesses, if, compelled by her regard for him, she disclosed what ought not to be revealed), that "when in service, she had gone into that place of worship, as an attendant on her mistress, but that, since she had obtained her liberty, she had never once gone near it: that she knew it to be the receptacle of all kinds of debaucheries; that it was well known that, for two years past, no one older than twenty had been initiated there. When any person was introduced he was delivered as a victim to the priests, who led him away to a place resounding with shouts, the sound of music, and the beating of cymbals and drums, lest his cries while suffering violation, should be heard abroad." She then entreated and besought him to put an end to that matter in some way or other; and not to plunge himself into a situation, where he must first suffer, and afterwards commit, everything that was abominable. Nor did she quit him until the young man gave her his promise to keep himself clear of those rites.

When he came home, and his mother made mention of such things pertaining to the ceremony as were to be performed on that day, and on the several following days, he told her that he would not perform any of them, nor did he intend to be initiated. His stepfather was present at this discourse. Immediately the woman observed that "he could not deprive himself of the company of Hispala for ten nights; that he was so fascinated by the caresses and baneful influence of that serpent, that he retained no respect for his mother or stepfather, or even the gods themselves." His mother on one side and his stepfather on the other loading him with reproaches, drove him out of the house, assisted by four slaves. The youth on this repaired to his aunt Aebutia, told her the reason of his being turned out by his mother, and the next day, by her advice, gave information of the affair to the consul Postumius, without any witnesses of the interview. The consul dismissed him, with an order to come again on the third day following. In the meantime, he inquired of his mother-in-law, Sulpicia, a woman of respectable character, "whether she knew an old matron called Aebutia, who lived on the Aventine hill?" When she had answered that "she knew her well, and that Aebutia was a woman of virtue, and of the ancient purity of morals;" he said that he required a conference with her, and that a messenger should be sent for her to come. Aebutia, on receiving the message, came to Sulpicia's house, and the consul, soon after, coming in, as if by accident, introduced a conversation about Aebutius, her brother's son. The tears of the woman burst forth, and she began to lament the unhappy lot of the youth: who after being robbed of his property by persons whom it least of all became, was then residing with her, being driven out of doors by his mother, because, being a good youth (may the gods be propitious to him), he refused to be initiated in ceremonies devoted to lewdness, as report goes.

The consul thinking that he had made sufficient inquiries concerning Aebutius, and that his testimony was unquestionable, having dismissed Aebutia, requested his mother-in-law to send again to the Aventine, and bring from that quarter Hispala, a freedwoman, not unknown in that neighborhood; for there were some queries which he wished to make of her. Hispala being alarmed because she was being sent for by a woman of such high rank and respectable character, and being ignorant of the cause, after she saw the lictors in the porch, the multitude attending to the consul and the consul himself, was very near fainting. The consul led her into the retired part of the house, and, in the presence of his mother-in-law, told her, that she need not be uneasy, if she could resolve to speak the truth. She might receive a promise of protection either from Sulpicia, a matron of such dignified character, or from himself. That she ought to tell him, what was accustomed to be done at the Bacchanalia, in the nocturnal orgies in the grove of Stimula. When the woman heard this, such terror and trembling of all her limbs seized her, that for a long time she was unable to speak; but recovering at length she said, that "when she was very young, and a slave, she had been initiated, together with her mistress; but for several years past, since she had obtained her liberty, she knew nothing of what was done there." The consul commended her so far, as not having denied that she was initiated, but charged her to explain all the rest with the same sincerity; and told her, affirming that she knew nothing further, that "there would not be the same tenderness or pardon extended to her, if she should be convicted by another person, and one who had made a voluntary confession; that there was such a person, who had heard the whole from her, and had given him a full account of it."

The woman, now thinking without a doubt that it must certainly be Aebutius who had discovered the secret, threw herself at Sulpicia's feet, and at first began to beseech her, "not to let the private conversation of a freedwoman with her lover be turned not only into a serious business, but even capital charge;" declaring that "she had spoken of such things merely to frighten him, and not because she knew anything of the kind." On this Postumius, growing angry, said "she seemed to imagine that then too she was wrangling with her gallant Aebutius, and not that she was speaking in the house of a most respectable matron, and to a consul." Sulpicia raised her, terrified, from the ground, and while she encouraged her to speak out, at the same time pacified her son-in-law's anger. At length she took courage, and, having censured severely the perfidy of Aebutius, because he had made such a return for the extraordinary kindness shown to him in that very instance, she declared that "she stood in great dread of the gods, whose secret mysteries she was to divulge; and in much greater dread of the men implicated, who would tear her asunder with their hands if she became an informer. Therefore she entreated this favor of Sulpicia, and likewise of the consul, that they would send her away some place out of Italy, where she might pass the remainder of her life in safety." The consul desired her to be of good spirits, and said that it should be his care that she might live securely in Rome.

Hispala then gave a full account of the origin of the mysteries. "At first," she said, "those rites were performed by women. No man used to be admitted. They had three stated days in the year on which such persons were initiated among the Bacchanalians, in the daytime. The matrons used to be appointed priestesses, in rotation. Paculla Minia, a Campanian, when priestess, made an alteration in every particular as if by the direction of the gods. For she first introduced men, who were her own sons, Minucius and Herrenius, both surnamed Cerrinius; changed the time of celebration, from day to night; and, instead of three days in the year, appointed five days of initiation in each month. From the time that the rites were thus made common, and men were intermixed with women, and the licentious freedom of the night was added, there was nothing wicked, nothing flagitious, that had not been practiced among them. There were more frequent pollution of men, with each other, than with women. If any were less patient in submitting to dishonor, or more averse to the commission of vice, they were sacrificed as victims. To think nothing unlawful, was the grand maxim of their religion. The men, as if bereft of reason, uttered predictions, with frantic contortions of their bodies; the women, in the habit of Bacchantes, with their hair dishevelled, and carrying blazing torches, ran down to the Tiber; where, dipping their torches in the water, they drew them up again with the flame unextinguished, being composed of native sulphur and charcoal. They said that those men were carried off by the gods, whom the machines laid hold of and dragged from their view into secret caves. These were such as refused to take the oath of the society or to associate in their crimes, or to submit to defilement. Their number was exceedingly great now, almost a second state in themselves and among them were many men and women of noble families. During the last two years it had been a rule, that no person above the age of twenty should be initiated, for they sought for people of such age as made them more liable to suffer deception and personal abuse." When she had completed her information, she again fell at the consul's knees, and repeated the same entreaties, that he might send her out of the country. The consul requested his mother-in-law to clear some part of the house, into which Hispala might remove; accordingly an apartment was assigned her in the upper part of it, of which the stairs, opening into the street, were stopped up, and the entrance made from the inner court. Thither all Fecenia's effects were immediately removed, and her domestics sent for. Aebutius, also, was ordered to remove to the house of one of the consul's clients.

When both the informers were by these means in his power, Postumius represented the affair to the senate, laying before them the whole circumstance, in due order; the information given to him at first, and the discoveries gained by his inquiries afterwards. Great consternation seized on the senators; not only on the public account, lest such conspiracies and nightly meetings might be productive of secret treachery and mischief, but, likewise, on account of their own particular families, lest some of their relations might be involved in this infamous affair. The senate voted, however, that thanks should be given to the consul because he had investigated the matter with singular diligence, and without exciting any alarm. They then commit to the consuls the holding an inquiry, out of the common course, concerning the Bacchanals and their nocturnal orgies. They ordered them to take care that the informers, Aebutius and Fecenia, might suffer no injury on that account; and to invite other informers in the matter, by offering rewards. They ordered that the officials in those rites, whether men or women, should be sought for, not only at Rome, but also throughout all the market towns and places of assembly, and be delivered over to the power of the consuls; and also that proclamation should be made in the city of Rome, and published through all Italy, that "no persons initiated in the Bacchanalian rites should presume to come together or assemble on account of those rites, or to perform any such kind of worship;" and above all, that search should be made for those who had assembled or conspired for personal abuse, or for any other flagitious practices. The senate passed these decrees. The consuls directed the curule aediles to make strict inquiry after all the priests of those mysteries, and to keep such as they could apprehend in custody until their trial; they at the same time charged the plebeian aediles to take care that no religious ceremonies should be performed in private. To the capital triumvirs the task was assigned to post watches in proper places in the city, and to use vigilance in preventing any meetings by night. In order likewise to guard against fires, five assistants were joined to the triumvirs, so that each might have the charge of the buildings in his own separate district, on this side the Tiber.

After despatching these officers to their several employments, the consuls mounted the rostrum; and, having summoned an assembly of the people, one of the consuls, when he had finished the solemn form of prayer which the magistrates are accustomed to pronounce before they address the people, proceeded thus: "Romans, to no former assembly was this solemn supplication to the gods more suitable or even more necessary: as it serves to remind you, that these are the deities whom your forefathers pointed out as the objects of your worship, veneration and prayers: and not those which infatuated men's minds with corrupt and foreign modes of religion, and drove them, as if goaded by the furies, to every lust and every vice. I am at a loss to know what I should conceal, or how far I ought to speak out; for I dread lest, if I leave you ignorant of any particular, I should give room for carelessness, or if I disclose the whole, that I should too much awaken your fears. Whatever I shall say, be assured that it is less than the magnitude and atrociousness of the affair would justify: exertions will be used by us that it may be sufficient to set us properly on our guard. That the Bacchanalian rites have subsisted for some time past in every country in Italy, and are at present performed in many parts of this city also, I am sure you must have been informed, not only by report, but by the nightly noises and the horrid yells that resound through the whole city; but still you are ignorant of the nature of that business. Part of you think it is some kind of worship of the gods; others, some excusable sport and amusement, and that whatever it may be, it concerns but a few. As regards the number if I tell you that there are many thousands, that you would be immediately terrified to excess is a necessary consequence; unless I further acquaint you who and what sort of persons they are. First, then, a great part of them are women, and this was the source of the evil; the rest are males, but nearly resembling women; actors and pathics in the vilest lewdness; night revellers, driven frantic by wine, noise of instruments, and clamors. The conspiracy, as yet, has no strength; but it has abundant means of acquiring strength, for they are becoming more numerous every day. Your ancestors would not allow that you should ever assemble casually without some good reason; that is, either when the standard was erected on the Janiculum, and the army led out on occasion of elections; or when the tribunes proclaimed a meeting of the commons, or some of the magistrates summoned you to it. And they judged it necessary, that wherever a multitude was, there should be a lawful govenor of that multitude present. Of what kind do you suppose are the meetings of these people? In the first place, held in the night, and in the next, composed promiscuously of men and women. If you knew at what ages the males are initiated, you would feel not only pity, but also shame for them. Romans, can you think youths initiated, under such oaths as theirs, are fit to be made soldiers? That arms should be intrusted with wretches brought out of that temple of obscenity? Shall these, contaminated with their own foul debaucheries and those of others, be champions for the chastity of your wives and children?

"But the mischief were less, if they were only effeminated by their practices; or that the disgrace would chiefly affect themselves; if they refrained their hands from outrage, and their thoughts from fraud. But never was there in the state an evil of so great magnitude, or one that extended to so many persons or so many acts of wickedness. Whatever deeds of villainy have, during late years been committed through lust; whatever through fraud; whatever through violence; they have all, be assured, proceeded from that association alone. They have not yet perpetrated all the crimes for which they combine. The impious assembly at present confines itself to outrages on private citizens; because it has not yet acquired force sufficient to crush the commonwealth: but the evil increases and spreads daily; it is already too great for the private ranks of life to contain it, and aims its views at the body of the state. Unless you take timely precautions, Romans, their nightly assembly may become as large as this, held in open day and legally summoned by a consul. Now they one by one dread you collected together in the assembly; presently, when you shall have separated and retired to your several dwellings, in town and country, they will again come together, and will hold a consultation on the means of their own safety, and, at the same time, of your destruction. Thus united, they will cause terror to every one of you. Each of you therefore, ought to pray that his kindred may have behaved with wisdom and prudence; and if lust, if madness, has dragged any of them into that abyss, to consider such a person as the relation of those with whom he has conspired for every disgraceful and reckless act, and not as one of your own. I am not secure, lest some even of yourselves may have erred through mistake; for nothing is more deceptive in appearance than false religion. When the authority of the gods is held out as a pretext to cover vice, fear enters our minds, lest in punishing the crimes of men, we may violate some divine right connected therewith. Numberless decisions of the pontiffs, decrees of the senate, and even answers of the aruspices, free you from religious scruples of this character. How often in the ages of our fathers was it given in charge to the magistrates, to prohibit the performances of any foreign religious rites; to banish strolling sacrificers and soothsayers from the Forum, the circus and the city; to search for and burn books of divination; and to abolish every mode of sacrificing that was not conformable to the Roman practice! For they, completely versed in every divine and human law, maintained that nothing tended so strongly to the subversion of religion as sacrifice, when we offered it not after the institutions of our forefathers, but after foreign customs. Thus much I thought necessary to mention to you beforehand, that no vain scruple might disturb your minds when you should see us demolishing the places resorted to by the Bacchanalians, and dispersing their impious assemblies. We shall do all these things with the favor and approbation of the gods; who, because they were indignant that their divinity was dishonored by those people's lust and crimes, have drawn forth their proceedings from hidden darkness into open light; and who have directed them to be exposed, not that they may escape with impunity, but in order that they may be punished and suppressed. The senate have committed to me and my colleague, an inquisition extraordinary concerning that affair. What is requisite to be done by ourselves, in person, we will do with energy. The charge of posting watches through the city, during the night, we have committed to the inferior magistrates; and, for your parts, it is incumbent on you to execute vigorously whatever duties are assigned you, and in the several places where each will be placed, to perform whatever orders you shall receive, and to use your best endeavors that no danger or tumult may arise from the treachery of the party involved in the guilt."

They then ordered the decrees of the senate to be read, and published a reward for any discoverer who should bring any of the guilty before them, or give information against any of the absent, adding, that "if any person accused should fly, they would limit a certain day upon which, if he did not answer when summoned, he would be condemned in his absence; and if anyone should be charged who was out of Italy, they would not allow him any longer time, if he should wish to come and make his defence." They then issued an edict, that "no person whatever should presume to buy or sell anything for the purpose of leaving the country; or to receive or conceal, or by any means aid the fugitives." On the assembly being dismissed, great terror spread throughout the city; nor was it confined merely within the walls, or to the Roman territory, for everywhere throughout the whole of Italy alarm began to be felt—when the letters from the guest-friends were received—concerning the decree of the senate, and what passed in the assembly and the edict of the consuls. During the night, which succeeded the day in which the affair was made public, great numbers attempting to fly, were seized and brought back by the triumvirs, who had posted guards at all the gates; and informations were lodged against many, some of whom, both men and women, put themselves to death. Above seven thousand men and women are said to have taken the oath of the association. But it appeared that the heads of the conspiracy were the two Catinii, Marcus and Caius, Roman plebeians; Lucius Opiturnius, a Faliscian; and Minius Cerrinius, a Campanian: that from these proceeded all their criminal practices, and that these were the chief priests and founders of the sect. Care was taken that they should be apprehended as soon as possible. They were brought before the consuls, and confessing their guilt, caused no delay to the ends of justice.

But so great were the numbers that fled from the city, that because the lawsuits and property of many persons were going to ruin, the praetors, Titius Maenius and Marcus Licinius were obliged, under the direction of the senate, to adjourn their courts for thirty days until the inquiries should be finished by the consuls. The same deserted state of the law courts, since the persons against whom charges were brought did not appear to answer, nor could be found in Rome, necessitated the consuls to make a circuit of the country towns, and there to make their inquisitions and hold the trials. Those who, as it appeared, had been only initiated, and had made after the priest, and in the most solemn form, the prescribed imprecations, in which the accursed conspiracy for the perpetration of every crime and lust was contained, but who had not themselves committed, or compelled others to commit, any of those acts to which they were bound by the oath—all such they left in prison. But those who had forcibly committed personal defilements or murders, or were stained with the guilt of false evidence, counterfeit seals, forged wills, or other frauds, all these they punished with death. A greater number were executed than thrown into prison; indeed the multitude of men and women who suffered in both ways, was very considerable. The consuls delivered the women who were condemned to their relations, or to those under whose guardianship they were, that they might inflict the punishment in private; but if there did not appear any proper person of the kind to execute the sentence, the punishment was inflicted in public. A charge was then given to demolish all the places where the Bacchanalians had held their meetings; first, in Rome, and then throughout all Italy; excepting those wherein should be found some ancient alter, or consecrated statue. With regard to the future, the senate passed a decree, "that no Bacchanalian rites should be celebrated in Rome or in Italy:" and ordering that, "in case any person should believe some such kind of worship incumbent upon him, and necessary; and that he could not, without offence to religion, and incurring guilt, omit it, he should represent this to the city praetor, and the praetor should lay the business before the senate. If permission were granted by the senate, when not less than one hundred members were present, then he might perform those rites, provided that no more than five persons should be present at the sacrifice, and that they should have no common stock of money, nor any president of the ceremonies, nor priest."

Another decree connected with this was then made, on a motion of the consul, Quintus Marcius, that "the business respecting the persons who had served the consuls as informers should be proposed to the senate in its original form, when Spurius Postumius should have finished his inquiries, and returned to Rome." They voted that Minus Cerrinius, the Campanian, should be sent to Ardea, to be kept in custody there; and that a caution should be given to the magistrates of that city, to guard him with more than ordinary care, so as to prevent not only his escaping, but his having an opportunity of committing suicide.

Spurius Postumius some time after came to Rome and on his proposing the question, concerning the reward to be given to Publius Aebutius and Hispala Fecenia, because the Bacchanalian ceremonies were discovered by their exertions, the senate passed a vote, that "the city quaestors should give to each of them, out of the public treasury, one hundred thousand asses; and that the consuls should desire the plebeian tribunes to propose to the commons as soon as convenient, that the campaigns of Publius Aebutius should be considered as served, that he should not become a soldier against his wishes, nor should any censor assign him a horse at the public charge." They voted also, that "Hispala Fecenia should enjoy the privileges of alienating her property by gift or deed; of marrying out of her rank, and of choosing a guardian, as if a husband had conferred them by will; that she should be at liberty to wed a man of honorable birth, and that there should be no disgrace or ignominy to him who should marry her; and that the consuls and praetors then in office, and their successors, should take care that no injury should be offered to that woman, and that she might live in safety. That the senate wishes, and thought proper, that all these things should be so ordered."—All these particulars were proposed to the commons, and executed, according to the vote of the senate; and full permission was given to the consuls to determine respecting the impunity and rewards of the other informers.[44]

The bacchanalian orgies were first suppressed nearly two hundred years before Christ. The above extract from Livy reminds us that at that time the Romans were still strong and virtuous, and that a proposal of their Consul to eradicate a vicious evil that threatened the existence of both domestic life and the State, met with warm approval and hearty support from both the Senate and the people. But the insidious infection was never completely eradicated; and the work of the "Greek from Etruria" bore bitter fruit in the centuries that followed. And when we consider that not only bacchanalian orgies, but Greek literature, painting, sculpture, tragedy and comedy, were the chief causes of the pollution of Roman morals and the destruction of the Roman State, should we be surprised that Juvenal, in an outburst of patriotic wrath, should have declaimed against "a Grecian capital in Italy";[45] and that he should have hurled withering scorn at

>The flattering, cringing, treacherous, artful race,
>Of fluent tongue and never-blushing face,
>A Protean tribe, one knows not what to call,
>That shifts to every form, and shines in all.

And, when we consider the state of the Roman world at the time of Christ, should we be surprised that St. Paul should have described Romans as "Being filled with all unrighteousness, fornication, wickedness, covetousness, maliciousness; full of envy, murder, debate, deceit, malignity; whisperers, backbiters, haters of God, despiteful, proud, boasters, inventors of evil things, disobedient to parents, without understanding, covenant-breakers, without natural affection, implacable, unmerciful"?[46]

Suffice it to say, in closing the chapter on Graeco-Roman paganism, that, at the beginning of the Christian era, the Roman empire had reached the limit of physical expansion. Roman military glory had culminated in the sublime achievements of Pompey and of Caesar. Mountains, seas, and deserts, beyond which all was barbarous and desolate, were the natural barriers of Roman dominion. Roman arms could go no farther; and Roman ambition could be no longer gratified by conquest. The Roman religion had fallen into decay and contempt; and the Roman conscience was paralyzed and benumbed. Disgusted with this world, the average Roman did not believe in any other, and was utterly without hope of future happiness. A gloomy despondency filled the hearts of men and drove them into black despair. When approaching death, they wore no look of triumph, expressed no belief in immortality, but simply requested of those whom they were leaving behind, to scatter flowers on their graves, or to bewail their early end. An epigram of the Anthology is this: "Let us drink and be merry; for we shall have no more of kissing and dancing in the kingdom of Proserpine: soon shall we fall asleep to wake no more." The same sentiments are expressed in epitaphs on Roman sepulchral monuments of the period. One of them reads thus: "What I have eaten and drunk, that I take with me; what I have left behind me, that have I forfeited." This is the language of another: "Reader, enjoy thy life; for after death there is neither laughter nor play, nor any kind of enjoyment." Still another: "Friend, I advise, mix thee a goblet of wine, and drink, crowning thy head with flowers. Earth and fire consume all that remains after death." And, finally, one of them assures us that Greek mythology is false: "Pilgrim, stay thee, listen and learn. In Hades there is no ferryboat, nor ferryman Charon; no Aeacus or Cerberus;—once dead, and we are all alike."[47]

Matthew Arnold has very graphically described the disgusting, sickening, overwhelming despair of the Roman people at the birth of Christ.

Ah! carry back thy ken,
    What, some two thousand years! Survey
The world as it was then.

Like ours it looked, in outward air,
    Its head was clear and true;
Sumptuous its clothing, rich its fare;
    No pause its action knew.

Stout was its arm, each thew and bone
    Seem'd puissant and alive—
But ah! its heart, its heart was stone
    And so it could not thrive.

On that hard pagan world disgust
    And secret loathing fell;
Deep weariness and sated lust
    Made human life a hell.

In his goodly hall with haggard eyes,
    The Roman noble lay;
He drove abroad in furious guise
    Along the Appian Way.

He made a feast, drank fierce and fast,
    And crowned his hair with flowers;
No easier, nor no quicker passed
    The impracticable hours.[48]

But the "darkest hour is just before the dawn," and "the fulness of the time was come." Already the first faint glimmers of the breaking of a grander and better day were perceptible to the senses of the noblest and finest of Roman intellects. Already Cicero had pictured a glorious millennium that would follow if perfect virtue should ever enter into the flesh and come to dwell among men.[49] Already Virgil, deriving inspiration from the Erythraean Sibylline prophecies, had sung of the advent of a heaven-born child, whose coming would restore the Golden Age, and establish enduring peace and happiness on the earth.[50] Already a debauched, degraded and degenerate world was crying in the anguish of its soul: "I know that my Redeemer liveth!" And, even before the Baptist began to preach in the wilderness, the ways had been made straight for the coming of the Nazarene.

APPENDICES

APPENDIX I

CHARACTERS OF THE SANHEDRISTS WHO TRIED JESUS

The following short biographical sketches of about forty of the members of the Sanhedrin who tried Jesus are from a work entitled "Valeur de l'assemblee qui prononca la peine de mort contre Jesus Christ" — Lemann. The English translation, under the title "Jesus Before the Sanhedrin," is by Julius Magath, Oxford, Georgia.

Professor Magath's translation is used in this work by special permission.—The Author.

THE MORAL CHARACTERS OF THE PERSONAGES WHO SAT AT THE TRIAL OF CHRIST

The members of the Sanhedrin that judged Christ were seventy-one in number, and were divided into three chambers; but we must know the names, acts, and moral characters of these judges. That such a knowledge would throw a great light on this celebrated trial can be easily understood. The characters of Caiaphas, Ananos, and Pilate are already well known to us. These stand out as the three leading figures in the drama of the Passion. But others have appeared in it; would it not be possible to produce them also before history? This task, we believe, has never yet been undertaken. It was thought that documents were wanting. But this in an error; such documents exist. We have consulted them; and in this century of historical study and research we shall draw forth from the places where they have been hidden for centuries, the majority of the judges of Christ.

Three kinds of documents have, in a particular manner, enabled us to discover the characters of these men: the books of the Evangelists, the valuable writings of Josephus the historian, and the hitherto unexplored pages of the Talmud. We shall bring to light forty of the judges, so that more than half of the Sanhedrin will appear before us; and this large majority will be sufficient to enable us to form an opinion of the moral tone of the whole assembly.

To proceed with due order, we will begin with the most important chamber—viz., the chamber of the priests.

I. The Chamber of the Priests

We use the expression "chamber of the *priests.*" In the Gospel narrative, however, this division of the Sanhedrin bears a more imposing title. Matthew, Mark, and the other Evangelists, designate it by the following names: the council *of the high priests,* and the council *of the princes of the priests.* [1]

But we may ask, Why is this pompous name given to this chamber by the Evangelists? Is this not an error on their part? An assembly of priests seems natural, but how can there be an assembly of high priests, since according to the Mosaic institution there could be only one high priest, whose office was tenable for life. There is, however, neither an error nor an undue amplification on the part of the Gospel narrators; and we may also add here that both Talmuds positively speak of an assembly of high priests.[2] But how, then, can we account for the presence of several high priests at the same time in the Sanhedrin? Here is the explanation, to the shame of the Jewish assembly:

For nearly a century a detestable abuse prevailed, which consisted in the arbitrary nomination and deposition of the high priest. The high priesthood, which for fifteen centuries had been preserved in the same family, being hereditary according to the divine command,[3] had at the time of Christ's advent become an object of commercial speculation. Herod commenced these arbitrary changes,[4] and after Judea became one of the Roman conquests the election of the high priest took place almost every year at Jerusalem, the procurators appointing and deposing them in the same manner as the praetorians later on made and unmade emperors.[5] The Talmud speaks sorrowfully of this venality and the yearly changes of the high priest.

This sacred office was given to the one that offered the most money for it, and mothers were particularly anxious that their sons should be nominated to this dignity.[6]

The expression, "the *council of the high priests,*" used by the Evangelists to designate this section of the Sanhedrin, is therefore rigorously correct; for at the time of the trial of Christ there were about twelve ex-high priests, who still retained the honorable title of their charge, and were, by the right of that title, members of the high tribunal. Several ordinary priests were also included in this chamber, but they were in most cases related to the high priests; for in the midst of the intrigues by which the sovereign pontificate was surrounded in those days, it was customary for the more influential of the chief priests to bring in their sons and allies as members of their chamber. The spirit of caste was very powerful, and as M. Derembourg, a modern Jewish savant, has remarked: "*A few priestly, aristocratic, powerful, and vain families, who cared for neither the dignity nor the interests of the altar, quarreled with each other respecting appointments, influence, and wealth.*"[7]

To sum up, we have, then, in this first chamber a double element—high priests and ordinary priests. We shall now make them known by their names and characters, and indicate the sources whence the information has been obtained.

CAIAPHAS, high priest then in office. He was the son-in-law of Ananos, and exercised his office for eleven years—during the whole term of Pilate's administration (25-36 A.D.). It is he who presided over the Sanhedrin during this trial, and the history of the Passion as given by the Evangelists is sufficient to make him known to us. (See Matt. xxvi. 3; Luke iii. 2, etc.; Jos., "Ant.," B. XVIII. C. II. 2.)

ANANOS held the office of high priest for seven years under Coponius, Ambivus, and Rufus (7-11 A.D.). This personage was the father-in-law of

Caiaphas, and although out of office was nevertheless consulted on matters of importance. It may be said, indeed, that in the midst of the instability of the sacerdotal office he alone preserved in reality its authority. For fifty years this high office remained without interruption in his family. Five of his sons successively assumed its dignity. This family was even known as the "sacerdotal family," as if this office had become hereditary in it. Ananos had charge also of the more important duties of the Temple, and Josephus says that he was considered the most fortunate man of his time. He adds, however, that the spirit of this family was haughty, audacious, and cruel. (Luke iii. 2; John xviii. 13, 24; Acts iv. 6; Jos., "Ant.," B. XV. C. III. 1; XX. IX. 1, 3; "Jewish Wars," B. IV. V. 2, 6, 7.)

ELEAZAR was high priest during one year, under Valerius Grattus (23-24 A.D.). He was the eldest son of Ananos. (Jos., "Ant.," B. XVIII. II. 2.)

JONATHAN, son of Ananos, simple priest at that time, but afterwards made high priest for one year in the place of Caiaphas when the latter was deposed, after the disgrace of Pilate, by Vitellius, Governor-general of Syria (37 A.D.). (Jos., "Ant.," B. XVIII. IV. 3.)

THEOPHILUS, son of Ananos, simple priest at that time, but afterwards made high priest in the place of his brother Jonathan, who was deposed by Vitellius. Theophilus was in office five years (38-42 A.D.). (Jos., "Ant.," B. XIX. VI. 2; Munk, "Hist. de la Palestine," p. 568.)

MATTHIAS, son of Ananos. Simple priest; afterwards high priest for two years (42-44 A.D.). He succeeded Simon Cantharus, who was deposed by King Herod Agrippa. (Jos., "Ant.," XIX. VI. 4.)

ANANUS, son of Ananos. Simple priest at the time; afterwards made high priest by Herod Agrippa after the death of the Roman governor, Portius Festus (63 A.D.). Being a Sadducee of extravagant zeal, he was deposed at the end of three months by Albanus, successor of Portius Festus, for having illegally condemned the apostle James to be stoned. (Acts xxiii. 2, xxiv. 1; Jos., "Ant.," B. XX. IX. 1.)

JOAZAR, high priest for six years during the latter days of Herod the Great and the first years of Archelaus (4 B.C.-2 A.D.). He was the son of Simon Boethus, who owed his dignity and fortune to the following dishonorable circumstance, as related by Josephus the historian: "There was one Simon, a citizen of Jerusalem, the son of Boethus, a citizen of Alexandria and a priest of great note there. This man had a daughter, who was esteemed the most beautiful woman of that time. And when the people of Jerusalem began to speak much in her commendation, it happened that Herod was much affected by what was said of her; and when he saw the damsel he was smitten with her beauty. Yet did he entirely reject the thought of using his authority to abuse her . . . so he thought it best to take the damsel to wife. And while Simon was of a dignity too inferior to be allied to him, but still too considerable to be despised, he governed his inclinations after the most prudent manner by augmenting the dignity of the family and making them more honorable. Accordingly he forthwith deprived

Jesus, the son of Phabet, of the high priesthood, and conferred that dignity of Simon." Such, according to Josephus, is the origin—not at all of a supernatural nature—of the call to the high priesthood of Simon Boethus and his whole family. Simon, at the time of this trial, was already dead; but Joazar figured in it with two of his brothers, one of whom was, like himself, an ex-high priest. (Jos., "Ant.," B. XV. IX. 3; XVII. VI. 4; XVIII. I. 1; XIX. VI. 2.)

ELEAZAR, second son of Simon Boethus. He succeeded his brother Joazar when the latter was deprived of that function by King Archelaus (2 A.D.). Eleazar was high priest for a short time only, the same king deposing him three months after his installation. (Jos., "Ant.," B. XVII. XIII. 1; XIX. VI. 2.)

SIMON CANTHARUS, third son of Simon Boethus. Simple priest at the time; was afterwards made high priest by King Herod Agrippa (42 A.D.), who, however, deposed him after a few months. (Jos., "Ant.," B. XIX. VI. 2, 4.)

JESUS ben SIE succeeded Eleazar to the high priesthood, and held the office for five or six years (1—6 A.D.) under the reign of Archelaus. (Jos., "Ant.," XVII. XIII. 1.)

ISMAEL ben PHABI. High priest for nine years under procurator Valerius Grattus, predecessor of Pontius Pilate. He was considered, according to the rabbins, the handsomest man of his time. The effeminate love of luxury of this chief priest was carried to such an extent that his mother, having made him a tunic of great price, he deigned to wear it once, and then consigned it to the public wardrobe, as a grand lady might dispose of a robe which no longer pleased her caprices. ("Talmud," "Pesachim," or "of the Passover," fol. 57, verso; "Yoma," or "the Day of Atonement," fol. 9, verso; 35, recto; Jos., "Ant.," XVIII. II. 2; XX. VIII. 11; Bartolocci, "Grand Bibliotheque Rabbinique," T. III. p. 297; Munk, "Palestine," pp. 563, 575.)

SIMON ben CAMITHUS, high priest during one year under procurator Valerius Grattus (24—25 A.D.). This personage was celebrated for the enormous size of his hand, and the Talmud relates of him the following incident: On the eve of the day of atonement it happened, in the course of a conversation which he had with Arathus, King of Arabia—whose daughter Herod Antipas had just married—that some saliva, coming out of the mouth of the king, fell on the robe of Simon. As soon as the king left him, he hastened to divest himself of it, considering it desecrated by the circumstance, and hence unworthy to be worn during the services of the following day. What a remarkable instance of Pharisaical purity and charity! ("Talmud," "Yoma," or "the Day of Atonement," fol. 47, verso; Jos., "Ant.," XVIII. II. 2; Derembourg, "Essai sur l'histoire," p. 197, n. 2.)

JOHN, simple priest. He is made known to us through the Acts of the Apostles. "And Annas the high priest, and Caiaphas, and John, and Alexander, and as many as were of the kindred of the high priest, were gathered together in Jerusalem." (Acts iv. 6.)

ALEXANDER, simple priest; also mentioned in the Acts of the Apostles in the passage above quoted. Josephus also makes mention of him, and says that he afterwards became an *Alabarch* —that is to say, first magistrate of the Jews in Alexandria. That he was very rich is to be learned from the fact that King Herod Agrippa asked and obtained from him the loan of two hundred thousand pieces of silver. (Acts iv. 6; Jos., "Ant.," XVIII. VI. 3; XX. V. 2; Petri Wesselingii, "Diatribe de Judaeorum Archontibus," Trajecti ad Rhenum, pp. 69—71.)

ANANIAS *ben* NEBEDEUS, simple priest at that time; was elected to the high priesthood under procurators Ventideus, Cumanus, and Felix (48—54 A.D.). He is mentioned in the Acts of the Apostles and by Josephus. It was this high priest who delivered the apostle Paul to procurator Felix. "Ananias the high priest descended with the elders, and with a certain orator named Tertullus, who informed the governor against Paul." (Acts xxiv. 1.) According to Jewish tradition, this high priest is chiefly known for his excessive gluttony. What the Talmud says of his voracity is quite phenomenal. It mentions three hundred calves, as many casks of wine, and forty pairs of young pigeons as having been brought together for his repast. ("Talmud," Bab., "Pesachim," or "of the Passover," fol. 57, verso; "Kerihoth," or "Sins which Close the Entrance to Eternal Life," fol. 28, verso; Jos., "Ant.," XX. V. 2; Derembourg, work quoted above, pp. 230, 234; Munk, "Palestine," p. 573, n. 1.)

HELCIAS, simple priest, and keeper of the treasury of the Temple. It is probably from him that Judas Iscariot received the thirty pieces of silver, the price of his treason. (Jos., "Ant.," XX. VIII. 11.)

SCEVA, one of the principal priests. He is spoken of in the Acts apropos of his seven sons, who gave themselves up to witchcraft. (Acts xix. 13, 14.)

Such are the chief priests that constituted the first chamber of the Sanhedrin at the time of the trial of Christ.

From the documents which we have consulted and the resume which we have just given, we gather:

1.   That several of the high priests were personally dishonorable.

2.   That all these high priests, who succeeded each other annually in the Aaronic office in utter disregard of the order established by God, were but miserable intruders. We trust that these expressions will not offend our dear Israelitish readers, for they are based on the statements of eminent and zealous Jewish writers.

To begin with Josephus the historian. Although endeavoring to conceal as much as possible the shameful acts committed by the priests composing this council, yet he was unable, in a moment of disgust, to refrain from stigmatizing them. "About this time," he says, "there arose a sedition between the high priests and the principal men of the multitude of Jerusalem, each of which assembled a company of the boldest sort of men, and of those that loved innovations, and became leaders to them. And when they struggled together they did it by casting reproachful words against one another, and by throwing stones also. And there was nobody to reprove them; but these disorders were done after a licentious manner in the city, as if it had no government over it. And such was the impudence and boldness that had seized on the high priests that they had the hardness to send their servants into the threshing-floors, to take away those tithes that were due the [simple] priests. Insomuch that the poorest priests died of want."[8] Such are the acts, the spirit of equity and kindness, that characterized the chief judges of Christ! But the Talmud goes farther still. This book, which ordinarily is not sparing of eulogies on the people of our nation, yet, considering separately and by name, as we have done, the high priests of that time, it exclaims: "What a plague is the family of Simon Boethus; cursed be their lances! What a plague is the family of Ananos; cursed be their hissing of vipers! What a plague is the family of Cantharus; cursed be their pens! What a plague is the family of Ismael ben Phabi; cursed be their fists! They are high priests themselves, their sons are treasurers, their sons-in-law are commanders, and their servants strike the people with staves."[9] The Talmud continues: "The porch of the sanctuary cried out four times. The first time, Depart from here, decandants of Eli;[10] ye pollute the Temple of the Eternal! The second time, Let Issachar ben Keifar Barchi depart from here, who polluteth himself and profaneth the victims consecrated to God![11] The third time, Widen yourselves, ye gates of the sanctuary, and let Israel ben Phabi the willful enter, that he may discharge the functions of the priesthood! Yet another cry was heard, Widen yourselves, ye gates, and let Ananias ben Nebedeus the gourmand enter, that he may glut himself on the victims!" In the face of such low morality, avowed by the least to be suspected of our own nation, is it possible to restrain one's indignation against those who sat at the trial of Christ as members of the chamber of priests? This indignation becomes yet more intense when one remembers that an ambitious hypocrisy, having for its aim the domineering over the people, had perverted the law of Moses in these men. The majority of the priests belonged, in fact, to the Pharisaic order, the members of which sect made religion subservient to their personal ambition; and in order to rule over the people with more ease, they used religion as a tool to effect this purpose, encumbering the law of Moses with exaggerated precepts and insupportable burdens which they strenuously imposed upon others, but failed to observe themselves. Can we, then, be astonished at the murderous hatred which these false and ambitious men conceived for Christ? When his words, sharper than a sword, exposed their hypocrisy and displayed the corrupt interior of these whitened sepulchers wearing the semblance of justice, the hatred they already cherished for him grew to a frenzied intensity. They never forgave him for having publicly unmasked them. Hypocrisy never forgives that.

Such were the men composing the council of priests, when the Sanhedrin assembled to judge Christ. Were we not justified in forming of them an unfavorable opinion? . . . But let us pass on to the second chamber, viz., the chamber of the scribes.

II. Chamber of the Scribes

Let us recall in a few words who the scribes were. Chosen indiscriminately among the Levites and laity, they formed the *corps savant* of the nation; they were doctors in Israel, and were held in high esteem and veneration. It is well known what respect the Jews, and the Eastern nations generally, have always had for their *wise men*.

Next to the chamber of the priests, that of the scribes was the most important. But from information gathered from the documents to which we have already referred, we are constrained to affirm that, with a few individual exceptions, this chamber was no better than that of the priests.

The following is a list of the names and histories of the *wise men* who composed the chamber of the scribes at the trial of Christ:

GAMALIEL, surnamed the ancient. He was a very worthy Israelite, and his name is spoken of with honor in the Talmud as well as in the Acts of the Apostles. He belonged to a noble family, being a grandson of the famous Hillel, who, coming from Babylon forty years before Christ, taught with such brilliant success in Jerusalem. Gamaliel acquired so great a reputation among his people for his scientific acquirements that the Talmud could say of him: *"With the death of Rabbi Gamaliel the glory of the law has departed."* It was at the feet of this doctor that Saul, afterwards Paul the apostle, studied the law and Jewish traditions, and we know how he gloried in this fact. Gamaliel had also among his disciples Barnabas and Stephen, the first martyr for the cause of Christ. When the members of the Sanhedrin discussed the expediency of putting the apostles to death, this worthy Israelite prevented the passing of the sentence by pronouncing these celebrated words: "Ye men of Israel, take heed to yourselves what ye intend to do as touching these men. . . . And now I say unto you, refrain from these men, and let them alone; for if this counsel be of men it will come to naught; but if it be of God ye cannot overthrow it; lest haply ye be found even to fight against God." Gamaliel died nineteen years after Christ (52 A.D.). (Acts v. 34—39; xxii. 3; Mishna, "Sotah," or "the Woman Suspected of Adultery," C. IX.; "Sepher Juchasin," or "the Book of the Ancestors," p. 53; David Ganz, "Germe de David ou Chronologie" to 4768; Bartolocci, "Bibliotheca magna Rabbinica," T. i. pp. 727—732.)

SIMON, son of Gamaliel, like his father, had a seat in the assembly. The rabbinical books speak of him in the highest terms of eulogy. The Mishna, for instance, attributes to him this sentence: "Brought up from my infancy among learned men, I have found nothing that is of greater value to man than silence. Doctrines are not the chief things, but work. He who is in the habit of much talking falls easily into error." This Simon became afterwards the intimate friend of the too celebrated bandit, John of Giscala, whose excesses and cruelty toward the Romans, and even the Jews, caused Titus to order the pillaging of Jerusalem. Simon was killed in the last assault in 70 A.D. (David Ganz, "Chronologie" to 4810; Mishna, "Aboth," or "of the Fathers," C. I.; "Talmud," Jerusalem, "Berachoth," or "of Blessings," fol. 6, verso; "Historia Doctorium Misnicorum," J. H. Otthonis, pp. 110—113; De Champagny, "Rome et la Judee," T. ii. 86—171.)

ONKELOS was born of heathen parents, but embraced Judaism, and became one of the most eminent disciples of Gamaliel. He is the author of the famous Chaldaic paraphrase of the Pentateuch. Although the rabbinical books do not mention him as a member of the Sanhedrin, yet it is highly probable that he belonged to that body, his writings and memory having always been held in great esteem by the Jews; even at the present day every Jew is enjoined to read weekly a portion of his version of the books of Moses. Onkelos carried the Pharisaical intolerance to the last degree. Converted from idolatry to Judaism, he hated the Gentiles to such an extent that he cast into the Dead Sea, as an object of impurity, the sum of money that he had inherited from his parents. We can easily understand how that, with such a disposition, he would not be favorably inclined toward Jesus, who received Gentiles and Jews alike. ("Talmud," 'Megilla," or "Festival of Esther," fol. 3, verso; "Baba-bathra," or "the Last Gate," fol. 134, verso; "Succa," or "the Festival of Tabernacles," fol. 28, verso; "Thosephthoth," or "Supplements to the Mishna," C. v.; Rabbi Gedalia, "Tzaltzeleth Hakkabalah," or "the Chain of the Kabalah," p. 28; "Histor. Doc. Misnic.," p. 110; De Rossi, "Dizionario degli Autori Ebrei," p. 81.)

JONATHAN *ben* UZIEL, author of a very remarkable paraphrase of the Pentateuch and the Prophets. There is a difference of opinion regarding the precise time at which he lived. Some place it several years before Christ; others at the time of Christ. We believe, however, that not only was he contemporary with Christ, but that he was also one of his judges. In support of our assertion we give the two following proofs, which we think indisputable: 1. Jonathan, the translator of the Prophets, has purposely omitted Daniel, which omission the Talmud explains as due to the special intervention of an angel who informed him that the manner in which the prophet speaks of the death of the Messiah coincided too exactly with that of Jesus of Nazareth. Now, since Jonathan has intentionally left out the prophecies of Daniel on account of their coincidence with the death of Christ, it proves that he could not have lived before Christ, but must have been contemporary with him. 2. In comparing the paraphrase of Onkelos with that of Jonathan, we find that the latter had made use of the work of the former, who lived in the time of Christ. Examples may be found in Deut. xxii. 5, Judges v. 26, Num. xxi. 28, 29. If, then, Jonathan utilized the work of Onkelos, who lived in the time of Christ, the fact proves beyond question that he could not have lived before Christ. The Talmudists, in order to reward this person for having, through his hatred of Christ, erased the name of Daniel from the roll of the prophets, eulogize him in the most absurd manner. They relate that while engaged in the study of the law of God, the atmosphere which surrounded him, and came in contact with the light of his understanding, so caught fire from his fervor that the birds, silly enough to be attracted toward it, were consumed immediately. ("Talmud," "Succa," or "the Festival of Tabernacles," fol. 28, verso; David Ganz, "Chronol." 4728; Gesenius, "Comm. on Isaiah," Part I. p. 65; Zunz, "Culte divin des Juifs," Berlin, 1832, p. 61; Derembourg, work quoted above, p. 276; Hanneburg, "Revelat Bibliq.," ii. 163, 432.)

SAMUEL HAKATON, or *the Less*. Surnamed to distinguish him from

Samuel the prophet. It was he who, some time after the resurrection of Christ, composed the famous imprecation against the Christians, called "Birchath Hamminim" (Benedictions of Infidels). The "Birchath Hamminim," says the Talmud, and the commentary of R. Jarchi, "was composed by R. Samuel Hakaton at Jabneh, where the Sanhedrin had removed after the misconduct of the Nazarene, who taught a doctrine contrary to the words of the living God." The following is the singular benediction: *"Let there be no hope for the apostates of religion, and let all heretics, whosoever they may be, perish suddenly. May the kingdom of pride be rooted out; let it be annihilated quickly, even in our days! Be blessed, O Lord, who destroyest the impious, and humblest the proud!"* As soon as Samuel Hakaton had composed this malediction, it was inserted as an additional blessing in the celebrated prayer of the synagogue, the "Shemonah-Essara" (the eighteen blessings). These blessings belonged to the time of Ezra—that is to say, five centuries before the Christian era; and every Jew has to recite it daily. St. Jerome was not ignorant of this strange prayer. He says: *"The Jews anathematize three times daily in their synagogue the name of the Christian, disguising it under the name of the Nazarene."* According to R. Gedalia, Samuel died before the destruction of Jerusalem, about fifteen or twenty years after Christ. ("Talmud," "Berachoth," or "of Prayers," fol. 28, verso; "Megilla," or "the Festival of Esther," fol. 28, verso; St. Jerome, "Comment. on Isaiam," B. II. C. V. 18, 19; Tom. iv. p. 81 of the "Valarsius," quarto edition; Vitringa, "de Synagoga vetr.," T. ii. p. 1036, 1047, 1051; Castellus, "Lexicon heptaglotton," art. Min.)

CHANANIA *ben* CHISKIA. He was a great conciliator in the midst of the doctrinal quarrels so common at that time; and it happened that the rival schools of Shammai and Hillel, which were not abolished with the death of their founders, often employed him as their arbitrator. This skillful umpire did not always succeed, however, in calming the disputants; for we read in the ancient books that in the transition from force of argument to argument of force, the members of the schools of Shammai and Hillel frequently came to blows. Hence the French expression *se chammailler*. It happened, however, according to the Talmud, that Chanania once departed from his usual system of equilibrium in favor of the prophet Ezekiel. It appears that on one occasion the most influential members of the Sanhedrin proposed to censure, and even reject, the book of this prophet, because, according to their opinion, it contained several passages in contradiction of the law of Moses; but Chanania defended it with so much eloquence that they were obliged to desist from their project. This fact alone, reported fully as it is in the Talmud, would be sufficient to show the laxity of the study of the prophecies at that time. Although the exact date of his death is uncertain, it is, nevertheless, sure that it took place before the destruction of the Temple. ("Talmud," "Chagiga," or "the obligations of the males to present themselves three times a year at Jerusalem," 2, 13; "Shabbath," or "of the Sabbath," C. I.; "Sepher Juchasin," or "the Book of Ancestors," p. 57.)

ISMAEL *ben* ELIZA, renowned for the depth of his mind and the beauty of his face. The rabbins record that he was learned in the most mysterious things;

for example, he could command the angels to descend from heaven and ascend thither. We have it also from the same authority that his mother held him in such high admiration that one day on his return from school she washed his feet, and, through respect for him, drank the water she had used for that purpose. His death was of a no less romantic nature. It appears that after the capture of Jerusalem, the daughter of Titus was so struck with his beauty that she obtained permission of her father to have the skin of his face taken off after his death, which skin she had embalmed, and, having perfumed it, she sent it to Rome to figure among the spoils as a trophy. ("Talmud," "Aboda Zarah," or "of Idolatry," C. I.; Rabbi Gedalia, "Tzaltzeleth Hakkabalah," or "the Chain of the Kabalah," p. 29; "Sepher Juchasin," or "the Book of Ancestors," p. 25; "Tosephoth Kiddushin," C. IV.)

RABBI ZADOK. He was about forty years old at the trial of Christ, and died after the burning of the Temple, aged over seventy. The Talmud relates that for forty years he ceased not from fasting, that God might so order it that the Temple should not be destroyed by fire. Upon this the question is propounded in the same book, but no answer given, as to how this rabbin could have known that the Temple was threatened with so great a calamity. We believe that Rabbi Zadok could have obtained information of this terrible event in one of the two ways—either from the prophetic voice of Daniel which proclaimed more than forty years previous to the occurrence that abomination and desolation should crush the Temple of Jerusalem when the Messiah should have been put to death; or by the voice of Jesus himself, who said forty years before the destruction of the Temple: "See ye not all these things?" (i.e., the buildings of the Temple) "verily, verily I say unto you, There shall not be left here one stone upon another that shall not be thrown down." (Mishna, "Shabbath," or "of the Sabbath," C. XXIV. 5 to end; "Eduth," or "of Testimony," C. VII. 1; "Aboth, or "of the Fathers of Tradition," IV. 5; David Ganz, "Chronol." 4785; "Seph. Juchasin," fol. 21, 26; Schikardi, "Jus Regium Hebraeorum," p. 468; Dan. ix. 25—27; Luke xxi. 6; Matt. xxvi. 2.)

JOCHANAN *ben* ZAKAI. The rabbinical books accord to this rabbi an extraordinary longevity. From their writings it would appear that, like Moses, he lived a hundred and twenty years, forty years of which he consecrated to manual labor; another forty to the study of the law; and the last forty years of his life he devoted to imparting his knowledge to others. His reputation as a savant was so well established that he was surnamed the *Splendor of Wisdom.* After the destruction of the Temple, he rallied together the remaining members of the Sanhedrin to Jabneh, where he presided over this remnant for the last four or five years of his life. He died in the year 73 A.D. When he breathed his last, says the Mishna, a cry of anguish was heard, saying: "With the death of Jochanan ben Zakai the splendor of wisdom has been quenched!" We have, however, other information regarding this rabbi which is, so to speak, like the reverse side of a medal. The Bereshith Rabba says that Rabbi Jochanan was in the habit of eulogizing himself in the most extravagant manner, and gives the following as a

specimen of the praises he bestowed upon himself: "If the skies were parchment, all the inhabitants of the world writers, and all the trees of the forest pens, all these would not suffice to transcribe the doctrines which he had learned from the masters." What humility of language! One day his disciples asked him to what he attributed his long life. "To my wisdom and piety," was his reply in his tone of habitual modesty. Besides, if we were to judge of his moral character by an ordinance of which he is the author, his morality might be equal to the standard of his humility. He abolished the Mosaical command of the ordeal of bitter waters, immorally isolating a passage in Isaiah from its context. Finally, to fill up the measure of his honesty, he became one of the lewdest courtiers of Titus, and the destroyer of his country. But while obsequious to human grandeur, he was obdurate to the warnings of God, and died proud and impenitent. ("Talmud," "Rosh Hashanah," or "of the New Year," fol. 20, recto; 31, recto; "Sotah," or "of the Woman Suspected," etc., IX. 9; "Yoma," or "the Day of Atonement," fol. 39, recto, and 43; "Gittin," or "of Divorce," fol. 56, verso and recto; "Succa," or "of the Festival of Tabernacles," fol. 28, verso; Mishna, Chapter, "Egla arupha"; "Sepher Juchasin," or "the Book of Ancestors," fol. 20, recto; "Seph. Hakkabalah"; Otthonis, "Hist. Doct. Misn.," pp. 93—103; Hosea iv. 14; Jos., "Wars," VI. V. 3; De Champagny, "Rome et la Judee," T. i. p. 158.)

ABBA SAUL. He was of prodigious height, and had the charge of superintending the burials of the dead, that everything might be done according to the law. The rabbins, who delight in the marvelous, affirm that in the exercise of his duties he found the thigh bone of Og, the King of Bashan, and the right eye of Absalom. By virtue of the marrow extracted from the thigh of Og, he was enabled to chase a young buck for three leagues; as for the eye of Absalom, it was so deep that he could have hidden himself in it as if in a cavern. These stories, no doubt, appear very puerile; and yet, according to a Talmudical book (Menorath-Hammoer, "the lighted candlestick"), which is considered of great authority even in the modern [orthodox] synagogue, we must judge of these matters in the following manner: "Everything which our doctors have taught in the Medrashim (allegoric or historical commentaries) we are bound to consider and believe in as the law of Moses our master; and if we find anything in it which appears exaggerated and incredible, we must attribute it to the weakness of our understandings, rather than to their teachings; and whoever turns into ridicule whatever they have said will be punished." According to Maimonides, Abba Saul died before the destruction of the Temple. (Mishna, "Middoth," or "of the Dimensions of the Temple," Chapter, "Har habbaith"; "Talmud," "Nidda," or "the Purification of Women," C. III. fol. 24, recto; Maimonides, "Proef ad zeraim"; Drach, "Harmonies entre l'Eglise et la Synagogue," T. ii. p. 375.)

R. CHANANIA, surnamed the Vicar of the Priests. The Mishna attributes to him a saying which brings clearly before us the social position of the Jewish people in the last days of Jerusalem. "Pray," said he, "for the Roman Empire; for should the terror of its power disappear in Palestine, neighbor will devour neighbor alive." This avowal shows the deplorable state of Judea, and the divisions to which she had become a prey. The Romans seem, however, to have cared very little for the sympathy of R. Chanania, for, having possessed themselves of the city, they put him to death. (Mishna, "Aboth," or "of the Fathers of Tradition," C. III. 2; "Zevachim," or "of Sacrifices," C. IX. 3; "eduth," or "of Testimony," C. II. 1; David Ganz, "Chronologie," 4826; "Sepher Juchasin," or "the Book of Ancestors," p. 57.)

RABBI ELEAZAR *ben* PARTAH, one of the most esteemed scribes of the Sanhedrin, on account of his scientific knowledge. Already very aged at the destruction of the Temple, he yet lived several years after that national calamity. ("Talmud," "Gittin," or "of Divorces," C. III. 4; "Sepher Juchasin," p. 31.)

RABBI NACHUM HALBALAR. He is mentioned in the rabbinical books as belonging to the Sanhedrin in the year 28 A.D., but nothing particular is mentioned of his history. ("Talmud," "Peah," or "of the Angle," C. II. 6, "Sanhedrin.")

RABBI SIMON HAMIZPAH. He also is said to have belonged to the Sanhedrin in the year 28 A.D. Beyond this but little is known. ("Talmud," "Peah," C. II. 6.)

These are, according to Jewish tradition, the principal scribes, or doctors, that composed the second chamber of the Sanhedrin at the time of the trial of Christ. The ancient books which speak of them are, of course, filled with their praises. Nevertheless, blended with these praises are some remarks which point to the predominant vice of these men—namely, pride. We read in Rabbi Nathan's book, "Aruch" (a Talmudical dictionary of great authority[12]): *"In the past and more honorable times the titles of rabbin, rabbi, or rav,[13] to designate the learned men of Babylon and Palestine, were unknown; thus when Hillel came from Babylon the title of rabbi was not added to his name. It was the same with the prophets, who were styled simply Isaiah, Haggai, etc., and not Rabbi Isaiah, Rabbi Haggai, etc. Neither did Ezra bring the title of rabbi with him from Babylon. It was not until the time of Gamaliel, Simon, and Jochanan ben Zackai that this imposing title was first introduced among the worthies of the Sanhedrin."*

This pompous appellation appears, indeed, for the first time among the Jews contemporary with Christ. "They love the uppermost rooms at feasts, and the chief seats in the synagogues, and greetings in the market-places, and to be called of men, Rabbi, Rabbi." Proud of their titles and learning, they laid claim to the foremost rank in society. *A wise man,* say they, *should be preferred to a king; the king takes the precedence of the high priest; the priest of the Levite; the Levite of the ordinary Israelite. The wise man should be preferred to the king, for if the wise man should die he could not easily be replaced; while the king could be succeeded by an Israelite of any order.[14]* Basing the social status on this maxim we are not astonished to find in the Talmud[15] that at a certain time twenty-four persons were excommunicated for having failed to render to the rabbi the reverence due his position. Indeed, a very small offense was often sufficient to call forth maledictions from this haughty and intolerant dignitary. Punishment was mercilessly inflicted wherever there was open violation of any one of the following rules established by the rabbis themselves:

If any one opposes his rabbi, he is guilty in the same degree as if he opposed God himself.[16]

If any one quarrels with his rabbi, it is as if he contended with the living God.[17]

If any one thinks evil of his rabbi, it is as if he thought evil of the Eternal.[18]

This self-sufficiency was carried to such an enormous extent that when Jerusalem fell into the hands of Titus, who came against it armed with the sword of vengeance of Jehovah, Rabbi Jehudah wrote with an unflinching pen: *"If Jerusalem was destroyed, we need look for no other cause than the people's want of respect for the rabbis."*[19]

We ask now of every sincere Israelite, What opinion can be formed of the members of the second chamber who are about to assist in pronouncing judgment upon Christ? Could impartiality be expected of those proud and selfish men, whose lips delighted in nothing so much as sounding their own praises? What apprehensions must one not have of an unjust and cruel verdict when he remembers it was of these very men that Christ had said: "Beware of the scribes, which desire to walk in long robes; they make broad their phylacteries and enlarge the borders of their garments; they love greetings in the market, and to be called Rabbi, Rabbi; which devour widows' houses; and for show make long prayers."[20] The remembrance of this rebuke, so galling to their pride, continually rankled in their minds; and when the opportunity came, with what remorseless hate did they wreak upon him their vengeance! We may, then, conclude from the foregoing facts that the members of the chamber of the scribes were no better than those composing the chamber of the priests. To this assertion, however, there is one exception to be made; for, as we have already seen, there was among those arrogant and unscrupulous men[21] one whose sense of justice was not surpassed by his great learning. That man was Gamaliel.

III. Chamber of the Elders

This chamber was the least influential of the three; hence, but few names of the persons composing it at the period to which we refer have been preserved.

JOSEPH OF ARIMATHEA. The Gospel makes of him the following eulogy: Rich man; honorable counselor; good and just man; the same had not consented to the counsel and deed of the others. Joseph of Arimathea is called in the Vulgate, or the Latin version of the Bible, "noble centurion," because he was one of the ten magistrates or senators who had the principal authority in Jerusalem under the Romans. His noble position is more clearly marked in the Greek version. That he was one of the seventy may be concluded, first, because it was common to admit senators who were considered the ancients of the people in this assembly; they were indeed the chiefs and the princes of the nation— *seniores populi, principes nostri;* second, because these words, "he had not consented to the counsel and deed of the others," proves that he had a right to be in the grand assembly and take part in the discussions. (Matt. xxvii. 57—59; Mark vx. 43—46; Luke xxiii. 50; John xix. 38; Jacobi Alting, "Schilo seu de Vaticinio patriarchae Jacobi," p. 310; Goschler, *Diction. Encyclopediq.;* word, "Arimathea"; Cornelius Lapidus, "Comment. in Script. sac.," edition Vives, T. xv. p. 638, second col.)

NICODEMUS. St. John the Evangelist says that he was by profession a Pharisee, a prince of the Jews, a master in Israel, and a member of the Sanhedrin, where he one day attempted to oppose his colleagues by speaking in defense of Jesus. This act brought down upon him the disdainful retort from the others, "Art thou also a Galilean?" He was one, it is true, but in secret. We know from the Gospel account of him that he possessed great riches, and that he used nearly a hundred pounds of myrrh and spices for the burial of Christ. The name of Nicodemus is mentioned in the Talmud also; and, although it was known that his attachment to Christ was great, he is, nevertheless, spoken of with honor. But this fact may be due to his great wealth. There were, says the Hebrew book, three eminent men in Jerusalem—Nicodemus ben Gurien, ben Tzitzith Hacksab, ben Kalba Shevuah—each of whom could have supported the whole city for ten years. (John iii. 1—10; vii. 50—52; xix. 39; "Talmud," "Gittin," or "of Divorces," C. V. fol. 56, verso; "Abadah Zarah," or "of Idolatry," C. II. fol. 25, verso; "Taanith," or "of the Fast Days," III. fol. 19, recto; fol. 20, verso; Midrash Rabbah on "Koheleth," VII. 11; David Ganz, "chron." 4757; Knappius, "Comment. in Colloquium Christi cum Nicodemo"; Cornelius Lapidus, "Comment. in Joann," Cap. III. *et seq.)*

BEN KALBA SHEVUAH. After stating that he was one of the three rich men of Jerusalem, the Talmud adds: "His name was given to him because whosoever entered his house as hungry as a dog came out filled." There is no doubt that his high financial position secured for him one of the first places in the chamber of the ancients. His memory, according to Ritter, is still preserved among the Jews in Jerusalem. ("Talmud," "Gittin," or "of Divorces," C. V. fol. 56, verso; David Ganz, "Chronol." 4757; Ritter, "Erdkunde," XVI. 478.)

BEN TZITZITH HACKSAB. The effeminacy of this third rich man is made known to us by the Talmud, where it is stated that the border of his pallium trained itself always on the softest carpets. Like Nicodemus and Kalba Shevuah, he no doubt belonged to the Sanhedrin. ("Talmud," "Gittin," C. V. fol. 56 verso; David Ganz, "Chron." 4757.)

SIMON. From Josephus the historian we learn that he was of Jewish parentage, and was highly esteemed in Jerusalem on account of the accurate knowledge of the law which he possessed. He had the boldness, one day, to convoke an assembly of the people and to bring an accusation against King Herod Agrippa, who, he said, deserved, on account of his bad conduct, that the entrance into the sacred portals should be forbidden him. This took place eight or nine years after Christ—that is to say, in the year 42 or 43 A.D. We may safely conclude that a man who had power enough to convoke an assembly and sufficient reputation and knowledge to dare accuse a king, must undoubtedly have belonged to the council of the Sanhedrin. Besides, his birth alone at a time when nobility of origin constituted, as we have already said, a right to honors, would have thrown wide open to him the doors of the assembly. (Jos., "Ant.," XIX. VII. 4; Derembourg, "Essai sur l'histoire et la geographie de la Palestine," p. 207, n. 1; Frankel, *Monatsschrift.,* III. 440.)

DORAS was a very influential citizen of Jerusalem, and is thus spoken of by Josephus. He was, however, a man of cruel and immoral character, not hesitating, for the sake of ingratiating himself with Governor Felix, to cause the assassination of Jonathan, the high priest who had made himself obnoxious to that ruler by some just remonstrances respecting his administration. Doras effected the assassination in cold blood by means of murderers hired at the expense of Felix (52 or 53 A.D.). The prominence which this man for a long time maintained in Jerusalem warrants the presumption that he was a member of the Sanhedrin. (Jos., "Ant.," XX. VIII. 5.)

JOHN, son of JOHN.

DOROTHEAS, son of NATHANAEL.

TRYPHON, son of THEUDION.

CORNELIUS, son of CERON.

These four personages were sent as ambassadors by the Jews of Jerusalem to Emperor Claudius in the year 44, when Cuspius Fadus was governor of Judea. Claudius mentions this fact in a letter sent by him to Cuspius Fadus, and which Josephus has preserved. It is very probable that either they themselves or their fathers were members of the chamber of the ancients; for the Jews appointed as their ambassadors only such members of the Sanhedrin as were distinguished for superior learning. (Jos., "Ant.," XX. I. 1, 2.)

The rabbinical books limit their information concerning the members of this chamber to the names we have just mentioned. To be guided, then, by the documents quoted, one would suppose that although this chamber was the least important of the three, yet its members were perhaps more just than those composing the other two, and consequently manifested less vehemence against Christ during His trial. But a statement made by Josephus the historian proves beyond doubt that this third chamber was made up of men no better than were to be found in the others. It was from among the wealthy element of Jewish society, says Josephus, that Sadduceeism received most of its disciples.[22] Since, then, the chamber of ancients was composed principally of the rich men of Jerusalem, we may safely conclude that the majority of its members were infected with the errors of Sadduceeism—that is to say, with a creed that taught that the soul dies before the body.[23] We are, then, in the presence of real materialists, who consider the destiny of man to consist in the enjoyment of material and worldly things,[24] and who are so carnally minded that it would seem as if the prophetic indignation of David had stigmatized them beforehand when he says: "They have so debased themselves as to become like the beasts that have no understanding."[25] Let not our readers imagine that in thus speaking we at all mean to do injustice to the memory of these men. A fact of great importance proves indisputably that Sadducees or Epicureans were numerous among the Sanhedrin. When, several years after the trial of Christ, the apostle Paul had in his turn to appear before that body, he succeeded by the skill of his oratory in turning the doctrinal differences of that assembly to his benefit. "Men and brethren," he exclaimed, "I am a Pharisee, the son of a Pharisee; of the hope and the resurrection of the dead I am called in question."[26] Hardly had the apostle pronounced these words when a hot discussion arose between the Sadducees and the Pharisees, all of them rising and speaking in great confusion—some for the resurrection, others against it—and it was in the tumult of recrimination and general uproar that the apostle was able peacefully to withdraw. Such was the state of things in the supreme council of the Hebrews; and men of notorious heresy, and even impiety, were appointed as judges to decide on questions of doctrine. Among these materialists there were, however, two just men; and, like Lot among the wicked inhabitants of Sodom, there were in this assembly Nicodemus and Joseph of Arimathea.

We shall now briefly sum up the contents of the preceding chapter. We possess certain information respecting more than one half of the seventy-one members of the Sanhedrin. We know almost all the high priests, who, as we have already said, formed the principal element of this council. This majority, as we have intimated, is sufficient for the forming of an estimate of the moral tone of all the judges; and before the debates begin, it is easy to foresee the issue of the trial of Christ.

What, indeed, could have been the issue of a trial before the first chamber, composed as it was of demoralized, ambitious, and scheming priests? of priests who were mostly Pharisees—that is to say, men of narrow minds, careful only of the external, haughty, overbearing, and self-satisfied, believing themselves to be both infallible and impeccable?[27] It is true they expected a Messiah; but their Messiah was to subdue unto them all their enemies, impose for their benefit a tax on all the nations of the earth, and uphold them in all the absurdities with which they have loaded the law of Moses.

But this man who is about to be brought before them has exposed their hypocritical semblance of piety, and justly stripped them of the undeserved esteem in which they were held by the people. He has absolutely denounced the precepts which they invented and placed above the law. He even desired to abolish the illegal taxes which they had imposed upon the people. Are not all these more than sufficient to condemn Him in their eyes and prove Him worthy of death?

Can a more favorable verdict be expected of the members of the second chamber, composed as it was of men so conceited and arrogant? These doctors expected a Messiah who would be another Solomon, under whose reign and with whose aid they would establish at Jerusalem an academy of learning that would attract all the kings, even as the Queen of Sheba was attracted to the court of the wisest king of Israel. But this Jesus, who claims to be the Messiah, has the boldness to declare blessed those who are humble in spirit. His disciples are but ignorant fishermen, chosen from the least of the tribes; his speech of a provoking simplicity, condemning before the multitude the haughty and pretentious language of the doctors. Are not these things sufficient to bring down upon him their condemnation?

And what justice can we expect, in fine, from the third chamber, when we remember that most of its members were depraved Sadducees, caring only for the enjoyment of the things of this world, heedless of the welfare of the soul, almost denying the existence of God, and disbelieving in the resurrection of the dead? According to their views, the mission of the Messiah was not to consist in the regenerating of Israel as well as of the whole human race, but in the making of Jerusalem the center of riches and worldly goods, which would be brought hither by the conquered and humbled Gentiles, who were to become the slaves of the Israelites. But the man upon whom they are called to pass judgment, far from attaching great importance to wealth and dignity, as did they, prescribes to his disciples the renunciation of riches and honors. He even despises those things which the Sadducees esteem most—viz., pedigree, silk attire, cups of gold, and sumptuous repast. What could have rendered his condemnation surer than such manifestations of contempt for the pride and voluptuousness of these men?

To limit our inquiry to the moral characters of the judges alone, the issue of the trial can be but fatal to the accused; and so, when the three chambers constituting the Sanhedrin council had entered into session, we can well imagine that there was no hope for the acquittal of Jesus; for are not all the high priests, as well as the majority of the scribes and ancients, against him?[28]

APPENDIX II

ACTS OF PILATE

The apocryphal Acts of Pilate are herewith given under Appendix II. The authenticity of these writings has never been finally settled by the scholarship of the world. It is safe to say, however, that the current of modern criticism is decidedly against their genuineness. Nevertheless, the following facts seem to be very generally conceded by the critics: That there are now in existence certain ancient documents called the "Acts of Pilate"; that they were probably discovered at Turin, in northern Italy, and were first used by the noted New Testament palaeographer, Dr. Constantine Tischendorf, who studied them in company with the celebrated orientalist, Victor Amadee Peyron, professor of oriental languages in the University of Turin; and, furthermore, that these documents that we now have are approximately accurate copies of the document mentioned by Justin Martyr about the year 138 A.D., and by Tertullian about the year 200 A.D.

But, admitting all these things, the question of *genuineness* and *authenticity* still remains to be settled. Was the document referred to by Justin as the "Acts of Pilate," and again as the "Acts recorded under Pontius Pilate," a genuine manuscript, written by or composed under the direction of Pilate, or was it a "pious fraud of some Christian," who gathered his prophecies from the Old, and his facts from the New Testament, and then embellished both with his imagination?

The subject is too vast and the space at our disposal is too limited to permit a discussion of the authenticity of the Acts of Pilate. We have deemed it sufficient to insert under Appendix II lengthy extracts from the writings of Tischendorf and Lardner, two of the most celebrated biblical critics, relating to the genuineness of these Acts. The reader would do well to peruse these extracts carefully before reading the Acts of Pilate.

LARDNER'S REMARKS ON THE ACTS OF PILATE

The Acts of Pontius Pilate, and his letter to Tiberius

"Justin Martyr, in his first Apology, which was presented to the emperor Antoninus Pius, and the Senate of Rome, about the year 140, having mentioned our Savior's crucifixion and some of the circumstances of it, adds: 'And that these things were so done you may know from the Acts made in the time of Pontius Pilate.'

"Afterwards in the same Apology, having mentioned some of our Lord's miracles, such as healing diseases and raising the dead, he adds: 'And that these things were done by him you may know from the Acts made in the time of Pontius Pilate.'

"Tertullian, in his Apology, about the year 200, having spoken of our Savior's crucifixion and resurrection, and his appearance to his disciples, who were ordained by him to preach the gospel over the world, goes on: 'Of all these things, relating to Christ, Pilate, in his conscience a Christian, sent an account to Tiberius, then emperor.'

"In another chapter or section of his Apology, nearer the beginning, he speaks to this purpose: 'There was an ancient decree that no one should be received for a deity unless he was first approved by the senate. Tiberius, in whose time the Christian religion had its rise, having received from Palestine in Syria an account of such things as manifested our Savior's divinity, proposed to the senate, and giving his own vote as first in his favor, that he should be placed among the gods. The senate refused, because he himself had declined that honor.'

" 'Nevertheless the emperor persisted in his own opinion, and ordered that if any accused the Christians they should be punished.' And then adds: 'Search,' says he, 'your own writings, and you will there find that Nero was the first emperor who exercised any acts of severity toward the Christians, because they were then very numerous at Rome.'

"It is fit that we should now observe what notice Eusebius takes of these things in his Ecclesiastical History. It is to this effect: 'When the wonderful resurrection of our Savior, and his ascension to heaven, were in the mouths of all men, it being an ancient custom for the governors of provinces to write the emperor, and give him an account of new and remarkable occurrences, that he might not be ignorant of anything; our Savior's resurrection being much talked of throughout all of Palestine, Pilate informed the emperor of it, as likewise of his miracles, which he had heard of, and that being raised up after he had been put to death, he was already believed by many to be a god. And it is said that Tiberius referred the matter to the senate, but that they refused their consent, under a pretence that it had not been first approved of by them; there being an ancient law that no one should be deified among the Romans without an order of the senate; but, indeed, because the saving and divine doctrine of the gospel needed not to be confirmed by human judgment and authority. However, Tiberius persisted in his former sentiment, and allowed not anything to be done that was prejudicial to the doctrine of Christ. These things are related by Tertullian, a man famous on other accounts, and particularly for his skill in the Roman laws. I say he speaks thus in his Apology for the Christians, written by him in the Roman tongue, but since (in the days of Eusebius) translated into the Greek.' His words are these: 'There was an ancient decree that no one should be consecrated as a deity by the emperor, unless he was first approved of by the senate. Marcus Aemilius knows this by his god Alburnus. This is to our purpose, forasmuch as among you divinity is bestowed by human judgment.'

"And if God does not please man, he shall not be God. And, according to this way of thinking, man must be propitious to God. Tiberius, therefore, in whose time the Christian name was first known in the world, having received an account of this doctrine out of Palestine, where it began, communicated that account to the senate; giving his own suffrage at the same time in favor of it. But the senate rejected it, because it had not been approved by themselves. 'Nevertheless the emperor persisted in his judgment, and threatened death to such as should accuse the Christians.' 'Which,' adds Eusebius, 'could not be other than the disposal of Divine Providence, that the doctrine of the gospel, which was then in its beginning, might be preached all over the world without molestation.' So Eusebius.

"Divers exceptions have been made by learned moderns to the original testimonies of Justin Martyr and Tertullian. 'Is there any likelihood,' say they, 'that Pilate should write such things to Tiberius concerning a man whom he had condemned to death? And if he had written them, is it probable that Tiberius should propose to the senate to have a man put among the gods upon the bare relation of a governor of a province? And if he had proposed it, who can make a doubt that the senate would not have immediately complied? So that though we dare not say that this narration is absolutely false, yet it must be reckoned as doubtful.' So says Du Pin.

"These and other difficulties shall not be considered.

"Now, therefore, I shall mention some observations:

"In the first place, I shall observe that Justin Martyr and Tertullian are early writers of good repute. That is an observation of Bishop Pearson. These testimonies are taken from the most public writings, Apologies for the Christian religion, presented, or at least proposed and recommended to the emperor and senate of Rome, or to magistrates of high authority and great distinction in the Roman empire.

Secondly: It certainly was the custom of governors of provinces to compose Acts or memoirs or commentaries of the remarkable occurrences in the places where they presided.

In the time of the first Roman emperors there were Acts of the Senate, Acts of the City, or People of Rome, Acts of other cities, and Acts of governors of provinces. Of all these we can discern clear proofs and frequent mention in ancient writers of the best credit. Julius Caesar ordered that Acts of the Senate, as well as daily Acts of the People, should be published. See Sueton. Jul. Caes. c. xx.

"Augustus forbade publishing Acts of the Senate.

"There was an officer, himself a senator, whose province it was to compose those Acts.

"The Acts of the Senate must have been large and voluminous, containing not only the question proposed, or referred to the senate by the consul, or the emperor, but also the debates and speeches of the senators.

"The Acts of the People, or City, were journals or registers of remarkable births, marriages, divorces, deaths, proceedings in courts of judicature, and other interesting affairs, and some other things below the dignity of history.

"To these Acts of each kind Roman authors frequently had recourse for information.

"There were such Acts or registers at other places besides Rome, particularly at Antium. From them Suetonius learned the day and place of the birth of

Caligula, about which were other uncertain reports. And he speaks of those Acts as public authorities, and therefore more decisive and satisfactory than some other accounts.

"There were also Acts of the governors of provinces, registering all remarkable transactions and occurrences.

"Justin Martyr and Tertullian could not be mistaken about this; and the learned bishop of Caesarea admits the truth of what they say. And in the time of the persecuting emperor Maximin, about the year of Christ 307, the heathen people forged Acts of Pilate, derogatory to the honor of our Savior, which were diligently spread abroad, to unsettle Christians, or discourage them in the profession of their faith. Of this we are informed by Eusebius in his Ecclesiastical History.

Thirdly: It was customary for the governors of provinces to send to the emperor an account of remarkable transactions in places where they presided.

"So thought the learned Eusebius, as we have seen.

"And Pliny's letters to Trajan, still extant, are a proof of it. Philo speaks of the Acts or Memoirs of Alexandria sent to Caligula, which that emperor read with more eagerness and satisfaction than anything else.

"Fourthly: It has been said to be very unlikely that Pilate should write such things to Tiberius, concerning a man whom he [Pilate] had condemned to death.

"To which it is easy to reply, that if he wrote to Tiberius at all, it is very likely that he should speak favorably and honorably of the Savior.

"That Pilate passed sentence of condemnation upon our Lord very unwillingly, and not without a sort of compulsion, appears from the history of the Evangelist: Matt. xxvii.; Mark xv.; Luke xxiii.; John xviii. Pilate was hard pressed. The rulers of the Jews vehemently accused our Lord to him. They said they had found him perverting the nation, and forbidding to give tribute to Caesar, saying that himself is Christ, a king, and the like; and all without effect for a while.

"Pilate still sought for expedients to set Jesus at liberty.

"As his reluctance had been very manifest and public in a court of judicature, in the chief city of the nation at the time of one of their great festivals, it is highly probable that when he sent to Rome he should make some apology for his conduct. Nor could anything be more proper than to allege some of our Savior's miracles which he had heard of, and to give an account to the zeal of those who professed faith in him after his ignominious crucifixion, and openly asserted that he had risen from the dead and ascended to heaven.

"Pilate would not dare in such a report to write falsehood, nor to conceal the most material circumstances of the case about which he was writing. At the trial he publicly declared his innocence: and told the Jews several times 'that he found no fault in him at all.'

"And when he was going to pronounce the sentence of condemnation, he took water and washed his hands before the multitude, saying: I am innocent of the blood of this just person: 'See ye to it.' Matt. xxvii. 24.

"When he wrote to Tiberius he would very naturally say something of our Lord's wonderful resurrection and ascension, which were much talked of and believed by many, with which he could not be possibly unacquainted. The mention of these things would be the best vindication of his inward persuasion, and his repeated declarations of our Lord's innocence upon trial notwithstanding the loud clamors and united accusations of the Jewish people and their rulers.

"Pilate, as has been said several times, passed condemnation upon Jesus very unwillingly, and not until after long trial.

"When he passed sentence upon him he gave orders that this title or inscription should be put upon the cross: 'Jesus of Nazareth, the king of the Jews.'

"When he had expired, application was made to Pilate, by Joseph of Arimathea, an honorable counsellor, that the body might be taken down and buried. To which he consented; but not till assurance from the centurion that he had been sometime dead. The next day some of the priests and pharisees came to him, saying: 'Sir, we remember that that deceiver said while he was yet alive, After three days I will rise again. Command, therefore, that the sepulchre be made sure, until the third day, lest his disciples come by night and steal him away, and say unto the people, He is risen from the dead.' 'So the last error shall be worse than the first.'

"Pilate said unto them: 'Ye have a watch; go your way, make it sure as you can'. So they went and made the sepulchre sure, sealing the stone and setting a watch.

"Whilst they were at the sepulchre there was a 'great earthquake,' the stone was rolled away by an Angel, 'whose countenance was like lightning, and for fear of whom the guards did shake and become as dead men.' Some of the guards went down into the City, and showed unto the chief priests all the things that were done.

"Nor can there be any doubt that these things came also to the governor's ears. Pilate, therefore, was furnished with materials of great importance relating to this case, very proper to be sent to the emperor. And very probably he did send them, for he could do no otherwise.

"Fifthly: it is said, 'That if Pilate had sent such things to Tiberius, it is nevertheless very unlikely that Tiberius should propose to the senate that our Savior might be put among the gods, because that emperor had little or no regard for things of religion.'

"But it is easy to answer that such observations are of little or no importance. Few princes are able to preserve uniformity in the whole of their conduct, and it is certain that Tiberius varied from himself upon many occasions and in different parts of his life.

"Sixthly: it is further urged, that if Tiberius had proposed the thing to the senate, there can be no doubt that the senate would have immediately complied.

"But neither is this difficulty insuperable; for we are assured by Suetonius that Tiberius let several things be decided by the senate contrary to his own opinion, without showing much uneasiness.

(It must be observed here that Dr. Lardner is very copious in quotations from the best authorities in proof of all his statements. The reader is referred to Vol. VI of his great works, pages 605-620, where will be found these quotations in foot-notes too lengthy to be transcribed here.)

"Seventhly: The right interpretation of the words of Tertullian will be of use to remove difficulties and to confirm the truth of the account.

"I have translated them in this manner: 'When Tiberius referred the matter to the senate, that our Lord should be placed in the number of gods, the senate refused, because he had himself declined that honor.'

"The words are understood to the like purpose by Pearson.

"There is another sense, which is that of the Greek translation of Tertullian's Apology, made use of by Eusebius: 'The senate refused because it had not itself approved of it.' But that sense, if it be any sense at all, is absurd, and therefore unlikely. If none beside the senate had a right to consecrate any for the deity, yet certainly the consul or the emperor might *refer* such a thing to that venerable body. According to Tertullian's account, the whole is in a fair way of legal proceeding." [And it may be remarked here that Tertullian, being well versed in Roman law, would hardly have passed by a blunder here or committed one in anything wherein he may have had to do with the statement.]

"By virtue of an ancient law, no one might be reckoned a god (at least by the Romans) without the approbation of the senate. Tiberius having been informed of some extraordinary things concerning Jesus, referred it to the senate, that he also might be placed in the number of deities. Was it possible after this that the senate should refuse it, under a pretense that Tiberius had bestowed divinity upon Jesus without their consent, when he had done no such thing, and at the very time was referring it to their judgment in the old legal way?

"Le Clerc objects that the true reading in Tertulian is not— *Non quia in se non probaverat,* but *quia non ipse probaverat.*

"Be it so. The meaning is the same. *Ipse* must intend the emperor, not the senate. The other sense is absurd, and next to a contradiction, and therefore not likely to be right, and at the same time it is a rude and needless affront. The other interpretation represents a handsome compliment, not without foundation. For it is very true that Tiberius had himself declined receiving divine honors.

"Eighthly: It has been objected that Tiberius was unfriendly to the Jewish people, and therefore it must be reckoned very improbable that he should be willing to put a man who was a Jew among the gods.

"But there is little or no ground for this objection. It was obviated long ago in the first part of this work, where beside other things it is said: In the reign of Tiberius the Jewish people were well used. They were indeed banished out of Italy by an edict; but it was for a misdemeanor committed by some villains of that nation. The great hardship was that many innocent persons suffered beside the guilty.

"Upon other occasions Tiberius showed the Jews all the favor that could be desired, especially after the death of Sejanus; and is much applauded for it by Philo.

"Ninthly: Still it is urged, 'Nothing can be more absurd than to suppose that Tiberius would receive for a deity a man who taught the worship of one God only, and whose religion decried all other deities as mere fiction.'

"Upon which I must say, nothing can be more absurd than this objection. Tertullian does not suppose Tiberius to be well acquainted with the Christian religion, our Savior's doctrine.

"All he says is, that, having heard of some extraordinary things concerning him, he had a desire to put him among the Roman deities.

"Tenthly: Tertullian proceeds: 'Nevertheless the emperor persisted in his opinion, and ordered that if any accused the Christians they should be punished.' This was very natural. Though the senate would not put Jesus in the number of deities, the emperor was still of opinion that it might have been done.

"And he determined to provide by an edict for the safety of those who professed a high regard for Jesus Christ. Which edict, as Eusebius reasonably supposes, was of use for securing the free preaching of the gospel in many places.

"But the authority of that edict would cease at the emperor's demise, if not sooner. Unfortunately, it could not be in force, or have any great effect, for a long season.

"Nor need we consider the ordering such an edict as in favor of the Christians as an incredible thing, if we observe what Philo says, who assures us that 'Tiberius gave orders to all the governors of provinces, to protect the Jews in the cities where they lived in the observation of their own rights and customs; and that they should bear hard on none of them, but such as were unpeaceable and transgressed the laws of the State.'

"Nor is it impossible that the Christians should partake of the like civilities, they being considered as a sect of the Jews. And it is allowed that the Roman empire did not openly persecute the Christians, till they became so numerous that the heathen people were apprehensive of the total overthrow of their religion.

"In the eleventh place, says a learned and judicious writer, 'It is probable that Pilate, who had no enmity toward Christ, and accounted him a man unjustly accused and an extraordinary person, might be moved by the wonderful circumstances attending and following his death, to hold him in veneration, and perhaps to think him a hero and the son of some deity. It is possible that he might send a narrative, such as he thought most convenient, of these transactions to Tiberius: but it is not at all likely that Tiberius proposed to the senate that Christ should be deified, and that the senate rejected it, and that Tiberius continued favorably disposed toward Christ, and that he threatened to punish those who should molest and accuse the Christians.' 'Observe also,' says the same learned writer, 'that the Jews persecuted the apostles, and slew Stephen, and that Saul made havoc of the church, entering into every house, and hailing men and women, committing them to prison, and that Pilate connived at all this violence, and was not afraid of the resentment of Tiberius on that account.'

"Admitting the truth of all these particulars just mentioned, it does not follow that no orders were given by Tiberius for the protection of the followers of Jesus.

"For no commands of princes are obeyed by all men everywhere. They are oftentimes transgressed.

"Nor was any place more likely than Judea, where the enmity of many against the disciples of Jesus was so great. Nor need it be supposed that Tiberius was very intent to have this order strictly regarded. For he was upon many occasions very indolent and dilatory; and he was well known to be so. Moreover, the death of Stephen was tumultuous, and not an act of the Jewish council. And further, the influence of Pilate in that country was not now at its full height. We perceive from the history of our Lord's trial before him, as recorded in the gospels, that he stood in fear of the Jews.

"He was apprehensive that, if he did not gratify them in that point, they might draw up a long list of maladministrations for the emperor's view. His condemnation of Jesus at the importunity of the Jews, contrary to his own judgment and inclination, declared to them more than once, was a point gained; and his government must have been ever after much weakened by so mean a condescension. And that Pilate's influence in the province continued to decline is manifest, in that the people of it prevailed at last to have him removed in a very ignominious manner by Vitellius, president of Syria.

"Pilate was removed from his government before the Passover in the year of Christ 36. After which there was no procurator or other person with the power of life and death, in Judea, before the ascension of Herod Agrippa, in the year 41.

"In that space of time the Jews would take an unusual license, and gratify their own malicious dispositions, beyond what they could otherwise have done, without control.

"Twelfth: Some have objected that Tertullian is so absurd as to speak of Christians in the time of Tiberius; though it be certain that the followers of Jesus were not known by that denomination till some time afterwards.

"But this is a trifling objection. Tertullian intends no more by Christians than followers of Jesus, by whatever name they were known or distinguished; whether that of Nazarenes, or Galileans, or disciples.

"And it is undoubted, that the Christian religion had its rise in the reign of Tiberius; though they who professed to believe in Jesus, as risen from the dead and ascended to heaven, were not called Christians till some time afterwards.

"So at the beginning of the paragraph he says, 'There was an ancient law that no god should be consecrated by the emperor, unless it was first approved by the senate.' Nevertheless, Tertullian was not so ignorant as not to know that there were not any emperors when the ancient decree was passed.

"His meaning is, that no one should be deified by any man, no, not by a consul or emperor, without the approbation of the senate.

"Finally: We do not suppose that Tiberius understood the doctrine of the Savior, or that he was at all inclined to be a Christian.

"Nor did Tertullian intend to say any such thing, for immediately after the passage first cited from him, he adds: 'But the Caesars themselves would have believed in Jesus Christ, if they had not been necessary for the world, or if Christians could have been Caesars.'

"Grotius appears to have rightly understood the importance of these passages of Tertullian; whose note upon Matthew xxiv. 2, I have transcribed below." The reader is referred to vol. VI. of Lardner's Works, where he will find the notes of this learned writer, as quoted from various ancients and moderns, in proof of all he has brought forward in these lengthy arguments, and which cannot be transcribed here.

"Admit, then, the right interpretation of Tertullian, and it may be allowed that what he says is not incredible or improbable. The Romans had almost innumerable deities, and yet they frequently added to that number and adopted new. As deifications were very frequent, Tiberius might have indulged a thought of placing Jesus among the established deities without intending to derogate from the worship or honor of those who were already received.

"But the senate was not in a humor to gratify him.

"And the reason assigned is, because the emperor himself had declined that honor, which is so plausible a pretense, and so fine a compliment, that we cannot easily suppose it to be Tertullian's own invention; which, therefore, gives credibility to his account.

"Eusebius, though he acknowledged the overruling providence of God in the favorable disposition of Tiberius toward the first followers of Jesus, by which means the Christian religion in its infancy was propagated over the world with less molestation, does also say, at the beginning of the chapter quoted, 'The senate refused their consent to the emperor's proposal, under a pretence that they had not been first asked, there being an ancient law, that no one should be deified without the approbation of the senate; but, indeed,' adds he, 'because the saving and divine doctrine of the gospel needed not to be ratified by human judgment and authority.'

Chyrsostom's observation is to like purpose, but with some inaccuracies. It is likely that he was not at all acquainted with Tertullian; and he was no admirer of Eusebius. Perhaps he builds upon general tradition only. 'The Roman senate,' says he, 'had the power of nominating and decreeing who should be gods. When, therefore, all things concerning Christ had been published, he who was the governor of the Jewish nation sent to them to know if they would be pleased to appoint him also to be a god. But they refused, being offended and provoked, that before their decree and judgment had been obtained, the power of the crucified one had shined out and had attracted all the world to the worship of him. But, by the overruling providence of God, this was brought to pass against their will, that the divinity of Christ might not be established by human appointment and that he might not be reckoned one of the many who were deified by them.'

"Some of which, as he proceeds to show, had been of infamous characters.

"I shall now transcribe below in his own words what Orosius, in the fifth century, says of this matter, that all my readers may have it at once before them without looking farther for it." This quotation from Orosius will be found in the

"Testimony of the Fathers," under the title, "Testimony of Orosius."

"And I refer to Zonoras and Nicephoras. The former only quotes Eusebius, and transcribes into his Annals the chapter of his Ecclesiastical History quoted by me. Nor has Nicephoras done much more."[1]

TISCHENDORF'S COMMENTS ON THE ACTS OF PILATE

"It is the same with the second apocryphal work brought under review above, the so-called Acts of Pilate, only with the difference that they refer as much to John as to the synoptical Gospels. Justin, in like manner as before, is the most ancient voucher for this work, which is said to have been written under Pilate's jurisdiction, and by reason of its specification of wonderful occurrences before, during, and after the crucifixion, to have borne strong evidence to the divinity of Christ. Justin saw as little reason as Tertullian and others for believing that it was a work of pious deception from a Christian hand." [As has been alleged by opponents.] "On the contrary, Justin appeals to it twice in his first Apology in order to confirm the accounts of the occurrences which took place at the crucifixion in accordance with prophecy, and of the miraculous healings effected by Christ, also the subject of prophetic announcement. He cites specifically (chap. 35) from Isaiah lxv. 2, and lviii. 2: 'I have spread out my hands all the day unto a rebellious people which walketh in a way that was not good. They ask of me the ordinances of justice, they take delight in approaching to God.' Further, from the 22d Psalm: 'They pierced my hands and my feet; they parted my garments upon them and cast lots upon my vesture.' With reference to this he remarks that Christ fulfilled this; that he did stretch forth his hands when the Jews crucified him—the men who contended against him and denied that he was Christ. 'Then,' he says further, 'as the prophet foretold, they dragged him to the judgment seat, set him upon it and said, Judge us.' The expression, however, 'they pierced,' etc., refers to the nails with which they fastened his feet and hands to the cross. And after they had crucified him they threw lots for his clothing, and they who had taken part in the act of crucifixion divided it among themselves. To this he adds: And you can learn from the Acts, composed during the governorship of Pontius Pilate, that these things really happened.

"Still more explicit is the testimony of Tertullian. It may be found in Apologeticus (chap. 2) where he says that out of envy Jesus was surrendered to Pilate by the Jewish ceremonial lawyers, and by him, after he had yielded to the cries of the people, given over for crucifixion; that while hanging on the cross he gave up the ghost with a loud cry, and so anticipated the executioner's duty; that at that same hour the day was interrupted by a sudden darkness; that a guard of soldiers was set at the grave for the purpose of preventing his disciples stealing his body, since he had predicted his resurrection, but that on the third day the ground was suddenly shaken and the stone rolled away from before the sepulchre; that in the grave nothing was found but the articles used in his burial; that the report was spread abroad by those who stood outside that the disciples had taken the body away; that Jesus spent forty days with them in Galilee, teaching them what their mission should be, and that after giving them their instructions as to what they should preach, he was raised in a cloud to heaven. Tertullian closes this account with the words, 'All this was reported to the Emperor at that time, Tiberius, by Pilate, his conscience having compelled even him to become a Christian.'

"The document now in our possession corresponds with this evidence of Justin and Tertullian. Even in the title it agrees with the account of Justin, although instead of the word *acta,* which he used, and which is manifestly must more Latin than Greek, a Greek expression is employed which can be shown to have been used to indicate genuine Acts. The details recounted by Justin and Tertullian are all found in our text of the Acts of Pilate, with this variation, that nothing corresponds to what is joined to the declaration of the prophet, 'They dragged him to the seat of judgment and set him upon it and said,' etc. Besides this, the casting lots for the vesture is expressed simply by the allusion to the division of the clothes. We must give even closer scrutiny to one point. Justin alludes to the miracles which were performed in fulfillment of Old Testament prophecy, on the lame, the dumb, the blind, the dead, and on lepers. In fact, in our Acts of Pilate there are made to appear before the Roman governor a palsied man who had suffered for thirty-eight years, and was brought in a bed by young men, and healed on the Sabbath day; a blind man cured by the laying on of hands; a cripple who had been restored; a leper who had been cleansed; the woman whose issue of blood had been stanched, and a witness of the raising of Lazarus from the dead. Of that which Tertullian cites we will adduce merely the passage found in no one of our gospels, that Jesus passed forty days after his resurrection in company with his disciples in Galilee.

"This is indicated in our Acts of Pilate at the end of the fifteenth chapter, where the risen man is represented as saying to Joseph: 'For forty days go not out of thy house, for behold I go to my brethren in Galilee.'

"Every one will perceive how strongly the argument that our Acts of Pilate are the same which Justin and Tertullian read is buttressed by these unexpected coincidences. The assertion recently made requires, consequently, no labored contradiction that the allusions to both men have grown out of their mere suspicion that there was such a record as the Acts of Pilate, or out of the circulation of a mere story about such a record, while the real work was written as the consequence of these allusions at the close of the third century. What an uncommon fancy it requires in the two men to coincide so perfectly in a single production, as is the case in the Acts to which I am now referring. And are we to imagine that they referred with such emphasis as they employed to the mere creations of their fancy?

"The question has been raised with more justice, whether the production in our possession may not have been a copy or a free revision of the old and primitive one. The modern change in the title has given support to this conjecture, for it has occasioned the work to be commonly spoken of as the Gospel of Nicodemus. But this title is borne neither by any Greek manuscript, the Coptic-Sahidian papyrus, nor the Latin manuscripts with the exception of a few of the most recent. It may be traced only subsequently to the twelfth century, although at a very early period, in one of the two prefaces attached to the work, Nicodemus is mentioned in one place as a Hebrew author and in another as a Greek translator. But aside from the title, the handwriting displays great variation, and the two prefaces alluded to above show clearly the work of two hands. Notwithstanding this, however, there are decisive grounds for holding that our Acts of Pilate contains in its main substance the documents drawn from Justin and Tertullian. The first of these to be noticed is, that the Greek text, as given in the version most widely circulated in the manuscripts, is surprisingly corroborated by two documents of the rarest character, and first used by myself—a Coptic-Sahidian papyrus manuscript and a Latin palimpsest—both probably dating from the fifth century. Such a documentary confirmation of their text is possessed by scarcely ten works of the collective Greek classic literature. Both of these ancient writings make it in the highest degree probable that the Egyptian and Latin translations which they contain were executed still earlier.

"But could a work which was held in great consideration in Justin's and Tertullian's time and down to the commencement of the fourth century, and which strenuously insists that the Emperor Maximin caused other blasphemous Acts of Pilate to be published and zealously circulated, manifestly for the purpose of displacing and discrediting the older Christian Acts—could such a work suddenly change its whole form, and from the fifth century, to which in so extraordinary a manner translators, wholly different in character, point back with such wonderful concurrence, continue in the new form? Contrary as this is to all historical criticism, there is in the contents of the work, in the singular manner in which isolated and independent details are shown to be related to the canonical books, no less than in the accordance with the earliest quotations found in Justin and Tertullian, a guaranty of the greatest antiquity.

"There are in the contents, also, matters of such a nature that we must confess that they are to be traced back to the primitive edition, as, for example, the narrative in the first chapter of the bringing forward of the accused.

"It is incorrect, moreover, to draw a conclusion from Justin's designation of the Acta which is not warranted by the whole character of the work. The Acta, the ὑπομνήματα, are specified in Justin's account not less than in the manuscripts which we possess, as being written *under* Pontius Pilate, and that can signify nothing else than that they were an official production composed under the direct sanction of the Roman governor. Their transmission to the emperor must be imagined as accompanied by a letter of the same character with that which has been brought down to us in the Greek and Latin edition, and yet not at all similar in purport to the notable Acts of Pilate."[2]

THE ACTS OF PILATE
(First Greek Form)

I, Ananias, of the propraetor's bodyguard, being learned in the law, knowing our Lord Jesus Christ from the Holy Scriptures, coming to Him by faith, and counted worthy of the holy baptism, searching also the memorials written at that time of what was done in the case of our Lord Jesus Christ, which the Jews had laid up in the time of Pontius Pilate, found these memorials written in Hebrew, and, by the favor of God, have translated them into Greek for the information of all who call upon the name of our Master Jesus Christ, in the seventeenth year of the reign of our lord Flavius Theodosius, and the sixth of Flavius Valentianus, in the ninth indiction.

All ye, therefore, who read and transfer into other books, remember me and pray for me, and pardon my sins which I have sinned against Him.

Peace be to those who read and those who hear, and to their households. Amen.

CHAP. 1.—Having called a council, the high priests and the scribes Annas and Caiaphas and Semes and Dathaes, and Gamaliel, Judas, Levi and Nepthalim, Alexander and Jairus, and the rest of the Jews, came to Pilate accusing Jesus about many things, saying: We know this man to be the son of Joseph the carpenter, born of Mary; and he says that he is the Son of God, and a king; moreover, profanes the Sabbath, and wishes to do away with the law of our fathers. Pilate says: And what are the things which he does, to show that he wishes to do away with it? The Jews say: We have a law not to cure anyone on the Sabbath; but this man has, on the Sabbath, cured the lame and the crooked, the withered and the blind and the paralytic, the dumb and the demoniac, by evil practices. Pilate says to them: What evil practices? They say to him: He is a magician, and by Beelzebub, prince of the demons, he casts out the demons, and all are subject to him. Pilate says to them: This is not casting out the demons by an unclean spirit, but by the god Esculapius.

The Jews say to Pilate: We entreat your highness that he stand at the tribunal and be heard. And Pilate, having called them, says: Tell me how I, being a procurator, can try a king? They say to him: We do not say that he is a king, but he himself says that he is. And Pilate, having called the runner, says to him: Let Jesus be brought in with respect. And the runner, going out and recognizing him, adored him, and took his cloak into his hand and spread it on the ground, and says to him: My Lord, walk on this and come in, for the procurator calls thee. And the Jews, seeing what the runner had done, cried out against Pilate, saying: Why hast thou ordered him to come in by a runner, and not by a crier? for assuredly the runner, when he saw him, adored him, and spread his doublet on the ground and made him walk like a king.

And Pilate, having called the runner, says to him: Why hast thou done this, and spread out thy cloak upon the earth and made Jesus walk upon it? The runner says to him: My Lord procurator, when thou didst send me to Jerusalem to Alexander, I saw him sitting upon an ass, and the sons of the Hebrews held branches in their hands and shouted; and others spread their clothes under him saying: Save now, thou who art in the highest; blessed is he that cometh in the name of the Lord.

The Jews cry out and say to the runner: The sons of the Hebrews shouted in Hebrew; whence, then, hast thou the Greek? The runner says to them: I asked one of the Jews, and said: What is it they are shouting in Hebrew? And he interpreted it for me. Pilate says to them: And what did they shout in Hebrew? The Jews say to him: *Hosanna membrome baruchamma adonai.* Pilate says to them: And this hosanna, etc., how is it interpreted? The Jews say to him: Save now in the highest; blessed is he that cometh in the name of the Lord. Pilate says to them: If you bear witness to the words spoken by the children, in what has the runner done wrong? And they were silent. And the procurator says to the runner: Go out and bring him in what way thou wilt. And the runner, going out, did in the same manner as before, and says to Jesus: My Lord, come in; the procurator calleth thee.

And Jesus, going in, and the standard bearers holding their standards, the tops of the standards bent down, and adored Jesus. And the Jews, seeing the bearing of the standards how they were bent down and adored Jesus, cried out vehemently against the standard bearers. And Pilate says to the Jews: Do you not wonder how the tops of the standards were bent down and adored Jesus? The Jews say to Pilate: We saw how the standard bearers bent them down and adored him. And the procurator, having called the standard bearers, says to them: Why have you done this? They say to Pilate: We are Greeks and temple slaves, and how could we adore him? and assuredly, as we were holding them up, the tops bent down of their own accord and adored him.

Pilate says to the rulers of the synagogue and the elders of the people: Do you choose for yourselves men strong and powerful, and let them hold up the standards, and let us see whether they will bend down with them. And the elders of the Jews picked out twelve men powerful and strong, and made them hold up the standards six by six; and they were placed in front of the procurator's tribunal. And Pilate says to the runner: Take him outside of the Pretorium, and bring him in again in whatever way may please thee. And Jesus and the runner went out of the Pretorium. And Pilate, summoning those who had formerly held up the standards, says to them: I have sworn by the health of Caesar, that if the standards do not bend down when Jesus comes in, I will cut off your heads. And the procurator ordered Jesus to come in the second time. And the runner did in the same manner as before, and made many entreaties to Jesus to walk on his cloak. And he walked on it and went in. And as he went in the standards were again bent down and adored Jesus.

CHAP. 2.—And Pilate, seeing this, was afraid, and sought to go away from the tribunal; but when he was still thinking of going away, his wife sent to him saying: Have nothing to do with this just man, for many things have I suffered on his account this night. And Pilate, summoning the Jews, says to them: You know that my wife is a worshiper of God, and prefers to adhere to the Jewish religion along with you. They say to him: Yes, we know. Pilate says to them: Behold, my wife has sent to me, saying, Have nothing to do with this just man, for many things have I suffered on account of him this night. And the Jews answering, say unto Pilate: Did we not tell thee that he was a sorcerer? Behold, he has sent a dream to thy wife.

And Pilate, having summoned Jesus, says to him: What do these witness against thee? Sayest thou nothing? And Jesus said: Unless they had the power, they would say nothing; for every one has the power of his own mouth to speak both good and evil. They shall see to it.

And the elders of the Jews answered, and said to Jesus: What shall we see? First, that thou wast born of fornication; secondly, that thy birth in Bethlehem was the cause of the murder of the infants; thirdly, that thy father Joseph and thy mother Mary fled into Egypt because they had no confidence in the people.

Some of the bystanders, pious men of the Jews, say: We deny that he was born of fornication; for we know that Joseph espoused Mary, and he was not born of fornication. Pilate says to the Jews who said he was of fornication: This story of yours is not true, because they were betrothed, as also these fellow-countrymen of yours say. Annas and Caiaphas say to Pilate: All the multitude of us cry out that he was born of fornication, and are not believed; these are proselytes and his disciples. And Pilate, calling Annas and Caiaphas, says to them: What are proselytes? They say to him: They are by birth children of the Greeks, and have now become Jews. And those that said that he was not born of fornication, viz.: Lazarus, Asterius, Antonius, James, Amnes, Zeras, Samuel, Isaac, Phinees, Crispus, Agrippas and Judas, say: We are not proselytes, but are children of the Jews, and speak the truth; for we were present at the betrothal of Joseph and Mary.

And Pilate, calling these twelve men who said that he was not born of fornication, says to them: I adjure you, by the health of Caesar, to tell me whether it be true that you say, that he was not born of fornication. They say to Pilate: We have a law against taking oaths, because it is a sin; but they will swear by the health of Caesar that it is not as we have said, and we are liable to death. Pilate says to Annas and Caiaphas: Have you nothing to answer to this? Annas and Caiaphas say to Pilate: These twelve are believed when they say that he was not born of fornication; all the multitude of us cry out that he was born of fornication, and that he is a sorcerer; and he says that he is the Son of God and a king, and we are not believed.

And Pilate orders all the multitude to go out, except the twelve men who said that he was not born of fornication, and he ordered Jesus to be separated from them. And Pilate says to them: For what reason do they wish to put him to death? They say to him: They are angry because he cures on the Sabbath. Pilate says: For a good work do they wish to put him to death? They say to him: Yes.

CHAP. 3.—And Pilate, filled with rage, went outside of the Pretorium and said to them: I take the sun to witness that I find no fault in this man. The Jews answered and said to the procurator: Unless this man were an evil-doer, we should not have delivered him to thee. And Pilate said: Do you take him and judge him according to your law. The Jews said to Pilate: It is not lawful for us to put anyone to death. Pilate said: Has God said that you are not to put to death, but that I am?

And Pilate went again into the Pretorium and spoke to Jesus privately, and said to him: Art thou the king of the Jews? Jesus answered Pilate: Dost thou say this of thyself, or have others said it to thee of me? Pilate answered Jesus: Am I also a Jew? Thy nation and the chief priests have given thee up to me. What hast thou done? Jesus answered: My kingdom is not of this world; for if my kingdom were of this world, my servants would fight in order that I should not be given up to the Jews: but now my kingdom is not from thence. Pilate said to him: Art thou, then, a king? Jesus answered him: Thou sayest that I am king. Because for this have I been born, and I have come, in order that everyone who is of the truth might hear my voice. Pilate says to him: What is truth? Jesus says to him: Truth is from heaven. Pilate says: Is truth not upon earth? Jesus says to Pilate: Thou seest how those who speak the truth are judged by those that have the power upon earth.

CHAP. 4.—And leaving Jesus within the Pretorium, Pilate went out to the Jews and said to them: I find no fault in him. The Jews say to him: He said, I can destroy this temple, and in three days build it. Pilate says: What temple? The Jews say: The one that Solomon built in forty-six years, and this man speaks of pulling it down and building it up in three days. Pilate says to them: I am innocent of the blood of this just man. See you to it. The Jews say: His blood be upon us and upon our children.

And Pilate, having summoned the elders and priests and Levites, said to them privately: Do not act thus, because no charge that you bring against him is worthy of death; for your charge is about curing and Sabbath profanation. The elders and the priests and the Levites say: If anyone speak evil against Caesar, is he worthy or death or not? Pilate says: He is worthy of death. The Jews say to Pilate: If anyone speak evil against Caesar, he is worthy of death; but this man has spoken evil against God.

And the procurator ordered the Jews to go outside of the Pretorium; and, summoning Jesus, he says to him: What shall I do to thee? Jesus says to Pilate: As it has been given to thee. Pilate says: How given? Jesus says: Moses and the prophets have proclaimed beforehand of my death and resurrection. And the Jews, noticing this and hearing it, say to Pilate: What more wilt thou hear of this blasphemy? Pilate says to the Jews: If these words be blasphemous, do you take him for the blasphemy, and lead him away to your synagogue and judge him according to your law. The Jews say to Pilate: Our law bears that a man who wrongs his fellow-men is worthy to receive forty save one: but he that blasphemeth God is to be stoned with stones.

Pilate says to them: Do you take him and punish him in whatever way you please. The Jews say to Pilate: We wish that he be crucified. Pilate says: He is not deserving of crucifixion.

And the procurator, looking round upon the crowds of the Jews standing by, sees many of the Jews weeping, and says: All the multitude do not wish him to die. The elders of the Jews say: For this reason all the multitude of us have come, that he should die. Pilate says to the Jews: Why should he die? The Jews say: Because he called himself the Son of God and King.

CHAP. 5.—And one Nicodemus, a Jew, stood before the procurator and said: I beseech your honor let me say a few words. Pilate says: Say on. Nicodemus says: I said to the elders and the priests and Levites, and to all the multitude of the Jews in the synagogue, What do you seek to do with this man? This man does many miracles and strange things, which no one has done or will do. Let him go and do not wish any evil against him. If the miracles which he does are of God, they will stand; but if of man, they will come to nothing. For assuredly Moses, being sent by God into Egypt, did many miracles, which the Lord commanded him to do before Pharaoh, king of Egypt. And there were Jannes and Jambres, servants of Pharaoh, and they also did not a few of the miracles which Moses did; and the Egyptians took them to be gods—this Jannes and Jambres. But, since the miracles which they did were not of God, both they and those who believed in them were destroyed. And now release this man, for he is not deserving of death.

The Jews say to Nicodemus: Thou hast become his disciple, and therefore thou defendest him. Nicodemus says to them: Perhaps, too, the procurator has become his disciple, because he defends him. Has the emperor not appointed him to this place of dignity? And the Jews were vehemently enraged, and gnashed their teeth against Nicodemus. Pilate says to them: Why do you gnash your teeth against him when you hear the truth? The Jews say to Nicodemus: Mayst thou receive his truth and his portion. Nicodemus says: Amen, amen; may I receive it, as you have said.

CHAP. 6.—One of the Jews, stepping up, asked leave of the procurator to say a word. The procurator says: If thou wishest to say anything, say on. And the Jew said: Thirty-eight years I lay in my bed in great agony. And when Jesus came, many demoniacs and many lying ill of various diseases were cured by him. And when Jesus saw me he had compassion on me, and said to me: Take up thy couch and walk. And I took up my couch and walked. The Jews say to Pilate: Ask him on what day it was when he was cured. He that had been cured says: On a Sabbath. The Jews say: Is not this the very thing we said, that on a Sabbath he cures and casts out demons?

And another Jew stepped up and said: I was born blind; I heard sounds, but saw not a face. And as Jesus passed by I cried out with a loud voice, Pity me, O son of David. And he pitied me and put his hands upon my eyes, and I instantly received my sight. And another Jew stepped up and said: I was crooked and he straightened me with a word. And another said: I was a leper, and he cured me with a word.

CHAP. 7.—And a woman cried out from a distance and said: I had an issue of blood, and I touched the hem of his garment, and the issue of blood, which I had had for twelve years, was stopped. The Jews say: We have a law that a woman's evidence is not received.

CHAP. 8.—And others, a multitude both of men and women, cried out, saying: This man is a prophet, and the demons are subject to him. Pilate says to them who said that the demons were subject to him: Why, then, were not your teachers also subject to him? They say to Pilate: We do not know. And others said: He raised Lazarus from the tomb after he had been dead four days. And the procurator trembled, and said to all the multitude of the Jews: Why do you wish to pour out innocent blood?

CHAP. 9.—And, having summoned Nicodemus and the twelve men that said he was not born of fornication, he says to them: What shall I do, because there is an insurrection among the people? They say to him: We know not; let them see to it. Again Pilate, having summoned all the multitude of the Jews, says: You know that it is customary, at the feast of unleavened bread, to release one prisoner to you. I have one condemned prisoner in the prison, a murderer named Bar Abbas, and this man standing in your presence, Jesus in whom I find no fault. Which of them do you wish me to release to you? And they cry out: Bar Abbas. Pilate says: What, then, shall we do to Jesus, who is called Christ? The Jews say: Let him be crucified. And others said: Thou art no friend of Caesar's if thou release this man, because he called himself the Son of God and King. You wish this man, then, to be a king, and not Caesar?

And Pilate, in a rage, says to the Jews: Always has your nation been rebellious, and you always speak against your benefactors. The Jews say: What benefactors? He says to them: Your God led you out of the land of Egypt from bitter slavery, and brought you safe through the sea as through dry land, and in the desert fed you with manna and gave you quails, and quenched your thirst with water from a rock, and gave you a law; and in all these things have you provoked your God to anger, and sought a molten calf. And you exasperated your God, and he sought to slay you. And Moses prayed for you, and you were not put to death. And now you charge me with hating the emperor.

And, rising up from the tribunal, he sought to go out. And the Jews cry out and say: We know that Caesar is king, and not Jesus. For assuredly the magi brought gifts to him as to a king. And when Herod heard from the magi that a king had been born, he sought to slay him; and his father, Joseph, knowing this, took him and his mother, and they fled into Egypt. And Herod, hearing of it, destroyed the children of the Hebrews that had been born in Bethlehem.

And when Pilate heard these words he was afraid; and, ordering the crowd to keep silence, because they were crying out, he says to them: So this is he whom Herod sought? The Jews say: Yes, it is he. And, taking water, Pilate washed his hands in the face of the sun, saying: I am innocent of the blood of this just man: see you to it. Again the Jews cry out: His blood be upon us and upon our children.

Then Pilate ordered the curtain of the tribunal where he was sitting to be drawn, and says to Jesus: Thy nation has charged thee with being a king. On this account, I sentence thee first to be scourged, according to the enactment of venerable kings, and then to be fastened on the cross in the garden where thou was seized. And let Dysmas and Gestas, the two malefactors, be crucified with thee.

CHAP. 10.—And Jesus went forth out of the Pretorium, and the malefactors with him. And when they came to the place they stripped him of his clothes and girded him with a towel, and put a crown of thorns on him round his head. And they crucified him; and at the same time, also, they hung up the two malefactors along with him. And Jesus said: Father, forgive them, for they know not what they do. And the soldiers parted his clothes among them; and the people stood looking at him. And the chief priests and the rulers with them mocked him, saying: He saved others; let him save himself. If he be the Son of God, let him come down from the cross. And the soldiers made sport of him, coming near and offering him vinegar mixed with gall, and said: Thou art the king of the Jews; save thyself.

And Pilate, after the sentence, ordered the charge against him to be inscribed as a superscription in Greek and Latin and Hebrew, according to what the Jews had said: He is king of the Jews.

And one of the malefactors hanging up spoke to him, saying: If thou be the Christ, save thyself and us. And Dysmas answering reproved him, saying: Dost thou not fear God, because thou art in the same condemnation? And we, indeed, justly, for we receive the fit punishment of our deeds; but this man has done no evil. And he said to Jesus: Remember me, Lord, in thy kingdom. And Jesus said to him: Amen, amen; I say to thee, Today shalt thou be with me in Paradise.

CHAP. 11.—And it was about the sixth hour, and there was darkness over the earth until the ninth hour, the sun being darkened; and the curtain of the temple was split in the middle. And, crying out with a loud voice, Jesus said: Father, *baddach ephkid ruel,* which is, interpreted, Into thy hands I commit my spirit. And, having said this, he gave up the ghost. And the centurion, seeing what had happened, glorified God and said: This was a just man. And all the crowds that were present at this spectacle, when they saw what had happened, beat their breasts and went away.

And the centurion reported what had happened to the procurator. And when the procurator and his wife heard it they were exceedingly grieved, and neither ate nor drank that day. And Pilate sent for the Jews and said to them: Have you seen what has happened? And they say: There has been an eclipse of the sun in the usual way.

And his acquaintances were standing at a distance, and the women who came with him from Galilee, seeing these things. And a man named Joseph, a councillor from the city of Arimathea, who also waited for the kingdom of God, went to Pilate and begged the body of Jesus. And he took it down and wrapped it in a clean linen, and placed it in a tomb hewn out of the rock, in which no one had ever lain.

CHAP. 12.—And the Jews, hearing that Joseph had begged the body of Jesus, sought him, and the twelve who said that Jesus was not born of fornication, and Nicodemus and many others who had stepped up before Pilate and declared his good works. And of all these that were hid Nicodemus alone was seen by them, because he was a ruler of the Jews. And Nicodemus says to them: How have you come into the synagogue? The Jews say to him: How hast thou come into the synagogue? for thou art a confederate of his, and his portion is with thee in the world to come. Nicodemus says: Amen, amen. And likewise Joseph also stepped out and said to them: Why are you angry against me because I begged the body of Jesus? Behold, I have put him in my new tomb, wrapping him in clean linen; and I have rolled a stone to the door of the tomb. And you have acted not well against the just man, because you have not repented of crucifying him, but also have pierced him with a spear. And the Jews seized Joseph and ordered him to be secured until the first day of the week, and said to him: Know that the time does not allow us to do anything against thee, because the Sabbath is dawning: and know that thou shalt not be deemed worthy of burial, but we shall give thy flesh to the birds of the air. Joseph says to them: These are the words of the arrogant Goliath, who reproached the living God and holy David. For God has said by the prophet, Vengeance is mine, and I will repay, saith the Lord. And now that he is uncircumcised in flesh, but circumcised in heart, has taken water and washed his hands in the face of the sun, saying, I am innocent of the blood of this just man; see ye to it. And you answered and said to Pilate: His blood be upon us and upon our children. And now I am afraid, lest the wrath of God come upon you and upon your children, as you have said. And the Jews, hearing these words, were embittered in their souls, and seized Joseph and locked him into a room where there was no window; and guards were stationed at the door, and they sealed the door where Joseph was locked in.

And on the Sabbath the rulers of the synagogue and the priests and the Levites made a decree that all should be found in the synagogue on the first day of the week. And, rising up early, all the multitude in the synagogue consulted by what death they should slay him. And when the Sanhedrin was sitting, they ordered him to be brought with much indignity. And, having opened the door, they found him not. And all the people were surprised and struck with dismay, because they found the seals unbroken, and because Caiaphas had the key. And they no longer dared to lay hands upon those who had spoken before Pilate in Jesus' behalf.

CHAP. 13.—And while they were still sitting in the synagogue and wondering about Joseph, there came some of the guard whom the Jews had begged of Pilate to guard the tomb of Jesus, that his disciples might not come and steal him. And they reported to the rulers of the synagogue, and the priests and Levites, what had happened: how there had been an earthquake; and we saw an angel coming down from heaven, and he rolled away the stone from the mouth of the tomb and sat upon it; and he shone like snow and like lightning. And we were very much afraid, and lay like dead men; and we heard the voice of the angel, saying to the women who remained beside the tomb, Be not afraid, for I know that you seek Jesus, who was crucified. He is not here. He has risen, as he said. Come, see the place where the Lord lay; and go quickly and tell his disciples that he is risen from the dead, and is in Galilee.

The Jews say: To what women did he speak? The men of the guard say: We know not who they were. The Jews say: At what time was this? The men of the guard say: At midnight. The Jews say: And wherefore did you not lay hold of them? The men of the guard say: We were like dead men from fear, not expecting to see the light of day, and how could we lay hold of them? The Jews say: As the Lord liveth, we do not believe you. The men of the guard say to the Jews: You have seen so great miracles in the case of this man, and have not believed; and how can you believe us? And assuredly you have done well to swear that the Lord liveth, for indeed he does live. Again the men of the guard say: We have heard that you have locked up the man that begged the body of Jesus, and put a seal on the door; and that you have opened it and not found him. Do you, then, give us the man whom you were guarding, and we shall give you Jesus. The Jews say: Joseph has gone away to his own city. The men of the guard say to the Jews: And Jesus has risen, as we heard from the angel, and is in Galilee.

And when the Jews heard these words they were very much afraid, and said: We must take care lest this story be heard, and all incline to Jesus. And the Jews called a council, and paid down a considerable money and gave it to the soldiers, saying: Say, while he slept, his disciples came by night and stole him; and if this come to the ears of the procurator we shall persuade him and keep you out of trouble. And they took it, and said as they had been instructed.

CHAP. 14.—And Phinees, a priest, and Adas, a teacher, and Haggai, a Levite, came down from Galilee to Jerusalem, and said to the rulers of the synagogue, and the priests and the Levites: We saw Jesus and his disciples sitting on the mountain called Mamilch; and he said to his disciples, Go into all the world, and preach to every creature: he that believeth and is baptized shall be saved, and he that believeth not shall be condemned. And these signs shall attend those who have believed: in my name they shall cast out demons, speak new tongues, take up serpents; and if they drink any deadly thing it shall by no means hurt them; they shall lay hands on the sick, and they shall be well. And while Jesus was speaking to his disciples we saw him taken up into heaven.

The elders and priests and Levites say: Give glory to the God of Israel, and confess to him whether you have heard and seen those things, of which you have given us an account. And those who had given the account said: As the Lord liveth, the God of our fathers, Abraham, Isaac, and Jacob, we heard these things, and saw him taken up into heaven. The elders and the priests and the Levites say to them: Have you come to give us this announcement, or to offer prayer to God? And they say: To offer prayer to God. The elders and the chief priests and the Levites say to them: If you have come to offer prayer to God, why, then, have you told these idle tales in the presence of all the people? Says Phinees, the priest, and Adas, the teacher, and Haggai, the Levite, to the rulers of the synagogues, and the priests and the Levites: If what we have said and seen be sinful, behold, we are before you; do to us as seems good in your eyes. And they took the law and made them swear upon it not to give any more an account of these matters to anyone. And they gave them to eat and drink and sent them out of the city, having given them also money, and three men with them; and they sent them away to Galilee.

And these men, having gone into Galilee, the chief priests and the rulers of the synagogue, and the elders came together in the synagogue and locked the door, and lamented with great lamentation, saying: Is this a miracle that has happened in Israel? And Annas and Caiaphas said: Why are you so much moved? Why do you weep? Do you not know that his disciples have given a sum of gold to the guards of the tomb, and have instructed them to say that an angel came down and rolled away the stone from the door of the tomb? And the priests and elders said: Be it that his disciples have stolen his body; how is it that the life has come into his body, and that he is going about in Galilee? And they, being unable to give an answer to these things, said, after great hesitation: It is not lawful for us to believe the uncircumcised.

CHAP. 15.—And Nicodemus stood up, and stood before the Sanhedrin, saying: You say well; you are not ignorant, you people of the Lord, of these men that come down from Galilee, that they fear God, and are men of substance, haters of covetousness, men of peace; and they have declared with an oath, we saw Jesus upon the mountain Mamilch with his disciples, and he taught what we heard from him, and we saw him taken up into heaven. And no one asked them in what form he went up. For assuredly, as the book of the Holy Scriptures taught us, Helias also was taken up into heaven, and Elissaeus cried out with a loud voice, and Helias threw his sheepskin upon Elissaeus, and Elissaeus threw his sheepskin upon the Jordan, and crossed and came into Jericho. And the children of the prophets met him and said, O Elissaeus, where is thy master Helias? And he said, He has been taken up into heaven. And they said to Elissaeus, Has not a spirit seized him, and thrown him upon one of the mountains? But let us take our servants with us and seek him. And they persuaded Elissaeus, and he went away with them. And they sought him three days, and did not find him; and they knew that he had been taken up. And now listen to me, and let us send into every district of Israel and see, lest, perchance, Christ has been taken up by a spirit and thrown upon one of the mountains. And this proposal pleased all. And they sent into every district of Israel and sought Jesus, and did not find him; but they found Joseph in Arimathea, and no one dared to lay hands on him.

And they reported to the elders and the priests and the Levites: We have gone round to every district of Israel, and have not found Jesus; but Joseph we have found in Arimathea. And hearing about Joseph they were glad and gave glory to the God of Israel. And the rulers of the synagogue, and the priests and the Levites, having held a council as to the manner in which they should meet with Joseph, took a piece of paper and wrote to Joseph as follows:

Peace to thee! We know that we have sinned against God, and against thee; and we have prayed to the God of Israel that thou shouldst deign to come to thy fathers and to thy children, because we all have been grieved. For, having opened the door, we did not find thee. And we know that we have counseled evil counsel against thee; but the Lord has defended thee, and the Lord himself has scattered to the winds our counsel against thee, O honorable father Joseph.

And they chose from all Israel seven men, friends of Joseph, whom, also, Joseph himself was acquainted with; and the rulers of the synagogue, and the priests and the Levites say to them: Take notice; if, after receiving our letter he read it, know that he will come with you to us. But if he do not read it, know that he is ill-disposed towards us. And, having saluted him in peace, return to us. And having blest the men, they dismissed them. And the men came to Joseph and did reverence to him, and said to him: Peace to thee! And he said: Peace to you and to all the people of Israel! And they gave him the roll of the letter. And Joseph, having received it, read the letter and rolled it up, and blessed God and said: Blessed be the Lord God, who has delivered Israel, that they should not shed innocent blood; and blessed be the Lord, who sent out his angel and covered me under his wings. And he set a table for them: and they ate and drank and slept there.

And they rose up early and prayed. And Joseph saddled his ass and set out with the men: and they came to the holy city Jerusalem. And all the people met Joseph and cried out: Peace to thee in thy coming in! And he said to all the people: Peace to you! and he kissed them. And the people prayed with Joseph, and they were astonished at the sight of him. And Nicodemus received him into his house and made a great feast, and called Annas and Caiaphas and the elders and the priests and the Levites to his house. And they rejoiced, eating and drinking with Joseph; and, after singing hymns, each proceeded to his own house. But Joseph remained in the house of Nicodemus.

And on the following day, which was the preparation, the rulers of the synagogue and the priests and the Levites went early to the house of Nicodemus; and Nicodemus met them and said: Peace to you! And they said: Peace to thee and to Joseph, and to all thy house and to all the house of Joseph! And he brought them into his house. And all the Sanhedrin sat down, and Joseph sat down between Annas and Caiaphas; and no one dared to say a word to him. And Joseph said: Why have you called me? And they signaled to Nicodemus to speak to Joseph. And Nicodemus, opening his mouth, said to Joseph: Father, thou knowest that the honorable teachers and the priests and the Levites seek to learn a word from thee. And Joseph said: Ask. And Annas and Caiaphas, having taken the law, made Joseph swear, saying: Give glory to the God of Israel, and give him confession; for Achar, being made to swear by the prophet Jesus, did not forswear himself, but declared unto him all, and did not hide a word from him. Do thou also, accordingly, not hide from us to the extent of a word. And Joseph said: I shall not hide from you one word. And they said to him: With grief were we grieved because thou didst beg the body of Jesus and wrap it in clean linen and lay it in a tomb. And on account of this we secured thee in a room where there was no window; and we put locks and seals upon the doors, and guards kept watching where thou wast locked in. And on the first day of the week we opened and found thee not, and were grieved exceedingly; and astonishment fell upon all the people of the Lord until yesterday. And now relate to us what happened to thee.

And Joseph said: On the preparation, about the tenth hour, you locked me up, and I remained all the Sabbath. And at midnight, as I was standing and praying, the room where you locked me in was hung up by the four corners, and I saw a light like lightning into my eyes. And I was afraid and fell to the ground. And some one took me by the hand and removed me from the place where I had fallen; and moisture of water was poured from my head even to my feet, and a smell of perfumes came about my nostrils. And he wiped my face and kissed me, and said to me, Fear not, Joseph: open thine eyes and see who it is that speaks to thee. And, looking up, I saw Jesus. And I trembled and thought it was a phantom; and I said the commandments, and he said them with me. Even so you are not ignorant that a phantom, if it meet anybody and hear the commandments, takes to flight. And seeing that he said them with me, I said to him, Rabbi Helias. And he said to me, I am not Helias. And I said to him, Who art thou, my lord? And he said to me, I am Jesus whose body thou didst beg from Pilate; and thou didst clothe me with clean linen, and didst put a napkin on my face, and didst lay me in thy new tomb, and didst roll a great stone to the door of the tomb. And I said to him that was speaking to me, Show me the place where I laid thee. And he carried me away and showed me the place where I laid him; and the linen cloth was lying in it, and the napkin for his face. And I knew that it was Jesus. And he took me by the hand and placed me, though the doors were locked, in the middle of my house, and led me away to my bed and said to me, Peace to thee! And he kissed me and said to me, For forty days go not forth out of thy house; for, behold, I go to my brethren in Galilee.

CHAP. 16.—And the rulers of the synagogue, and the priests and the Levites when they heard these words from Joseph, became as dead, and fell to the ground, and fasted until the ninth hour. And Nicodemus, along with Joseph, exhorted Annas and Caiaphas, the priests and the Levites, saying: Rise up and stand upon your feet, and taste bread and strengthen your souls, because tomorrow is the Sabbath of the Lord. And they rose up and prayed to God, and ate and drank, and departed every man to his own house.

And on the Sabbath our teachers and the priests and Levites sat questioning each other and saying: What is this wrath that has come upon us? for we know his father and mother. Levi, a teacher, says: I know that his parents fear God, and do not withdraw themselves from the prayers, and give the tithes thrice a year. And when Jesus was born his parents brought him to this place and gave sacrifices and burnt offerings to God. And when the great teacher, Symeon, took him into his arms, he said, Now thou sendest away thy servant, Lord, according to thy word, in peace; for mine eyes have seen thy salvation, which thou hast prepared before the face of all the peoples; a light for the revelation of the Gentiles, and the glory of thy people Israel. And Symeon blessed them, and said to Mary his mother, I give thee good news about this child. And Mary said, It is well, my lord. And Symeon said to her, It is well; behold, he lies for the fall and the rising again of many in Israel, and for a sign spoken against; and of thee thyself a sword shall go through the soul, in order that the reasoning of many hearts may be revealed.

They say to the teacher Levi: How knowest thou these things? Levi says to them: Do you not know that from him I learned the law? The Sanhedrin say to him: We wish to see thy father. And they sent for his father. And they asked him, and he said to them: Why have you not believed my son? The blessed and just Symeon himself taught him the law. The Sanhedrin says to Rabbi Levi: Is the word that you have said true? And he said: It is true. And the rulers of the synagogue, and the priests and the Levites said to themselves: Come, let us send into Galilee to the three men that came and told about his teaching and his taking up, and let them tell us how they saw him taken up. And this saying pleased all. And they sent away the three men who had already gone away into Galilee with them; and they say to them: Say to Rabbi Adas and Rabbi Phinees and Rabbi Haggai, Peace to you and all who are with you! A great inquiry having taken place in the Sanhedrin, we have been sent to you to call you to this holy place, Jersualem.

And the men set out into Galilee and found them sitting and considering the law: and they saluted them in peace. And the men who were in Galilee said to those who had come to them: Peace unto all Israel! And they said: Peace to you! And they again said to them: Why have you come? And those who had been sent said: The Sanhedrin call you to the holy city Jerusalem. And when the men heard that they were sought by the Sanhedrin they prayed to God, and reclined with the men and ate and drank, and rose up and set out in peace to Jerusalem.

And on the following day the Sanhedrin sat in the synagogue, and asked them, saying: Did you really see Jesus sitting on the mountain Mamilch teaching his eleven disciples, and did you see him taken up? And the men answered them and said: As we saw him taken up, so also we said.

Annas says: Take them away from one another and let us see whether their account agrees. And they took them away from one another. And first they call Adas and say to him: How didst thou see Jesus taken up? Adas says: While he was yet sitting on the mountain Mamilch and teaching his disciples, we saw a cloud overshadowing both him and his disciples. And the cloud took him up into heaven, and his disciples lay upon their faces upon the earth. And they call Phinees, the priest, and ask him also, saying: How didst thou see Jesus taken up? And he spoke in like manner. And they again asked Haggai, and he spoke in like manner. And the Sanhedrin said: The law of Moses holds: At the mouth of two or three every word shall be established. Buthem, a teacher, says: It is written in the law, And Enoch walked with God, and is not, because God took him. Jairus, a teacher, said: And the death of holy Moses we have heard of, and have not seen it; for it is written in the law of the Lord, and Moses died from the mouth of the Lord, and no man knoweth of his sepulchre unto this day. And Rabbi Levi said: Why did Rabbi Symeon say, when he saw Jesus, "Behold, he lies for the fall and rising again of many in Israel, and for a sign spoken against"? And Rabbi Isaac said: It is written in the law, Behold, I send my messenger before thy face, who shall go before thee to keep thee in every good way, because my name has been called upon him.

Then Amas and Caiaphas said: Rightly have you said what is written in the law of Moses, that no one saw the death of Enoch, and no one has named the death of

Moses; but Jesus was tried before Pilate, and we saw him receiving blows and spittings on his face, and the soldiers put about him a crown of thorns, and he was scourged and received sentence from Pilate, and was crucified upon the Cranium, and two robbers with him; and they gave him to drink vinegar with gall, and Longinus, the soldier, pierced his side with a spear; and Joseph, our honorable father, begged his body, and he says he is risen; and as the three teachers say, We saw him taken up into heaven; and Rabbi Levi has given evidence of what was said by Rabbi Symeon, and that he said, Behold, he lies for the fall and rising again of many in Israel, and for a sign spoken against. And all the teachers said to all the people of the Lord: If this was from the Lord, and is wonderful in your eyes, knowing you shall know, O house of Jacob, that it is written, Cursed is every one that hangeth upon a tree. And another scripture teaches: The gods which have not made the heaven and the earth shall be destroyed. And the priests and the Levites said to each other: If this memorial be until the year that is called Jobel, know that it shall endure forever, and he hath raised for himself a new people. Then the rulers of the synagogue, and the priests and the Levites, announced to all Israel, saying: Cursed is that man who shall worship the work of man's hand, and cursed is the man who shall worship the creatures more than the Creator. And all the people said, Amen, amen.

And all the people praised the Lord, and said: Blessed is the Lord, who hath given rest to his people Israel, according to all that he hath spoken; there hath not fallen one word of every good word of his that he spoke to Moses, his servant. May the Lord our God be with us, as he was with our fathers; let him not destroy us. And let him not destroy us, that we may incline our hearts to him, that we may walk in all his ways, that we may keep his commandments and his judgments which he commanded to our fathers. And the Lord shall be for a king over all the earth in that day; and there shall be one Lord, and his name one. The Lord is our king; he shall save us. There is none like thee, O Lord. Great art thou, O Lord, and great is thy name. By thy power heal us, O Lord, and we shall be healed; save us, O Lord, and we shall be saved, because we are thy lot and heritage. And the Lord will not leave his people, for his great name's sake; for the Lord has begun to make us into his people.

And all, having sung praises, went away each man to his own house glorifying God; for his is the glory forever and ever. Amen.

NOTES TO VOLUME II

PART I THE ROMAN TRIAL

CHAPTER II NUMBER OF REGULAR TRIALS

1 Mommsen, "Romisches Staatsrecht," III. I. p. 748.
2 "The Jewish People in the Time of Jesus Christ," 2d Div., I. p. 185.
3 "The Jewish People in the Time of Jesus Christ," 2d Div., I. p. 187.
4 Josephus, "Wars of the Jews," II. 8, i.
5 Josephus, "Ant.," XX. 9, i.
6 John xix. 10.
7 John xviii. 31.

CHAPTER III POWERS AND DUTIES OF PILATE

1 Acts xxv., xxvi.
2 "The Trial of Jesus," p. 77.
3 "The Jewish People in the Time of Jesus Christ," 1st Div., II. p. 74.
4 "The Legal Procedure of Cicero's Time," p. 118.
5 "The Legal Procedure of Cicero's Time," p. 118.
6 "The Trial of Jesus," p. 293.
7 "The Legal Procedure of Cicero's Time," p. 413.
8 "Geschichte des romischen Criminal-Processes."
9 "The Trial of Jesus," pp. 291-93.

CHAPTER IV MODE OF TRIAL IN ROMAN CAPITAL CASES

1 Dionysius II. 14.
2 Liv. II. iv. 5.
3 Heuzey, "Miss. archeol. de Maced.," p. 38.
4 Accusatores multos esse in civitate utile est, ut metu contineatur audacia (pro Roscio Amer. 20).
5 Persa V. 63 *seq.*

CHAPTER V ROMAN FORMS OF PUNISHMENT

1 Fiske, "Manual of Classical Literature," III. Sec. 264.
2 Gibbon, "The Decline and Fall of the Roman Empire," Chap. XLIV.
3 Const. crim. Theres., Art. 5, par. 2.
4 Keim, "Jesus of Nazara," vol. vi. p. 250.
5 Keim, "Jesus of Nazara," vol. vi. p. 250.
6 John xix. 38-41.
7 "History of Madagascar," vol. i. pp. 371, 372.
8 "Records of Travel in Turkey and Greece," vol. i. p. 447.
9 "The Celtic Druids," p. 126; "Anacalypsis," vol. i. p. 317.
10 "Anacalypsis," vol. i. p. 217.
11 Colenso's "Pentateuch Examined," vol. vi. p. 115.
12 Baring-Gould, "Curious Myths," p. 291.
13 "Octavius," Chap. XXIX.
14 "Ancient Art and Mythology," p. 30.
15 Brinton, "The Myths of the New World," p. 95.
16 Baring-Gould, "Curious Myths," p. 299.
17 Vol. iii. Art., "Cross."
18 Kingsborough, "Mexican Antiquities," vol. vi. 166. p.
19 "Curious Myths," p. 311.

CHAPTER VI ROMAN LAW APPLICABLE TO THE TRIAL OF JESUS

1 "Digest," XLVIII. 4.
2 "De Inventione," II. 17.
3 Tacitus, "Annals," p. 215.
4 Dio, Lib. LVIII.
5 "Annals," B. VI. Chap. II.
6 Dollinger, "The Gentile and the Jew," vol. ii. p. 33.
7 Dollinger, "The Gentile and the Jew," vol. ii. p. 172.
8 "Liberty, Equality, Fraternity," pp. 89, 90.
9 De Legibus.
10 Correspondence between Pliny and Trajan, Letters XCVII, XCVIII.

CHAPTER VII PONTIUS PILATE

1 Suet., "Caesar Augustus," Chap. LXIV.
2 Philo, "De Legatione ad Cajum," Sec. 38, ed. Mangey, II. 589 *seq.* *NP **3** Josephus, "Ant.," XVIII. 3, 1.
4 Apol. c. 21 ("jam pro sua conscientia Cristianum").
5 "Historical Lectures," 6th ed. p. 350.
6 Josephus, "Ant.," XVIII. 3, 2.
7 Scott, "Anne of Geierstein," Chap. I.
8 Gessner, "Descript. Mont. Pilat," Zurich, 1555.
9 Golbery, "Univers Pittoresque de la Suisse," p. 327.

CHAPTER VIII JESUS BEFORE PILATE

1 Matt. xxvii. 1, 2.
2 Mark xv. 1. *NP **3** Keim, "Jesus of Nazara," vol. vi. p. 84.
4 Josephus, "Wars of the Jews," II. 14, 8; II. 15, 1.
5 Keim, "Jesus of Nazara," vol. vi. p. 87.
6 Geikie, "The Life and Words of Christ," vol. ii. p. 533.
7 Acts xxiv. 1.
8 Acts xxv. 16.
9 John xviii. 30.
10 John xviii. 31.
11 Act IV. Scene i.
12 Luke xxiii. 2.
13 Acts xviii. 14, 15.
14 Matt. xxii. 21.
15 Matt. xvii. 24, 25.
16 Matt. xxvi. 18, 19.
17 Josephus, "Ant.," XVII. 10, 5.
18 Josephus, "Ant.," XVII. 10, 6.
19 Josephus, "Ant.," XVII. 10, 7.
20 John xviii. 33.
21 Matt. xx. 25.
22 Matt. xi. 8.
23 John xviii. 34.
24 John xviii. 36.
25 John xviii. 37.
26 John xviii. 38.
27 Luke xxiii. 5.

CHAPTER IX JESUS BEFORE HEROD

1 Luke xiii. 32.
2 Luke xxiii. 8.
3 Josephus, "Ant.," XVIII. 7, 1, 2.
4 Luke xxiii. 9.
5 Luke xxxii. 10.
6 Luke xxiii. 11.
7 Tacitus, "Hist.," II. 89.
8 Luke xxiii. 12.

CHAPTER X JESUS AGAIN BEFORE PILATE

1 Luke xxiii. 13-16.
2 Luke xxiii. 17.
3 Livy v. 13: "Vinctis quoque demptu vincula."
4 Matt. xxvii. 16-18.
5 Matt. xxvii. 20-22.
6 Vie, par. 131.
7 Luke xxvii. 19.
8 John xix. 7.
9 John xix. 9.
10 John xix. 15.
11 John xix. 15.
12 John xix. 12.
13 Matt. xxvii. 24.
14 Matt. xxvii. 26-31.

CHAPTER XI LEGAL ANALYSIS AND SUMMARY OF THE ROMAN TRIAL OF JESUS

1 Keim, "Jesus of Nazara, vol. vi. p. 87.
2 Geikie, "The Life and Words of Christ," vol. ii. p. 533.
3 Geikie, "The Life and Words of Christ," vol. ii. p. 532.
4 Acts xxiv; xxv. 11; xxvi. 32.
5 Matt. xxvii. 11.
6 Mark xv. 2.
7 Luke xxiii. 3.
8 John xviii. 37.
9 Luke xxiii. 4-16.
10 Luke xxiii. 23, 24.
11 "Liberty, Equality, Fraternity," p. 87.
12 "Liberty, Equality, Fraternity," pp. 93-95.
13 L. 12, Cod. De poenis, ix. 47: "Vanae voces populi non sunt audiendae, nec enim vocibus eorum credi oportet quando aut noxium crimine absolvi aut innocentem condemnari desiderant."
14 John xix. 10.
15 Dr. Smith's "History of Greece," Chap. XXXV. p. 418.
16 I Tim. iii. 16.
17 See Dict. Philos. Art. "Religion."
18 "Emile."
19 "Sartor Resartus," 137, 140.
20 "Herzog's Encyc." vol. v. 751. Art. "Herder."
21 "Vergangl. u. Bleibendes im Christenthum," 132.
22 "Etudes d'Hist. Rel.," pp. 213, 214.

23 "Jesus of Nazara," vol. vi. pp. 430, 431.

24 Montholon, "Recit de la Captivite de l'Emp. Napoleon."

25 Bertrand's "Memoirs" Paris, 1844.

26 "Je meurs dans la religion catholique, apostolique et romaine, dans le sein de laquelle je suis ne, il y a plus de cinquante ans."

PART II GRAECO—ROMAN PAGANISM

1 Dollinger, "The Gentile and the Jew," vol. ii. p. 29.

2 "Preparation of the World for Christ," pp. 380, 381.

3 Suetonius, "Caesar Augustus," Chap. XCV.

4 Matt. i. 20.

5 Matt. ii. 13.

6 Suetonius, "Caesar Augustus," Chap. XCIV.

7 Suetonius, "Caesar Augustus," Chap. XCII.

8 Dollinger, "The Gentile and the Jew," vol. ii. p. 185.

9 Liv. xl. 59.

10 Ap. Aug. C. D. VI. 2.

11 Dollinger, vol. ii. p. 183.

12 Suetonius, "Caligula," Chap. V.

13 Mabillon, "Iter. Ital." p. 77.

14 Pausanias, ix. 17. 1.

15 De Superst. 6.

16 M. Dic, quaeso, num te illa terrent? Triceps apud inferos Cerberus? Cocyti fremitus? travectio Acherontis?

"Mento summam aquam attingens enectus siti,

Tantalus, tum illud quod,

Sisiphus versat

Saxum sudans nitendo neque proficit hilum," fortasse etiam inexorabiles judices Minor et Rhadamanthus? apud quos nec te L. Crassus defendet, nec M. Antonius; nec, quoniam apud Graecos judices res agetur, poteris adhibere Demosthenen; tibi ipsi pro te erit maxima corona causa dicenda. Haec fortasse metuis, et idcirco mortem censes esse sempiternum malum. A. Adeone me delirare censes, ut ista esse credam? M. An tu haec non credis? A. Minime vero. M. Male hercule narras. A. Cur, quaeso. M. Quia disertus esse possem, si contra ista dicerem.

17 Sallust, "Bellum Catilinarium, 50."

18 Renan, "Les Apotres."

19 "Hamlet," Act III, Scene i.

20 Dollinger, vol. ii. pp. 175-79.

21 Dion. ii. 25.

22 Dollinger, vol. ii. pp. 267-69.

23 Suetonius "Julius Caesar," l-li.

24 Xen. de Rep. Lac. i. 8.

25 "Polyb. Fragm." in Scr. Vet. Nov. Coll. ed. Mav. ii. 384.

26 Dollinger, vol. ii. p. 249.

27 "Xen. Mem. Socr." iii. 13.

28 Plutarch, "Life of Lucullus."

29 Fisher, "The Beginnings of Christianity," p. 205.

30 "Encyc. Brit." vol. iii. p. 436.

31 Plutarch, "Life of Cato."

32 Cicero, "Pro Cluent." 66.

33 Tacitus, "Annals," 42-44.

34 De Pressense, "The Religions Before Christ," p. 158.

35 Milman's "Gibbon's Rome," vol. i. p. 51.

36 Suetonius, "Caligula," Chap. V.

37 Fisher, "The Beginnings of Christianity," p. 213.

38 Pliny, Ep. X. 38.

39 Suetonius, "Julius Caesar," Chap. XLIX.

40 Dollinger, vol. ii. pp. 253, 254.

41 Dollinger, vol. ii. pp. 205, 206.

42 Dollinger, vol. ii. p. 207.

43 Dollinger, vol. ii. p. 208.

44 Livy, b. xxxix. Chaps. VII.-XX.

45 "——non possum ferre, Quirites, Graecam urbem." (Sat. III.)

46 Romans i. 29-31.

47 Dollinger, vol. ii. pp. 155, 156.

48 Matthew Arnold's Poems—"Obermann Once More."

49 Cicero, "De Fin." v. pp. 24, 69.

50 Eclogue IV.

APPENDICES

APPENDIX I CHARACTERS OF THE SANHEDRISTS WHO TRIED JESUS

1 Matt. ii. 4; xxi. 15; xxvi. 3, 47, 59; Mark xi. 18; xv. 11; Luke xix. 47; xx. 1; John xi. 47; xii. 20.

2 Derembourg, "Essai sur l'histoire et la geographie de la Palestine," p. 231, note 1.

3 Josephus, "Ant.," Book XX. Chap. X. 1; XV. III. 1.

4 Josephus, "Ant.," Book XV. Chap. III. 1.

5 Josephus, "Ant.," Book XVIII. Chap. II. 3; Book XX. Chap. IX. 1, 4.

6 See "Talmud," "Yoma," or "the Day of Atonement," fol. 35, recto; also Derembourg, work above quoted, p. 230, note 2.

7 "Essai sur l'histoire et la geographie de la Palestine," p. 232.

8 Jos., "Ant.," XX. VIII. 8.

9 "Talmud," "Pesachim," or "of the Passover," fol. 57, verso.

10 The high priests designated under the name of the descendants of Eli are those who, as sons of the high priest Eli, polluted the Temple by their immorality. (See 1 Kings iii. 22-25.)

11 This Issacher was a priest of such a dainty nature that in order to touch the sacrifices he covered his hands with silk. ("Talmud," "Pesachim," or "of the Passover," fol. 57, verso.)

12 Rabbi Nathan, son of Rabbi Yechiel, was the disciple of the celebrated Moses, the preacher and first rabbi of the synagogue at Rome in the ninth century. His work forms a large folio volume, and contains some minute explanations of the most difficult passages in the "Talmud."

13 I. e., lord.

14 "Talmud," Jerus., "Horayoth," or "Regulations of Justice," fol. 84, recto.

15 "Talmud," Jerus., "Shevuoth," or "of Oaths," fol. 19, verso.

16 "Tanchumah," or "Book of Consolation," fol. 68, recto.

17 "Tanchumah," or "Book of Consolation," fol. 68, recto.

18 "Tanchumah," or "Book of Consolation," fol. 68, recto, and "Sanhedrin," fol. 110, verso.

19 "Talmud," "Shabbath," or "of the Sabbath," fol. 119, recto.

20 Luke xx. 46; Matt. xxiii. 5-7; Mark xii. 38, 39.

21 Some remarkable pages respecting the pride of the Jewish scribes and doctors may be found in Bossuet's "Meditations on the Gospel."

22 Jos., "Ant.," XVIII. I. 4.

23 Jos., "Ant.," XVIII. I. 4.

24 Munk, "Palestine," p. 515.

25 Psalms.

26 Acts xxiii. 6.

27 Matt. vi. 2, 5, 16; ix. 11, 14; xii. 2; xxiii. 5, 15, 23; Luke v. 30; vi. 2, 7; xi. 39, etc.; xviii. 12; John

ix. 16; "Perkeh Avoth," or "Sentences of the Fathers," I. 16; Jos., "Ant.," XVII. II. 4; XVIII. I. 3; "Vita," 38; "Talmud," Bab., "Sotah," fol. 22, recto.

28 "From that time forth began Jesus to show unto his disciples, how that he must go unto Jerusalem, and suffer many things of the elders and chief priests and scribes." (Matt. xvi. 21.)

APPENDIX II ACTS OF PILATE

1 "The Credibility of the Gospel History," in the chapter on "Testimonies of Ancient Heathens," vol. vi. p. 605 *et seq.*

2 "Origin of the Four Gospels," pp. 141-50.

BIBLIOGRAPHY

MAIN AUTHORITIES

THE BIBLE.   English Authorized Version of 1611.

THE TALMUD.   Babylonian Recension, translated into English by Michael L. Rodkinson. New Talmud Publishing Company, New York, 1896.

THE MISHNA.   Edition of Surenhusius. Amsterdam, 1698-1703. Consulted by the author in the Astor Library, New York City.

MINOR AUTHORITIES

ABBOTT.   Jesus of Nazareth, by Lyman Abbott. Harper Brothers, New York, 1882.

ANDREWS.   The Life of Our Lord, by Samuel J. Andrews. Charles Scribner's Sons, New York, 1906.

BARING-GOULD.   Curious Myths of the Middle Ages, by S. Baring-Gould. Roberts Brothers, Boston, 1880.

BAUR.   The Church History of the First Three Centuries, by F. C. Baur. Translated from German by A. Mendies. London, 1878.

BENNY.   The Criminal Code of the Jews, by Philip Berger Benny. Smith, Elder & Company, London, 1880.

BLACKSTONE.   Commentaries on the Laws of England, by Sir William Blackstone. Edited and annotated by Thomas M. Cooley. Callaghan & Company, Chicago, 1884.

CICERO.   M. Tullii Ciceronis orationes. Whittaker & Company, London, 1855.

DEUTSCH.   The Talmud, by Emanuel Deutsch. The Jewish Publication Society of America, Philadelphia, 1896.

DOLLINGER.   The Gentile and the Jew, by John J. I. Dollinger. Two volumes. Gibbings & Company, London, 1906.

EDERSHEIM.   The Life and Times of Jesus the Messiah, by Alfred Edersheim. Two volumes. Longmans, Green & Company, New York, 1905.

FARRAR.   The Life of Christ, by Frederic W. Farrar. E. P. Dutton & Company, New York, 1883.

FISHER.   The Beginnings of Christianity, by George P. Fisher. Charles Scribner's Sons, New York, 1906.

GEIB.   Geschichte des romischen Criminalprocesses, von Dr. Gustav Geib. Weidmann'sche Buchhandlung. Leipzig, 1842.

GEIKIE.   The Life and Words of Christ, by Cunningham Geikie.

Two volumes. Henry S. King & Company. London, 1877.

GIBBON. The History of the Decline and Fall of the Roman Empire, by Edward Gibbon. With notes by Rev. H. H. Milman. Phillips, Sampson & Company, Boston, 1853.

GRAETZ. History of the Jews, by Heinrich Graetz. Six volumes. The Jewish Publication Society of America, Philadelphia, 1891.

GREENLEAF. The Testimony of the Evangelists, by Simon Greenleaf. Soney & Sage, Newark, N. J., 1903.

GREENIDGE. The Legal Procedure of Cicero's Time, by A. H. J. Greenidge. Stevens & Sons, London, 1901.

HARNACK. Reden und Aufsatze, von Adolf Harnack. J. Ricker'sche Verlagsbuchhandlung, Giessen, 1904.

HIGGINS. Anacalypsis: An Enquiry into the Origin of Languages, Nations and Religions, by Godfrey Higgins. Longman, Brown & Longman, London, 1827.

HODGE. Systematic Theology, by Charles Hodge. Charles Scribner's Sons, New York, 1892.

INNES. The Trial of Jesus Christ, by A. Taylor Innes. T. & T. Clark, Edinburgh, 1905.

JOSEPHUS. The Works of Flavius Josephus, Whiston's Translation.

JOST. Geschichte des Judenthums, von I. M. Jost. Dorffling und Francke, Leipzig, 1857.

JUVENAL. The Satires of Juvenal. George Bell & Sons, London, 1904.

KEIM. Jesus of Nazara, by Theodor Keim. Six volumes. Williams & Norgate, London, 1883.

LARDNER. Works of Nathaniel Lardner. Ten volumes. William Ball, London, 1838.

LEMANN. Valeur de l'assemblee qui prononca la peine de mort contre Jesus Christ, par MM. Lemann. Peine de mort contre Jesus Christ, par MM. Lemann. Translated from the French into English under the title "Jesus Before the Sanhedrin," by Prof. Julius Magath, of Oxford, Ga., in 1899.

LIVY. The History of Rome, by Titus Livius. George Bell & Sons, London, 1906.

LOISY. Les Evangiles Synoptiques, par Alfred Loisy. Librairie Fishbacher, Paris, 1907.

MENDELSOHN. The Criminal Jurisprudence of the Ancient Hebrews, by S. Mendelsohn. M. Curlander, Baltimore, 1891.

MOMMSEN. The Provinces of the Roman Empire, by Theodor Mommsen. Two volumes. Charles Scribner' Sons, New York, 1899.

MONTESQUIEU.	De l'Esprit Des Lois, par Montesquieu. Garnier Freres, Paris, 1905.
PALEY.	Evidences of Christianity, by William Paley. The Religious Tract Society, London, 1794.
RABBINOWICZ.	Legislation Criminelle du Talmud, par I. J. M. Rabbinowicz. Chez l'auteur, Paris, 1876.
RENAN.	Histoire des origines du christianisme, par Joseph Ernest Renan. Paris, 1863. Livres 1-6: 1. Vie de Jesus. 2. Les apotres. 3. Saint Paul. 4. L'Antichrist. 5. Les evangiles et la seconde generation chretienne. 6. L'eglise chretienne.
ROSADI.	The Trial of Jesus, by Giovanni Rosadi. Dodd, Mead & Company, New York, 1905.
SALVADOR.	Histoire des Institutions de Moise, par J. Salvador. Michel Levy-Freres, Paris, 1862.
SCHURER.	The Jewish People in the Time of Jesus Christ, by Emil Schurer. Charles Scribner's Sons, New York, 1906.
STEPHEN.	Liberty, Equality, Fraternity, by James Fitzjames Stephen. Henry Holt & Company, New York, 1873.
SUETONIUS.	The Lives of the Twelve Caesars, by C. Suetonius Tranquillus. George Bell & Sons, London, 1906.
TACITUS.	The Works of Tacitus. American Book Company, New York, 1904.
WISE.	The Martyrdom of Jesus, by Isaac M. Wise. The Bloch Publishing and Printing Company, Cincinnati & Chicago, 1888.

In addition to the above, many other authorities have been consulted in the preparation of the two volumes of this work. Quotations from them are frequently found in the text, and citations are given in the notes. The author, in closing the article, entitled "Bibliography," wishes to express his sense of great indebtedness and appreciation to the numerous very valuable encyclopedias that adorn the shelves of the various libraries of New York City; and especially to The Jewish Encyclopedia, published by Funk & Wagnalls, New York and London, 1901.

INDEX

Composed by the Computer Composition System of The Harrison Company, Norcross, Georgia. Cover designed by the late W. Harrell Brooks. Covers crafted by Kingsport Press, book lithographed and bound by Kingsport Press, Kingsport, Tennessee, under the direction of Jean Haynes and Jim Sams. Printed in brown ink on Warren's Olde Style Wove. Bound in Whitman's Blue Skivertex, with End Papers in Blue Elephant Hide.